W9-BOM-136

WELCOME TO SAN FRANCISCO

With its myriad hills and spectacular bay, San Francisco beguiles with natural beauty, vibrant neighborhoods, and contagious energy. From the hipster Mission District to the sassy Castro, from bustling Union Square to enduring Chinatown, this dynamic town thrives on variety. The city makes it wonderfully easy to tap into the good life, too: between San Francisco's hot arts scene, tempting boutiques, parks perfect for jogging or biking, and all those stellar locavore restaurants and cocktail bars, it's the ultimate destination for relaxed self-indulgence.

TOP REASONS TO GO

★ **Foodie heaven:** Top restaurants, hip ethnic favorites, farmers' markets, food trucks.

★ **Distinctive neighborhoods:** Buzzing, walkable streets invite discovery.

★ **Golden Gate Bridge:** Electric orange and towering, this glorious span inspires awe.

★ **Waterfront activities:** Whether you hike, bike, or stroll it, the bay is magnetic.

★ **Accessible art:** From famous street murals to top-notch museums, art is everywhere.

Fodor's SAN FRANCISCO

Editorial: Douglas Stallings, *Editorial Director*; Salwa Jabado and Margaret Kelly, *Senior Editors*; Alexis Kelly, Jacinta O'Halloran, and Amanda Sadlowski, *Editors*; Teddy Minford, *Associate Editor*; Rachael Roth, *Content Manager*

Design: Tina Malaney, *Associate Art Director*

Photography: Jennifer Arnow, *Senior Photo Editor*

Maps: Rebecca Baer, *Senior Map Editor*; Mark Stroud (Moon Street Cartography), David Lindroth, *Cartographers*

Production: Jennifer DePrima, *Editorial Production Manager*; Carrie Parker, *Senior Production Editor*; Elyse Rozelle, *Production Editor*; David Satz, *Director of Content Production*

Business & Operations: Chuck Hoover, *Chief Marketing Officer*; Joy Lai, *Vice President and General Manager*; Stephen Horowitz, *Head of Business Development and Partnerships*

Public Relations: Joe Ewaskiw, *Manager*

Writers: Amanda Kuehn Carroll, Denise Leto, Danny Mangin, Rebecca Flint Marx, Andrea Powell, Jerry James Stone

Editor: Margaret Kelly

Production Editor: Jennifer DePrima

Production Design: Liliana Guia

29th Edition

ISBN 978-0-1475-4692-0

ISSN 1525–1829

PRINTED IN THE UNITED STATES OF AMERICA

10 9 8 7 6 5 4 3 2 1

Fodor's
SAN FRANCISCO

CONTENTS

Fodor's Features

MAPS

ABOUT THIS GUIDE

Fodor's Recommendations

Everything in this guide is worth doing—we don't cover what isn't—but exceptional sights, hotels, and restaurants are recognized with additional accolades. **Fodor's**Choice★ indicates our top recommendations. Care to nominate a new place? Visit Fodors.com/contact-us.

Trip Costs

We list prices wherever possible to help you budget well. Hotel and restaurant price categories from **$** to **$$$$** are noted alongside each recommendation. For hotels, we include the lowest cost of a standard double room in high season. For restaurants, we cite the average price of a main course at dinner or, if dinner isn't served, at lunch. For attractions, we always list adult admission fees; discounts are usually available for children, students, and senior citizens.

Hotels

Our local writers vet every hotel to recommend the best overnights in each price category, from budget to expensive. Unless otherwise specified, you can expect private bath, phone, and TV in your room. For expanded hotel reviews, facilities, and deals visit Fodors.com.

Top Picks
- ★ **Fodor's**Choice

Listings
- ✉ Address
- ✉ Branch address
- ☎ Telephone
- 📠 Fax
- 🌐 Website
- 📧 E-mail
- 🎟 Admission fee
- 🕒 Open/closed times
- [M] Subway
- ✥ Directions or Map coordinates

Hotels & Restaurants
- 🏨 Hotel
- 🛏 Number of rooms
- 🍽 Meal plans
- 🍴 Restaurant
- ✍ Reservations
- 👔 Dress code
- 💳 No credit cards
- [$] Price

Other
- ⇨ See also
- ☞ Take note
- 🏌 Golf facilities

Restaurants

Unless we state otherwise, restaurants are open for lunch and dinner daily. We mention dress code only when there's a specific requirement and reservations only when they're essential or not accepted.

Credit Cards

The hotels and restaurants in this guide typically accept credit cards. If not, we'll say so.

EUGENE FODOR

Hungarian-born Eugene Fodor (1905–91) began his travel career as an interpreter on a French cruise ship. The experience inspired him to write *On the Continent* (1936), the first guidebook to receive annual updates and discuss a country's way of life as well as its sights. Fodor later joined the U.S. Army and worked for the OSS in World War II. After the war, he kept up his intelligence work while expanding his guidebook series. During the Cold War, many guides were written by fellow agents who understood the value of insider information. Today's guides continue Fodor's legacy by providing travelers with timely coverage, insider tips, and cultural context.

EXPERIENCE
SAN FRANCISCO

SAN FRANCISCO TODAY

The quintessential boomtown, San Francisco has been alternately riding high and crashing since the gold rush. Those who lost out during the heady days of the dot-com bubble had barely finished dancing on the grave of the Internet economy when biotech rode into town, turning bust to boom. So which San Francisco will you find? A reversal of fortune is always possible, but here's a snapshot of what the city's like—for now, anyway.

Revitalized Neighborhoods

Long the domain of drug addicts and homeless people smack-dab in the heart of downtown, **Mid-Market**—Market Street between 5th and 9th Streets south to Mission Street—resisted the best efforts of a string of San Francisco mayors to revitalize the area. In the end it took more than City Hall muscle to get the ball rolling; it took Twitter, the social media heavyweight lured here by the promise of a payroll tax break in 2013. Since then a bevy of companies, including Uber, Microsoft, and Square, have followed. Restaurants like Equator Coffee and Popsons Burgers have also begun to change the vibe on the street. American Conservatory's new Strand Theater opened across from U.N. Plaza in 2015, while the Hall, a pop-up indoor food market and event space, has become a kind of community living room on one of the area's more stubborn blocks. But housing has lagged, languishing for years in the approval process before ever breaking ground. And without residents, the sidewalks roll up at night, killing a string of restaurants that opened here with high hopes only to shutter again for lack of business. Without residents, big retail is hesitating, leaving even almost-completed projects without tenants. The next couple of years, as residential projects finally come online and commercial projects fail or fly, will tell whether Mid-Market will fulfill the dreams of city planners and developers or stagnate, busy with office workers by day but abandoned and sketchy at night.

Still one of the poorest and most dangerous neighborhoods in the city, with visible drug and prostitution activity and a grimy, gritty feel, the **Tenderloin** today is also obviously on the rise. And why not? It's cheek-by-jowl with downtown, and a short hop to SoMa, and in the most expensive city in the country, it looks like location location location is finally conquering the sketch factor that's kept many away. New, young residents—many of them well-paid tech workers with offices nearby in Mid-Market—now patronize urbane new retail such as Japanese spa Onsen and trendy bars and restaurants like Black Cat, the Saratoga, and Huxley. The Tenderloin Museum—opened by neighborhood housing advocates to inspire neighborhood cohesion and, let's face it, attract hipsters and their money—gives new residents the feeling that they're in the vanguard, rediscovering a storied hood. And concrete improvements are good for everyone; the neighborhood is slated to get 100 new streetlights in a bid to improve both safety and environment. On the cultural front, the Tenderloin may become home to the nation's first swath dedicated to transgender culture. City supervisors are set to vote on the creation of Compton's Transgender Lesbian Bisexual Gay District, encompassing six blocks of the Tenderloin (in addition to two blocks of 6th Street across Market) that include sites important to trans history. Three years before Stonewall at Compton's Cafe (Turk and Taylor Streets), transgender customers fought back against police harassment, sparking a two-day riot and the birth of a movement. Unlike the Mission, which has battled wave after wave of gentrification and struggles mightily (and increasingly unsuccessfully) to maintain its workaday Latino roots, the Tenderloin is poised to weather the transition without completely losing its character. Among the factors that help is Glide Memorial, the radically inclusive church community and neighborhood giant that's provided daily services, housing, and after-school care—not to mention acupuncture and meditation—to the neighborhood's down-and-out for more than 50 years. Led by local hero Cecil Williams, who counts among his friends Bono, the Obamas, and Warren Buffett, Glide bridges the gap between the street's poorest and the relatively wealthy young tech workers trying to find their way here: Google donated the money for the church's digital storage system, Twitter's CEO helps prep the soup kitchen's lunch, and Zendesk employees donate time making clean-needle kits. In another bid to keep the Tenderloin from going the way of the Mission, the city voted to restrict Airbnb incursion by requiring a 30-day minimum stay in the neighborhood's Single Occupancy Residences, the one-room apartments that stand between a lot of folks and homelessness, or at least a quick ticket out of the city. But it remains to be seen whether the neighborhood's history, character, and poorest residents can withstand the tsunami of money heading their way.

When **Bayview–Hunters Point**—devastated by the closing of the shipyards in the 1990s, stung by the abandonment of Candlestick Park in 2014, and still marred by one of the highest murder rates in the city—can claim new Starbucks, Peet's, and the artisanal Craftsman & Wolves coffee shop The Den, you know the neighborhood is ripe for gentrification.

Living on the Street

With housing costs skyrocketing, San Francisco has finally surpassed New York with the highest rents in the country: $4,650 for a two-bedroom apartment. In a city of about 800,000 and bounded by water on three sides, San Francisco's housing stock has been steady for decades—there's nowhere to go but up. And the towers are slowly rising, but only a few lucky people without very deep pockets will have access to one. San Francisco is also one of the most popular tourist destinations in the country, bringing in over $9 billion annually. Folks come to see the lovely city cascading down its hills to the bay, the Golden Gate Bridge, and photo-worthy Victorians. But they also see panhandlers holding signs that say "Anything helps"; people sleeping on the sidewalk in the middle of the day; tent cities stretching down city blocks; and the disheveled, mentally ill wandering the streets. It's a shocking contrast, especially in a city of such wealth. Upward of 6,700 people are homeless in the city, and almost half of them sleep outside. The city spends over $240 million in homeless services annually, and in 2016 even created a Department of Homelessness and Supportive Housing, which provides on-site social services and mental health support. But there simply aren't enough spots. And while the city works to create housing and gather funding, the homeless population increases. The president's threat to cut all federal funding to sanctuary cities like San Francisco, which receives $1 billion in federal money annually, adds a new layer of uncertainty to an already intractable issue.

SAN FRANCISCO PLANNER

When to Go

You can visit San Francisco comfortably any time of year. Possibly the best time is September and October, when the city's summerlike weather brings outdoor concerts and festivals. The climate here always feels Mediterranean and moderate—with a foggy, sometimes chilly bite. The temperature rarely drops below 40°F, and anything warmer than 80°F is considered a heat wave. Be prepared for rain in winter, especially December and January. Winds off the ocean can add to the chill factor. That old joke about summer in San Francisco feeling like winter is true at heart, but once you move inland, it gets warmer. (And some locals swear that the thermostat has inched up in recent years.)

Weather

Thanks to its proximity to the Pacific Ocean, San Francisco has remarkably consistent weather throughout the year. The average high is 63°F and the average low is 51°F. Summer comes late in San Francisco, which sees its warmest days in September and October. On average, the city gets 20 inches of rainfall a year, most of it in the December-to-March period.

Getting Around

Walking: San Francisco rewards walking, and the areas that most visitors cover are easy (and safe) to reach on foot. However, many neighborhoods have steep— make that *steep*—hills. In some areas the sidewalk is carved into steps; a place that seems just a few blocks away might be a real hike, depending on the grade. When your calves ache, you're that much closer to being a local.

By Subway: BART is San Francisco's subway, limited to one straight line through the city. Within the city, it's a handy way to get to the Mission or perhaps Civic Center. BART is most useful for reaching the East Bay or SFO and Oakland's airport. There are no special visitor passes for BART; within town a ticket runs $1.95.

On Muni: Muni includes the city's extensive system of buses, electric streetcars, nostalgic F-line trolleys, and cable cars. The trolleys and cable cars are a pleasure for the ride alone, and they run in well-traveled areas like Market Street and, in the case of the cable cars, the hills from Union Square to Fisherman's Wharf. Basic fare for the bus, streetcars, and trolleys is $2.50; cable-car tickets cost $7 one-way. At $21, a one-day Visitor Passport, which includes cable car rides, is a good deal.

By Car or Taxi: Considering its precipitous hills, one-way streets, and infuriating dearth of parking, San Francisco is not a good place to drive yourself. Taxis, however, can come in very handy. Call one or hail one on the street; they tend to cluster around downtown hotels. Ride companies like Lyft and Uber now do most of the taxi business in the city; hail one with their respective phone apps.

Festivals and Parades

San Francisco's major parades and festivals are notoriously creative, energetic, and often off-the-wall. Among the hundreds of events on the city's annual calendar, here are the ones that are especially characteristic and fun.

Chinese New Year, February. This celebration in North America's largest Chinatown lasts for almost three weeks. The grand finale is the spectacularly loud, crowded, and colorful Golden Dragon Parade, which rocks with firecrackers. If you don't want to stand on the sidewalk for hours in advance, buy bleacher seats. Contact the **Chinese Chamber of Commerce** (☎ *415/982–3071* ⊕ *www.chineseparade. com*) for more info.

St. Stupid's Day Parade, April. The First Church of the Last Laugh (⊕ *www.saint-stupid.com*) holds this fantastically funny event on—when else?—April 1. Hundreds of people wander through the Financial District dressed in elaborate costumes (although there are fewer drag queens than on Halloween). Parade goers toss singular socks at the Stock Exchange, lob losing lottery tickets at the Federal Reserve, and sing their way down Columbus Avenue.

San Francisco International Film Festival, April and May. The country's longest-running film festival packs in audiences with premieres, international films, and rarities. Check the listings (☎ *415/561–5000* ⊕ *festival.sffs.org*) well in advance; screenings can sell out quickly.

Lesbian, Gay, Bisexual, and Transgender Pride Celebration, June. More than half a million people come to join the world's largest pride event, with a downtown parade roaring to a start by leather-clad Dykes on Bikes. If you're visiting around this time—usually the last weekend of June—book your hotel *far* ahead (☎ *415/864–0831* ⊕ *www.sfpride.org*).

San Francisco Open Studios, October and November. More than 800 artists open their studios to the public. It's a great window into the local fine-arts scene (☎ *415/861–9838* ⊕ *www.artspan.org*).

Dance-Along Nutcracker, December. This holiday tradition, part spoof and part warmhearted family event, was started by the San Francisco Lesbian/Gay Freedom Band (⊕ *www.sflgfb.org*). You can join the dancers onstage or simply toss snowflakes from the audience.

Helpful San Francisco Websites

Check out these online options—besides our own ⊕ *www.fodors.com*

⊕ *www.sftravel.com* for the San Francisco visitor bureau.

⊕ *www.sfgate.com* from the major daily newspaper, especially ⊕ *www.sfgate.com/sfguide* (for city neighborhoods and events) and ⊕ *www.sfgate.com/entertainment* (for entertainment articles and listings).

⊕ *sf.funcheap.com* for a daily listing of free and inexpensive events in the city.

⊕ *sfist.com* for a daily feed of local news, gossip, and SF preoccupations.

⊕ *www.sfstation.com* for daily listings on all sorts of events, restaurants, clubs, and so on.

⊕ *www.7x7.com* for the skinny on shopping, eating, playing, and following art in the city.

⊕ *www.thebolditalic.com* for a photo-heavy, hip take on life in the city, from microhoods to microbrews.

⊕ *burritojustice.com* for opinionated takes on San Francisco burritos and some history thrown in for kicks.

⊕ *www.sfgirlbybay.com*, a design blog that spans the globe, but shows plenty of love to San Francisco attractions and shops.

WHAT'S WHERE

1 Chinatown. Live fish flopping around on ice; the scent of incense, cigarettes, and vanilla; bargains announced in myriad Chinese dialects ... you'll feel like you should've brought your passport.

2 SoMa. Anchored by SFMOMA and Yerba Buena Gardens, SoMa is a once-industrial neighborhood that's in transition. Luxury condos and stylish restaurants abound and cool dance clubs draw the bridge-and-tunnel crowd, but some parts are still gritty.

3 Civic Center. Monumental city government buildings and performing arts venues dominate, but it's also a chronic homeless magnet. Locals love Hayes Valley, the chic little neighborhood west of City Hall.

4 Nob Hill. Topped by staid and elegant behemoths, hotels that ooze reserve and breeding, Nob Hill is old-money San Francisco.

5 Russian Hill. These steep streets hold a vibrant, classy neighborhood that's very au courant. Locals flock to Polk and Hyde Streets, the hill's main commercial avenues, for excellent neighborhood eateries and fantastic window-shopping.

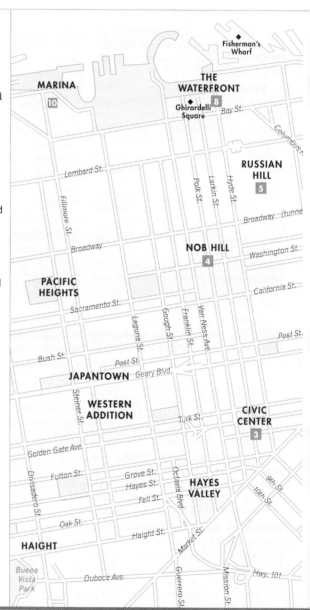

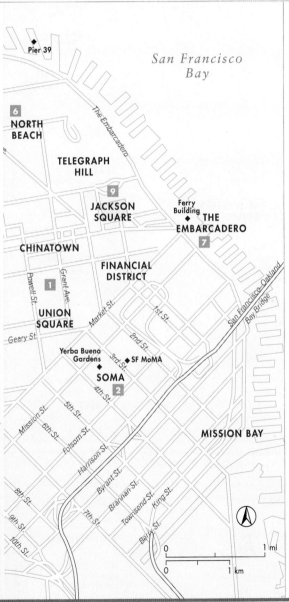

6 North Beach. The city's small Italian neighborhood makes even locals feel as if they're on holiday. In the morning, fresh focaccia beckons, and there are few better ways to laze away an afternoon than in one of North Beach's cafés.

7 Embarcadero. The city's northeastern waterfront is anchored at the foot of Market Street by the exquisite Ferry Building marketplace. The promenade that starts in back has great views of the bay and the Bay Bridge.

8 The Waterfront. If you wander the shops and attractions of Fisherman's Wharf, Pier 39, and Ghirardelli Square, the only locals you'll meet will be the ones with visitors in tow. Everything here is designed for tourists.

9 Jackson Square. For history buffs and antiques lovers, this upscale corner of the Financial District is a pleasant diversion.

10 The Marina. With fine-wine shops, trendy boutiques, fashionable cafés and restaurants, and pricey waterfront homes, the Marina is San Francisco's yuppiest neighborhood. It's also home to the exquisite 1915 Palace of Fine Arts.

WHAT'S WHERE

11 The Presidio. Locals come to the Presidio, the wooded shoreline park just west of the Marina, for a quick in-town getaway, the spirit lift only an amble on the sand in the shadow of the Golden Gate Bridge can provide.

12 Golden Gate Park. Covering more than 1,000 acres of greenery, with sports fields, windmills, museums, gardens, and a few bison thrown in for good measure, Golden Gate Park is San Francisco's backyard.

13 The Western Shoreline. A natural gem underappreciated by locals and visitors alike, the city's windswept Pacific shore stretches for miles.

14 The Haight. If you're looking for '60s souvenirs, you can find them here, along with some of the loveliest Victorians in town (and aggressive panhandling). Hip locals come for the great secondhand shops, cheap brunch, and low-key bars and cafés.

15 The Castro. Yes, it's proudly rainbow-flag-waving, in-your-face fab, but the Castro is a friendly neighborhood that welcomes visitors of all stripes. Shop the trendy boutiques, and catch a film at the truly noteworthy Castro Theatre.

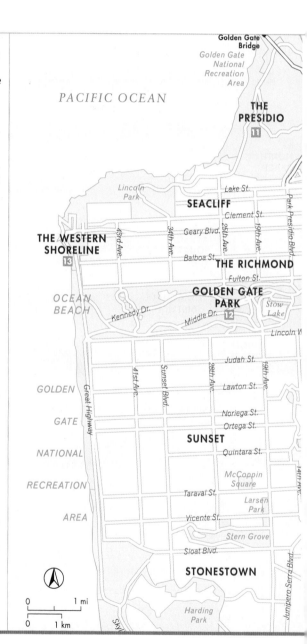

1

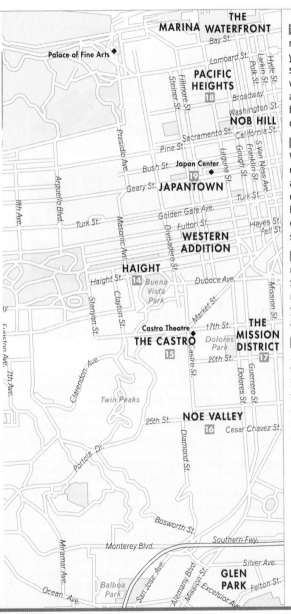

16 Noe Valley. A cute, pricey neighborhood favored by young families. The main strip, 24th Street, is lined with coffee shops, eateries, and boutiques selling fancy bath products and trendy children's clothing.

17 The Mission District. When the sun sets, people descend on the Mission from all over the Bay Area for destination restaurants, excellent bargain-price ethnic eateries, and the hippest bar scene around.

18 Pacific Heights. This neighborhood has some of San Francisco's most opulent real estate—but in most cases you'll have to be content with an exterior view.

19 Japantown. A tight-knit Japanese-American population supports this area, of interest to outsiders mostly for the ethnic shopping and dining opportunities of the Japan Center and the small streets just north.

SAN FRANCISCO TOP ATTRACTIONS

Golden Gate Bridge

(A) San Francisco's signature International Orange entryway is the city's majestic background, and about 10 million people a year head to the bridge for an up-close look. Walking the 1.7 miles to Marin County—inches from roaring traffic, steel shaking beneath your feet, and only a railing between you and the water 200 feet below—is much more than a superlative photo op (though it's that, too).

Alcatraz

(B) Considering how many movies have been set here, you might feel that you've already "been there, done that"—but you really shouldn't miss a trip to America's most infamous federal pen. Husky-throated onetime inmates and grizzled former guards bring the Rock to life on the wonderful audio tour; you'll hear yarns about desperate escape attempts and notorious crooks like Al Capone while you walk the cold cement cell block. But it's not all doom and gloom: you'll enjoy stunning views of the city skyline on the ferry ride to and from the island.

Golden Gate Park

(C) It may be world-famous, but first and foremost the park is the city's backyard. Come here any day of the week and you'll find a microcosm of San Francisco, from the Russian senior citizens feeding the pigeons at Stow Lake and the moms pushing strollers through the botanical gardens to school kids exploring the fabulous California Academy of Sciences and arts boosters checking out the latest at the de Young Museum. Be sure to visit the park's iconic treasures, including the serene Japanese Tea Garden and the beautiful Victorian Conservatory of Flowers. If you have the time to venture farther into this urban oasis, you'll discover less-accessible gems like the Beach Chalet and the wild western shores of Ocean Beach.

Cable Cars

(D) You've already seen them (on the big screen, in magazines, and, admit it, on the Rice-a-Roni box). And considering a ticket costs $7 a pop, do you really need to ride a cable car? Yes, you do, at least once during your visit. Flag down a Powell–Hyde car along Powell Street, grab the pole, and clatter and jiggle up mansion-topped Nob Hill. Crest the hill, and hold on for the hair-raising descent to Fisherman's Wharf, with sun glittering off the bay and Alcatraz bobbing in the distance. Don't deny it—this would be a deal at twice the price.

Ferry Building

(E) Foodies, rejoice! The historic Ferry Building is stuffed to the brim with all things tasty, including cafés, restaurants, a farmers' market, and merchants peddling everything from wine and olive oil to oysters and mushrooms. The building backs up to the bay, so the views are great—but they're even better from the decks of the departing ferries.

Wine Country

(F) You don't need to be a connoisseur to enjoy a trip to Napa or Sonoma … or both (hey, you're on vacation). But there's more to a Wine Country visit than vineyard tours and tastings: landmark restaurants, breathtaking scenery, fantastic artwork, hot-air-balloon rides, and secluded boutique hotels. And when you're ready for a break, a great glass of wine is never that far out of reach.

LOCAL FOR A DAY

Want to get a slice of local life by just hanging out and skipping the sightseeing? These experiences will let you pretend you're a San Franciscan, without a whopping rent check.

Shop the Ferry Plaza Farmers' Market

Roll out of bed and make your way to the Ferry Building—preferably on a Saturday—to join locals and celebrity chefs on a taste bud–driven raid. Out front, farmer-run stands showcase the Bay Area's finest organic, free-range, locavore goods. The indoor stalls will keep your mouth watering with artisanal cheeses, chocolates, and luscious pastries. Snag some takeaway food and perfectly ripe fruit for a picnic.

Stretch Your Legs in the Presidio

Spend a few hours wandering around this former military base at the foot of the Golden Gate Bridge. From gorgeous lookout points and the only campsite in the city to exhibition spaces and restaurants in restored military buildings, the Presidio has a sweeping natural beauty that brushes up against man-made diversions. Join people walking their dogs on the wooded hiking trails, or amble the paths along the sand of Crissy Field, then get in line for a cocoa at the Warming Hut.

Hang Out in Hayes Valley

Long beloved of artsy, cutting-edge locals, this quarter of cool cafés and high-design boutiques is finally on the radar of most San Franciscans. Browse your socks off, then grab a coffee from local cult microroasters Blue Bottle Coffee or a brew at the Biergarten and check out the latest temporary art installation in Patricia's Green, the petite community park.

Find a Quiet Beach

Leave the beach near Fisherman's Wharf far behind and seek out these two instead: Breezy Baker Beach, tucked against the cliffs just south of the Golden Gate Bridge, is known for its bridge and ocean views—and its nudists, those hardy souls. A bit farther south, nestled in ultrapricey Seacliff, is China Beach, a smaller, more secluded spot that's never crowded.

Linger over Breakfast

Notoriously food-centric San Franciscans are big on the most important meal of the day. The lines at popular breakfast places can be just as long as those at the hottest nightspots. Some favorites include:

Dottie's True Blue Café. The wait is worth it here for the blueberry pancakes or smoked whiskey-fennel sausage, mushroom, and baby spinach scramble.

Kate's Kitchen. Heaping plates of Southern-inspired fare take the edge off a hairy-tongued Lower Haight morning after. Go for the cornmeal pancakes.

Mama's. The line forms early at this tried-and-true diner.

Sweet Maple. Famous for its Millionaire's Bacon (bacon with brown sugar, black pepper, and cayenne), this stylish diner also serves what many claim is the city's best French toast.

Nurse a Coffee

Spend a few hours in the right independent café or coffeehouse and you'll feel as if you're in a neighbor's living room. Come for a jolt of java, sometimes a reasonably priced meal, and usually Wi-Fi. Stay all afternoon—nobody minds—and you'll see the best reflection of a microcommunity.

SAN FRANCISCO WITH KIDS

On the Move

Adventure Cat Sailing. Them: playing on the trampoline at the bow of this 55-foot catamaran. You: enjoying a drink and the bay sunset on the stern deck.

Cable Cars. This one's a no-brainer. But don't miss the **Cable Car Terminus** at Powell and Market Streets, where conductors push the iconic cars on giant turntables, and the **Cable Car Museum**, where you can see how cable cars work.

F-Line Trolleys. Thomas the Tank Engine fan in tow? Hop on one of the F-line's neat historic streetcars. ■TIP➜ Bonus: this line connects other kid-friendly sights, like Fisherman's Wharf, Pier 39, and the San Francisco Railway Museum.

Sneak in Some Culture

ODC/San Francisco. Best known for its holiday production of *The Velveteen Rabbit*, the dance troupe also holds other performances throughout the year.

San Francisco Mime Troupe. We know, it sounds lame. But these aren't your father's mimes, or mimes at all. In fact, they're a vocal political theater troupe that gives family-friendly outdoor performances.

Stern Grove Festival. Enjoying a delicious picnic in a eucalyptus grove, your kids might not even complain that they're listening to—gasp—classical music (or Latin jazz or opera).

The Great Outdoors

Aquatic Park Beach. Does your brood include a wannabe Michael Phelps? Then head to this popular beach, one of the few places around the city where it's safe to swim. ■TIP➜ Many other Bay Area beaches have powerful currents that make swimming dangerous.

Golden Gate Promenade. If your kids can handle a 3.3-mile walk, this one's a beauty—winding from Aquatic Park Beach, through the Presidio, to Fort Point Pier near the base of the Golden Gate Bridge.

Muir Woods. If these massive trees look tall to you, imagine seeing them from 2 or 4 feet lower.

Stow Lake. When feeding bread to the ducks gets old (like that's ever going to happen), you can rent a rowboat or pedal boat.

Just Plain Fun

AT&T Park. Emerald grass, a sun-kissed day, a hot dog in your hand … and suddenly, you're 10 again, too.

Dim Sum. A rolling buffet from which kids point and pick—likely an instant hit.

Fisherman's Wharf, Hyde Street Pier, Ghirardelli Square, and Pier 39. The phrase "tourist trap" may come to mind, but in this area you can get a shrimp cocktail, clamber around old ships, snack on chocolate, and laugh at the sea lions.

Musée Mécanique. How did people entertain themselves before Wii (or TV)? Come here to find out.

Yerba Buena Gardens. Head here for ice-skating, bowling, a carousel, a playground, and the Children's Creativity Museum, a hands-on arts-and-technology center.

San Francisco Zoo. Between Grizzly Gulch, Lemur Forest, and Koala Crossing, you can make a day of it.

Learn a Thing or Two

California Academy of Sciences. Dinosaurs, penguins, free-flying rain-forest butterflies, giant snakes … what's not to like?

Exploratorium. A very hands-on science museum, including the full-immersion Tactile Dome.

TOP WALKING TOURS

All About Chinatown. On a delightful behind-the-scenes look at the neighborhood, owner Linda Lee and her guides stop in Ross Alley and at a Buddhist temple. At herbal and food markets, you'll learn the therapeutic benefits of fish stomachs and ponder uses for live partridges. ☎ 415/982–8839 ⊕ www.allaboutchinatown.com ✆ From $35.

Chinatown Alleyway Tours. To learn about the modern Chinatown community, join up with one of these young guides. Tour leaders, who all grew up here, discuss Chinatown's history and current social issues. ☎ 415/984–1478 ⊕ www.chinatownalleywaytours.org ✆ From $23.

Discover Walks. These free, hour-long tours of Chinatown, Fisherman's Wharf, and North Beach by enthusiastic young locals conveniently happen every day, so you can book one when it suits your schedule. The guides are paid in tips, so be sure to show them some love. Free tours run April through October; the rest of the year paid tours are available by reservation. ✉ San Francisco ☎ 415/494–9255 ⊕ www.discoverwalks.com/san-francisco-walking-tours ✆ Free, gratuity expected.

Don Herron's Dashiell Hammett Tour. Brush up on your noir slang and join trench-coated guide Herron for a walk by the mystery writer's haunts and the locations from some of Hammett's novels. At four hours for $20, it's one of the best deals going. See the website for tours or arrange one of your own. ✉ Civic Center ⊕ www.donherron.com ✆ $20.

Local Tastes of the City Tours. If you want to aggressively snack your way through a neighborhood as you walk it, consider hanging with cookbook author Tom Medin or one of his local guides. You'll learn why certain things just taste better in San Francisco—like coffee and anything baked with sourdough—and you'll get tips about how to find good food once you get back home. Along the way, you'll gorge yourself into oblivion: the North Beach tour, for instance, might include multiple stops for coffee and baked goods. ☎ 415/665–0480, 888/358–8687 ⊕ www.sffoodtour.com ✆ From $69.

Precita Eyes Mural Walks. For an insider's look at the Mission District's vibrant murals, this is the place to call. The nonprofit organization has nurtured this local art form from the get-go, and the folks here stay on top of the latest additions. ☎ 415/285–2287 ⊕ www.precitaeyes.org ✆ From $20.

San Francisco City Guides. An outstanding free service supported by the San Francisco Public Library, these walking tours have themes that range from individual neighborhoods to local history (the gold rush, the 1906 quake, ghost walks) to architecture. Each May and October additional walks are offered. Although the tours are free and the knowledgeable guides are volunteers, it's appropriate to make a $5 donation for these nonprofit programs. Tour schedules are available online, at library branches, and at the San Francisco Visitor Information Center at Powell and Market Streets. ☎ 415/557–4266 ⊕ www.sfcityguides.org ✆ Free.

Wok Wiz Chinatown Tour. The late cookbook author and Chinatown booster Shirley Fong-Torres founded Wok Wiz, and her team continues to lead these walks. Conversation topics include folklore and, of course, food. The version called "I Can't Believe I Ate My Way Through Chinatown!" includes breakfast and lunch. ☎ 650/355–9657 ⊕ www.wokwiz.com ✆ From $35.

OFFBEAT SF

Looking for an unusual San Francisco experience that'll give you bragging rights? Try one of these quirky choices—even a local would be impressed.

16th Avenue Steps. Just standing at the base of this glorious mosaic of a stairway in the Inner Sunset is a treat: its underwater theme gives way to daytime dragonflies and butterflies, eventually transitioning to a starry, bat-studded night sky. Hike to the top, and you may have tiny Grand View Park all to yourself. The view (after a further climb) is grand. (*Moraga St., between 15th and 16th Aves.*)

ATA. Dedicated to getting anyone's art in front of an audience, Artists' Television Access has been showing films by local artists for more than 20 years. An open-minded crowd comes to ATA's tiny space, where about 10 bucks gets you a peek at what might be the next groundbreaker. ⊕ *www.atasite.org*

Audium. Billed as a "theater of sound-sculptured space," Audium is an experience like no other. Every Friday and Saturday a few dozen participants sit in concentric circles in a completely soundproofed room in utter darkness, and music plays over the 169 speakers strategically placed, well, everywhere. ⊕ *www.audium.org*

Mt. Davidson. Ask San Franciscans what the highest point in town is and they'll most will likely say Twin Peaks, but it's actually this "mountain," the next hill over. Visible from all over town but rarely visited, Mt. Davidson is topped with a eucalyptus-filled park. Finding the road up here is tricky (entrance at Dalewood and Myra Ways), but once you get there you'll have amazing views—while all those tourists are still waiting for a parking space on Twin Peaks.

Nightlife at the Cal Academy of Sciences. Supersize snakes, waddling penguins, and taxidermy are cool anytime, but throw in a cash bar and a DJ and this science club gets even cooler. Join the trendiest of geek crowds knocking back drinks and getting up close and personal with wild animals (with help from the academy's staffers) Thursdays from 6 pm to 10 pm; 21 and over. ⊕ *www.calacademy.org*

Nontraditional holiday celebrations. If you find yourself in town on a holiday, chances are the locals are commemorating it in an unorthodox way. Valentine's Day and you want to do something special with your honey? How about the mass pillow fight at Ferry Plaza? Easter Sunday after Mass? Check out BYOBW; at Bring Your Own Big Wheel—yes, those plastic ride-ons from grade-school days—often costumed grown-ups fly down the windy bit of Vermont Street with knees akimbo. Celebrations here are a bit of a non sequitur, but that's all part of the fun.

Red Hots Burlesque. Venerable gay SoMa hot spot The Stud is hopping most any night, but the saucy ladies of Red Hots Burlesque absolutely pack the house Friday evenings with their sexy, funny, body-positive show. You can even visit their School of Shimmy and take some new moves home with you.

Seward Street Slides. Wander a few blocks off the beaten path in the Castro to the unassuming Seward Minipark (Seward Street, off Douglass Street) and its unbelievably awesome, steep concrete slides. They may be intended for kids, but grown-ups are just as likely to hop on a cardboard box and take a ride.

A WATERFRONT WALK: THE FERRY BUILDING TO FISHERMAN'S WHARF

One of the great pleasures of San Francisco is a stroll along the bay, with its briny scent, the cry of the gulls, and boats bobbing on the waves. The flat, 2-mile walk along the Embarcadero from the Ferry Building offers a chance to take in some of the city's blockbuster sights, along with spectacular bay vistas.

The Ferry Building: Foodie Mecca

Standing sentry at the foot of Market Street, the **Ferry Building** offers organic, seasonal delights from such local treasures as Cowgirl Creamery and Prather Ranch Meat Company. Take your picnic to a bench out back and take in the bay and the Bay Bridge.

Embarcadero: New Life for Old Piers

Heading north on the Embarcadero as the piers go up in number, watch for a mélange of historical info on black-and-white pillars, engraved in the sidewalk, and on plaques. These line **Pier 1,** where the giant paddle wheeler *San Francisco Belle* docks. **Pier 7** juts out far into the bay; an evening stroll here is lovely (if chilly) under the street lamps.

Just two blocks beyond at Pier 15 is the city's excellent hands-on science museum, the **Exploratorium.**

North Beach Detour: Levi's and Coit Tower

Near Pier 17, a left on Union and a right on Battery leads to **Levi Strauss headquarters,** where visitors can shop for jeans or peruse artifacts such as miners' jeans from the 1880s. Back across Battery, **Levi's Plaza** is one of the most manicured parks in town.

Consider heading west on Filbert or Greenwich and ascending one of the steep staircases clinging to **Telegraph Hill** for spectacular views and a peek into the lush stairway gardens along the way up to **Coit Tower.** Then return down the stairs to continue along the Embarcadero.

Embarcadero North End: Tourist San Francisco

Continuing north up the Embarcadero, **Alcatraz Landing** (Pier 33) is a good spot to pick up souvenirs even if you're not taking the highly recommended tour. **Pier 39** is just around the corner, with its cornucopia of souvenir vendors; thankfully, sea lion–watching is still free.

A few blocks farther north is **Fisherman's Wharf,** at Pier 45. Bypass the wax museum and make a beeline for the fabulous vintage arcade **Musée Mécanique** (at the foot of Taylor Street). For crab- and bunny-shape sourdough loaves, stop by Boudin Bakery, just down Taylor on Jefferson.

Last Stop: Historic Vessels at the Hyde Street Pier

Follow the towering masts to the foot of Hyde Street and the collection of exquisitely restored ships there. Afterward, head up Hyde to the **cable-car turnaround,** where you can grab an Irish coffee at the **Buena Vista.**

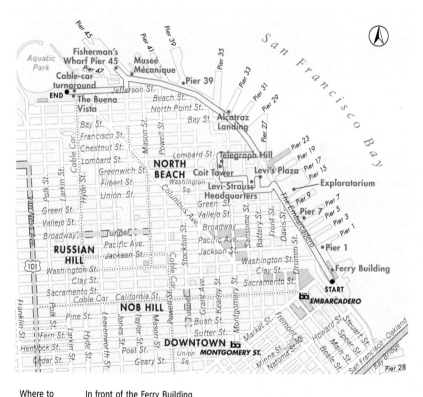

Where to Start:	In front of the Ferry Building.
Time/Length:	30–60 minutes at a moderate pace, without stops. With a picnic and park breaks, this walk could be a three-hour affair. The total distance is 2 miles.
Where to Stop:	At the cable-car turnaround or resting your feet at the Buena Vista.
Best Time to Go:	Sunny days are best for strolling the waterfront. Start off at the Ferry Building in the morning, ideally on a Saturday, when farmers' market stalls fill the plaza. The street-theater scene from Pier 39 to Fisherman's Wharf is liveliest on weekends, too.
Worst Time to Go:	Rain puts a huge damper on this walk, which is all about being outside. Weekends are bustling, but they can mean large crowds at the big-ticket attractions—Alcatraz and Fisherman's Wharf.
Getting Around:	If you're driving, park at the north end—it's much cheaper—and do the walk backward from north to south. Pedicabs will offer rides along the way, and the F-line is always available for the weary.

GREAT ITINERARIES

Compared to other major cities, San Francisco is quite a small town, with just a handful of major sights and museums. Much of the city's charm is in its neighborhoods, so look beyond the big names and explore the stairways and alleyways that are the heart of the city.

SAN FRANCISCO IN 1 DAY

Start your first day in **Union Square,** but don't be too early: the focus of this neighborhood is shopping, and most doors don't open until 10 am (11 am on Sundays). At the cable-car turnaround at Powell and Market Streets, hop aboard either line and ride over Nob Hill and into **Chinatown.** Browse the produce stalls and markets, peruse herb shops, and explore alleyways. Have your camera ready as you pass from Chinatown into **North Beach,** the old Italian quarter: Broadway looking down Columbus and Grant is one of the most interesting cultural intersections of the city. Walk Columbus Avenue—stopping for espresso, of course—then head toward Coit Tower up Filbert Street, which becomes the Filbert Steps, one of the city's many stairways. Keep your eyes—and ears—open for **Telegraph Hill** 's famous wild parrots. Take in the views at the top and the tower's WPA-era murals of California's history, then head back into North Beach for dinner or cocktails.

SAN FRANCISCO IN 2 DAYS

Day 1: Ferry Building, Alcatraz, and Fisherman's Wharf

Get up early and head to the gourmet marketplace at the **Ferry Building;** Saturday morning's picture-perfect farmers' market is the best time to visit. Gather provisions and head north along the Embarcadero to Pier 33, stopping to read the historical markers along the way. You should buy tickets to the next stop, **Alcatraz,** in advance since tours frequently sell out; plan to spend a few hours exploring the former prison island. Afterward, head north to **Pier 39,** where you can browse through the overpriced stores if you're on a kitschy-souvenir hunt. Otherwise, follow the barking to the sea lions basking just north of the pier. At **Fisherman's Wharf,** return to early-20th-century San Francisco at the delightful **Musée Mécanique,** then grab an Irish coffee at the Buena Vista. As tempting as it might be to dine on the water, most restaurants here have less-than-spectacular food. A better and cheaper option is to pick up some to-go Dungeness crabs from one of the outdoor vendors and eat as you stroll along the waterfront. Or hop on the Powell–Hyde or Powell–Mason cable-car line for better dining on Russian Hill or in North Beach, respectively.

Day 2: South of Market, Civic Center, Golden Gate Park, and Golden Gate Bridge

The spectacular San Francisco Museum of Modern Art (or SFMOMA, as it's known) reopened in 2016 after construction that made it the largest modern-art museum in the country and the true cultural anchor of the **South of Market** neighborhood. Check out the striking **Contemporary Jewish Museum** or the **Museum of the African Diaspora,** and then consider a short stop at the **California Historical Society.** Take a break in expansive **Yerba Buena Gardens,** then hop a beautifully restored vintage F-Line streetcar down Market Street to **Civic Center** and the superlative **Asian Art Museum.** Now head to the city's favorite green space: **Golden Gate Park.** Explore the park's eastern end, where you'll find the Conservatory of Flowers, the California Academy of Sciences, the de Young Museum, and the San Francisco Botanical Garden. In the afternoon head north to the **Golden Gate Bridge** (wear layers—that wind can be brutal!) for a quick photo op. The adventurous may choose to bike or even walk across the bridge to Sausalito (a 5- to 6-mile trip), a Mediterranean jewel of a small town. Have drinks along the boardwalk, then hop a ferry back to the city; be sure to check the schedule; the last ferry usually leaves before 7 pm.

SAN FRANCISCO IN 5 DAYS

Day 3: The Castro and the Mission

Ride the antique trolleys to the western end of the F-Line in the **Castro.** Stroll down Castro Street, under the giant rainbow flag and past the art-deco **Castro Theatre,** window-shopping and stopping at any café that might tempt you. You can go north to the **Haight** and see its beautiful Victorians while treasure hunting in the many vintage shops. Otherwise, head east on 18th Street to the **Mission** and **Dolores Park,** one of the city's favorite hangouts, then visit Mission Dolores and wander rows of centuries-old gravestones in the tiny cemetery. Be sure to hit the "Valencia Corridor" (Valencia Street between 16th and 20th Streets), dipping into independent bookstores, hipster cafés, and quirky shops. Don't miss the area's vibrant, often politically charged murals. Stay in the Mission for dinner and drinks; this is the city's best neighborhood for restaurants and watering holes.

Days 4 and 5: Other Neighborhoods

These lesser known areas can be visited in a day, or spread out over two days. In **Japantown,** visit the two-building Japan Center mall, with traditional Japanese restaurants, toy stores, and tea shops— the Kinokuniya Bookstore is a favorite. Contrast that with a visit to the J-Pop Center on Post Street, with funky shops that reflect modern Japanese pop culture. Head north on Fillmore and explore another world: swanky **Pacific Heights,** with its wineshops, high-end boutiques, and elegant home-decor stores. Cross Van Ness to Polk Street and see the transformation **Polk Gulch** is making, from gritty bars and doughnut shops to fancy lounges and unique stores. Continue north to **Russian Hill** and terraced Ina Coolbrith Park for broad vistas of the bay. Ascend the Vallejo Steps and you're within easy reach of the hill's best hidden lanes, including Macondray Lane. Continue north to zigzag down crooked Lombard Street. Finally, head back to Hyde Street for dinner at one of Russian Hill's trendy eateries.

If You Have More Time

With more than five days, you can begin to explore the Bay Area. Cross the bay to **Oakland** or **Berkeley** and check out Oakland's Chinatown or spend an afternoon scouting the university. Alternatively, you can head north from the city to majestic Muir Woods; if you've never seen the redwoods—the largest living things on earth—this is a must. World-famous Napa Valley or lower-key Sonoma Valley both merit an overnight stay.

FREE AND ALMOST FREE

Despite—or perhaps because of—the astronomical cost of living here, San Francisco offers loads of free diversions. Here are our picks for the best free things to do in the city, in alphabetical order. Also check out ⊕ *sf.funcheap.com* for a calendar of random, offbeat, and often free one-offs.

Free Museums and Galleries

■ Fort Point National Historic Site

■ Octagon House

■ San Francisco Cable Car Museum

■ San Francisco Railway Museum

■ Wells Fargo History Museum

Free Museum Times

The first week of every month brings a bonanza of free museum times.

■ Asian Art Museum, first Sunday of every month

■ Chinese Historical Society of America, first Sunday of every month

■ Contemporary Jewish Museum, first Tuesday of every month

■ de Young Museum, first Tuesday of every month

■ Legion of Honor, first Tuesday of every month

■ Yerba Buena Center for the Arts (galleries), first Tuesday of every month

Free Concerts

■ The Golden Gate Park Band plays free public concerts on Sunday afternoon, April through October, on the Music Concourse in the namesake park.

■ Stern Grove Festival concerts, held on Sunday afternoon from June through August, ranging from opera to jazz to pop music. The amphitheater is in a beautiful eucalyptus grove, so come early and picnic before the show.

■ Yerba Buena Gardens Festival hosts many concerts and performances from May through October, including Latin jazz, global music, dance, and even puppet shows.

Free Tours

■ The free San Francisco City Guides walking tours are easily one of the best deals going. Knowledgeable, enthusiastic guides lead walks that focus on a particular neighborhood, theme, or historical period, like Victorian architecture in Alamo Square or the bawdy days of the Barbary Coast.

■ City Hall offers free tours of its grandiose HQ on weekdays.

More Great Experiences for $7 or Less

■ See some baseball at AT&T Park, for free! Go to the stadium's Portwalk, beyond the outfield wall, and you'll have a standing-room view of the game through the open fence.

■ Do your own walking tour of the Mission District's fantastic outdoor murals, then grab a bite at a taqueria or food truck.

■ Choose a perfect treat at the Ferry Building's fabulous marketplace—maybe a scoop of Ciao Bella gelato or a croissant from Miette—and stroll the waterfront promenade.

■ Hike up to the top of Telegraph Hill for sweeping city and bay views.

SAN FRANCISCO'S CABLE CARS

The moment it dawns on you that you severely underestimated the steepness of the San Francisco hills will likely be the same moment you look down and realize those tracks aren't just for show—or just for tourists.

Sure, locals rarely use the cable cars for commuting these days. (That's partially due to the $7 fare—hear that, Muni?) So you'll likely be packed in with plenty of fellow sightseers. You may even be approaching cable-car fatigue after seeing its image on so many souvenirs. But if you fear the magic is gone, simply climb on board, and those jaded thoughts will dissolve. Grab the pole and gawk at the view as the car clanks down an insanely steep grade toward the bay. Listen to the humming cable, the clang of the bell, and the occasional quip from the gripman. It's an experience you shouldn't pass up, whether on your first trip or your fiftieth.

HOW CABLE CARS WORK

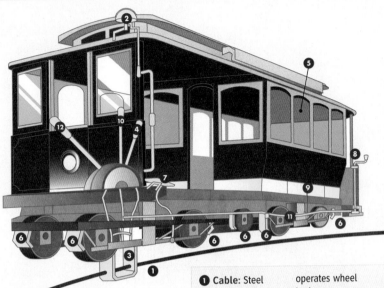

The mechanics are pretty simple: cable cars grab a moving subterranean cable with a "grip" to go. To stop, they release the grip and apply one or more types of brakes. Four cables, totaling 9 miles, power the city's three lines. If the gripman doesn't adjust the grip just right when going up a steep hill, the cable will start to slip and the car will have to back down the hill and try again. This is an extremely rare occurrence—imagine the ribbing the gripman gets back at the cable car barn!

Gripman: Stands in front and operates the grip, brakes, and bell. Favorite joke, especially at the peak of a steep hill: "This is my first day on the job folks..."

Conductor: Moves around the car, deals with tickets, alerts the grip about what's coming up, and operates the rear wheel brakes.

❶ Cable: Steel wrapped around flexible sisal core; 2 inches thick; runs at a constant 9½ mph.

❷ Bells: Used for crew communication; alerts other drivers and pedestrians.

❸ Grip: Vice-like lever extends through the center slot in the track to grab or release the cable.

❹ Grip Lever: Left-hand lever; operates grip.

❺ Car: Entire car weighs 8 tons.

❻ Wheel Brake: Steel brake pads on each wheel.

❼ Wheel Brake Lever: Foot pedal; operates wheel brakes.

❽ Rear Wheel Brake Lever: Applied for extra traction on hills.

❾ Track Brake: 2-foot-long sections of Monterey pine push down against the track to help stop the car.

❿ Track Brake Lever: Middle lever; operates track brakes.

⓫ Emergency Brake: 18-inch steel wedge, jams into street slot to bring car to an immediate stop.

⓬ Emergency Brake Lever: Right-hand lever, red; operates emergency brake.

ROUTES

Powell–Hyde line: Most scenic, with classic Bay views. Begins at Powell and Market streets, then crosses Nob Hill and Russian Hill before a white-knuckle descent down Hyde Street, ending near the Hyde Street Pier.

Powell–Mason line: Also begins at Powell and Market streets, but winds through North Beach to Bay and Taylor streets, a few blocks from Fisherman's Wharf.

California line: Runs from the foot of Market Street, at Drumm Street, up Nob Hill and back. Great views (and aromas and sounds) of Chinatown on the way up. Sit in back to catch glimpses of the Bay. ■TIP→ Take the California line if it's just the cable-car experience you're after—the lines are shorter, and the grips and conductors say it's friendlier and has a slower pace.

Cars run at least every 15 minutes, from around 6 AM to about 1 AM.

RULES OF THE RIDE

Tickets. There are ticket booths at all three turnarounds, or you can pay the conductor after you board (they can make change). Try not to grumble about the price—they're embarrassed enough as it is.

■TIP→ If you're planning to use public transit a few times, or if you'd like to ride back and forth on the cable car without worrying about the price, consider a one-day Muni passport. You can get passports online, at the Powell Street turnaround, the TIX booth on Union Square, or the Fisherman's Wharf cable-car ticket booth at Beach and Hyde streets.

All Aboard. You can board on either side of the cable car. It's legal to stand on the running boards and hang on to the pole, but keep your ears open for the gripman's warnings. ■TIP→ Grab a seat on the outside bench for the best views.

Most people wait (and wait) in line at one of the cable car turnarounds, but you can also hop on along the route. Board wherever you see a white sign showing a figure climbing aboard a brown cable car; wave to the approaching driver, and wait until the car stops.

Riding on the running boards can be part of the thrill.

CABLE CAR HISTORY

HALLIDIE FREES THE HORSES

In the 1850s and '60s, San Francisco's streetcars were drawn by horses. Legend has it that the horrible sight of a car dragging a team of horses downhill to their deaths roused Andrew Smith Hallidie to action. The English immigrant had invented the "Hallidie Ropeway," essentially a cable car for mined ore, and he was convinced that his invention could also move people. In 1873, Hallidie and his intrepid crew prepared to test the first cable car high on Russian Hill. The anxious engineer peered down into the foggy darkness, failed to see the bottom of the hill, and promptly turned the controls over to Hallidie. Needless to say, the thing worked . . . but rides were free for the first two days because people were afraid to get on.

SEE IT FOR YOURSELF

The **Cable Car Museum** is one of the city's best free offerings and an absolute must for kids. (You can even ride a cable car there, since all three lines stop between Russian Hill and Nob Hill.) The museum, which is inside the city's last cable-car barn, takes the top off the system to let you see how it all works. Eternally humming and squealing, the massive powerhouse cable wheels steal the show. You can also climb aboard a vintage car and take the grip, let the kids ring a cable-car bell (briefly, please!), and check out vintage gear dating from 1873.

■ TIP → The gift shop sells cable car paraphernalia, including an authentic gripman's bell for $600 (it'll sound like Powell Street in your house every day). For significantly less, you can pick up a key chain made from a piece of worn-out cable.

CHAMPION OF THE CABLE CAR BELL

Each September the city's best and brightest come together to crown a bell-ringing champion at Union Square. The crowd cheers gripmen and conductors as they stomp, shake, and riff with the rope. But it's not a popularity contest; the ringers are judged by former bell-ringing champions who take each ping and gong very seriously.

UNION SQUARE
AND CHINATOWN

Getting Oriented

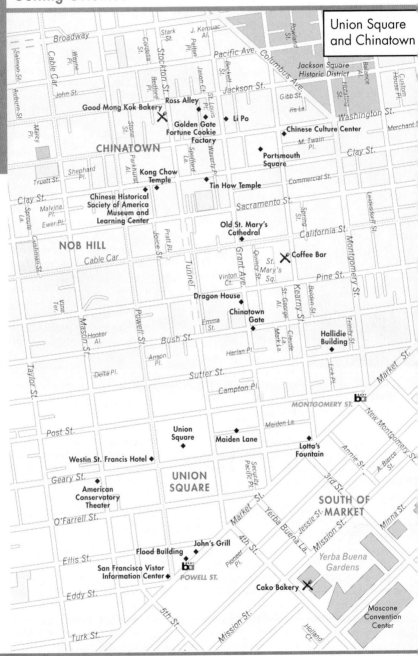

Union Square
and Chinatown

Broadway

Stark St.

J. Kerouac Al.

Rowland St.

Pacific Ave.

Columbus Ave.

Jackson Square
Historic District

Custom
House Pl.

Cable Car

Wayne Pl.

Cordelia St.

Stockton St.

Jason Ct.

Pelton Pl.

Beckett St.

Balance Al.

Hotaling St.

Salmon St.

Auburn St.

John St.

Bedford Pl.

Jackson St.

Gibb St.

Merchant.

Good Mong Kok Bakery

Ross Alley

St. Louis Pl.

Hs La.

Washington St.

Marcy Pl.

Stone St.

✗

Li Po

Golden Gate
Fortune Cookie
Factory

Chinese Culture Center

CHINATOWN

Waverly Pl.

Spofford La.

Portsmouth
Square

M. Twain Pl.

Clay St.

Truett St.

Shephard Pl.

Parkhurst Al.

Kong Chow
Temple

Tin How Temple

Commercial St.

Clay St.

Sproule La.

Malvina Pl.

Ewer Pl.

Cushman St.

Chinese Historical
Society of America
Museum and
Learning Center

Sacramento St.

Spring St.

Leidesdorff St.

NOB HILL

Joice St.

Old St. Mary's
Cathedral

California St.

Montgomery St.

Cable Car

Pratt Pl.

Grant Ave.

Quincy St.

St. Mary's Sq.

✗ Coffee Bar

Tunnel

Vinton Ct.

Pine St.

Vine Ter.

Mason St.

Powell St.

Hooker Al.

Dragon House

Emma St.

Chinatown
Gate

St. George Al.

Kearny St.

Belden St.

Trinity St.

Hallidie
Building

Taylor St.

Bush St.

Anson Pl.

Harlan Pl.

Claude La.

Mark La.

Lick Pl.

Market St.

Delta Pl.

Sutter St.

Campton Pl.

MONTGOMERY ST. 🚇

New Montgomery St.

Post St.

Union
Square

Maiden La.

Maiden Lane

Lotta's
Fountain

Annie St.

A. Bierce St.

Westin St. Francis Hotel ◆

Geary St.

American
Conservatory
Theater

**UNION
SQUARE**

Security Pacific Pl.

3rd St.

**SOUTH OF
MARKET**

Minna St.

O'Farrell St.

Market St.

Yerba Buena La.

Jessie St.

Mission St.

Ellis St.

John's Grill

4th St.

Flood Building

San Francisco Vistor
Information Center ◆

🚇

POWELL ST.

Pioneer Pl.

*Yerba Buena
Gardens*

Eddy St.

Cako Bakery ✗

Moscone
Convention
Center

5th St.

Mission St.

Holland Ct.

Turk St.

TOP REASONS TO GO

Ross Alley, Chinatown: Breathe in the scented air as you watch the nimble hands at Golden Gate Fortune Cookie Factory, then kick back with a cocktail at Li Po around the corner, rumored to be haunted by the ghost of an opium junkie still looking to score.

Return to noir San Francisco: Have a late martini lunch under the gaze of the Maltese Falcon at John's Grill, then swing through the lobby of the Flood Building and nod to the other Maltese Falcon there.

Shop the square: Prime your credit cards and dive right in, from Bloomie's to the boutiques of Maiden Lane.

Tin How Temple: Climb the narrow stairway to this space with hundreds of red lanterns, then step onto the tiny balcony and take in the alley scene below.

Elevator at the St. Francis: Ride a glass elevator to the sky (or the 32nd floor) for a gorgeous view of the cityscape, especially in the evening when the lights come up.

QUICK BITES

Cako Bakery. Only the hardiest souls pass by Cako without succumbing to the siren call of the perfect cupcake. ⊠ *211 O'Farrell St., Union Sq.* ☎ *415/404–7303* ⊕ *www.cako.com* ▭ *No credit cards.*

Coffee Bar. When you need some seriously good local roast, head to this tiny storefront in St. Mary's Square Garage. ⊠ *433 Kearny St., between Pine and California Sts., Chinatown* ☎ *415/795–1214* ⊕ *www.coffeebarsf.com.*

Good Mong Kok Bakery. You'll feel like a local at this line-around-the-corner, cash-only, no-English-spoken bakery. The delicious dim sum is strictly to-go, so picnic a block west at Woh Hei Yuen Park on Powell Street. ⊠ *1039 Stockton St., near Jackson St., Chinatown* ☎ *415/397–2688* ▭ *No credit cards.*

GETTING THERE

In these two neighborhoods, cars equal hassle. Traffic is slow and parking is pricey. Save yourself the frustration and take advantage of the confluence of public transit at Powell and Market Streets: buses, Muni light-rail vehicles (Powell Street Station for both), cable cars, and F-line streetcars run here.

For the love of Buddha, don't drive in Chinatown! The steep, narrow, one-way streets are difficult to navigate by car. It's an easy walk from Union Square, and both Powell lines of the cable-car system pass through. You can also take the 30–Stockton bus; this route is a virtual "Chinatown Express," running from Fisherman's Wharf down Stockton Street through Chinatown to Union Square.

PLANNING YOUR TIME

Set aside at least an hour to scope out the stores and sights in and around Union Square—or most of the day if you're a shopper—but don't bother arriving before 10 am, when the first shops open. Sunday is a bit quieter.

Give yourself at least two hours to tour compact Chinatown. If possible, come on a weekday (it's less crowded) and before lunchtime (busiest with locals). You won't need more than 15 or 20 minutes at any of the sights themselves, but exploring the shops and alleys is, indeed, the whole point.

Sightseeing
★★★
Nightlife
★
Dining
★★★
Lodging
★★★★★
Shopping
★★★★★

The Union Square area bristles with big-city bravado, while just a stone's throw away is a place that feels like a city unto itself, Chinatown. The two areas share a strong commercial streak, although manifested very differently. In Union Square—a plaza but also the neighborhood around it—the crowds zigzag among international brands, trailing glossy shopping bags. A few blocks north, people dash between small neighborhood stores, their arms draped with plastic totes filled with groceries or souvenirs.

UNION SQUARE

Updated by
Denise M. Leto

The city's finest department stores put on their best faces in Union Square, along with such exclusive emporiums as Tiffany & Co. and Bulgari, and such big-name franchises as Nike, the Apple Store, H&M, Barney's, and Uniqlo. Visitors lay their heads at several dozen hotels within a three-block walk of the square, and the downtown theater district is nearby. Union Square is shopping-centric; nonshoppers will find fewer enticements here.

TOP ATTRACTIONS

Maiden Lane. Known as Morton Street in the raffish Barbary Coast era, this former red-light district reported at least one murder a week during the late 19th century. Things cooled down after the 1906 fire destroyed the brothels, and these days Maiden Lane is a chic, boutique-lined pedestrian mall (favored by brides-to-be) stretching two blocks, between Stockton and Kearny Streets. Wrought-iron gates close the street to traffic most days between 11 and 5, when the lane becomes a patchwork of umbrella-shaded tables. At **140 Maiden Lane** is the only Frank Lloyd Wright building in San Francisco, fronted by a large brick archway. The graceful, curving ramp and skylights of the interior are said to have been his model for the Guggenheim Museum in New York. ⊠ *Between Stockton and Kearny Sts., Union Sq.*

Union Square. Ground zero for big-name shopping in the city and within walking distance of many hotels, Union Square is home base for many visitors. The Westin St. Francis Hotel and Macy's line two of the square's sides, and Saks, Neiman-Marcus, and Tiffany & Co. edge the other two. Four globular lamp sculptures by the artist R. M. Fischer preside over the landscaped, 2½-acre park, which has a café with outdoor seating, an open-air stage, and a visitor-information booth—along with a

> ## SAN FRANCISCO'S FANTASY FOUNTAIN
>
> In front of the Grand Hyatt hotel at 345 Stockton Street gurgles an intricate bronze fountain depicting San Francisco. It's one of many local public works by Ruth Asawa, the city's "fountain lady." Look closely at this one and you can find an amorous couple behind one of the Victorian bay windows.

familiar kaleidoscope of characters: office workers sunning and brown-bagging, street musicians, shoppers taking a rest, kids chasing pigeons, and a fair number of homeless people. The constant clang of cable cars traveling up and down Powell Street helps maintain a festive mood.

The heart of San Francisco's downtown since 1850, the square takes its name from the violent pro-Union demonstrations staged here before the Civil War. At center stage, Robert Ingersoll Aitken's *Victory Monument* commemorates Commodore George Dewey's victory over the Spanish fleet at Manila in 1898. The 97-foot Corinthian column, topped by a bronze figure symbolizing naval conquest, was dedicated by Theodore Roosevelt in 1903 and withstood the 1906 earthquake. After the earthquake and fire of 1906, the square was dubbed "Little St. Francis" because of the temporary shelter erected for residents of the St. Francis Hotel. Actor John Barrymore (grandfather of actress Drew Barrymore and a notorious carouser) was among the guests pressed into volunteering to stack bricks in the square. His uncle, thespian John Drew, remarked, "It took an act of God to get John out of bed and the United States Army to get him to work." ✉ *Bordered by Powell, Stockton, Post, and Geary Sts., Union Sq.*

WORTH NOTING

American Conservatory Theater (*A.C.T.*). Celebrated local architects Bliss and Faville, also responsible for the nearby St. Francis Hotel, designed the neoclassical home of San Francisco's premier repertory theater company. The 1910 structure, which replaced one destroyed in the 1906 earthquake, sustained heavy damage in the 1989 quake but was beautifully restored. A.C.T. is renowned for productions by playwrights such as Tony Kushner (*Angels in America*) and company favorite Tom Stoppard (*The Invention of Love* and *Indian Ink* premiered here), and cutting-edge works such as *The Black Rider* by Tom Waits, William S. Burroughs, and Robert Wilson. ✉ *415 Geary St., box office at 405 Geary St., Union Sq.* ☎ *415/749–2228* ⊕ *www.act-sf.org.*

Hallidie Building. Named for cable-car inventor Andrew S. Hallidie, this 1918 structure is best viewed from across the street. Willis Polk's revolutionary glass-curtain wall—believed to be the world's first such

Union Square is the city's epicenter of high-end shopping.

facade—hangs a foot beyond the reinforced concrete of the frame. The reflecting glass, decorative exterior fire escapes that appear to be metal balconies, and Venetian Gothic cornice are notably lovely. ⊠ *130 Sutter St., between Kearny and Montgomery Sts., Union Sq.*

Lotta's Fountain. Saucy gold rush–era actress, singer, and dancer Lotta Crabtree so aroused the city's miners that they were known to shower her with gold nuggets and silver dollars after her performances. The peculiar, rather clunky fountain was her way of saying thanks to her fans. Given to the city in 1875, the fountain became a meeting place for survivors after the 1906 earthquake. Each April 18, the anniversary of the quake, San Franciscans gather at this quirky monument. An image of redheaded Lotta herself, in a very pink, rather risqué dress, appears in one of the Anton Refregier murals in Rincon Center. ⊠ *Traffic triangle at intersection of 3rd, Market, Kearny, and Geary Sts., Union Sq.*

San Francisco Visitor Information Center. Head downstairs from the cable-car terminus to the visitor center, where multilingual staffers answer questions and provide maps and pamphlets. Muni Passports are sold here, and you can pick up discount coupons—the savings can be significant, especially for families. If you're planning to hit the big-ticket stops like the California Academy of Sciences and the Exploratorium and ride the cable cars, consider purchasing a CityPass (*www. citypass.com/san-francisco*) here. ■TIP→ **The CityPass ($94, $69 ages 5–11), good for nine days, including seven days of transit, will save you 50%.** The pass is also available at the attractions it covers, though if you choose the pass that includes Alcatraz—an excellent deal— you'll have to buy it directly from Alcatraz Cruises. ⊠ *Hallidie Plaza,* *lower level, 900 Market St., at Market and Powell Sts., Union Sq.* ☎ *415/391–2000,* ⊕ *www.sftravel. com* ☯ *Closed Sun. Nov.–Apr.*

Westin St. Francis Hotel. Built in 1904 and barely established as the most sumptuous hotel in town before it was ravaged by fire following the 1906 earthquake, this grande-dame hotel designed by Walter Danforth Bliss and William Baker Faville reopened in 1907 with the addition of a luxurious Italian Renaissance–style residence designed to attract loyal clients from among the world's rich and powerful. The hotel's checkered past includes the ill-fated 1921 bash in the suite of the silent-film superstar Fatty Arbuckle, at which a woman became ill and later died. Arbuckle endured three sensational trials for rape and murder before being acquitted, by which time his career was kaput. In 1975, Sara Jane Moore, standing among a crowd outside the hotel, attempted to shoot then-president Gerald Ford. Of course the grand lobby contains no plaques commemorating these events. ■TIP→ **Some visitors make the St. Francis a stop whenever they're in town, soaking up the lobby ambience or enjoying a cocktail in Clock Bar or a meal at the Oak Room Restaurant.** ⊠ *335 Powell St., at Geary St., Union Sq.* ☎ *415/397–7000* ⊕ *westinstfrancis.com.*

CHINATOWN

A few blocks uphill from Union Square is the abrupt beginning of dense and insular Chinatown—the oldest such community in the country. When the street signs have Chinese characters, produce stalls crowd pedestrians off the sidewalk, and whole roast ducks hang in deli windows, you'll know you've arrived. (The neighborhood huddles together in the 17 blocks and 41 alleys bordered roughly by Bush, Kearny, and Powell Streets and Broadway.) Chinatown has been attracting the curious for more than 100 years, and no other neighborhood in the city absorbs as many tourists without seeming to forfeit its character. Join the flow and step into another world. Good-luck banners of crimson and gold hang beside dragon-entwined lampposts and pagoda roofs, while honking cars chime in with shoppers bargaining loudly in Cantonese or Mandarin.

TOP ATTRACTIONS

Chinatown Gate. This is the official entrance to Chinatown. Stone lions flank the base of the pagoda-topped gate; the lions, dragons, and fish up top symbolize wealth, prosperity, and other good things. The four Chinese characters immediately beneath the pagoda represent the philosophy of Sun Yat-sen (1866–1925), the leader who unified China in the early 20th century. Sun Yat-sen, who lived in exile in San Francisco

Locals snap up flowers from an outdoor vendor in Chinatown.

for a few years, promoted the notion of friendship and peace among all nations based on equality, justice, and goodwill. The vertical characters under the left pagoda read "peace" and "trust," the ones under the right pagoda "respect" and "love." The whole shebang telegraphs the internationally understood message of "photo op." Immediately beyond the gate, dive into souvenir shopping on Grant Avenue, Chinatown's tourist strip. ⊠ *Grant Ave. at Bush St., Chinatown.*

Dragon House. A veritable museum, the store sells authentic, centuries-old antiques like ivory carvings and jade figures (including a naughty statue or two). ⊠ *455 Grant Ave., Chinatown* ☎ *415/421–3693.*

Fodor's Choice
★
Tin How Temple. Duck into the inconspicuous doorway, climb three flights of stairs, and be assaulted by the aroma of incense in this tiny, altar-filled room. In 1852, Day Ju, one of the first three Chinese to arrive in San Francisco, dedicated this temple to the Queen of the Heavens and the Goddess of the Seven Seas, and the temple looks largely the same today as it did more than a century ago. In the entry-way, elderly ladies can often be seen preparing "money" to be burned as offerings to various Buddhist gods or as funds for ancestors to use in the afterlife. Hundreds of red-and-gold lanterns cover the ceiling; the larger the lamp, the larger its donor's contribution to the temple. Gifts of oranges, dim sum, and money left by the faithful, who kneel mumbling prayers, rest on altars to different gods. Tin How presides over the middle back of the temple, flanked by one red and one green lesser god. Take a good look around, since taking photographs is not allowed. ⊠ *125 Waverly Pl., between Clay and Washington Sts., Chinatown* ☒ *Free, donations accepted.*

Continued on page 45

CHINATOWN

Chinatown's streets flood the senses. Incense and cigarette smoke mingle with the scents of briny fish and sweet vanilla. Rooflines flare outward, pagoda-style. Loud Cantonese bargaining and honking car horns rise above the sharp clack of mah-jongg tiles and the eternally humming cables beneath the street.

Most Chinatown visitors march down Grant Avenue, buy a few trinkets, and call it a day. Do yourself a favor and dig deeper. This is one of the largest Chinese communities outside Asia, and there is far more to it than buying a back-scratcher near Chinatown Gate. To get a real feel for the neighborhood, wander off the main drag. Step into a temple or an herb shop and wander down a flag-draped alley. And don't be shy: residents welcome guests warmly, though rarely in English.

Whatever you do, don't leave without eating something. Noodle houses, bakeries, tea houses, and dim sum shops seem to occupy every other storefront. There's a feast for your eyes as well: in the market windows on Stockton and Grant, you'll see hanging whole roast ducks, fish, and shellfish swimming in tanks, and strips of shiny, pink-glazed Chinese-style barbecued pork.

CHINATOWN'S HISTORY

Sam Brannan's 1848 cry of "Gold!" didn't take long to reach across the world to China. Struggling with famine, drought, and political upheaval at home, thousands of Chinese jumped at the chance to try their luck in California. Most came from the Pearl River Delta region, in the Guangdong province, and spoke Cantonese dialects. From the start, Chinese businesses circled around Portsmouth Square, which was conveniently central. Bachelor rooming houses sprang up, since the vast majority of new arrivals were men. By 1853, the area was called Chinatown.

The Street of Gamblers (Ross Alley), 1898 (top). The first Chinese telephone operator in Chinatown (bottom).

COLD WELCOME

The Chinese faced discrimination from the get-go. Harrassment became outright hostility as first the gold rush, then the work on the Transcontinental Railroad petered out. Special taxes were imposed to shoulder aside competing "coolie labor." Laws forbidding the Chinese from moving outside Chinatown kept the residents packed in like sardines, with nowhere to go but up and down—thus the many basement establishments in the neighborhood. State and federal laws passed in the 1870s deterred Chinese women from immigrating, deeming them prostitutes. In the late 1870s, looting and arson attacks on Chinatown businesses soared.

The coup de grace, though, was the Chinese Exclusion Act, passed by the U.S.

Chinatown's Grant Avenue.

Women and children flooded into the neighborhood after the Great Quake.

Congress in 1882, which slammed the doors to America for "Asiatics." This was the country's first significant restriction on immigration. The law also prevented the existing Chinese residents, including American-born children, from becoming naturalized citizens. With a society of mostly men (forbidden, of course, from marrying white women), San Francisco hoped that Chinatown would simply die out.

OUT OF THE ASHES

When the devastating 1906 earthquake and fire hit, city fathers thought they'd seize the opportunity to kick the Chinese out of Chinatown and get their hands on that desirable piece of downtown real estate. Then Chinatown businessman Look Tin Eli had a brainstorm of Disneyesque proportions.

He proposed that Chinatown be rebuilt, but in a tourist-friendly, stylized, "Oriental" way. Anglo-American architects would design new buildings with pagoda roofs and dragon-covered columns. Chinatown would attract more tourists—the curious had been visiting on the sly for decades—and add more tax money to the city's coffers. Ka-ching: the sales pitch worked.

PAPER SONS

For the Chinese, the 1906 earthquake turned the virtual "no entry" sign into a flashing neon "welcome!" All the city's immigration records went up in smoke, and the Chinese quickly began to apply for passports as U.S. citizens, claiming their old ones were lost in the fire. Not only did thousands of Chinese become legal overnight, but so did their sons in China, or "sons," if they weren't really related. Whole families in Chinatown had passports in names that weren't their own; these "paper sons" were not only a windfall but also an uncomfortable neighborhood conspiracy. The city caught on eventually and set up an immigration center on Angel Island in 1910. Immigrants spent weeks or months being inspected and interrogated while their papers were checked. Roughly 250,000 people made it through. With this influx, including women and children, Chinatown finally became a more complete community.

A GREAT WALK THROUGH CHINATOWN

■ Start at the Chinatown Gate and walk ahead on Grant Avenue, entering the souvenir gauntlet. (You'll also pass Old St. Mary's Cathedral.)

■ Make a right on Clay Street and walk to Portsmouth Square. Sometimes it feels like the whole neighborhood's here, playing chess and exercising.

■ Head up Washington Street to the Old Chinese Telephone Exchange building, now the EastWest Bank. Across Grant, look left for Waverly Place. Here Free Republic of China (Taiwanese) flags flap over some of the neighborhood's most striking buildings, including Tin How Temple.

■ At the Sacramento Street end of Waverly Place stands the First Chinese Baptist Church of 1908. Just across the way, the Clarion Music Center is full of unusual instruments, as well as exquisite lion-dance sets.

■ Head back to Washington Street and check out the many herb shops.

■ Follow the scent of vanilla down Ross Alley (entrance across from Superior Trading Company) to the Golden Gate Fortune Cookie Factory. Then head across the alley to Sam Bo Trading Co., where religious

items are stacked in the narrow space. Tell the owners your troubles and they'll prepare a package of joss papers, joss sticks, and candles, and tell you how and when to offer them up.

■ Turn left on Jackson Street; ahead is the real Chinatown's main artery, Stockton Street, where most residents do their

grocery shopping. Vegetarians will want to avoid Luen Fat Market (No. 1135), with tanks of live frogs, turtles, and lobster as well as chickens and ducks. Look toward the back of stores for Buddhist altars with offerings of oranges and grapefruit. From here you can loop one block east back to Grant.

WORTH NOTING

Chinese Culture Center. Chiefly a place for the community to gather for calligraphy and Mandarin classes, the center operates a gallery with occasionally interesting temporary exhibits by Chinese and Chinese-American artists. Excellent two-hour walking tours of Chinatown depart from the gallery on Thursdays, Fridays, and Saturdays; call the center or visit its website for details. ⊠ *Hilton Hotel, 750 Kearny St., 3rd fl., Chinatown* ☎ *415/986–1822* ⊕ *www.c-c-c.org* ⬚ *Center and gallery free ($5 suggested donation), tour $30* ⊙ *Closed Sun.*

Chinese Historical Society of America Museum and Learning Center. The displays at this small, light-filled gallery document the Chinese-American experience—from 19th-century agriculture to 21st-century food and fashion trends—and include a thought-provoking collection of racist games and toys. The facility also has temporary exhibits of works by contemporary Chinese-American artists. ⊠ *965 Clay St., between Stockton and Powell Sts., Chinatown* ☎ *415/391–1188* ⊕ *www.chsa. org* ⬚ *$15, free 1st Sun. of month* ⊙ *Closed Mon.*

FAMILY **Golden Gate Fortune Cookie Factory.** Follow your nose down Ross Alley to this tiny but fragrant cookie factory. Two workers sit at circular motorized griddles and wait for dollops of batter to drop onto a tiny metal plate, which rotates into an oven. A few moments later out comes a cookie that's pliable and ready for folding. It's easy to peek in for a moment, and hard to leave without a few free samples. A bagful of cookies—with mildly racy "adult" fortunes or more benign ones—costs under $5. ⊠ *56 Ross Alley, off Washington or Jackson St. west of Grant Ave., Chinatown* ☎ *415/781–3956* ⬚ *Free.*

Kong Chow Temple. This ornate temple sets a somber, spiritual tone right away with a sign warning visitors not to touch *anything.* The god to whom the members of this temple pray represents honesty and trust. Chinese stores and restaurants often display his image because he's thought to bring good luck in business. Chinese immigrants established the temple in 1851; its congregation moved to this building in 1977. Take the elevator up to the fourth floor, where incense fills the air. You can show respect by placing a dollar or two in the donation box and by leaving your phone stowed. Amid the statuary, flowers, and richly colored altars (red wards off evil spirits and signifies virility, green symbolizes longevity, and gold connotes majesty), a couple of plaques announce that "Mrs. Harry S. Truman came to this temple in June 1948 for a prediction on the outcome of the election … this fortune came true." ■ TIP→ **The temple's balcony has a good view of Chinatown.** ⊠ *855 Stockton St., 4th fl., Chinatown* ☎ *415/788–1339* ⬚ *Free.*

Old St. Mary's Cathedral. Dedicated in 1854, this served as the city's Catholic cathedral until 1891. The verse below the massive clock face beseeched naughty Barbary Coast boys: "Son, observe the time and fly from evil." Across the street from the church in **St. Mary's Square,** a statue of Sun Yat-sen towers over the site of the Chinese leader's favorite reading spot during his years in San Francisco. ■ TIP→ **A surprisingly peaceful spot, St. Mary's Square also has a**

couple of small, well-kept playgrounds, perfect for a break from the hustle and bustle of Chinatown. ⊠ *660 California St., at Grant Ave., Chinatown* ⊕ *oldsaintmarys.org.*

Portsmouth Square. Chinatown's living room buzzes with activity. The square, with its pagoda-shape structures, is a favorite spot for morning tai chi; by noon dozens of men huddle around Chinese chess tables, engaged in competition. Kids scamper about the square's two grungy playgrounds (warning: the bathrooms are sketchy). Back in the late 19th century this land was near the waterfront. The square is named for the USS *Portsmouth*, the ship helmed by Captain John Montgomery, who in 1846 raised the American flag here and claimed the then-Mexican land for the United States. A couple of years later, Sam Brannan kicked off the gold rush at the square when he waved his loot and proclaimed, "Gold from the American River!" Robert Louis Stevenson, the author of *Treasure Island,* often dropped by, chatting up the sailors who hung out here. Some of the information he gleaned about life at sea found its way into his fiction. A bronze galleon sculpture, a tribute to Stevenson, anchors the square's northwest corner. A plaque marks the site of California's first public school, built in 1847. ⊠ *Bordered by Walter Lum Pl. and Kearny, Washington, and Clay Sts., Chinatown.*

3

SOMA AND
CIVIC CENTER

with the Tenderloin and Hayes Valley

Getting Oriented

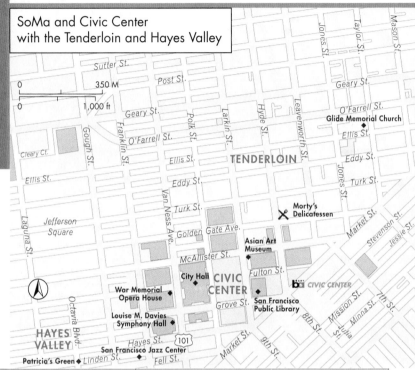

SoMa and Civic Center
with the Tenderloin and Hayes Valley

GETTING THERE	QUICK BITES
For most SoMa visitors who stick close to the area around Yerba Buena Gardens and the Moscone Center, getting here is a matter of walking roughly 10 minutes from Union Square, less from Market Street transit. It's best to reach the Civic Center by Muni light rail, bus, or F-line. Hoofing it from Union Square requires walking through the unsavory Tenderloin area, and from SoMa it's a long, ugly haul. After dark, safety concerns dictate a cab for both of these neighborhoods.	**Blue Bottle Coffee.** If you're in Hayes Valley and see a clutch of people gathered around what looks like a garage, you've stumbled upon the original kiosk of Blue Bottle Coffee; the company's "artisanal microroasting" philosophy holds that coffee should be brewed within 24 hours of roasting. ✉ *315 Linden St., at Gough St., Hayes Valley* ☎ *415/252–7535* ⊕ *bluebottlecoffee.com.* **Morty's Delicatessen.** The sandwiches and salads are piled high, the folks are friendly, and vegetarians have reasonable options at this super-casual spot on the edge of the Tenderloin. ✉ *280 Golden Gate Ave., at Hyde St., Civic Center* ☎ *415/567–3354* ⊕ *www.mortysdeli.com* ☾ *Closed Sun.* **Samovar Tea Lounge.** Above the Martin Luther King Jr. memorial in the Yerba Buena Gardens, the lounge is a serene retreat with glass walls overlooking an infinity pool. Especially on a blustery day, the organic and fair-trade teas hit the spot. ✉ *730 Howard St., at 4th St., SoMa* ☎ *415/227–9400* ⊕ *www.samovarlife.com.*

KEY

bⓐ *BART station*

Systems
mural

TOP REASONS TO GO

SFMOMA: Explore the vast trove of modern masterpieces at this newly expanded museum, the country's largest dedicated to modern art.

Asian Art Museum: Stand face-to-face with a massive gold Buddha in one of the world's largest collections of Asian art.

Club-hopping in SoMa: Shake it with the cool, friendly crowd that fills SoMa's dance clubs until the wee hours, and all weekend long at the EndUp.

Yerba Buena Gardens: Gather picnic provisions and choose a spot on the grass in downtown's oasis.

Hanging out at Patricia's Green: Grab a cup of coffee or an ice cream—Blue Bottle and Smitten Ice Cream are just around the corner—and head to the narrow swath of park that serves as hopping Hayes Valley's living room.

San Francisco Jazz Center: Experience the amazing acoustics at Hayes Valley's intimate temple to jazz.

PLANNING YOUR TIME

You could spend all day museum-hopping in SoMa. Allow at least two hours for gigantic SFMOMA. An hour each should do it for the Museum of the African Diaspora, the Contemporary Jewish Museum, and the Center for the Arts, a little less than that for the smaller museums.

SoMa after dark is another adventure entirely. More interested in Merlot or megaclubs than Matisse? Start here around 8 pm for dinner, then move on to a bar or dance spot. *See Where to Eat and Nightlife for our top recommendations.*

Plan on spending at least two hours at the Asian Art Museum and no more than a half hour at City Hall. Except for these two mainstays, you'll have little reason to visit the Civic Center area unless you have tickets to the opera, symphony, or other cultural event. Hayes Valley and its shops and boutiques merit a leisurely one-hour look-see.

Sightseeing
★★★
Nightlife
★★★★
Dining
★★★
Lodging
★★★★
Shopping
★

To a newcomer, SoMa (short for "south of Market") and the Civic Center may look like cheek-by-jowl neighbors— they're divided by Market Street. To locals, though, these areas are separate entities, especially since Market Street itself is considered such a strong demarcation line. Both neighborhoods have a core of cultural sights but more than their share of sketchy blocks. North of the Civic Center lies the western section of the frisky Tenderloin neighborhood, while to the east is hip Hayes Valley.

SOMA

Updated by
Denise M. Leto

SoMa is less a neighborhood than a sprawling area of wide, traffic-heavy boulevards lined with office skyscrapers and ultrachic condo high-rises. Aside from the fact that many of them work in the area, locals are drawn to the cultural offerings, destination restaurants, and concentration of dance clubs. In terms of sightseeing, gigantic and impressive SFMOMA tops the list, followed by the specialty museums of the Yerba Buena arts district.

SoMa was once known as South of the Slot (read: the Wrong Side of the Tracks) in reference to the cable-car slot that ran up Market Street. Ever since gold-rush miners set up their tents here in 1848, SoMa has played a major role in housing immigrants to the city.

The most recent influx of techies (and their money) is changing the neighborhood again: the skid row of 6th Street, between Market and Mission Streets, now coexists with trendy bars and cafés that cater to Twitter's workforce; once a scary section of SoMa, the neighborhood is trying hard to rebrand itself as Mid-Market.

TOP ATTRACTIONS

Contemporary Jewish Museum. Daniel Liebeskind designed the postmodern CJM, whose impossible-to-ignore diagonal blue cube juts out of a painstakingly restored power substation. A physical manifestation of the Hebrew phrase *l'chaim* (to life), the cube may have obscure philosophical origins, but Liebeskind created a unique, light-filled space that merits a stroll through the lobby even if current exhibits don't entice you into the galleries. ■ TIP➜ San Francisco's best Jewish deli, Wise Sons, recently opened a counter in the museum, giving you a chance to sample the company's wildly popular smoked trout. ⊠ *736 Mission St., between 3rd and 4th Sts., SoMa* 🕾 *415/655–7800* ⊕ *www.thecjm.org* 🎟 *$14; $5 Thurs. after 5 pm, free 1st Tues. of month* 🕓 *Closed Wed.*

Fodor'sChoice **San Francisco Museum of Modern Art.** Founded in 1935, the San Francisco
★ Museum of Modern Art was the first museum on the West Coast dedicated to modern and contemporary art. In 2016, after a major three-year building expansion designed by Snøhetta, SFMOMA emerged as the largest modern art museum in the country and the revitalized anchor of the Yerba Buena arts district. Nearly tripling its gallery space over seven floors, the museum displays 1,900 of its 33,000-work collection, including a daunting 20-plus temporary exhibits. It can be overwhelming—you could easily spend a day taking it all in, but allow at least two hours; three is better. The original 3rd Street entrance remains, but use the new entrance on Howard Street to experience Richard Serra's gigantic *Sequence,* a gorgeous 15-foot-tall metal walk-through spiral. The museum's expanded collection, showcased on floors three through seven, includes a heavy dose of new art from the Doris and Donald Fisher Collection, one of the greatest private collections of modern and contemporary art in the world. Highlights include a deep collection of German abstract expressionist Gerhard Richter, American painter Ellsworth Kelly, and a tranquil gallery of Agnes Martin. Photography has long been one of the museum's strong suits, and the third floor is dedicated to it. Also look for seminal works by Diego Rivera, Alexander Calder, Chuck Close, Matisse, and Picasso. More than one visitor has been fooled by Duane Hanson's lifelike *Policeman.* Don't miss the new second-floor sculpture terrace with its striking living wall. The first floor is free to the public and contains four large works, as well as the museum's wonderful shop and expensive restaurant. If you don't have hours, save the steep entrance fee and take a spin through here. Ticketing, information, and one gallery are on the second floor; save time and reserve timed tickets online. Take advantage of the variety of well-done audio tours, which focus on specific exhibits or subjects and use positioning technology to locate you in the museum and talk about what you're seeing. Daily guided tours—a quick 25 minutes or 45 minutes—are an excellent way to get a foothold in this expansive space. And if you start to fade, grab a cup of Sightglass coffee at the café on the third floor; another café/restaurant is located by the fifth-floor sculpture garden. The monochromatic bathrooms—a different color on each floor—are surprising and fun. ⊠ *151 3rd St., SoMa* 🕾 *415/357–4000* ⊕ *www.sfmoma.org* 🎟 *$25.*

FAMILY
Fodor's Choice
★

Yerba Buena Gardens. There's not much south of Market Street that encourages lingering outdoors—or indeed walking at all—with this notable exception. These two blocks encompass the Center for the Arts, the Metreon, and Moscone Convention Center, but the gardens themselves are the everyday draw. Office workers escape to the green swath of the East Garden, the focal point of which is the memorial to Martin Luther King Jr. Powerful streams of water surge over large, jagged stone columns, mirroring the enduring force of King's words that are carved on the stone walls and on glass blocks behind the waterfall. Moscone North is behind the memorial, and an overhead walkway leads to Moscone South and its rooftop attractions. ■ TIP→ The gardens are liveliest during the week and especially during the Yerba Buena Gardens Festival, from May through October (www. ybgfestival.org), with free performances of everything from Latin music to Balinese dance.

Atop the Moscone Convention Center perch a few lures for kids. The historic Looff carousel (*$4 for two rides*) twirls daily 10–5. South of the carousel is the Children's Creativity Museum (*415/820–3320 creativity.org*), a high-tech, interactive arts-and-technology center (*$12*) geared to children ages 3–12. Just outside, kids adore the excellent slides, including a 25-foot tube slide, at the play circle. Also part of the rooftop complex are gardens, an ice-skating rink, and a bowling alley. ⊠ *Bordered by 3rd, 4th, Mission, and Folsom Sts., SoMa* ⊕ *yerbabuenagardens.com* ✉ *Free.*

WORTH NOTING

California Historical Society. If you're not a history buff, the CHS might seem like an obvious skip—who wants to look at fading old photographs and musty artifacts?—but these airy galleries are worth a stop. The thoughtful and relevant shows here draw from the society's vast repository of Californiana—hundreds of thousands of photographs, publications, paintings, and gold-rush paraphernalia. ■ TIP→ From out front, take a look across the street: this is the best view of the Museum of the African Diaspora's three-story photo mosaic. ⊠ *678 Mission St., SoMa* ☎ *415/357–1848* ⊕ *www.californiahistoricalsociety.org* ✉ *$5* ⊗ *Closed Mon.*

Museum of the African Diaspora (MoAD). Dedicated to the influence that people of African descent have had all over the world, MoAD focuses on temporary exhibits in its three galleries over two upper floors. With floor-to-ceiling windows onto Mission Street, the museum fits perfectly into the cultural scene of Yerba Buena and is well worth a 30-minute foray. Most striking is its front-window exhibit: a three-story mosaic, made from thousands of photographs, that forms the image of a young girl's face. ■ TIP→ Walk up the stairs inside the museum to view the photographs up close—Malcolm X is there, Muhammad Ali, too, along with everyday folks—but the best view is from across the street. ⊠ *685 Mission St., SoMa* ☎ *415/358–7200* ⊕ *www.moadsf.org* ✉ *$10* ⊗ *Closed Mon. and Tues.*

Palace Hotel. The city's oldest hotel, a Sheraton property, has a storied past. It opened in 1875, but fire destroyed the original structure after the 1906 earthquake, despite the hotel's 28,000-gallon reservoir. The current building dates from 1909. President Warren Harding died here while still in office in 1923, and the body of King Kalakaua of Hawaii spent a night at the Palace after he died in San Francisco in 1891. The managers play up this ghoulish history with talk of a haunted guest room, but the opulent surroundings are this genteel hostelry's real draw. Maxfield Parrish's spectacular wall-size painting *The Pied Piper*, in the bar/restaurant of the same name, is well worth a look. ⊠ *2 New Montgomery St., SoMa* ☎ *415/512–1111* ⊕ *www.sfpalace.com.*

Rincon Center. The only reason to visit what is basically a modern office building is the striking Works Project Administration mural by Anton Refregier in the lobby of the streamlined moderne-style former post office on the building's Mission Street side. The 27 panels depict California life from the days when Native Americans were the state's sole inhabitants through World War I. Completion of this significant work was interrupted by World War II (which explains the swastika in the final panel) and political infighting. The latter led to some alteration in Refregier's "radical" historical interpretations; they exuded too much populist sentiment for some of the politicians who opposed the artist. ⊠ *Bordered by Steuart, Spear, Mission, and Howard Sts., SoMa.*

Systems mural. On a sound wall along the Caltrain tracks is Brian Barneclo's behemoth *Systems* (2011), exploring everything from the nervous system to the ecosystem. At 24,000 square feet, the city's largest mural is also among its most high-profile artworks, visible from passenger trains and the freeway. ⊠ *7th and Townsend Sts., SoMa* ⊕ *sfmural.com.*

Yerba Buena Center for the Arts. You never know what's going to be on display at this facility in Yerba Buena Gardens, but whether it's an exhibit of Mexican street art (graffiti to laypeople), innovative modern dance, or a baffling video installation, it's likely to be memorable. The productions here, which lean toward the cutting edge, tend to draw a young, energetic crowd. ■**TIP→** **Present any public library card or public transit ticket to receive a 10% discount.** ⊠ *701 Mission St., SoMa* ☎ *415/978–2787* ⊕ *www.ybca.org* 🎟 *Galleries $10, free 1st Tues. of month* ⊗ *Closed Mon.*

CIVIC CENTER

The eye-catching, gold-domed City Hall presides over this patchy neighborhood bordered roughly by Franklin, McAllister, Hyde, and Grove Streets. The optimistic "City Beautiful" movement of the early 20th century produced the Beaux Arts–style complex for which the area is named, including City Hall, the War Memorial Opera House, the Veterans Building, and the old public library, now the home of the Asian Art Museum. The wonderful Main Library on Larkin Street between Fulton and Grove Streets is a modern variation on the Civic Center's architectural theme.

The Civic Center area may have been set up on City Beautiful principles, but illusion soon gives way to reality. The buildings are grand, but many of the city's most destitute residents eke out an existence on the neighborhood's streets and plazas. Still, areas of interest on either side of City Hall include the Asian Art Museum, the Main Library, United Nations Plaza, the War Memorial Opera House, Davies Symphony Hall, and ACT's Strand Theater. Tickets to a show at one of the grand performance halls are the main reason many venture here, and major city events like the Pride parade and Giants' victory celebrations draw big crowds; the Asian Art Museum and City Hall are worthy sightseeing stops, too.

TOP ATTRACTIONS

Fodor'sChoice **Asian Art Museum.** You don't have to be a connoisseur of Asian art to
★   appreciate a visit to this museum whose monumental exterior conceals a light, open, and welcoming space. The fraction of the Asian's collection on display (about 2,500 pieces out of 15,000-plus total) is laid out thematically and by region, making it easy to follow historical developments.

Begin on the third floor, where highlights of Buddhist art in Southeast Asia and early China include a large, jewel-encrusted, exquisitely painted 19th-century Burmese Buddha, and clothed rod puppets from Java. On the second floor you can find later Chinese works, as well as pieces from Korea and Japan. The joy here is all in the details: on a whimsical Korean jar, look for a cobalt tiger jauntily smoking a pipe, or admire the delicacy of the Japanese tea implements. The ground floor is devoted to temporary exhibits and the museum's wonderful gift shop. During spring and summer, visit the museum the first Thursday evening of the month for extended programs and sip drinks while a DJ spins tunes. ⊠ *200 Larkin St., between McAllister and Fulton Sts., Civic Center* ☎ *415/581–3500* ⊕ *www.asianart.org* ⌛ *$20 weekdays, $25 weekends, free 1st Sun. of month; $10 Thurs. 5–9* ⊙ *Closed Mon.*

City Hall. This imposing 1915 structure with its massive gold-leaf dome—higher than the U.S. Capitol's—is about as close to a palace as you're going to get in San Francisco. The classic granite-and-marble behemoth was modeled after St. Peter's Basilica in Rome. Architect Arthur Brown Jr., who also designed Coit Tower and the War Memorial Opera House, designed an interior with grand columns and a sweeping central staircase. San Franciscans were thrilled, and probably a bit surprised, when his firm built City Hall in just a few years. The 1899 structure it replaced had taken 27 years to erect, as corrupt builders and politicians lined their pockets with funds earmarked for it. That building collapsed in about 27 seconds during the 1906 earthquake, revealing trash and newspapers mixed into the construction materials.

City Hall was spruced up and seismically retrofitted in the late 1990s, but the sense of history remains palpable. Some noteworthy events that have taken place here include the marriage of Marilyn

Monroe and Joe DiMaggio (1954); the hosing—down the central staircase—of civil-rights and freedom-of-speech protesters (1960); the murders of Mayor George Moscone and openly gay supervisor Harvey Milk (1978); the torching of the lobby by angry members of the gay community in response to the light sentence given to the former supervisor who killed both men (1979); and the registrations of scores of gay couples in celebration of the passage of San Francisco's Domestic Partners Act (1991). In 2004, Mayor Gavin Newsom took a stand against then-current state law by issuing marriage licenses to same-sex partners.

On display in the South Light Court are city artifacts including maps, documents, and photographs. That enormous, 700-pound iron head once crowned the *Goddess of Progress* statue, which topped the old City Hall building until it crumbled during the 1906 earthquake.

Across Polk Street from City Hall is **Civic Center Plaza,** with lawns, walkways, seasonal flower beds, a playground, and an underground parking garage. This sprawling space is generally clean but somewhat grim. Many homeless people hang out here, so the plaza can feel dodgy. ⊠ *Bordered by Van Ness Ave. and Polk, Grove, and McAllister Sts., Civic Center* ☎ *415/554–6023 recorded tour info, 415/554–6139 tour reservations* ⊕ *sfgov.org/cityhall/city-hall-tours* 🎫 *Free* ☉ *Closed weekends.*

WORTH NOTING

Louise M. Davies Symphony Hall. Fascinating and futuristic-looking, this 2,750-seat hall is the home of the San Francisco Symphony. The glass wraparound lobby and pop-out balcony high on the southeast corner are visible from outside, as is the Henry Moore bronze sculpture that sits on the sidewalk at Van Ness Avenue and Grove Street. The hall's 59 adjustable Plexiglas acoustical disks cascade from the ceiling like hanging windshields. Concerts range from typical symphonic fare to more unusual combinations, such as performers like Al Green and Arlo Guthrie. Scheduled tours (about 75 minutes) on Mondays take in Davies and the nearby War Memorial Opera House. ⊠ *201 Van Ness Ave., Civic Center* ☎ *415/552–8338* ⊕ *www.sfwmpac.org* 🎫 *Tours $7.*

San Francisco Public Library. Topped with a swirl like an art-deco nautilus, the library's seven-level glass atrium fills the building with light. Local researchers take advantage of centers dedicated to gay and lesbian, African-American, Chinese, and Filipino history, and everyone appreciates the basement-level café, Wi-Fi, and 15-minute Internet-terminal access. ■ **TIP➜ The sixth-floor San Francisco History Center has fun exhibits of city ephemera, including—a treat for fans of noir fiction— novelist Dashiell Hammett's typewriter.** ⊠ *100 Larkin St., at Grove St., Civic Center* ☎ *415/557–4400* ⊕ *sfpl.org.*

THE TENDERLOIN

Stretching west of Union Square and north of Civic Center, the Tenderloin could be the city's poster child for urban challenges: low-income families huddle in tiny apartments; single-room-occupancy hotels offer shelter a step up from living on the street; drug dealing and prostitution are rampant and visible; and very few green spaces break up the monotony of high-rises. So why in the world would anyone go out of the way to come here? Well, exceptional Vietnamese food, for one thing, but these days more than just the great *pho* is luring people to the Tenderloin. Trendy watering holes and coffee shops are springing up, with a handful of intrepid hipsters moving into the hood after them. The Tenderloin may be on its way to becoming the next Mission, but for now it remains a gritty slice of San Francisco: come hungry and take a cab, especially at night.

■ **TIP→ Some parts of the Tenderloin are more dangerous than others, and a single street can change from block to block. Little Saigon's Larkin Street corridor is relatively safe during the day, as are most streets north of Eddy (an area that realtors insist on calling the TenderNob for its proximity to Nob Hill). Absolutely avoid the last two blocks of Turk Street and Golden Gate Avenue before they meet Market Street.**

EXPLORING

Glide Memorial Church. For a rockin' gospel concert and an inclusive, feel-good vibe, head to Glide, where Reverend Cecil Williams, a bear of a man and a local celeb do-gooder, leads a hand-clapping, shout-it-out, get-on-your-feet "celebration." The diverse crowd—gay and straight, all colors of the rainbow, religious and not—is large and enthusiastic. You might recognize the church from the Will Smith film *The Pursuit of Happyness.* ✉ *330 Ellis St., at Taylor St., Tenderloin* ☎ *415/674–6000* ⊕ *www.glide.org.*

▌ QUICK BITES

Un Cafecito. Experience the new Tenderloin at this airy space that serves café fare—bagels, sandwiches—with a Mexican twist. Regulars love the tamales and breakfast burritos, and the Mexican mocha is not-too-sweet perfection. ✉ *335 Jones St., Tenderloin* ☎ *415/674–1769* ☉ *Closed Sun.*

HAYES VALLEY

A chic neighborhood due west of Civic Center, Hayes Valley has terrific eateries, cool watering holes, and great browsing in its funky clothing, home-decor, and design boutiques. Locals love this quarter, but without any big-name draws it remains off the radar for many visitors.

EXPLORING

SFJAZZ Center. Devoted entirely to jazz, the center hosts performances by jazz greats such as McCoy Tyner, Joshua Redman, Regina Carter, and Chick Corea. Walk by and the street-level glass walls will make you feel as if you're inside; head indoors and the acoustics will knock your socks off. ✉ *201 Franklin St., at Fell St., Hayes Valley* ☎ *866/920–5299* ⊕ *www.sfjazz.org.*

NOB HILL AND
RUSSIAN HILL

with Polk Gulch

Getting Oriented

Nob Hill and Russian Hill
with Polk Gulch

TOP REASONS TO GO

Macondray Lane: Duck into this secret, lush garden lane and walk its narrow, uneven cobblestones.

Vallejo Steps area: Make the steep climb up to lovely Ina Coolbrith Park, then continue up along the glorious garden path of the Vallejo Steps to a spectacular view at the top.

San Francisco Art Institute: Contemplate a Diego Rivera mural and stop at the café for cheap organic coffee and a priceless view of the city and the bay. It may be the best—and cheapest—way to spend an hour in the neighborhood.

Cable Car Museum: Ride a cable car all the way back to the barn, hanging on tight as it clack-clack-clacks its way up Nob Hill, then go behind the scenes at the museum.

Play "Bullitt" on the steepest streets: For the ride of your life, take a drive up and down the city's steepest streets on Russian Hill. A trip over the precipice of Filbert or Jones will make you feel as if you're falling off the edge of the world.

QUICK BITES

The Boy's Deli. Tucked in the back of a tiny produce market is a counter serving up some of the biggest, juiciest, best sandwiches in town—strictly to go—along with traditional sides. If you like yours spicy, go for the Sandlot, which features the deli's delicious rotisserie chicken. ⊠ *Polk & Green Produce Market, 2222 Polk St., between Green and Vallejo Sts., Russian Hill* ☎ *415/776–3099.*

Swensen's Ice Cream. The original Swensen's has been a neighborhood favorite since it opened in 1948. An antique sign still fronts the tiny shop, but concessions to the times include such ice-cream flavors as green tea and lychee. ⊠ *1999 Hyde St., at Union St., Russian Hill* ☎ *415/775–6818* ⊕ *www.swensensicecream.com* ⊟ *No credit cards.*

GETTING THERE

The thing about Russian and Nob Hills is that they're both especially steep hills. If you're not up for the hike, a cable car is certainly the most exciting way to reach the top. Take the California line for Nob Hill and the Powell–Hyde line for Russian Hill. Buses serve the area as well, such as the 1–California bus for Nob Hill, but the routes run only east–west. Only the cable cars tackle the steeper north–south streets. Driving yourself is a hassle, since parking is a challenge on these crowded, precipitous streets.

PLANNING YOUR TIME

Since walking Nob Hill is (almost) all about gazing at exteriors, touring the neighborhood during daylight hours is a must. The sights here don't require a lot of visiting time—say a half hour each at the Cable Car Museum and Grace Cathedral—but allow time for the walk itself. An afternoon visit is ideal for Russian Hill, so you can browse the shops. You could cover both neighborhoods in three or four hours. If you time it just right, you can finish up with a sunset cocktail at a swanky hotel lounge or the retro-tiki Tonga Room.

4

Sightseeing
★★
Nightlife
★
Dining
★★★
Lodging
★★★
Shopping
★★

In place of the quirky charm and cultural diversity that mark other San Francisco neighborhoods, Nob Hill exudes history and good breeding. Topped with some of the city's most elegant hotels, Gothic Grace Cathedral, and private blue-blood clubs, it's the pinnacle of privilege. One hill over, across Pacific Avenue, is another old-family bastion, Russian Hill. It may not be quite as wealthy as Nob Hill, but it's no slouch—and it's got jaw-dropping views.

NOB HILL

Updated by
Denise M. Leto

Nob Hill was officially dubbed during the 1870s when "the Big Four"—Charles Crocker, Leland Stanford, Mark Hopkins, and Collis P. Huntington, who were involved in the construction of the transcontinental railroad—built their hilltop estates. The lingo is thick from this era: those on the hilltop were referred to as "nabobs" (originally meaning a provincial governor from India) and "swells," and the hill itself was called Snob Hill, a term that survives to this day. By 1882 so many estates had sprung up on Nob Hill that Robert Louis Stevenson called it "the hill of palaces." But the 1906 earthquake and fire destroyed all the palatial mansions except for portions of the James Flood brownstone. History buffs may choose to linger here, but for most visitors, a casual glimpse from a cable car will be enough.

⇨ *For more details on the Cable Car Museum, see the Cable Cars feature in Experience San Francisco.*

TOP ATTRACTIONS

FAMILY **Cable Car Museum.** One of the city's best free offerings, this museum is an absolute must for kids. You can even ride a cable car here—all three lines stop between Russian Hill and Nob Hill. The facility, which is inside the city's last cable-car barn, takes the top off the system to let you see how it all works. Eternally humming and squealing, the massive powerhouse cable wheels steal the show. You can also climb aboard a vintage car and take the grip, let the kids ring a cable-car bell (briefly), and check out vintage gear dating from 1873. ⊠ *1201 Mason St., at Washington St., Nob Hill* ☎ *415/474–1887* ⊕ *www.cablecarmuseum.org* ☞ *Free.*

> ### CLOSE-UPS ON THE BROCKLEBANK
>
> The grand Brocklebank Apartments, on the northeast corner of Sacramento and Mason Streets across from the Fairmont hotel, might look eerily familiar. In 1958 the complex was showcased in Alfred Hitchcock's *Vertigo* (Jimmy Stewart starts trailing Kim Novak here), and in the 1990s it popped up in the miniseries *Tales of the City.*

Grace Cathedral. Not many churches can boast an altarpiece by Keith Haring and not one but two labyrinths. The seat of the Episcopal Church in San Francisco, this soaring Gothic-style structure, erected on the site of the 19th-century railroad baron Charles Crocker's mansion, took 53 years to build, wrapping up in 1964. The gilded bronze doors at the east entrance were taken from casts of Lorenzo Ghiberti's incredible Gates of Paradise, which are on the Baptistery in Florence, Italy. A black-and-bronze stone sculpture of St. Francis by Beniamino Bufano greets you as you enter.

The 35-foot-wide limestone labyrinth is a replica of the 13th-century stone maze on the floor of Chartres Cathedral. All are encouraged to walk the ¼-mile-long labyrinth, a ritual based on the tradition of meditative walking. There's also a terrazzo outdoor labyrinth on the church's north side. The AIDS Interfaith Chapel, to the right as you enter Grace, contains a metal triptych by the late artist Keith Haring and panels from the AIDS Memorial Quilt. ■TIP→ Especially dramatic times to view the cathedral are during Thursday-night evensong (5:15 pm) and during special holiday programs. ⊠ *1100 California St., at Taylor St., Nob Hill* ☎ *415/749–6300* ⊕ *www.gracecathedral.org* ☞ *Free; tours $25.*

WORTH NOTING

Collis P. Huntington Park. The elegant park west of the Pacific Union Club and east of Grace Cathedral occupies the site of a mansion owned by the "Big Four" railroad baron Collis P. Huntington. He died in 1900, the mansion was destroyed in the 1906 fire, and in 1915 his widow—by then married to Huntington's nephew—donated the land to the city for use as a park. The Huntingtons' neighbors, the Crockers, once owned the *Fountain of the Tortoises,* based on the original in Rome's Piazza Mattei. ■TIP→ The benches around the fountain offer a welcome break after climbing Nob Hill. ⊠ *Taylor and California Sts., Nob Hill.*

WALKING THE HILLS

Start a tour of Nob Hill and Russian Hill with a cable-car ride up to **California** and **Powell Streets** on Nob Hill (all lines go here). Walking two blocks east you can pass all the Big Four mansions-cum-hotels on the hill. Peek at the Keith Haring triptych in impressive **Grace Cathedral**; grab a Peet's coffee in the basement café if you need a lift. Next, head down to the **Cable Car Museum** to see the machinery in action. Then make your way to Russian Hill—a cable car is a fine way to reach the peak—to visit some of the city's loveliest hidden lanes and stairways. At **Mason** and **Vallejo Streets,** head up the **Vallejo Steps,** passing contemplative, terraced **Ina Coolbrith Park** and beautifully tended private gardens. Take in the sweeping city and bay view from the top of the hill, then head right on **Jones Street** and duck right under the trellis to wooded and shady **Macondray Lane.** From here it's a six-block hike to crooked **Lombard Street.** If you've still got some steam, be sure to go another block to see **Diego Rivera's mural** and the surprise panoramic view from the **San Francisco Art Institute.**

Fairmont San Francisco. The hotel's dazzling opening was delayed a year by the 1906 quake, but since then, the marble palace has hosted presidents, royalty, movie stars, and local nabobs. Things have changed since its early days, however: on the eve of World War I, you could get a room for as low as $2.50 per night, meals included. Nowadays, prices go as high as $20,000, which buys a night in the eight-room, contemporary art–filled penthouse suite. Swing through the opulent lobby on your way to tea (served on weekends from 1:30 to 3) at the Laurel Court restaurant; peek through the foyer's floor-to-ceiling windows for a glimpse of the hotel's garden and beehives, where the honey served with tea is produced. Don't miss an evening cocktail (a mai tai is in order) in the kitschy Tonga Room, complete with tiki huts, a sporadic tropical rainstorm, and a floating bandstand. ⊠ *950 Mason St., Nob Hill* ☎ *415/772–5000* ⊕ *www.fairmont.com/san-francisco.*

InterContinental Mark Hopkins Hotel. Built on the ashes of railroad tycoon Mark Hopkins's grand estate (constructed at his wife's urging; Hopkins himself preferred to live frugally), this 19-story hotel went up in 1926. A combination of French château and Spanish Renaissance architecture, with noteworthy terra-cotta detailing, it has hosted statesmen, royalty, and Hollywood celebrities. The 11-room penthouse was turned into a glass-wall cocktail lounge in 1939: the Top of the Mark is remembered fondly by thousands of World War II veterans who jammed the lounge before leaving for overseas duty. Wives and sweethearts watching the ships depart gave the room's northwest nook its name—Weepers' Corner. ■ TIP➜ With its 360-degree views, the lounge is a wonderful spot for a nighttime drink. ⊠ *999 California St., at Mason St., Nob Hill* ☎ *415/392–3434* ⊕ *www.intercontinentalmarkhopkins.com.*

Nob Hill Masonic Center. Erected by Freemasons in 1957, the hall is familiar to locals mostly as a concert and lecture venue, where such notables as

Van Morrison and Al Gore have appeared. But you don't need a ticket to check out artist Emile Norman's impressive lobby mosaic. Mainly in rich greens and yellows, it depicts the Masons' role in California history. ✉ *1111 California St., Nob Hill* ☎ *415/776-7457* ⊕ *sfmasonic.com.*

Pacific Union Club. The former home of silver baron James Flood cost a whopping $1.5 million in 1886, when even a stylish Victorian like the Haas-Lilienthal House cost less than $20,000. All that cash did buy some structural stability. The Flood residence (to be precise, its shell) was the only Nob Hill mansion to survive the 1906 earthquake and fire. The Pacific Union Club, a bastion of the wealthy and powerful, purchased the house in 1907 and commissioned Willis Polk to redesign it; the architect added the semicircular wings and third floor. (The ornate fence design dates from the mansion's construction.) ✉ *1000 California St., Nob Hill.*

RUSSIAN HILL

Essentially a tony residential neighborhood of spiffy pieds-à-terre, Victorian flats, Edwardian cottages, and boxlike condos, Russian Hill has some of the city's loveliest stairway walks, hidden garden ways, and steepest streets—not to mention those bay views. Several stories explain the origin of Russian Hill's name. One legend has it that Russian farmers raised vegetables here for Farallon Islands seal hunters; another attributes the name to a Russian sailor of prodigious drinking habits who drowned when he fell into a well on the hill. A plaque at the top of the Vallejo Steps gives credence to the version that says sailors of the Russian-American company were buried here in the 1840s. Be sure to visit the sign for yourself—its location offers perhaps the finest vantage point on the hill.

TOP ATTRACTIONS

Fodor's Choice ★ **Ina Coolbrith Park.** If you make it all the way up here, you may have the place all to yourself, or at least feel like you do. The park's terraces are carved from a hill so steep that it's difficult to see if anyone else is there or not. Locals love this park because it feels like a secret no one else knows about—one of the city's magic hidden gardens, with a meditative setting and spectacular views of the bay peeking out from among the trees. A poet, Oakland librarian, and niece of Mormon prophet Joseph Smith, Ina Coolbrith (1842–1928) introduced Jack London and Isadora Duncan to the world of books. For years she entertained literary greats in her Macondray Lane home near the park. In 1915 she was named poet laureate of California. ✉ *Vallejo St. between Mason and Taylor Sts., Russian Hill.*

Lombard Street. The block-long "Crookedest Street in the World" makes eight switchbacks down the east face of Russian Hill between Hyde and Leavenworth Streets. Residents bemoan the traffic jam outside their front doors, but the throngs continue. Join the line of cars waiting to drive down the steep hill, or avoid the whole mess and walk down the steps on either side of Lombard. You take in super views of North Beach and Coit Tower whether you walk or drive—though if you're the one behind the wheel, you'd better keep your eye on the road lest you become yet another of the many folks who ram the garden barriers.

■ TIP ➜ **Can't stand the traffic? Thrill seekers of a different stripe may want to head two blocks south of Lombard to Filbert Street. At a gradient of 31.5%, the hair-raising descent between Hyde and Leavenworth Streets is the city's steepest. Go slowly!** ⊠ *Lombard St. between Hyde and Leavenworth Sts., Russian Hill.*

Fodor's Choice
★

Macondray Lane. San Francisco has no shortage of impressive, grand homes, but Macondray Lane is the quintessential hidden garden. Enter under a lovely wooden trellis and proceed down a quiet, cobbled pedestrian lane lined with Edwardian cottages and flowering plants and trees. A flight of steep wooden stairs at the end of the lane leads to Taylor Street—on the way down you can't miss the bay views. If you've read any of Armistead Maupin's *Tales of the City* books, you may find the lane vaguely familiar. It's the thinly disguised setting for part of the series' action. ⊠ *Between Jones and Taylor Sts., and Union and Green Sts., Russian Hill.*

San Francisco Art Institute. The number-one reason for a visit is Mexican master Diego Rivera's *The Making of a Fresco Showing the Building of a City* (1931), in the student gallery to your immediate left inside the entrance. Rivera himself is in the fresco—his broad behind is to the viewer—and he's surrounded by his assistants. They in turn are surrounded by a construction scene, laborers, and city notables such as sculptor Robert Stackpole and architect Timothy Pflueger. *Making* is one of three San Francisco murals painted by Rivera. The number-two reason to come here is the café, or more precisely the eye-popping, panoramic view from the café, which serves surprisingly decent food for a song.

The **Walter & McBean Galleries** (*415/749–4563; Tues. 11–7, Wed.–Sat. 11–6*) exhibit the often provocative works of established artists. ⊠ *800 Chestnut St., Russian Hill* ☎ *415/771–7020* ⊕ *www.sfai.edu* ⌨ *Galleries free.*

Fodor's Choice
★

Vallejo Steps area. Several Russian Hill buildings survived the 1906 earthquake and fire and remain standing. Patriotic firefighters saved what's become known as the **Flag House** (*1652–56 Taylor St.*) when they spotted the American flag on the property and doused the flames with seltzer water and wet sand. The owner, a flag collector, fearing the house would burn to the ground, wanted it to go down in style, with "all flags flying." The Flag House, at the southwest corner of Ina Coolbrith Park, is one of a number of California shingle–style homes in this neighborhood, several of which the architect Willis Polk designed.

Polk drew up the plans for the nearby **Polk-Williams House** (*Taylor and Vallejo Sts.*) and lived in one of its finer sections, and he was responsible for **1034–1036 Vallejo,** across the street. He also laid out the Vallejo Steps themselves, which climb the steep ridge across Taylor Street from the Flag House. Though very steep, the walk up to Ina Coolbrith Park and beyond is possibly the most pleasurable thing to do while on Russian Hill, rewarding you as it does with glorious views. ■ TIP ➜ **If the walk up the steps will be too taxing, park at the top of the steps by heading east on Vallejo from Jones and enjoy the scene from there.** ⊠ *Taylor and Vallejo Sts., steps lead up toward Jones St., Russian Hill.*

NORTH BEACH

Getting Oriented

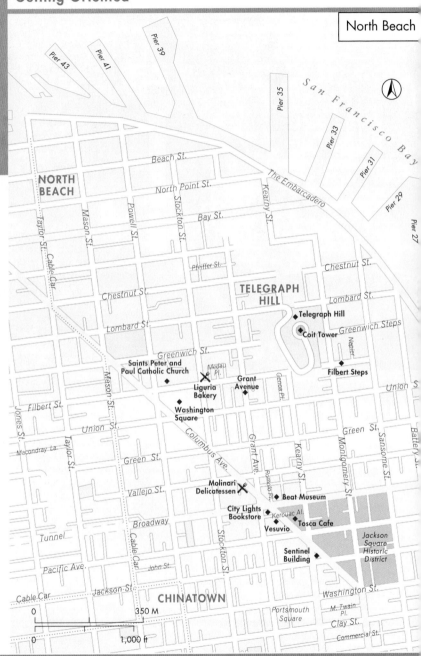

North Beach

Pier 43
Pier 41
Pier 39
Pier 35
Pier 33
Pier 31
Pier 29
Pier 27

San Francisco Bay

The Embarcadero

NORTH BEACH

Beach St.
North Point St.
Bay St.
Chestnut St.
Lombard St.

Taylor St. Cable Car
Mason St.
Powell St.
Stockton St.
Keamy St.

Pfeiffer St.

Chestnut St.

TELEGRAPH HILL

Telegraph Hill

Lombard St.

Coit Tower   Greenwich Steps

Napier

Greenwich St.

Saints Peter and Paul Catholic Church

Medau Pl.

Filbert Steps

Liguria Bakery

Grant Avenue

Genoa Pl.

Union S

Washington Square

Filbert St.

Jones St.

Union St.

Mason St.

Green St.

Grant Ave.

Keamy St.

Montgomery St.

Sansome St.

Battery St.

Macondray La.

Taylor St.

Green St.

Columbus Ave.

Vallejo St.

Romolo Pl.

Molinari Delicatessen

Beat Museum

City Lights Bookstore

Kerouac Al.

Tosca Cafe

Broadway

Vesuvio

Jackson Square Historic District

Tunnel

Cable Car

Stockton St.

Sentinel Building

Pacific Ave.

John St.

Cable Car   Jackson St.

CHINATOWN

Washington St.

Portsmouth Square

M. Twain Pl.

Clay St.

0   350 M

0   1,000 ft

Commercial St.

TOP REASONS TO GO

Espresso, espresso, espresso: Or cappuccino, americano, mocha—however you take your caffeine, this is the neighborhood for it. Hanging out in a café constitutes sightseeing here, so find a chair and get to work.

Colorful watering holes: The high concentration of bars with character, like Tosca Café and Vesuvio, makes North Beach the perfect neighborhood for a pub crawl.

Filbert Steps: Walk down this dizzying stairway from Telegraph Hill's Coit Tower, past lush private gardens and jaw-dropping bay views—and listen for the hill's famous screeching parrots.

Grant Avenue: Check out vanguard boutiques, rambling antiques shops, and cavernous old-time bars, all chockablock on narrow Grant Avenue. The best stuff is crowded into the four blocks between Columbus Avenue and Filbert Street.

Browsing books at City Lights: Illuminate your mind at this Beat-era landmark. Its great book selection, author events, and keen staff make it just as cool as ever.

QUICK BITES

Liguria Bakery. The Soracco family has been baking focaccia in North Beach for more than a century, and many consider their fresh-from-the-oven bread the neighborhood's best. Arrive before noon: when the focaccia is gone, the bakery closes. ⊠ *1700 Stockton St., at Filbert St., North Beach* ☎ *415/421–3786* ▭ *No credit cards* ⊘ *Closed Sun. and Mon.*

Molinari Delicatessen. The friendly *paesans* behind the counter have been serving up the most delicious, and quite possibly the biggest, sandwiches in town for over 100 years in this location alone. Take a number, grab your bread from the bin, and gaze upon the sandwich board. ⊠ *373 Columbus Ave., at Vallejo St., North Beach* ☎ *415/421–2337* ⊕ *www.molinarisalame.com* ⊘ *Closed Sun.*

GETTING THERE

The Powell–Mason cable-car line can drop you within a block of Washington Square Park, in the heart of North Beach. The 30–Stockton and 15–3rd Street buses run to the neighborhood from Market Street. Once you're here, North Beach is a snap to explore on foot. Most of it is relatively flat—but climbing Telegraph Hill to reach Coit Tower is another story entirely.

PLANNING YOUR TIME

There's no bad time of day to visit this quarter. The cafés buzz from morning to night, the shops along main drags Columbus Avenue and Broadway tend to stay open until at least 6 or 7 pm, and late-night revelers don't start checking their watches until about 2 am. Sunday is quieter, since some shops close (though City Lights is open daily, until midnight).

Plan to spend a few hours here. It's all about lingering, and the only major "sightseeing" spot is Coit Tower. The walk up to the tower is strenuous but rewarding; if you can tough it, make time for it. If you're driving, keep in mind that parking is difficult, especially at night.

Sightseeing
★★
Nightlife
★★★★
Dining
★★★
Lodging
★
Shopping
★★★

San Francisco novelist Herbert Gold calls North Beach "the longest-running, most glorious, American bohemian operetta outside Greenwich Village." Indeed, to anyone who's spent some time in its eccentric old bars and cafés, North Beach evokes everything from the Barbary Coast days to the no-less-rowdy Beatnik era.

Updated by
Denise M. Leto

Italian bakeries appear frozen in time, homages to Jack Kerouac and Allen Ginsberg pop up everywhere, and strip joints, the modern equivalent of the Barbary Coast's "houses of ill repute," do business on Broadway. With its outdoor café tables, throngs of tourists, and holiday vibe, this is probably the part of town Europeans are thinking of when they say San Francisco is the most European city in America.

The neighborhood truly was a beach at the time of the gold rush—the bay extended into the hollow between Telegraph and Russian Hills. Among the first immigrants to Yerba Buena during the early 1840s were young men from the northern provinces of Italy. The Genoese started the fishing industry in the newly renamed boomtown of San Francisco, as well as a much-needed produce business. Later, Sicilians emerged as leaders of the fishing fleets and eventually as proprietors of the seafood restaurants lining Fisherman's Wharf. Meanwhile, their Genoese cousins established banking and manufacturing empires.

Once almost exclusively Italian American, today's North Beach has only a small percentage of Italians (many of them elderly), with growing Chinese and San Francisco yuppie populations. But walk down narrow Romolo Place (off Broadway east of Columbus) or Genoa Place (off Union west of Kearny) or Medau Place (off Filbert west of Grant) and you can feel the immigrant Italian roots of this neighborhood. Locals know that the city's finest Italian restaurants are elsewhere, but North Beach is the place that puts folks in mind of Italian food, and there are many decent options to choose from. Bakeries sell focaccia fresh from the oven; eaten warm or cold, it's the perfect portable food. Many other aromas fill the air: coffee beans, deli meats and cheeses, Italian pastries, and—always—pungent garlic. ⇨ *For more on the North Beach food scene, see the Where to Eat chapter.*

A NORTH BEACH WALK

To hit the highlights of the neighbor-hood, start off with a browse at Beat landmark **City Lights Bookstore**. For cool boutique shopping, head north up **Grant Avenue**. Otherwise, it's time to get down to the serious business of hanging out. Make a left onto **Columbus Avenue** when you leave the bookstore and walk the strip until you find a café table or pastry display that calls your name.

Fortified, continue down Colum-bus to **Washington Square**, where you can walk or take the 39 bus up **Telegraph Hill** to Coit Tower's views. Be sure to take in the gorgeous gardens along the **Filbert Steps** on the way down. Finally, reward yourself by returning to **Columbus Avenue** for a drink at one of the atmosphere-steeped watering holes like **Tosca** or **Specs**.

TOP ATTRACTIONS

5

Fodor's Choice
★

City Lights Bookstore. Take a look at the exterior of the store: the replica of a revolutionary mural destroyed in Chiapas, Mexico, by military forces; the art banners hanging above the windows; and the sign that says "Turn your sell [sic] phone off. Be here now." This place isn't just doling out best sellers. Designated a city landmark, the hangout of Beat-era writers—Allen Ginsberg and store founder Law-rence Ferlinghetti among them—and independent publisher remains a vital part of San Francisco's literary scene. Browse the three levels of poetry, philosophy, politics, fiction, history, and local zines, to the tune of creaking wood floors. ■ TIP➜ **Be sure to check the calendar of literary events.**

Back in the day, the basement was a kind of literary living room, where writers like Ginsberg and Jack Kerouac would read and even receive mail. Ferlinghetti cemented City Lights' place in history by publishing Ginsberg's *Howl and Other Poems* in 1956. The small volume was ignored in the mainstream…until Ferlinghetti and the bookstore man-ager were arrested for obscenity and corruption of youth. In the land-mark First Amendment trial that followed, the judge exonerated both men, declaring that a work that has "redeeming social significance" can't be obscene. *Howl* went on to become a classic.

Stroll Kerouac Alley, branching off Columbus Avenue next to City Lights, to read the quotes from Ferlinghetti, Maya Angelou, Confu-cius, John Steinbeck, and the street's namesake embedded in the pave-ment. ✉ *261 Columbus Ave., North Beach* ☎ *415/362–8193* ⊕ *www.citylights.com.*

Coit Tower. Whether or not you agree that it resembles a fire-hose nozzle, this 210-foot tower is among San Francisco's most distinctive skyline sights. Although the monument wasn't intended as a tribute to firemen, it's often considered as such because of the donor's special attachment to the local fire company. As the story goes, a young gold rush–era girl, Lillie Hitchcock Coit (known as Miss Lil), was a fervent admirer of her local fire company—so much so that she once deserted a wedding party

Lolling around Washington Square, post-espresso, is a fine use of a sunny afternoon.

and chased down the street after her favorite engine, Knickerbocker No. 5, while clad in her bridesmaid finery. She became the Knickerbocker Company's mascot and always signed her name "Lillie Coit 5." When Lillie died in 1929 she left the city $125,000 to "expend in an appropriate manner...to the beauty of San Francisco."

You can ride the elevator to the top of the tower—the only thing you have to pay for here—to enjoy the view of the Bay Bridge and the Golden Gate Bridge; due north is Alcatraz Island. Most visitors saunter right past the 19 fabulous Depression-era murals inside the tower that depict California's economic and political life, but take the time to appreciate the first New Deal art project supported by taxpayer money. The federal government commissioned the paintings from 25 local artists, and ended up funding a controversy. The radical Mexican painter Diego Rivera inspired the murals' socialist-realist style, with its biting cultural commentary, particularly about the exploitation of workers. At the time the murals were painted, clashes between management and labor along the waterfront and elsewhere in San Francisco were widespread. ✉ *Telegraph Hill Blvd. at Greenwich St. or Lombard St., North Beach* ☎ *415/362–0808* 🌐 *sfrecpark.org* 🎫 *Free; elevator to top $8.*

Fodor's Choice ★ **Telegraph Hill.** Residents here have some of the city's best views, as well as the most difficult ascents to their aeries. The hill rises from the east end of Lombard Street to a height of 284 feet and is capped by Coit Tower. Imagine lugging your groceries up that! If you brave the slope, though, you can be rewarded with a "secret treasure" San Francisco moment. Filbert Street starts up the hill, then becomes the **Filbert Steps** when the going gets too steep. You can cut between the Filbert Steps

CLOSE UP

The Birds

While on Telegraph Hill, you might be startled by a chorus of piercing squawks and a rushing sound of wings. No, you're not about to have a Hitchcock bird-attack moment. These small, vivid green parrots with cherry-red heads number in the hundreds; they're descendants of former pets that escaped or were released by their owners. (The birds dislike cages, and they bite if bothered ... must've been some disillusioned owners along the way.)

The parrots like to roost high in the aging cypress trees on the hill, chattering and fluttering, sometimes taking wing en masse. They're not popular with some residents, but they did find a champion in local bohemian Mark Bittner, a former street musician. Bittner began chronicling their habits, publishing a book and battling the homeowners who wanted to cut down the cypresses. A documentary, *The Wild Parrots of Telegraph Hill*, made the issue a cause célèbre. In 2007, City Hall, which recognizes a golden goose when it sees one, stepped in and brokered a solution to keep the celebrity birds in town. The city would cover the homeowners' insurance worries and plant new trees for the next generation of wild parrots.

5

and another flight, the **Greenwich Steps**, on up to the hilltop. As you climb, you can pass some of the city's oldest houses and be surrounded by beautiful, flowering private gardens. In some places the trees grow over the stairs so it feels like you're walking through a green tunnel; elsewhere, you'll have wide-open views of the bay. The cypress trees that grow on the hill are a favorite roost of local avian celebrities the wild parrots of Telegraph Hill; you'll hear the cries of the cherry-headed conures if they're nearby. And the telegraphic name? It comes from the hill's status as the first Morse code signal station back in 1853. ⌧ *Bordered by Lombard, Filbert, Kearny, and Sansome Sts., North Beach*.

WORTH NOTING

Beat Museum. "Museum" might be a stretch for this tiny storefront that's half bookstore, half memorabilia collection. You can see the 1949 Hudson from the movie version of *On the Road* and the shirt Neal Cassady wore while driving Ken Kesey's Merry Prankster bus, "Further." There are also manuscripts, letters, and early editions by Jack Kerouac, Allen Ginsberg, and Lawrence Ferlinghetti, but the true treasure here is the passionate and well-informed staff, which often includes the museum's founder, Jerry Cimino: your short visit may turn into an hours-long trip through the Beat era. ■ TIP→ **The excellent Saturday walking tour goes beyond the museum to take in favorite Beat watering holes and hangouts in North Beach.** ⌧ *540 Broadway, North Beach* ☎ *415/399–9626* ⊕ *www.thebeatmuseum.org* ⌧ *$8; walking tours $25.*

Grant Avenue. Originally called Calle de la Fundación, Grant Avenue is the oldest street in the city, but it's got plenty of young blood. Here dusty bars such as the Saloon and perennial favorites like the Savoy

Tivoli mix with hotshot boutiques, odd curio shops like the antique jumble that is Aria, atmospheric cafés such as the boho haven Caffè Trieste, and authentic Italian delis. While the street runs from Union Square through Chinatown, North Beach, and beyond, the fun stuff in this neighborhood is crowded into the four blocks between Columbus Avenue and Filbert Street. ⊠ *North Beach.*

O PIONEERS!

The corner of Broadway and Columbus Avenue witnessed an unusual historic breakthrough. Here stood the Condor Club, where in 1964 Carol Doda became the country's first dancer to break the topless barrier. A bronze plaque honors the milestone (only in SF).

Saints Peter and Paul Catholic Church.
Camera-toting visitors focus their lenses on the Romanesque splendor of what's often called the Italian Cathedral. Completed in 1924, the church has Disneyesque stone-white towers that are local landmarks. Mass reflects the neighborhood; it's given in English, Italian, and Chinese. (This is one of the few churches in town where you can hear Mass in Italian.) Following their 1954 City Hall wedding, Marilyn Monroe and Joe DiMaggio had their wedding photos snapped here. ■ TIP→ **On the first Sunday of October, a Mass followed by a parade to Fisherman's Wharf celebrates the Blessing of the (Fishing) Fleet. Also in October is the Italian Heritage Parade in North Beach. The country's oldest Italian celebration, it began in 1869.** ⊠ *666 Filbert St., at Washington Sq., North Beach* ☎ *415/421–0809* ⊕ *www.salesiansspp.org.*

Sentinel Building. A striking triangular shape and a gorgeous green patina make this 1907 flatiron building at the end of Columbus Avenue a visual knockout. In the 1970s local filmmaker Francis Ford Coppola bought the building to use for his production company. The ground floor houses Coppola's stylish wine bar, **Café Zoetrope.** Stop in for wines from the Coppola vineyards in Napa and Sonoma, simple Italian dishes, and foodie gifts. ⊠ *916 Kearny St., at Columbus Ave., North Beach.*

Washington Square. Once the daytime social heart of Little Italy, this grassy patch has changed character numerous times over the years. The Beats hung out here in the 1950s, hippies camped out in the 1960s and early '70s, and nowadays you're more likely to see elderly Asians doing tai chi than Italian folks reminiscing about the old country. You might also see homeless people hanging out on the benches and young locals sunbathing or running their dogs. Lillie Hitchcock Coit, in yet another show of affection for San Francisco's firefighters, donated the statue of two firemen with a child they rescued. ⊠ *Bordered by Columbus Ave. and Stockton, Filbert, and Union Sts., North Beach.*

ON THE WATERFRONT

Getting Oriented

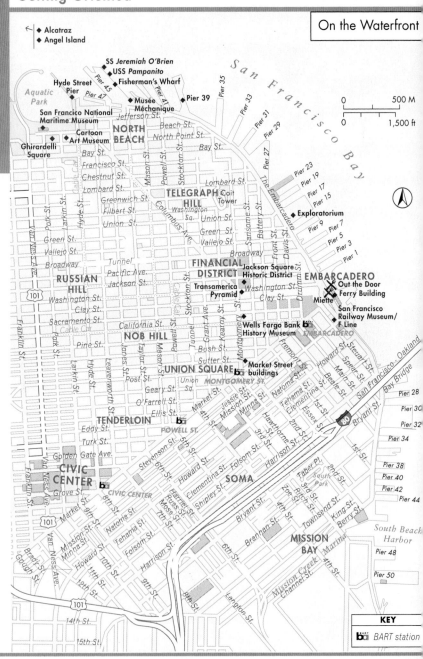

On the Waterfront

◆ Alcatraz
◆ Angel Island

SS Jeremiah O'Brien
USS Pampanito
Hyde Street   Fisherman's Wharf
Pier
Pier 45
Pier 47
◆ Pier 39
Pier 35
Pier 33
Aquatic Park
Musée Mechanique
San Francisco National Maritime Museum
Jefferson St.
Pier 31
Pier 29
Beach St.
North Point St.
Cartoon Art Museum
NORTH BEACH
Bay St.
Pier 27
Ghirardelli Square
Bay St.
Pier 23
Pier 19
Francisco St.
Pier 17
Chestnut St.
Lombard St.
Pier 15
Lombard St.
TELEGRAPH HILL
Coit Tower
Greenwich St.
◆ Exploratorium
Filbert St.
Washington Sq.
Pier 9 Pier 7
Green St.
Union St.
Union St.
Green St.
Pier 5
Vallejo St.
Pier 3
Green St.
Broadway
Pier 1
Vallejo St.
Broadway
Tunnel
Pacific Ave.
FINANCIAL DISTRICT
Jackson Square Historic District
EMBARCADERO
RUSSIAN HILL
Jackson St.
Transamerica Pyramid
Washington St.
Out the Door
Ferry Building
101
Washington St.
Clay St.
Miette
Clay St.
San Francisco Railway Museum/ F Line
Sacramento St.
California St.
NOB HILL
Wells Fargo Bank History Museum
EMBARCADERO
Cable Car
Pine St.
Bush St.
Sutter St.
Market Street buildings
UNION SQUARE
MONTGOMERY ST.
Post St.
Union Sq.
Geary St.
Pier 28
O'Farrell St.
Pier 30
Ellis St.
TENDERLOIN
POWELL ST.
Pier 32
Eddy St.
Pier 34
Turk St.
Golden Gate Ave.
San Francisco–Oakland Bay Bridge
Pier 38
CIVIC CENTER
Pier 40
Grove St.
CIVIC CENTER
SOMA
South Park
Pier 42
Pier 44
101
Market St.
MISSION BAY
South Beach Harbor
Pier 48
Mission Creek Channel St.
Marina
Pier 50
14th St.
15th St.

0   500 M
0   1,500 ft

KEY
🅱 BART station

GETTING THERE

The Powell–Hyde and Powell–Mason cable-car lines both end near Fisherman's Wharf. The walk from downtown through North Beach to the northern waterfront is lovely, and if you stick to Columbus Avenue, the incline is relatively gentle. F-line trolleys run all the way down Market to the Embarcadero, then north to the wharf, but a packed trolley or two may pass by before one with room stops.

TOP REASONS TO GO

Ferry Building: Join locals eyeing luscious produce and foods prepared by some of the city's best chefs at San Francisco's premier farmers' market on Saturday morning.

Alcatraz: Go from a scenic bay tour to "the hole"—solitary confinement in absolute darkness—while inmates and guards tell you stories about what life was really like on the Rock.

F-line: Grab a polished wooden seat aboard one of the city's vintage streetcars and clatter down the tracks toward the Ferry Building's spire.

Exploratorium: Play with the ultimate marble run, touch your way through the pitch-black Tactile Dome, or explore yourself in the Science of Sharing at the city's beloved hands-on science museum in its spectacular bay-side home.

QUICK BITES

The Ferry Building is a favorite spot for a bite on the Embarcadero.

Miette. If you need a sweet treat, head to pink Miette, where the cakes and pastries are absolute organic perfection. ✉ 1 Ferry Bldg., Embarcadero ☎ 415/837-0300 ⊕ www.miette.com.

Out the Door. Grab something to go from the beloved Vietnamese restaurant Slanted Door's takeout counter. ✉ 1 Ferry Bldg., Embarcadero ☎ 415/321-3740 ⊕ www.outthedoors.com.

PLANNING YOUR TIME

If you're planning to go to Alcatraz, be sure to buy your tickets in advance, as tours frequently sell out. Alcatraz ferries leave from Pier 33—so there isn't a single good reason to suffer Pier 39's tacky, overpriced attractions. If you're a sailor at heart, though, definitely spend an hour with the historic ships of the Hyde Street Pier.

FERRIES

The bay is a huge part of San Francisco's charm, and getting out on the water gives you an attractive and unique (though windy) perspective on the city. ■TIP➜ A ride on a commuter ferry is cheaper than a cruise, and just as lovely.

Blue & Gold Fleet. This ferry operator offers bay cruises and, in summer, high-speed Rocket-Boat rides, as well as commuter service to Oakland, Alameda, Tiburon, Sausalito, Vallejo, and Angel Island. ✉ Pier 39, Fisherman's Wharf ☎ 415/705-5555 ⊕ www.blueandgoldfleet.com.

Red and White Fleet. Choose from among the widest range of tour options, including sunset cruises from April to October. ✉ Pier 43½, Fisherman's Wharf ☎ 415/673-2900 ⊕ www.redandwhite.com.

6

Sightseeing
★★★
Nightlife
—
Dining
★★★
Lodging
★★★★
Shopping
★★

San Francisco's waterfront neighborhoods have fabulous views and utterly different personalities. Kitschy, overpriced Fisherman's Wharf struggles to maintain the last shreds of its existence as a working wharf, while Pier 39 is a full-fledged consumer circus. The Ferry Building draws well-heeled locals with its culinary pleasures, firmly connecting the Embarcadero and downtown. Between the Ferry Building and Pier 39, a former maritime no-man's-land now houses the relocated Exploratorium, a $90-million cruise-ship terminal, Alcatraz Landing, fashionable waterfront restaurants, and restored, pedestrian-friendly piers.

FISHERMAN'S WHARF

Updated by
Denise M. Leto

The crack of fresh Dungeness crab, the aroma of sourdough warm from the oven, the cry of the gulls—in some ways you can experience Fisherman's Wharf today as it has been for more than 100 years. Italians began fishing these waters in the 19th century as immigrants to booming Barbary Coast San Francisco. Family businesses established generations ago continue to this day—look for the Alioto-Lazio Fish Company, selling crab fresh off the boat here for more than 70 years, and Castagnola's restaurant, serving Italian food and seafood since 1916.

As the local fishing industry has contracted and environmental awareness has changed fishing regulations, Fisherman's Wharf has morphed. Fewer families make a living off the sea here, fewer fishing boats go out, and more of the wharf survives on tourist dollars. You'll see more schlock here than in any other neighborhood in town: overpriced food alongside discount electronics stores, bargain-luggage outlets, and cheap T-shirts and souvenirs.

It's enough to send locals running for the hills, but there are things here worth experiencing. Explore maritime history aboard the fabulous ships of the Hyde Street Pier, amuse yourself early-20th-century style with the mechanical diversions at Musée Mécanique, and grab a bowl of chowder or some Dungeness crab from one of the stands along Jefferson Street to get a taste of what made Fisherman's Wharf what it is in the first place. If you come early, you can avoid the crowds and get a sense of the Wharf's functional side: it's not entirely an amusement-park replica.

TOP ATTRACTIONS

FAMILY
Fodor'sChoice
★

Hyde Street Pier. Cotton candy and souvenirs are all well and good, but if you want to get to the heart of the Wharf—boats—there's no better place to do it than at this pier, one of the Wharf area's best bargains. Depending on the time of day, you might see boatbuilders at work or children pretending to man an early-1900s ship.

Don't pass up the centerpiece collection of historic vessels, part of the **San Francisco Maritime National Historic Park**, almost all of which can be boarded. The *Balclutha*, an 1886 full-rigged three-masted sailing vessel that's more than 250 feet long, sailed around Cape Horn 17 times. Kids especially love the *Eureka*, a side-wheel passenger and car ferry, for her onboard collection of vintage cars. The *Hercules* is a steam-powered tugboat, and the *C.A. Thayer* is a beautifully restored three-masted schooner.

Across the street from the pier and a museum in itself is the maritime park's **Visitor Center** (*499 Jefferson St., 415/447–5000; June–Aug., daily 9:30–5:30; Sept.–May, daily 9:30–5*), whose fun, large-scale exhibits make it an engaging stop. See a huge First Order Fresnel lighthouse lens and a shipwrecked boat. Then stroll through time in the exhibit "The Waterfront," where you can touch the timber from a gold rush–era ship recovered from below the Financial District, peek into 19th-century storefronts, and see the sails of an Italian fishing vessel. ⊠ *Hyde and Jefferson Sts., Fisherman's Wharf* ☎ *415/561–7100* ⊕ *www.nps.gov/safr* 🚢 *Ships $10 (ticket good for 7 days).*

QUICK
BITES

Buena Vista Café. Locals love the cheery Buena Vista Café, which claims to be the first place in the United States to have served Irish coffee. The bartenders serve about 2,000 Irish coffees a day, so it's always crowded; try for a table overlooking Victorian Park and its cable-car turntable. ■ TIP➔ The café dishes up great breakfasts all day, including crab omelets and crab Benedict. ⊠ *2765 Hyde St., Fisherman's Wharf* ☎ *415/474–5044* ⊕ *www.thebuenavista.com.*

FAMILY
Fodor'sChoice
★

Musée Mécanique. Once a staple at Playland-at-the-Beach, San Francisco's early 20th-century amusement park, the antique mechanical contrivances at this time-warped arcade—including peep shows and nickelodeons—make it one of the most worthwhile attractions at the Wharf. Some favorites are the giant and rather creepy "Laffing Sal," an arm-wrestling machine, the world's only steam-powered motorcycle,

ESCAPE FROM ALCATRAZ

Federal-prison officials liked to claim that it was impossible to escape Alcatraz, and for the most part, that assertion was true. For seasoned swimmers, though, the trip has never posed a problem—in fact, it's been downright popular.

In the 1930s, in an attempt to dissuade the feds from converting Alcatraz into a prison, a handful of schoolgirls made the swim to the city. At age 60, native son Jack LaLanne did it (for the second time) while shackled and towing a 1,000-pound rowboat. Every year a couple of thousand participants take the plunge during the annual Escape from Alcatraz Triathlon. Heck, a dog made the crossing in 2005 and finished well ahead of most of the (human) pack. And since 2006, seven-year-old Braxton Bilbrey remains the youngest "escapee" on record. Incidentally, those reports of shark-infested waters are true, but the sharks are almost never dangerous species.

and mechanical fortune-telling figures that speak from their curtained boxes. Note the depictions of race that betray the prejudices of the time: stoned Chinese figures in the "Opium-Den" and clown-faced African Americans eating watermelon in the "Mechanical Farm." ■TIP→ Admission is free, but you'll need quarters to bring the machines to life. ⊠ *Pier 45, Shed A, Fisherman's Wharf* ☎ *415/346–2000* ⊕ *museemecaniquesf.com* 🔖 *Free.*

FAMILY **Pier 39.** The city's most popular waterfront attraction draws millions of visitors each year, who come to browse through its shops and concessions hawking every conceivable form of souvenir. The pier can be quite crowded, and the numerous street performers may leave you feeling more harassed than entertained. Arriving early in the morning ensures you a front-row view of the sea lions that bask here, but if you're here to shop—and make no mistake about it, Pier 39 wants your money—be aware that most stores don't open until 9:30 or 10 (later in winter).

Brilliant colors enliven the double-decker **San Francisco Carousel** (*$5 per ride*), decorated with images of such city landmarks as the Golden Gate Bridge and Lombard Street.

Follow the sound of barking to the northwest side of the pier to view the **sea lions** that flop about the floating docks. During the summer, orange-clad naturalists answer questions and offer fascinating facts about the playful pinnipeds—for example, that most of the animals here are males.

At the **Aquarium of the Bay** (*415/623–5300 or 888/732–3483, www. aquariumofthebay.org; $19.95, hrs vary but at least 10–6 daily*) moving walkways transport you through a space surrounded on three sides by water filled with indigenous San Francisco Bay marine life, from fish and plankton to sharks. Many find the aquarium overpriced; if you can, take advantage of the family rate (*$70 for 2 adults and 2 kids under 12*). ⊠ *Beach St. at Embarcadero, Fisherman's Wharf* ⊕ *www.pier39.com.*

SS *Jeremiah O'Brien*. A participant in the D-Day landing in Normandy during World War II, this Liberty Ship freighter is one of two such vessels (out of more than 2,700 built) still in working order. On board you can peek at the crew's living quarters—bedding and personal items make it look as if they've just stepped away for a moment—and the officers' mess hall. The large display of the Normandy invasion, one of many exhibits on board, was a gift from France. To keep the 1943 ship in sailing shape, the steam engine—which appears in the film *Titanic*—is operated dockside seven times a year on special "steaming weekends." Cruises take place several times a year between May and October, and the vessel is open to visitors daily. ⊠ *Pier 45, Fisherman's Wharf* ☎ *415/544–0100* ⊕ *www.ssjeremiahobrien.org* ⌨ *$20 (family pass $40).*

OFF THE BEATEN PATH

WORTH NOTING

Angel Island. For an outdoorsy adventure and some fascinating history, consider a day at this island northwest of Alcatraz. Discovered by Spaniards in 1775 and declared a U.S. military reserve 75 years later, the island was used as a screening ground for Asian, mostly Chinese, immigrants—who were often held for months, even years, before being granted entry—from 1910 until 1940. You can visit the restored Immigration Station, from the dock where detainees landed to the barracks where you can see the poems in Chinese script they etched onto the walls. In 1963 the government designated Angel Island a state park. Today people come for picnics, hikes along the scenic 5-mile path that winds around the island's perimeter, and tram tours that explain the park's history. Blue & Gold Fleet is the only Angel Island ferry service with departures from San Francisco; boats leave from Pier 41. ⊠ *Pier 41, Fisherman's Wharf* ☎ *415/435–1915 park information and ferry schedules, 415/705–5555, 800/426–8687 tickets* ⊕ *angelisland.com* ⌨ *$18 round-trip.*

6

Cartoon Art Museum. Krazy Kat, Zippy the Pinhead, Batman, and other colorful cartoon icons greet you at the Cartoon Art Museum, established with an endowment from cartoonist-icon Charles M. Schulz and ensconced in its Fisherman's Wharf home in 2017. The museum's strength is its changing exhibits, which explore such topics as America from the perspective of international political cartoons, and the output of women and African-American cartoonists. Serious fans of cartoons—especially those on the quirky underground side—will likely enjoy the exhibits; those with a casual interest may be bored. The store here carries cool titles to add to your collection. Consult the museum's website for open hours and admission. ⊠ *781 Beach St., Fisherman's Wharf* ☎ *415/227–8666* ⊕ *www.cartoonart.org.*

Ghirardelli Square. Most of the redbrick buildings in this early-20th-century complex were once part of the Ghirardelli factory. Now tourists come here to pick up the famous chocolate, though you can purchase it all over town and save yourself a trip to what is essentially a mall. But this is the only place to watch the cool chocolate manufactory in action. Placards throughout the square describe the factory's history. ⊠ *900 N. Point St., Fisherman's Wharf* ☎ *415/775–5500* ⊕ *www.ghirardellisq.com.*

FAMILY **San Francisco National Maritime Museum.** You'll feel as if you're out to sea when you step aboard, er, inside this sturdy, round, ship-shape structure dubbed the Bathhouse Building. The first floor of the museum, part of the **San Francisco Maritime National Historical Park,** has stunningly restored undersea dreamscape murals and some of the museum's intricate ship models. The first-floor balcony overlooks the beach and has lovely WPA-era tile designs. ■TIP➔ **If you've got young kids in tow, the museum makes a great quick, free stop. Then pick up ice cream at Ghirardelli Square across the street and enjoy it on the beach or next door in Victorian Park, where you can watch the cable cars turn around.** ✉ *Aquatic Park, foot of Polk St., Fisherman's Wharf* ☎ *415/447–5000* ⊕ *www.nps.gov/safr* ⊡ *Donation suggested.*

USS Pampanito. Get an intriguing, if mildly claustrophobic, glimpse into life on a submarine during World War II on this small, 80-man sub, which sank six Japanese warships and damaged four others. ■TIP➔ **There's not much in the way of interpretive signs, so opt for the audio tour to learn about what you're seeing.** ✉ *Pier 45, Fisherman's Wharf* ☎ *415/775–1943* ⊕ *www.maritime.org/pamphome.htm* ⊡ *$20 (family pass $45).*

EMBARCADERO

Stretching from below the Bay Bridge to Fisherman's Wharf, San Francisco's flat, accessible waterfront invites you to get up close and personal with the bay, the picturesque and constant backdrop to this stunning city. For decades the Embarcadero was obscured by a terrible raised freeway and known best for the giant buildings on its piers that further cut off the city from the bay. With the freeway gone and a few piers restored for public access, the Embarcadero has been given a new lease on life. Millions of visitors may come through the northern waterfront every year, lured by Fisherman's Wharf and Pier 39, but locals tend to stop short of these, opting instead for the gastronomic pleasures of the Ferry Building. Between the two, though, you'll find tourists and San Franciscans alike soaking up the sun, walking out over the water on a long pier to see the sailboats, savoring the excellent restaurants and old-time watering holes, watching the street performers that crowd Justin Herman Plaza on a sunny day—these are the simple joys that make you happy you're in San Francisco, whether for a few days or a lifetime.

TOP ATTRACTIONS

Fodor'sChoice **Alcatraz.** *See the highlighted feature at the end of the chapter.*
      ★

FAMILY **Exploratorium.** Walking into this fascinating "museum of science, art, Fodor'sChoice and human perception" is like visiting a mad-scientist's laboratory.
      ★   Most of the exhibits are supersize, and you can play with everything. Signature experiential exhibits include the Tinkering Studio and a glass Bay Observatory building, where the exhibits inside help visitors better understand what they see outside.

Get an *Alice in Wonderland* feeling in the distortion room, where you seem to shrink and grow as you walk across the slanted, checkered floor. In the shadow room, a powerful flash freezes an image of your shadow on the wall; jumping is a favorite pose. "Pushover" demonstrates cow-tipping, but for people: stand on one foot and try to keep your balance while a friend swings a striped panel in front of you (trust us, you're going to fall).

More than 650 other exhibits focus on sea and insect life, computers, electricity, patterns and light, language, the weather, and more. "Explainers"—usually high-school students on their days off—demonstrate cool scientific tools and procedures, like DNA-sample collection and cow-eye dissection. One surefire hit is the pitch-black, touchy-feely Tactile Dome ($8–$15 extra; reservations required). In this geodesic dome strewn with textured objects, you crawl through a course of ladders, slides, and tunnels, relying solely on your sense of touch. Lovey-dovey couples sometimes linger in the "grope dome," but be forewarned: the staff will turn on the lights if necessary. ■TIP→ Patrons must be at least seven years old to enter the Tactile Dome, and the space is not for the claustrophobic. ✉ *Piers 15–17, Embarcadero* ☎ *415/561–0360 general information, 415/561–0362 Tactile Dome reservations* ⊕ *www.exploratorium.edu* 🖅 *$30.*

Fodor's Choice
★

Ferry Building. The jewel of the Embarcadero, erected in 1896, is topped by a 230-foot clock tower modeled after the campanile of the cathedral in Seville, Spain. On the morning of April 18, 1906, the tower's four clock faces, powered by the swinging of a 14-foot pendulum, stopped at 5:17—the moment the great earthquake struck—and stayed still for 12 months.

Today San Franciscans flock to the street-level marketplace, stocking up on supplies from local favorites such as Acme Bread, Scharffen Berger Chocolate, Cowgirl Creamery, Blue Bottle Coffee, and Humphry Slocombe ice cream. Slanted Door, the city's beloved high-end Vietnamese restaurant, is here, along with highly regarded Bouli Bar. The seafood bar at Hog Island Oyster Company has fantastic bay view panoramas. On the plaza side, the outdoor tables at Gott's Roadside offer great people-watching with their famous burgers. On Saturday morning the plazas outside the building buzz with an upscale farmers' market where you can buy exotic sandwiches and other munchables. Extending south from the piers north of the building all the way to the Bay Bridge, the waterfront promenade out front is a favorite among joggers and picnickers, with a front-row view of sailboats plying the bay. True to its name, the Ferry Building still serves actual ferries: from its eastern flank they sail to Sausalito, Larkspur, Tiburon, and the East Bay. ✉ *Embarcadero at foot of Market St., Embarcadero* ☎ *415/983–8030* ⊕ *www.ferrybuildingmarketplace.com.*

F-line. The city's system of vintage electric trolleys, the F-line, gives the cable cars a run for their money as a beloved mode of transportation. The beautifully restored streetcars—some dating from the 19th century—run from the Castro District down Market Street to the Embarcadero, then north to Fisherman's Wharf. Each car is unique, restored to the colors of its city of origin, from New Orleans and Philadelphia to Moscow and Milan. ■TIP→ Purchase tickets on board; exact change is required. ✉ *San Francisco* ⊕ *www.streetcar.org* 🖅 *$2.50.*

6

WORTH NOTING

FAMILY **San Francisco Railway Museum.** A labor of love brought to you by the same vintage-transit enthusiasts responsible for the F-line's revival, this one-room museum and store celebrates the city's streetcars and cable cars with photographs, models, and artifacts. The permanent exhibit includes the replicated end of a streetcar with a working cab—complete with controls and a bell—for kids to explore; the cool, antique Wiley birdcage traffic signal; and models and display cases to view. Right on the F-line track, just across from the Ferry Building, this is a great quick stop. ⊠ *77 Steuart St., Embarcadero* ☏ *415/974–1948* ⊕ *www. streetcar.org* ⊠ *Free.*

FINANCIAL DISTRICT

During the latter half of the 19th century, when San Francisco was a brawling, extravagant gold-rush town, today's Financial District was underwater. Yerba Buena Cove reached all the way up to Montgomery Street, and what's now Jackson Square was the heart of the Barbary Coast, bordering some of the roughest wharves in the world. These days, Jackson Square is a genteel and upscale neighborhood wedged between North Beach and the Financial District, but buried below Montgomery Street lies a remnant of these wild days: more than 100 ships abandoned by frantic crews and passengers caught up in gold fever lie under the foundations of buildings here.

The Financial District of the 21st century is a decidedly less exciting affair, and safer, too: no one's going to slip you a Mickey and ship you off to Shanghai. It's all office towers packed with mazes of cubicles now, and folks in suits and "office casual" fill the sidewalks at lunchtime. When the sun sets, this quarter empties out fast. The few sights here will appeal mainly to gold-rush history enthusiasts; others can safely steer clear.

EXPLORING

Jackson Square Historic District. This was the heart of the Barbary Coast of the Gay '90s—the 1890s, that is. Although most of the red-light district was destroyed in the fire that followed the 1906 earthquake, the remaining old redbrick buildings, many of them now occupied by advertising agencies, law offices, and antiques firms, retain hints of the romance and rowdiness of San Francisco's early days.

With its gentrified gold rush–era buildings, the 700 block of **Montgomery Street** just barely evokes the Barbary Coast days, but this was a colorful block in the 19th century and on into the 20th. Writers Mark Twain and Bret Harte were among the contributors to the spunky *Golden Era* newspaper, which occupied No. 732 (now part of the building at No. 744). From 1959 to 1996, the late ambulance-chaser extraordinaire, lawyer Melvin Belli, had his headquarters at Nos. 722 and 728–730. There was never a dull moment in Belli's world; he represented clients from the actress Mae West to Gloria

Sykes (who in 1964 claimed that a cable-car accident turned her into a nymphomaniac) to the disgraced televangelists Jim and Tammy Faye Bakker. Whenever he won a case, he fired a cannon and raised the Jolly Roger. Belli was also known for receiving a letter from the never-caught Zodiac killer.

Restored 19th-century brick buildings line Hotaling Place, which connects Washington and Jackson Streets. The lane is named for the **A.P. Hotaling Company whiskey distillery** (*451 Jackson St., at Hotaling Pl.*), the largest liquor repository on the West Coast in its day. The exceptional City Guides (*415/557–4266, www.sfcityguides. org*) Gold Rush City walking tour covers this area and brings its history to life. ⊠ *Bordered by Columbus Ave., Broadway, and Washington and Sansome Sts., San Francisco.*

> ### WHISKEY RHYME
>
> The Italianate Hotaling building survived the disastrous 1906 quake and fire—a miracle considering the thousands of barrels of inflammable liquid inside. A plaque on the side of the structure repeats a famous query: "If, as they say, god spanked the town for being over frisky, why did he burn the churches down and save Hotaling's whiskey?"

6

Market Street buildings. The street, which bisects the city at an angle, has consistently challenged San Francisco's architects. One of the most intriguing responses to this challenge sits diagonally across Market Street from the Palace Hotel. The tower of the **Hobart Building** (No. 582) combines a flat facade and oval sides and is considered one of Willis Polk's best works in the city. East on Market Street is Charles Havens's triangular **Flatiron Building** (Nos. 540–548), another classic solution. At Bush Street, the **Donahue Monument** holds its own against the skyscrapers that tower over the intersection. This homage to waterfront mechanics, which survived the 1906 earthquake (a famous photograph shows Market Street in ruins around the sculpture), was designed by Douglas Tilden, a noted California sculptor. The plaque in the sidewalk next to the monument marks the spot as the location of the San Francisco Bay shoreline in 1848. Telltale nautical details such as anchors, ropes, and shells adorn the gracefully detailed **Matson Building** (No. 215), built in the 1920s for the shipping line Matson Navigation. ⊠ *Between New Montgomery and Beale Sts., Financial District.*

Transamerica Pyramid. It's neither owned by Transamerica nor is it a pyramid, but this 853-foot-tall obelisk *is* the most photographed of the city's high-rises. Excoriated in the design stages as "the world's largest architectural folly," the icon was quickly hailed as a masterpiece when it opened in 1972. Today it's probably the city's most recognized structure after the Golden Gate Bridge. Visit the small, street-level visitor center to see the virtual view from the top, watch videos about the building's history, and perhaps pick up a T-shirt. ■ TIP➜ A fragrant redwood grove along the east side of the building, replete with benches and a cheerful fountain, is a placid patch in which to unwind. ⊠ *600 Montgomery St., Financial District* ⊕ *www.pyramidcenter.com.*

Alcatraz as Native Land

In the 1960s, Native Americans attempted to reclaim Alcatraz, citing an 1868 treaty that granted Native Americans any surplus federal land. Their activism crested in 1969, when several dozen Native Americans began a 19-month occupation, supported by public opinion and friendly media.

The group offered to buy the island from the government for $24 worth of beads and other goods—exactly what Native Americans had been paid for Manhattan in 1626. In their Proclamation to the Great White Father and His People, the group laid out the 10 reasons why Alcatraz would make an ideal Indian reservation, among them: "There is no industry and so unemployment is very great," and "The soil is rocky and nonproductive, and the land does not support game." Federal agents removed the last holdouts in 1971, but each Thanksgiving Native Americans and others gather on the island to commemorate the takeover. In 2013 the park service restored the protesters' fading graffiti on the water tower, and today's visitors are still greeted with the huge message: "Indians Welcome. Indian Land."

Wells Fargo Bank History Museum. There were no formal banks in San Francisco during the early years of the gold rush, and miners often entrusted their gold dust to saloon keepers. In 1852, Wells Fargo opened its first bank in the city on this spot, and the company soon established banking offices in mother-lode camps throughout California. At the fun two-story museum, you can pick up a free ticket and climb aboard a stagecoach—the projected driver will tell you about the ride and the scenery passing by on the wall—or take the reins and experience a trip out west. Have your picture taken in front of the gorgeous red Concord stagecoach (collect your souvenir photo at the desk), the likes of which carried passengers from St. Joseph, Missouri, to San Francisco in just three weeks during the 1850s. The museum also displays samples of nuggets and gold dust from mines, an old telegraph machine on which you can practice sending codes, and tools the '49ers used to coax the precious mineral from the ground. ✉ *420 Montgomery St., Financial District* ☎ *415/396–2619* ⊕ *www.wellsfargohistory.com* 🎫 *Free.*

ALCATRAZ

"They made that place purely for punishment, where men would rot. It was designed to systematically destroy human beings . . . Cold, gray, and lonely, it had a weird way of haunting you—there were those dungeons that you heard about, but there was also the city . . . only a mile and a quarter away, so close you could almost touch it. Sometimes the wind would blow a certain way and you could smell the Italian cooking in North Beach and hear the laughter of people, of women and kids. That made it worse than hell."

—Jim Quillen, former Alcatraz inmate

Gripping the rail as the ferryboat pitches gently in the chilly breeze, you watch formidable Alcatraz rising ahead. Imagine making this trip shackled at the ankle and waist, the looming fortress on the craggy island ahead, waiting to swallow you whole. Thousands of visitors come every day to walk in the footsteps of Alcatraz's notorious criminals. The stories of life and death on "the Rock" may sometimes be exaggerated, but it's almost impossible to resist the chance to wander the cellblock that tamed the country's toughest gangsters and saw daring escape attempts of tremendous desperation.

LIFE ON THE ROCK

The federal penitentiary's first warden, James A. Johnston, was largely responsible for Alcatraz's (mostly false) hell-on-earth reputation. A tough but relatively humane disciplinarian, Johnston strictly limited the information flow to and from the prison when it opened in 1934. Prisoners' letters were censored, newspapers and radios were forbidden, and no visits were allowed during a convict's first three months in the slammer. Understandably, imaginations ran wild on the mainland.

A LIFE OF PRIVILEGE

Monotony was an understatement on Alcatraz; the same precise schedule was kept daily. The rulebook stated, "You are entitled to food, clothing, shelter, and medical attention. Anything else you get is a privilege." These privileges, from the right to work to the ability to receive mail, were earned by following the prison's rules. A relatively minor infraction meant losing privileges. A serious breach, like fighting, brought severe punishments like time in the Hole (a.k.a. the Strip Cell, since the prisoner had to strip) or the Oriental (an absolutely dark, silent cell with a hole in the ground for a toilet).

THE SPAGHETTI RIOT

Johnston knew that poor food was one of the major causes of prison riots, so he insisted that Alcatraz serve the best chow in the prison system. But the next warden at Alcatraz slacked off, and in 1950, one spaghetti meal too many sent the inmates over the edge. Guards deployed tear gas to subdue the rioters.

A PRISONER'S DAY

6:30 AM: Wake-up call. Prisoners get up, get dressed, and clean cells.

6:50 AM: Prisoners stand at cell doors to be counted.

7:00 AM: Prisoners march single-file to mess hall for breakfast.

7:20 AM: Prisoners head to work or industries detail; count.

9:30 AM: 8-minute break; count.

11:30 AM: Count; prisoners march to mess hall for lunch.

12:00 PM: Prisoners march to cells; count; break in cells.

12:20 PM: Prisoners leave cells, march single-file back to work; count.

2:30 PM: 8-minute break; count.

4:15 PM: Prisoners stop work, two counts.

4:25 PM: Prisoners march into mess hall and are counted; dinner.

4:45 PM: Prisoners return to cells and are locked in.

5:00 PM: Prisoners stand at their doors to be counted.

8:00 PM: Count.

9:30 PM: Count; lights out.

12:01 AM—5 AM: Three counts.

INFAMOUS INMATES

Fewer than 2,000 inmates ever did time on the Rock; though they weren't necessarily the worst criminals, they were definitely the worst prisoners. Most were escape artists, and others, like Al Capone, had corrupted the prison system from the inside with bribes.

Name Al "Scarface" Capone

On the Rock 1934–1939

In for Tax evasion

Claim to fame Notorious Chicago gangster and bootlegger who arranged the 1929 St. Valentine's Day Massacre.

Hard fact Capone was among the first transfers to the Rock and arrived smiling and joking. He soon realized the party was over. Capone endured a few stints in the Hole and Warden Johnston's early enforced-silence policy; he was also stabbed by a fellow inmate. The gangster eventually caved, saying "it looks like Alcatraz has got me licked," thus cementing the prison's reputation.

Name Robert "The Birdman" Stroud

On the Rock 1942–1959

In for Murder, including the fatal stabbing of a prison guard

Claim to fame Subject of the acclaimed but largely fictitious 1962 film *Birdman of Alcatraz*.

Hard fact Stroud was actually known as the "Bird Doctor of Leavenworth." While incarcerated in Leavenworth prison through the 1920s and 30s, he became an expert on birds, tending an aviary and writing two books. The stench and mess in his cell discouraged the guards from searching it—and finding Stroud's homemade still. His years on the Rock were birdless.

Name George "Machine Gun" Kelly

On the Rock 1934–1951

In for Kidnapping

Claim to fame Became an expert with a machine gun at the urging of his wife, Kathryn. Kathryn also encouraged his string of bank robberies and the kidnapping for ransom of oilman Charles Urschel. While stashed in Leavenworth on a life sentence, Kelly boasted that he would escape and then free Kathryn. That got him a one-way ticket to Alcatraz.

Hard fact Was an altar boy on Alcatraz and was generally considered a model prisoner.

NO ESCAPE

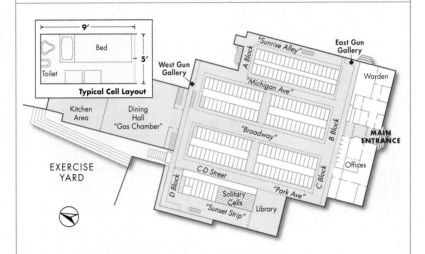

Alcatraz was a maximum-security federal penitentiary with one guard for every three prisoners. The biggest deterrent to escape, though, was the 1.4 miles of icy bay waters separating the Rock from the city. Only a few prisoners made it off the island, and only one is known to have survived. And that story about the shark-infested waters? There are sharks in the bay, but they're not the man-eating kind.

Bloodiest Attempt: In 1946, six prisoners hatched a plan to surprise a guard, seize weapons, and escape through the recreation yard. They succeeded up to a point, arming themselves and locking several guards into cells, but things got ugly when the group couldn't find the key that opened the door to the prison yard. Desperate, they opened fire on the trapped guards. Warden Johnston called in the Marines, who shelled the cell house for two days in the so-called Battle of Alcatraz. Three ringleaders were killed in the fighting; two were executed for murder; and one, who was just 19 years old, got 99 years slapped on to his sentence.

Craftiest Attempt: Over six months, three convicts stole bits and pieces from the kitchen and machine shop to make drills and digging pieces. They used these basic tools to widen a vent into the utility corridor. They also gathered bits of cardboard, toilet paper, and hair from the prison's barbershop to make crude models of their own heads. Then, like teenagers sneaking out, they put the decoy heads in their cots and walked away—up the pipes in the utility corridor to the roof, then down a drainpipe to the ground. They set sail in a raft made from prison raincoats, and are officially presumed dead.

Most Anticlimactic: In 1962, one prisoner spent an entire year loosening the bars in a window. Then he slipped through and managed to swim all the way to Fort Point, near the Golden Gate Bridge. He promptly fell asleep there and was found an hour later by some teenagers.

6 TIPS FOR ESCAPING TO ALCATRAZ

"Broadway," once the cell blocks' busiest corridor.

1. Buy your ticket in advance. Visit the website for Alcatraz Cruises (☎ 415/981–7625 ⊕ www.alcatrazcruises.com) to scout out available departure times for the ferry. Prepay by credit card—the ticket price covers the boat ride and the audio tour—and print your ticket at home. Bring it to Pier 33 up to an hour before sailing and experience just a touch of schadenfreude as you overhear attendants tell scores of too-late passengers that your tour is sold out.

2. Dress smart. Bring that pullover you packed to ward off the chill from the boat ride and Alcatraz Island. Also: sneakers. Some Alcatraz guides are fanatical about making excellent time.

3. Go for the evening tour. You'll get even more out of the experience if you do it at night. The evening tour has programs not offered during the day, the bridge-to-bridge view of the city twinkles at night, and your "prison experience" will be amplified as dark-ness mournfully falls while you shuffle around the cell block.

4. Unplug and go against the flow. If you miss a cue on the excellent audio tour and find yourself out of synch, don't sweat it—use it as an opportunity to switch off the tape and walk against the grain of the people following the tour. No one will stop you if you walk back through a cell block on your own, taking the time to listen to the haunting sound of your own footsteps on the concrete floor.

5. Be mindful of scheduled and limited-capacity talks. Some programs only happen once a day (the schedule is posted in the cell house). Certain talks have limited capacity seating, so keep an eye out for a cell house staffer handing out passes shortly before the start time.

6. Talk to the staff. One of the island's greatest resources is its staff, who practically bubble over with information. Pick their brains, and draw them out about what they know.

PRACTICALITIES

Visitors at the Alcatraz dock waiting to depart "Uncle Sam's Devil's Island."

GETTING THERE
All cruises are operated by Alcatraz Cruises, the park's authorized concessionaire.

TIMING
The boat ride to Alcatraz is only about 15 minutes long, but you should allow about three hours for your entire visit. The delightful F-line vintage streetcars are the most direct public transit to the dock; on weekdays the 10-Townsend bus will get you within a few blocks of Pier 33.

FOOD
The prisoners might have enjoyed good food on Alcatraz, but you won't—unless you pack a picnic. Food is not available on the island, so be sure to stock up before you board the boat. Sandwich fare is available at Alcatraz Landing, at Pier 33, and the Ferry Building's bounty is just a 20-minute walk from Pier 33. In a pinch, you can also pony up for the underwhelming snacks on the boat.

STORM TROOPER ALERT!

When he was filming *Star Wars,* George Lucas recorded the sound of Alcatraz's cell doors slamming shut and used the sound bite in the movie whenever Darth Vader's star cruiser closed its doors.

KIDS ON THE ROCK
Parents should be aware that the audio tour, while engaging and worthwhile, includes some startlingly realistic sound effects. (Some children might not get a kick out of the gunshots from the Battle of Alcatraz—or the guards' screams, for that matter.) If you stay just one minute ahead in the program, you can always fast forward through the violent moments on your little one's audio tour.

THE MARINA AND THE PRESIDIO

with Cow Hollow

Getting Oriented

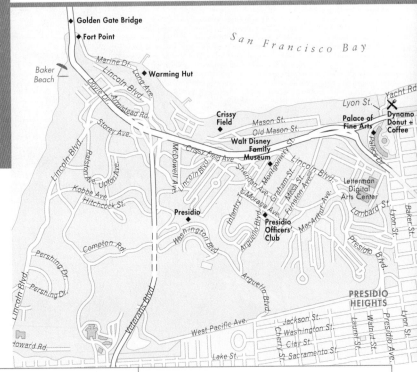

PLANNING YOUR TIME	TOP REASONS TO GO
Walking across the Golden Gate Bridge takes about 30 minutes, but leave some time to take in the view on the other side. If you aren't in a hurry, plan to spend at least two to three hours in the Presidio, and be sure to allow 15 minutes to stroll around the stunning Palace of Fine Arts. In a pinch, make a 30- to 45-minute swing-through for the views. Shoppers can burn up an entire day browsing the Marina's Chestnut Street and Cow Hollow's Union Street. Weekends are liveliest, while Mondays are quiet, since some shops close.	**Golden Gate Bridge:** Get a good look at the iconic span from the Presidio, then bundle up and walk over the water. **Shop Cow Hollow and the Marina:** Browse hip boutiques and lavish antiques shops on Union Street, Cow Hollow's main drag. Then head north to Chestnut Street. **Palace of Fine Arts:** Bring a picnic to this movingly beautiful faux-Greek remnant of the 1915 Panama-Pacific International Exposition and travel back in time to the city's post-earthquake-and-fire coming-out party. **Crissy Field:** Join jogging, cycling, and kitesurfing locals along this beautifully restored strip of sand and marshland where the bay laps the shore, a stone's throw from the Golden Gate Bridge. **Presidio wanderings:** Lace up your walking shoes and follow one of the wooded trails; the city will feel a hundred miles away.

The Marina, Cow Hollow, and The Presidio

GETTING THERE

The Marina and the Presidio are great for biking and easily reached along the Embarcadero. The Presidio, vast and with plenty of parking, is one area where it pays to have a car. If you're driving to either the Marina or the Presidio, parking isn't too bad—the Palace of Fine Arts and Crissy Field both have lots. For those without wheels, the free year-round shuttle PresidiGo, which runs two routes through the Presidio every half hour, is a dream; ride both loops for a good one-hour overview. Pick up the shuttle at the transit center at Lincoln Boulevard and Graham Street. Weekdays from 9:30 to 4, a free shuttle runs from the Embarcadero BART/Muni station and the Transbay Temporary Terminal downtown to the Presidio (Muni Passport holders can ride this shuttle during commuter hours as well). For a map and schedule, check ⊕ www.presidio.gov. The only public transportation to this part of town is the bus; the 30–Stockton runs to Chestnut and Laguna in the Marina, two blocks south of Fort Mason.

QUICK BITES

Dynamo Donut & Coffee. This tiny kiosk on the Marina's yacht harbor is the perfect spot to grab a pick-me-up before a stroll to the Palace of Fine Arts or along the beach. The donuts are extra special, from the vanilla bean standby to scrumptious gluten-free options, and Dynamo serves local Four Barrel Coffee. Grab them by 1, when the kiosk closes. ⊠ 110 Yacht Rd., Marina 🕾 415/920–1978 ⊕ www.dynamo-donut.com ⊘ Closed Mon.

Greens to Go. The takeout counter of the famous vegetarian restaurant carries mouthwatering premade salads, sandwiches, and soups. Eat at picnic tables outside or head up a steep flight of stairs to a grassy park with splendid Marina views. ⊠ Fort Mason, Bldg. A, Marina 🕾 415/771–6330 ⊕ www.greensrestaurant.com.

7

THE GOLDEN GATE BRIDGE

Two red towers reach into the sky, floating above the mist like ghost ships on foggy days. If there's one image that instantly conjures San Francisco, it's the majestic Golden Gate Bridge, one of the most recognizable sights in the world.

Spanning the Golden Gate—the mouth of the San Francisco Bay, after which the bridge was named—between San Francisco and pastoral Marin County, the bridge has won both popular and critical acclaim, including being named one of the seven wonders of the modern world. With its simple but powerful art-deco design, the 1.7-mile suspension span and its 750-foot towers were built to withstand winds of more than 100 mph. It's also not a bad place to be in an earthquake: designed to sway almost 28 feet, the Golden Gate Bridge (unlike the Bay Bridge) was undamaged by the 1989 Loma Prieta quake. If you're on the bridge when it's windy, stand still and you can feel it swaying a bit.

Lincoln Blvd. near Doyle Dr. and Fort Point, Presidio 415/921-5858 www. goldengatebridge.org

Pedestrians: Mar.–Oct., daily 5 am–9 pm; Nov.–Feb., daily 5 am–6:30 pm; hrs change with daylight saving time. Bicyclists: daily 24 hrs.

A DAY OVER THE BAY
Crossing the Golden Gate Bridge under your own power is a sensation that's hard to describe. Especially as you approach midspan, hovering more than 200 feet above the water makes you feel as though you're outside of time—exhilarating, a little scary, definitely chilly. From the bridge's eastern-side walkway, the only side pedestrians are allowed on,

you can take in the San Francisco skyline and the bay islands; look west for the wild hills of the Marin Headlands, the curving coast south to Lands End, and the Pacific Ocean. On sunny days, sailboats dot the water, and brave windsurfers test the often-treacherous tides beneath the bridge. A vista point on the Marin County side provides a spectacular city panorama. The views are fantastic however you cross—by foot, bicycle, or motorized vehicle—but driving or cycling will allow you to fully appreciate the bridge from multiple vantage points in and around the Presidio.

THE MAN WHO BUILT THE BRIDGE

In the early 1900s, San Francisco was behind the times. Sure, the city had the engineering marvel of the cable car and hundreds of streetcar lines, but as the largest U.S. city served mainly by ferries, this town needed a bridge. Enter Joseph Strauss, a structural engineer, dreamer, and poet who promised that not only could he build a bridge, but he could also do it on the cheap. At 5 feet 3 inches tall, Strauss was a force of nature. He worked tirelessly over the next 20-odd years, first as a bridge booster and then overseeing its design and construction. Though the final structure bore little resemblance to his original plan, Strauss guarded his legacy jealously, refusing to recognize the seminal contributions of engineer Charles A.

Ellis. In 2007, the Golden Gate Bridge District finally recognized Ellis's role, though Strauss, who died less than a year after opening day in 1937, would doubtless be pleased with the inscription on his statue, which stands sentry in the southern parking lot: "The Man Who Built the Bridge."

VISITING THE BRIDGE TODAY

The bridge has been standing for three-quarters of a century, but the visitor's experience got an upgrade to coincide with the 75th-anniversary celebration in 2012. You can grab a snack at the art deco–style Bridge Café. The recently erected Bridge Pavilion sells attractive, high-quality souvenirs and has a small display of historical artifacts: look for an original brush used to paint the bridge. At the outdoor exhibits, you can see the bridge rise before your eyes on hologram panels, learn about the features that make it art deco, and read about the personalities behind its design and construction. Kids favor the hands-on displays that let them raise the deck with a pulley and make the bridge sway, as it does in high winds and earthquakes. City Guides offers free walking tours of the bridge every Thursday and Sunday at 11 am.

Sightseeing
★★★★
Nightlife
★★
Dining
★★★
Lodging
★★★
Shopping
★★★★

Yachts bob at their moorings, satisfied-looking folks jog along the Marina Green, and multimillion-dollar homes overlook the bay in the picturesque, if somewhat sterile, Marina neighborhood. Does it all seem a bit too perfect? Well, it got this way after the hard knock of Loma Prieta—the current pretty face was put on after hundreds of homes collapsed in the 1989 earthquake. Just west of this waterfront area is a more natural beauty: the Presidio. Once a military base, this beautiful, sprawling park is mostly green space, with hills, woods, and the marshlands of Crissy Field.

THE MARINA

Updated by
Denise M. Leto

Well-funded postcollegiates and the nouveau riche flooded the Marina after the 1989 Loma Prieta earthquake had sent many residents running for more-solid ground, changing the tenor of this formerly low-key neighborhood. The number of yuppie coffee emporiums skyrocketed, a bank became a Williams-Sonoma store, and the local grocer gave way to a Pottery Barn. On weekends a young, fairly homogeneous, well-to-do crowd floods the cafés and bars. (Some things don't change—even before the quake, the Marina Safeway was a famed pickup place for straight singles, hence the nickname "Dateway.") South of Lombard Street is the Marina's affluent neighbor, Cow Hollow, whose main drag, Union Street, has some of the city's best boutique shopping and a good selection of restaurants and cafés. Joggers and kite-flyers head to the Marina Green, the strip of lawn between the yacht club and the mansions of Marina Boulevard.

TOP ATTRACTIONS

Fodor's Choice
★
Palace of Fine Arts. At first glance this stunning, rosy rococo palace seems to be from another world, and indeed, it's the sole survivor of the many tinted-plaster structures (a temporary classical city of sorts) built for the 1915 Panama-Pacific International Exposition, the world's fair that celebrated San Francisco's recovery from the 1906 earthquake and fire. The expo buildings originally extended about a mile along the shore. Bernard Maybeck designed this faux-Roman classic beauty, which was reconstructed in concrete and reopened in 1967. A victim of the elements, the Palace required a piece-by-piece renovation that was completed in 2008.

The pseudo-Latin language adorning the Palace's exterior urns continues to stump scholars. The massive columns (each topped with four "weeping maidens"), great rotunda, and swan-filled lagoon have been used in countless fashion layouts, films, and wedding photo shoots. After admiring the lagoon, look across the street to the house at 3460 Baker St. If the maidens out front look familiar, they should—they're original casts of the "garland ladies" you can see in the Palace's colonnade. ⊠ *3301 Lyon St., at Beach St., Marina* ☎ ⊠ *Free.*

OFF THE
BEATEN
PATH
Wave Organ. Conceived by environmental artist Peter Richards and fashioned by master stonecutter George Gonzales, this unusual wave-activated acoustic sculpture gives off subtle harmonic sounds produced by seawater as it passes through 25 tubes. The sound is loudest at high tide. The granite and marble used for walkways, benches, and alcoves that are part of the piece were salvaged from a gold rush–era cemetery. ⊠ *North of Marina Green at end of jetty by Yacht Rd., park in lot north of Marina Blvd. at Lyon St., Marina.*

7

WORTH NOTING

Fort Mason Center. Originally a depot for the shipment of supplies to the Pacific during World War II, the fort was converted into a cultural center in 1977. Here you can find the vegetarian restaurant Greens and shops, galleries, and performance spaces, most of which are closed on Mondays.

The **Museo Italo-Americano** (*Bldg. C, 415/673–2200, museoitaloamericano.org; Tues.–Sun. noon–4*) is a small gallery that hosts one exhibit at a time, worth a glance if you're already at Fort Mason.

The temporary exhibits downstairs at the **SFMOMA Artists Gallery** (*Bldg. A, 415/441–4777, www.sfmoma.org/visit/artists_gallery; Tues.–Sat. 10:30–5*) can be great, but head upstairs and check out the paintings, sculptures, prints, and photographs for sale or rent. You won't find a Picasso or a Rembrandt, but where else can you get a $50,000 work of art to hang on your wall for $400 (a month)?

From March to October, Friday evenings at Fort Mason mean **Off the Grid** (*offthegridsf.com*); the city's food-truck gathering happens at locations around town, and this is one of the oldest and most popular. ⊠ *Buchanan St. and Marina Blvd., Marina* ☎ *415/345–7500 event information* ⊕ *www.fortmason.org.*

COW HOLLOW

Between old-money Pacific Heights and the well-heeled, postcollegiate Marina lies comfortably upscale Cow Hollow. The neighborhood's name harks back to the 19th-century dairy farms whose owners eked out a living here despite the fact that there was more sand than grass. A patch of grass remains a scarce commodity in this mostly residential area, but Cow Hollow does have one heck of a commercial strip, centered around Union Street (⇨ *Chapter 18, Shopping and Spas*). To get a feel for this accessible bastion of affluence, stroll down Union. Browse the cosmetics and jewelry stores, snazzy clothing boutiques, and shops selling home decor for every taste (if not budget), then rest your feet at one of the many good restaurants or sidewalk cafés.

EXPLORING

Octagon House. This eight-sided home sits across the street from its original site on Gough Street; it's one of two remaining octagonal houses in the city (the other is on Russian Hill), and the only one open to the public. White quoins accent each of the eight corners of the pretty blue-gray exterior, and a colonial-style garden completes the picture. The house is full of antique American furniture, decorative arts (paintings, silver, rugs), and documents from the 18th and 19th centuries, including the contents of a time capsule left by the original owners in 1861 that was discovered during a 1950s renovation. A deck of Revolutionary-era hand-painted playing cards takes an anti-monarchist position: in place of kings, queens, and jacks, the American upstarts substituted American statesmen, Roman goddesses, and Indian chiefs. ✉ *2645 Gough St., near Union St., Cow Hollow* ☎ *415/441–7512* ⊕ *nscda-ca.org/octagon-house/* ✆ *Free, donations encouraged.*

Vedanta Society Old Temple. A pastiche of colonial, Queen Anne, Moorish, and Hindu opulence, lavender with turrets battling red-top onion domes, and Victorian detailing everywhere, this 1905 structure was the first Hindu temple in the West. Vedanta, an underlying philosophy of Hinduism, maintains that all religions are paths to one goal. ✉ *2963 Webster St., Cow Hollow* ☎ *415/922–2323* ⊕ *www.sfvedanta.org.*

Wedding Houses. These identical white double-peak homes (joined in the middle) were erected in the late 1870s or early 1880s by dairy rancher James Cudworth as wedding gifts for his two daughters, down the street from his own house at 2040 Union Street. These days the buildings house a bar and a restaurant. ✉ *1980 Union St., Cow Hollow.*

PRESIDIO

At the foot of the Golden Gate Bridge, one of city residents' favorite in-town getaways is the 1,400-plus-acre Presidio, which combines accessible nature-in-the-raw with a window into the past. For more than 200 years and under the flags of three nations—Spain, Mexico, and the United States—the Presidio served as an army post, but in 1995 the U.S. Army officially handed over the keys to the National Park Service. The

PARK IT HERE

Since 2010, San Francisco has been reclaiming parking spaces and turning them into parklets, tiny parks open to the public. These dot the city—more than three dozen and counting—from mobile, red-metal containers with built-in benches and plantings to Powell Street's eight-section high-design aluminum parklet. The Mission has the highest concentration, mostly along Valencia Street, but one of the most creative—an old Citroën van turned into seating and planters—is in front of the Rapha bike shop on Filbert near Fillmore in Cow Hollow. And even if everyone in that parklet in front of a café is clutching a to-go cup, remember these are public spaces; look for the "Public Parklet" sign and grab a seat. For a parklet map, visit ⊕ *pavementtoparks.org.*

keys came without sufficient federal funding, though, and it seemed the Presidio would be sold piecemeal to developers.

An innovative plan combining public and private monies and overseen by the Presidio Trust, the federal agency created to run the park, was hatched to help the Presidio become self-sufficient, which it did in 2013. The trust has found paying tenants such as George Lucas's Industrial Light and Magic, the Walt Disney Family Museum, and a few thousand lucky San Franciscans who live in restored army housing. Now this spectacular corner of the city—surrounded by sandy beaches and rocky shores, and with windswept hills of cypress dotted with historical buildings—is a thriving urban park. The Presidio has superb views and some of the best hiking and biking areas in San Francisco; even a drive through this lush area is a treat.

TOP ATTRACTIONS

Fodor'sChoice
★
Presidio. When San Franciscans want to spend a day in the woods, they come here. The Presidio has 1,400 acres of hills and majestic woods, two small beaches, and stunning views of the bay, the Golden Gate Bridge, and Marin County. Famed environmental artist Andy Goldsworthy's work greets visitors at the Arguello Gate entrance. The 100-plus-foot *Spire,* made of 37 cypress logs reclaimed from the Presidio, looks like a rough, natural version of a church spire. ■TIP➤ **The Presidio's best lookout points lie along Washington Boulevard, which meanders through the park.**

Part of the **Golden Gate National Recreation Area,** the Presidio was a military post for more than 200 years. Don Juan Bautista de Anza and a band of Spanish settlers first claimed the area in 1776. It became a Mexican garrison in 1822, when Mexico gained its independence from Spain; U.S. troops forcibly occupied the Presidio in 1846. The U.S. Sixth Army was stationed here until 1994.

The Presidio is now a thriving community of residential and nonresidential tenants, who help to fund its operations by rehabilitating and leasing its more than 700 buildings. Bay Area filmmaker George Lucas's 23-acre **Letterman Digital Arts Center,** a digital studio "campus," along

The Presidio with Kids

If you're in town with children (and you have a car), the sprawling, bayside Presidio offers enough kid-friendly diversions for one very full day. Start off at **Julius Kahn Park**, on the Presidio's southern edge, which has a disproportionate number of structures that spin. Swing by George Lucas's **Letterman Digital Arts Center** to check out the Yoda fountain; then head to the **Immigrant Point Lookout** on Washington Boulevard, with views of the bay and the ocean. Children love the pet cemetery, with its sweet, leaning headstones; it's near the stables, where you might glimpse some of the park police's equestrian members. Older kids might enjoy a stop at the **Walt Disney Family Museum** (⊠ *104 Montgomery St.* ☎ *415/345–6800*) to see the model of Disneyland and a replica of the ambulance jeep Walt Disney drove during World War I. The last stop is **Crissy Field**, where kids can ride bikes, skate, or run along the beach and clamber over the rocks; the view of the Golden Gate Bridge from below is captivating. Two nature centers here have fun, hands-on exhibits for kids. Finally, stop by the **Warming Hut**, at the western end of Crissy Field, for sandwiches and hot chocolate. You can also do a version of this day using the PresidiGo shuttle, but you'll need to adapt your route according to the shuttle stops.

the eastern edge of the land, is exquisitely landscaped and largely open to the public. If you have kids in tow or are a *Star Wars* fan yourself, sidle over to the **Yoda Fountain** (Letterman Drive at Dewitt Road), between two of the arts-center buildings, then take your picture with the life-size Darth Vader statue in the lobby, open to the public on weekdays.

The Presidio Trust, created to manage the Presidio and guide its transformation from military post to national park, has now turned its focus to rolling out the welcome mat to the public. The Presidio's visitor-serving tenants, such as the Asian-theme SenSpa, the House of Air Trampoline Park, Planet Granite climbing gym, the Walt Disney museum, and a fabulous lodge at the Main Post, have helped with this goal. The rental of old military houses and apartments helps too, with top rents pushing $20,000 a month.

Especially popular is **Crissy Field**, a stretch of restored marshland along the sand of the bay. Kids on bikes, folks walking dogs, and joggers share the paved path along the shore, often winding up at the Warming Hut, a combination café and fun gift store at the end of the path, for a hot chocolate in the shadow of the Golden Gate Bridge. Midway along the Golden Gate Promenade that winds along the shore is the Gulf of the Farallones National Marine Sanctuary Visitor Center, where kids can get a close-up view of small sea creatures and learn about the rich ecosystem offshore. Just across from the Palace of Fine Arts, Crissy Field Center offers great children's programs and has cool science displays. West of the Golden Gate Bridge is sandy **Baker Beach**, beloved for its spectacular views and laid-back vibe (read: you'll see naked people here). This is one of those places that inspires local pride.

The Presidio also has a golf course, picnic sites, and the only camp-ground in the city; the views from the many overlooks are sublime. For background and to help plan your time here, stop at the high-tech **Visitor Center** *(210 Lincoln Blvd., 415/561–4323). ⊠ Between Marina and Lincoln Park, Presidio ⊕ www.presidio.gov.*

WORTH NOTING

FAMILY **Fort Point.** Dwarfed today by the Golden Gate Bridge, this brick for-tress constructed between 1853 and 1861 was designed to protect San Francisco from a Civil War sea attack that never materialized. It was also used as a coastal-defense fortification post during World War II, when soldiers stood watch here. This National Historic Site is now a sprawling museum of military memorabilia. The building, which surrounds a lonely, windswept courtyard, has a gloomy air and is suitably atmospheric. It's usually chilly, too, so bring a jacket. The top floor affords a unique angle on the bay. ■TIP→ **Take care when walking along the front side of the building, as it's slippery, and the waves have a dizzying effect.**

On the days when Fort Point is staffed (on Friday and weekends), guided group tours and cannon drills take place. The popular, guided candlelight tours, available only in winter, book up in advance, so plan ahead. Living-history days take place throughout the year, when Union soldiers perform drills, a drum-and-fife band plays, and a Civil War–era doctor shows his instruments and describes his surgical tech-nique (gulp). ⊠ *Marine Dr. off Lincoln Blvd., Presidio* ☎ *415/556–1693 ⊕ www.nps.gov/fopo* ⊠ *Free.*

Presidio Officers' Club. An excellent place to begin a historical tour of the Presidio, the Officers' Club offers a walk through time from the Presidio's earliest days as the first nonnative outpost in present-day San Francisco to more than a century as a U.S. army post. For a richer experience, visit the Presidio Heritage Gallery upstairs before explor-ing the building. Start with the excellent short film about life here from the time of the Ohlone to the present, then peruse the displays of artifacts including uniforms and weaponry. Head back downstairs to the Mesa Room, where you can literally see layers of history: part of the painstakingly preserved original adobe wall from the 1790s, the brick fireplace from the 1880s commander's office, and the mission revival fireplace from the 1930s billiard room. You can imagine the brass mingling under giant wrought-iron chandeliers in the Moraga Room. Excavation of the Presidio continues: outside, a canopy covers the Presidio Archaeology Field Station, where you can watch archae-ologists at work from May to September. ■TIP→ **Also at the club, the outdoor seating at Mexican-influenced Arguello, by local favorite chef Traci des Jardins, is lovely on a sunny day.** ⊠ *50 Moraga Ave., Presidio* ☎ *415/561–4400 ⊕ www.presidioofficersclub.com* ⊠ *Free.*

Walt Disney Family Museum. This beautifully refurbished brick bar-racks house is a tribute to the man behind Mickey Mouse, the Dis-ney Studios, and Disneyland. The smartly organized displays include hundreds of family photos, and well-chosen videos play throughout.

Disney's legendary attention to detail becomes particularly evident in the cels and footage of *Fantasia, Sleeping Beauty,* and other animation classics. "The Toughest Period in My Whole Life" exhibit sheds light on lesser-known bits of history: the animators' strike at Disney Studios, the films Walt Disney made for the U.S. military during World War II, and his testimony before the House Un-American Activities Committee during its investigation of Communist influence in Hollywood. The liveliest exhibit and the largest gallery documents the creation of Disneyland with a fun, detailed model of what Disney imagined the park would be. Teacups spin, the Matterhorn looms, and that world-famous castle leads the way to Fantasyland. You won't be the first to leave humming "It's a Small World." In the final gallery, titled simply "December 16, 1966," a series of sweet cartoons chronicles the world's reaction to Disney's sudden death. ⊠ *Main Post, 104 Montgomery St., off Lincoln Blvd., Presidio* ☎ *415/345–6800* ⊕ *www.waltdisney.org* ✉ *$25.*

8

THE WESTERN
SHORELINE

Getting Oriented

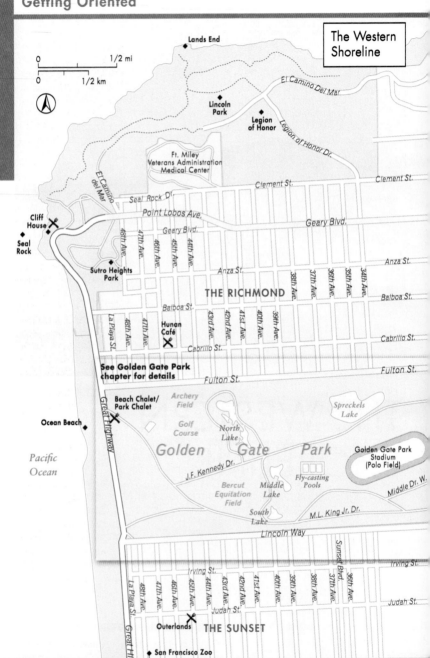

The Western Shoreline

Lands End

1/2 mi

1/2 km

El Camino Del Mar

Lincoln Park

Legion of Honor

Legion of Honor Dr.

Ft. Miley Veterans Administration Medical Center

Clement St.

Clement St.

Seal Rock Dr.

Point Lobos Ave.

Geary Blvd.

Geary Blvd.

Cliff House

Seal Rock

Sutro Heights Park

48th Ave.
47th Ave.
46th Ave.
45th Ave.
44th Ave.

Anza St.

Anza St.

38th Ave.
37th Ave.
36th Ave.
35th Ave.
34th Ave.

THE RICHMOND

Balboa St.

Balboa St.

La Playa St.
48th Ave.
47th Ave.

Hunan Café

43rd Ave.
42nd Ave.
41st Ave.
40th Ave.
39th Ave.

Cabrillo St.

Cabrillo St.

See Golden Gate Park chapter for details

Fulton St.

Fulton St.

Beach Chalet/ Park Chalet

Archery Field

Spreckels Lake

Ocean Beach

Great Highway

Golf Course

North Lake

Golden   Gate   Park

Golden Gate Park Stadium (Polo Field)

Pacific Ocean

J.F. Kennedy Dr.

Bercut Equitation Field

Middle Lake

Fly-casting Pools

Middle Dr. W.

South Lake

M.L. King Jr. Dr.

Lincoln Way

Sunset Blvd.

La Playa St.
48th Ave.
47th Ave.
46th Ave.
45th Ave.
44th Ave.
43rd Ave.
42nd Ave.
41st Ave.
40th Ave.
39th Ave.
38th Ave.
37th Ave.
36th Ave.

Irving St.

Irving St.

Judah St.

Great Hi

Judah St.

Outerlands   THE SUNSET

San Francisco Zoo

MAKING THE MOST OF YOUR TIME

Despite low-lying fog and often biting chill, the premier sights of the Western Shoreline are outdoors—gorgeous hiking trails and sandy stretches of coastline. Bundle up and start off on the Coastal Trail, which passes by the Legion of Honor. Continue west to catch the sunset from the Cliff House or the Beach Chalet. If you don't want to do the entire 3-mile hike, you can spend an hour touring the museum, catch the stunning views just below it, and head to the beach.

TOP REASONS TO GO

Lands End: Head down the gorgeous Coastal Trail near the Cliff House; you'll quickly find yourself in a forest with unparalleled views of the Golden Gate Bridge.

Toast the sunset at the Beach Chalet: Top off a day of exploring with a cocktail overlooking Ocean Beach.

Legion of Honor: Tear yourself away from the spectacular setting and eye-popping view and travel back to 18th-century Europe through the paintings, drawings, and porcelain collected here.

Ocean Beach: Wrap up warm and stroll along the strand on a brisk, cloudy day and you'll feel like a gritty local. Then thaw out over a bowl of steaming pho in the Richmond.

Old-time San Francisco: Wandering among the ruins of the Sutro Baths below the Cliff House, close your eyes and imagine vintage San Francisco: the monumental baths, popular amusement park Playland at the Beach, and that great, old, teetering, Victorian Cliff House of days gone by.

GETTING THERE

To reach the Western Shoreline from downtown by Muni light rail, take the N–Judah to Ocean Beach or the L–Taraval to the zoo. From downtown by bus, take the 38–Geary, which runs all the way to 48th and Point Lobos Avenues, just east of the Cliff House. Along the Western Shoreline, the 18–46th Avenue runs between the Legion of Honor and the zoo (and beyond).

QUICK BITES

Beach Chalet and Park Chalet. The gorgeous setting often overshadows the upscale comfort food at the upstairs Beach Chalet and its downstairs sister, Park Chalet, across from Ocean Beach, on the western edge of Golden Gate Park. ⊠ 1000 Great Hwy., at JFK Dr., Golden Gate Park ☎ 415/386–8439 ⊕ www.beachchalet.com.

Cliff House. On the Western Shoreline, the Cliff House may be more about the view than the food, but what a view! At the casual upstairs bistro, big windows face west toward the sea. Downstairs is the fancier, pricier Sutro's, with two-story-tall glass walls overlooking the Pacific and the Marin Headlands. Both places appropriately emphasize seafood dishes. ⊠ 1090 Point Lobos Ave., Richmond ☎ 415/386–3330 ⊕ www.cliffhouse.com.

8

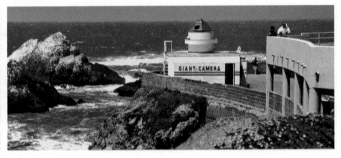

Sightseeing
★★★
Nightlife
—
Dining
★★★
Lodging
—
Shopping
—

Few American cities provide a more intimate and dramatic view of the power and fury of the surf attacking the shore than San Francisco does along its wild Western Shoreline. From Lincoln Park in the north, along Ocean Beach from the Richmond south to the Sunset, a different breed of San Franciscan chooses to live in this area: surfers who brave the heaviest fog to ride the waves; writers who seek solace and inspiration in this city outpost; and dog lovers committed to giving their pets a good workout each day.

THE RICHMOND

Updated by
Denise M. Leto

In the mid-19th century, the western section of town just north of Golden Gate Park was known as the Outer Lands, covered in sand dunes and seen fit for cemeteries and little else. Today it's the Richmond, comprised of two distinct neighborhoods: the Inner Richmond, from Arguello Boulevard to about 20th Avenue, and the Outer Richmond, from 20th to the ocean. Clement Street, packed with solid dining options, from French to Burmese, and with numerous Chinese groceries, is the Inner Richmond's favorite commercial strip. The street makes for great strolling and even better eating. The Outer Richmond has its share of restaurants—most along Geary Boulevard, some along Clement—including the city's highest concentration of Russian eateries and bakeries. But this mostly residential neighborhood is about the foggy hinterlands that stretch west to the coast: dramatic Lincoln Park with Golden Gate views, the Cliff House, and often-chilly, uncrowded Ocean Beach.

From Lands End in Lincoln Park you have some of the best views of the Golden Gate—the name was given to the opening of San Francisco Bay long before the bridge was built—and the Marin Headlands. From the historic Cliff House south to the sprawling San Francisco Zoo, the

Great Highway and Ocean Beach run along the western edge of the city (south of Golden Gate Park, you're in the Sunset). If you're here in winter or spring, keep your eyes peeled for migrating gray whales. The wind is often strong along the shoreline, summer fog can blanket the ocean beaches, and the water is cold and usually too rough for swimming. Don't forget your jacket!

TOP ATTRACTIONS

Legion of Honor. The old adage of real estate—location, location, location—is at full force here. You can't beat the site of this museum of European art atop cliffs overlooking the ocean, the Golden Gate Bridge, and the Marin Headlands. A pyramidal glass skylight in the entrance court illuminates the lower-level galleries, which exhibit prints and drawings, English and European porcelain, and ancient Assyrian, Greek, Roman, and Egyptian art. The 20-plus galleries on the upper level display the permanent collection of European art (paintings, sculpture, decorative arts, and tapestries) from the 14th century to the present day.

The noteworthy Auguste Rodin collection includes two galleries devoted to the master and a third with works by Rodin and other 19th-century sculptors. An original cast of Rodin's *The Thinker* welcomes you as you walk through the courtyard. As fine as the museum is, the setting and view outshine the collection and also make a trip here worthwhile. ✉ *34th Ave. at Clement St., Richmond* ☎ *415/750–3600* ⊕ *legionofhonor.famsf.org* ✍ *$15, free 1st Tues. of month.*

Fodor'sChoice **Lincoln Park.** Although many of the city's green spaces are gentle and
★ welcoming, Lincoln Park is a wild, 275-acre park in the Outer Richmond with windswept cliffs and panoramic views. The Coastal Trail, the park's most dramatic one, leads out to **Lands End**; pick it up west of the Legion of Honor (at the end of El Camino del Mar) or from the parking lot at Point Lobos and El Camino del Mar. Time your hike to hit Mile Rock at low tide, and you might catch a glimpse of two wrecked ships peeking up from their watery graves. ⚠ **Be careful if you hike here; landslides are frequent, and people have fallen into the sea by standing too close to the edge of a crumbling bluff top.**

On the tamer side, large Monterey cypresses line the fairways at Lincoln Park's 18-hole golf course, near the Legion of Honor. At one time this land was the Golden Gate Cemetery, where the dead were segregated by nationality; most were indigent and interred without ceremony in the potter's field. In 1900 the Board of Supervisors voted to ban burials within city limits, and all but two city cemeteries (at Mission Dolores and the Presidio) were moved to Colma, a small town just south of San Francisco. When digging has to be done in the park, bones occasionally surface again. ✉ *Entrance at 34th Ave. at Clement St., Richmond.*

8

Visitors enjoy the rough beauty of the Pacific from the Cliff House.

WORTH NOTING

Cliff House. A meal at the Cliff House isn't just about the food—the spectacular ocean view is what brings folks here—but the cuisine won't leave you wanting. The vistas, which include offshore Seal Rock (the barking marine mammals who reside there are actually sea lions), can be 30 miles or more on a clear day—or less than a mile on foggy days. ■TIP→ **Come for drinks just before sunset; then head back into town for dinner.**

Three buildings have occupied this site since 1863. The current building dates from 1909; a 2004 renovation has left a strikingly attractive restaurant and a squat concrete viewing platform out back. The complex, owned by the National Park Service, includes a gift shop.

Sitting on the observation deck is the **Giant Camera,** a camera obscura with its lens pointing skyward housed in a cute yellow-painted wooden shack. Built in the 1940s and threatened many times with demolition, it's now on the National Register of Historic Places. Step into the dark, tiny room inside (for a $3 fee); a fascinating 360-degree image of the surrounding area—which rotates as the "lens" on the roof rotates—is projected on a large, circular table. ■TIP→ **In winter and spring you may also glimpse migrating gray whales from the observation deck.**

To the north of the Cliff House lie the ruins of the once grand glass-roof **Sutro Baths,** which you can explore on your own (they look a bit like water-storage receptacles). Adolph Sutro, eccentric onetime San Francisco mayor and Cliff House owner, built the bath complex, including a train out to the site, in 1896, so that everyday folks could enjoy the benefits of swimming. Six enormous baths (some freshwater and some seawater), more than 500 dressing rooms, and several restaurants covered 3 acres north of the Cliff House and accommodated 25,000 bathers. Likened to Roman baths in a European glass palace, the baths were for decades the favorite destination of San Franciscans in search of entertainment. The complex fell into disuse after World War II, was closed in 1952, and burned down (under questionable circumstances) during demolition in 1966. ⊠ *1090 Point Lobos Ave., Richmond* ☎ *415/386–3330* ⊕ *www.cliffhouse.com* ☜ *Free.*

Ocean Beach. Stretching 3 miles along the western side of the city from the Richmond to the Sunset, this sandy swath of the Pacific coast is good for jogging or walking the dog—but not for swimming. The water is so cold that surfers wear wet suits year-round, and riptides are strong, so only brave the waves if you are a strong swimmer or surfer—drownings are not infrequent. As for sunbathing, it's rarely warm enough here; think meditative walking instead of sun worshipping.

Paths on both sides of the Great Highway lead from Lincoln Way to Sloat Boulevard (near the zoo); the beachside path winds through landscaped sand dunes, and the paved path across the highway is good for biking and in-line skating (though you have to rent bikes elsewhere). The **Beach Chalet** restaurant and brewpub is across the Great Highway from Ocean Beach, about five blocks south of the Cliff House. ⊠ *Along Great Hwy. from Cliff House to Sloat Blvd. and beyond, San Francisco.*

Sutro Heights Park. Crows and other large birds battle the heady breezes at this cliff-top park on what were once the grounds of the home of Adolph Sutro, an eccentric mining engineer and former San Francisco mayor. An extremely wealthy man, Sutro may have owned about 10% of San Francisco at one point, but he couldn't buy good taste: a few remnants of his gaudy, faux-classical statue collection still stand (including the lions at what was the main gate). Monterey cypresses and Canary Island palms dot the park, and photos on placards depict what things looked like before the house burned down in 1896, from the greenhouse to the ornate carpet-bed designs.

All that remains of the main house is its foundation. Climb up for a sweeping view of the Pacific Ocean and the Cliff House below (which Sutro owned), and try to imagine what the perspective might have been like from one of the upper floors. San Francisco City Guides (*415/557–4266, www.sfcityguides.org*) runs a free Saturday tour of the park that starts at 2 (meet at the lion statue at 48th and Point Lobos Avenues). ⊠ *Point Lobos and 48th Aves., Richmond.*

THE SUNSET

Hugging the southern edge of Golden Gate Park and built atop the sand dunes that covered much of western San Francisco into the 19th century, the Sunset is made up of two distinct neighborhoods—the popular Inner Sunset, from Stanyan Street to 19th Avenue, and the foggy Outer Sunset, from 19th to the beach. The Inner Sunset is perhaps the perfect San Francisco "suburb": not too far from the center of things, reachable by public transit, and home to main streets—Irving Street and 9th Avenue just off

Golden Gate Park—packed with excellent dining options, with Asian food particularly well represented. Long the domain of surfers and others who love the laid-back beach vibe and the fog, the slow-paced Outer Sunset finds itself newly on the radar of locals, with high-quality cafés and restaurants and quirky shops springing up along Judah Street between 42nd and 46th Avenues. The zoo is the district's main tourist attraction.

EXPLORING

FAMILY **San Francisco Zoo.** Occupying prime oceanfront property, the zoo is touting its metamorphosis into the "New Zoo," a wildlife-focused recreation center that inspires visitors to become conservationists. Integrated exhibits group different species of animals from the same geographic areas together in enclosures that don't look like cages. More than 250 species reside here, including endangered species such as the snow leopard, Sumatran tiger, grizzly bear, and a Siberian tiger.

The zoo's superstar exhibit is **Grizzly Gulch,** where orphaned grizzly bear sisters Kachina and Kiona enchant visitors with their frolicking and swimming. When the bears are in the water, the only thing between you and them is (thankfully thick) glass. Grizzly feedings are at 10:30 am daily.

New in 2016, the **Mexican Gray Wolf grotto** houses three males: David Bowie, Jerry Garcia, and Prince. Hunted down to seven animals in the 20th century, the wolves are making a comeback due to conservation and breeding programs at zoos like this one. The **Lemur Forest** has four varieties of the bug-eyed, long-tailed primates from Madagascar. You can help hoist food into the lemurs' feeding towers and watch the fuzzy creatures climb up to chow down. African Kikuyu grass carpets the circular outer area of **Gorilla Preserve,** one of the largest and most natural gorilla habitats of any zoo in the world. Trees and shrubs create communal play areas.

Ten species of rare primates—including black howler monkeys, emperor tamarins, and lion-tailed macaques—live and play at the two-tier **Primate Discovery Center,** which contains 23 interactive learning exhibits on the ground level.

Magellanic penguins waddle about the rather sad concrete **Penguin Island,** splashing and frolicking in its 200-foot pool. Feeding time is 3:30. Koalas peer out from among the trees in **Koala Crossing,** and kangaroos and wallabies headline the **Australian Walkabout** exhibit. The 7-acre **Puente al Sur** (Bridge to the South) re-creates habitats in South America, replete with giant anteaters and capybaras.

An **African Savanna** exhibit mixes giraffes, zebras, kudus, ostriches, and many other species, all living together in a 3-acre section with a central viewing spot accessed by a covered passageway.

The 6-acre **Children's Zoo** has about 300 mammals, birds, and reptiles, plus an insect zoo, a meerkat and prairie-dog exhibit, a nature trail, a nature theater, a huge playground, a restored 1921 Dentzel carousel, and a mini–steam train. A ride on the train costs $5, and you can hop astride one of the carousel's 52 hand-carved menagerie animals for $3. ⊠ *Sloat Blvd. and 47th Ave., Sunset* ☎ *415/753–7080* ⊕ *www.sfzoo.org* ⊠ *$19, $1 off with Muni transfer (take Muni L–Taraval streetcar from downtown).*

GOLDEN GATE PARK

A GREEN RETREAT

Stretching more than 1,000 acres from the ocean to the Haight, Golden Gate Park is a place to slow down and smell the eucalyptus. Stockbrokers and gadget-laden parents stroll the Music Concourse, while speedy tattooed cyclists and wobbly, training-wheeled kids cruise along shaded paths. Stooped seniors warm the garden benches, hikers search for waterfalls, and picnickers lounge in the Rhododendron Dell. San Franciscans love their city streets, but the park is where they come to breathe.

PLANNING A PARK VISIT

ORIENTATION

The park breaks down naturally into three chunks. The eastern end attracts the biggest crowds with its cluster of blockbuster sights. It's also the easiest place to dip into the park for a quick trip. Water hobbyists come to the middle section's lake-speckled open space. Sporty types head west to the coastal end for its soccer fields, golf course, and archery range. This windswept western end is the park's least visited and most naturally landscaped part. ⊙ Daily 6 am—10 pm ⊕ www.sfrecpark.org.

WALKING TOURS

San Francisco Botanical Garden (☎ 415/661–1316) has free botanical tours every day (admission not included). Tours start near the main gate daily at 1:30 pm. Additional tours meet at the Friend Gate (at the northern entrance) Apr.–Sept., Fri.–Sun. at 2 pm.

San Francisco City Guides (☎ 415/557–4266) offers free year-round tours of the park's eastern end, its western end, and the Japanese Tea Garden.

BEST TIMES TO VISIT

Time of day: It's best to arrive early at the Conservatory of Flowers, the de Young Museum, and the Japanese Tea Garden to avoid crowds. At sunset, the only place to be is the park's western end, watching the sun dip into the Pacific.

Time of year: Visit during the week if you can. The long, Indian summer days of September and October are the warmest times to visit, and many special weekend events are held then.

Blooms: The rhododendrons bloom between February and May. The Queen Wilhelmina Tulip Garden blossoms in February and March. Cherry trees in the Japanese Tea Garden bloom in April, and the Rose Garden is at its best from mid-May to mid-June, in the beginning of July, and during September

(opposite) Conservatory of Flowers. (top left) The San Francisco Botanical Garden in bloom.

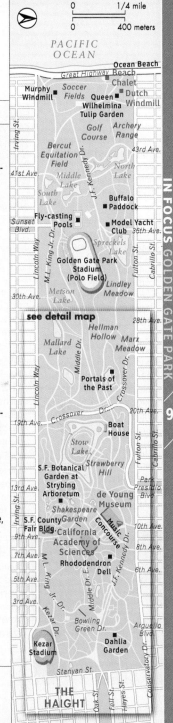

TIPS

■ Carry a map—the park's sightlines usually prevent you from using city landmarks as reference points. Posted maps are few and far between, and they're sometimes out of date. Paths aren't always clear, so stick to well-marked trails.

■ In Golden Gate Park, free public restrooms are fairly common and mostly clean, especially around the eastern end's attractions. Facilities are available behind the Conservatory of Flowers or in the de Young Museum at the sculpture garden and café patio. Farther west, behind Stow Lake's boathouse and near the Koret Children's Quarter are facilities.

■ Check out goldengatepark. com for a calendar of park events. This unofficial site also has maps and parking info.

BEST WAYS TO SPEND YOUR TIME

The park stretches 3 miles east to west and is a half-mile wide, so it's possible to cover the whole thing in a day—by car, public transportation, bike, or even on foot. But to do so might feel more like a forced march than a pleasure jaunt. Weigh your time and your interests, choose your top picks, then leave at least an extra hour to just enjoy being outdoors.

Two hours: Swing by the exquisite Conservatory of Flowers for a 20-minute peek, then head to the de Young Museum. Spend a few minutes assessing its controversial exterior and perhaps glide through some of the galleries before heading to the observation tower for a panoramic view of the city. Cross the music concourse to the spectacular Academy of Sciences.

Half day: Spend a little extra time at the sights described above, then head to the nearby Japanese Tea Garden to enjoy its perfectionist landscape. Next, cross the street to the San Francisco Botanical Garden at Strybing Arboretum and check out the intriguing Primitive Garden. If you brought supplies, this is a great place for a picnic; you can also grab lunch at the de Young Café.

Full day: After the half-day tour (above) continue on to the children's playground if you have kids in tow. Once your little ones see the playground's tree house–like play structures and climbing opportunities, you may be here for the rest of the day. Alternatively, make your way to the serene National AIDS Memorial Grove. Then head west, stopping at Stow Lake to climb Strawberry Hill. Wind up at the Beach Chalet for a sunset drink.

(top) Amateur musicians entertain passersby. (middle) Sundays are ideal biking days. (bottom) The meandering paths are perfect for strolling.

GETTING AROUND THE PARK

WALKING
The most convenient entry point is on the eastern edge at Stanyan Street, continuing into the park on JFK Drive, which points you directly toward the Conservatory of Flowers. It's a 10-minute walk there; allow another 10–15 minutes to reach the California Academy of Sciences, de Young Museum, Japanese Tea Garden, and San Francisco Botanical Garden. Stow Lake is another 10 minutes west from these four sights.

BY BIKE
The park is fantastic for cycling, especially on Sunday when cars are barred from John F. Kennedy Drive. Biking the park round trip is about a 7-mile trip, which usually takes 1–2 hours. The route down John F. Kennedy Drive takes you past the prettiest, well-maintained sections of the park on a mostly flat circuit. The most popular route continues all the way to the beach. Keep in mind that the ride is downhill toward the ocean, uphill heading east.

BY CAR
If you have a car, you'll have no trouble hopping from sight to sight. (But remember, the main road, John F. Kennedy Drive, is closed to cars on Sunday.) Parking within the park is often free and is usually easy to find especially beyond the eastern end. On Sundays or anytime the eastern end is crowded, head for the residential streets north of the park or the underground parking lot; enter on 10th and Fulton (northern edge of the park) or MLK and Concourse (in the park).

BY SHUTTLE
The free Golden Gate Park shuttle runs 9-6 weekends and holidays. It loops through the park every 15-20 minutes, stopping at 14 sights from McLaren Lodge to the Dutch Windmill. If you're driving, leave your car in the free spaces along Ocean Beach (Great Hwy. between Lincoln and Fulton) and wait at the green shuttle stop sign.

(top) Water lilies adorn the Japanese Tea Garden.

WHERE TO RENT

Parkwide Bike Rentals & Tours (☎ 415/671–8989). The only rental shop in the park is behind the band-shell on the music concourse. For an extra $10 you can return your bike to the Embarcadero/Ferry Building, the Marina, or Union Square. **Golden Gate Park Skate & Bike** (✉ 3038 Fulton St. ☎ 415/668–1117). On the northern edge of the park; good deals on rentals. **San Francisco Bicycle Rentals** (✉ 425 Jefferson St. ☎ 415/922–4537). Customers rave about excellent service and good deals at this Fisherman's Wharf outfit. Pick up a bike at **Golden Gate Tours & Bike Rentals** (✉ 1816 Haight St. ☎ 415/922–4537). Return by ferry and drop your bike at the Fisherman's Wharf shop for an extra $6.

BEST PLACES TO PICNIC ON WEEKENDS

■ Lawn in front of the Conservatory of Flowers.

■ By the pond in the San Francisco Botanical Garden.

■ The benches overlooking the Rustic Bridge at Stow Lake.

■ Rhododendron Dell.

DON'T-MISS SIGHTS

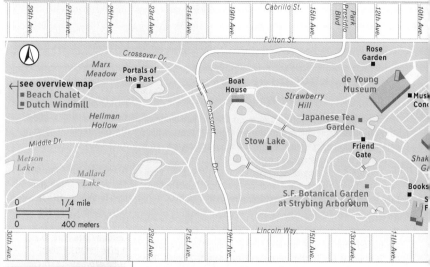

Conservatory of Flowers

✉ John F. Kennedy Dr. at
Conservatory Dr.

☎ 415/666-7001

💲 $8, free 1st Tues. of
month

🕑 Tues.-Sun. 9-5; 10-4 in
winter

🌐 www.conservatoryof
flowers.org

CONSERVATORY OF FLOWERS

Whatever you do, be sure to at least drive by the Conservatory of Flowers—it's just too darn pretty to miss. The gorgeous, white-framed, 1878 glass structure is topped with a 14-ton glass dome. Stepping inside the giant greenhouse is like taking a quick trip to the rainforest; it's humid, warm, and smells earthy. The undeniable highlight is the Aquatic Plants section, where lily pads float and carnivorous plants dine on bugs to the sounds of rushing water. On the east side of the conservatory (to the right as you face the building), cypress, pine, and redwood trees surround the **Dahlia Garden,** which blooms in summer and fall. To the west is the **Rhododendron Dell,** which contains 850 varieties, more than any other garden in the country. It's a favorite local Mother's Day picnic spot.

STOW LAKE

Russian seniors feed the pigeons, kids watch turtles sunning themselves, and joggers circle this placid body of water, Golden Gate Park's largest lake. Early park superintendent John McLaren may have snarked that manmade Stow Lake was "a shoestring around a watermelon," but for more than a century visitors have come to walk its paths and bridges, paddle boats, and climb Strawberry Hill (the "watermelon"). Cross one of the bridges—the 19th-century stone bridge on the southwest side is lovely—and ascend the hill; keep your eyes open for the waterfall and an elaborate Chinese Pavilion.

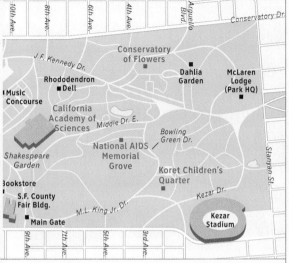

Stow Lake

- ✉ Off John F. Kennedy Dr.
- ☎ Boat rental 415/752–0347
- ⊙ Boat rentals daily 10-4.

San Francisco Japanese Tea Garden

- ✉ Hagiwara Tea Garden Dr.
- ☎ 415/752-4227
- 💲 $8, free Mon., Wed., and Fri. with entry by 10 am
- ⊙ Mar.–Oct., daily 9–6; Nov.–Feb., daily 9–4:45.
- 🌐 www.japaneseteagardensf.com

Koret Children's Quarter

- ✉ Bowling Green Dr., off Martin Luther King Jr. Dr
- ☎ 415/831-2700
- 💲 Playground free, carousel $2, kids 6–12 $1
- ⊙ Playground daily dawn-dusk; carousel Memorial Day–Labor Day, daily 10–4:30, Labor Day–Memorial Day, Fri.–Sun. 10–4:30.

SAN FRANCISCO JAPANESE TEA GARDEN

As you amble through the manicured landscape, past Japanese sculptures and perfect miniature pagodas, over ponds of huge, ancient carp, you may be transported to a more peaceful plane. Or maybe the shrieks of kids clambering over the almost vertical "humpback" bridges will keep you firmly in the here and now. Either way, this garden is one of those tourist spots that's truly worth a stop (a half-hour will do). And at 5 acres, it's large enough that you'll always be able to find a bit of serenity, even when the tour buses drop by. ■TIP→ The garden is especially lovely in April, when the cherry blossoms are in bloom.

KORET CHILDREN'S QUARTER

The country's first public children's playground has wave-shaped climbing walls, old-fashioned cement slides, and a 20-plus-foot rope climbing structure that kids love and parents fear, as well as a beautiful, handcrafted 1912 Herschell-Spillman Carousel. The lovely stone Sharon Building, next to the playground, offers kids' art classes. Bring a picnic or pick up grub nearby on 9th Avenue and you could spend the entire day here. Be aware that the playground, which has separate areas for toddlers and bigger kids, is unenclosed and sight-lines can be obstructed.

DE YOUNG MUSEUM

✉ 50 Hagiwara Tea
   Garden Dr.

☎ 415/750–3600

🌐 deyoung.famsf.org

🎟 $15; free 1st Tues.
   of month

🕐 Tues.–Sun. 9:30–5:15

TIPS

■ Admission at the de Young is good for same-day admission to the Legion of Honor and vice-versa.

■ The de Young is famous these days first and foremost for its striking and controversial building and tree-topping tower. These are accessible to the public for free, so if it's not the art you're interested in seeing, save the cost of admission and head up the elevator to 360-degree views from the glass-walled observation floor.

■ When it's time for a nosh, head to the de Young Café and dine in the lovely outdoor sculpture garden on tableware fit for MOMA.

Everyone in town has a strong opinion about the de Young. Some adore the striking copper façade, while others grimace and hope that the green patina of age will mellow the effect. The building almost overshadows the museum's respected collection of American, African, and Oceanic art.

HIGHLIGHTS

Head through the sprawling concourse level and begin your visit on the upper level, where you'll find textiles; art from Africa, Oceana, and New Guinea; and highlights of the 20th-century American painting collection (such as Wayne Thiebaud, John Singer Sargent, Winslow Homer, and Richard Diebenkorn). These are the don't-miss items, so take your time. Then head back downstairs to see art from the Americas and contemporary work.

The de Young has had some major international coups, scoring exhibits such as *Tutankhamun and the Golden Age of the Pharoahs*; *Van Gogh, Gaugin, Cezanne, and Beyond: Post-Impressionist Masterpieces from the Musée d'Orsay*; and *Picasso: Masterpieces from the Musée National Picasso, Paris.* Be sure to check for traveling exhibits while you're visiting. Recent shows have included the stunning Jean Paul Gaultier exhibition (extra fees apply).

CALIFORNIA ACADEMY OF SCIENCES

✉ 55 Music Concourse Dr.

☎ 415/379–8000

🌐 www.calacademy.org

💳 $35, free one Sun. per quarter, $3 off for visitors who walk, bike, or take public transit.

🕐 Mon.–Sat. 9:30–5, Sun. 11–5

IN FOCUS GOLDEN GATE PARK 9

With its native plant–covered living roof, retractable ceiling, three-story rainforest, gigantic planetarium, living coral reef, and frolicking penguins, the Cal Academy is one of the city's most spectacular treasures. Dramatically designed by Renzo Piano, it's an eco-friendly, energy-efficient adventure in biodiversity and green architecture. The roof's large mounds and hills mirror the local topography, and Piano's audacious design completes the dramatic transformation of the park's Music Concourse. Moving away from a restrictive role as a backward-looking museum that catalogued natural history, the new academy is all about sustainability and the future, but you'll still find those beloved dioramas in African Hall.

HIGHLIGHTS

By the time you arrive, hopefully you've decided which shows and programs to attend, looked at the academy's floorplan, and designed a plan to cover it all in the time you have. And if not, here's the quick version: Head left from the entrance to the wooden walkway over otherworldly rays in the Philippine Coral Reef, then continue to the Swamp to see Claude, the famous albino alligator. Swing through African Hall and gander at the penguins, take the elevator up to the living roof, then return to the main floor and get in line to explore the Rainforests of the World, ducking free-flying butterflies and watching for other live surprises. You'll end up below ground in the Amazonian Flooded Rainforest, where you can explore the academy's other aquarium exhibits. Phew.

TIPS

■ The academy often hosts gaggles of schoolchildren. Arrive early and allow plenty of time to wait in line.

■ Plan ahead: check Planetarium show times, animal feeding times, etc, before you arrive.

■ Visitors complain about the high cost of food here; consider bringing a picnic.

■ Free days are tempting, but the tradeoff includes extremely long lines and the possibility that you won't get in.

■ With antsy kids, visit Early Explorers Cove and use the academy's in-and-out privileges to run around outside.

■ Take time to examine the structure itself, from denim insulation to weather sensors.

ALSO WORTH SEEING

San Francisco Botanical Garden at Strybing Arboretum

SAN FRANCISCO BOTANICAL GARDEN AT STRYBING ARBORETUM

One of the best picnic spots in a very picnic-friendly park, the 55-acre arboretum specializes in plants from areas with climates similar to that of the Bay Area. Walk the Eastern Australian garden to see tough, pokey shrubs and plants with cartoon-like names, such as the hilly-pilly tree. Kids gravitate toward the large shallow fountain and the pond with ducks, turtles, and egrets. Free tours meet at the main gate daily at 1:30. ⊠ *Enter the park at 9th Ave. at Lincoln Way* ☎ *415/661–1316* ⊕ *sfbotanicalgarden.org* ✉ *$8* ⊙ *Mar.–Sept., daily 9–7; Oct.–early Nov. and Feb.–Mar., daily 9–5. Nov.–Jan., daily 9–4.*

NATIONAL AIDS MEMORIAL GROVE

This lush, serene 7-acre grove was conceived as a living memorial to the disease's victims. Coast live oaks, Monterey pines, coast redwoods, and other trees flank the grove. There are also two stone circles, one recording the names of the dead and their loved ones, the other engraved with a poem. Free 20-minute tours are available some Saturdays. ⊠ *Middle Dr. E, west of tennis courts* ☎ *415/765-0497* ⊕ *www.aidsmemorial.org.*

Beach Chalet

BEACH CHALET

Hugging the park's western border, this 1925 Willis Polk-designed structure houses gorgeous depression-era murals of familiar San Francisco scenes, while verses by local poets adorn niches here and there. Stop by the ground-floor visitors center on your way to indulge in a microbrew upstairs, ideally at sunset. ⊠ *1000 Great Hwy.* ☎ *restaurant 415/386-8439* ⊕ *www.beachchalet.com* ⊙ *Restaurant Mon.–Thurs. 9 am–10 pm, Fri. 9 am–11 pm, Sat. 8 am–11 pm, Sun. 8 am–10 pm.*

Dutch Windmill

DUTCH WINDMILL

It may not pump water anymore, but this carefully restored windmill, built in 1903 to irrigate the park, continues to enchant visitors. The Queen Wilhelmina Tulip Garden here is a welcoming respite, particularly lovely during its February and March bloom. The Murphy Windmill is just south of the Dutch Windmill and has a refurbished copper dome; swing by for an interesting comparison. ⊠ *Northwest corner of the park* ☎ *No phone* ⊙ *Dawn–dusk.*

THE HAIGHT, THE CASTRO, AND NOE VALLEY

10

Getting Oriented

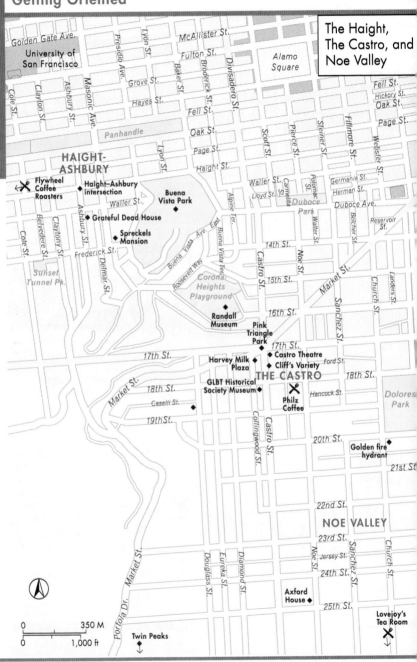

The Haight,
The Castro, and
Noe Valley

PLANNING YOUR TIME

The Upper Haight is only a few blocks long, and although there are plenty of shops and amusements, an hour or so should be enough unless you're into vintage shopping. Many restaurants here cater to the morning-after crowd, so this is a great place for brunch. With the prevalence of panhandling in this area, you may be most comfortable here during the day.

The Castro, with its fun, sometimes adult-theme storefronts, invites unhurried exploration; allot at least 60 to 90 minutes. Visit in the evening to check out the lively nightlife, or in the late morning—especially on weekends—when the street scene is hopping.

A loop through Noe Valley takes about an hour. With its popular breakfast spots and cafés, this neighborhood is a good place for a morning stroll. After you've filled up, browse the shops along 24th and Church Streets.

TOP REASONS TO GO

Castro Theatre: Take in a film at this gorgeous throwback and join the audience shouting out lines, commentary, and songs. Come early and let the Wurlitzer set the mood.

Sunday brunch in the Castro: Recover from Saturday night (with the entire community) at one of the area's favorite brunch spots.

Vintage shopping in the Haight: Find the perfect 1930s afternoon dress at Relic Vintage, a pristine faux-leopard coat at Held Over, or the motorcycle jacket of your dreams at Buffalo Exchange.

24th Street stroll: Take a leisurely ramble down lovable Noe Valley's main drag, lined with unpretentious cafés, comfy eateries, and cute one-of-a-kind shops.

QUICK BITES

Flywheel Coffee Roasters. Family-owned, this light-filled café with a view of Golden Gate Park roasts its beans in-house for a great cuppa. ✉ *672 Stanyan St., Haight* ☏ *415/682–4023* ⊕ *www.flywheelcoffee.com.*

Lovejoy's Tea Room. The tearoom is a homey jumble, with its lace-covered tables, couches, and mismatched chairs set among the antiques for sale. High tea and cream tea are served, along with traditional English-tearoom "fayre." ✉ *1351 Church St., at Clipper St., Noe Valley* ☏ *415/648–5895* ⊕ *www. lovejoystearoom.com.*

Philz Coffee. One of the city's most-popular places for the serious coffee drinker serves up the strongest handcrafted cup of joe in town. ✉ *4023 18th St., Castro* ☏ *415/875–9656* ⊕ *www.philzcoffee.com.*

GETTING THERE

F-line trolleys serve the Castro; Muni light rail K-Ingleside, L-Taraval, M-Ocean View, and T-Third cars stop at Castro station; and the J–Church serves the Castro and Noe Valley. The 71–Haight/Noriega bus from Union Square and the 6–Parnassus from Market and Van Ness serve the Haight. If on foot, know that the hill between the Castro and Noe Valley is steep.

10

Sightseeing
★

Nightlife
★★★

Dining
★★★

Lodging
★

Shopping
★★★

These distinct neighborhoods wear their personalities large and proud, and all are perfect for just strolling around. Like a slide show of San Franciscan history, you can move from the Haight's residue of 1960s counterculture to the Castro's connection to 1970s and '80s gay life to 1990s gentrification in Noe Valley. Although historic events thrust the Haight and the Castro onto the international stage, both are anything but stagnant—they're still dynamic areas well worth exploring.

THE HAIGHT

Updated by
Denise M. Leto

During the 1960s the siren song of free love, peace, and mind-altering substances lured thousands of young people to the Haight, a neighborhood just east of Golden Gate Park. By 1966 the area had become a hot spot for rock artists, including the Grateful Dead, Jefferson Airplane, and Janis Joplin. Some of the most infamous flower children, including Charles Manson and People's Temple founder Jim Jones, also called the Haight home.

Today the '60s message of peace, civil rights, and higher consciousness has been distilled into a successful blend of commercialism and progressive causes: the Haight Ashbury Free Clinic, founded in 1967, survives at the corner of Haight and Clayton, while throwbacks like Bound Together Books (the anarchist book collective), the head shop Pipe Dreams, and a bevy of tie-dye shops all keep the Summer of Love alive in their own way. The Haight's famous political spirit—it was the first neighborhood in the nation to lead a freeway revolt, and it continues to host regular boycotts against chain stores—survives alongside some of the finest Victorian-lined streets in the city. And the kids continue to come: this is where young people who end up on San Francisco's streets most often gather.

CLOSE UP

Hippie History

The eternal lure for twentysome-things, cheap rent, first helped spawn an indelible part of SF's history and public image. In the early 1960s young people started streaming into the sprawling, inexpensive Victorians in the area around the University of San Francisco, earnestly seeking a new era of communal living, individual empowerment, and expanded consciousness.

Golden Gate Park's Panhandle, a green strip on the Haight's northern edge, was their gathering spot—the site of protests, concerts, food giveaways, and general hanging out. In 1967, George Harrison strolled up the park's Hippie Hill, borrowed a guitar, and played for a while before being recognized. He led the crowd, Pied Piper–style, into the Haight.

A HIPPIE STATE OF MIND

At first the counterculture was all about sharing and taking care of one another—a good thing, considering most hippies were either broke or had renounced money. The daily free "feeds" in the Panhandle were a staple for many. The Diggers, an anarchist street-theater group, were known for handing out bread shaped like the big coffee cans they baked it in. (The Diggers also gave us immortal phrases such as "Do your own thing.")

At the time, the U.S. government, Harvard professor Timothy Leary, a Stanford student named Ken Kesey, and the kids in the Haight were all experimenting with LSD. Acid was legal, widely available, and usually given away for free. At Kesey's all-night parties, called "acid tests," a buck got you a cup of "electric" Kool-Aid, a preview of psychedelic art, and an earful of the house band, the

Grateful Dead. When LSD was made illegal in 1966, the kids responded by staging a Love Pageant Rally, where they dropped acid tabs en masse and rocked out to Janis Joplin and the Dead.

THE PEAK OF THE PARTY

Things crested early in 1967, when between 10,000 and 50,000 people ("depending on whether you were a policeman or a hippie," according to one hippie) gathered at the Polo Field in Golden Gate Park for the Human Be-In of the Gathering of the Tribes. Allen Ginsberg and Timothy Leary spoke, the Dead and Jefferson Airplane played, and people costumed with beads and feathers waved flags, clanged cymbals, and beat drums. A parachutist dropped onto the field, tossing fistfuls of acid tabs to the crowd. America watched via satellite, gape-mouthed—it was every conservative parent's nightmare.

BURN OUT

Later that year, thousands heeded Scott McKenzie's song "San Francisco," which promised "For those who come to San Francisco, Summertime will be a love-in there." The Summer of Love swelled the Haight's population from 7,000 to 75,000; people came both to join in and to ogle. But degenerates soon joined the gentle people, heroin replaced LSD, crime became rampant, and the Haight began a fast slide.

Hippies will tell you the Human Be-In was the pinnacle of their scene, while the Summer of Love came from outside—a media creation that turned their movement into a monster. Still, the idea of that fictional summer lingers, and to this day pilgrims from all over the world come to the Haight to search for a past that never was.

10

TWO HAIGHTS

The Haight is actually composed of two distinct neighborhoods: the Lower Haight runs from Divisadero to Webster; the Upper Haight, immediately east of Golden Gate Park, is the part people tend to call Haight-Ashbury (and the part that's covered here). San Franciscans come to the Upper Haight for the myriad vintage clothing stores concentrated in its few blocks, bars with character, restaurants where huge breakfast portions take the edge off a hangover, and Amoeba, the best place in town for new and used CDs and vinyl. The Lower Haight is a lively, grittier stretch with several well-loved pubs and a smattering of niche music shops.

TOP ATTRACTIONS

Haight-Ashbury Intersection. On October 6, 1967, hippies took over the intersection of Haight and Ashbury Streets to proclaim the "Death of Hip." If they thought hip was dead then, they'd find absolute confirmation of it today, what with the only tie-dye in sight on the famed corner being Ben & Jerry's storefront. ⊠ *Haight.*

WORTH NOTING

Buena Vista Park. If you can manage the steep climb, this eucalyptus-filled park has great city views. Dog walkers and homeless folks make good use of the park, the only green area in the Haight. Be sure to scan the stone rain gutters lining many of the park's walkways for inscribed names and dates; these are the remains of gravestones left unclaimed when the city closed the Laurel Hill cemetery around 1940. A new pit stop includes a portable toilet and disposal for used needles and condoms; definitely avoid the park after dark, when these items are left behind. ⊠ *Haight St. between Lyon St. and Buena Vista Ave. W, Haight.*

QUICK BITES

Cha Cha Cha. Boisterous Cha Cha Cha serves island cuisine, a mix of Cajun, Southwestern, and Caribbean influences. The decor at this Haight Street institution is Technicolor tropical plastic, and the food is hot and spicy. Try the fried calamari or chili-spiked shrimp, and wash everything down with a pitcher of Cha Cha Cha's signature sangria. Reservations are not accepted, so expect a wait for dinner. ⊠ *1801 Haight St., at Shrader St., Haight* ☎ *415/386-7670* ⊕ *www.cha3.com.*

Grateful Dead House. On the outside, this is just one more well-kept Victorian on a street that's full of them, but true fans of the Dead may find some inspiration at this legendary structure. The three-story house (closed to the public) is tastefully painted in sedate mauves, tans, and teals—no bright tie-dye colors here. ⊠ *710 Ashbury St., just past Waller St., Haight.*

A colorful mosaic mural in the Castro

Spreckels Mansion. Not to be confused with the Spreckels Mansion of Pacific Heights, this house was built for sugar baron Richard Spreckels in 1887. Jack London and Ambrose Bierce both lived and wrote here, while more recent residents included musician Graham Nash and actor Danny Glover. The boxy, putty-color Victorian—today a private home—is in mint condition. ⊠ *737 Buena Vista Ave. W, Haight.*

THE CASTRO

The brash and sassy Castro district—the social, political, and cultural center of San Francisco's thriving gay (and, to a much lesser extent, lesbian) community—stands at the western end of Market Street. This neighborhood is one of the city's liveliest and most welcoming, especially on weekends. Streets teem with folks out shopping, pushing political causes, heading to art films, and lingering in bars and cafés. It's also one of the city's most expensive neighborhoods, with an influx of tech money exacerbating an identity crisis that's been simmering for a couple of decades. But you'll still see hard-bodied men in painted-on T-shirts cruising the cutting-edge clothing and novelty stores, and pairs of all genders and sexual persuasions hold hands. Brightly painted, intricately restored Victorians line the streets here, making the Castro a good place to view striking examples of the architecture San Francisco is famous for.

CLOSE UP

The Early Days of Gay San Francisco

San Francisco's gay community has been a part of the city since its earliest days. As a port city and a major hub during the 19th-century gold rush, San Francisco became known for its sexual openness along with all of its other liberalities. But a major catalyst for the rise of a gay community was World War II.

STATIONED IN SAN FRANCISCO

During the war, hundreds of thousands of servicemen cycled through "Sodom by the Sea," and for most, San Francisco's permissive atmosphere was an eye-opening experience. The army's "off-limits" lists of forbidden establishments unintentionally (but effectively) pointed the way to the city's gay bars. When soldiers were dishonorably discharged for homosexual activity, many stayed on.

MAKING THE CITY HOME

Scores of these newcomers found homes in what was then called Eureka Valley. When the war ended, the predominantly Irish-Catholic families in that neighborhood began to move out, heading for the 'burbs. The new arrivals snapped up the Victorians on the main drag, Castro Street.

BEGINNING OF THE MOVEMENT

The establishment pushed back. In the 1950s, San Francisco's police chief vowed to crack down on "perverts," and the city's gay, lesbian, bisexual, and transgender residents lived in fear of getting caught in police raids. (Arrest meant being outed in the morning paper.) But harassment helped galvanize the community. The Daughters of Bilitis lesbian organization was founded in the city in 1955; the gay male Mattachine Society, started in Los Angeles in 1950, followed suit with a San Francisco branch.

THE TIDE BEGINS TO TURN

By the mid-1960s these clashing interests gave the growing gay population a national profile. The police upped their policy of harassment but overplayed their hand. In 1965 they dramatically raided a New Year's benefit event, and the tide of public opinion began to turn. The police were forced to appoint the first-ever liaison to the gay community. Local gay organizations began to lobby openly. As one gay participant noted, "We didn't go back into the woodwork."

THE 1970S AND HARVEY MILK

The 1970s—thumping disco, raucous street parties, and gay bashing—were a tumultuous time for the gay community. Thousands from across the country flocked to San Francisco's gay scene. Eureka Valley had more than 60 gay bars, the bathhouse scene in SoMa (where the leather crowd held court) was thriving, and graffiti around town read "Save San Francisco—Kill a Fag." When the Eureka Valley Merchants Association refused to admit gay-owned businesses in 1974, camera shop owner Harvey Milk founded the Castro Valley Association, and the neighborhood's new moniker was born. Milk was elected to the city's Board of Supervisors in 1977, its first openly gay official (and the inspirational figure for the Oscar-winning film *Milk*).

TOP ATTRACTIONS

Fodor'sChoice **Castro Theatre.** Here's a classic way to join in the Castro community:
★ grab some popcorn and catch a flick at this 1,500-seat art-deco theater; opened in 1922, it's the grandest of San Francisco's few remaining movie palaces. The neon marquee, which stands at the top of
the Castro strip, is the neighborhood's great landmark. The Castro
was the fitting host of 2008's red-carpet preview of Gus Van Sant's
film *Milk*, starring Sean Penn as openly gay San Francisco supervisor
Harvey Milk. The theater's elaborate Spanish baroque interior is fairly
well preserved. Before many shows the theater's pipe organ rises from
the orchestra pit and an organist plays pop and movie tunes, usually
ending with the Jeanette McDonald standard "San Francisco" (go
ahead, sing along). The crowd can be enthusiastic and vocal, talking back to the screen as loudly as it talks to them. Classics such as
Who's Afraid of Virginia Woolf? take on a whole new life, with the
assembled beating the actors to the punch and fashioning even snap-
pier comebacks for Elizabeth Taylor. Head here to catch sing-along
classics like *Mary Poppins*, a Fellini film retrospective, or the latest
take on same-sex love. ⊠ *429 Castro St., Castro* ☏ *415/621–6120*
⊕ *www.castrotheatre.com.*

WORTH NOTING

Clarke's Mansion. Built for attorney Alfred "Nobby" Clarke, this 1892
off-white baroque Queen Anne home was dubbed Clarke's Folly.
(His wife refused to inhabit it because it was in an unfashionable part
of town—at the time, anyone who was anyone lived on Nob Hill.)
The greenery-shrouded house (now apartments) is a beauty, with
dormers, cupolas, rounded bay windows, and huge turrets topped
by gold-leaf spheres. ⊠ *250 Douglass St., between 18th and 19th
Sts., Castro.*

QUICK
BITES

Dinosaurs. Most folks think of the Tenderloin or the Richmond for Vietnamese sandwiches, but this small Castro storefront serves up exceptionally
fresh bánh mì and rockin' spring rolls. Service is quick, and a couple of
outdoor tables take in the scene on Market Street. ⊠ *2275 Market St., near
16th St., Castro* ☏ *415/503–1421* ⊕ *eatdinosaurs.com.*

10

Thorough Bread and Pastry. Parisian pastry chef Michel Suas, founder
of the San Francisco Baking Institute, offers perfectly executed French
pastries—such as his near-legendary almond croissant—at this sweet
Castro storefront. Exposed-brick walls and cement floors give the interior
an arty-industrial feel, but don't overlook the leafy back patio. ⊠ *248
Church St., Castro* ☏ *415/558–0690* ⊕ *thoroughbreadandpastry.com*
🕘 *Closed Mon.*

CASTRO AND NOE WALK

The Castro and Noe Valley are both neighborhoods that beg to be walked—or ambled through, really, without time pressure or an absolute destination. Hit the Castro first, beginning at **Harvey Milk Plaza** under the gigantic rainbow flag. If you're going on to Noe Valley, first head east down **Market Street** for the cafés, bistros, and shops, then go back to **Castro Street** and head south, past the glorious art-deco **Castro Theatre,** checking out boutiques and cafés along the way (Cliff's Variety, at 479 Castro Street, is a must). To tour Noe Valley, go east down **18th Street** to Church (at Dolores Park), and then either strap on your hiking boots and head south over the hill or hop the J–Church to **24th Street,** the center of this rambling neighborhood.

GLBT Historical Society Museum. The small, two-gallery Gay, Lesbian, Bisexual, and Transgender (GLBT) Historical Society Museum, the first of its kind in the United States, presents multimedia exhibits from its vast holdings covering San Francisco's queer history. In the main gallery, you might hear the audiotape Harvey Milk made for the community in the event of his assassination; explore artifacts from "Gayborhoods," lost landmarks of the city's gay past; or flip through a memory book with pictures and thoughts on some of the more than 20,000 San Franciscans lost to AIDS. Though certainly not for the faint of heart (those offended by sex toys and photos of lustily frolicking naked people may, well, be offended), the museum offers an inside look at these communities so integral to the fabric of San Francisco life. ✉ *4127 18th St., near Castro St., Castro* ☎ *415/621–1107* ⊕ *www.glbthistory.org* ✇ *$5, free 1st Wed. of the month.*

Harvey Milk Plaza. An 18-foot-long rainbow flag, the symbol of gay pride, flies above this plaza named for the man who electrified the city in 1977 by being elected to its Board of Supervisors as an openly gay candidate. In the early 1970s Milk had opened a camera store on the block of Castro Street between 18th and 19th Streets. The store became the center for his campaign to open San Francisco's social and political life to gays and lesbians.

The liberal Milk hadn't served a full year of his term before he and Mayor George Moscone, also a liberal, were shot in November 1978 at City Hall. The murderer was a conservative ex-supervisor named Dan White, who had recently resigned his post and then became enraged when Moscone wouldn't reinstate him. Milk and White had often been at odds on the board, and White thought Milk had been part of a cabal to keep him from returning to his post. Milk's assassination shocked the gay community, which became infuriated when the infamous "Twinkie defense"—that junk food had led to diminished mental capacity—resulted in a manslaughter verdict for White. During the so-called White Night Riot of May 21, 1979, gays and their allies stormed City Hall, torching its lobby and several police cars.

Milk, who had feared assassination, left behind a tape recording in which he urged the community to continue the work he had begun. His legacy is the high visibility of gay people throughout city government; a bust of him was unveiled at City Hall on his birthday in 2008, and the 2008 film *Milk* gives insight into his life. A plaque at the base of the flagpole lists the names of past and present openly gay and lesbian state and local officials. ⊠ *Southwest corner of Castro and Market Sts., Castro.*

Pink Triangle Park. On a median near the Castro's huge rainbow flag stands this memorial to the gays, lesbians, bisexual, and transgender people whom the Nazis forced to wear pink triangles. Fifteen triangular granite columns, one for every 1,000 gays, lesbians, bisexual, and transgender people estimated to have been killed during and after the Holocaust, stand at the tip of a pink-rock-filled triangle—a reminder of the gay community's past and ongoing struggle for civil rights. ⊠ *Corner of Market, Castro, and 17th Sts., Castro.*

FAMILY **Randall Museum.** One of the best things about visiting this free nature museum for kids may be its tremendous views of San Francisco. Younger kids who are still excited about petting a rabbit, touching a snakeskin, or seeing a live hawk will enjoy a trip here. The museum sits beneath a hill variously known as Red Rock, Museum Hill, and, correctly, Corona Heights; hike up the steep but short trail for great, unobstructed city views. ⊠ *199 Museum Way, off Roosevelt Way, Castro* ☎ *415/554–9600* ⊕ *www.randallmuseum.org* 🖼 *Free.*

> **SISTER ACT!**
>
> If you're lucky enough to happen upon a cluster of cheeky cross-dressing nuns while in the Castro, meet the legendary Sisters of Perpetual Indulgence. They're decked out in white face-paint, glitter, and fabulous jewels. Renowned for their wit and charity fund-raising bashes, the Sisters—Sister Mary MaeHimm, Sister Bea Attitude, Sister Farrah Moans, and the gang—are the pinnacle of Castro color.

NOE VALLEY

This upscale but relaxed enclave just south of the Castro (also known as Stroller Valley for its relatively high concentration of little ones) is among the city's most desirable places to live, with laid-back cafés, kid-friendly restaurants, and comfortable, old-time shops along Church Street and 24th Street, its main thoroughfares. You can also see remnants of Noe Valley's agricultural beginnings: Billy Goat Hill (at Castro and 30th Streets), a wild-grass hill often draped in fog and topped by one of the city's best rope-swinging trees, is named for the goats that grazed here right into the 20th century.

EXPLORING

Axford House. This mauve house was built in 1877 by William Axford, a Scottish immigrant and metalsmith whose Mission Iron Works made cannonballs for the Union Army during the Civil War. The house, perched several feet above the sidewalk, was built when Noe Valley was still a rural area, as evidenced by the hayloft in the gable of the adjacent carriage house. The original iron fence, made in Axford's foundry, remains. ⊠ *1190 Noe St., at 25th St., Noe Valley.*

Golden fire hydrant. When all the other fire hydrants went dry during the fire that followed the 1906 earthquake, this one kept pumping. Noe Valley and the Mission District were thus spared the devastation wrought elsewhere in the city, which explains the large number of pre-quake homes here. Every year on April 18 (the anniversary of the quake), folks gather here to share stories about the earthquake, and the famous hydrant gets a fresh coat of gold paint. ⊠ *Church and 20th Sts., southeastern corner, across from Dolores Park, Noe Valley.*

OFF THE
BEATEN
PATH

Twin Peaks. Windswept and desolate Twin Peaks yields sweeping vistas of San Francisco and the neighboring East and North Bay counties. You can get a real feel for the city's layout here, but you'll share it with busloads of other admirers; in summer, arrive before the late-afternoon fog turns the view into pea soup. To drive here, head west from Castro Street up Market Street, which eventually becomes Portola Drive. Turn right (north) on Twin Peaks Boulevard and follow the signs to the top. Muni Bus 37–Corbett heads west to Twin Peaks from Market Street. Catch this bus above the Castro Street Muni light-rail station on the island west of Castro at Market Street. ⊠ *Noe Valley.*

Getting Oriented

Mission District

Market St.

Church St.

Dolores St.

Guerrero St.

Valencia St.

Mission St.

Capp St.

South Van Ness Ave.

Shotwell St.

Folsom St.

Harrison St.

Alabama St.

Florida St.

Bryant St.

Four Barrel Coffee

Food Chain mural

15th St.

16th St.

16th St.

Mission Dolores

Creativity Explored

16th ST. MISSION

Frankli Square

17th St.

17th St.

Clarion Alley murals

18th St.

18th St.

Tartine Bakery and Café

Maestrapeace mural

Dolores Park

19th St.

19th St.

826 Valencia mural

20th St.

21st St.

Sanchez St.

Hill St.

Church St.

Dolores St.

Guerrero St.

Valencia St.

Bartlett St.

Mission St.

Capp St.

South Van Ness Ave.

Shotwell St.

Treat St.

Harrison St.

Alabama St.

Florida St.

Bryant St.

York St.

22nd St.

POTRERO → HILL

MISSION

Pan-Lido Salvadoreño

23rd St.

DOGPATCH →

23rd St.

Museum of ◆→ Craft and Design

NOE VALLEY

24th St.

24TH ST. MISSION

Balmy Alley murals ◆

Precita Eyes Mural Arts and Visitors Center

Galería o la Raza

Osage Ave.

Lilac St.

Cypress St.

Jersey St.

25th St.

25th St.

Clipper St.

26th St.

26th St.

Cesar Chavez St. (Army)

Cesar Chavez St.

San Jose Ave.

27th St.

Precita Ave.

Duncan St.

28th St.

Mission St.

Coleridge St.

Prospect St.

Winfield St.

Folsom St.

Alabama St.

0   1/2 mile

0   500 meters

Ripley St.

Bernal Heights Park

KEY

🅱️ *BART station*

TOP REASONS TO GO

Bar-hop: Embrace your inner (or not-so-inner) hipster. Grab a cocktail at Trick Dog, whose mixologists mix up some of the Mission's finest drinks, then head over to the stylish Nihon Whisky Lounge or stop by the Chapel, where live music often accompanies the cocktails.

Chow down on phenomenal, cheap ethnic food: Keen appetites and thin wallets will meet their match here. Just try to decide between deliciously fresh burritos, garlicky falafel, thin-crust pizza, savory samosas, and more.

One-of-a-kind shopping: Barter for buried treasure at 826 Valencia and its Pirate Supply Store, then hop next door and say hello to the giraffe's head at the mad taxidermy–cum-garden store hodgepodge that is Paxton Gate.

Vivid murals: Check out dozens of energetic, colorful public artworks in alleyways and on building exteriors.

Hang out in Dolores Park: Join Mission locals and their dogs on this hilly expanse of green that has a glorious view of downtown and, if you're lucky, the Bay Bridge. On sunny days the whole neighborhood comes out to play.

QUICK BITES

Four Barrel Coffee. The pastries may be fresh, the space may be light and inviting, and the parklet out front may beckon you, but come to Four Barrel for the coffee: house-roasted beans make for one of the best cups of coffee in town, and you'll be in and out while others are still in line at Tartine. ⊠ *375 Valencia St., Mission District* ☎ *415/252–0800* ⊕ *fourbarrelcoffee.com.*

Pan-Lido Salvadoreño. Trays of Salvadoran treats such as the quesadilla—a tasty cornmeal muffin with a sweet, cream-cheese filling (not a cheese-stuffed tortilla)—await at what many consider the best Latin-American bakery in town. ⊠ *3147 22nd St., Mission District* ☎ *415/282–3350* ⊟ *No credit cards.*

GETTING THERE

After climbing the hills downtown, you'll find the Mission to be welcomingly flat. BART's two Mission District stations drop you right in the heart of the action. Get off at 16th Street for Mission Dolores and the shopping, nightlife, and restaurants of the Valencia Corridor or 24th Street to see the neighborhood murals and the increasingly trendy Calle 24 district. The busy 14–Mission bus runs all the way from downtown into the neighborhood, but BART is a much faster and more direct route. Parking can be a drag, especially on weekend evenings. If you're heading out in the evening, your safest bet would be taking a cab, since some blocks are sketchy.

PLANNING YOUR TIME

A walk that includes Mission Dolores and the neighborhood's murals takes about two hours. If you plan to go on a mural walk with the Precita Eyes organization, or if you're a window-shopper, add at least another hour. The Mission is a neighborhood that sleeps in. In the afternoon and evening, the main drags—Mission, Valencia, and 24th Streets—really come to life.

From Sunday through Tuesday it's relatively quiet here, especially in the evening—a great time to get a café table with no wait.

 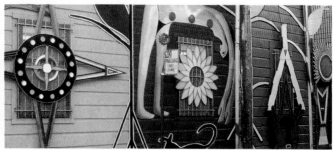

Sightseeing
★★
Nightlife
★★★★★
Dining
★★★★★
Lodging
—
Shopping
★★★

The Mission has a number of distinct personalities: it's the Latino neighborhood, where working-class folks raise their families and where gangs occasionally clash; it's the hipster hood, where tattooed and pierced twenty- and thirty-somethings hold court in the coolest cafés and bars in town; it's a culinary epicenter, with the strongest concentration of destination restaurants and affordable ethnic cuisine; it's the face of gentrification, where high-tech money prices out longtime commercial and residential renters; and it's the artists' quarter, where murals adorn literally blocks of walls long after the artists have moved to cheaper digs. It's also the city's equivalent of the Sunshine State—this neighborhood's always the last to succumb to fog.

Updated by
Denise M Leto

Packed with destination restaurants, hole-in-the-wall ethnic eateries, and hip watering holes—plus taquerías, pupuserías, and produce markets—the city's hottest hood strikes an increasingly precarious balance between cutting-edge hot spot and working-class enclave. With longtime businesses being forced out by astronomical rents and city agencies coming together with community groups to create an action plan to reverse gentrification in the neighborhood, the Mission is in flux once again, a familiar state for almost 100 years.

The eight blocks of Valencia Street between 16th and 24th Streets—what's become known as the Valencia Corridor—typify the Mission District's diversity. Businesses on the block between 16th and 17th Streets, for instance, include an upscale Peruvian restaurant, a tattoo parlor, a Belgian eatery beloved for its fries, the yuppie-chic bar Blondie's, a handful of funky home-decor stores, a pizzeria, a Vietnamese kitchen, a trendy Italian place, a sushi bar, bargain and pricey thrift shops, and the Puerto Alegre restaurant, a near dive with pack-a-punch margaritas locals revere. As prices rise, this strip has lost some of its edge as even international publications proclaim its hipness. At the same time, nearby Mission Street is morphing from a down-at-the-heels row of check-cashing parlors, dollar stores, and residential hotels into overflow for the Valencia Corridor's restaurant explosion.

Italian and Irish in the early 20th century, the Mission became heavily Latino in the late 1960s, when immigrants from Mexico and Central America began arriving. Since the 1970s, groups of muralists have transformed walls and storefronts into canvases, creating art accessible to everyone. Following the example set by the Mexican liberal artist and muralist Diego Rivera, many of the Latino artists address political and social justice issues in their murals. More recently, artists of varied backgrounds, some of whom simply like to paint on a large scale, have expanded the conversation.

The actual conversations you'll hear on the street these days might unfold in Chinese, Vietnamese, Arabic, and other tongues of the non-Latino immigrants who began settling in the Mission in the 1980s and 1990s, along with a young bohemian crowd enticed by cheap rents and the burgeoning arts-and-nightlife scene. These newer arrivals made a diverse and lively neighborhood even more so, setting the stage for the Mission's current hipster cachet. With the neighborhood flourishing, rents have gone through the roof, but the Mission remains scruffy in patches, so as you plan your explorations, take into account your comfort zone.

■TIP➜ Be prepared for homelessness and drug use around the BART stations, prostitution along Mission Street, and raucous bar-hoppers along the Valencia Corridor. The farther east you go, the sketchier the neighborhood gets.

TOP ATTRACTIONS

Balmy Alley murals. Mission District artists have transformed the walls of their neighborhood with paintings, and Balmy Alley is one of the best-executed examples. Many murals adorn the one-block alley, with newer ones continually filling in the blank spaces. In 1971, artists began teaming with local children to create a space to promote peace in Central America, community spirit, and (later) AIDS awareness; since then dozens of artists have added their vibrant works. ⚠ Be alert here: the 25th Street end of the alley adjoins a somewhat dangerous area. ✉ *24th St. between and parallel to Harrison and Treat Sts., alley runs south to 25th St., Mission District.*

Clarion Alley murals. Inspired by the work in Balmy Alley, a new generation of muralists began creating a fresh alley-cum-gallery here in 1992. The works by the loosely connected artists of the Clarion Alley Mural Project (CAMP) represent a broad range of styles and imagery, an exuberant, flowery exhortation to Tax the Rich; a lesbian celebration including donkey heads, skirts, and Donald Trump with hair

BETHANY

DID YOU KNOW?

San Francisco is chockablock with murals—around 2,000—and the Mission District is the epicenter of all the artistic fervor.

of flames bookended by a white hooded figure holding a gavel. The alley's murals offer a quick but dense glimpse at the Mission's contemporary art scene. ⊠ *Between Valencia and Mission Sts. and 17th and 18th Sts., Mission District.*

Fodor's Choice
★

Dolores Park. A two-square-block microcosm of life in the Mission, Dolores Park is one of San Francisco's liveliest green spaces: dog lovers and their pampered pups congregate, kids play at the extravagant, recently reconstructed playground, and hipsters hold court, drinking beer on sunny days. During the summer, the park hosts movie nights; performances by Shakespeare in the Park, the San Francisco Mime Troupe, and the San Francisco Symphony; and any number of pop-up events and impromptu parties. Spend a warm day here—maybe sitting at the top of the park with a view of the city and the Bay Bridge—surrounded by locals and that laid-back San Francisco energy, and you may well find yourself plotting your move to the city. ⊠ *Between 18th and 20th Sts. and Dolores and Church Sts., Mission District.*

Maestrapeace mural. The towering mural that seems to enclose the Women's Building celebrates women around the world who work for peace. Created by seven main artists and numerous helpers, this is one of the city's don't-miss murals. If the building's open, you can pick up a key to the mural's figures and symbols. ⊠ *Women's Bldg., 3543 18th St., between Valencia and Guerrero Sts., Mission District* ☎ *415/431–1180* ⊕ *www.womensbuilding.org.*

Mission Dolores. Two churches stand side by side here, including the small adobe **Mission San Francisco de Asís**, which, along with the Presidio's Officers' Club, is the oldest standing structure in San Francisco. Completed in 1791, it's the sixth of the 21 California missions founded by Franciscan friars in the 18th and early 19th centuries. Its ceiling depicts original Ohlone Indian basket designs, executed in vegetable dyes. The tiny chapel includes frescoes and a hand-painted wooden altar.

There's a hidden treasure here, too. In 2004 an archaeologist and an artist crawling along the ceiling's rafters opened a trapdoor behind the altar and rediscovered the mission's original mural, painted with natural dyes by Native Americans in 1791. The centuries have taken their toll, so the team photographed the 20-by-22-foot mural and began digitally restoring the photographic version. Among the images is a dagger-pierced Sacred Heart of Jesus.

The small museum here covers the mission's founding and history, and the pretty little cemetery—which appears in Alfred Hitchcock's film *Vertigo*—contains the graves of mid-19th-century European immigrants. The remains of an estimated 5,000 Native Americans lie in unmarked graves. Services are held in both the old mission and next door in the handsome multidome basilica. ⊠ *Dolores and 16th Sts., Mission District* ☎ *415/621–8203* ⊕ *www.missiondolores.org* ✉ *Suggested donation $7.*

Vivid public art provides a backdrop for the Mission District.

WORTH NOTING

826 Valencia mural. Fans of graphic novelist Chris Ware will want to take a good look at the facade of 826 Valencia, the nonprofit organization established by writer Dave Eggers and educator Nínive Calegari to help students in elementary, middle, and high school develop their writing skills. Ware designed the intricate mural for the group's storefront as a meditation on the evolution of human communication. ✉ *826 Valencia St., between 19th and 20th Sts., Mission District* ⊕ *826valencia.org.*

Creativity Explored. Joyous, if chaotic, creativity pervades the workshops of this art-education center and gallery for developmentally disabled adults. Several dozen adults work at the center each day—guided by a staff of working artists—painting, working in the darkroom, producing videos, and crafting prints, textiles, and ceramics. On weekdays you can drop by and see the artists at work. The art produced here is striking, and some of it is for sale; this is a great place to find a unique San Francisco masterpiece to take home. ✉ *3245 16th St., Mission District* ☎ *415/863–2108* ⊕ *www.creativityexplored.org* ✉ *Free.*

Food Chain mural. Brian Barneclo's gigantic *Food Chain* is a retro, 1950s-style celebration of the city's many neighborhoods—and the food chain—complete with an ant birthday party and worms finishing off a human skull. But in a cute way. Barneclo fans can see more of his work at Rye bar and the restaurants Nopa and farmerbrown (as well as the Facebook headquarters in Menlo Park). ✉ *Foods Co, 1800 Folsom St., Shotwell St. side of store between 14th and 15th Sts., Mission District.*

CLOSE UP

San Francisco on Film

11

With its spectacular cityscape, atmospheric fog, and a camera-ready iconic bridge, it's little wonder that San Francisco has been the setting for hundreds of films. While you're running around town, you might have the occasional sense of déjà vu, sparked by a scene from a Hitchcock or Clint Eastwood thriller. *Here are a few of the city's favorite cinematic sites:*

■ *Zodiac*, a 2007 drama about a legendary Bay Area serial killer, filmed scenes at the real-life locations where victims were gunned down. It also re-created the *San Francisco Chronicle* offices, but down south in L.A.

■ City Hall shows up in the Clint Eastwood cop thrillers *Dirty Harry* and *Magnum Force*, and is set aflame in the James Bond flick *A View to a Kill*. Its interior became a nightclub for Robin Williams's *Bicentennial Man* and a courthouse in *Tucker: The Man and His Dream*.

■ Streets in Russian Hill, Potrero Hill, and North Beach were used for the supreme car-chase sequence in *Bullitt*. The namesake detective, played by Steve McQueen, lived in Nob Hill at 1153–57 Taylor Street. And the "King of Cool" did much of his own stunt driving, thank you very much.

■ Brocklebank Apartments, at Mason and Sacramento Streets in Nob Hill, appears in several films, most notably as the posh residence of Kim Novak in Alfred Hitchcock's *Vertigo*. Other key *Vertigo* locations include

the cemetery of Mission Dolores and the waterfront at Fort Point.

■ The great Bogie-and-Bacall noir film *Dark Passage* revolves around the art-deco apartment building at 1360 Montgomery Street and the nearby Filbert Steps.

■ Dashiell Hammett's *Thin Man* characters, Nick and Nora Charles, do much of their sleuthing in the city, especially in films like *After the Thin Man*, in which the base of Coit Tower stands in as the entrance to the Charles' home.

■ North Beach's Tosca Café, at 242 Columbus Avenue, is the bar where Michael Douglas unwinds in *Basic Instinct*.

■ The Hilton Hotel at 333 O'Farrell Street became the "Hotel Bristol," the scene of much of the mayhem caused by Barbra Streisand in *What's Up, Doc?*

■ At 2640 Steiner Street in Pacific Heights is the elegant home that Robin Williams infiltrates while disguised as a nanny in *Mrs. Doubtfire*.

■ The Castro of the 1970s comes alive in *Milk*, Gus Van Sant's film starring Sean Penn as slain San Francisco supervisor Harvey Milk.

■ And, of course, there are plenty of movies about the notorious federal prison on Alcatraz Island, including Burt Lancaster's redemption drama *Birdman of Alcatraz*, Clint Eastwood's suspenseful *Escape from Alcatraz*, the goofy *So I Married an Axe Murderer*, and the Sean Connery and Nicolas Cage action flick, *The Rock*.

Galería de la Raza. San Francisco's premier showcase for contemporary Latino art, the gallery exhibits the works of mostly local artists. Events include readings and spoken word by local poets and writers, screenings of Latin American and Spanish films, and theater works by local minority theater troupes. The gallery may close between exhibits, so call ahead. Just across the street, murals and mosaics festoon the 24th Street/York Street Minipark, a tiny urban playground. A mosaic-covered Quetzalcoatl serpent plunges into the ground and rises, creating hills for little ones to clamber over, and mural-covered walls surround the space. ⊠ *2857 24th St., at Bryant St., Mission District* ☎ *415/826–8009* ⊕ *www.galeriadelaraza.org.*

Precita Eyes Mural Arts and Visitors Center. The muralists of this nonprofit arts organization design and create murals and lead guided walks of area murals. Tours start with a 45-minute slide presentation before participants head outside to view murals on Balmy Alley and 24th Street. You can pick up a map of 24th Street's murals at the center and buy art supplies, T-shirts, postcards, and other mural-related items. ⊠ *2981 24th St., Mission District* ☎ *415/285–2287* ⊕ *www.precitaeyes. org* ☛ *Center free, tours $20.*

DOGPATCH

East of the Mission District and Potrero Hill and a short T-Third Muni light-rail ride from SoMa, the Dogpatch neighborhood has been on the rise for the last decade. Red-hot galleries have hit a critical mass, decamping from aging Union Square and even New York to fill the Minnesota Street Project, a giant warehouse of art space; the Museum of Craft and Design is another neighborhood anchor. Artisans, designers, and craftspeople eager to protect the area's historical industrial legacy have all moved here in recent years, providing a solid customer base for shops, boutique restaurants, and artisanal food producers (but no grocery store or bank). At or near the intersection of 3rd and 22nd Streets, you'll find neighborhood breakfast favorite Just for You Café, locally sourced Italian food at sunny yellow Piccino, and small-batch organic ice cream at Mr. and Mrs. Miscellaneous.

EXPLORING

Museum of Craft and Design. Right at home in this once-industrial neighborhood now bursting with creative energy, this small, four-room space—definitely a quick view—mounts temporary art and design exhibitions. The focus might be sculpture, metalwork, furniture, or jewelry—or industrial design, architecture, or other topics. The MakeArt Lab gives kids the opportunity to create their own exhibit-inspired work, and the beautifully curated shop sells tempting textiles, housewares, jewelry, and other well-crafted items. ⊠ *2569 3rd St., near 22nd St., Dogpatch* ☎ *415/773–0303* ⊕ *sfmcd.org* ☛ *$8, free 1st Tues. of month.*

PACIFIC HEIGHTS
AND JAPANTOWN

Getting Oriented

Pacific Heights and Japantown

Marina Blvd

Gashouse Cove

Beach St.

Fort Mason

North Point St.

Cervantes Blvd

North Point St.

Bay St.

Capra Way

Avila St.

MARINA

Francisco St.

Chestnut St.

Hyde St.

Toledo Way

George R. Moscone Rec. Center

Lombard St.

FILLMORE

Magnolia St.

[101]

RUSSIAN HILL

Lombard St.

Moulton St.

Greenwich St.

COW HOLLOW

Greenwich St.

Pixley St.

Filbert St.

Polk St.

Larkin St.

[101]

Filbert St.

Laguna St.

Octavia St.

Green St.

Union St.

Vallejo St.

Green St.

Scott St.

Pierce St.

Steiner St.

Fillmore St.

Webster St.

Buchanan St.

Gough St.

Franklin St.

Van Ness Ave.

PACIFIC HEIGHTS

Broadway

Broadway

✕ Broadway and Webster Street estates

Whittier ◆ Mansion

Pacific Ave.

Jackson St.

Haas-Lilienthal ◆ House

NOB HILL

Spreckels Mansion ◆

Washington St.

Clay St.

Alta Plaza Park ◆

WEBSTER ST. HISTORIC DISTRICT

Lafayette Park

Franklin Street ◆ buildings

Clay St.

Sacramento St.

Atherton House ◆

Italianate ◆ Victorians

Perine Pl.

✕ Jane

California St.

Laguna St.

Octavia St.

California St.

Pine St.

Austin St.

California St.

✕ b Patisserie

Pine St.

Webster St.

Laguna St. ◆ Victorians

Bush St.

Fern St.

Sutter St.

Hemlock St.

Divisadero St.

Wilmot St.

Bush St.

JAPANTOWN

✕ Yasukochi's Sweet Stop

Franklin St.

Van Ness Ave.

Cedar St.

Sutter St.

Crown & Crumpet Tea Stop Cafe

✕ ◆ Buchanan Mall

Geary St.

Post St.

New People

Myrtle St.

Kabuki Springs & Spa ◆

◆ Japan Center

Geary Blvd.

St. Francis Square

Starr King Way

O'Farrell St.

Olive St.

Ellis St.

O'Farrell St.

Steiner St.

Fillmore St.

Ellis St.

Willow St.

Laguna St.

Ellis St.

Gough St.

Franklin St.

[101]

Willow St.

Eddy St.

Polk St.

Ellis St.

Scott St.

Pierce St.

Willow St.

Jefferson Square

Larch St.

Elm St.

Broderick

Turk St.

Elm St.

Golden Gate Ave.

McAllister St.

0   1/4 mile

0   400 meters

TOP REASONS TO GO

Chic shopping on Fillmore Street: Browse the superfine shops along Pacific Heights' main drag.

Picnic with a view at Lafayette Park: Gather supplies along Fillmore Street and climb to the top of this park. It's surrounded by grand homes and has a sweeping view of the city.

Asian shops galore in the Japan Center: Grab a quick bean-paste snack at May's Coffee Shop or browse the wonderful Kinokuniya Bookstore and the tea implements at Asakichi.

Spa serenity at Kabuki Springs: Enter the peaceful lobby and prepare to be transported at the Japanese-style communal baths.

See how the other half lives: Check out the grand, historic homes along the tree-lined streets of Pacific Heights.

QUICK BITES

b Patisserie. Your search for the perfect *kouign-amann* (Breton cake) ends here. Varieties include black sesame and maple bacon, but you can't go wrong with plain. Grab a seat in the bright interior and watch the action in the pastry kitchen, or take your treasure and a cup of Four Barrel Coffee to go. ⊠ *2821 California St., Pacific Heights* ☎ *415/440–1700* ⊕ *bpatisserie.com* ⊗ *Closed Mon.*

Crown & Crumpet Tea Stop Cafe. In the lobby of the New People building, this little tea shop looks like a little girl's fantasy, with pretty flowered and polka-dotted tablecloths and fancy settings. Stop in for a warm panini or salad, or have high tea with scones, crumpets, and finger sandwiches. ⊠ *New People, 1746 Post St., Japantown* ☎ *415/771–4252* ⊕ *crownandcrumpet.com.*

Jane. Stop in this bright, two-story spot for their famous avocado mash, mile-high quiche, homemade baked goods, and a cup of Stumptown coffee. ⊠ *2123 Fillmore St., Pacific Heights* ☎ *415/931–5263* ⊕ *www.itsjane.com.*

GETTING THERE

12

Steep streets in Pacific Heights make for impressive views and rough walking; unless you're in decent shape, consider taking a car or taxi to this neighborhood.

The only public transit that runs through the area is the bus. For Pacific Heights proper, take the 12–Folsom to its terminus at Van Ness and Pacific Avenues and walk west. For shopping on Union Street in Cow Hollow (lower Pacific Heights), catch the 41–Union or the 45–Union bus.

Buses that run to Japantown from downtown include the 2–Clement, 3–Jackson, and the very busy 38–Geary.

PLANNING YOUR TIME

Give yourself an hour to wander Fillmore Street, more if you're planning to have a meal here or picnic in Lafayette or Alta Plaza park. Checking out the stunning homes in Pacific Heights is best done by car, unless you have serious stamina; a half hour should be enough.

Shops and restaurants are the highlights of Japantown, so plan a daytime visit for a meal and some window-shopping; lunchtime is ideal.

Sightseeing
★★
Nightlife
★★
Dining
★★★
Lodging
★
Shopping
★★★

Pacific Heights and Japantown are something of an odd couple: privileged, old-school San Francisco and the workaday commercial center of Japanese American life in the city, stacked virtually on top of each other. The sprawling, extravagant mansions of Pacific Heights gradually give way to the more modest Victorians and unassuming housing tracts of Japantown. The most interesting spots in Japantown huddle in the Japan Center, the neighborhood's two-block centerpiece, and along Post Street. You can find plenty of authentic Japanese treats in the shops and restaurants.

PACIFIC HEIGHTS

Updated by
Denise M. Leto

Pacific Heights defines San Francisco's most expensive and dramatic real estate. Grand Victorians line the streets, mansions and town houses are priced in the millions, and there are magnificent views from almost any point in the neighborhood. Old money and new, personalities in the limelight and those who prefer absolute media anonymity live here, and few outsiders see anything other than the pleasing facades of Queen Anne charmers, English Tudor imports, and baroque bastions. Nancy Pelosi and Dianne Feinstein, Larry Ellison, and Gordon Getty all own impressive homes here, but not even pockets as deep as those can buy a large garden—space in the city is simply at too much of a premium. The boutiques and restaurants along Fillmore Street, which range from glam to funky, are a draw for the whole city.

12

A PACIFIC HEIGHTS WALK

Start at **Broadway and Webster Street,** where four notable estates stand within a block of one another. Two are on the north side of Broadway west of the intersection, one is on the same side to the east, and the last is half a block south on Webster. Head south down Webster and hang a right onto Clay to **Alta Plaza Park,** or skip the park and turn left on Jackson to the **Whittier Mansion,** at Jackson and Laguna Streets. Head south down Laguna and cross Washington Street to **Lafayette Park.** Walk on Washington along the edge of the park, past the formal French **Spreckels Mansion** at the corner of Octavia Street, and continue east two more blocks to Franklin Street. Turn left (north); halfway down the block stands the handsome **Haas-Lilienthal House.** Head back south on Franklin Street, stopping to view several **Franklin Street buildings.** At California Street, turn right (west) to see two **Italianate Victorians** and the **Atherton House.** Continue west to Laguna Street and turn left (south); past Pine Street sits a sedate block of **Laguna Street Victorians.**

TOP ATTRACTIONS

Haas-Lilienthal House. A small display of photographs on the bottom floor of this elaborate, gray 1886 Queen Anne house makes clear that despite its lofty stature and striking, round third-story tower, the house was modest compared with some of the giants that fell victim to the 1906 earthquake and fire. The Foundation for San Francisco's Architectural Heritage operates the home, whose carefully kept rooms provide a glimpse into late-19th-century life through period furniture, authentic details (antique dishes in the kitchen built-in), and photos of the family that occupied the house until 1972. ■TIP→ **You can admire hundreds of gorgeous San Francisco Victorians from the outside, but this is the only one that's open to the public, and it's worth a visit.** Volunteers conduct one-hour house tours three days a week, and informative two-hour walking tours of Pacific Heights on Sunday afternoon (call or check website for schedule). ⊠ *2007 Franklin St., between Washington and Jackson Sts., Pacific Heights* ☎ *415/441–3004* ⊕ *www.sfheritage.org* ⊡ *Tours $8.*

WORTH NOTING

FAMILY **Alta Plaza Park.** Golden Gate Park's longtime superintendent, John McLaren, designed Alta Plaza in 1910, modeling its terracing on that of the Grand Casino in Monte Carlo, Monaco. From the top you can see Marin to the north, downtown to the east, Twin Peaks to the south, and Golden Gate Park to the west. ■TIP→ **Kids love the many play structures at the large, enclosed playground at the top; everywhere else is dog territory.** ⊠ *Bordered by Clay, Steiner, Jackson, and Scott Sts., Pacific Heights.*

SAN FRANCISCO'S ARCHITECTURE

San Francisco's architecture scene underwent a dramatic growth spurt in the first decade of the new millennium. Boldface international architects spearheaded major projects like the de Young Museum, the California Academy of Sciences, and the Contemporary Jewish Museum. And with those additions came heated local debates.

The development flurry is thrown into sharp relief by the previous decades spent carefully preserving the city's historic buildings. Genteel Victorian homes are a city signature, and this residential legacy is fiercely protected.

Residents aren't shy about voicing opinions on the "starchitect" plans, either. As high-profile designs unfold and new condo neighborhoods break ground, criticism will surely escalate. One thing that gratifies everyone: the impressive advances made in eco-friendly building practices. As *Chronicle* columnist John King put it, San Francisco has gotten "a crash course

in contemporary architecture. One that is long, long overdue."

SAN FRANCISCO MUSEUM OF MODERN ART (SFMOMA)

Renowned Swiss architect Mario Botta's first shot at designing a museum resulted in the distinctive, sturdy geometrical forms that reflected his signature style. Here a black-and-white cylindrical tower anchors the brick structure. Botta called the huge, slanted skylight the "city's eye, like the Cyclops." A new wing, designed by Snøhetta, a Norwegian architecture firm noted for its cultural projects, opened in 2016. The expansion, which adds more than 100,000 square feet of gallery and public space, accommodates the recently acquired modern art collection of late Gap founder Don Fisher, a must for modern-art lovers.

DE YOUNG MUSEUM OF FINE ART

Love it or hate it, the structure is a must-see destination in Golden Gate Park. After the original Egyptian-revival edifice was deemed seismically unsafe following the Loma Prieta quake in 1989, the Pritzker-winning Swiss team Herzog & de Meuron won the commission to rebuild. Their design's copper facade and, in particular, the 144-foot observation tower—a twisted parallelogram grazing the tree-tops—drew fire from critics, who compared the design to a "rusty aircraft carrier." But the copper hue is mellowing with age, and the panoramic view from the ninth-floor observation deck is a hit—shifting any controversy to the museum's internal politics.

CALIFORNIA ACADEMY OF SCIENCES

An eco-friendly, energy-efficient adventure in biodiversity, Renzo Piano's audacious design for this natural history museum comes equipped with a rain forest, a planetarium, skylights, and a retractable ceiling over the central courtyard. But it's the "living roof," covered in native plants, that generates the most comment.

MISSION BAY, RINCON HILL, AND THE TRANSBAY DISTRICT

San Francisco's cityscape is undergoing tremendous change, especially moving south from Market Street along the waterfront. Don't expect old-school gingerbread here. Instead, glass-sheathed, condo-crammed high-rises are taking over what was a working-class area of warehouses and lofts, studded by the AT&T Ballpark. The first phase of an ultramodern Transbay Terminal is slated for 2017. A new University of California, San Francisco (UCSF) biotech campus has changed the landscape of Mission Bay, with a blocky Campus Conference Center by Mexican architect Ricardo Legorreta.

PRESIDIO

The development of this parkland continues at a relatively slow pace. Its historic military-base buildings are being put to new uses—everything from a printing press to a spa. Additions include a digital arts center by George Lucas, a Walt Disney Museum, and the hip Inn at the Presidio boutique hotel.

Left: California Academy of Sciences; top right: Painted ladies; bottom right: de Young Museum of Fine Art

DID YOU KNOW?

These soft-colored Victorian homes in Pacific Heights are closer to the original hues sported back in the 1900s. It wasn't until the 1960s that the bold, electric colors now seen around San Francisco gained popularity. Before that, the most typical house paint color was a standard gray.

Atherton House. The mildly daffy design of this Victorian-era house incorporates Queen Anne, Stick-Eastlake, and other architectural elements. Many claim the house—now apartments—is haunted by the ghosts of its 19th-century residents, who regularly whisper, glow, and generally cause a mild fuss. ⊠ *1990 California St., Pacific Heights.*

Broadway and Webster Street estates. Broadway uptown, unlike its garish North Beach stretch, has plenty of prestigious addresses. The three-story palace at 2222 Broadway, which has an intricately filigreed doorway, was built by Comstock silver-mine heir James Flood and later donated to a religious order. The Convent of the Sacred Heart purchased the **Grant House** at 2220 Broadway. These two buildings, along with a Flood property at 2120 Broadway, are used as school quarters. A gold-mine heir, William Bourn II, commissioned Willis Polk to build the nearby brick mansion at 2550 Webster Street. ⊠ *Pacific Heights.*

Franklin Street buildings. The three blocks south of the Haas-Lilienthal House contain a few curiosities of interest to architecture buffs. What at first looks like a stone facade on the **Golden Gate Church** (*1901 Franklin St.*) is actually redwood painted white. A handsome Georgian-style residence built in the early 1900s for a coffee merchant sits at 1735 Franklin. On the northeast corner of Franklin and California Streets is a **Christian Science church**; built in the Tuscan revival style, it's noteworthy for its terra-cotta detailing. The **Coleman House** (*1701 Franklin St.*) is an impressive twin-turret Queen Anne mansion that was built for a gold-rush mining and lumber baron. Don't miss the large, brilliant-purple stained-glass window on the house's north side. ⊠ *Franklin St. between Washington and California Sts., Pacific Heights.*

Italianate Victorians. Two Italianate Victorians stand out on the 1800 block of California. The beauty at 1834, the Wormser-Coleman house, was built in the 1870s. Coleman bought the lot next door, giving this property an unusually spacious yard for the city, even in this luxurious neighborhood. ⊠ *1818 and 1834 California St., Pacific Heights.*

Lafayette Park. Clusters of trees dot this four-block-square oasis for sunbathers and dog-and-Frisbee teams. On the south side of the park, squat but elegant **2151 Sacramento**, a private condominium, is the site of a home occupied by Sir Arthur Conan Doyle in the late 19th century. Coats of arms blaze in the front stained-glass windows. The park itself is a lovely neighborhood space, where Pacific Heights residents laze in the sun or exercise their pedigreed canines while gazing at downtown's skyline in the distance. ⊠ *Bordered by Laguna, Gough, Sacramento, and Washington Sts., Pacific Heights.*

Laguna Street Victorians. On the west side of the 1800 block of Laguna Street, these oft-photographed houses cost between $2,000 and $2,600 when they were built in the 1870s. No bright colors here, though—most of the paint jobs are in soft beiges or pastels. ⊠ *Between Bush and Pine Sts., Pacific Heights.*

Spreckels Mansion. Shrouded behind tall juniper hedges at the corner of winding, redbrick Octavia Street, overlooking Lafayette Park, the estate was built for sugar heir Adolph Spreckels and his wife, Alma.

12

Mrs. Spreckels was so pleased with her house that she commissioned George Applegarth to design another building in a similar vein: the Legion of Honor. One of the city's great iconoclasts, Alma Spreckels was the model for the bronze figure atop the Victory Monument in Union Square. These days an iconoclast of another sort owns the mansion: romance novelist Danielle Steel, whose dust-up with local columnists over the size of those hedges entertained aficionados of local gossip in 2014. ⊠ *2080 Washington St., at Octavia St., Pacific Heights.*

Whittier Mansion. With a Spanish-tile roof and scrolled bay windows on all four sides, this is one of the most elegant 19th-century houses in the state. Unlike other grand mansions lost in the 1906 quake, the Whittier Mansion was built so solidly that only a chimney toppled over during the disaster. Built by William Franklin Whittier, the founder of (what became) PG&E, the house served as the German consulate during the Nazi period. Legend has it that the house is haunted. ⊠ *2090 Jackson St., Pacific Heights.*

JAPANTOWN

Though still the spiritual center of San Francisco's Japanese American community, Japantown feels somewhat adrift. The Japan Center mall, for instance, comes across as rather sterile, and whereas Chinatown is densely populated and still largely Chinese, Japantown struggles to retain its unique character.

Also called Nihonmachi, Japantown is centered on the southern slope of Pacific Heights, north of Geary Boulevard between Fillmore and Laguna Streets. The Japanese community in San Francisco started around 1860; after the 1906 earthquake and fire many of these newcomers settled in the Western Addition. By the 1930s they had opened shops, markets, meeting halls, and restaurants and established Shinto and Buddhist temples. But during World War II the area was virtually gutted when many of its residents, including second- and third-generation Americans, were forced into so-called relocation camps. During the 1960s and 1970s redevelopment further eroded the neighborhood, and most Japanese Americans now live elsewhere in the city.

Still, when several key properties in the neighborhood were sold in 2007, a group rallied to "save Japantown," and some new blood finally infused the area with energy: Robert Redford's Sundance corporation revived the Kabuki Theatre; the local, hip hotel group Joie de Vivre took over the Hotel Kabuki; and the J-Pop Center, New People, brought Japanese pop culture and a long-missing youthful vibe. ■ TIP→ **Japantown is a relatively safe area, but the Western Addition, south of Geary Boulevard, can be dangerous even during the daytime. Also avoid going too far west of Fillmore Street on either side of Geary.**

TOP ATTRACTIONS

Japan Center. Cool and curious trinkets, noodle houses and sushi joints, a destination bookstore, and a peek at Japanese culture high and low await at this 5-acre complex designed in 1968 by noted American architect Minoru Yamasaki. The Japan Center includes the shop- and restaurant-filled Kintetsu and Kinokuniya buildings; the excellent Kabuki Springs & Spa; the Hotel Kabuki; and the Sundance Kabuki, Robert Redford's fancy, reserved-seating cinema/restaurant complex.

The Kinokuniya Bookstore, in the Kinokuniya Building, has an extensive selection of Japanese-language books, *manga* (graphic novels), books on design, and English-language translations and books on Japanese topics. Just outside, follow the Japanese teenagers to Pika Pika, where you and your friends can step into a photo booth and then use special effects and stickers to decorate your creation. On the bridge connecting the center's two buildings, check out Shige Antiques for *yukata* (lightweight cotton kimonos) for kids and lovely silk kimonos, and Asakichi and its tiny incense shop for tinkling wind chimes and display-worthy teakettles. Continue into the Kintetsu Building for a selection of Japanese restaurants.

Between the Miyako Mall and the Kintetsu Building are the five-tier, 100-foot-tall **Peace Pagoda** and the Peace Plaza, where seasonal festivals are held. The pagoda, which draws on the 1,200-year-old tradition of miniature round pagodas dedicated to eternal peace, was designed in the late 1960s by Yoshiro Taniguchi to convey the "friendship and goodwill" of the Japanese people to the people of the United States. The plaza itself is a shadeless, unwelcoming space with little seating. Continue into the Miyako Mall to Ichiban Kan, a Japanese dollar store where you can pick up fun Japanese kitchenware, tote bags decorated with hedgehogs, and erasers shaped like food. ✉ *Bordered by Geary Blvd. and Fillmore, Post, and Laguna Sts., Japantown.*

Fodor'sChoice **Kabuki Springs & Spa.** This serene spa is one Japantown destination that
★ draws locals from all over town, from hipster to grandma, Japanese-American or not. Balinese urns decorate the communal bath area of this house of tranquility.

The extensive service menu includes facials, salt scrubs, and mud and seaweed wraps, in addition to massage. You can take your massage in a private room with a bath or in a curtained-off area.

The communal baths ($25) contain hot and cold tubs, a large Japanese-style bath, a sauna, a steam room, and showers. Bang the gong for quiet if your fellow bathers are speaking too loudly. The clothing-optional baths are open for men only on Monday, Thursday, and Saturday; women bathe on Wednesday, Friday, and Sunday. Bathing suits are required on Tuesday, when the baths are coed.

Men and women can reserve private rooms daily. ✉ *1750 Geary Blvd., Japantown* ☎ *415/922–6000* ⊕ *www.kabukisprings.com.*

WORTH NOTING

Buchanan Mall. The shops lining this open-air mall are geared more toward locals—travel agencies, electronics shops—but there are some fun Japanese-goods stores here, too. Arrive early in the day and you may score some fabulous *mochi* (a soft, sweet Japanese rice treat) at **Benkyodo Company** (*1747 Buchanan St., 415/922–1244, www.benkyodocompany.com*). It's easy to spend hours among the fabulous origami and craft papers at **Paper Tree** (*1743 Buchanan St., 415/921–7100, paper-tree.com*). For lunch head to **Hinodeya Ramen** (*1737 Buchanan St., 415/757–0552*), serving light-tasting dashi (clear-broth) ramen, a rarity in the city. Have a seat on local artist Ruth Asawa's twin origami-style fountains, which sit in the middle of the mall. ⊠ *Buchanan St. between Post and Sutter Sts., Japantown.*

New People. The kids' counterpart to the Japan Center, this fresh shopping center combines a cinema, a tea parlor, and shops with a successful synergy. The downstairs cinema shows classic and cutting-edge Asian (largely Japanese) films and is home to the San Francisco Film Society. Upstairs you can peruse Japanese pop-culture items and anime-inspired fashion, like handmade, split-toe shoes at Sou Sou and Lolita fashion at Baby, the Stars Shine Bright. ⊠ *1746 Post St., Japantown* ⊕ *www.newpeopleworld.com.*

WHERE TO EAT

HOW TO EAT LIKE A LOCAL

San Francisco may well be the most piping-red-hot dining scene in the nation now. After all, with a booming tech industry, there are mouths to feed. Freedom to do what you want. Innovation. Eccentricity. These words define the culture, the food, and the cuisine of the city by the bay. Get in on what locals know by enjoying their favorite foods.

FOOD TRUCKS

This is where experimentation begins, where the overhead is low, and risk-taking is fun. From these mobile kitchens careers are launched. A food meet-up called "Off the Grid" happens in season at Fort Mason where you can do a progressive dinner among the 25 or so trucks. Year-round the convoy roams to different locations, selling things like Korean poutine, Indian burritos, and Vietnamese burgers. Each dish seems to reflect a refusal to follow the norm.

DIM SUM

The tradition of dim sum took hold in San Francisco when Chinese immigrants from Guangdong Province arrived with Cantonese cuisine. These earlier settlers eventually established teahouses and bakeries that sold dim sum, like the steamed dumplings stuffed with shrimp (*har gow*) or pork (*shao mai*). Now carts roll from table to table in Chinatown restaurants—and other parts of the city. Try the grilled and fried bite-size savories but also the sweets like *dan tat*, an egg custard tart.

BARBECUE

Whaaa? San Francisco barbecue? And what would that be? You can bet it's meat from top purveyors nearby. The city is surrounded by grazing lands,

13

where the animals and their minders, the ranchers, are king. Until now, meats came simply plated. Now it's messy, with smokiness, charred crusts, and gorgeous marbling. But you may never hear of a San-Fran-style barbecue, because, in the words of one chef, we're "nondenominational." You'll see it all: Memphis, Texas, Carolina, and Kansas City.

ICE CREAM

How ice cream became so popular in a place that probably spends many of its 365 days below the 75 degree mark is a mystery. But the lines attest to the popularity of the frozen dessert that gets its own San Francisco twist. This is the vanilla-bean vanilla and Tcho chocolate crowd. Bourbon and cornflakes? Reposado tequila? Cheers to that. Diversity and local produce is blended into flavors like ube (purple yam), yuzu, and Thai latte. Vegans, we got you covered, too.

BURRITOS

This stuffed tortilla got its Bay Area start in the 1960s in the Mission District. Because the size and fillings distinguish it from other styles, it became known as the Mission burrito. Look for rice (Southern Californians are cringing), beans, salsa, and enough meat in the burrito for two meals. The aluminum foil keeps the interior neat, in theory. Popular choices are *carne asada* (beef)

and *carnitas* (pork). But then there's *lengua* (beef tongue) and *birria* (goat). This is a hands-on meal. No utensils, please.

COFFEE

Coffee roasters here are like sports teams in other cities. You pick one of the big five or six to be loyal to, and defend it tirelessly. San Francisco favorites source impeccably and blend different beans as if they were winemaking. In addition, a few of the big names—Four Barrel, Sightglass, Ritual, Blue Bottle—roast their own to control what they grind and pour at their outlets across the city—and now nationally and internationally.

FARMERS' MARKETS

These are our new grocery stores. They're the places to discover the latest in fruits, vegetables, and dried beans— much of it grown within a 60-mile radius. Cheeses, cured salami, breads, and nuts are sampled. Then there are the local ready-to-eat snacks, like pizza and *huevos rancheros*. The most popular market is the one on Saturday at the Ferry Plaza.

Left: Several farmers' markets occupy the Ferry Building; top right: Dim sum being served at a local restaurant; bottom right: One of the many farmers' markets in the city.

Updated by Rebecca Flint Marx

San Francisco is one of America's top food cities. Some of the biggest landmarks are restaurants; and for some visitors, chefs like Daniel Patterson are just as big a draw as Alcatraz. In fact, on a Saturday, the Ferry Building—a temple to local eating—may attract more visitors than the Golden Gate Bridge.

Chefs are drawn to the superb ingredients plucked from the soils. Chances are that the Meyer lemons, fava beans, or strawberries on your plate that are preserved, pureed, or pickled were harvested this morning or within the last 48 hours. The briny abalone, crab, oysters, squid, and tuna that are poached, seared, smoked, or carpaccio'ed are caught just off shore. You will also get to taste unusual varieties, like lollipop kale, agretti greens, and yuzu citrus. (The biggest downside is that some San Francisco menus come across as precious not delicious, a name-dump of ingredients.) But this is definitely post-carrot-and-peas paradise, unless, of course, you're talking heirloom carrot sorbet.

Today the most interesting kitchens are using these ingredients in regional cuisines, like Korean, Japanese, Italian, or South American. So get ready to dig into kung pao pastrami, porcini doughnuts with raclette béchamel, and yucca gnocchi. That fig-on-a-plate reputation? That's so last decade—as is foie gras, the sale of which is incredibly controversial throughout the state.

But the playground isn't just in haute cuisine kitchens. Culinary hot spots are just as likely to be a burger, pizza, or barbecue joint— with a few classically trained chefs dedicating their lives to making a better margherita pizza. And you can just as easily find superb *bánh mì*, ramen noodles, and juicy *al pastor* tacos in the kitchens of Little Saigon, Japantown, or the Mission District, with allegiances running strong. A *carnitas* burrito can cause serious family feuds (especially, say, if your husband likes El Farolito and you're more a La Taqueria diehard).

SAN FRANCISCO DINING PLANNER

RESERVATIONS

Snagging reservations at restaurants with a lot of buzz has gotten notoriously difficult, with 5:30 and 9:30 often the pick. These choices aren't terrible if you plan on it. For a reservation at peak eating hours, though, our best advice is to call as far in advance as possible—try dining there earlier in the week if the Friday and Saturday tables are all full. You can also try calling a restaurant in the early afternoon the day of, because that's when they're making their reservation confirmation calls. If you're calling a few days ahead of time, ask if you can be put on a waiting list. Also, ask whether there's a bar or counter you can dine at—these are usually offered first-come, first-served. It's worth noting that several places set aside many tables for walk-in business (and not for advance reservations), in which case you can just show up and make the most of the waits. As a last resort, many popular San Francisco restaurants are also open for lunch.

HOURS

Unless otherwise noted, the restaurants listed in this guide are open daily for lunch and dinner. Prime time for dinner is around 7:30 or 8 pm, and although there are places for night owls to fuel up, most restaurants stop serving around 10 pm. Restaurants, along with bars and clubs, may serve alcohol between the hours of 6 am and 2 am.

WHAT TO WEAR

In general, San Franciscans are neat but casual dressers; only at the top-notch dining rooms do you see a more formal style. But the way you look can influence how you're treated—and where you're seated. Generally speaking, jeans will suffice at most table-service restaurants in the $ to $$$ range. A few pricier restaurants require jackets, and some insist on ties. In reviews, we mention dress only when men are required to wear a jacket or a jacket and tie. Note that shorts, sweatpants, and sports jerseys are rarely appropriate. When in doubt, call the restaurant and ask.

PRICES

If you're watching your budget, be sure to ask the price of daily specials. The charge for these dishes can sometimes be out of line with the menu. If you eat early or late, you may be able to take advantage of a prix-fixe deal not offered at peak hours. Many upscale restaurants offer lunch deals with special menus at bargain prices. Credit cards are widely accepted, but some restaurants (particularly smaller ones) accept only cash. Also, keep in mind that a restaurant listed as $$$ may actually have a good deal or two, such as an early prix-fixe dinner or a great bar scene and good, reasonably priced bar food to go with it.

WHAT IT COSTS				
	$	$$	$$$	$$$$
Restaurants	under $15	$15–$22	$23–$30	over $30

Restaurant prices are the average cost of a main course at dinner, or if dinner is not served, at lunch.

TIPPING AND TAXES

In most restaurants, tip the waiter 18%–20%. (To figure out a 20% tip quickly, just move the decimal spot one place to the left and double that.) Bills for parties of six or more sometimes include the tip. A few restaurants in the Bay Area are experimenting with a gratuity-included policy for all parties. There are only about six such places, and the movement is led by some of the best chefs.

Tip at least $1 per drink at the bar; $2 if it's a labor-intensive cocktail. Also be aware that some restaurants, now required to fund the city's new universal health-care ordinance, are passing these costs along to their customers instead of raising prices—usually in the form of a 3%–4% surcharge or a $1–$3.50-per-head charge. (San Francisco sales tax is currently at 8.5%.)

PARKING

Most high-end restaurants offer valet parking—worth considering in crowded neighborhoods such as North Beach, Russian Hill, Union Square, and the Mission. There's often a nominal charge and a time restriction on validated parking.

USING THE MAPS

Throughout the chapter, you'll see mapping symbols and coordinates (3:F2) after property names or reviews. To locate the property on a map, turn to the San Francisco Dining and Lodging Atlas at the end of the chapter. The first number after the symbol indicates the map number. Following that is the property's coordinate on the map grid.

RESTAURANT REVIEWS

Listed alphabetically within neighborhood.

UNION SQUARE

Tourists are attracted to this neighborhood for its many hotels and theater houses but primarily for its first-rate shopping. What is harder to find here is authentic San Francisco eating (locals dislike battling the crowds). But if you know where to look, you can find good places tucked away into narrow side alleys or in the lobbies of hotels.

$$$$ SEAFOOD ✕ **Farallon.** Even though San Francisco is right on the Bay, it can be surprisingly hard to find great menus that focus on fish. But this white-linen restaurant delivers. **Known for:** freshly shucked shellfish; sustainably caught fish; happy hour oysters. [$] *Average main: $32* ✉ *450 Post St., Union Sq.* ☎ *415/956–6969* 🌐 *www.farallonrestaurant.com* ✥ *4:E3.*

$ JAPANESE 🍴 **Katana-Ya.** There's a line in front of this hole-in-the-wall ramen house from the moment it opens, and no wonder: it serves some of the most authentic noodles in town. Hand-drawn pictures of specials punctuate a colorful interior with too-close tables and a couple of stools around the bar. **Known for:** great ramen; long waits. [$] *Average main: $11* ✉ *430 Geary St., Union Sq.* ☎ *415/771–1280* ✣ *4:E4.*

$$$$ THAI Fodor's Choice ★ 🍴 **Kin Khao.** Casual eaters of Americanized Thai food probably won't recognize much at this modern, low-lit restaurant, but travelers to Thailand—the chef-owner is a native—will likely see a few familiars on the short, focused menu. The *yum kai dao*, a spicy fried egg salad, runs with yolk and is spiked with cilantro. **Known for:** authentic dishes; explosive flavors. [$] *Average main: $32* ✉ *55 Cyril Magnin St., corner of Mason and Ellis Sts., Union Sq.* ✣ *Located off the lobby of the Parc 55 Hotel* ☎ *415/362–7456* 🌐 *kinkhao.com* ✣ *4:E5.*

$$$$ MODERN AMERICAN Fodor's Choice ★ 🍴 **Liholiho Yacht Club.** Big-hearted, high-spirited cooking has made Chef Ravi Kapur's lively restaurant one of the toughest reservations in town. The menu is inspired but not defined by the chef's native Hawaii. **Known for:** poke; Hawaiian-inspired food; lively buzz. [$] *Average main: $35* ✉ *871 Sutter St., Union Sq.* ☎ *415/440–5446* 🌐 *www.lycf.com* 🕒 *Closed Sun. No lunch.* ✣ *4:C3.*

$$$ CHINESE 🍴 **M.Y. China.** Hand-pulled noodles are the real star at celebrity chef Martin Yan's show palace. Whether or not Yan is there, you'll be sure to watch his cooks stretch, twist, toss, and drop them into a beef short-rib soup flavored with star anise. **Known for:** hand-pulled noodles; celebrity chef. [$] *Average main: $25* ✉ *Westfield Mall, 845 Market St., Union Sq.* ☎ *415/580–3001* 🌐 *tastemychina.com* ✣ *4:F5.*

CHINATOWN

Once you step beneath the gateway on Grant Street and meander the alleyways, into the restaurants and bakeries along Jackson, Clay, and Washington Streets, you might be surprised at what you'll find. A food market, along Stockton, is a riot of exotic fruits, vegetables, and other delicacies. Restaurants feature the cuisine of (mostly) China's Guangdong Province, or Cantonese style. A lot of the Chinese, though, have moved out and into the Richmond and Sunset neighborhoods. This is a trek from downtown, set against the breakers and not the bay, but if you want the real deal, venture there. Not far from Chinatown is also Little Saigon, in the Tenderloin—many restaurants are run by ethnic Chinese who emigrated from Vietnam.

$$ CHINESE FAMILY 🍴 **Great Eastern.** Fresh, simply prepared Cantonese-style cuisine is the reason to dine here. Seafood is a particular strength—it hails from tanks that occupy a corner of the street-level main dining room. **Known for:** seafood; Cantonese food; dim sum. [$] *Average main: $19* ✉ *649 Jackson St., Chinatown* ☎ *415/986–2500* 🌐 *www.greateasternsf.com* ✣ *1:D4.*

$$$ CHINESE 🍴 **Mister Jiu's.** Brandon Jew's ambitious, graceful restaurant offers the chef's contemporary, farm-to-table interpretation of Chinese cuisine. This is the place for hot-and-sour soup garnished with nasturtiums and pot stickers made with Swiss chard and local chicken. **Known for:**

modern Chinese food; cocktails. [$] *Average main: $30* ✉ *28 Waverly Pl., Chinatown* ☎ *415/857–9688* 🌐 *www.misterjius.com* 🕓 *Closed Sun. and Mon. No lunch.* ✣ *1:D4.*

$$ CHINESE FAMILY 🍴 **R&G Lounge.** Salt-and-pepper Dungeness crab is a delicious draw at this bright, three-level Cantonese eatery that excels in the crustacean. A menu with photographs will help you sort through other HK specialties, including Peking duck and shrimp-stuffed bean curd. **Known for:** crab; Cantonese specialties; extensive menu. [$] *Average main: $19* ✉ *631 Kearny St., Chinatown* ☎ *415/982–7877* 🌐 *www.rnglounge.com* ✣ *1:E4.*

SOMA

Hip SoMa covers a large area that swings from chic residential lofts and 19th-century warehouses–turned–trendy eateries to slightly dingy sidewalk scenes, particularly near the police station and in the higher numbers (7th through 10th nearer to Market). It has the rowdy ballpark and the genteel South Park within its fold. And restaurants near here fuel the mostly young and single local crowd who work in tech (Pinterest, Yelp, Twitter, and Adobe are nearby and so is the train to Silicon Valley). Also, interesting chef-owned restaurants are finding their footing here, like AQ, Una Pizza Napoletana, Benu, Saison, and Citizen's Band.

$$$ MODERN AMERICAN 🍴 **Bar Agricole.** Thanks to celebrated bartender/owner Thad Vogler, this sleek LEED-certified spot is a haven for cocktail hounds. Be sure to enjoy the creative libations, but don't neglect the terrific food, either. **Known for:** cocktails; green design; California-Mediterranean cuisine. [$] *Average main: $27* ✉ *355 11th St., SoMa* ☎ *415/355–9400* 🌐 *www.baragricole.co* ✣ *3:G3.*

$$$$ MODERN AMERICAN Fodor's Choice ★ 🍴 **Benu.** Chef Corey Lee's three-Michelin-star fine-dining mecca is a must-stop for those who hop from city to city, collecting memorable meals. Each of the tasting menu's 15-plus courses is impossibly meticulous, a marvel of textures and flavors. **Known for:** high-end dining; tasting menu; good service. [$] *Average main: $285* ✉ *22 Hawthorne St., SoMa* ☎ *415/685–4860* 🌐 *www.benusf.com* 🕓 *Closed Sun. and Mon. No lunch* ✣ *1:F6.*

$$$ MODERN BRITISH 🍴 **The Cavalier.** British pub grub gets a Nor Cal makeover at this Anna Weinberg–Jennifer Puccio production. Like the pair's other collaborations (Marlowe, Park Tavern, Leo's Oyster Bar), it's insanely popular and loud, yet deliciously comforting. **Known for:** Brit-inspired food; cocktails; lively atmosphere. [$] *Average main: $30* ✉ *Hotel Zetta, 360 Jessie St., SoMa* ☎ *415/321–6000* 🌐 *thecavaliersf.com* ✣ *4:G6.*

$$$ MEDITERRANEAN 🍴 **The Fly Trap.** The pistachio meatballs put this place on the San Francisco culinary map. It continues to attract SoMa crowds with Cal-Med fare like braised short ribs and saffron *arancini* (rice balls). **Known for:** Mediterranean-influenced food; cocktails. [$] *Average main: $23* ✉ *606 Folsom St., SoMa* ☎ *415/243–0580* 🌐 *flytrapsf.com* 🕓 *Closed Sun. No lunch* ✣ *1:F6.*

$$$ CONTEMPORARY Fodor's Choice ★ 🍴 **In Situ.** Benu chef Corey Lee's restaurant at SFMOMA is an exhibition of its own, with a rotating menu comprised of dishes from 80 famous chefs around the world. You might taste David Chang's sausage and rice cakes, Rene Redzepi's wood sorrel granita, or Wylie Dufresne's

shrimp grits. **Known for:** global influences; originality; museum location. $ *Average main: $30* ⊠ *151 3rd St., SoMa* ☎ *415/941–6050* ⊕ *insitu.sfmoma.org* ⊙ *Closed Wed. No dinner Mon. and Tues.* ✛ *1:E6.*

$$$
AMERICAN
Fodor'sChoice
★

✕ **Marlowe.** Hearty American bistro fare and hip design draw crowds to this Anna Weinberg–Jennifer Puccio production. The menu boasts one of the city's best burgers, and the dining room gleams with white penny tile floors and marble countertops. **Known for:** burgers; strong drinks; festive atmosphere. $ *Average main: $27* ⊠ *500 Brannan St., SoMa* ☎ *415/777–1413* ⊕ *www.marlowesf.com* ⊙ *No lunch weekends* ✛ *1:E6.*

$$$$
MODERN
AMERICAN

✕ **Saison.** This Michelin-starred restaurant always begs the question, what exactly do you get for $398 per person? The answer is a culinary adventure of many courses impeccably prepared by chef Joshua Skenes, who teases deepest flavors from premium ingredients. **Known for:** splurgy dining; unique, inventive menu. $ *Average main: $398* ⊠ *178 Townsend St., SoMa* ☎ *415/828–7990* ⊕ *www.saisonsf.com* ⊙ *Closed Sun. and Mon.* ✛ *1:G6.*

$$$
MODERN
AMERICAN

✕ **Town Hall.** American fare with a Southern flair is the headline at chefs Mitchell and Steven Rosenthal's power broker's pit stop. Barbecue gulf shrimp, juicy fried chicken, and butterscotch-chocolate *pot de crème* highlight a menu that has enough variety to satisfy nearly everyone, and portions to satisfy almost every appetite. **Known for:** hearty food; lunchtime scene. $ *Average main: $30* ⊠ *342 Howard St., SoMa* ☎ *415/908–3900* ⊕ *www.townhallsf.com* ⊙ *No lunch weekends* ✛ *1:F5.*

$$$
MODERN
AMERICAN
Fodor'sChoice
★

✕ **Trou Normand.** Thad Vogler's second endeavor (Bar Agricole was the first) delivers a fun boozy evening in stunning surroundings. Located off the lobby of the art-deco-era Pacific Telephone building, it excels at house-cured salami and charcuterie and classic brandy-based cocktails. **Known for:** house-made charcuterie; brandy-based cocktails. $ *Average main: $26* ⊠ *140 New Montgomery St., SoMa* ☎ *415/975–0876* ⊕ *www.trounormandsf.com* ✛ *1:E6.*

$$$$
MODERN
AMERICAN

✕ **Twenty Five Lusk.** Tucked off an alley, this sleek two-story bastion of American cuisine serves a hefty helping of glamour with its food. The lights are low, the wines are well chosen, and the grilled-cheese canapés are served with caviar. **Known for:** sexy ambience; top-notch ingredients. $ *Average main: $33* ⊠ *25 Lusk St., SoMa* ☎ *415/495–5875* ⊕ *www.25lusk.com* ✛ *1:G6.*

$$$
PIZZA

✕ **Una Pizza Napoletana.** Inside this bare-bones SoMa spot you'll find one of the best Neapolitan-style pizzas outside of Italy. Chef-owner and Manhattan transplant Anthony Mangieri is an obsessive artisan, carefully making each and every pizza by hand. **Known for:** Neapolitan-style pizza; brief menu. $ *Average main: $25* ⊠ *210 11th St., SoMa* ☎ *415/861–3444* ⊕ *www.unapizza.com* ⊙ *Closed Sun.–Tues.* ✛ *3:G3.*

$$
ITALIAN

✕ **Zero Zero.** You can visit this popular and comfortable California-Italian place almost any time of day, whether you're craving a thin-crust "Cali-politan" pizza for lunch or house-made pasta for dinner. Ingredients are fresh and seasonal, and portions are affordable and easy to share. **Known for:** thin-crust pizza; lively bar. $ *Average main: $20* ⊠ *826 Folsom St., SoMa* ☎ *415/348–8800* ⊕ *www.zerozerosf.com* ✛ *1:F6.*

13

TENDERLOIN

A land of dive bars, package-liquor stores, panhandlers, and ... some of the best pho and bánh mì in the city, this seedy district of low rents encompasses Little Saigon. Locals know to come here for great cheap eats, including not just Vietnamese but naans and masalas. This is San Francisco's rougher neighborhood—one of the last holdouts.

$$
VIETNAMESE
✕**Bodega Bistro.** Located in the Tenderloin's Little Saigon quarter, this casual Vietnamese bistro brims at lunchtime with fans of its steaming bowls of pho (the beef version is particularly good). For dinner, the round tables are overloaded with signature specialties like roast squab and *bun cha Hanoi* (broiled pork over rice vermicelli). **Known for:** outstanding pho; Hanoi street food. $ *Average main: $18* ✉ *607 Larkin St., Polk Gulch* ☎ *415/580–7965* ⊕ *www.bodegabistro.co* ✣ *4:A6.*

$$
THAI
✕**Lers Ros.** Skip the "same old" pad thai and try something new at this authentic Thai standby. Thai herb sausage and papaya salad with salted egg are good appetizers to share, while the pork belly with crispy rind and basil leaves and *duck larb* (meat salad) come packed with flavor and heat. **Known for:** authentic Thai; extensive menu. $ *Average main: $15* ✉ *730 Larkin St., Tenderloin* ☎ *415/931–6917* ⊕ *www.lersros.com* ✣ *4:A5.*

HAYES VALLEY

Hayes Valley is sprouting several hip and haute dining destinations around its main stem, Hayes Street, upping choices for pretheater dining. The low-key vibe in the wine bars and cafés makes it easy to feel like a local.

$$$
MODERN
AMERICAN
Fodor's Choice
★
✕**Alta CA.** The creation of lauded chef Daniel Patterson, this pretty restaurant has creativity to rival that of Patterson's Michelin-starred Coi, but a much less formal vibe. A 25-seat circular bar dominates the dining room, while small plates dominate the menu. **Known for:** homemade pierogi with seasonal fillings; creative cuisine; good cocktails. $ *Average main: $30* ✉ *1420 Market St., Civic Center* ☎ *415/590–2585* ⊕ *altaca.co* ☾ *Closed Sun.* ✣ *3:F2.*

$$$$
MODERN
AMERICAN
✕**Jardinière.** Famed chef Traci Des Jardins's restaurant is so sophisticated you may as well be eating at the nearby Opera House. An eye-catching curving staircase leads to an oval atrium, where locals and out-of-towners alike indulge in French-Californian dishes, such as foie gras terrine or sorrel soup. **Known for:** French technique; pre-opera dining. $ *Average main: $33* ✉ *300 Grove St., Hayes Valley* ☎ *415/861–5555* ⊕ *www.jardiniere.com* ☾ *No lunch* ✣ *3:F2.*

$$
JAPANESE
✕**Nojo Ramen.** For a little bonhomie before the symphony, it's hard to go wrong with this buzzy (and typically crowded) ramen spot. Noodles are the star of the menu, and deservedly so, but you'll also find izakaya-style small plates and comfort food like chicken teriyaki. **Known for:** ramen with chicken-based (paitan) broth; Japanese comfort foods; long lines. $ *Average main: $17* ✉ *231 Franklin St., Hayes Valley* ☎ *415/896–4587* ⊕ *www.nojosf.com* ☾ *Closed Mon. No lunch.* ✣ *3:F2.*

$$$$ FRENCH

🍴 **Petit Crenn.** Chef Dominique Crenn's sequel to her Michelin-starred Atelier Crenn is more casual but no less accomplished. Here, the French chef keeps her focus on seafood and vegetables, inspired by her family home on the French coastal region of Brittany and presented as a seven-course prix fixe menu. **Known for:** seafood focus; seven-course prix fixe menu. [$] *Average main: $87* ✉ *609 Hayes St., Hayes Valley* ☎ *415/864–1744* 🌐 *www.petitcrenn.com* 🕒 *Closed Mon.* ✣ *3:E2.*

$$$ SWEDISH

🍴 **Pläj.** The only Swedish restaurant in San Francisco is tucked behind the lobby of the Inn at the Opera and serves refreshing cuisine—fishes pickled, smoked, and cured in-house. Case in point is the beet-cured gravlax, which is complemented by sorrel sorbet and lemon crème fraîche. **Known for:** authentic Swedish cuisine; homemade aquavits (Scandinavian spirits). [$] *Average main: $26* ✉ *333 Fulton St., Hayes Valley* ☎ *415/294–8925* 🌐 *www.plajrestaurant.com* 🕒 *No lunch* ✣ *3:E2.*

$$$$ MODERN AMERICAN Fodor's Choice ★

🍴 **Rich Table.** Sardine potato chips and porcini doughnuts are the most popular bites at co-chefs Evan and Sarah Rich's lively restaurant—and the most indicative of its creativity. The mains are also clever stunners: try one of the proteins or pastas, like the Douglas fir gnocchi. **Known for:** creative food; freshly baked bread. [$] *Average main: $34* ✉ *199 Gough St., Hayes Valley* ☎ *415/355–9085* 🌐 *www.richtablesf.com* 🕒 *No lunch* ✣ *3:E3.*

$$ GERMAN

🍴 **Suppenküche.** Nobody goes hungry—and no beer drinker goes thirsty—at this lively, hip outpost of simple German cooking in Hayes Valley. When the room gets crowded, which it regularly does, strangers sit together at unfinished pine tables. **Known for:** generous beer selection; authentic German food. [$] *Average main: $20* ✉ *525 Laguna St., Hayes Valley* ☎ *415/252–9289* 🌐 *www.suppenkuche.com* 🕒 *No lunch Mon.–Sat.* ✣ *3:E2.*

$$$ MEDITERRANEAN Fodor's Choice ★

🍴 **Zuni Café.** After one bite of Zuni's succulent brick-oven-roasted whole chicken with Tuscan bread salad, you'll understand why the two-floor café is a perennial star. Its long copper bar is a hub for a disparate mix of patrons who commune over oysters on the half shell and cocktails and wine. **Known for:** famous roast chicken; classic San Francisco dining. [$] *Average main: $30* ✉ *1658 Market St., Hayes Valley* ☎ *415/552–2522* 🌐 *www.zunicafe.com* 🕒 *Closed Mon.* ✣ *3:F3.*

NOB HILL AND RUSSIAN HILL

NOB HILL

Nob Hill, the most famous hill in a city of hills, is known for its iconic hotels—the Fairmont, the Mark, the Ritz-Carlton, the Huntington—and for its views. Unfortunately, the food isn't as unparalleled as the scenic outlooks. Real estate is expensive, so it's not the place for chefs to roll the dice on a new venture. But what you will find are hotel dining rooms and established institutions.

$$$$ ITALIAN Fodor's Choice ★

🍴 **Acquerello.** Chef-co-owner Suzette Gresham has elicited plenty of swoons over the years with her high-end but soulful Italian cooking. Her Parmesan *budino* (pudding) is a star of the menu, which features both classic and cutting-edge dishes. **Known for:** prix-fixe dining;

Parmesan budino; extensive Italian wine list. [$] *Average main: $95* ✉ *1722 Sacramento St., Polk Gulch* ☎ *415/567–5432* 🌐 *www.acquerello.com* ⏱ *Closed Sun. and Mon. No lunch* ✥ *2:H5.*

$$ SEAFOOD Fodor's Choice ★ 🍴 **Swan Oyster Depot.** Half fish market and half diner, this small, slim, family-run seafood operation, open since 1912, has no tables, just a narrow marble counter with about 18 stools. Most people come in to buy perfectly fresh salmon, halibut, crabs, and other seafood to take home. **Known for:** fresh seafood; long lines. [$] *Average main: $18* ✉ *1517 Polk St., Polk Gulch* ☎ *415/673–1101* ▭ *No credit cards* ⏱ *Closed Sun. No dinner* ✥ *2:H5.*

RUSSIAN HILL

Despite its name, don't expect Russian food here. Instead, this area bordering Nob Hill caters to the postcollege crowds, who want to live near the buzzy Polk and Larkin Streets. They mix in with the upper-crust San Franciscans who live in the art-deco high-rises with views. Many romantic bistros are tucked away on tree-lined Hyde Street.

$$ AFGHAN 🍴 **Helmand Palace.** This handsomely outfitted spot will introduce you to the aromas and tastes of Afghan cooking. The sauces and spices recall India's cuisine, while the emphasis on lamb brings to mind Turkey and Greece. **Known for:** traditional Afghani cuisine; neighborhood gem. [$] *Average main: $16* ✉ *2424 Van Ness Ave., Russian Hill* ☎ *415/345–0072* 🌐 *www.helmandpalacesf.com* ⏱ *No lunch* ✥ *2:H3.*

$$$$ FRENCH 🍴 **La Folie.** Chef-owner Roland Passot's whimsical cuisine takes center stage at this small, *très* Parisian establishment. The dining room is decorated in warm woods and copper tones, while the prix-fixe menus are served in three, four, or five courses. **Known for:** creative French cuisine; prix-fixe menus. [$] *Average main: $100* ✉ *2316 Polk St., Russian Hill* ☎ *415/776–5577* 🌐 *www.lafolie.com* ⏱ *Closed Sun. and Mon. No lunch* ✥ *2:H3.*

$$ TAPAS 🍴 **Zarzuela.** Full-blooded Spaniards swear by the paella at this tiny old-world-style bistro, complete with matador posters on the wall. Also not to be missed is the homemade sangria—or any of the impressive roster of tapas prepared by Madrid-bred chef Lucas Gasco. **Known for:** authentic tapas; not-to-be-missed sangria. [$] *Average main: $21* ✉ *2000 Hyde St., Russian Hill* ☎ *415/346–0800* ⏱ *Closed Sun. and Mon. No lunch* ✥ *1:B3.*

NORTH BEACH

One of the city's oldest neighborhoods, North Beach continues to speak Italian, albeit in fewer households than it did when Joe DiMaggio was hitting home runs at the local playground.

Columbus Avenue, North Beach's primary commercial artery, and nearby side streets boast dozens of moderately priced Italian restaurants and coffee bars that San Franciscans flock to for a dose of strong community feeling. But beware, there are a few tourist traps that are after the college crowd who flock here for cheap drinks then want to fill up on cheap food.

$$$$ MODERN AMERICAN Fodor's Choice ★ 🍴 **Coi.** Although Daniel Patterson no longer presides over the kitchen, his restaurant is still a can't-miss destination for exquisite, rarefied dining. Under chef Matthew Kirkley, the eight-course tasting menu now focuses on seafood, but still prizes obsessively sourced, highly seasonal ingredients. **Known for:** fine dining; seasonal ingredients and fresh seafood. [$] *Average main: $250* ✉ *373 Broadway, North Beach* ☎ *415/393–9000* 🌐 *www.coirestaurant.com* 🕒 *Closed Tues. and Wed. No lunch.* ✥ *1:E3.*

$$ ITALIAN 🍴 **L'Osteria del Forno.** Pass through the door of this modest storefront and you'll feel as if you've stumbled into a trattoria in Italy. The aromas of Northern Italian cooking permeate the sunny yellow dining room, which is overseen by its native Italian owners. **Known for:** thin-crust pizza; small plates; all-Italian wine list. [$] *Average main: $15* ✉ *519 Columbus Ave., North Beach* ☎ *415/982–1124* 🌐 *www.losteriadel-forno.com* 💳 *No credit cards* 🕒 *Closed Tues.* ✥ *1:D3.*

$$ MIDDLE EASTERN 🍴 **Maykadeh.** The authentic Persian cooking has a large and faithful following of homesick Iranian émigrés—and locals in the know. Lamb dishes with rice are the specialties, served in a warm and attractive dining room. **Known for:** delicious lamb dishes; traditional Persian cooking. [$] *Average main: $20* ✉ *470 Green St., North Beach* ☎ *415/362–8286* 🌐 *www.maykadehrestaurant.com* ✥ *1:D3.*

$$$ AMERICAN 🍴 **Original Joe's.** Nostalgia isn't just in the decor but also on the menu at this retro North Beach institution, where you'll find a '50s-era disregard for calorie counts—and a perfectly seasoned hamburger steak. Roasted prime rib and six different veal dishes add to the mid-century meat-heavy menu. **Known for:** classic Cal-Ital food; meat-heavy menu; retro dining. [$] *Average main: $26* ✉ *601 Union St., North Beach* ☎ *415/775–4877* 🌐 *www.originaljoessf.com* ✥ *1:D3.*

$$$ AMERICAN 🍴 **Park Tavern.** This upscale American tavern on pretty Washington Square has been a hit from the day it opened. Its appeal lies in both its handsome dining room and the hearty food consumed there. **Known for:** meaty American food; tasty bar bites. [$] *Average main: $30* ✉ *1652 Stockton St., North Beach* ☎ *415/989–7300* 🌐 *www.parktavernsf.com* 🕒 *No lunch Mon.–Thurs.* ✥ *1:D3.*

$$ PIZZA FAMILY 🍴 **Tommaso's.** San Francisco's first wood-fired brick pizza oven was installed here in 1935. The oven is still here, and the pizzas' delightfully chewy crusts, creamy mozzarella, and full-bodied house-made sauce have kept legions returning for decades. **Known for:** North Beach institution; legendary pizza; classic pasta dishes. [$] *Average main: $22* ✉ *1042 Kearny St., North Beach* ☎ *415/398–9696* 🌐 *www.tommasos.com* 🕒 *Closed Mon. No lunch* ✥ *1:D3.*

$$$ PIZZA FAMILY 🍴 **Tony's Pizza Napoletana.** Locals hotly debate who makes the city's best pizza, and for many Tony Gemignani takes the prize. Repeatedly crowned the World Champion Pizza Maker at the World Pizza Cup in Naples, he's renowned here for his flavorful dough and impressive range. **Known for:** World Champion Pizza chef; multiple pizza ovens and pie styles; family dining. [$] *Average main: $27* ✉ *1570 Stockton St., North Beach* ☎ *415/835–9888* 🌐 *www.tonyspizzanapoletana.com* 🕒 *Closed Tues.* ✥ *1:D3.*

$$$ ITALIAN 🍴 **Tosca Cafe.** Following a much-heralded revamp, this 1919 boho classic continues to attract both celebs and local scenesters. The room is dark and clubby, and the food skews Italian, with a raft of pastas and antipasti. **Known for:** Italian-American comfort food; tasty cocktails; signature roast chicken for two. [$] *Average main: $28* ✉ *242 Columbus Ave., North Beach* ☎ *415/986–9651* 🌐 *www.toscacafesf.com* 🕓 *No lunch* ✣ *1:D3.*

THE WATERFRONT

FISHERMAN'S WHARF

To the north of the Ferry Building lies Fisherman's Wharf, a jumbled mix of seafood dining rooms, sidewalk vendors, and trinket shops that visitors religiously trudge through and San Franciscans invariably dismiss as a tourist trap. But even locals may come for a cracked crab.

$$$$ AMERICAN 🍴 **Gary Danko.** This San Francisco classic has earned a legion of fans—and a Michelin star—for its namesake chef's refined and creative cooking. The cost of a meal is pegged to the number of courses, from three to five, and the menu spans a classic yet Californian style that changes seasonally. **Known for:** prix-fixe menu; fine dining; extensive wine list. [$] *Average main: $87* ✉ *800 N. Point St., Fisherman's Wharf* ☎ *415/749–2060* 🌐 *www.garydanko.com* 🕓 *No lunch* 👔 *Jacket required* ✣ *1:A1.*

EMBARCADERO

Locals and visitors alike flock here for gorgeous bay views, a world-class waterfront esplanade, and a Ferry Building that's much better known for its food than its boat rides. Some of the best bakers and cooks in the city have their satellites here, or this is where they start up.

$$$$ AMERICAN 🍴 **Boulevard.** Two local restaurant celebrities—chef Nancy Oakes and designer Pat Kuleto—are behind this high-profile, high-priced eatery in the historic 1889 Audiffred Building. The Belle Époque interior and sophisticated American food with a French accent attract well-dressed locals and flush out-of-towners. **Known for:** sophisticated French-Californian food; generous portions; excellent desserts. [$] *Average main: $38* ✉ *1 Mission St., Embarcadero* ☎ *415/543–6084* 🌐 *www.boulevardrestaurant.com* 🕓 *No lunch weekends* ✣ *1:G4.*

$$$$ SPANISH 🍴 **Coqueta.** With its Embarcadero perch, Bay Bridge views, and stellar Spanish tapas, celebrity chef Michael Chiarello's first San Francisco restaurant has been a big hit. Equal parts rustic and chic, it's a lively destination for both small bites and larger meals. **Known for:** Spanish tapas; water views; creative cocktails. [$] *Average main: $33* ✉ *Pier 5, on the Embarcadero, near Broadway, Embarcadero* ☎ *415/704–8866* 🌐 *coquetasf.com* 🕓 *No lunch Mon.* ✣ *1:F3.*

$$ AMERICAN FAMILY 🍴 **Fog City.** All but hidden on a far-flung stretch of the Embarcadero, this 21st-century diner is well worth the hike. It's best known for its updated classics, like a short-rib BLT with kimchi mayo and corn bread that emerges hot from the wood-fired oven. **Known for:** updated diner food; excellent cocktails; views of Battery St. and the Embarcadero.

§ *Average main: $21* ✉ *1300 Battery St., Embarcadero* ☎ *415/982–2000* ⊕ *www.fogcitysf.com* ✛ *1:E2.*

$ ✕ **Gott's Roadside.** A lunchtime favorite, this Ferry Building stalwart
BURGER boasts a view of Coit Tower and crowd-pleasing grub. This is a burger
FAMILY chain that cares about details: its dressings are house-made, its patties
use freshly ground Niman Ranch beef, and its menu includes a wine
list. **Known for:** organic meats; elevated fast food; wine list and good
shakes. § *Average main: $13* ✉ *1 Ferry Bldg., Suite 6, Embarcadero*
☎ *415/318–3423* ⊕ *www.gotts.com* ✛ *1:G4.*

$$ ✕ **Hog Island Oyster Company.** A thriving oyster farm north of San Fran-
SEAFOOD cisco in Tomales Bay serves up its harvest at this raw bar and restaurant
in the Ferry Building. Devotees come here for impeccably fresh oysters
and clams on the half shell. **Known for:** fresh oysters; first-rate seafood
stew; busy raw bar. § *Average main: $17* ✉ *Ferry Bldg., Embarcadero*
at Market St., Embarcadero ☎ *415/391–7117* ⊕ *www.hogislandoysters.*
com ✛ *1:G4.*

$$$$ ✕ **La Mar Cebicheria Peruana.** Right on the water's edge, this casually chic
PERUVIAN outpost, the chain's first outside Peru, imports real Peruvian flavors to
San Francisco. Fresh seafood is a big draw here, though not the only
one. **Known for:** fresh seafood; authentic Peruvian food; tasty empana-
das and causas. § *Average main: $34* ✉ *Pier 1½, between Washington*
and Jackson Sts., Embarcadero ☎ *415/397–8880* ⊕ *lamarsf.com* ✛ *1:F3.*

$$$ ✕ **Slanted Door.** If you're looking for homey Vietnamese food served
VIETNAMESE in a down-to-earth dining room at a bargain-basement price, *don't*
stop here. Celebrated chef-owner Charles Phan has mastered the
upmarket, Western-accented Vietnamese menu. **Known for:** upscale
Vietnamese food; great cocktails. § *Average main: $30* ✉ *Ferry Bldg.,*
Embarcadero at Market St., Embarcadero ☎ *415/861–8032* ⊕ *www.*
slanteddoor.com ✛ *1:G4.*

FINANCIAL DISTRICT

The center of commerce, with some very good restaurants (housed in
old Barbary Coast buildings), FiDi caters to the business elite with prices
to match. But there are some new faces in San Francisco's economy:
engineers and software developers looking for a fast lunch head to
modest Indian and Chinese places, as well as superb sandwich shops.

$$ ✕ **Barbacco.** The busy sister restaurant to neighboring Perbacco offers
ITALIAN affordable small plates to let you try a little of this and a little of that.
Thanks to the extensive menu, a meal here is like grazing through
the different regions of Italy. **Known for:** regional Italian food; quality
food in casual setting; curated wine list. § *Average main: $18* ✉ *220*
California St., Financial District ☎ *415/955–1919* ⊕ *www.barbaccosf.*
com ⊗ *Closed Sun. No lunch weekends* ✛ *1:E4.*

$$ ✕ **Bocadillos.** The name means "sandwiches," and this sleek little spot
SPANISH has them in spades. Here you'll find plump rolls (pick two for $14) filled
with everything from smoked salmon to Catalan sausage. **Known for:**
tasty tapas; variety of wines by the glass. § *Average main: $15* ✉ *710*
Montgomery St., Financial District ☎ *415/982–2622* ⊕ *www.bocasf.*
com ▬ *No credit cards* ⊗ *Closed Sun. No lunch Sat.* ✛ *1:E4.*

13

$$$ FRENCH 🍴 **Café Claude.** Francophiles congregate here for that *je ne sais quoi,* right down to the delicious croque monsieur, escargots, steak tartare, and coq au vin. If you think this place looks straight out of Paris, it mostly is. **Known for:** French bistro food; live jazz. [$] *Average main: $24* ✉ *7 Claude La., Financial District* ☎ *415/392–3505* 🌐 *www.cafe-claude.com* 🕓 *No lunch Sun.* ✥ *4:H2.*

$$$ ITALIAN 🍴 **Cotogna.** This urban trattoria is just as in demand as its fancier big sister, Quince, next door. The draw here is Chef Michael Tusk's flavorful, rustic, seasonally driven Italian cooking. **Known for:** rustic Italian; fantastic wine list. [$] *Average main: $25* ✉ *490 Pacific Ave., Financial District* ☎ *415/775–8508* 🌐 *www.cotognasf.com* ✥ *1:E3.*

$$$ MEDITERRANEAN 🍴 **Gitane.** With its lush hot-house decor—red lamps, tuffeted curved seats, and oversized art—this romantic spot is a Valentine's Day favorite. It's also a great place for conversation, sangrias, and Mediterranean-inspired cooking. **Known for:** romantic vibe; bacon bonbons; creative cocktails. [$] *Average main: $27* ✉ *6 Claude La., Financial District* ☎ *415/788–6686* 🌐 *www.gitanerestaurant.com* 🕓 *Closed Sun. and Mon. No lunch* ✥ *4:H2.*

$$$$ GREEK 🍴 **Kokkari.** Satisfy your craving for outstanding Greek taverna food—albeit at steak-house prices. The menu hits all of the classics and then some, starting with a dizzying selection of *mezethes* (small plates) like stuffed grape leaves. **Known for:** Greek cuisine and hospitality; inviting rustic-chic space; semolina custard wrapped in phylo. [$] *Average main: $36* ✉ *200 Jackson St., Financial District* ☎ *415/981–0983* 🌐 *www.kokkari.com* 🕓 *No lunch weekends* ✥ *1:F3.*

$$$$ MODERN AMERICAN 🍴 **Michael Mina.** The flagship outpost for this acclaimed chef remains a beacon of refined dining. The New American menu includes luxurious renditions of shabu-shabu (boiled beef) and lobster potpie with cognac cream and baby root vegetables. **Known for:** prix-fixe menu; white-tablecloth dining. [$] *Average main: $33* ✉ *252 California St., Financial District* ☎ *415/397–9222* 🌐 *www.michaelmina.net* 🕓 *No lunch weekends* ✥ *1:E4.*

$$$ ITALIAN 🍴 **Perbacco.** Chef Staffan Terje understands the cuisine of northern Italy. From the complimentary basket of skinny, brittle breadsticks to the pappardelle with short rib ragu, his entire menu is a delectable paean to the region. **Known for:** pasta stuffed with meat and cabbage; house-made cured meats; authentic Northern Italian cuisine. [$] *Average main: $30* ✉ *230 California St., Financial District* ☎ *415/955–0663* 🌐 *www.perbaccosf.com* 🕓 *Closed Sun. No lunch Sat.* ✥ *1:E4.*

$$$$ MODERN AMERICAN 🍴 **Quince.** Although Michael Tusk's fine-dining mecca underwent a major renovation in 2014, the quality of his Michelin-starred contemporary Californian cuisine has gone unchanged. But to enjoy it, you'll have to splurge on a 9- to 12-course chef's tasting menu. **Known for:** prix-fixe menu; highly seasonal ingredients; strong wine list. [$] *Average main: $220* ✉ *470 Pacific Ave., Financial District* ☎ *415/775–8500* 🌐 *www.quincerestaurant.com* 🕓 *Closed Sun. No lunch* ✥ *1:E3.*

$ RAMEN 🍴 **The Ramen Bar.** Acclaimed chef Michael Mina has gotten on the ramen train with a big assist from Tokyo native and chef Ken Tominaga. Their FiDi collaboration is a popular lunchtime spot known as much for fast service as for Tokyo-style noodles. **Known for:** Tokyo-style noodles;

poke bowl; elevated ramen. $ *Average main: $14* ✉ *101 California St., Financial District* ☎ *415/684–1570* ⊕ *www.theramenbar.com* ☉ *Closed weekends* ✣ *1:F4.*

$$$ ✕ **Tadich Grill.** Locations and owners have changed more than once since
SEAFOOD this old-timer started as a coffee stand on the waterfront in 1849, but the crowds keep coming. Seafood is—and has always been—the name of the game here. **Known for:** seafood focus; crab dishes; dedicated following. $ *Average main: $27* ✉ *240 California St., Financial District* ☎ *415/391–1849* ⊕ *www.tadichgrill.com* ☉ *Closed Sun.* ✣ *1:E4.*

13

$$$ ✕ **Wayfare Tavern.** This energetic and upscale American tavern owned
AMERICAN by TV chef and personality Tyler Florence is rich with turn-of-the-20th-century Americana, including brick walls, comfortable booths, and a billiards room. The approachable menu also tips its hat to tradition—and comfort. **Known for:** comfort food; stand-out burger; lively scene. $ *Average main: $25* ✉ *558 Sacramento St., Financial District* ☎ *415/722–9060* ⊕ *www.wayfaretavern.com* ✣ *1:E4.*

$$ ✕ **Yank Sing.** This bustling teahouse serves some of San Francisco's best
CHINESE dim sum to office workers on weekdays and boisterous families on
FAMILY weekends. The several dozen varieties prepared daily include both the classic and the creative. **Known for:** classic dim sum; Shanghai soup dumplings. $ *Average main: $16* ✉ *49 Stevenson St., Financial District* ☎ *415/541–4949* ⊕ *www.yanksing.com* ☉ *No dinner* ✣ *1:E5.*

THE MARINA

On a sunny day, the Marina is perhaps one of the most cheerful places in the city, with sweeping views of Marin and the Golden Gate Bridge and plenty of joggers and bicyclists. Residents tend to be a mix of the just-graduated who are still very much into the nightclub scene. Mixed in are the affluent of the spectacular waterfront properties who hit Chestnut Street after dark for good food.

$$$ ✕ **A16.** Named after a highway that runs through Southern Italy, this
ITALIAN trattoria specializes in the food from that region, done very, very well. The menu is stocked with pizza and rustic pastas like *maccaronara* with *ragu napoletana* and house-made salted ricotta, as well as entrées like roasted chicken with sage salsa verde. **Known for:** excellent Southern Italian food; mostly Southern Italian wine list; lively bar. $ *Average main: $25* ✉ *2355 Chestnut St., Marina* ☎ *415/771–2216* ⊕ *www. a16pizza.com* ☉ *No lunch Mon. and Tues.* ✣ *2:D3.*

$$$ ✕ **Greens.** Owned and operated by the San Francisco Zen Center, this
VEGETARIAN legendary vegetarian restaurant gets some of its fresh produce from the center's organic Green Gulch Farm. Despite the lack of meat, hearty dishes from chef Annie Somerville—such as green curry and wild-mushroom-leek pizza—really satisfy. **Known for:** sweeping views; hearty vegetarian food. $ *Average main: $24* ✉ *Bldg. A, Fort Mason, 2 Marina Blvd., Marina* ☎ *415/771–6222* ⊕ *www.greensrestaurant.com* ☉ *No lunch Mon.* ✣ *2:G1.*

$$ ✕ **Tacolicious.** Tacos and tequila draw a young and energetic crowd to
MEXICAN this lively Marina hot spot. Tables are usually laden with made-to-order guacamole and platters of well-stuffed tortillas (the *carnitas*

and short-rib tacos are especially full of flavor). **Known for:** stuffed tacos; potent drinks; festive atmosphere. $ *Average main: $15* ✉ *2250 Chestnut St., Marina* ☎ *415/346–1966* ⊕ *www.tacolicious. com* ✦ *2:E2.*

COW HOLLOW

Just up the hill from the Marina—and slightly quieter with more young families—is Cow Hollow. Union Street is the main strip, dense with restaurants, cafés, and boutiques that mostly cater to the trendy A-list crowd. Wander even farther up the hills and you'll be in the thick of the manses of Pacific Heights.

$$$

ITALIAN

FAMILY

✕ **Rose's Café.** Although it's open morning until night, this cozy café is most synonymous with brunch. Sleepy-headed locals turn up for delights like the breakfast pizza of smoked ham, eggs, and fontina and the French toast with caramelized apples. **Known for:** popular Sunday brunch; breakfast pizza; top-notch ingredients. $ *Average main: $28* ✉ *2298 Union St., Cow Hollow* ☎ *415/775–2200* ⊕ *www.rosescafesf. com* ✦ *2:E3.*

THE RICHMOND AND SUNSET DISTRICT

THE RICHMOND

The Richmond encompasses the land on the north side of Golden Gate Park, running to the ocean's edge. As for architecture eye-candy, there isn't much, but this is the land of authentic Asian food, particularly in Inner Richmond, known as the new Chinatown, covering Clement Street from about 2nd to 13th Avenues. On the main thoroughfares of Clement, Balboa, and Geary Streets, you'll find bargain dim sum, Burmese, Korean barbecue, and noodle soups of all persuasions.

$$

ASIAN

✕ **Burma Superstar.** Locals make the trek to the "Avenues" for this perennially crowded spot's flavorful, well-prepared Burmese food. Its signature dish is the extraordinary tea leaf salad, a combo of spicy, salty, crunchy, and sour that is mixed table-side. **Known for:** tea leaf salad; samusa soup; long lines. $ *Average main: $15* ✉ *309 Clement St., Richmond* ☎ *415/387–2147* ⊕ *www.burmasuperstar. com* ✦ *2:A6.*

$

VIETNAMESE

FAMILY

✕ **Good Noodle.** The menu at this no-frills Formica-and-linoleum spot is big and remarkably cheap. You can order everything from Vietnamese salads to rice dishes and noodle plates. **Known for:** two dozen varieties of pho; no frills, affordable dining. $ *Average main: $10* ✉ *239 Clement St., Richmond* ☎ *415/379–9008* ⊕ *www.good-noodlesf.com* ✦ *2:A6.*

$$

PIZZA

✕ **Pizzetta 211.** This shoebox-size spot puts together thin-crust pies topped with the kinds of ingredients that are worth the (almost) constant wait. Almost half the menu changes on a biweekly basis. **Known for:** thin-crust pies; long lines. $ *Average main: $16* ✉ *211 23rd Ave., Richmond* ☎ *415/379–9880* ⊕ *www.pizzetta211.com* ☾ *Closed Tues.* ✦ *3:A1.*

$ ✕ **Tenglong.** This tidy space lures plenty of locals with its dry chicken
CHINESE   wings, fried in garlic and roasted red peppers. Run by two former restaurant owners from Hong Kong, it specializes in mostly Southern-style
Chinese like Cantonese and has a few Sichuan specialties, too. **Known
for:** Cantonese food; chicken wings; local hotspot. $ *Average main: $12*
✉ *208 Clement St., Richmond* 🕾 *415/666–3515* ⊕ *www.tenglongsf.
com* ⊘ *Closed Tues.* ✛ *2:A6.*

$$ ✕ **Ton Kiang.** This local favorite specializes in the lightly seasoned Hakka
CHINESE   cuisine of southern China, rarely found in this country and even obscure
FAMILY   to many Chinese. Its hallmarks here include salt-baked chicken, braised
Fodor'sChoice   stuffed tofu, steamed fresh bacon with dried mustard greens, and clay
★   pots of meats and seafood. **Known for:** Hakka cuisine; delicious dim
sum. $ *Average main: $15* ✉ *5821 Geary Blvd., Richmond* 🕾 *415/752–
4440* ⊕ *www.tonkiangsf.com* ⊘ *Closed Wed.* ✛ *2:A6.*

SUNSET DISTRICT

The Sunset neighborhood encompasses the land south of Golden Gate
Park, running all the way to the ocean's edge, and has a surf-town or
small-town vibe. It's known for its fog, yes, but also bargain eats (UCSF
is here) that range from pizzas and salads to Eritrean *injera* (flatbread)
and Chinese dumplings, concentrated along Irving Street.

$$$ ✕ **Outerlands.** This cozy, wood-lined restaurant is as infamous for its
MODERN   lines as it is famous for its brunch. The food here is thoroughly North-
AMERICAN   ern California, from the granola with goat's milk yogurt to the avocado
toast drizzled with Meyer lemon vinaigrette. **Known for:** brunch; cast-
iron grilled cheese; long waits. $ *Average main: $25* ✉ *4001 Judah St.,
Sunset* 🕾 *415/661–6140* ⊕ *www.outerlandssf.com* ✛ *3:A4.*

$$ ✕ **Park Chow.** What do spaghetti and meatballs, Thai noodles with
AMERICAN   chicken and steak, salads in three sizes, and big burgers have in com-
FAMILY   mon? They're all on the eclectic comfort-food menu at this neigh-
borhood standby. **Known for:** ginger cake with pumpkin ice cream;
classic comfort food. $ *Average main: $18* ✉ *1240 9th Ave., Sunset*
🕾 *415/665–9912* ⊕ *www.chowfoodbar.com* ✛ *3:A6.*

$ ✕ **San Tung.** The food of China's northeastern province of Shandong is
CHINESE   the draw at this bare-bones storefront restaurant. Specialties include
FAMILY   steamed dumplings—shrimp and leek dumplings are the most popu-
lar—and hand-pulled noodles, in soup or stir-fried. **Known for:** chicken
wings with cult following; steamed dumplings. $ *Average main: $12*
✉ *1031 Irving St., Sunset* 🕾 *415/242–0828* ⊘ *Closed Wed.* ✛ *3:A6.*

THE HAIGHT, THE WESTERN ADDITION, THE CASTRO, AND NOE VALLEY

THE HAIGHT

Haight-Ashbury was home base for the country's famed 1960s coun-
terculture, and its café scene still reflects that colorful past. For ethnic
flavors, go to the neighborhoods on either side of Golden Gate Park.

Over time, the Haight has become two distinct neighborhoods. The
Upper Haight is an energetic commercial stretch from Masonic Avenue
to Stanyan Street, where head shops and tofu-burger joints still thrive.

Meanwhile, the modestly gritty Lower Haight has emerged as a lively bohemian quarter of sorts, with mostly ethnic eateries lining the blocks between Webster and Pierce Streets.

$$
THAI

× **Thep Phanom.** This cozy Thai restaurant has been a neighborhood stalwart for over three decades. Lemongrass chicken, seafood, and rich curries are among the specialties. **Known for:** rich curries; tasty seafood dishes; local favorite. $ *Average main: $15* ⊠ *400 Waller St., Haight* ☏ *415/431–2526* ⊕ *www.thepphanom.com* ☉ *No lunch* ✛ *3:D3.*

$$
ITALIAN

× **Uva Enoteca.** This casual Italian wine bar hits all the right notes. The mood is convivial, the food is solid, and there's plenty of wine—more than 15 by the glass (available in 2- or 8-ounce pours) and a long list of bottles. **Known for:** simple but delicious dining; variety of wines by the glass. $ *Average main: $17* ⊠ *568 Haight St., Haight* ☏ *415/829–2024* ⊕ *www.uvaenoteca.com* ☉ *No lunch weekdays. No dinner Sun.* ✛ *3:D3.*

THE WESTERN ADDITION

This is a patchwork of culturally and economically diverse neighborhoods bordering the Lower Haight, the Fillmore District, and Japantown, where you can find Italian, Japanese, and Indian restaurants housed in 1950s-era and Victorian buildings in the span of a couple of city blocks. Tucked between some cheap-knockoff stores and national chains are a couple of dining heavies (and one of the most well-known city parks, Alamo Square).

$$
BARBECUE

× **4505 Burgers & BBQ.** Noted butcher Ryan Farr is behind the tender, deliciously charred brisket at this hipster-chic barbecue shack. The smoker here works overtime, churning out an array of meats that can be had by the plate and pound. **Known for:** smoked meats; delicious sides; juicy burgers. $ *Average main: $17* ⊠ *705 Divisadero, at Grove St., Western Addition* ☏ *415/231–6993* ⊕ *www.4505meats. com* ✛ *3:B2.*

$$$
AMERICAN

× **Nopa.** This is the good-food granddaddy of the hot corridor of the same name (NoPa equals North of the Panhandle). The Cali-rustic fare here draws dependable crowds, especially on the weekends. **Known for:** California cooking; flatbread topped with bacon and Treviso cheese; lively crowd. $ *Average main: $24* ⊠ *560 Divisadero St., Western Addition* ☏ *415/864–8643* ⊕ *www.nopasf.com* ☉ *No lunch weekdays* ✛ *3:B3.*

$$$
MEXICAN
FAMILY
Fodor's Choice
★

× **Nopalito.** Those in the mood for Mexican will find authentic flavors at this NoPa offshoot. That authenticity is matched by creativity and fresh ingredients. **Known for:** creative Mexican food; fresh tortillas; delicious empanadas. $ *Average main: $23* ⊠ *306 Broderick St., Western Addition* ☏ *415/437–0303* ⊕ *www.nopalitosf.com* ✛ *3:B3.*

$$$$
MODERN
AMERICAN

× **The Progress.** This second restaurant from the chef-owners of State Bird Provisions is one of the more coveted reservations in town. The lure is inventive, Michelin-starred California cooking, served family-style. **Known for:** inventive California cooking; family-style dining; prix-fixe menu. $ *Average main: $62* ⊠ *1525 Fillmore St., Western Addition* ☏ *415/673–1294* ⊕ *www.theprogress-sf.com* ☉ *No lunch* ✛ *3:C1.*

$$$
MODERN
AMERICAN
Fodor's Choice
★
✕ **State Bird Provisions.** It's more or less impossible to nab a reservation at Stuart Brioza and Nicole Krasinski's game-changing, Michelin-starred restaurant. But if you do walk in and brave the 90-plus-minute wait, you'll eventually be rewarded with inventive bites served from dim sum–style carts. **Known for:** dim sum–style dining; long waits. $ *Average main: $30* ✉ *1529 Fillmore St., Western Addition* ☎ *415/795–1272* ⊕ *www.statebirdsf.com* ⊘ *No lunch* ✚ *3:C1.*

THE CASTRO

The Castro neighborhood, the epicenter of the city's gay community, is chockablock with restaurants and bars. Market Street between Church and Castro Streets is a great stretch for people-watching and café- or bistro-hopping.

$$$
MODERN
AMERICAN
✕ **Frances.** Still one of the hottest tickets in town, chef Melissa Perello's simple, sublime restaurant is a consummate date-night destination. Perello's seasonal California-French cooking is its own enduring love affair. **Known for:** seasonal menu; neighborhood gem; tough reservation. $ *Average main: $30* ✉ *3870 17th St., Castro* ☎ *415/621–3870* ⊕ *www.frances-sf.com* ⊘ *Closed Mon. No lunch* ✚ *3:C5.*

$$
SEAFOOD
FAMILY
✕ **Woodhouse Fish Co.** New Englanders hungry for a lobster roll fix need look no further than this super-friendly spot, where the rolls are utterly authentic and accompanied with slaw and fries. Seafood fans will find plenty else to love on the menu, which is stocked with everything from cioppino to crab melts. **Known for:** fresh seafood; dollar oysters on Tuesday; legendary lobster roll. $ *Average main: $19* ✉ *2073 Market St., Castro* ☎ *415/437–2722* ⊕ *www.woodhousefish.com* ✚ *3:D4.*

NOE VALLEY

Also called Stroller Valley for its high quota of young families, Noe has seen a change in demographic lately, with many newly minted Facebook millionaires moving into this area and neighboring Mission Dolores (heard of Mark Zuckerberg?). Despite hungry, wealthy residents, Noe has been mysteriously slow to welcome good restaurants. A few standouts are along the main strip of 24th Street from Church to Castro Streets, and on Church Street from 24th to 30th Streets.

$$$
ITALIAN
✕ **La Ciccia.** This charming neighborhood trattoria is the only restaurant in the city exclusively serving Sardinian food. The island's classics are all represented—octopus stew in a spicy tomato sauce; spaghetti with *bottarga* (cured roe); and *fregola* (pebble-shape pasta) with sea urchin and cured tuna heart. **Known for:** Sardinian food; industry favorite; extensive wine list. $ *Average main: $28* ✉ *291 30th St., Noe Valley* ☎ *415/550–8114* ⊕ *www.laciccia.com* ⊘ *Closed Sun. and Mon. No lunch* ✚ *3:D6.*

13

MISSION DISTRICT AND POTRERO HILL

MISSION DISTRICT

You'll never go hungry here, in San Francisco's most jam-packed restaurant neighborhood. From dirt-cheap taquerias to hip tapas joints, city dwellers know this sector as the go-to area for a great meal. The Valencia Street corridor has been particularly hot, opening new restaurants at a milestone pace, with many declaring this to be the best food neighborhood in the city.

$$ MODERN AMERICAN

🍴 **AL's Place.** AL is Chef Aaron London, and his place is a sunny, whitewashed corner spot that serves inventive, Michelin-starred vegetable-forward cooking. London's menu changes frequently, but some dishes, like lightly cured trout and grits with seasonal produce, stick around. **Known for:** seasonal cooking; inventive vegetable-heavy menu; fries with cult following. [$] *Average main: $17* ✉ *1499 Valencia St., Mission* ☎ *415/416–6136* 🌐 *www.alsplacesf.com* 🕓 *Closed Mon. and Tues. No lunch.* ✥ *3:E6.*

$ CAMBODIAN

🍴 **Angkor Borei.** Lemongrass and softly sizzling chilies perfume this modest neighborhood favorite, opened by Cambodian refugees in the late 1980s. The menu includes an array of curries, salads of squid or cold noodles with ground fish, and lightly curried fish mousse cooked in a banana leaf basket. **Known for:** Cambodian food; variety of curries. [$] *Average main: $13* ✉ *3471 Mission St., Bernal Heights* ☎ *415/550–8417* 🌐 *www.cambodiankitchen.com* 🕓 *Closed Wed. No lunch Sun.* ✥ *3:F6.*

$$ ITALIAN

🍴 **Beretta.** A young crowd flocks to this perennially popular neighborhood favorite. Its formula is simple: excellent cocktails, affordable Italian food, and late dining until 1 am. **Known for:** thin-crust pizza; excellent cocktails; lively and loud crowd. [$] *Average main: $18* ✉ *1199 Valencia St., Mission District* ☎ *415/695–1199* 🌐 *www.berettasf.com* 🕓 *No lunch weekdays* ✥ *3:E6.*

$$$ MODERN AMERICAN Fodor's Choice ★

🍴 **Central Kitchen.** Californian cuisine in all of its freshness is on display in this offshoot of Flour + Water. You might taste charred brussels sprouts with fermented scallions and fish sauce, or one of chef Thomas McNaughton's famous pastas. **Known for:** famous pasta dishes; family-style dining; pretty courtyard. [$] *Average main: $28* ✉ *3000 20th St., Mission District* ☎ *415/826–7004* 🌐 *www.centralkitchensf.com* 🕓 *Closed Sun. No lunch Mon.–Sat.* ✥ *3:H6.*

$$$ ITALIAN Fodor's Choice ★

🍴 **Delfina.** To find Craig and Annie Stoll's cultishly adored Northern Italian spot, just look for the crowds. They're a constant fixture here, as are deceptively simple, exquisitely flavored dishes like the signature spaghetti with plum tomatoes. **Known for:** signature spaghetti with plum tomatoes; long waits; much-lauded panna cotta. [$] *Average main: $27* ✉ *3621 18th St., Mission District* ☎ *415/552–4055* 🌐 *www.delfinasf.com* 🕓 *No lunch* ✥ *3:E6.*

$$ INDIAN Fodor's Choice ★

🍴 **Dosa on Valencia.** If you like Indian food but crave more than chicken tikka masala and naan, this cheerful temple of South Indian cuisine is for you. Aside from the large, thin savory namesake pancake, the kitchen also prepares curries, *uttapam* (open-face pancakes), and various starters, breads, rice dishes, and chutneys. **Known for:** Southern

Indian food; Indian street food dishes; tasty curries. $ *Average main: $18 ⊠ 995 Valencia St., at 21st St., Mission District* ☎ 415/642–3672 ⊕ *www.dosasf.com* ☉ *No lunch weekdays* ✛ *3:E6.*

$$$ ✕ **Flour + Water.** This hot spot is synonymous with pasta, though its

ITALIAN blistery thin-crust Neapolitan pizzas are also top notch. The grand experience here is the seven-course pasta-tasting menu (extra for wine pairings). **Known for:** difficult to get a reservation; delicious pizzas and pastas; noisy scene. $ *Average main: $26 ⊠ 2401 Harrison St., Mission District* ☎ 415/826–7000 ⊕ *www.flourandwater.com* ☉ *No lunch* ✛ *3:G6.*

13

$$$ ✕ **Foreign Cinema.** Forget popcorn: In this hip, loftlike space "dinner and

MODERN a movie" become one joyous event. Classic films are projected on a wall

AMERICAN in a large inner courtyard while you're served stellar seasonal California

FAMILY cooking. **Known for:** seasonal and flavorful California cooking; date night; weekend brunch. $ *Average main: $27 ⊠ 2534 Mission St., Mission District* ☎ 415/648–7600 ⊕ *www.foreigncinema.com* ☉ *No lunch weekdays* ✛ *3:F6.*

$ ✕ **La Santaneca de la Mission.** The El Salvadorans who live in the Mission

LATIN AMERICAN head here for *pupusas*, the stuffed cornmeal rounds that are more or

FAMILY less the hamburger of their homeland. You'll find them filled with meat, cheese, and beans at this friendly, family-run place. **Known for:** classic Salvadoran fare; variety of pupusas; good value. $ *Average main: $7 ⊠ 2815 Mission St., Mission District* ☎ 415/285–2131 ▬ *No credit cards* ☉ *Closed Wed.* ✛ *3:F6.*

$$$$ ✕ **Lazy Bear.** There's no end to the buzz of chef David Barzelay's pop-

MODERN up turned permanent, or the quest for a ticket to one of his modern

AMERICAN American dinners. A reservation for the 14-plus-course prix-fixe menu that changes monthly is required. **Known for:** hot-ticket often resold; communal dining; dinner party setup. $ *Average main: $160 ⊠ 3416 19th St., Mission District* ☎ 415/874–9921 ⊕ *www.lazybearsf.com* ☉ *Closed Sun. and Mon. No lunch.* ✛ *3:F6.*

$$ ✕ **Limón Rotisserie.** Cooks in Peru and Ecuador have long argued over

PERUVIAN which country invented ceviche. Most diners at Limón would probably

FAMILY line up with the Peruvians after eating the myriad delicious versions served here. **Known for:** Peruvian ceviche; marinated roasted chicken; creative cocktails. $ *Average main: $18 ⊠ 524 Valencia St., Mission District* ☎ 415/252–0918 ⊕ *www.limonrotisserie.com* ✛ *3:E5* ✛ *3:F6.*

$$$ ✕ **Locanda.** The owners of lauded Delfina channel the culinary tradi-

ITALIAN tions of Rome at this lively osteria. Carbs get glorious treatment: chewy *pizza bianca* is an addictive starter, while peppery and creamy *tonnarelli cacio e pepe* is a signature. **Known for:** delicious pasta and antipasti; busy bar. $ *Average main: $26 ⊠ 557 Valencia St., Mission District* ☎ 415/863–6800 ⊕ *www.locandasf.com* ☉ *No lunch* ✛ *3:F5.*

$$ ✕ **Lolinda.** Argentine fare, a convivial atmosphere, and good bartenders

ARGENTINE help explain the appeal of this contemporary steak house. This sprawl-ing two-level former nightclub space is scene-y with a capital S, with two bars and a rooftop deck (El Techo) that offers captivating views. **Known for:** modern Argentine food; lively scene; tasty cocktails. $ *Average main: $22 ⊠ 2518 Mission St., Mission District* ☎ 415/550–6970 ⊕ *www.lolindasf.com* ☉ *No lunch* ✛ *3:F6.*

$ CHINESE 🍴 **Mission Chinese Food.** While the setting is somewhat one-star, the food draws throngs for its bold, cheerfully inauthentic riffs on Chinese cuisine. The kitchen pumps out some fine and super-fiery kung pao pastrami as well as other dishes made with quality meats and ingredients, like salt cod fried rice with mackerel confit, and sour chili chicken. **Known for:** kung pao pastrami; salt cod fried rice; to-go spot due to long waits. [$] *Average main: $14* ✉ *2234 Mission St., Mission District* ☎ *415/863–2800* 🌐 *www.missionchinesefood.com* 🕒 *Closed Wed.* ✣ *3:F6.*

$$ KOREAN FUSION FAMILY 🍴 **Namu Gaji.** Chef Dennis Lee's innovative, satisfying cooking is inspired both by Korean tradition and Northern Californian ingredients. At this primo location across from Dolores Park, mushrooms are accompanied by tofu and ricotta, and pickled daikon and bacon jam anoint the burger. **Known for:** innovative Korean cuisine; stonepot serving dishes; local ingredients. [$] *Average main: $19* ✉ *499 Dolores St., Mission District* ☎ *415/431–6268* 🌐 *www.namusf.com* 🕒 *Closed Mon. No lunch Tues.* ✣ *3:E6.*

$ RAMEN 🍴 **Orenchi Beyond.** After years of heading an hour down the peninsula to satisfy their ramen cravings at Orenchi, San Franciscans now have their own Mission location. Though the space has a hipster slant, the namesake ramen bowl still boasts the *tonkotsu* broth base that cooks for 18 hours, and chewy noodles that attract the harshest of critics. **Known for:** authentic ramen; long waits. [$] *Average main: $13* ✉ *174 Valencia St., at Duboce, Mission District* ☎ *415/431–3971* 🌐 *www.orenchi-beyond.com* 🕒 *Closed Mon. No dinner Tues.–Thurs.* ✣ *3:E4.*

$$ PIZZA FAMILY 🍴 **Pizzeria Delfina.** As one of the contenders for the city's best pizza, this offshoot of Delfina is known for perfectly blistered thin crusts and near-constant crowds. Besides its roster of pizzas, the menu also offers super-fresh salads and antipasti. **Known for:** European-style pizzeria; sidewalk seating; long waits for pizza to go. [$] *Average main: $17* ✉ *3621 18th St., Mission District* ☎ *415/437–6800* 🌐 *www.pizzeriadelfina.com* 🕒 *No lunch Tues.* ✣ *3:E6.*

$ DELI 🍴 **Salumeria.** When chef Thomas McNaughton isn't hosting dinner guests at Central Kitchen, that restaurant's courtyard turns into a casual hangout for lunch goers who order from this larder and deli. A half-dozen sandwiches as well as salads are on the menu, with daily specials. **Known for:** tasty sandwiches and salads; courtyard hangout; grocery. [$] *Average main: $13* ✉ *3000 20th St., Mission District* ☎ *415/471–2998* 🌐 *salumeriasf.com* 🕒 *No dinner* ✣ *3:H6.*

$ MEXICAN FAMILY 🍴 **SanJalisco.** This colorful old-time, sun-filled, family-run restaurant is a neighborhood favorite, and not only because it serves breakfast all day—though the hearty *chilaquiles* hit the spot. On weekends, adventurous eaters may opt for *birria,* a spicy barbecued goat stew, or *menudo,* a tongue-searing soup made from beef tripe. **Known for:** breakfast all day; beef-tripe menudo; delicious sangria. [$] *Average main: $11* ✉ *901 S. Van Ness Ave., Mission District* ☎ *415/648–8383* 🌐 *www.sanjalisco.com* ✣ *3:F6.*

$ BAKERY Fodor's Choice ★ 🍴 **Tartine Bakery & Café.** Chad Robertson is America's first modern cult baker, and this tiny Mission District outpost is where you'll find his famed loaves of tangy country bread. You'll also find beloved pastries like croissants and morning buns—and near-constant lines out the door.

Known for: bread with cult following; delicious pastries; long lines. [$] *Average main: $10* ✉ *600 Guerrero St., at 18th St., Mission District* ☎ *415/487–2600* 🌐 *www.tartinebakery.com* ✣ *3:E6.*

$$$$ MODERN AMERICAN FAMILY
🍴 **Tartine Manufactory.** Little Tartine bakery has expanded big time, with this sunny, cathedral-like space in the Heath Ceramics building. This is where you come for Chad Robertson's bread and Liz Prueitt's pastries, but also for breakfast, lunch, and dinner. **Known for:** Chad Robertson's bread; Liz Prueitt's pastries; seasonal salads. [$] *Average main: $32* ✉ *595 Alabama St., Mission District* ☎ *415/757–0007* 🌐 *www.tartinemanufactory.com* ⏲ *No dinner Mon. and Tues.* ✣ *3:H6.*

13

$ DELI FAMILY Fodor's Choice ★
🍴 **Wise Sons Jewish Delicatessen.** Jewish comfort food is the order of the day (and night) at this simple deli counter decorated with old family portraits. Old-school classics are made with new-wave sensibilities: the pastrami and corned beef are hormone- and antibiotic-free. **Known for:** contemporary Jewish cuisine; pastrami on rye; breakfast all day. [$] *Average main: $14* ✉ *3150 24th St., at Shotwell, Mission District* ☎ *415/787–3354* 🌐 *wisesonsdeli.com* ✣ *3:F6.*

POTRERO HILL AND DOGPATCH

East of the Mission, Potrero Hill is home to a cluster of casual, often reasonably priced dining rooms in the blocks around Connecticut and 18th Streets and is one of the more elevated places in the city (like Nob Hill), so be prepared to work your calves. Hot now is historic Dogpatch—a neighborhood of dilapidated warehouses and the Hell's Angels headquarters. Because the 22nd Street Caltrain Station is here, the terminus for trains that go south to Silicon Valley, the neighborhood is filling up with transplanted techies, along with restaurants and bars to feed and water them.

$$ BARBECUE FAMILY
🍴 **The Magnolia Brewing Co.'s Smokestack.** One of the city's best Wagyu beef briskets is served in an unassuming (from the exterior) former factory in trendy Dogpatch. Several American styles—Kansas City, Texas, and the Carolinas—are showcased on an extra-large chalkboard that lists daily specials, priced by the pound. **Known for:** barbecue, beer, and whiskey; industrial-cool space. [$] *Average main: $15* ✉ *2505 3rd St., Dogpatch* ☎ *415/864–7468* 🌐 *www.magnoliasmokestack.com* ✣ *3:H6.*

$$ MODERN AMERICAN FAMILY
🍴 **Plow.** The breakfast lines are as constant as the excellent fluffy lemon-ricotta pancakes, scrambles, and biscuits served at this former architect's studio. The atmosphere is also winning—bright and pastoral, with rustic wood floors and huge windows. **Known for:** in-demand breakfast; Little Plowers menu; long lines. [$] *Average main: $15* ✉ *1299 18th St., Potrero Hill* ☎ *415/821–7569* 🌐 *www.eatatplow.com* ⏲ *No dinner.* ✣ *3:H6.*

PACIFIC HEIGHTS AND JAPANTOWN

PACIFIC HEIGHTS

Pacific Heights may well be one of the city's better-known neighborhoods, thanks to Hollywood movies and jaw-dropping mansions. More down-to-earth, and down the hill, is Lower Pac Heights, which attracts professionals and postgrads who flock to Fillmore Street's many casual eateries.

$$$ VIETNAMESE FAMILY

🍴 **Out the Door.** A casual offshoot of Charles Phan's Slanted Door, this spot is actually where locals prefer to go for his version of Vietnamese. The look is chic and simple, with an open kitchen, a communal table, counter seating, and an eclectic crowd. **Known for:** Phan classics; weekend brunch; communal table. [$] *Average main: $24* ✉ *2232 Bush St., Pacific Heights* ☎ *415/923–9575* 🌐 *www.outthedoors.com* ✥ *2:F6.*

$ BURGER FAMILY

🍴 **Roam Artisan Burgers.** All the burgers at this laid-back spot are responsibly sourced, and the beef is 100% grass-fed. Choose a patty (beef, bison, vegetarian, or turkey), then apply preset toppings, or invent your own. **Known for:** specialty patties; sustainable ingredients. [$] *Average main: $11* ✉ *1923 Fillmore St., Pacific Heights* ☎ *415/800–7801* 🌐 *www.roamburgers.com* ✥ *2:F5.*

$$$ ITALIAN Fodor's Choice ★

🍴 **SPQR.** Brought to you by the same team that operates the Marina's wildly popular A16, SPQR is a modern Italian spot known for Chef Matthew Accarrino's inventive, hyperseasonal cooking. You'll find antipasti (the chicken liver is a favorite), superlative pastas like smoked fettuccine with sea urchin, and mains, like suckling pork. **Known for:** inventive and seasonal cuisine; Italian wine list; neighborhood hot spot. [$] *Average main: $30* ✉ *1911 Fillmore St., Pacific Heights* ☎ *415/771–7779* 🌐 *www.spqrsf.com* ⏲ *No lunch weekdays* ✥ *2:F6.*

JAPANTOWN

The epicenter of Japantown, which covers about six city blocks, may well be the Kintetsu Mall, with kitschy Japanese gift shops (a Hello Kitty shop and a bookstore) and restaurants dishing out ramen, donburi, and mochi. There's also a glut of restaurants, sushi shops, and izakayas along Buchanan Street's pedestrian way, between Post and Sutter.

$ JAPANESE FAMILY

🍴 **Mifune Don.** Thin brown soba and thick white udon are the stars at this long-popular outpost of a celebrated Osaka restaurant. There's usually a line, but the house-made noodles, served both hot and cold and with a score of toppings, are worth the wait (and the line moves quickly). **Known for:** house-made soba and udon; savory Japanese pancakes; long lines. [$] *Average main: $12* ✉ *22 Peace Plaza, Suite 560, Japantown* ☎ *415/346–1993* ⏲ *Closed Tues.* ✥ *2:F6.*

DINING AND
LODGING ATLAS

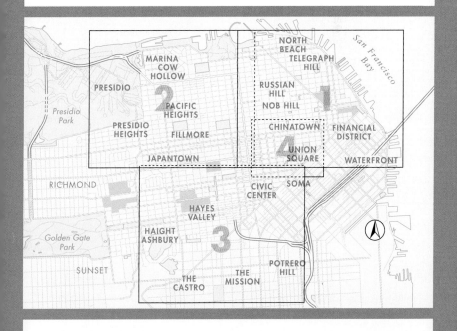

MARINA
COW
HOLLOW

PRESIDIO

2
PACIFIC
HEIGHTS

Presidio
Park

PRESIDIO
HEIGHTS

FILLMORE

JAPANTOWN

NORTH
BEACH
TELEGRAPH
HILL

RUSSIAN
HILL
NOB HILL

CHINATOWN

1

FINANCIAL
DISTRICT

4
UNION
SQUARE

WATERFRONT

San Francisco Bay

RICHMOND

Golden Gate
Park

SUNSET

HAYES
VALLEY

HAIGHT
ASHBURY

3

THE
CASTRO

THE
MISSION

CIVIC
CENTER

SOMA

POTRERO
HILL

KEY
☐ Hotels
■ Restaurants
■ Restaurant in Hotel
Embarcadero
BART Station
Bay Area Rapid Transit

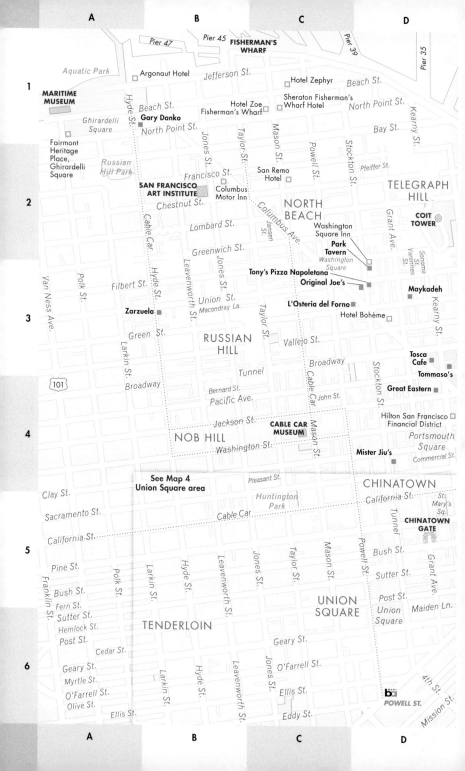

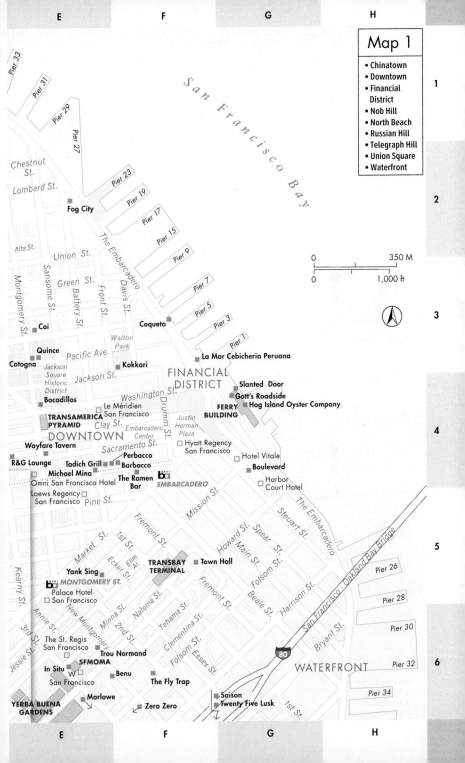

Map 1

- Chinatown
- Downtown
- Financial District
- Nob Hill
- North Beach
- Russian Hill
- Telegraph Hill
- Union Square
- Waterfront

San Francisco Bay

Pier 33
Pier 31
Pier 29
Pier 27
Chestnut St.
Lombard St.
Pier 23
Pier 19
Fog City
Pier 17
Pier 15
Alta St.
Union St.
Pier 9
Green St.
Pier 7
Pier 5
Pier 3
Coqueta
Pier 1
Coi
Walton Park
Quince
Pacific Ave.
La Mar Cebicheria Peruana
Cotogna
Jackson Square Historic District
Kokkari
FINANCIAL DISTRICT
Jackson St.
Slanted Door
Washington St.
Gott's Roadside
Bocadillos
Le Méridien San Francisco
FERRY BUILDING
Hog Island Oyster Company
TRANSAMERICA PYRAMID
Clay St.
DOWNTOWN
Embarcadero Center
Justin Herman Plaza
Wayfare Tavern
Sacramento St.
Hyatt Regency San Francisco
R&G Lounge
Perbacco
Hotel Vitale
Tadich Grill
Barbacco
Boulevard
Michael Mina
The Ramen Bar
Omni San Francisco Hotel
EMBARCADERO
Harbor Court Hotel
Loews Regency San Francisco
Pine St.
Mission St.
Market St.
Fremont St.
Howard St.
Spear St.
Steuart St.
San Francisco - Oakland Bay Bridge
TRANSBAY TERMINAL
Town Hall
Yank Sing
Ecker St.
Elim Al.
Folsom St.
Beale St.
Pier 26
MONTGOMERY ST.
Fremont St.
Palace Hotel San Francisco
Minna St.
Natoma St.
Harrison St.
Pier 28
Kearny St.
New Montgomery
2nd St.
Tehama St.
Pier 30
Annie St.
Clementina St.
The St. Regis San Francisco
Folsom St.
Essex St.
Pier 32
3rd St.
Trou Normand
In Situ
SFMOMA
Benu
Bryant St.
WATERFRONT
Pier 34
Jessie St.
San Francisco
The Fly Trap
YERBA BUENA GARDENS
Marlowe
Zero Zero
Saison
Twenty Five Lusk
1st St.

0   350 M
0   1,000 ft

E   F   G   H
1
2
3
4
5
6

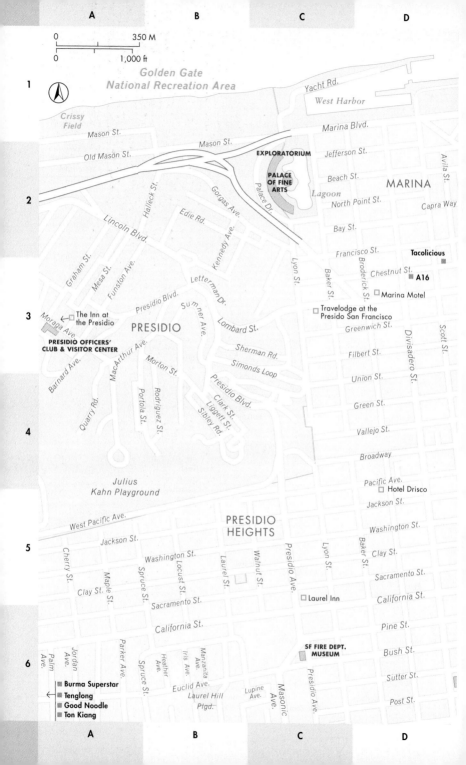

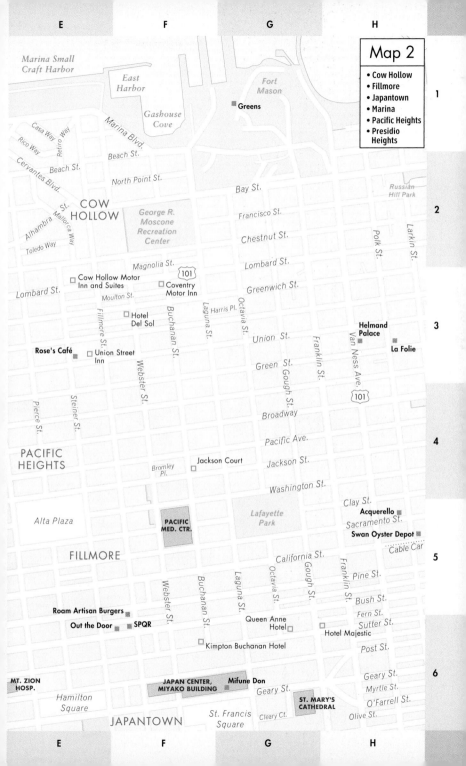

Map 2

• Cow Hollow
• Fillmore
• Japantown
• Marina
• Pacific Heights
• Presidio Heights

1

Marina Small Craft Harbor

East Harbor

Gashouse Cove

Fort Mason

Greens

Casa Way Way

Rico Way

Retiro Way

Cervantes Blvd.

Marina Blvd.

Beach St.

Beach St.

North Point St.

Bay St.

Russian Hill Park

2

Alhambra St.

Mallorca Way

COW HOLLOW

Francisco St.

Toledo Way

George R. Moscone Recreation Center

Chestnut St.

Polk St.

Larkin St.

Lombard St.

Magnolia St.

Cow Hollow Motor Inn and Suites

101

Coventry Motor Inn

Lombard St.

Moulton St.

Hotel Del Sol

Harris Pl.

Greenwich St.

Lombard St.

Union St.

Helmand Palace

La Folie

3

Rose's Café

Union Street Inn

Fillmore St.

Buchanan St.

Laguna St.

Octavia St.

Green St.

Gough St.

Franklin St.

Van Ness Ave.

101

Pierce St.

Steiner St.

Webster St.

Broadway

Pacific Ave.

4

PACIFIC HEIGHTS

Bromley Pl.

Jackson Court

Jackson St.

Washington St.

Clay St.

Acquerello

Alta Plaza

PACIFIC MED. CTR.

Lafayette Park

Sacramento St.

Swan Oyster Depot

Cable Car

FILLMORE

California St.

5

Roam Artisan Burgers

Out the Door   SPQR

Webster St.

Buchanan St.

Laguna St.

Octavia St.

Gough St.

Franklin St.

Pine St.

Bush St.

Fern St.

Sutter St.

Queen Anne Hotel

Hotel Majestic

Kimpton Buchanan Hotel

Post St.

MT. ZION HOSP.

Hamilton Square

JAPAN CENTER, MIYAKO BUILDING

Mifune Don

Geary St.

Geary St.

Myrtle St.

6

ST. MARY'S CATHEDRAL

O'Farrell St.

JAPANTOWN

St. Francis Square

Cleary Ct.

Olive St.

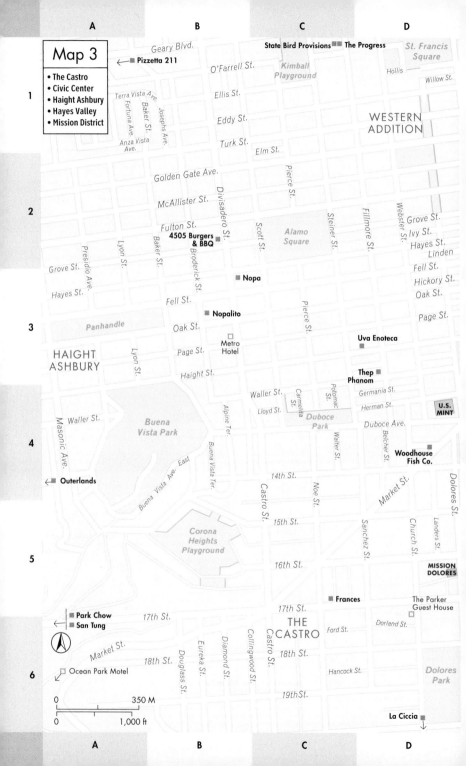

Map 3

- The Castro
- Civic Center
- Haight Ashbury
- Hayes Valley
- Mission District

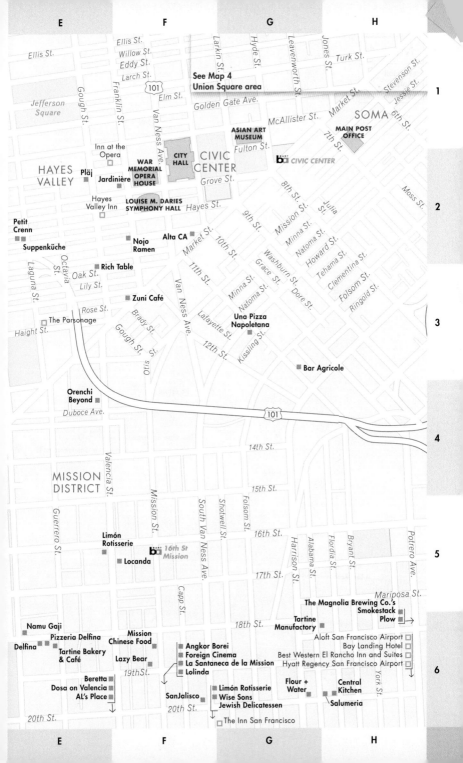

Map 4

- Nob Hill
- SoMa
- Union Square

A

B

C

D

1

Kimball Pl.

Sacramento St.

Golden Ct.

Leroy Pl.

Lysette St.

Taylor St.

Cushman St.

Huntington Park

Acorn Al.

Cable Car

The Scarlet Huntington Hotel

California St.

Helen St.

2

Pine St.

Touchard St.

Jones St.

Taylor St.

Mulford Al.

Hyde St.

Leavenworth St.

Petite Auberge

Bush St.

Hotel Beresford

3

Hotel Vertigo

Liholiho Yacht Club

Sutter St.

Cosmo Pl.

The Andrews Hotel

Larkin St.

Post St.

Beresford Arms

Colin Pl.

Shannon St.

Warwick San Francisco

Meacham Pl.

Hotel Adagio

The Alise San Francisco

4

Geary St.

The Marker San Francisco

Clift San Francisco

Amity Al.

Harlem Al.

Ada Ct.

Myrtle St.

O'Farrell St.

Antonio St.

Steveloe Pl.

5

Lers Ros

Olive St.

TENDERLOIN

Ellis St.

Cohen Pl.

Willow St.

Bodega Bistro

Eddy St.

Wagner Al.

6

Phoenix Hotel

Turk St.

A

B

C

D

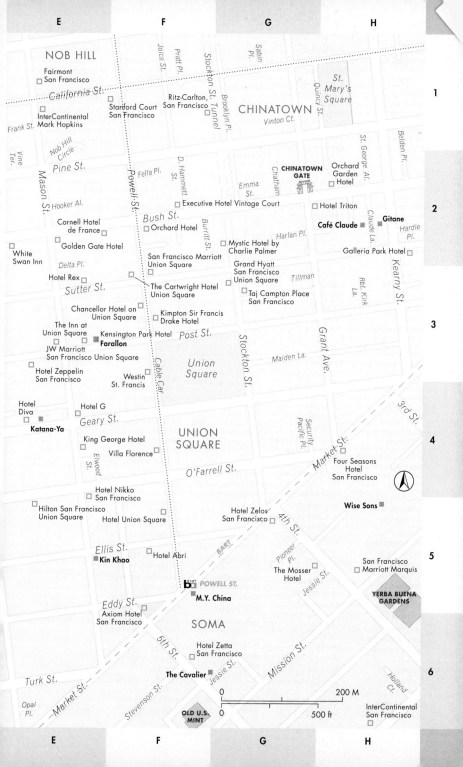

WHERE TO STAY

Updated by
Daniel Mangin

San Francisco accommodations are diverse, ranging from cozy bed-and-breakfasts and kitschy motels to chic boutique hotels, grande dames, and sleek high-rises. Though the tech boom has skyrocketed the prices of even some of the most dependable low-cost options, some Fodor's faves still offer fine accommodations without prices that rival the city's steep hills. In fact, the number of reasonably priced accommodations is impressive.

The Hotel Nikko, Hotel Drisco, Tuscan (now the Hotel Zoe), and other city stalwarts received a sprucing up in 2017, along with other hotels initiating upgrades during the expected period of low occupancy during the Moscone Center convention facility expansion project, which continues into 2018. San Francisco hotels also continue to "go green" in a big way, cutting electrical and water consumption and expanding recycling, composting, and other eco-friendly strategies. In addition to helping the properties cut costs, market research shows that their customers, especially millennials, respond favorably to such initiatives.

When contemplating a stay in San Francisco, consider timing. Many business-oriented hotels offer great weekend deals (such properties are busiest from Monday through Thursday), with the opposite often true at lodgings geared more to leisure travelers. Though a mini building boom in hotel construction should alleviate room shortages, when there's a big convention in town, even the humblest accommodations can triple in price or more.

Once you settle into your perfect room, remember this advice: when in doubt, ask the concierge. This holds true for almost any request, whether you have special needs or burning desires—if anyone can get you tickets to that sold-out show or a table at the hottest restaurant, it's the concierge.

WHERE SHOULD I STAY?

	Neighborhood Vibe	Pros	Cons
Union Square/ Downtown	Union Square is a hub for visitors; you'll find a wide range of choices—and prices—for lodging.	Excellent shopping. Home to the theater district, great transit access to other neighborhoods.	Often crowded and noisy. Many panhandlers. Close to Tenderloin, a still-seedy part of town. Take cabs at night.
SoMa	Square one for the business set. Offers luxury high-rises, old classics, and a few bargains.	Near the museums and Yerba Buena Gardens. Steps from the convention center. Many fine eateries.	Construction in the area may mean traffic snarls. As with many changing neighborhoods, street life takes many forms. Be cautious walking around at night.
Financial District	A mini Midtown Manhattan where properties cater to business travelers.	Excellent city and bay views, which are spectacular by night. Easy access to restaurants and nightclubs.	Some streets are iffy at night. Hotels are on the pricey side. Many businesses close at night and on weekends.
Nob Hill	Synonymous with San Francisco's high society, this area contains some of the city's best-known luxury hotels.	Many hotels boast gorgeous views and notable restaurants. Easy access to Union Square and Chinatown.	Hotels here will test your wallet, while the area's steep hills may try your endurance.
Civic Center/ Van Ness	A wide mix of lodgings scattered throughout this area.	Many cultural offerings and government offices surround this central hub. Not too far from Union Square.	Away from touristy areas. A large homeless population lives in the area.
Fisherman's Wharf/North Beach	Mostly chain hotels by the wharf; lodgings get funkier and smaller in North Beach.	Near attractions like Ghirardelli Square and Pier 39. Cable-car lines and bay-cruise piers are nearby.	City ordinances limit wharf hotels to four stories, so good views are out. Very touristy.
Pacific Heights/Cow Hollow/The Marina	A few tony accommodations in quietly residential Pacific Heights. Mostly motels along Lombard Street, a busy traffic corridor.	Away from the more tourist-oriented areas; visitors have a chance to explore where locals eat and shop. Lots of free parking.	Getting downtown can be challenging via public transportation. Some complain of the fraternity-like bar scene.

14

SAN FRANCISCO LODGING PLANNER

FACILITIES

When pricing accommodations, always ask what facilities are included and what entails an additional charge. One big unexpected extra might be parking fees, which are off the charts in San Francisco. A seemingly expensive hotel that provides free parking and a hearty breakfast, for instance, can end up costing you less than one that charges for parking and breakfast. All the hotels listed have private baths, central heating, and private phones unless otherwise noted. Many places don't have air-conditioning, but you probably won't need it. Even in September and October, when the city sees its warmest days, the temperature rarely climbs above 70°F.

Nearly all hotels have Wi-Fi available, and though many offer the service for free, some charge for quicker connections, multiple devices, or both. Larger hotels often have video or high-speed checkout capability. Pools are a rarity, but most large properties have gyms or health clubs, and sometimes full-scale spas; hotels without facilities usually have arrangements for guests at nearby gyms, sometimes for a fee. At the end of each review, we state whether any meals (and in San Francisco, this means breakfast) are included in the room rate. Mirroring a trend elsewhere in the country, some hotels no longer provide room service, so if that's an amenity you require, be sure to inquire.

FAMILY TRAVEL

San Francisco attracts many family vacationers, and hotels have followed the family-friendly trend. Some properties provide diversions like in-room video games, suites with kitchenettes, and foldout sofa beds; some, like Hotel Diva, have even decked-out special kids' suites with toys, games, and karaoke machines. Many full-service San Francisco hotels provide rollaway beds, babysitting recommendations, and stroller rentals, but make arrangements when booking the room, not when you arrive. When booking at older downtown hotels, many of which are small, don't assume there will be room for a rollaway bed; sometimes fire-safety regulations won't allow one to be used.

PARKING

Several properties on Lombard Street and in the Civic Center area have free parking (but not always in a covered garage). And, occasionally hotel package deals include parking. Hotels in the Union Square and Nob Hill areas charge $30 to $70 per day for garage parking; many hotels charge extra fees for SUVs. Some bed-and-breakfasts have limited free parking available, but many don't, requiring you to park on the street. Depending on the neighborhood, this can be easy or quite difficult, so ask for realistic parking information when you call. Some hotels offer a choice of valet parking with unlimited in-out privileges or self-parking. The cost is generally less for the latter in part because no tip is involved). Given the expense of parking, and the ease of getting around San Francisco on public transportation, you may well want to leave the car at home or wait to rent one until you're ready to leave town.

PRICES

San Francisco hotel prices rank among the highest in the country. Weekend rates for double rooms in high season average about $250 a night citywide except during large conventions such as Oracle's and Salesforce's, when even the humblest downtown lodgings command $500 or more. At other times, even in high season, decent lower-cost accommodations are relatively plentiful, especially in comparison to New York, Washington, and other big cities. Most hotels price rooms dynamically, with rates for dates a few days forward or months down the line fluctuating from hour to hour depending on availability—if you have your heart set on a particular property and its prices are high for your desired dates, it's wise to check back often either online or by phone.

You'll sometimes, but not always, find a hotel's best rates on its website. If looking for a same-day room, check out apps such as Hotel Tonight or access the last-minute pages of Expedia and other travel sites for the best deals. Whenever you're making a reservation, inquire about special rates and packages. The lodgings we list are the cream of the crop in each price category.

WHAT IT COSTS

	$	$$	$$$	$$$$
Hotels	under $150	$150–$249	$250–$350	over $350

Prices are the lowest cost of a standard double room in high season.

RESERVATIONS

Reservations are always advised, especially during the peak seasons—from August through November, during the Oracle Convention week in fall, and weekends in December. Celebrations like Chinese New Year (late January or early February), Mother's Day and Bay to Breakers (mid-May), and gay pride (June) also require reservations.

USING THE MAPS

Throughout, you'll see mapping symbols and coordinates (3:F2) after property names or reviews. To locate the property on a map, turn to the San Francisco Dining and Lodging Atlas at the end of Where to Eat. The first number after the symbol indicates the map number. Following that is the property's coordinate on the map grid.

LODGING REVIEWS

Listed alphabetically within neighborhoods. Hotel reviews have been shortened. For full information, visit Fodors.com.

UNION SQUARE AND CHINATOWN

UNION SQUARE

$$ HOTEL Fodor's Choice ★

The Alise San Francisco. Three blocks west of Union Square and loaded with high- and low-tech amenities, this Pineapple Hospitality boutique property delivers value in a stylish package, starting with the lobby's paintings and sculptures and the glass-on-panel wall installations above the adjacent Pineapple Bistro and Bar. Inside a renovated 1913 structure, the hotel, which opened in 2016, has four room types, all with bright-yellow curtains, light-colored walls, and Carrara marble–tiled bathrooms. **Pros:** bright-yellow decor; loaded with amenities; let's-have-fun vibe. **Cons:** many rooms are small; some visitors find hotel's neighborhood intimidating after dark. [$] *Rooms from: $239* ✉ *580 Geary St., Union Sq.* ☎ *415/441–2700, 800/227–4223* 🌐 *www.thealise.com* 🛏 *93 rooms* 🍴 *No meals* ✥ 4:D4.

$$ **The Andrews Hotel.** Two blocks west of Union Square, this Queen
HOTEL Anne–style property debuted in 1905 as the Sultan Turkish Baths
for gentlemen. **Pros:** intimate; moderate prices; restaurant's praise-
worthy service and Italian fare. **Cons:** small rooms; old-style decor;
no breakfast area. $ *Rooms from: $219* ⊠ *624 Post St., Union Sq.*
☎ *415/563–6877, 800/926–3739* ⊕ *www.andrewshotel.com* ↩ *48
rooms* ◯ *Breakfast* ✦ *4:D3.*

$$ **Axiom Hotel San Francisco.** Green, pet-friendly, and equipped with
HOTEL fiber-optic wireless Internet, the tech-oriented Axiom—a splashy
Fodor's Choice refresh of a 1908 hotel—nimbly provides a boutique experience
★ business and leisure travelers applaud. **Pros:** tech-friendly amenities;
polite, intuitive, efficient staff; splashy public spaces. **Cons:** smallish rooms; somewhat congested area; some guests find street people
intimidating. $ *Rooms from: $221* ⊠ *28 Cyril Magnin St., at 5th
and Market Sts., Union Sq.* ☎ *415/392–9466* ⊕ *www.axiomhotel.com*
↩ *155 rooms* ◯ *No meals* ✦ *4:F5.*

$$ **Beresford Arms.** Fancy molding and 10-foot-tall windows grace the
HOTEL red-carpeted lobby of this brick Victorian listed on the National Regis-
FAMILY ter of Historic Places. **Pros:** moderately priced; suites with kitchenettes
and Murphy beds are a plus for families with kids; three blocks from
Union Square. **Cons:** no air-conditioning; cramped standard rooms;
can be noisy at night. $ *Rooms from: $179* ⊠ *701 Post St., Union Sq.*
☎ *415/673–2600, 800/533–6533* ⊕ *www.beresford.com* ↩ *95 rooms*
◯ *Breakfast* ✦ *4:C3.*

$$ **The Cartwright Hotel Union Square.** A relatively inexpensive Union
HOTEL Square–area option (look for online specials), this 1913 Edwardian
is part of the Best Western chain's Premier Collection, and it retains
a period feel, especially in the tile-floor lobby and adjoining wood-
paneled bar. **Pros:** great location; spacious closets; staff that cares. **Cons:**
small rooms; small baths; uninspired decor. $ *Rooms from: $233* ⊠ *524
Sutter St., Union Sq.* ☎ *415/421–2865, 800/780–7234* ⊕ *www.cart-
wrightunionsquare.com* ↩ *114 rooms* ◯ *No meals* ✦ *4:F3.*

$$$ **Chancellor Hotel on Union Square.** Built to accommodate visitors to the
HOTEL 1915 Panama-Pacific International Exposition, this favorite of budget
travelers has views of Powell Street cable cars from its modest lobby.
Pros: free Wi-Fi; good value for Union Square; friendly staff, some of
whom have worked here for decades. **Cons:** small bathrooms; noise
from cable cars; no air-conditioning (ceiling fans). $ *Rooms from: $269*
⊠ *433 Powell St., Union Sq.* ☎ *415/362–2004, 800/428–4748* ⊕ *www.
chancellorhotel.com* ↩ *137 rooms* ◯ *No meals* ✦ *4:F3.*

$$$ **Clift San Francisco.** The entrance to this 1915 classic is so nondescript,
HOTEL you could walk right past without a hint of what's inside—a seriously
sexy hotel, all the more so since guest-room renovations commenced in
2017. **Pros:** discreet and helpful staff; surreal interior design; close to
public transportation, shopping, and theaters. **Cons:** street noise (book
on upper floors to avoid); pricey during major conventions; aesthetic
too over-the-top for some guests. $ *Rooms from: $284* ⊠ *495 Geary
St., Union Sq.* ☎ *415/775–4700* ⊕ *www.clifthotel.com* ↩ *363 rooms*
◯ *No meals* ✦ *4:D4.*

14

$ | HOTEL | Fodor's Choice ★

🏨 **Cornell Hotel de France.** Discovering this enchanting family-operated small hotel is like finding a bit of Paris a few blocks from Union Square. **Pros:** a bit of Paris in San Francisco; individually decorated rooms; special packages and discounts. **Cons:** several blocks from the center of things; surrounding area mildly dodgy after dark; small lobby. [$] *Rooms from: $149* ✉ *715 Bush St., Union Sq.* ☎ *415/421–3154* 🌐 *www.cornellhotel.com* 🛏 *48 rooms* 🍴 *Breakfast* ✥ 4:E2.

$$ | HOTEL

🏨 **Executive Hotel Vintage Court.** These Napa Valley–inspired rooms, just two blocks from Union Square, are named after California wineries and feature large writing desks and dark-wood venetian blinds; some have sunny window seats. **Pros:** complimentary local wines; corner rooms offer plenty of light; bathrooms renovated in 2016. **Cons:** small bathrooms, a few with stall showers only; up a hill from downtown; service can seem perfunctory. [$] *Rooms from: $239* ✉ *650 Bush St., Union Sq.* ☎ *415/392–4666, 800/654–1100* 🌐 *www.executivehotels.net/vintagecourt* 🛏 *106 rooms* 🍴 *Breakfast* ✥ 4:F2.

$ | B&B/INN | FAMILY | Fodor's Choice ★

🏨 **Golden Gate Hotel.** Budget seekers looking for accommodations around Union Square will enjoy this four-story Edwardian with bay windows, an original birdcage elevator, hallways lined with historical photographs, and rooms decorated with antiques, wicker pieces, and Laura Ashley bedding and curtains. **Pros:** friendly staff; free Wi-Fi; spotless rooms; comfortable bedding; good location if you're a walker. **Cons:** some rooms share a bath; resident cat and dog, so not good for guests with allergies; some rooms on small side. [$] *Rooms from: $145* ✉ *775 Bush St., Union Sq.* ☎ *415/392–3702, 800/835–1118* 🌐 *www.goldengatehotel.com* 🛏 *23 rooms* 🍴 *Breakfast* ✥ 4:E2.

$$$ | HOTEL | FAMILY

🏨 **Grand Hyatt San Francisco Union Square.** Rooms done in warm autumnal tones, with textured custom furniture, original artwork, and teak beds, are all high-tech: windows can be blacked out from your bed, and you can stream from your mobile or other device to a swiveling flatscreen. **Pros:** stellar views from upper floors; good-size workstations; weekend deals. **Cons:** small bathrooms; corporate feel. [$] *Rooms from: $269* ✉ *345 Stockton St., Union Sq.* ☎ *415/398–1234* 🌐 *sanfrancisco.grand.hyatt.com* 🛏 *685 rooms* 🍴 *No meals* ✥ 4:G3.

$$ | HOTEL

🏨 **Hilton San Francisco Union Square.** With 1,919 rooms and suites, this is the largest hotel in California—sometimes the lobby feels like downtown at rush hour—but there is a positive side to all that size: many rooms in the silvery tower enjoy views that rank among San Francisco's finest. **Pros:** super views; excellent service; full-service spa. **Cons:** area is dodgy after dark; there can be a wait at check-in. [$] *Rooms from: $239* ✉ *333 O'Farrell St., Union Sq.* ☎ *415/771–1400* 🌐 *www.hiltonsanfranciscohotel.com* 🛏 *1,919 rooms* 🍴 *No meals* ✥ 4:E5.

$$ | HOTEL

🏨 **Hotel Abri.** Near Union Square shops, theaters, and restaurants, this appealing hotel has small but tastefully appointed rooms with smart TVs, iPod docking stations, comfortable bedding, and fancy bath products. **Pros:** tasteful rooms; free Wi-Fi; near the Powell Street cable-car turnaround, shops, and eateries. **Cons:** most rooms have showers only; on-street parking nearly impossible; $30 "urban fee" for amenities not all guests require. [$] *Rooms from: $219* ✉ *127 Ellis St., Union Sq.* ☎ *866/823–4669, 415/392–8800* 🌐 *www.hotel-abri.com* 🛏 *91 rooms* 🍴 *No meals* ✥ 4:F5.

$$ HOTEL **Hotel Adagio.** The Spanish-colonial facade of this 16-story theater-row hotel complements its chic interior, while the decent-sized rooms excite the eye with hues of fog, spring grasses, and Merlot grapes. **Pros:** Marriott-run property with boutique-hotel charm; close to theater district on a bus route; good drinks and scene at lobby bar The Mortimer. **Cons:** street noise; area can be dodgy at night; adjacent to a popular outdoor bar. [$] *Rooms from: $249* ✉ *550 Geary St., Union Sq.* ☎ *415/775–5000, 800/228–8830* 🌐 *www.hoteladagiosf.com* 🛏 *171 rooms* 🍴 *No meals* ⊕ 4:D4.

$$ HOTEL **Hotel Beresford.** For many budget travelers the Beresford's pluses—reasonable prices, sightseeing assistance, and a central location—outweigh minuses that include the small rooms, so-so decor, and no air-conditioning. **Pros:** reasonably priced; close to Union Square; free Wi-Fi. **Cons:** no air-conditioning; small rooms; traditional decor can be stuffy. [$] *Rooms from: $165* ✉ *635 Sutter St., Union Sq.* ☎ *415/673–9900, 800/533–6533* 🌐 *www.beresford.com* 🛏 *114 rooms* 🍴 *Breakfast* ⊕ 4:D3.

$$ HOTEL FAMILY **Hotel Diva.** Entering this magnet for urbanites craving modern decor requires stepping over footprints, handprints, and autographs embedded in the sidewalk by visiting stars; in the rooms, designer carpets complement mid-century-modern chairs and brushed-steel headboards whose shape mimics that of ocean waves. **Pros:** punchy design; in the heart of the theater district; accommodating staff. **Cons:** few frills; tiny bathrooms (but equipped with eco-friendly bath products); many rooms are small. [$] *Rooms from: $189* ✉ *440 Geary St., Union Sq.* ☎ *415/885–0200, 800/553–1900* 🌐 *www.hoteldiva.com* 🛏 *130 rooms* 🍴 *No meals* ⊕ 4:E4.

$$$ HOTEL **Hotel G.** This Union Square hotel manages to feel both homey and innovative with creative touches throughout and bountiful technological amenities. **Pros:** fun design; on-site dining and drinking; great central location. **Cons:** street noise; wooden or concrete flooring can be loud. [$] *Rooms from: $270* ✉ *386 Geary St., Union Sq.* ☎ *877/828–4478* 🌐 *www.hotelgsanfrancisco.com* 🛏 *149 rooms* 🍴 *No meals* ⊕ 4:E4.

$$$ HOTEL FAMILY Fodor's Choice ★ **Hotel Nikko San Francisco.** Known for impeccable service and satin-smooth style, this youngish grande dame celebrated her 30th birthday in 2017 with a $60 million makeover that took its visual cues from traditional kimonos and Japanese calligraphy. **Pros:** polished multilingual staff; tastefully designed rooms; large indoor pool. **Cons:** slightly formal vibe doesn't work for some travelers; expensive during busy convention weeks; so-so surrounding neighborhood. [$] *Rooms from: $284* ✉ *222 Mason St., Union Sq.* ☎ *415/394–1111, 800/248–3308* 🌐 *www.hotelnikkosf.com* 🛏 *532 rooms* 🍴 *No meals* ⊕ 4:E5.

$$ HOTEL **Hotel Rex.** At this literary-themed hotel—named after San Francisco Renaissance poet, translator, and essayist Kenneth Rexroth and frequented by artists and writers—paintings and shelves of antiquarian books line the lobby lounge and small rooms evoke the spirit of salon society with restored period furnishings and striped carpeting. **Pros:** convenient location; good free Wi-Fi; solicitous staffers. **Cons:** many rooms are small; lacks fitness center and similar amenities; older-property smell in hallways and some rooms. [$] *Rooms from: $249* ✉ *562 Sutter St., Union Sq.* ☎ *415/433–4434, 800/433–4434* 🌐 *www.thehotelrex.com* 🛏 *94 rooms* 🍴 *No meals* ⊕ 4:E3.

$$ 🏨 **Hotel Triton.** One of San Francisco's early concept boutique hotels,
HOTEL the Triton may have been eclipsed by newcomers in both style and
substance, but its staff remains attentive and the hotel's location at the
convergence of Chinatown, the Financial District, and Union Square
keeps it worthy of consideration. **Pros:** attentive service; arty environs;
good location. **Cons:** rooms and baths are on the small side; hallways
feel cramped; needs a reboot. $ *Rooms from: $219* ✉ *342 Grant Ave.,
Union Sq.* ☎ *415/394–0500, 877/793–9931* ⊕ *www.hoteltriton.com*
⌁ *140 rooms* ¡O¡ *No meals* ✛ *4:H2.*

$$ 🏨 **Hotel Union Square.** The design-centric interiors of this hotel erected
HOTEL for the 1915 Panama-Pacific International Exposition evoke art-deco
style but feel strictly contemporary. **Pros:** stylish rooms; central location;
free Wi-Fi. **Cons:** at 120–170 square feet, Economy Petite rooms are
small indeed; street noise can be loud at night. $ *Rooms from: $236*
✉ *114 Powell St., Union Sq.* ☎ *415/397–3000* ⊕ *www.hotelunion-
square.com* ⌁ *131 rooms* ¡O¡ *No meals* ✛ *4:F5.*

$$$ 🏨 **Hotel Zeppelin San Francisco.** San Francisco's reputation for political and
HOTEL artistic rebellion inspired the design team that transformed the former
Fodor'sChoice Prescott Hotel into a frothy homage to 1950s Beat writers, 1960s hippies
★ and rockers, and other local agents of change. **Pros:** plucky design; com-
munal lobby and game room; gung-ho staff. **Cons:** smallish rooms; some
guests find pace too frenetic; service can seem too informal. $ *Rooms
from: $299* ✉ *545 Post St., Union Sq.* ☎ *415/563–0303, 888/539–7510*
⊕ *www.hotelzeppelin.com* ⌁ *196 rooms* ¡O¡ *No meals* ✛ *4:E3.*

$$$ 🏨 **The Inn at Union Square.** Built in 1922, this six-story inn started as an
B&B/INN antiquarian bookstore with accommodations, but with amenities that
include high-quality bath products, soft robes, free high-speed Wi-Fi,
and in-room service tablets, the experience is strictly 21st century. **Pros:**
comfortable rooms; upgraded bathrooms; lounges with complimentary
snacks. **Cons:** some rooms can be noisy; interiors feel stuffy; cramped
hallways. $ *Rooms from: $289* ✉ *440 Post St., Union Sq.* ☎ *800/288–
4346* ⊕ *www.unionsquare.com* ⌁ *30 rooms* ¡O¡ *Breakfast* ✛ *4:E3.*

$$$$ 🏨 **JW Marriott San Francisco Union Square.** Bullet elevators whisk guests
HOTEL skyward from the third-floor marble lobby of this 1987 John Portman–
designed hotel to contemporary guest rooms outfitted with business-
oriented clientele in mind. **Pros:** large rooms; luxurious bathrooms;
full-service business center. **Cons:** lacks character; service is polite but
not particularly warm; expensive parking. $ *Rooms from: $362* ✉ *500
Post St., Union Sq.* ☎ *415/771–8600* ⊕ *www.jwmarriottunionsquare.
com* ⌁ *337 rooms* ¡O¡ *No meals* ✛ *4:E3.*

$$ 🏨 **Kensington Park Hotel.** Built in the mid-1920s in a Moorish and Gothic
HOTEL style, this former Elks Club retains its period feel and features, with rich
marble and dark-wood accents, crystal chandeliers, vaulted ceilings, and
antique furnishings in the lobby and vintage touches in the comfortable
guest rooms. **Pros:** friendly personal service; unbeatable location; period
feel. **Cons:** some rooms have street noise; rooms average 220 square
feet; bathrooms are small. $ *Rooms from: $220* ✉ *450 Post St., Union
Sq.* ☎ *415/788–6400, 800/553–1900* ⊕ *www.kensingtonparkhotel.com*
⌁ *93 rooms* ¡O¡ *No meals* ✛ *4:E3.*

14

$$$ HOTEL 🏨 **Kimpton Sir Francis Drake Hotel.** Beefeater-costumed doormen welcome guests into the ornate high-ceilinged lobby of this 1928 landmark whose rooms are equipped with 21st-century tech amenities but evoke the hotel's heyday with regal headboards and plush white comforters. **Pros:** first-rate Powell Street location; ornate lobby; Starlight Room drag show. **Cons:** small rooms and baths; slow elevators; dated room decor. [$] *Rooms from: $299* ✉ *450 Powell St., Union Sq.* ☎ *415/392–7755, 800/546–7866* 🌐 *www.sirfrancisdrake.com* 🛏 *416 rooms* 🍴 *No meals* ✥ 4:F3.

$$ HOTEL 🏨 **King George Hotel.** Though attractively furnished in classic English style, the compact rooms at the King George can feel dark and stuffy, but service and hospitality have more than made up for it and have been points of pride since the hotel's 1914 opening. **Pros:** service and hospitality; convenient to Union Square and SoMa; rooms often at a very good rate. **Cons:** low ceilings in hallways; location on the edge of the Tenderloin unnerves some guests; baths and some closets are minuscule. [$] *Rooms from: $249* ✉ *334 Mason St., Union Sq.* ☎ *415/781–5050, 800/288–6005* 🌐 *www.kinggeorge.com* 🛏 *153 rooms* 🍴 *No meals* ✥ 4:E4.

$$ HOTEL 🏨 **The Marker San Francisco.** Behind a cheery 1910 Beaux-Arts facade, The Marker, formerly the Hotel Monaco, delivers a comfortable experience amid the theater district. **Pros:** near theater district; self-parking option at garage across street; local art in public spaces. **Cons:** close to sketchy Tenderloin neighborhood; some discount-rate rooms very small. [$] *Rooms from: $229* ✉ *501 Geary St., Union Sq.* ☎ *415/292–0100, 844/736–2753* 🌐 *www.jdvhotels.com/the-marker-san-francisco* 🛏 *201 rooms* 🍴 *No meals* ✥ 4:D4.

$$$ HOTEL 🏨 **Mystic Hotel by Charlie Palmer.** Chef-hotelier Charlie Palmer serves up art and style at this historic property that survived the 1906 earthquake. **Pros:** online specials especially off-season; fun on-site bar; artsy decor. **Cons:** smallish rooms (but large suites have soaking tubs); city noise. [$] *Rooms from: $279* ✉ *417 Stockton St., Union Sq.* ☎ *415/400–0500* 🌐 *www.mystichotel.com* 🛏 *82 rooms* 🍴 *Breakfast* ✥ 4:G2.

$$ HOTEL Fodor's Choice ★ 🏨 **Orchard Garden Hotel.** Feel virtuous and eco-friendly while enjoying a junior terrace room with private outdoor space and views of downtown at this service-oriented boutique hotel close to the Financial District and Chinatown. **Pros:** close to the Financial District and Chinatown; clean rooms; capable service. **Cons:** pricey during high season; lacks character of older establishments; minimalist aesthetic won't appeal to all travelers. [$] *Rooms from: $229* ✉ *466 Bush St., Union Sq.* ☎ *415/399–9807* 🌐 *www.theorchardgardenhotel.com* 🛏 *86 rooms* 🍴 *No meals* ✥ 4:H2.

$$$ HOTEL 🏨 **Orchard Hotel.** Rooms done in a soft palette of relaxing colors create a soothing refuge from Union Square's bustle, nicely blending Silicon Valley chic with classic European touches. **Pros:** cutting-edge technology; sizable rooms; green pedigree. **Cons:** can be pricey (but look for deals on hotel website); uphill from Union Square; area outside hotel safe but a tad grungy. [$] *Rooms from: $269* ✉ *665 Bush St., Union Sq.* ☎ *415/362–8878, 888/717–2881* 🌐 *www.theorchardhotel.com* 🛏 *113 rooms* 🍴 *No meals* ✥ 4:F2.

$$$ B&B/INN 🏨 **Petite Auberge.** The provincial room decor of Petite Auberge—bright flowered wallpaper and an armoire that compensates for little or no closet space—recalls an intimate country inn and pleases Francophiles seeking Old World charm after a hectic day of business or touring. **Pros:** Old World charm; breakfast buffet; provincial decor. **Cons:** most rooms short on closet space; a bit of a climb from Union Square; though reasonably safe, the inn's block feels gritty at night. [$] *Rooms from: $299* ✉ *863 Bush St., Union Sq.* ☎ *415/928–6000, 800/365–3004* 🌐 *www.petiteaubergesf.com* 🛏 *26 rooms* 🍴 *Breakfast* ✥ 4:D2.

$$ HOTEL 🏨 **San Francisco Marriott Union Square.** Business travelers appreciate the 30-floor Marriott's attention to their needs with easily accessible plugs, movable desks, ergonomic chairs, and laptop connectors to flat-screen TVs—and its prime location near shopping, restaurants, nightspots, and public transportation. **Pros:** convenient location; in-room amenities for business travelers; generally solid service. **Cons:** noisy street; lacking in atmosphere; not worth it if not on sale. [$] *Rooms from: $237* ✉ *480 Sutter St., Union Sq.* ☎ *415/398–8900, 866/912–0973* 🌐 *www.marriott.com/hotels/travel/sfous* 🛏 *500 rooms* 🍴 *No meals* ✥ 4:F3.

$$$$ HOTEL 🏨 **Taj Campton Place San Francisco.** Beauty and highly attentive service remain the hallmarks of this top-tier hotel, whose rooms are elegantly decorated in a contemporary Italian style, with sandy earth tones and handsome pearwood paneling and cabinetry. **Pros:** discreet, attentive service; first-class restaurant; abundant natural light. **Cons:** pricey (but worth it); smallest rooms 250 square feet. [$] *Rooms from: $425* ✉ *340 Stockton St., Union Sq.* ☎ *415/781–5555, 866/332–1670* 🌐 *www.tajcamptonplace.com* 🛏 *110 rooms* 🍴 *No meals* ✥ 4:G3.

$$$ HOTEL 🏨 **Villa Florence.** A stylish refuge amid the Powell Street whirlwind, this boutique hotel welcomes guests to rooms that feel comfortable, upbeat, and expansive—brown hues from light to chocolate predominate, with magenta accents and polished chrome adding 21st-century style. **Pros:** easy access to shopping, theater, and public transportation; business meeting room named for Machiavelli (imagine the possibilities). **Cons:** excess fees; noise from cable cars; crowded street. [$] *Rooms from: $256* ✉ *225 Powell St., Union Sq.* ☎ *415/397–7700, 877/564–2086 for reservations* 🌐 *www.villaflorence.com* 🛏 *189 rooms* 🍴 *No meals* ✥ 4:F4.

$$ HOTEL 🏨 **Warwick San Francisco.** The handsome, if small, rooms at this 1913 theater district hotel evoke an aristocratic feel with geometric wallpaper, black-and-white framed historic photos curated by the San Francisco Public Library, and ornate wooden furnishings. **Pros:** artsy rooms with historic photos; on-site restaurant and bar; good online rates for families. **Cons:** older property with thin walls; small rooms. [$] *Rooms from: $237* ✉ *490 Geary St., Union Sq.* ☎ *415/928–7900* 🌐 *warwickhotels.com/san-francisco* 🛏 *74 rooms* 🍴 *No meals* ✥ 4:D4.

$$$$ HOTEL 🏨 **Westin St. Francis.** The survivor of two major earthquakes, some headline-grabbing scandals, and even an attempted presidential assassination, this grande dame that dates to 1904 remains ever above the fray. **Pros:** prime Union Square location; great views from some rooms; special weekend rates part of year. **Cons:** rooms in original building can be small; public spaces lack the panache of days gone by. $\boxed{S}$ *Rooms from: $356* ⊠ *335 Powell St., Union Sq.* ☎ *415/397–7000, 800/917–7458* ⊕ *www.westinstfrancis.com* ⤳ *1,195 rooms* �‖O❙ *No meals* ✛ *4:F3.*

$$$
B&B/INN
⬚ **White Swan Inn.** A cozy library with a crackling fireplace and comfortable chairs and sofas is the heart of this inviting English-style bed-and-breakfast. **Pros:** cozy antidote to nearby chain hotels; nice lounge and patio area; caring staff members. **Cons:** thin walls can make for noisy rooms; nearby streets can feel gritty at night. $\boxed{S}$ *Rooms from: $284* ⊠ *845 Bush St., Union Sq.* ☎ *415/775–1755, 800/999–9570* ⊕ *www. whiteswaninnsf.com* ⤳ *26 rooms* ❖O❙ *Breakfast* ✛ *4:E2.*

SOMA

$$$$
HOTEL
⬚ **Four Seasons Hotel San Francisco.** Occupying floors 5 through 17 of a skyscraper, the Four Seasons delivers subdued elegance in rooms with contemporary artwork, fine linens, floor-to-ceiling windows that overlook Yerba Buena Gardens or downtown, and bathrooms with deep soaking tubs and glass-enclosed showers. **Pros:** near museums, galleries, restaurants, shopping, and clubs; terrific fitness facilities; luxurious rooms and amenities. **Cons:** pricey; rooms can feel sterile. $\boxed{S}$ *Rooms from: $525* ⊠ *757 Market St., SoMa* ☎ *415/633–3000, 800/332–3442, 800/819–5053* ⊕ *www.fourseasons.com/sanfrancisco* ⤳ *277 rooms* ❖O❙ *No meals* ✛ *4:H4.*

$$$
HOTEL
⬚ **Hotel Zelos San Francisco.** A high-style haven on the top five floors of the green-tiled 1907 Pacific Place Building, the Zelos offers a luxurious oasis above the busiest part of town, with spacious rooms decked out in muted alligator-pattern carpeting, bold taupe-and-cream striped drapes, and sleek furniture echoing a 1930s sensibility. **Pros:** snappy design; convenient to public transit including cable cars; in-room spa service. **Cons:** rates soar during large conventions; too much of a scene for some guests; some rooms have no street views. $\boxed{S}$ *Rooms from: $270* ⊠ *12 4th St., SoMa* ☎ *415/348–1111, 888/459–3303* ⊕ *hotelzelos.com* ⤳ *202 rooms* ❖O❙ *No meals* ✛ *4:G5.*

$$$
HOTEL
Fodor's Choice
★
⬚ **Hotel Zetta San Francisco.** With a playful lobby lounge, the London-style Cavalier brasserie, and slick-yet-homey tech-friendly rooms, this trendy redo behind a stately 1913 neoclassical facade is a leader in the SoMa hotel scene. **Pros:** tech amenities and arty design; fine restaurant and lounge; noteworthy fitness center. **Cons:** lots of hubbub and traffic; no bathtubs; aesthetic mildly too frenetic for some guests. $\boxed{S}$ *Rooms from: $289* ⊠ *55 5th St., SoMa* ☎ *415/543–8555* ⊕ *hotelzetta.com* ⤳ *116 rooms* ❖O❙ *No meals* ✛ *4:F6.*

$$$
HOTEL
⬚ **InterContinental San Francisco.** The arctic-blue glass exterior and subdued, Zen-like lobby may mimic an airport concourse, but it's merely a prelude to expansive, spectacularly thought-out guest rooms supplied with all the ultramodern conveniences sophisticated travelers expect. **Pros:** well-equipped gym; near Moscone Center; destination restaurant. **Cons:** decor short on character; borders a rough neighborhood; a few blocks off the major tourist path. $\boxed{S}$ *Rooms from: $269* ⊠ *888 Howard St., SoMa* ☎ *415/616–6500, 866/781–2364* ⊕ *www.intercontinental-sanfrancisco.com* ⤳ *550 rooms* ❖O❙ *No meals* ✛ *4:H6.*

$ HOTEL **The Mosser Hotel.** A compatible pairing of contemporary decor and original 1913 architectural elements entices a budget-minded clientele to this family-owned eight-floor hotel just south of Market Street. **Pros:** convenient, lively location; lowest-priced rooms a bargain for downtown; music-themed rooms. **Cons:** some rooms share a bath; coffee, tea, and muffins served free in morning but no breakfast; service can be brusque. [$] *Rooms from: $129* ✉ *54 4th St., SoMa* ☎ *415/986–4400, 800/227–3804* 🌐 *www.themosser.com* 🛏 *166 rooms* 🍴 *No meals* ⊕ 4:G5.

$$$$ HOTEL **Palace Hotel, San Francisco.** When it opened in 1875, the Palace was the world's largest and most luxurious hotel, but it needed to be completely rebuilt after the 1906 earthquake and fire. **Pros:** oozes history; well-trained staff; state-of-the-art fitness center and indoor lap pool. **Cons:** smallish rooms with even smaller baths; west-facing rooms can be warm and stuffy; street noise (ask for an upper-floor room). [$] *Rooms from: $399* ✉ *2 New Montgomery St., SoMa* ☎ *415/512–1111, 888/627–7196* 🌐 *www.sfpalace.com* 🛏 *566 rooms* 🍴 *No meals* ⊕ 1:E5.

14

$$$$ HOTEL **San Francisco Marriott Marquis.** The distinctive design of the 40-story Marriott has been compared to a parking meter and a jukebox, but the guest rooms, decorated in tasteful neutrals, satisfy the business set with ergonomic chairs, wide desks, and a host of technological amenities. **Pros:** stunning views from upper-floor rooms; in the cultural district; staffed full-service business center. **Cons:** pricey parking; frenetic lobby; rooms fill quickly during conferences. [$] *Rooms from: $352* ✉ *780 Mission St., SoMa* ☎ *415/896–1600, 888/236–2427* 🌐 *www.marriott.com/sfodt* 🛏 *1,500 rooms* 🍴 *No meals* ⊕ 4:H5.

$$$$ HOTEL Fodor's Choice ★ **The St. Regis San Francisco.** Across from Yerba Buena Gardens and SFMOMA, the luxurious and modern St. Regis is favored by celebrities such as Lady Gaga and Al Gore. **Pros:** excellent views; stunning lap pool; luxe spa. **Cons:** expensive rates; small front-desk area; cramped space for passenger unloading. [$] *Rooms from: $358* ✉ *125 3rd St., SoMa* ☎ *415/284–4000* 🌐 *www.stregis.com/sanfrancisco* 🛏 *260 rooms* 🍴 *No meals* ⊕ 1:E6.

$$$ HOTEL FAMILY **W San Francisco.** Chic, urban, and compact, the W's colorful guest rooms come with such homey comforts as upholstered window seats, pillow-top mattresses, goose-down comforters and pillows, and sleek baths. **Pros:** sophisticated digs; in the heart of the cultural district; Bliss spa and fitness center. **Cons:** on-the-go vibe not for everyone; at a busy intersection; area's street people unsettle some guests. [$] *Rooms from: $314* ✉ *181 3rd St., SoMa* ☎ *415/777–5300* 🌐 *www.wsanfrancisco.com* 🛏 *404 rooms* 🍴 *No meals* ⊕ 1:E6.

THE TENDERLOIN

$$ HOTEL **Phoenix Hotel.** A magnet for the boho crowd, the Phoenix is retro and low-key, with bamboo furniture, white bedspreads, and original pieces by local artists, as well as modern amenities like iHome docking stations. **Pros:** mellow staffers set boho tone; cheeky design, hip restaurant/bar; free parking. **Cons:** somewhat seedy location; no elevators; can be loud in the evenings. [$] *Rooms from: $249* ✉ *601 Eddy St., Tenderloin* ☎ *415/776–1380, 800/248–9466* 🌐 *www.thephoenixhotel.com* 🛏 *44 rooms* 🍴 *Breakfast* ⊕ 4:A6.

HAYES VALLEY

$ 🖵 **Hayes Valley Inn.** Offering "European charm in the heart of Hayes Val-
B&B/INN ley," the modest, clean rooms of this hotel come with sinks and vanities; a couple of spotless shared bathrooms are down the hall. **Pros:** inexpensive; free Wi-Fi; close to shopping, restaurants, and theater. **Cons:** no in-room bathrooms; no elevator; some street noise. $ *Rooms from: $129 ✉ 417 Gough St., Hayes Valley* ☎ *415/431–9131, 800/930–7999* ⊕ *www.hayesvalleyinn.com* ⇱ *28 rooms* ❑ *Breakfast* ✛ 3:E2.

$$ 🖵 **Inn at the Opera.** Within walking distance of Davies Symphony Hall
B&B/INN and the War Memorial Opera House, these small rooms with dark wood furnishings cater to season-ticket holders for the opera, ballet, and symphony; they've also been the choice for stars of the music, dance, and opera worlds, from Luciano Pavarotti to Mikhail Barysh-nikov. **Pros:** staff goes the extra mile; intimate restaurant. **Cons:** smallish rooms and bath; sold out far in advance during opera season; so-so neighborhood, difficult parking. $ *Rooms from: $229 ✉ 333 Fulton St., Hayes Valley* ☎ *415/863–8400, 800/325–2708* ⊕ *www.shellhospitality. com/inn-at-the-opera* ⇱ *48 rooms* ❑ *Breakfast* ✛ 3:E2.

$ 🖵 **Metro Hotel.** These tiny rooms, with simple yet modern decor and
HOTEL equipped with private, if small, bathrooms, are within walking distance
Fodor's Choice to the lively Haight, Hayes Valley, Panhandle, NoPa, and Castro neigh-
★ borhoods. **Pros:** can't beat the price; out-of-downtown location; friendly staffers. **Cons:** small rooms and bathrooms; street noise; only difficult street parking available. $ *Rooms from: $107 ✉ 319 Divisadero St., Hayes Valley* ☎ *415/861–5364* ⊕ *www.metrohotelsf.com* ⇱ *24 rooms* ❑ *No meals* ✛ 3:B3.

$$ 🖵 **The Parsonage.** The two owners of this 1883 Victorian, a National
B&B/INN Historic Landmark, have created a one-of-a-kind bed-and-breakfast
Fodor's Choice steps from the lower Haight and Hayes Valley, with many of the original
★ mantlepieces, fireplaces, and mirrors, and ornate ceiling molding still intact. **Pros:** step back in time and sleep on antique beds; outstanding breakfast; innkeepers treat visitors like houseguests. **Cons:** street parking only; bygone-era feel not for everyone; guests with allergies may not appreciate presence of resident dog. $ *Rooms from: $240 ✉ 198 Haight St., Hayes Valley* ☎ *415/863–3699* ⊕ *www.theparsonage.com* ⇱ *5 rooms* ❑ *Breakfast* ✛ 3:E3.

NOB HILL

$$$$ 🖵 **Fairmont San Francisco.** Dominating the top of Nob Hill like a Euro-
HOTEL pean palace, the Fairmont indulges guests in luxury—rooms in the main building, adorned in sapphire blues with platinum and pewter accents, have high ceilings, decadent beds, and marble bathrooms; rooms in the newer Tower, many with fine views, have a neutral color palette with bright-silver notes. **Pros:** huge bathrooms; stunning lobby; great location. **Cons:** some older rooms are small; hills can be challenging for those on foot. $ *Rooms from: $459 ✉ 950 Mason St., Nob Hill* ☎ *415/772–5000, 800/257–7544* ⊕ *www.fairmont.com/san-francisco* ⇱ *592 rooms* ❑ *No meals* ✛ 4:E1.

$$ HOTEL **Hotel Vertigo.** Scenes in Alfred Hitchcock's classic thriller *Vertigo* were shot in this ornate hotel (it was a speakeasy during Prohibition), and designer Thomas Schoos has infused the guest rooms with a reckless, whimsical tribute—consider the tangerine highlights and the horse-head lamps, not to mention the classic *Vertigo* swirl logo along the walls. **Pros:** tons of personality; artsy decor. **Cons:** borderline neighborhood; no air-conditioning. [$] *Rooms from: $229* ✉ *940 Sutter St., between Leavenworth and Hyde Sts., Nob Hill* ☎ *415/885–6800, 800/553–1900* 🌐 *www.hotelvertigosf.com* 🛏 *110 rooms* 🍴 *No meals* ✛ 4:B3.

$$$ HOTEL **InterContinental Mark Hopkins.** The circular redbrick drive of this towering 1926 architectural landmark leads to an opulent, mirrored, marble-floor lobby that's the gateway to luxurious rooms aglow with gold, cream, and yellow tones. **Pros:** spectacular views; steeped in history; last-minute deals often possible online. **Cons:** decor too old-style for some guests; small bathrooms in some rooms and suites; steep climb from Union Square. [$] *Rooms from: $299* ✉ *1 Nob Hill, Nob Hill* ☎ *415/392–3434, 800/662–4455* 🌐 *www.intercontinentalmarkhopkins.com* 🛏 *380 rooms* 🍴 *No meals* ✛ 4:E1.

14

$$$$ HOTEL Fodor's Choice ★ **Ritz-Carlton, San Francisco.** A tribute to beauty and attentive, professional service, the Ritz-Carlton emphasizes luxury and elegance, which is evident in the Ionic columns that grace the neoclassical facade and the crystal chandeliers that illuminate marble floors and walls in the lobby. **Pros:** terrific service; beautiful surroundings; Parallel 37 restaurant and Lobby Lounge. **Cons:** expensive; hilly location; no pool. [$] *Rooms from: $570* ✉ *600 Stockton St., at California St., Nob Hill* ☎ *415/296–7465, 800/542–8680* 🌐 *www.ritzcarlton.com/sanfrancisco* 🛏 *336 rooms* 🍴 *No meals* ✛ 4:F1.

$$$ HOTEL Fodor's Choice ★ **The Scarlet Huntington Hotel.** Stars from Bogart and Bacall to Picasso and Pavarotti have stayed in this hotel famed for its spacious high-ceilinged rooms and suites, most of which have great views of Grace Cathedral and Huntington Park or the bay and the fog rolling across the city skyline. **Pros:** spacious rooms; first-rate spa with city views; impressive service from greeting to farewell. **Cons:** up a steep hill from downtown; expensive restaurant; ultracontemporary aesthetic doesn't work for some guests. [$] *Rooms from: $329* ✉ *1075 California St., Nob Hill* ☎ *415/474–5400, 800/227–4683* 🌐 *www.thescarlethotels.com/sf* 🛏 *134 rooms* 🍴 *No meals* ✛ 4:D1.

$$$ HOTEL **Stanford Court San Francisco.** Railroad baron Leland Stanford's mansion once stood where the Stanford is today, and the warm tones and handsome leather chairs are reminiscent of a grander time. **Pros:** attention to technological detail; classic yet modern; off-season packages. **Cons:** up a steep hill from Union Square and Financial District; many rooms are small. [$] *Rooms from: $300* ✉ *905 California St., Nob Hill* ☎ *415/989–3500* 🌐 *www.stanfordcourt.com* 🛏 *393 rooms* 🍴 *No meals* ✛ 4:F1.

NORTH BEACH

$$ HOTEL FAMILY **Columbus Motor Inn.** Close to Chinatown and Fisherman's Wharf, this affordable lodging is a great pick if you have a family and a car to park. **Pros:** free parking; affordable rooms deep-cleaned every three months; lively location. **Cons:** lacks amenities; decor is not stylish; street-facing

accommodations can be noisy. $ *Rooms from: $188* ⊠ *1075 Columbus Ave., North Beach* ☎ *415/885–1492* ⊕ *www.columbusmotorinn.com* ⌁ *45 rooms* ⋮○⋮ *No meals* ✛ *1:B2.*

$$
HOTEL

⌂ **Hotel Bohème.** This small hotel in historic North Beach takes you back in time with cast-iron beds, large mirrored armoires, and memorabilia recalling the Beat generation—whose leading light, Allen Ginsberg, often stayed here (legend has it that in his later years he could be seen sitting in a window, typing away on his typewriter). **Pros:** North Beach location with literary pedigree; stylish rooms; helpful staff. **Cons:** street parking is scarce; no air-conditioning; small rooms. $ *Rooms from: $195* ⊠ *444 Columbus Ave., North Beach* ☎ *415/433–9111* ⊕ *www.hotelboheme.com* ⌁ *15 rooms* ⋮○⋮ *No meals* ✛ *1:D3.*

$
HOTEL
Fodor's Choice
★

⌂ **San Remo Hotel.** A few blocks from Fisherman's Wharf, this three-story 1906 Italianate Victorian—once home to longshoremen and Beat poets—has a narrow stairway from the street leading to the front desk and labyrinthine hallways. **Pros:** inexpensive rates; free Wi-Fi; rooftop penthouse (reserve way ahead) has private deck with Coit Tower views. **Cons:** some rooms are dark; only the penthouse suite has a private bath; parking (discounted fee) is off-site. $ *Rooms from: $119* ⊠ *2237 Mason St., North Beach* ☎ *415/776–8688, 800/352–7366* ⊕ *www.san-remohotel.com* ▭ *No credit cards* ⊗ *64 rooms* ⋮○⋮ *No meals* ✛ *1:C2.*

$$
B&B/INN

⌂ **Washington Square Inn.** Surrounded by fine shops and cafés, this inn overlooks North Beach's tree-lined Washington Square Park. **Pros:** central location with many restaurants nearby; reasonable (off-site) parking fees; free Wi-Fi, local calls, and afternoon tea, wine, and hors d'oeuvres. **Cons:** no air-conditioning; some rooms are small; old-style decor. $ *Rooms from: $224* ⊠ *1660 Stockton St., at Filbert St., North Beach* ☎ *415/981–4220, 800/388–0220* ⊕ *www.wsisf.com* ⌁ *15 rooms* ⋮○⋮ *Breakfast* ✛ *1:D2.*

THE WATERFRONT

FISHERMAN'S WHARF

$$$
HOTEL
FAMILY
Fodor's Choice
★

⌂ **Argonaut Hotel.** The Argonaut's spacious guest rooms have exposed-brick walls, wood-beam ceilings, and best of all, windows that open to the sea air and the sounds of the waterfront; many rooms enjoy Alcatraz and Golden Gate Bridge views. **Pros:** bay views; near Hyde Street cable car; toys for the kids. **Cons:** nautical theme isn't for everyone; cramped public areas; far from crosstown attractions. $ *Rooms from: $269* ⊠ *495 Jefferson St., at Hyde St., Fisherman's Wharf* ☎ *415/563–0800, 866/415–0704* ⊕ *www.argonauthotel.com* ⌁ *252 rooms* ⋮○⋮ *No meals* ✛ *1:A1.*

$$$$
RENTAL
FAMILY

⌂ **Fairmont Heritage Place, Ghirardelli Square.** Located in the former Ghirardelli chocolate factory, one- to-three-bedroom apartments deliver comfort and style, with fully equipped gourmet kitchens, brick walls, plush bedding, laundry facilities, modern furniture in chocolate and lavender hues, and views of Alcatraz and the bay. **Pros:** luxurious and historic; gigantic apartments with many amenities; bay views from most accommodations. **Cons:** a bit of a trek from downtown; expensive; limited food and beverage service. $ *Rooms from: $1,100* ⊠ *950 N. Point St., Fisherman's Wharf* ☎ *415/268–9900* ⊕ *www.fairmont.com/ghirardelli* ⌁ *53 rooms* ⋮○⋮ *Breakfast* ✛ *1:A1.*

$$$ HOTEL FAMILY **Hotel Zephyr.** Directly facing Alcatraz with unobstructed bay and prison vistas, this block-long Fisherman's Wharf hotel pays edgy but playful tribute to San Francisco's shipyard past. **Pros:** lively decor and views; indoor game room and The Yard outdoor "adult playground"; The Camper grab-and-go food option. **Cons:** touristy area; expensive parking; some housekeeping lapses. [$] *Rooms from: $269* ✉ *250 Beach St., Fisherman's Wharf* ☎ *415/617–6555, 844/617–6555* 🌐 *www.hotelzephyrsf.com* 🛏 *361 rooms* 🍴 *No meals* ✣ 1:C1.

$$$ HOTEL **Hotel Zoe Fisherman's Wharf.** Multimillion-dollar renovations in 2017 transformed the dowdy former Best Western Tuscan into a smart-looking boutique hotel with guest-room interiors inspired by luxury Mediterranean yachts. **Pros:** cozy feeling; steps from Fisherman's Wharf; smart-looking contemporary design. **Cons:** congested touristy area; small rooms. [$] *Rooms from: $279* ✉ *425 N. Point St., at Mason St., Fisherman's Wharf* ☎ *415/561–1100, 800/648–4626* 🌐 *www.hotelzoesf.com* 💳 *No credit cards* 🛏 *221 rooms* 🍴 *No meals* ✣ 1:C1.

$$$ HOTEL FAMILY **Sheraton Fisherman's Wharf Hotel.** It might not look like much from the street, but from the fire pits lining the parking area to the lobby's mood lighting, this Sheraton is one festive gal. **Pros:** in the heart of Fisherman's Wharf; fun colors; outdoor pool. **Cons:** touristy area; feels corporate despite festive atmosphere; far from downtown and crosstown sights. [$] *Rooms from: $319* ✉ *2500 Mason St., Fisherman's Wharf* ☎ *415/362–5500, 888/627–7024* 🌐 *www.sheratonatthewharf.com* 🛏 *531 rooms* 🍴 *No meals* ✣ 1:C1.

EMBARCADERO

$$$ HOTEL **Harbor Court Hotel.** This Spanish Colonial Revival–style Embarcadero hotel was once an Army-Navy YMCA residence. **Pros:** convenient quiet location; friendly professional staffers; Bay Bridge and Ferry Building views from some rooms. **Cons:** many rooms are small given the rates; some rooms lack views; fee for amenities they don't require irks some guests. [$] *Rooms from: $275* ✉ *165 Steuart St., Embarcadero* ☎ *415/882–1300, 877/989–5861* 🌐 *www.harborcourthotel.com* 🛏 *131 rooms* 🍴 *No meals* ✣ 1:G5.

$$$$ HOTEL FAMILY Fodor's Choice ★ **Hotel Vitale.** The emphasis on luxury and upscale relaxation at this eight-story bay-front property is apparent in every thoughtful detail: little vases of lavender mounted outside each room; limestone-lined baths stocked with top-of-the-line products; the penthouse-level day spa with soaking tubs set in a rooftop bamboo forest. **Pros:** family-friendly studios; great waterfront views; penthouse spa. **Cons:** some rooms feel cramped; "urban fee" adds further expense to an already pricey property; only partial bay views from some rooms. [$] *Rooms from: $385* ✉ *8 Mission St., Embarcadero* ☎ *415/278–3700, 888/890–8688* 🌐 *www.hotelvitale.com* 🛏 *200 rooms* 🍴 *No meals* ✣ 1:G4.

$$$$ HOTEL **Hyatt Regency San Francisco.** This waterfront property's 17-story atrium lobby starred in several 1970s flicks, most notably the disaster epic *The Towering Inferno,* but the entire hotel is ready for new close-ups after a 2016 makeover. **Pros:** elegant design plus grand bay views; near restaurants, shopping, and the Ferry Building; even the smallest rooms a decent size. **Cons:** soaring room rates in high season; geared

toward business travelers; lacks intimacy. $ *Rooms from: $429* ⊠ *5 Embarcadero Center, Embarcadero* ☎ *415/788–1234, 800/233–1234* ⊕ *sanfranciscoregency.hyatt.com* ⊟ *No credit cards* ⟋ *804 rooms* ⦿ *No meals* ✛ *1:G4.*

FINANCIAL DISTRICT

$$$
HOTEL

⊤ **Galleria Park Hotel.** Though the Galleria Park's rooms are small, they provide all the technological amenities modern travelers require, and this green-certified hotel manages to be both hip and welcoming. **Pros:** convenient location one block from BART; friendly management; in-house Gaspar French brasserie. **Cons:** small rooms and bathrooms; city noise. $ *Rooms from: $339* ⊠ *191 Sutter St., Financial District* ☎ *415/781–3060, 800/792–9639* ⊕ *www.galleriapark.com* ⟋ *177 rooms* ⦿ *No meals* ✛ *4:H2.*

$$
HOTEL
FAMILY

⊤ **Hilton San Francisco Financial District.** Business travelers patronize this hoppin' Hilton for its airy guest rooms and large work desks, but even in high season the weekend rates drop significantly, luring leisure travelers. **Pros:** abundant parking; bay and city views; playground across the street. **Cons:** congested downtown area; rooms could use sprucing up; feels very corporate. $ *Rooms from: $229* ⊠ *750 Kearny St., Financial District* ☎ *415/433–6600* ⊕ *www.sanfranciscohiltonhotel.com* ⟋ *543 rooms* ⦿ *No meals* ✛ *1:D4.*

$$$
HOTEL

⊤ **Le Méridien San Francisco.** The stylishly contemporary Le Méridien scores well on both form and function, with compelling artworks and installations throughout the lobby and guest rooms outfitted with polished granite sinks, California-inspired photographs, and handy in-room safes with outlets for recharging electronic devices. **Pros:** spacious rooms, many with good views; interesting artwork throughout; accommodating staff. **Cons:** after dark this Financial District neighborhood grows sleepy; restaurant and bar merely okay; high rates during major conventions. $ *Rooms from: $258* ⊠ *333 Battery St., Financial District* ☎ *415/296–2900* ⊕ *www.lemeridien.com/ sanfrancisco* ⟋ *360 rooms* ⦿ *No meals* ✛ *1:E4.*

$$$$
HOTEL

⊤ **Loews Regency San Francisco.** Every room has spectacular city and bay views at this hotel, which occupies the top 11 floors in two towers of one of San Francisco's tallest buildings; glass-enclosed sky bridges with amazing vistas themselves connect the towers. **Pros:** spectacular "bridge-to-bridge" views; among the city's most comfortable beds; complimentary seasonal Saturday-at-sunset rooftop champagne toast. **Cons:** in a business area that's quiet at night and on weekends; pricey. $ *Rooms from: $449* ⊠ *222 Sansome St., Financial District* ☎ *415/276–9888, 844/271–6289* ⊕ *www.loewshotels.com/regency-san-francisco* ⟋ *155 rooms* ⦿ *No meals* ✛ *1:E4.*

$$$$
HOTEL
Fodor's Choice
★

⊤ **Omni San Francisco Hotel.** In a 1926 Florentine Renaissance–style structure that once housed banks and other financial enterprises, the Omni draws travelers seeking historical flavor and a downtown location. **Pros:** immaculate rooms; historical flavor; good weekend rates. **Cons:** weekday stays can be pricey; expensive restaurant; not much to do in immediate area at night and on weekends. $ *Rooms from: $355* ⊠ *500 California St., Financial District* ☎ *415/677–9494* ⊕ *www.omni-sanfrancisco.com* ⟋ *362 rooms* ⦿ *No meals* ✛ *1:E4.*

THE MARINA AND THE PRESIDIO

THE MARINA

$$ HOTEL FAMILY Fodor'sChoice ★ **Cow Hollow Motor Inn and Suites.** The suites at this modern motel resemble typical San Francisco apartments and are more spacious than average, featuring big living rooms, one or two bedrooms, hardwood floors, sitting and dining areas, marble wood-burning fireplaces, and fully equipped kitchens. **Pros:** free covered parking in building for one vehicle; good value and location especially for families; well-run sister properties nearby if this one full. **Cons:** congested neighborhood; standard rooms face a loud street; average decor. [$] *Rooms from: $195* ✉ *2190 Lombard St., Marina* ☎ *415/921–5800* 🌐 *www.cowhollowmotorinn.com* 🛏 *129 rooms* 🍴 *No meals* ✥ 2:E3.

$ HOTEL Fodor'sChoice ★ **Marina Motel.** Bougainvillea, fuchsia, and other foliage real and trompe l'oeil add color and verve to this 1939 motor court operated by the granddaughters of the original owners—when everything's in bloom and hummingbirds flit through the quiet courtyard the mood is magical. **Pros:** within walking distance of Marina District restaurants, bars, and shops; quiet courtyard rooms; a delight for the price. **Cons:** on a busy street; no air-conditioning (usually not a problem in the Marina). [$] *Rooms from: $149* ✉ *2576 Lombard St., Marina* ☎ *415/921–9406, 800/346–6118* 🌐 *www.marinamotel.com* 🛏 *39 rooms* 🍴 *No meals* ✥ 2:D3.

THE PRESIDIO

$$$ B&B/INN Fodor'sChoice ★ **The Inn at the Presidio.** Built in 1903 and opened as a hotel in 2012, this two-story, Georgian Revival–style structure once served as officers' quarters but now has 26 guest rooms—most of them suites—complete with gas fireplaces and modern-meets-salvage-store finds such as wrought-iron beds, historic black-and-white photos, and Pendleton blankets. **Pros:** Golden Gate Bridge views; away-from-it-all feeling yet still in the city; Presidio's hiking and biking trails, Disney museum, and other attractions. **Cons:** no on-site restaurant; no elevator; challenging to get a taxi; far from downtown attractions. [$] *Rooms from: $295* ✉ *42 Moraga Ave., Presidio* ☎ *415/800–7356* 🌐 *www.innatthepresidio.com* 🛏 *26 rooms* 🍴 *Breakfast* ✥ 2:A3.

$$ HOTEL **Travelodge at the Presidio San Francisco.** The tan-and-green Travelodge stands three stories tall near the Lombard Street entrance to the woodsy Presidio, and the beautifully manicured park of Lucasfilm's Letterman Digital Arts complex is just two blocks away. **Pros:** a block off Lombard, so less traffic noise than similar options; near public transportation and natural beauty; free parking and strong Wi-Fi. **Cons:** limited number of parking spaces; far from downtown attractions; room noise sometimes carries; no frills. [$] *Rooms from: $199* ✉ *2755 Lombard St., Presidio* ☎ *415/931–8581, 800/578–7878* 🌐 *www.travelodgepresidio.com* 🛏 *27 rooms* 🍴 *No meals* [M] ✥ 2:C3.

14

COW HOLLOW

$$ **Coventry Motor Inn.** Among the many motels on busy Lombard Street,
HOTEL   this is one of the cleanest and quietest, and the unusually spacious rooms have quality beds and well-lighted dining and work areas that make this a favorite for those looking for comfort without a hefty price tag. **Pros:** good value; free parking in building; spacious rooms. **Cons:** busy street; few amenities; far from downtown sights. $ *Rooms from: $158* ✉ *1901 Lombard St., Cow Hollow* ☎ *415/567–1200* ⊕ *www.coventrymotorinn.com* ⤴ *69 rooms* |○| *No meals* ✛ 2:F3.

$$ **Hotel Del Sol.** This beach-themed 1950s motor lodge is close to Fort
HOTEL   Mason, the Walt Disney Family Museum, Crissy Field, and Chestnut
FAMILY   Street's kids-oriented businesses, making it a great option for families. **Pros:** nearby places to eat and shop; heated pool; walk-in closets, docking stations. **Cons:** far from downtown; exterior walkways could use sprucing up; parking fee high for this area where there's often no charge. $ *Rooms from: $229* ✉ *3100 Webster St., Cow Hollow* ☎ *415/921–5520, 877/433–5765* ⊕ *www.jdvhotels.com/hotel-del-sol* ⤴ *57 rooms* |○| *Breakfast* ✛ 2:F3.

$$ **Union Street Inn.** Antiques, unique artwork, and such touches as
B&B/INN   candles, fresh flowers, wineglasses, and fine linens make rooms in this
Fodor's Choice   green-and-cream 1902 Edwardian popular with honeymooners and
★   those looking for a romantic getaway with an English countryside ambience. **Pros:** personal service; excellent full breakfast; romantic setting. **Cons:** parking is difficult; no air-conditioning; no elevator. $ *Rooms from: $249* ✉ *2229 Union St., Cow Hollow* ☎ *415/346–0424* ⊕ *www.unionstreetinn.com* ⤴ *6 rooms* |○| *Breakfast* ✛ 2:E3.

MISSION DISTRICT

$$ **The Inn San Francisco.** No other San Francisco bed-and-breakfast is
B&B/INN   as steeped in local lore as this Italianate Victorian mansion decked out in ornate poster beds, opulent Oriental rugs, and precious Victorian artifacts. **Pros:** charming antiques; location on city's sunny side; free street parking. **Cons:** neighborhood can be sketchy at night; some rooms are a tight squeeze; a couple of rooms lack a private bath. $ *Rooms from: $165* ✉ *943 S. Van Ness Ave., Mission District* ☎ *415/641–0188, 800/359–0913* ⊕ *www.innsf.com* ⤴ *21 rooms* |○| *Breakfast* ✛ 3:G6.

$$ **The Parker Guest House.** Two yellow 1909 Edwardian houses enchant
B&B/INN   travelers wanting an authentic San Francisco experience; dark hall-
Fodor's Choice   ways and steep staircases lead to bright earth-toned rooms with private
★   tiled baths (most with tubs), comfortable sitting areas, and cozy linens. **Pros:** handsome affordable rooms; just steps from Dolores Park and the vibrant Castro District on a Muni line; elaborate gardens. **Cons:** stairs can be challenging for those with limited mobility. $ *Rooms from: $179* ✉ *520 Church St., Mission District* ☎ *415/621–4139* ⊕ *parkerguesthouse.com* ⤴ *21 rooms* |○| *Breakfast* ✛ 3:D5.

PACIFIC HEIGHTS AND JAPANTOWN

PACIFIC HEIGHTS

$$$$
HOTEL
Fodor'sChoice
★
🏨 **Hotel Drisco.** Pretend you're a denizen of one of San Francisco's wealthiest residential neighborhoods while you stay at this understated, elegant 1903 Edwardian hotel. **Pros:** full renovation of property in 2017; great service and many amenities; quiet residential retreat. **Cons:** far from downtown (but free weekday-morning chauffeur service); room-rate uptick since renovation; on a steep hill. $ *Rooms from: $499* ✉ *2901 Pacific Ave., Pacific Heights* ☎ *415/346–2880, 800/634–7277* ⊕ *www.hoteldrisco.com* 🛏 *48 rooms* ⫿○⫿ *Breakfast* ✢ 2:D4.

$
HOTEL
🏨 **Hotel Majestic.** Open in 1902, the five-story Majestic is the city's oldest continually operating hotel; its elegant lobby is a graceful haven of antique chandeliers, plush Victorian chairs, and antiquarian French books. **Pros:** quintessential San Francisco hotel; spacious rooms; good rates for extended stays. **Cons:** bus ride or 20-minute walk to downtown; old style won't appeal to all guests; cramped entryway. $ *Rooms from: $135* ✉ *1500 Sutter St., Pacific Heights* ☎ *415/441–1100, 800/869–8966* ⊕ *www.thehotelmajestic.com* 🛏 *58 rooms* ⫿○⫿ *No meals* ✢ 2:H6.

$$
B&B/INN
🏨 **Jackson Court.** The bright and spacious rooms at this 1900 mansion—a combination bed-and-breakfast and time-share—contain a mix of antiques and contemporary furnishings; some even have fireplaces and window seats. **Pros:** pleasant residential area; games for rainy days; rooms are constantly refreshed. **Cons:** no air-conditioning; small and dated bathrooms; no tubs. $ *Rooms from: $239* ✉ *2198 Jackson St., Pacific Heights* ☎ *415/929–7670* ⊕ *www.jacksoncourt.com* 🛏 *10 rooms* ⫿○⫿ *Breakfast* ✢ 2:F4.

$$
HOTEL
FAMILY
🏨 **Laurel Inn.** The blue-and-tan facade of this small hotel, punctuated on two sides by garage entrances, hints at its 1963 motor-inn origins, yet the spacious rooms, renovated in 2017, feel modern. **Pros:** spacious; family- and pet-friendly rooms; fun design. **Cons:** no air-conditioning; quite a distance from downtown. $ *Rooms from: $209* ✉ *444 Presidio Ave., Pacific Heights* ☎ *415/567–8467, 800/552–8735* ⊕ *www.jdvhotels.com/hotels/california/san-francisco-hotels/laurel-inn* 🛏 *49 rooms* ⫿○⫿ *Breakfast* ✢ 2:C5.

$$
B&B/INN
🏨 **Queen Anne Hotel.** Built in the 1890s as a girls' finishing school, this Victorian mansion has a large parlor and guest rooms with such touches as painted cherub murals and, in some, wood-burning fireplaces. **Pros:** lots of character; free weekday car service. **Cons:** 20-minute walk to downtown; slightly dated feel; some guests complain of stuffy, airless rooms. $ *Rooms from: $249* ✉ *1590 Sutter St., Pacific Heights* ☎ *415/441–2828* ⊕ *www.queenanne.com* 🛏 *48 rooms* ⫿○⫿ *Breakfast* ✢ 2:G6.

JAPANTOWN

$$$
HOTEL
🏨 **Kimpton Buchanan Hotel.** Local designer Nicole Hollis created a mildly opulent apartmentlike feel in the Kimpton Buchanan's rooms and public areas. **Pros:** apartmentlike feel; away from downtown bustle yet still convenient; complimentary yoga mats in rooms, bicycles at front desk. **Cons:** too far from the action for some travelers; some perks Kimpton regulars expect not offered here; hallways could be brighter and

14

less somber in tone. $ *Rooms from: $298* ✉ *1800 Sutter St., Japantown* ☎ *415/921–4000, 855/454–4644* ⊕ *www.thebuchananhotel.com* ⊃ *131 rooms* ❘⊘❘ *No meals* ✛ 2:F6.

THE SUNSET

$$ ⌖ **Ocean Park Motel.** This 1930s art-deco motel lures families, dog lovers,
HOTEL surfers, and locals wanting to escape the hustle of the city and retreat to
FAMILY these quiet, spacious, wood-paneled rooms in the Outer Sunset neighborhood. **Pros:** free parking; kitchens in many rooms; quiet neighborhood. **Cons:** far from tourist sites and downtown; in a foggy part of town. $ *Rooms from: $165* ✉ *2690 46th Ave., Sunset* ☎ *415/566–7020* ⊕ *www.oceanparkmotel.com* ⊃ *25 rooms* ❘⊘❘ *No meals* ✛ 3:A6.

BY THE AIRPORT

Reasonably priced—and occasionally posh—digs can make this area a fine choice for budget seekers or travelers who disdain the urban bustle.

$ ⌖ **Aloft San Francisco Airport.** On the southern edge of SFO's runway, this
HOTEL Starwood-branded property has comfortable, compact rooms with triple-paned windows and blackout curtains that help diminish the noise. **Pros:** hip, affordable hotel; indoor heated pool; jogging trail. **Cons:** can be noisy; pricey for smallish rooms outside the city. $ *Rooms from: $149* ✉ *401 E. Millbrae Ave., Millbrae* ☎ *650/443–5500, 866/716–8143* ⊕ *www.aloftsanfranciscoairport.com* ⊃ *253 rooms* ❘⊘❘ *No meals* ✛ 3:H6.

$$ ⌖ **Bay Landing Hotel.** The European-country style of this airport hotel—
HOTEL think poster beds and heavy wooden furnishings—is pleasant enough, but the selling point is the bayfront address, promising unsurpassed views out of the double-paned windows. **Pros:** unsurpassed bayfront views; breakfast included in rate; weekend online specials. **Cons:** a trek from the city; decor feels a bit stuffy. $ *Rooms from: $209* ✉ *1550 Bayshore Hwy., Burlingame* ☎ *650/259–9000* ⊕ *www.baylandinghotel.com* ⊃ *133 rooms* ❘⊘❘ *Breakfast* ✛ 3:H6.

$$ ⌖ **Best Western El Rancho Inn and Suites.** Utilizing quintessential California
HOTEL landscaping standards like redwoods, bougainvilleas, and palms sets
FAMILY this well-maintained inn's exterior apart from its peers. **Pros:** affordable; outdoor pool; package to park at inn while traveling. **Cons:** Caltrain noise; 20-minute drive to San Francisco; dated decor. $ *Rooms from: $155* ✉ *1100 El Camino Real, Millbrae* ☎ *650/588–8500, 800/780–7234* ⊕ *www.elranchoinn.com* ⊃ *219 rooms* ❘⊘❘ *Breakfast* ✛ 3:H6.

$ ⌖ **Hyatt Regency San Francisco Airport.** Located 2 miles south of SFO,
HOTEL the Hyatt Regency is one of the largest airport convention hotels in Northern California, but the spectacular 10-story, 29,000-square-foot lobby atrium sets it apart for those seeking more than the typical business-center ambience. **Pros:** free transportation to Burlingame and SFO; heated outdoor pool and whirlpool; bay views from many rooms. **Cons:** driving into the city takes 20 or 30 minutes (more at rush hour); large convention hotel; sometimes lackluster service. $ *Rooms from: $129* ✉ *1333 Bayshore Hwy., Burlingame* ☎ *650/347–1234* ⊕ *www.sanfranciscoairport.hyatt.com* ⊃ *789 rooms* ❘⊘❘ *No meals* ✛ 3:H6.

PERFORMING
ARTS

Updated by
Jerry James
Stone

Sophisticated, offbeat, and often ahead of the curve, San Francisco's performing arts scene supports world-class opera, ballet, and theater productions, along with alternative-dance events, avant-garde plays, groundbreaking documentaries, and a slew of spoken-word and other literary happenings.

The heart of the mainstream theater district lies on or near Geary Street, mostly west of Union Square, though touring Broadway shows land a little farther afield at big houses like the Orpheum and Golden Gate. But theater can be found all over town. For a bit of culture shock, slip out to eclectic districts like the Mission or Haight, where smaller theater companies reside and short-run and one-night-only performances happen on a regular basis.

The city's opera house and symphony hall present the musical classics, and venues like the Fillmore and the Warfield host major rock and jazz talents, but the city's extensive festival circuit broadens the possibilities considerably. Stern Grove is the nation's oldest summer music festival that remains free to this day; Noise Pop is the premier alt-rock showcase putting such acts like Modest Mouse on the map; and Hardly Strictly Bluegrass is a beloved celebration of bluegrass, country, and roots music, attracting hundreds of thousands of attendees from all over the nation every year.

The range of offerings is just as eclectic on the film front. San Francisco moviegoers love blockbuster hits like everyone else, but they also champion little-known indie and art-house flicks and flock to the interactive sing-along musicals presented at Castro Theatre. Nearly every month an important film festival takes place. During warmer months, many of the city's parks host free movie nights outdoors showcasing film classics or pop-culture favorites.

San Francisco also has a rich dance scene, from classical dancers to jugglers. And it doesn't take stadium seating to make a performance space. Cafés, clubs, and bookstores often host poetry readings or author lectures.

PERFORMING ARTS PLANNER

TICKETS 101

The opera, symphony, the San Francisco Ballet's *The Nutcracker,* and touring hit musicals are often sold out in advance. Tickets are usually available for other shows within a day of the performance.

City Box Office. This charge-by-phone service sells tickets for many performances and lectures. You can also buy tickets online, or in person on weekdays from 9:30 to 5:30. ⌧ *180 Redwood St., Suite 100, off Van Ness Ave., between Golden Gate Ave. and McAllister St., Civic Center* ☎ *415/392–4400* ⊕ *www.cityboxoffice.com.*

San Francisco Performances. SFP brings an eclectic array of top-flight global music and dance talents to various venues—mostly the Yerba Buena Center for the Arts, Davies Symphony Hall, and Herbst Theatre. Artists have included Yo-Yo Ma, Edgar Meyer, the Paul Taylor Dance Company, and Midori. Tickets can be purchased in person through City Box Office, online, or by phone. ⌧ *500 Sutter St., Suite 710, Financial District* ☎ *415/392–2545* ⊕ *www.sfperformances.org.*

Tickets.com. You can charge tickets for everything from jazz concerts to Giants games by phone or online. ☎ *800/352–0212* ⊕ *www.tickets.com.*

TIX Bay Area. Half-price, same-day tickets for many local and touring shows go on sale (cash only) at the TIX booth in Union Square, which is open daily from 10 to 6. Discount purchases can also be made online. ⌧ *350 Powell St., at Geary St., Union Sq.* ☎ *415/433–7827* ⊕ *www.tixbayarea.org.*

LISTING INFORMATION

The best guide to the arts is printed in the "Datebook" section and the "96 Hours" section of the *San Francisco Chronicle* (⊕ *www.sfgate. com*). Also check out the city's free alternative weeklies, including *SF Weekly* (⊕ *sfweekly.com*) and the *San Francisco Bay Guardian* (⊕ *sfbg.com*).

Online, SF Station (⊕ *sfstation.com*) has a frequently updated arts and nightlife calendar. *San Francisco Arts Monthly* (⊕ *sfarts.org*), which is published at the end of the month, has arts features and events listings, plus a helpful "Visiting San Francisco?" section. For offbeat, emerging-artist performances, consult CounterPULSE (⊕ *counterpulse.org*).

DANCE

San Francisco has always been a hotbed of dance. Local groups such as Alonzo King's LINES Ballet tour extensively and are well regarded by national dance critics. And classical-ballet lovers won't be left out; the highly regarded San Francisco Ballet excels at both traditional and contemporary repertoires. **Dancers' Group** (⊕ *www.dancersgroup.org*) is a website with events and resource listings for dancers and dance aficionados. The Web-only **DanceView Times** (⊕ *www.danceviewtimes. com*) reviews productions and events.

Alonzo King LINES Ballet. Since 1982 this company has been staging the fluid and gorgeous ballets of choreographer and founder Alonzo King, sometimes in collaboration with top-notch world musicians such as Zakir Hussain and Hamza El Din. Ballets incorporate both classical and modern techniques, with experimental set design, costumes, and music. The San Francisco season is in spring. ⊠ *26 7th St., SoMa* ☏ *415/863–3040* ⊕ *www.linesballet.org.*

FAMILY **ODC/Dance.** Highly popular with kids, this 10-person dance troupe holds an annual Yuletide version of *The Velveteen Rabbit* (mid-November to mid-December), at the Yerba Buena Center for the Arts, that ranks among the city's best holiday-season performances. The group's main repertory season generally runs intermittently between January and June. ⊠ *351 Shotwell St., Mission District* ☏ *415/863–9834* ⊕ *www.odc.dance.*

RAWdance CONCEPT Series. A modern-day salon is made for both dance aficionados and those just ballet-curious. The semiregular series takes place in a small and awkward space, but it's perfect for making new friends. The choreography is colorful and "outside the lines" of your usual dance troupe. In true bohemian spirit, admission is pay-what-you-can, and sometimes food is served as well. ⊠ *105 Sanchez St., Haight* ☏ *415/686–0728* ⊕ *www.rawdance.org.*

Fodor's Choice ★ **San Francisco Ballet.** For ballet lovers, the nation's oldest professional company is reason alone to visit the Bay Area. SFB's performances, for the past three decades under the direction of Helgi Tomasson, have won critical raves. The primary season runs from February through May. The repertoire includes full-length ballets such as *Don Quixote* and *Sleeping Beauty*; the December presentation of *The Nutcracker* is truly spectacular. The company also performs bold new dances from star choreographers such as William Forsythe and Mark Morris, alongside modern classics by George Balanchine and Jerome Robbins. Tickets are available at the **War Memorial Opera House.** ⊠ *War Memorial Opera House, 301 Van Ness Ave., at Grove St., Civic Center* ☏ *415/865–2000* ⊕ *www.sfballet.org.*

FILM

Films of every stripe—3-D blockbusters, art-house indies, classic revivals—find an audience in the Bay Area. The Alamo Drafthouse and Kabuki Cinema are great spots for enjoying a cocktail (or meal) with your movie. Check out Filmnight in the Park for a BYOB type experience.

MOVIE THEATERS

Alamo Drafthouse Cinema. For a dinner and movie combo, visit this art-deco landmark theater, which features new American cuisine, craft beers, and a hip selection of films, including new releases, indie favorites, and cult classics. Be sure to save room for a boozy milk shake, like the Alpine Lift. ⊠ *2550 Mission St, at 21st St., Mission District* ☏ *415/549–5959* ⊕ *www.drafthouse.com/sf.*

Balboa Theatre. This historic theater, which just celebrated its 88th birthday, features a combination of classic movies, second-run hits, local documentaries, and art-house favorites. ⊠ *3630 Balboa St., at 37th St., Richmond* ☎ *415/221–8184* ⊕ *www.balboamovies.com.*

Fodor's Choice **Castro Theatre.** A large neon sign marks the exterior of this 1,400-plus-
★ seat art-deco movie palace whose exotic interior transports you back to 1922, when the theater first opened. High-profile festivals present films here, along with classic revivals and foreign flicks. There are a few cult-themed drag shows every month. ■ TIP➔ **Lines for the Castro's popular sing-along movie musicals often trail down the block.** ⊠ *429 Castro St., near Market St., Castro* ☎ *415/621–6120* ⊕ *www.castrotheatre.com.*

The Clay. This small but comfortable single-screen theater dates to 1910 and shows first-run art-house films. ⊠ *2261 Fillmore St., at Clay St., Pacific Heights* ☎ *415/561–9921.*

Embarcadero Center Cinemas. Shows often sell out at this extremely popular five-screen theater, which screens the best in first-run independent, art-house, and foreign films. ⊠ *1 Embarcadero Center, promenade level, Embarcadero* ☎ *415/352–0835.*

Roxie Theater. This is San Francisco's oldest continually operating theater, which turned 100 back in 2009. Film noir and indie features and documentaries, as well as first-run movies and classic foreign cinema, are the specialties. It's also home to the city's Noise Pop Festival. ■ TIP➔ **Monday nights are discounted.** ⊠ *3117 16th St., between Valencia and Guerrero Sts., Mission District* ☎ *415/863–1087* ⊕ *www.roxie.com.*

San Francisco Cinematheque. In the spotlight are experimental film and digital media. Cinematheque hosts screenings throughout the city, but most are at the Yerba Buena Center for the Arts. ⊠ *SoMa* ☎ *415/552–1990* ⊕ *www.sfcinematheque.org.*

Sundance Kabuki Cinema. Moviegoing here is a first-class experience. The seating is comfy and spaced out, and you can reserve your seat in advance online, so you don't need to arrive an hour early to snag one. The standard concession items are available, along with food options that are borderline gourmet. Beer and wine—which you can take into the theater!—are also served. Film screenings run the gamut from mainstream blockbusters to offbeat indies. ⊠ *1881 Post St., at Fillmore St., Japantown* ☎ *415/346–3243* ⊕ *www.sundancecinemas.com.*

FILM FESTIVALS

Area film festivals, especially the popular San Francisco International Film Festival, often attract sell-out crowds; many screenings feature Q&A sessions with directors and actors from around the world. Smaller niche events duplicate the format on a more intimate scale. During the summer months, you can even catch festival screenings outdoors in the city's many parks.

American Indian Film Festival. Presented by the American Indian Film Institute, this event has been based in San Francisco since 1977. Each November the festival takes over various venues, including the Palace of Fine Arts Theatre. ⊠ *San Francisco* ☎ *415/554–0525* ⊕ *www.aifisf.com.*

Film Night in the Park. One of the best times you can have watching a movie in San Francisco—and it's free—the Film Night in the Park is wildly popular. Put on by the San Francisco Neighborhood Theater Foundation, the event shows free films throughout the city from mid to late summer. Films like *The Graduate, JAWS 3 in 3D, Sixteen Candles,* and *Citizen Kane* are screened in outdoor spaces such as Union Square or Dolores Park. All shows begin at dusk. ■TIP➔ Bring a picnic, but chairs are not welcome. ✉ *San Francisco* ⊕ *www.sfntf.org.*

San Francisco CAAMFest. Asian and Asian-American cinema is the focus of this March festival, presented by the Center for Asian American Media (CAAM). The lineup includes feature and short films and videos—everything from animation to documentaries. ✉ *San Francisco* ☎ *415/863–0814* ⊕ *www.caamedia.org.*

San Francisco IndieFest & DocFest. This popular event presents a slate of movies that are defiantly out of the mainstream. IndieFest caters to a younger demographic and specializes in oddball fare rarely programmed at other festivals; DocFest performs the same service for documentaries that you won't find at the local multiplex. ✉ *San Francisco* ☎ *415/552–5580* ⊕ *www.sfindie.com.*

San Francisco International Film Festival. For two weeks at the end of spring, the San Francisco Film Society—which also sponsors year-round screenings and film series—takes over several theaters, including the Castro Theatre, the Sundance Kabuki Cinema, and Pacific Film Archive, to launch this festival. The event schedules about 300 films, documentaries, and videos from 50 countries; many are U.S. premieres. ✉ *San Francisco* ⊕ *www.sffs.org.*

San Francisco International LGBTQ Film Festival. The world's oldest and largest festival honoring gay and lesbian films takes place at various venues for two weeks in late June. ✉ *San Francisco* ☎ *415/703–8655* ⊕ *www.frameline.org/festival.*

San Francisco Jewish Film Festival. In late July and early August, the Castro Theatre and other Bay Area venues screen films as part of this event. Parties on the opening and closing nights of the festival celebrate the films and filmmakers. ✉ *San Francisco* ☎ *415/621–0556* ⊕ *www.jfi.org.*

MUSIC

San Francisco's symphony and opera perform in the Civic Center area, but musical ensembles can be found all over the Bay Area in smaller spaces, churches, museums, restaurants, and parks.

CONCERTS

42nd Street Moon. This group produces delightful "semistaged" concert performances of rare chestnuts from Broadway's golden age of musical theater, such as *L'il Abner* and *The Boys From Syracuse.* ✉ *Eureka Theatre, 215 Jackson St., Financial District* ☎ *415/255–8207* ⊕ *www.42ndstmoon.org.*

Eureka Theatre. The Eureka Theatre hosts most 42nd Street Moon shows. ⊠ *215 Jackson St., between Front and Battery Sts., Financial District* ☎ *415/788–7469* ⊕ *www.theeurekatheatre.com.*

Chanticleer. A Bay Area treasure, this all-male a-cappella ensemble stages lively and technically flawless performances that show off a repertoire ranging from sacred medieval music to show tunes to contemporary avant-garde works. ⊠ *San Francisco* ☎ *415/252–8589* ⊕ *www.chanticleer.org.*

Kronos Quartet. Twentieth-century works and a number of premieres make up the programs for this always entertaining, Grammy Award–winning string ensemble, which spends much of the year traveling throughout the United States and abroad. ⊠ *San Francisco* ⊕ *www. kronosquartet.org.*

Noontime Concerts at Old St. Mary's Cathedral. This Gothic Revival church, completed in 1872 and rebuilt after the 1906 earthquake, hosts a notable chamber-music series on Tuesday at 12:30. ⊠ *660 California St., Financial District* ☎ *415/777–3211* ⊕ *www.noontimeconcerts.org.*

Old First Concerts. The well-respected Friday-evening and Sunday-afternoon series includes chamber music, choral works, vocal soloists, new music, and jazz. ⊠ *Old First Presbyterian Church, 1751 Sacramento St., at Van Ness Ave., Polk Gulch* ☎ *415/474–1608* ⊕ *www.oldfirstconcerts.org.*

Fodor's Choice ★ **San Francisco Symphony.** One of America's top orchestras performs from September through May, with additional summer performances of light classical music and show tunes. The orchestra and its charismatic music director, Michael Tilson Thomas, known for his daring programming of 20th-century American works, often perform with soloists of the caliber of Andre Watts, Gil Shaham, and Renée Fleming. The symphony's adventurous projects include its collaboration with the heavy-metal band Metallica. ■TIP→ Deep discounts on tickets are often available through Travelzoo, Groupon, and other vendors. ⊠ *Davies Symphony Hall, 201 Van Ness Ave., at Grove St., Civic Center* ☎ *415/864–6000* ⊕ *www.sfsymphony.org.*

SFJAZZ Center. Jazz legends Branford Marsalis and Herbie Hancock have performed at the snazzy center, as have Rosanne Cash and world-music favorite Esperanza Spaulding. The sight lines and acoustics here impress. Shows often sell out quickly. ⊠ *201 Franklin St., Hayes Valley* ☎ *866/920–5299* ⊕ *www.sfjazz.org.*

MUSIC FESTIVALS

Hardly Strictly Bluegrass Festival. The city's top free music event, as well as one of the greatest gatherings for bluegrass, country, and roots music in the country, takes place in late September or early October. Roughly 50,000 fans turn out to see the likes of Willie Nelson, Emmylou Harris, Jimmie Dale Gilmore, and Del McCoury at Hellman Hollow (formerly Speedway Meadows) in Golden Gate Park. ⊠ *Hellman Hollow, Lindley & Marx Meadows in Golden Gate Park* ⊕ *www. hardlystrictlybluegrass.com.*

How Weird Street Faire. Home to 10-plus music stages, ranging from drum and bass to techno-pop, this music festival for up-and-coming DJs is part Mardis Gras, part Burning Man, and *all* San Francisco. ⊠ *Howard St., near 2nd St., SoMa* ⊕ *www.howweird.org.*

Noise Pop Festival. This weeklong festival in February or March is widely considered to be one of the country's top showcases for what's new in indie-pop and alt-rock and is held at Slim's, the Great American Music Hall, The Independent, and other cool clubs. Founded in 1993, the low-key festival has helped local fans discover such talented acts as Modest Mouse, Kristin Hersh, and Bettie Serveert. (Phone info about the event is best obtained by calling the individual venues.) ⊠ *San Francisco* ☎ *415/375–3370* ⊕ *www.noisepop.com.*

San Francisco Jazz Festival. Every year starting in October, concert halls, clubs, and churches throughout the city host this acclaimed two-week festival. The popular event, which got its start in 1983, has featured such big-name acts as Ornette Coleman, Sonny Rollins, and McCoy Tyner, as well as newer jazz stars like Brad Mehldau and Chris Botti. ⊠ *San Francisco* ☎ *866/920–5299* ⊕ *www.sfjazz.org.*

Fodor's Choice ★ **Stern Grove Festival.** The nation's oldest continual free summer music festival hosts Sunday-afternoon performances of symphony, opera, jazz, pop music, and dance. The amphitheater is in a beautiful eucalyptus grove, perfect for picnicking before the show. World-music favorites such as Ojos de Brujas, Seu Jorge, and Shuggie Otis get the massive crowds dancing. ■TIP➔ Shows generally start at 2 pm, but arrive hours earlier if you want to see the performances up close—and dress for cool weather, as the fog often rolls in. ⊠ *Sigmund Stern Grove, Sloat Blvd. at 19th Ave., Sunset* ☎ *415/252–6252* ⊕ *www.sterngrove.org.*

OPERA

Pocket Opera. A lively, modestly priced alternative to grand opera, this company's concert performances of popular and seldom-heard works are mostly in English. Offenbach's operettas are frequently on the bill during the season, which runs from February through July. Concerts are held at various locations, including the Legion of Honor. ⊠ *San Francisco* ☎ *415/972–8934* ⊕ *www.pocketopera.org.*

Fodor's Choice ★ **San Francisco Opera.** Founded in 1923, this internationally recognized organization has occupied the War Memorial Opera House since the building's completion in 1932. From September through January and June through July, the company presents a dozen or so operas. SF opera frequently collaborates with European companies and presents unconventional, sometimes edgy projects designed to attract younger audiences. Translations are projected above the stage during most non-English productions. ⊠ *War Memorial Opera House, 301 Van Ness Ave., at Grove St., Civic Center* ☎ *415/864–3330 tickets* ⊕ *www. sfopera.com* ☞ *Box office: 199 Grove St., at Van Ness Ave.; open Mon. 10–5, Tues.–Fri. 10–6.*

PERFORMING ARTS CENTERS

Fodor'sChoice ★ **War Memorial Opera House.** With its soaring vaulted ceilings and marble foyer, this elegant 3,146-seat venue, built in 1932, rivals the Old World theaters of Europe. Part of the San Francisco War Memorial and Performing Arts Center, which also includes Davies Symphony Hall and Herbst Theatre, this is the home of the San Francisco Opera and the San Francisco Ballet. ⊠ *301 Van Ness Ave., at Grove St., Civic Center* ☎ *415/621–6600* ⊕ *www.sfwmpac.org.*

Fodor'sChoice ★ **Yerba Buena Center for the Arts.** Across the street from the San Francisco Museum of Modern Art and abutting a lovely urban garden, this performing arts complex schedules interdisciplinary art exhibitions, touring and local dance troupes, music, film programs, and contemporary theater events. You can depend on the quality of the productions at Yerba Buena. Film buffs often come here to check out the San Francisco Cinematheque (*www.sfcinematheque.org*), which showcases experimental film and digital media. And dance enthusiasts can attend concerts by a roster of city companies that perform here, including Smuin Ballet/SF (*www.smuinballet.org*), ODC/San Francisco (*www. odcdance.org*), the Margaret Jenkins Dance Company (*www.mjdc.org*), and Alonzo King's Lines Ballet (*www.linesballet.org*). The Lamplighters (*www.lamplighters.org*), an alternative opera that specializes in Gilbert and Sullivan, also performs here. ⊠ *3rd and Howard Sts., SoMa* ☎ *415/978–2787* ⊕ *www.ybca.org.*

15

SPOKEN WORD AND READINGS

Aspiring and established writers, poets, and performers step up to the mike all over town and put their words and egos on the line. Check listings in the alternative weeklies or the *San Francisco Sunday Chronicle* (⊕ *www.sfgate.com*).

Cafe International. An open-mike session follows one or more featured readers here every Friday night at 8. Spoken-word performances are interspersed with acoustic musical acts. ⊠ *508 Haight St., at Fillmore St., Haight* ☎ *415/552–7390.*

Fodor'sChoice ★ **City Arts & Lectures.** Each year this program includes more than 20 fascinating conversations with writers, composers, actors, politicians, scientists, and others. The Nourse Theater, in the Performing Arts Center, is usually the venue. Past speakers have included Salman Rushdie, Ken Burns, and Linda Ronstadt. ⊠ *Nourse Theater, 275 Hayes St., Haight* ☎ *415/392–4400* ⊕ *www.cityarts.net.*

Commonwealth Club of California. The nation's oldest public-affairs forum hosts speakers as diverse as Erin Brockovich and Bill Gates; every president since Teddy Roosevelt has addressed the club. Topics range from culture and politics to economics and foreign policy. Events are open to nonmembers; contact the club for the current schedule of events. Venues vary by speaker. Lectures are broadcast on NPR. ⊠ *555 Post St, at Mason St., Financial District* ☎ *415/597–6700* ⊕ *www.commonwealthclub.org.*

West Coast Live. Billed as "San Francisco's Live Radio Show to the World," the program invites an audience to its weekly broadcasts, many from the San Francisco Ferry Building or the Freight & Salvage Coffeehouse in Berkeley. The eclectic guest list includes personalities such as Craig Newmark, Rita Moreno, Jamaica Kincaid, and Adam Savage and Jamie Hyneman (the *Mythbusters* guys). ⊠ *San Francisco* ☎ *415/664–9500* ⊕ *www.wcl.org.*

Writers with Drinks. This quirky, oft-madcap, and hilariously funny spoken-word event is part reading, part circus variety show. Writers range from unknowns to rising stars and the occasional well-known author. Writers with Drinks usually takes place at the Make-Out Room, at 3225 22nd Street in the Mission. ⊠ *Usually takes place at Make-Out Room, 3225 22nd St., Mission District* ⊕ *www.writerswithdrinks.com.*

THEATER

The three major commercial theaters—the Curran, Golden Gate, and Orpheum—are operated by the Shorenstein-Nederlander organization, which books touring plays and musicals, some before they open on Broadway. Theatre Bay Area (⊕ *www.theatrebayarea.org*) lists most Bay Area performances online.

American Conservatory Theater. One of the nation's leading regional theater companies presents about eight plays a year, from classics to contemporary works, often in repertory. The season runs from early fall to late spring. In December ACT stages a beloved version of Charles Dickens's *A Christmas Carol.* ⊠ *415 Geary St., Union Sq.* ☎ *415/749–2228* ⊕ *www.act-sf.org.*

Curran Theater. Fresh from a makeover, some of the biggest touring shows come to this local gem, which has hosted classical music, dance, and stage performances since its 1925 opening. Shows are of the long-running Broadway musical variety, such as *Stomp* and *Jersey Boys,* and the seasonal *A Christmas Carol.* ⊠ *445 Geary St., at Mason St., Union Sq.* ☎ *415/358–1220* ⊕ *www.sfcurran.com/.*

EXIT Theatre. *The* place for absurdist and experimental theater, this three-stage venue also presents the annual **Fringe Festival** in September. ⊠ *156 Eddy St., between Mason and Taylor Sts., Union Sq.* ☎ ⊕ *www.theexit.org.*

Golden Gate Theater. This stylishly refurbished movie theater is now primarily a musical house. Touring productions of popular Broadway shows and revivals are its mainstays. ⊠ *1 Taylor St., at Golden Gate Ave., Tenderloin* ☎ *888/746–1799* ⊕ *www.shnsf.com.*

Magic Theatre. Once Sam Shepard's favorite showcase, the pint-size Magic presents works by rising American playwrights such as Matthew Wells, Karen Hartman, and Claire Chafee. ⊠ *Fort Mason, Bldg. D, Laguna St. at Marina Blvd., Marina* ☎ *415/441–8822* ⊕ *www.magictheatre.org.*

The Marsh. Experimental works, including one-man and one-woman shows, works in progress, and new-vaudeville shows can be seen here. ⊠ *1062 Valencia St., at 22nd St., Mission District* ☎ *415/282–3055* ⊕ *www.themarsh.org.*

CLOSE UP

Arts and Culture Beyond the City

Although most folks from outlying areas drive *into* San Francisco to enjoy the performing arts, there are plenty of reasons to head *out* of the city.

FILM

Pacific Film Archive. Affiliated with the University of California, this theater screens a comprehensive mix of classics, American, and foreign films. ✉ 2155 Center St., at Oxford St., Berkeley ☎ 510/642–0808 ⊕ www.bampfa.org.

Paramount Theatre. The spectacular art-deco Paramount screens a few vintage flicks (*The Sting, Casablanca*) every month and presents live events. ✉ 2025 Broadway, near 19th St. BART station, Oakland ☎ 510/465–6400 ⊕ www.paramounttheatre.com.

MUSIC

Berkeley Symphony Orchestra. The Berkeley Symphony Orchestra rose to prominence under Kent Nagano's baton and continues to prosper with Joana Carneiro at the helm. The emphasis is on 20th-century composers. The orchestra plays a few concerts each year, in the University of California–Berkeley's Zellerbach Hall and elsewhere in Berkeley. ■TIP➜ The acoustics in Zellerbach Hall are poor; sit in the front or middle orchestra for the best sound. ☎ 510/841–2800 ⊕ www.berkeleysymphony.org.

Freight & Salvage Coffeehouse. Some of the most talented practitioners of folk, blues, Cajun, and bluegrass perform at the alcohol-free venue. ✉ 2020 Addison St., Berkeley ☎ 510/644–2020 ⊕ www.thefreight.org.

Yoshi's. This popular Oakland club is one of the nation's best jazz venues. ✉ 510 Embarcadero St., between Washington and Clay Sts., Oakland ☎ 510/238–9200 ⊕ www.yoshis.com.

THEATER

Berkeley Repertory Theatre. This Tony Award–winning group is the American Conservatory Theater's major rival for leadership among the region's resident professional companies. It performs an adventurous mix of classics and new plays from fall to spring in its theater complex, near BART's Downtown Berkeley Station. Parking is difficult, so arrive early if you're coming by car. ✉ 2025 Addison St., Berkeley ☎ 510/647–2949 ⊕ www.berkeleyrep.org.

Cal Performances. Held at various venues on the University of California–Berkeley campus from September through May, this popular series offers the Bay Area's most varied bill of internationally acclaimed artists in all disciplines. ☎ 510/642–9988 ⊕ www.calperformances.org.

15

New Conservatory Theatre Center. This three-stage complex hosts the annual **Pride Season,** focusing on contemporary gay- and lesbian-themed works, as well as other events, including educational plays for young people. ✉ *25 Van Ness Ave., between Fell and Oak Sts., Civic Center* ☎ *415/861–8972* ⊕ *www.nctcsf.org.*

FAMILY **New Pickle Circus.** The acrobatically inclined group generally performs at the Circus Center around Christmastime, with fire-breathing jugglers and high-flying trapeze artists. There are a few smaller productions in

San Francisco and the Bay Area throughout the year. ⊠ *755 Frederick St.* ☎ *415/759–8123* ⊕ *www.circuscenter.org.*

Orpheum Theater. The biggest touring shows, such as *Hamilton* and *The Lion King,* are performed at this gorgeously restored 2,500-seat venue. The theater, opened in 1926 as a vaudeville stage, is as much an attraction as the shows. It was modeled after the Spanish baroque palaces and is considered one of the most beautiful theaters in the world; the interior walls have ornate cathedral-like stonework, and the gilded plaster ceiling is perforated with tiny lights. ⊠ *1192 Market St., at Hyde St., Tenderloin* ☎ *888/746–1799* ⊕ *www.shnsf.com.*

FAMILY **San Francisco Mime Troupe.** The politically leftist, barbed satires of this Tony Award–winning troupe are hardly mime in the Marcel Marceau sense. The group performs afternoon musicals at area parks from the July 4 weekend through September, and taking one in is a perfect way to spend a sunny summer day. ⊠ *San Francisco* ☎ *415/285–1717* ⊕ *www.sfmt.org.*

Theatre Rhinoceros. Gay and lesbian performers and playwrights are showcased at various venues. ⊠ *1 Sansome St., Suite 3500, Financial District* ☎ *800/838–3006 tickets, 415/552–4100 offices* ⊕ *www. therhino.org.*

NIGHTLIFE

Updated by
Jerry James
Stone

After hours, the city's business folk and workers give way to costume-clad partygoers, hippies and hipsters, downtown divas, frat boys, and those who prefer something a little more clothing-optional. Downtown and the Financial District remain pretty serious even after dark, and Nob Hill is staid, though you can't beat views from penthouse lounges, the most famous being the Top of the Mark (Hopkins). Nearby North Beach is an even better starting point for an evening out.

Always lively, North Beach's options include family-friendly dining spots, historic bars from the city's bohemian past (among them Jack Kerouac's old haunts), and even comedy clubs where stars such as Robin Williams and Jay Leno cut their teeth. In SoMa there are plenty of places to catch a drink before a Giants game and brewpubs to celebrate in afterward. SoMa also hosts some of the hottest dance clubs, along with some saucy gay bars. While Union Square can be a bit trendy, even the swanky establishments have loosened things up in recent years.

Heading west to Hayes Valley, a more sophisticated crowd dabbles in the burgeoning "culinary cocktail movement." Up-and-coming singles gravitate north of here to Cow Hollow and the Marina. Polk Street was the gay mecca before the Castro and still hosts some wild bars, but things get downright outlandish in the Castro district. Indie hipsters of all persuasions populate the Mission and Haight districts by night. Keep in mind, though, that some of the best times San Francisco has to offer are off the beaten path. And a good party can still be found in even the sleepiest of neighborhoods, such as Bernal Heights and Dogpatch.

NIGHTLIFE PLANNER

HOURS

Sports bars and hotel bars tend to be open on Sundays, but others may be closed. A few establishments—especially wine bars and restaurant bars—also close on Monday. Last call is typically at 1:30 am; Financial District bars catering to the after-work crowd, however, may stop serving as early as 9 or 10 pm, and generally close by midnight at the latest. Bands and performers usually take the stage between 8 and 11 pm. A few after-hours clubs are open until 4 am or all night.

MONEY

While larger establishments will take everything from Visa to Apple Pay, payment options can vary by neighborhood. It's easy to get by on plastic in Union Square or the Marina, but the Castro and Mission are hard cash only.

LATE-NIGHT TRANSPORTATION

You're better off taking public transportation or taxis on weekend nights, unless you're heading downtown (Financial District or Union Square) and are willing to park in a lot. There's only street parking in North Beach, the Mission, Castro, and the Haight, and finding a spot can be practically impossible. Muni stops running between 1 am and 5 am but has its limited Owl Service on a few lines—including the K, N, L, 90, 91, 14, 24, 38, and 22—every 30 minutes. Service cuts have put a dent in frequency; check ⊕ *www.sfmuni.com* for current details. You can sometimes hail a taxi on the street in well-trodden nightlife locations like North Beach or the Mission, but you can also call for one (☎ *415/626–2345 Yellow Cab, 415/648–3181 Arrow*). The best option by far is booking a taxi with a smartphone-based app (⊕ *www.uber. com*, ⊕ *www.lyft.com*). ■TIP➔ Cabs in San Francisco are more expensive than in other areas of the United States; expect to pay at least $15 to get anywhere within the city. Keep in mind that BART service across the bay stops shortly after midnight.

LOCAL LISTINGS

Entertainment information is printed in the "Datebook" section and the more calendar-based "96 Hours" section of the *San Francisco Chronicle* (⊕ *www.sfgate.com*). Also consult any of the free alternative weeklies, notably the *SF Weekly* (⊕ *www.sfweekly.com*), which blurbs nightclubs and music, and the *San Francisco Bay Guardian* (⊕ *www. sfbg.com*), which lists neighborhood, avant-garde, and budget events. SF Station (⊕ *www.sfstation.com*; online only) has an up-to-date calendar of entertainment goings-on.

SMOKING

By law, bars and clubs are smoke-free, except for the very few that are staffed entirely by the owners.

TICKETS AND COVERS

The cover charge at smaller, less popular clubs ranges from $5 to $10, and credit cards are rarely accepted for this. Covers at larger venues may spike to $30, and tickets usually can be purchased through ⊕ *www.*

16

TOP 5 BARS

■ **Cliff House:** Granted, it's pricey and the interior is ho-hum, but huge picture windows with views of the rolling Pacific remind you why you came here in the first place.

■ **El Rio:** The perfect dive, with inexpensive drink specials, a stellar patio, and an ever-changing calendar of events (free oysters on Friday, salsa Sunday).

■ **Smuggler's Cove:** Despite the gaudy (and distracting) pirate theme, this joint serves superb cocktails.

Rum is king, with more than 200 different styles available.

■ **Vesuvio Café:** This is one of those rare bars with a fleet of regulars but is also a place that everyone knows about. It's in one of the most touristy parts of town, but still manages to be cool.

■ **Yield:** Planet-friendly wines and reclaimed decor, plus small plates using locally sourced ingredients are just a few reasons to visit this off-the-beaten-path wine bar.

tickets.com or ⊕ *www.ticketweb.com*. Bars often have covers for live music—usually $5 to $15.

WHAT TO WEAR

Except for a few skyline lounges, you're not expected to dress up. Still, San Franciscans are a stylish bunch. For women, dressed-up jeans with heels and cute tops are one popular uniform; for guys it's button-up shirts or designer tees and well-tailored jeans. Of course, stylish means a black designer outfit at one place and funky thrift-store togs at another, so you have to use your judgment.

UNION SQUARE AND CHINATOWN

UNION SQUARE

Known mostly for high-end shopping and the surrounding theater district, the square has its own share of nightlife. You'll find places pouring interesting cocktails, a good mix of locals and tourists, and nods to nightspots and eras past. PCH is the perfect stop for cocktails crafted from locally grown ingredients.

BARS

Harry Denton's Starlight Room. Forget low-key drinks—the only way to experience Harry Denton's is to go for a show. Cough up the cover charge and enjoy the opulent, over-the-top decor and entertainment (some of the best cover bands in the business, usually playing Top 40 hits from the '60s, '70s, and '80s). Velvet booths and romantic lighting help re-create the 1950s high life on the 21st floor of the Sir Francis Drake Hotel, and the small dance floor is packed on Friday and Saturday nights. Jackets are preferred for men. Call ahead—the room is sometimes closed for private events on weekdays. ⊠ *Sir Francis Drake Hotel, 450 Powell St., between Post and Sutter Sts., Union Sq.* ☎ *415/395–8595* ⊕ *www.starlightroomsf.com.*

Le Colonial. Down an easy-to-miss alley off Taylor Street is what appears to be a two-story plantation house in the center of the city. Without being kitschy, the top-floor bar successfully evokes French-colonial Vietnam, thanks to creaky wooden floors, Victorian sofas, a patio with potted palms, and tasty French-Vietnamese food and tropical cocktails. You'll find local jazz bands playing early in the week, but come the weekend this is a full-on DJ-driven dance party. When you arrive, sweep past the café tables and the hostess and head up the stairs to your left. ⊠ *20 Cosmo Pl., off Taylor St., between Post and Sutter Sts., Union Sq.* ☎ *415/931–3600* ⊕ *www.lecolonialsf.com.*

Pacific Cocktail Haven. PCH for short, this neighborhood hangout has taken over the space that once belonged to the Latin sensation Cantina. Having a convivial aura and industrial-chic decor, PCH hits all the right notes. Plus the well-chosen and unique ingredients mean there's a little something for everyone. And the glassware is as dazzling as the elixirs inside. ■ TIP➡ The must-try cocktail is the Oh Snap!, a concoction of gin, sugar snap peas, citrus, and absinthe. ⊠ *580 Sutter St., at Mason St., Union Sq.* ☎ *415/398–0195* ⊕ *www.pacificcocktailsf.com* ☉ *Closed Sun.*

Redwood Room. Opened in 1933 and updated by designer Philippe Starck in 2001, this lounge at the Clift Hotel is a San Francisco icon. The entire room, floor to ceiling, is paneled with the wood from a single redwood tree, giving the place a rich, monochromatic look. The gorgeous original art-deco sconces and chandeliers still hang, but bizarre video installations on plasma screens also adorn the walls. It's packed on weekend evenings after 10, when young scenesters swarm in; for maximum glamour, visit on a weeknight. ⊠ *Clift Hotel, 495 Geary St., at Taylor St., Union Sq.* ☎ *415/929–2372 for table reservations, 415/775–4700 for hotel* ⊕ *www.clifthotel.com.*

Romper Room. If you weren't of legal drinking age during the '80s, now's your chance to experience the era's ambience. The Romper Room, bubbling over with neon pink and leopard print, is a funky little bar and quasi-dance club located in the city's somewhat cookie-cutter and label-driven Union Square district. The cocktail menu is small and simple, but they guarantee you won't have to wait longer than 90 seconds to get one. ⊠ *25 Maiden La., at Kearny St., Union Sq.* ☎ *415/275–3418* ⊕ *www.romperroom.com.*

Slide. During Prohibition, one of the city's more notorious speakeasies was accessible only via a secret-wall passage and a 15-foot slide that whisked patrons into the basement "restaurant" known as Coffee Dan's (it wasn't really a restaurant). That space has been reclaimed, restored, and aptly renamed Slide. A swanky, modern version of its former self, the place still has a slide, though stairs are also available. On the weekends, DJs spin a mix of hip-hop, downtempo, and Rat Pack–era hits from a 1920s baby grand piano that has been converted to a DJ booth. Like similar-themed bars within the city, the facility is completely unmarked. ⊠ *430 Mason St., at Geary St., Union Sq.* ☎ *415/421–1916* ⊕ *www.slidesf.com.*

16

CHINATOWN

Chinatown's streets are fast-paced and teeming with people, which makes the district's famous alleyways so charming and welcoming. Away from the bustle (and the hustle), you'll find sake bars and beer pubs filled with locals and tourists.

GAY NIGHTLIFE

Bow Bow Cocktail Lounge. At this quirky, inclusive, divey karaoke bar, you can get your kicks performing in front of a sometimes rowdy but nearly always supportive audience of hip young things and Asian businessmen. ⊠ *1155 Grant Ave., near Broadway, Chinatown* ☎ *415/421–6730.*

SOMA AND CIVIC CENTER

SOMA

In modern, industrial SoMa you'll find everyone from loyal Giants fans celebrating with locally made brews at 21st Amendment to the gay biker crowd that explodes onto the patio of the Lone Star Saloon, with everyone else apt to wind up at one of The Stud's diverse dance parties. The headliners head to Slim's or the DNA Lounge.

BARS

21st Amendment Brewery. This popular brewery is known for its range of beer types, with multiple taps going at all times. In the spring, the Hell or High Watermelon—a wheat beer—gets rave reviews. ■ TIP→ Serious beer drinkers should try the Back in Black, a black IPA-style beer this brewpub helped pioneer. The space has an upmarket warehouse feel, though exposed wooden ceiling beams, framed photos, whitewashed brick walls, and hardwood floors make it feel cozy. It's a good spot to warm up before a Giants game and an even better place to party after they win. ⊠ *563 2nd St., between Federal and Brannan Sts., SoMa* ☎ *415/369–0900* ⊕ *www.21st-amendment.com.*

City Beer Store. Called CBS by locals, this friendly tasting room cum liquor mart has a wine-bar's sensibility. Perfect for connoisseurs and the merely beer curious, CBS stocks more than 300 different bottled beers, and more than a dozen are on tap. The indecisive can mix and match six-packs to go. ■ TIP→ Come early: The small space fills up quickly on event nights. ⊠ *1168 Folsom St., at 8th St., SoMa* ☎ *415/503–1033* ⊕ *www.citybeerstore.com.*

MoMo's. This stylish American restaurant and trendy bar has an outdoor patio perfect for sunny days; it's the most popular pre- and postgame bar. The individual pizzas are tasty—and big enough to share. ⊠ *760 2nd St., at King St., SoMa* ☎ *415/227–8660* ⊕ *www.sfmomos.com.*

Terroir. The focus at this quaint wine bar is on natural (and mostly Old World) vintages, though it's not impossible to find local offerings, too. And while the space may be small, the selection is not: more than 700 different wines, stacked literally to the ceiling, compete for your attention. Don't let the owners' French accents intimidate you: the staff here is helpful. Terroir serves a small selection of artisanal cheeses and charcuterie to pair with the wines. ■TIP➔ Go on a weekday and head to the candlelit loft above the bar. It's the best seat in the house. ⊠ *1116 Folsom St., at 7th St., SoMa* ☎ *415/558–9946* ⊕ *www.terroirsf.com.*

Thirsty Bear. This eco-friendly brewpub is the perfect pit stop for those on a budget who don't want to compromise. Thirsty Bear is the only certified organic brewery within the city limits, and the beers here are handcrafted variations on traditional styles. ■TIP➔ If you can't decide which beer to start with, sample all on tap. The bar's tapas menu features seasonal meats and produce (mostly local) and sustainably harvested seafood. The upstairs pool hall is ideal for large groups. ⊠ *661 Howard St., at Hawthorne St., SoMa* ☎ *415/974–0905* ⊕ *www.thirstybear.com.*

View Lounge. Art-deco-influenced floor-to-ceiling windows frame superb views on the 39th floor of the San Francisco Marriott. You won't feel out of place here just getting a drink or two rather than dinner. It can get crowded here on weekends. ⊠ *San Francisco Marriott, 780 Mission St., between Mission and Market Sts., SoMa* ☎ *415/442-6003* ⊕ *sfviewlounge.com.*

CABARET

AsiaSF. Saucy, sexy, and fun, this is one of the hottest places in town for a drag-show virgin. The entertainment, as well as gracious food service, is provided by some of the city's most gorgeous "gender illusionists," who strut in impossibly high heels on top of the catwalk bar, vamping to tunes like "Cabaret" and "Big Spender." The creative Asian-influenced cuisine is surprisingly good. ■TIP➔ Go on a weekday to avoid the bachelorette parties. Make reservations, or risk being turned away. Oh, and bring a camera. ⊠ *201 9th St., at Howard St., SoMa* ☎ *415/255–2742* ⊕ *www.asiasf.com.*

DANCE CLUBS

111 Minna Gallery. Gallery by day, bar–dance club by night, this warehouse space on a small side street just south of Mission Street is usually full of hipsters and artsy youngsters. Dance events typically take place on Fridays and Saturdays from 9 pm until 2 am, though the bar opens around 5. ⊠ *111 Minna St., between 2nd and New Montgomery Sts., SoMa* ☎ *415/974–1719* ⊕ *www.111minnagallery.com* ☉ *Gallery closed weekends.*

DNA Lounge. The music changes nightly at the venerable DNA Lounge, and one of the highlights is **Bootie.** Every Saturday night, this popular mash-up unites hard-core and indie rockers, hip-hop devotees, and emo fans. Three bars and dance floors on two levels mean that DNA is rarely uncomfortably crowded. ■TIP➔ The action spills into the pizza joint next door, so you don't have to stop dancing if you suddenly get hungry. ⊠ *375 11th St., between Harrison and Folsom Sts., SoMa* ☎ *415/626–1409* ⊕ *www.dnalounge.com.*

The EndUp. Sometimes 2 am is way too early. And with a 30-hour dance party starting at 10 pm on Saturday, the EndUp is by far SF's most popular after-hours place, with possibly the best sound system in the city. ■TIP➔ Said system is cranked. Even the cool kids wear earplugs. It's open nonstop from 10 pm Saturday until 4 am Monday, and generally 10 pm–4 am weekdays It can be a bit of a meat market, but this San Francisco institution doesn't adhere to any particular scene. ⊠ *401 6th St., at Harrison St., SoMa* ☎ *415/646–0999.*

16

GAY NIGHTLIFE

Lone Star Saloon. This watering hole is popular with bikers, bears, and the men who love them. The inside bar has an old-style-tavern feel, with barrels (not bowls) of peanuts, a pool table, a tiny dance floor, and a long wooden bar you half expect the bartender to sling a beer down. Weekend "Beer Busts" unfold on the great outdoor patio bar. Expect a big crowd on a sunny day. The scene here isn't particularly female-friendly, and the action can get steamy during events like gay-pride day or the Folsom Street Fair. ⊠ *1354 Harrison St., at 9th St., SoMa* ☎ *415/863–9999* ⊕ *www.lonestarsf.com.*

SF Eagle. This spacious indoor-outdoor leather bar is a holdover from the days before AIDS and SoMa's gentrification. The Sunday-afternoon "Beer Busts" (3 pm–6 pm) remain a high point of the leather set's week, and Thursday nights are given over to live music. This remains a welcoming place for people from all walks of life. ⊠ *398 12th St., at Harrison St., SoMa* ⊕ *www.sf-eagle.com.*

The Stud. Glam trans women, gay bears, tight-teed pretty boys, ladies and their ladies, and a handful of straight onlookers congregate here to dance to live DJ sounds and watch world-class drag performers on the small stage. The entertainment is often campy, pee-your-pants funny, and downright fantastic. Each night's music is different—from funk, soul, and hip-hop to '80s tunes and disco favorites. ■TIP➔ **At Frolic, the Stud's most outrageous party (second Saturday of the month), club goers dance the night away dressed as bunnies, kittens, and even stranger creatures.** ⊠ *399 9th St, at Harrison St., SoMa* ☎ *415/863–6623* ⊕ *www.studsf.com* ☽ *Closed Mon.*

MUSIC CLUBS

Slim's. National touring acts—mostly along the pop-punk and hard- and alt-rock lines but including metal and bluegrass—are the main draws at this venue, one of SoMa's most popular nightclubs. Co-owner Boz Scaggs helps bring in the crowds and famous headliners like Dressy Bessy and Dead Meadow. ⊠ *333 11th St., between Harrison and Folsom Sts., SoMa* ☎ *415/255–0333* ⊕ *www.slimspresents.com.*

CIVIC CENTER

Lawyers, politicians, and others in the government biz populate this neighborhood by day, and at night the scene tends to remain buttoned-up.

MUSIC CLUBS

Warfield. This former movie palace—a "palace" in every sense of the word—is now one of the city's largest rock-and-roll venues, with tables and chairs downstairs and theater seating upstairs. The historic venue has booked everyone from Prince and the Grateful Dead to the Pretenders and the Killers. ⊠ *982 Market St., at Taylor St., Civic Center* ☎ *415/345–0900* ⊕ *thewarfieldtheatre.com.*

THE TENDERLOIN

This neighborhood is best known for its grit and realism, but despite this The Loin is centrally located and, depending on your reservation time at Bourbon & Branch, the perfect place to start (or end) your night on the town.

BARS

Fodor'sChoice ★ **Bourbon & Branch.** Bourbon & Branch reeks of Prohibition-era speakeasy cool. It's not exclusive, though: everyone is granted a password. The place has sex appeal, with tin ceilings, bordello-red silk wallpaper, intimate booths, and low lighting; loud conversations and cell phones are not allowed. The menu of expertly mixed cocktails and quality bourbon and whiskey is substantial, though the servers aren't always authorities. ■TIP➔ Your reservation dictates your exit time, which is strictly enforced. There's also a speakeasy within the speakeasy called Wilson & Wilson, which is more exclusive, but just as funky. ⊠ *501 Jones St., at O'Farrell St., Tenderloin* ☎ *415/346-1735* ⊕ *www.bourbonandbranch.com.*

Edinburgh Castle. Work off your fish-and-chips and Scottish brew with a turn at the dartboard or pool table at this cavernous pub. It's popular with locals and Brits who congregate at the long bar or in the scattered seating areas, downing single-malt Scotch or pints of Fuller's. The pub holds weekly trivia nights (the toughest in town) and occasional Scottish cultural events (January's Robert Burns celebration is a favorite). Be aware that the surrounding neighborhood is gritty. ⊠ *950 Geary St., between Larkin and Polk Sts., Tenderloin* ☎ *415/885-4074* ⊕ *http://www.thecastlesf.com/.*

MUSIC CLUBS

Fodor'sChoice ★ **Great American Music Hall.** You can find top-drawer entertainment at this eclectic nightclub. Acts range from the best in blues, folk, and jazz to up-and-coming college-radio and American-roots artists to indie rockers such as OK Go, Mates of State, and the Cowboy Junkies. The colorful marble-pillared emporium (built in 1907 as a bordello) also accommodates dancing at some shows. Pub grub is available on most nights. ⊠ *859 O'Farrell St., between Polk and Larkin Sts., Tenderloin* ☎ *415/885-0750* ⊕ *www.slimspresents.com.*

HAYES VALLEY

Chic Hayes Valley takes nighttime seriously but not at the expense of having a good time. Look for fine wines at Hôtel Biron, learn a thing or three about rum at Smuggler's Cove, and compete at karaoke at The Mint.

BARS

Absinthe. The popular restaurant's 30-plus specialty cocktails—or even just a plain old Manhattan—make a trip just to the bar worthwhile. ⊠ *398 Hayes St., at Gough St., Hayes Valley* ☎ *415/551-1590* ⊕ *www.absinthe.com.*

Hôtel Biron Wine Bar and Art Gallery. Sharing an alleylike block with the backs of Market Street restaurants, this tiny, cavelike (in a good way) spot displays artworks of the Mission School aesthetic on its brick

16

walls. The well-behaved twenty- to thirtysomething clientele enjoys the off-the-beaten-path quarters, the wines from around the world, the soft lighting, and the hip music. ⊠ *45 Rose St., off Market St. near Gough St., Hayes Valley* ☎ *415/703–0403* ⊕ *www.hotelbiron.com.*

Fodor's Choice **Smuggler's Cove.** With the decor of a pirate ship and a slew of rum-based cocktails, you half expect Captain Jack Sparrow to sidle up next to you at this offbeat, Disney-esque hangout. But don't let the kitschy ambience fool you. The folks at Smuggler's Cove take rum so seriously they even make their own, which you can sample along with more than 200 other offerings, some of them vintage and very hard to find. A punch card is provided so you can try all 70 cocktails and remember where you left off without getting shipwrecked. The small space fills up quickly, so arrive early. ⊠ *650 Gough St., at McAllister St., Hayes Valley* ☎ *415/869–1900* ⊕ *www.smugglerscovesf.com.*

GAY NIGHTLIFE

The Mint Karaoke Lounge. A mixed gay-straight crowd that's drop-dead serious about its karaoke—to the point where you'd think an *American Idol* casting agent was in attendance—comes here seven nights a week. Regulars sing everything from Simon and Garfunkel songs to disco classics in front of an attentive audience. Do *not* walk onstage unprepared! Check out the songbook online to perfect your debut before you attempt to take the mike. ⊠ *1942 Market St., between Duboce Ave. and Laguna St., Hayes Valley* ☎ *415/626–4726* ⊕ *www.themint.net.*

NOB HILL

Whether you're out on the streets or inside a bar, Nob Hill serves up fantastic city views, the very best of which can be experienced from the Top of the Mark.

BARS

Tonga Room and Hurricane Bar. Since the 1940s the Tonga Room has supplied its city with high Polynesian kitsch. Fake palm trees, grass huts, a lagoon (three-piece combos play pop standards on a floating barge), and faux monsoons—courtesy of sprinkler-system rain and simulated thunder and lightning—grow more surreal as you quaff the bar's signature mai tais and other too-too fruity cocktails. ■TIP→ **Looking for an evening chock-full of bad decision making? Order the Scorpion Bowl and let the drunk dialing begin!** ⊠ *Fairmont San Francisco, 950 Mason St., at California St., Nob Hill* ☎ *415/772–5278* ⊕ *www.tongaroom.com.*

Top of the Mark. A famous magazine photograph immortalized the bar atop the Mark Hopkins as a hot spot for World War II servicemen on leave or about to ship out. The view remains sensational. Entertainment ranges from solo jazz piano to six-piece jazz ensembles. Cover charges vary, and shows begin at 7 pm weekdays and 9 pm weekends. ⊠ *Mark Hopkins InterContinental, 999 California St., at Mason St., Nob Hill* ☎ *415/392-3434* ⊕ *www.topofthemark.com.*

The Wreck Room. Shuffleboard, arcade basketball, a jukebox, and plenty of flat-screen TVs make this spacious yet divey place feel like a time machine back to your college days. On weekends the crowd is a sea of popped collars, baseball caps, and chest bumps, so get there early if you yearn for a turn at one of the games. ✉ *1390 California St., at Hyde St., Nob Hill* ☎ *415/932–6715* ⊕ *www.thewreckroomsf.com.*

POLK GULCH

Sassy, vibrant, and even a little crass, Lower Gulch, the southern half of this neighborhood—Polk Street from Geary Street to a little beyond California Street—was the heart of San Francisco's pre-Castro gay mecca. Things mostly settle down north of California in the Upper Gulch section, though even straight bars like Kozy Kar live up to this hood's feisty reputation.

BARS

Amélie. A slice of modern French life, this cozy and romantic wine bar is an ideal spot for European oenophiles. Vintage-theater seating is available up front—perfect for mingling with strangers. The prices are reasonable, the pours handsome. ■ **TIP→** Sit at the red-lacquer bar **to learn about wine and pick up a French phrase or two.** ✉ *1754 Polk St., at Washington St., Polk Gulch* ☎ *415/292–6916* ⊕ *www.ameliewinebar.com.*

Kozy Kar. Outrageous and full of sexual energy, this tiny space with an even tinier dance floor may be the heterosexual equivalent of San Francisco's gay bar scene. The drinks are stiff, but if they overwhelm you—or you just want to have fun—there's a waterbed for you to lounge on. Cartoons and '80s movies play on various televisions. Pay attention and you'll catch frames of porn mixed in for good measure, but if you miss them, don't worry: the bar and the floors are lined with vintage centerfolds. It may all be on the racy side, but it's never creepy or uncomfortable. ✉ *1548 Polk St., at Sacramento St., Polk Gulch* ☎ *415/346–5699* ⊕ *www.kozykar.com.*

GAY NIGHTLIFE

The Cinch. This Wild West–themed neighborhood bar has pinball machines, pool tables, and a smoking patio. It's not the least bit trendy, which is part of the charm for regulars. ✉ *1723 Polk St., between Washington and Clay Sts., Polk Gulch* ☎ *415/776–4162* ⊕ *www.cinchsf.com.*

NORTH BEACH

The heterosexual counterpart to the gay Castro, North Beach contains a suave mixture of watering holes, espresso cafés, late-night gelato ops, and strip clubs. Vesuvio Cafe is a must-visit for literary fans.

BARS

15 Romolo. Easy to miss and overshadowed by the neighboring girlie shows, this watering hole serves up artisanal drinks—including riffs off your own suggestions—and intriguing fare like hot dogs stuffed with cheddar and wrapped in tortillas. With a non-Internet jukebox and a photo booth, we're talking strictly old school. ✉ *15 Romolo Pl., between Broadway St. and Fresno St., North Beach* ☎ *415/398–1359* ⊕ *www.15romolo.com.*

16

Specs Twelve Adler Museum Cafe. If you're bohemian at heart, you can groove on this hidden hangout for artists, poets, and heavy-drinking lefties. It's one of the few remaining old-fashioned watering holes in North Beach that still smack of the Beat years and the 1960s. Though it's just off a busy street, Specs is strangely immune to the hustle and bustle outside. ⊠ *12 William Saroyan Pl., off Columbus Ave., between Pacific Ave. and Broadway St., North Beach* ☎ *415/421–4112.*

Tosca Café. Like Specs and Vesuvio nearby, this historic charmer holds a special place in San Francisco lore. It has an Italian flavor, with opera, big-band, and Italian standards on the jukebox, an antique espresso machine that's nothing less than a work of art, and lived-in red leather booths. With Francis Ford Coppola's Zoetrope just across the street, celebrities and hip film-industry types often stop by when they're in town; locals, like Sean Penn, have been known to shoot pool in the back room. ⊠ *242 Columbus Ave., near Broadway, North Beach* ☎ *415/986–9651* ⊕ *toscacafesf.com.*

Fodor'sChoice
★
Vesuvio Cafe. If you're hitting only one bar in North Beach, it should be this one. The low-ceiling second floor of this raucous boho hangout, little altered since its 1960s heyday (when Jack Kerouac frequented the place), is a fine vantage point for watching the colorful Broadway Street and Columbus Avenue intersection. Another part of Vesuvio's appeal is its diverse clientele, from older neighborhood regulars and young couples to Bacchanalian posses. ⊠ *255 Columbus Ave., at Broadway St., North Beach* ☎ *415/362–3370* ⊕ *www.vesuvio.com.*

CABARET

Fodor'sChoice
★
Club Fugazi. The claim to fame here is *Beach Blanket Babylon*, a wacky musical send-up of San Francisco moods and mores that has been going strong since 1974, making it the longest-running musical revue anywhere. Although the choreography is colorful, the singers brassy, and the satirical songs witty, the real stars are the comically exotic costumes and famous ceiling-high "hats"—which are worth the price of admission alone. The revue sells out as early as a month in advance, so order tickets as far ahead as possible. Those under 21 are admitted only to the Sunday matinee. ■TIP➔ If you don't shell out the extra money for reserved seating, you won't have an assigned seat—so get your cannoli to go and arrive at least 30 minutes prior to showtime to get in line. ⊠ *678 Green St., at Powell St., North Beach* ☎ *415/421–4222* ⊕ *www. beachblanketbabylon.com.*

COMEDY

Cobb's Comedy Club. Stand-up comics such as Bill Maher, Paula Poundstone, and Sarah Silverman have appeared at this club. You can also see sketch comedy and comic singer-songwriters here. No one under 18 is admitted. ⊠ *915 Columbus Ave., at Lombard St., North Beach* ☎ *415/928–4320* ⊕ *www.cobbscomedyclub.com.*

Purple Onion. This funny house ranks right up there with Bimbo's and the Fillmore on the list of San Francisco's most famous clubs, and people seem to love it or hate it. Regardless, the Onion is a historic, quintessential San Francisco institution that provided an early platform for both folk-music troubadours such as the Kingston Trio and comedic acts like Robin Williams. In addition to stand-up, you can catch sketch comedy, open mike, and improv shows. ✉ *530 Jackson St., between Kearny St. and Columbus Ave., North Beach* ☎ *415/730–2359* ⊕ *purpleonionatkells.com.*

MUSIC CLUBS

Bimbo's 365 Club. The plush main room and adjacent lounge of this club, here since 1951, retain a retro vibe perfect for the "Cocktail Nation" programming that keeps the crowds entertained. For a taste of the old-school San Francisco nightclub scene, you can't beat it. Indie low-fi and pop bands such as Stephen Malkmus and the Jicks and Camera Obscura play here. ✉ *1025 Columbus Ave., at Chestnut St., North Beach* ☎ *415/474–0365* ⊕ *www.bimbos365club.com.*

The Saloon. Hard-drinkin' in-the-know locals favor this raucous spot, known for great blues. Built in the 1860s, the onetime bordello is purported to be the oldest bar in the city. This is not the place to order a mixed drink. You've been warned. ✉ *1232 Grant Ave., near Columbus Ave., North Beach* ☎ *415/989–7666* ⊕ *www.sfblues.net/Saloon.html.*

THE WATERFRONT

16

FISHERMAN'S WHARF

Come nightfall, the crowds that throng the northern waterfront during the day tend to thin out, and the nightlife scene here is almost quaint.

BARS

Buena Vista Café. At the end of the Hyde Street cable-car line, the Buena Vista packs 'em in for its famous Irish coffee—which, according to owners, was the first served stateside (in 1952). The place oozes nostalgia, drawing devoted locals as well as out-of-towners relaxing after a day of sightseeing. It's narrow and can get crowded, but this spot provides a fine alternative to the overpriced tourist joints nearby. ✉ *2765 Hyde St., at Beach St., Fisherman's Wharf* ☎ *415/474–5044* ⊕ *www.thebuenavista.com.*

EMBARCADERO

The waterfront's eastern section stays busy at night, not a surprise given its expansive bay views and proximity to Union Square, Chinatown, the Financial District, and SoMa.

BARS

Hard Water. This waterfront restaurant and bar with stunning bay views pays homage to America's most iconic spirit—bourbon—with a wall of whiskeys and a lineup of specialty cocktails. The menu, crafted by Charles Phan of Slanted Door fame, includes spicy pork-belly cracklings, corn-bread-crusted alligator, and other fun snacks. ✉ *Pier 3, Suite 3–102, at Embarcadero, Embarcadero* ☎ *415/392–3021* ⊕ *www.hardwaterbar.com.*

Hog Island Oyster Bar. On a sunny day, is there anything better than sipping wine and eating oysters? Only if it's here, on a waterside patio, with the looming Bay Bridge and the Oakland and Berkeley hills as a backdrop. The oysters are from Marin County, and many of the wines are from Sonoma and Napa. ⊠ *Ferry Bldg., 1 Embarcadero Plaza, Financial District* ☎ *415/391–7117* ⊕ *www.hogislandoysters.com.*

Pier 23 Cafe. Beer arrives at your table in buckets at this waterfront bar, which has ample seating at plastic tables on a wooden deck. Although you'd expect to sit elbow-to-elbow with fishermen, you're more likely to share the space with twenty- and thirtysomethings drawn by the beer and food specials. ⊠ *Pier 23, The Embarcadero, Embarcadero* ☎ *415/362–5125* ⊕ *www.pier23cafe.com.*

FINANCIAL DISTRICT

Not surprisingly, the nightlife scene here revolves around suits recovering from extended workdays or still trying to seal the deal. Wiggle in among the shop talkers and enjoy a stiff martini.

BARS

Harrington's Bar and Grill. The epicenter for downtown festivities on St. Patrick's Day, this family-owned Irish saloon (closed Sunday) is an attitude-free place for the well-tailored-suit set to have an after-work drink the rest of the year. The restaurant serves American fare, with the occasional Irish special, and has a good selection of imported beers. Another local favorite, the Royal Exchange, is next door and eerily similar. ⊠ *245 Front St., near Sacramento St., Financial District* ☎ *415/392–7595* ⊕ *www.harringtonsbarandgrill.com.*

The Hidden Vine. True to its name, this cozy wine bar is in a little alley (just north of Market Street) and the location is part of the appeal, but the wines and amuse-bouches make it truly worthwhile. A jumble of velvet chairs and love seats fills the space, and the owner, who serves most nights, acts as your sommelier. The space also features its very own boccie court. ⊠ *408 Merchant St., at Battery St., Financial District* ☎ *415/674–3567* ⊕ *www.thehiddenvine.com.*

COMEDY

Punchline. A launch pad for the likes of Jay Leno and Whoopi Goldberg, this place books some of the nation's top talents. Headliners have included Dave Chappelle, Margaret Cho, and Jay Mohr. No one under 18 is admitted. ⊠ *444 Battery St., between Clay and Washington Sts., Financial District* ☎ *415/397–7573* ⊕ *www.punchlinecomedyclub.com.*

THE MARINA

The young up-and-comers of the Marina district check each other out over high-end cocktails at a few semifancy, see-and-be-seen establishments.

BARS

Nectar. This small, classy, storefront lounge has reasonable tasting flights (around $20) and decent food that looks more impressive than it tastes. No complaints about the wine choices, though, which are consistently excellent. Warm lighting accents modern furnishings, including a signature beehive-shape wine display. On weekends the decibel level rises considerably and space is at a premium. ⊠ *3330 Steiner St., between Chestnut and Lombard Sts., Marina* ☎ *415/345–1377* ⊕ *www.nectarwinelounge.com.*

COW HOLLOW

In between the Marina and Pacific Heights, this small yet affluent neighborhood has a similar scene to the bordering Marina district but without the hefty price tags.

BARS

Balboa Cafe. Here you'll spy young (thirtysomething) and upwardly mobile former frat boys and sorority girls munching on tasty burgers—considered by some to be the best in town—while trying to add a few new names to their iPhones. ✉ *3199 Fillmore St., at Greenwich St., Cow Hollow* ☎ *415/921–3944* ⊕ *www.balboacafe.com.*

Bus Stop. Popular with frat boys and stockbrokers alike, this Marina/Cow Hollow favorite has 18 screens and two pool tables. If you want to meet the local diehards, this is the place. It's also one of the few spots in this neighborhood where you'll feel comfortable dressed down. Order food from neighboring restaurants; the bar provides menus. ✉ *1901 Union St., at Laguna St., Cow Hollow* ☎ *415/567–6905* ⊕ *www.busstop-sf.com.*

Perry's. One of San Francisco's oldest singles bars still packs 'em in. You can dine on great hamburgers (and a stellar Reuben) as well as more substantial fare while gabbing about the game with the well-scrubbed, khaki-clad, baseball-cap-wearing crowd. ✉ *1944 Union St., at Laguna St., Cow Hollow* ☎ *415/922–9022* ⊕ *www.perryssf.com.*

16

THE WESTERN SHORELINE

THE RICHMOND AND SUNSET

The nightlife in these practical, comfy neighborhoods center more on reasonably priced restaurants—including Clement Street's good Chinese, Thai, Burmese, and Vietnamese ones—than on bars and nightclubs. What bar scene there is, you'll find low-key and welcoming. Fierce waves and mesmerizing sunsets are just a few of the reasons to make your way to the district's western reaches.

BARS

Fodor's Choice ★ **Cliff House.** Classier than the nearby Beach Chalet, with a more impressive view of Ocean Beach, this is our pick if you must choose just one oceanfront restaurant/bar. Sure, it's the site of many high-school prom dates, and you could argue that the food and drinks are overpriced, and some say the sleek facade seems more suitable for a mausoleum—but the views are terrific. The best window seats are reserved for diners, but there's a small upstairs lounge where you can watch gulls sail high above the vast blue Pacific. ■**TIP→ Come before sunset.** ✉ *1090 Point Lobos, at Great Hwy., Richmond* ☎ *415/386–3330* ⊕ *www.cliffhouse.com.*

The Riptide. A cozy cabin bar that's the perfect finale for beachgoers, Riptide is a surfer favorite, but you don't have to own a board to feel at home. You'll find classic beers, good food, and all at wallet-friendly prices. There's live music most nights, which swings somewhere between bluegrass to karaoke. Many tourists fooled by San Francisco's definition of summer end up warming their popsicle toes at the bar's fireplace. Sunday's feature a bacon Bloody Mary great for hangovers. ✉ *3639 Taraval St, Sunset* ☎ *415/681–8433* ⊕ *www.riptidesf.com.*

MUSIC CLUBS

The Plough and Stars. This decidedly unglamorous pub, where crusty old-timers swap stories over pints of Guinness, is the city's best bet for traditional Irish music. Bay Area musicians (and, once in a while, big-name bands) perform every night except Monday. Talented locals gather to play on Tuesday and Sunday *seisiúns*, informal "sessions" where musicians sit around a table and drink and eat while chiming in; anyone skilled at Irish traditional music can join in. ✉ *116 Clement St., at 2nd Ave., Richmond* ☎ *415/751–1122* ⊕ *www.theploughandstars.com.*

GOLDEN GATE PARK

Often shrouded by the city's famous fog and always scented by crisp eucalyptus, Golden Gate Park provides a suitably mellow nightlife experience.

BARS

Beach Chalet. This restaurant-microbrewery, on the second floor of a historic building filled with 1930s Works Project Administration murals, has a stunning view of the Pacific Ocean, so you may want to time your visit to coincide with the sunset. ■ TIP→ **Arrive at least 30 minutes before sunset to beat the dinner crowd.** If you come right at dinnertime or even at lunchtime on weekends, diners with reservations will be given first dibs on the window seats (and on tables in general). The bar is toward the back, with a so-so view of the action. The American bistro food—which, for appetizers, includes ahi tuna tartare and fried calamari—is decent, the house brews are rich and flavorful, and there's a good selection of California wines by the glass. The seasonal Oktoberfest brew is a highlight of the beer menu. The cheaper Park Chalet on the ground floor has park, rather than ocean, views. ✉ *1000 Great Hwy., near John F. Kennedy Dr., Golden Gate Park* ☎ *415/386–8439* ⊕ *www.beachchalet.com.*

Park Chalet. You'll feel like you're in a cabin in the woods as you relax in an Adirondack chair under a heat lamp, enclosed by the greenery of Golden Gate Park. In addition to serving pub food such as burgers, salads, steaks, and fish-and-chips, the brewery churns out its own beer. The Park Chalet shares a building with the Beach Chalet—but it isn't waterside, so you won't freeze if it's overcast. ✉ *1000 Great Hwy., near John F. Kennedy Dr., Golden Gate Park* ☎ *415/386–8439* ⊕ *www.parkchalet.com.*

THE HAIGHT AND THE CASTRO

THE HAIGHT

The hippie joints that made the Haight famous may be long gone, but this neighborhood retains a countercultural vibe. Beer connoisseurs should head directly to the Toronado.

BARS

The Alembic. This dark-wood and low-lit space has a certain swagger that is at once charming and classy. It serves full meals but is also a good choice for cocktails and small plates—the jerk-spiced duck hearts, pork-belly sliders, and pickled quail eggs are all winners. ■TIP➡ Carnivores: check out the bone-marrow plate. ✉ *1725 Haight St., at Cole St., Haight* ☎ *415/666–0822* ⊕ *www.alembicsf.com.*

Noc Noc. A cross between a Tim Burton film and an Oingo Boingo album, this funky cavelike bar has been making every day Halloween since 1986. Noc Noc's bartenders serve up about 20 or so beers on tap, sake (even unfiltered), and unique twists on traditional drinks, like the P&P, a blend of hefeweizen and pear cider. The house DJ plays acid jazz, industrial, and ambient tunes. When the nearby Toronado gets too busy, head over here. ✉ *557 Haight St., at Steiner St., Haight* ☎ *415/861–5811* ⊕ *nocnocs.com.*

Fodor's Choice ★ Toronado. You come to what may be the city's most popular dive bar for one thing and one thing only: the reasonably priced beers, about four dozen of them on tap. The menu, which hangs from the ceiling, will put a kink in your neck as you try to decide. The bar opens in the late morning and has a good-size crowd by early afternoon, so show up early to sit at one of the highly coveted tables. ■TIP➡ Don't worry about eating beforehand. It's okay to bring in outside food. ✉ *547 Haight St., at Fillmore St., Haight* ☎ *415/863–2276* ⊕ *www.toronado.com.*

THE CASTRO

The gay district is as outrageous as one might expect, if not more so. Leather daddies, costumed club kids, and those who defy recently passed "no nudity" laws are among the characters you'll stumble across day or night. The party never seems to stop at popular Badlands.

BARS

Blackbird. This neighborhood hangout tries too hard to be hip and cool, but it's a lot of fun. The crowd is less casual than others in the Castro, though no one will judge you for wearing Chuck Taylors. Blackbird serves up a good selection of craft beers, along with seasonal cocktails. The chipotle Bloody Mary is a must-try. ✉ *2124 Market St., at Church St., Castro* ☎ *415/503–0630* ⊕ *www.blackbirdbar.com.*

Lucky 13. Greasers, hipsters, Betty Page wannabes, anyone looking for a good beer in the Castro, and assorted other patrons make Lucky 13 a fun place indeed. The drink prices are reasonable, the beer selection is huge, and there's high-end root beer on tap for the designated driver with a discriminating palate. The best seats are upstairs overlooking the crowd. ✉ *2140 Market St., at Church St., Castro* ☎ *415/487–1313.*

16

CLOSE UP

Gay and Lesbian Nightlife

In the days before the gay liberation movement, bars were more than mere watering holes—they also served as community centers where members of a mostly underground minority could network and socialize. In the 1960s the bars became hotbeds of political activity; by the 1970s other social opportunities had become available to gay men and lesbians, and the bars' importance as centers of activity decreased.

Old-timers may wax nostalgic about the vibrancy of pre-AIDS, 1970s bar life, but you can still have plenty of fun. The one difference is the one-night-a-week operation of some of the best clubs, which may cater to a different (sometimes straight) clientele on other nights. This type of club tends to come and go, so it's best to pick up one of the two main gay papers to check the latest happenings.

Bay Area Reporter. The weekly *Bay Area Reporter* covers gay and lesbian events in its entertainment pages and calendar and has a nightlife website (⊕ *www.bartabsf.com*).

San Francisco Bay Times. The biweekly *Bay Times* (⊕ *www.sfbaytimes.com*) runs features and extensive calendar listings of lesbian and gay events.

For a place known as a gay mecca, San Francisco has always suffered from a surprising drought of lesbian bars. The Lexington Club, in the nightlife-filled Mission District, is the best-known bar. The Café is probably the most lesbian-friendly Castro bar, though you'll find queer gals (and many more queer guys) at the Mint and The Stud, too.

GAY NIGHTLIFE

Badlands. Shirts off! If a sweaty muscle sandwich sounds like your idea of a good time, head to Badlands, where serious party boys come to grind to throbbing music on a packed dance floor. The lines can be ridiculous on weekends; those in the know go on Wednesday or Thursday. Tight-teed patrons range from twenties to forties. ⊠ *4121 18th St., between Castro and Collingwood Sts., Castro* ☎ *415/626–9320* ⊕ *www.sfbadlands.com.*

The Café. Always comfortable and often packed with a mixed gay, lesbian, and straight crowd, this is a place where you can dance to house or disco music, shoot pool, or meet guys in their twenties at the bar. The outdoor deck—a rarity—makes it a favorite destination for smokers. There's a small weekend cover; expect a line to get in. ⊠ *2369 Market St., at 17th St., Castro* ☎ *415/523–0133* ⊕ *www. cafesf.com.*

THE MISSION

Once a vibrant mix of Latino street culture and twentysomething dot-com action, the Mission is defined these days by its hipster crowd. This neighborhood rarely sleeps.

BARS

Elbo Room. This popular two-story space has a little something for everyone. The main bar downstairs is quaint and swanky with tables, booths, and classic arcade games. Hit the upstairs to see up-and-coming artists before they hit the big time. The music includes Afro-Cuban, indie rock, jazz, and more. ⊠ *647 Valencia St., between 17th St. and 18th St., Mission District* ☎ *415/552–7788* ⊕ *www.elbo.com.*

Elixir. The cocktails are well crafted and affordable at the city's second-oldest saloon location—various watering holes have operated on this site since 1858. ■TIP➔ Sunday's do-it-yourself Bloody Mary bar is a local favorite. ⊠ *3200 16th St., at Guerrero St., Mission District* ☎ *415/552–1633* ⊕ *www.elixirsf.com.*

Fodor'sChoice
★
El Rio. A dive bar in the best sense has a calendar chock-full of events, from free bands and films to Salsa Sunday (seasonal), all of which keep Mission kids coming back. Bands play several nights a week, and there are plenty of other events. No matter what day you attend, expect to find a diverse gay-straight crowd. When the weather's warm, the large patio out back is especially popular, and the midday dance parties are *the* place to be. ⊠ *3158 Mission St., between César Chavez and Valencia Sts., Mission District* ☎ *415/282–3325* ⊕ *www.elriosf.com.*

Nihon. Whiskey lovers *need* to check this place out, if only to drool over the 150 or so bottles behind the bar. Nihon attracts a super-swank, youngish crowd for decent (if pricey) Japanese tapas; the whiskeys pair with sushi surprisingly well. The dramatic lighting, close quarters, and blood-red tuffets make the bar more suitable for romance than business. ⊠ *1779 Folsom St., near 14th St., Mission District* ☎ *415/552–4400* ⊕ *dajanigroup.net/establishments/nihon-whisky-lounge.*

Rite Spot Cafe. A Mission tradition for more than 50 years, this classy and casual charmer is like a cabaret club in an aging mobster's garage. Quirky lounge singers and other musicians entertain most nights. A small menu of affordable sandwiches and Italian food beats your average bar fare. Rite Spot is in a mostly residential and somewhat desolate part of the Mission, so you may feel like you're entering a no-man's-land. ⊠ *2099 Folsom St., at 17th St., Mission District* ☎ *415/552–6066* ⊕ *www.ritespotcafe.net.*

Urban Putt. While the city's only miniature golf course is kid-friendly during the day, this 14-hole indoor course really lights up at night. The bar features cocktails inspired by Bay Area attractions, as does the fairway. So you'll be putting through the Transamerica Pyramid and those famous Painted Ladies. And Urban Putt is complete with theme park cuisine, such as corn dogs and organic soft-serve ice cream. Those seeking more substantial eats should head upstairs to the restaurant. ⊠ *1096 S. Van Ness Ave., at 22nd St., Mission District* ☎ *415/341–1080* ⊕ *www.urbanputt.com.*

16

Zeitgeist. It's a bit divey, a bit rock and roll, but a good place to relax with a cold one or an ever-popular (and ever-strong) Bloody Mary in the large beer "garden" (there's not much greenery) on a sunny day. Grill food is available, and if you're lucky. one of the city's most famous food-cart operators, the Tamale Lady, will drop by. If you own a trucker hat, a pair of Vans, and a Pabst Blue Ribbon T-shirt, you'll fit right in. ⊠ *199 Valencia St., at Duboce Ave., Mission District* ☎ *415/255–7505* ⊕ *www.zeitgeistsf.com.*

DANCE CLUBS

Make-Out Room. Are you ready to dance? At this tiny Latin club the beats are always fresh, if not downright nasty—this place is called the Make-Out Room for a reason. With the small bar and just a few cushiony booths, don't expect to sit for long. Most nights are free, but expect a small cover charge on weekends when bands like Thee Swank Bastards or Grave Bros Deluxe play. ⊠ *3225 22nd St., at Mission St., Mission District* ☎ *415/647–2888* ⊕ *www.makeoutroom.com.*

GAY NIGHTLIFE

Martuni's. A mixed crowd enjoys cocktails in the semi-refined environment of this bar where the Castro, the Mission, and Hayes Valley intersect; variations on the martini are a specialty. In the intimate back room a pianist plays nightly, and patrons take turns boisterously singing show tunes. Martuni's often gets busy after symphony and opera performances—Davies Hall and the Opera House are both within walking distance. ■TIP➔ **The Godiva Chocolate Martini is a crowd favorite.** ⊠ *4 Valencia St., at Market St., Mission District* ☎ *415/241–0205.*

DOGPATCH

The historic Dogpatch neighborhood was once mostly residential, but some of the city's best off-the-beaten-path joints can be found here. Yield Wine Bar is one of several shining stars at or near 3rd and 22nd Streets. If dinner is on the agenda, consider Serpentine. Directly across 3rd from Yield, it serves up amazing food and even better cocktails.

BARS

Magnolia Pub & Brewery. Outfitted in industrial-chic, this brewhouse has a little something for everyone, except maybe hungry vegetarians. Its huge on-site brewing system can produce up to 30 barrels of beer and is equally matched by Magnolia's unique cocktail menu, featuring off-the-wall ingredients like beef bouillon. The love affair with meat doesn't stop there, as they even craft their own sausages. ⊠ *2505 3rd St., Between 22nd & 23rd Sts., Dogpatch* ☎ *415/864–7468* ⊕ *www.magnoliapub.com.*

Fodor's Choice ★ **Yield.** A stone's throw from the bay, the city's greenest wine bar serves up sustainable, organic, and biodynamic wines from around the world. Small plates are also available, usually vegetarian, and change weekly, as does the wine menu. The commitment to a healthier planet isn't reflected only in the food and drink, but also the decor, a mixture of reused wine bottles and wood reclaimed from nearby piers. ■TIP➔ **Public transportation shuts down early at night, so expect to need a taxi back and to wait about 30 minutes for it to arrive.** ⊠ *2490 3rd St., at 22nd St., Dogpatch* ☎ *415/401–8984* ⊕ *http://www.yieldandpause.com/.*

SAFETY AFTER DARK

San Franciscans sometimes seem to get a perverse thrill out of the grittiness of their city. Some of the best nightlife options are in sketchy locations; in the areas we've listed below you're better off cabbing it. Bartenders can call you a ride when you're ready to leave.

■ **The Tenderloin:** Many locals walk to Tenderloin bars, but take a cab if addicts and lowlifes loitering in front of hourly rate hotels give you the jitters. The edges east of Jones Street and north of Sutter Street aren't too bad.

■ **SoMa:** More than five blocks or so south of Market Street is an industrial no-man's-land, though this area becomes more developed and inhabited by flashy residential skyscrapers with each passing year.

■ **Civic Center:** Don't stray north, east, or south of the performing arts venues. The one safe corridor is west to Gough Street, which will bring you into Hayes Valley. Avoid Market Street between 6th and 10th Streets.

■ **Western Addition:** If coming to this neighborhood's music clubs, take a cab or opt for valet parking if it's available.

■ **The Outer Mission (south of 24th Street):** On Mission Street, don't stray below 24th. If you're feeling nervous between 16th and 24th Streets, walk a block west to Valencia Street.

It's safe to walk around the Financial District, Union Square, Haight Street and Cole Valley, Nob Hill, the Mission (above 24th Street), and SoMa north of Howard.

POTRERO HILL

One of the city's less walkable neighborhoods and far from the center of the nightlife scene sometimes feels downright sleepy. But a strip of 18th Street near Connecticut Street has good food and cocktails, and the Bottom of the Hill music club has a loyal clientele.

DANCE CLUBS
Bottom of the Hill. This is a great live-music dive—in the best sense of the word—and truly the epicenter for Bay Area indie rock. The club has hosted some great acts over the years, including the Strokes and the Throwing Muses. Rap and hip-hop acts occasionally make it to the stage. ⊠ *1233 17th St., at Texas St., Potrero Hill* ☎ *415/621–4455* ⊕ *www.bottomofthehill.com.*

PACIFIC HEIGHTS

One of the city's most exclusive enclaves has city and bay views, though most of these are from posh residences. The nightlife here is generally tasteful and discreet.

WESTERN ADDITION

The Western Addition was among San Francisco's earliest multicultural neighborhoods, and it remains ethnically and economically diverse, if also pretty rough in many spots. The jazz, rock, and blues clubs here book high-profile performers.

BARS

Tsunami Sushi Panhandle. This place next to a jointly owned sake shop has a small but very good sushi menu, as well as a list of more than 100 sakes. The staffers know their stuff—including how to make killer sake-tinis. ⊠ *1306 Fulton St., at Divisadero St., Western Addition* ☎ *415/567–7664* ⊕ *dajanigroup.net.*

MUSIC CLUBS

BooM BooM RooM. John Lee Hooker's old haunt has been an old-school blues haven for years, attracting top-notch acts from all around the country. Luck out with legendary masters like James "Super Chikan" Johnson, or discover new blues and funk artists. ⊠ *1601 Fillmore St., at Geary Blvd., Western Addition* ☎ *415/673–8000* ⊕ *www.boom-boomroom.com.*

The Fillmore. This is *the* club that all the big names, from Coldplay to Clapton, want to play. San Francisco's most famous rock-music hall presents national and local acts: rock, reggae, grunge, jazz, folk, acid house, and more. Go upstairs to view the amazing collection of rock posters lining the walls. At the end of each show, free apples are set near the door, and staffers hand out collectible posters. ■TIP➔ **Avoid steep service charges by purchasing tickets at the club's box office on Sunday from 10 to 4.** ⊠ *1805 Geary Blvd., at Fillmore St., Western Addition* ☎ *415/346–6000* ⊕ *www.thefillmore.com.*

The Independent. Originally called the Box for its giant cube-shape interior, this off-the-beaten-path music venue showcases rock, heavy metal, folk, soul, reggae, hip-hop, and even comedy acts. There's a big dance floor. ⊠ *628 Divisadero St., at Hayes St., Western Addition* ☎ *415/771–1421* ⊕ *www.theindependentsf.com.*

BERNAL HEIGHTS

Atop a steep hill, Bernal Heights is a section of town many San Franciscans have yet to visit. Its few bars have a cozy, neighborhood feel.

GAY NIGHTLIFE

Wild Side West. A friendly pool game is always going on at this mellow, slightly out-of-the-way hangout, where all are welcome. Outside is a large deck and one of San Francisco's best bar gardens, where acoustic-guitar sing-alongs are not uncommon. Rumor has it that Janis Joplin was a regular here. Ask the bartender for the scoop. ⊠ *424 Cortland Ave., at Wool St., Bernal Heights* ☎ *415/647–3099* ⊕ *www.wildsidewest.com.*

SPORTS AND
THE OUTDOORS

Updated
by Andrea
Powellt

San Francisco's surroundings—the bay, ocean, mountains, and forests—make getting outdoors away from the city a no-brainer. Muir Woods, Point Reyes, and Stinson Beach in Marin County offer dozens of opportunities for exploring the natural beauty of the Bay Area. But the peninsular city— with its many green spaces, steep inclines, and breathtaking views—has plenty to offer itself.

Bikers and hikers traverse the majestic Golden Gate Bridge, bound for the Marin Headlands or the winding trails of the Presidio. Runners, strollers, and cyclists head for Golden Gate Park's wooded paths, and water lovers satisfy their addictions by kayaking, sailing, kite-surfing, and even swimming, in the bay and along the rugged Pacific coast.

Prefer to watch from the sidelines? The Giants (baseball) are San Francisco's professional sports team; the A's (baseball) and the Golden State Warriors (basketball) play in Oakland; and the 49ers (football) are based in Santa Clara. But the city has plenty of other periodic sporting events to watch, including that roving costume party, the Bay to Breakers race in May. For events listings and local perspectives on Bay Area sports, pick up a copy of the *San Francisco Chronicle* (⊕ *www.sfgate. com*) or the *San Francisco Examiner* (⊕ *www.examiner.com*).

BASEBALL

San Francisco Giants. Three World Series titles (2010, 2012, and 2014) and the classic design of AT&T Park lead to sellouts for nearly every home game the National League team plays. ⊠ *AT&T Park, 24 Willie Mays Plaza, between 2nd and 3rd Sts., SoMa* ☎ *415/972–2000, 800/734–4268* ⊕ *sanfrancisco.giants.mlb.com.*

GETTING TICKETS

There are 31,000 season-ticket holders (for just over 41,000 seats), so tickets for popular games routinely sell out quickly. If tickets aren't available at Tickets.com, try the team-approved reseller StubHub! (⊕ *www.stubhub.com*) or just show up on game day—there are usually plenty of scalpers, some even selling at reasonable prices.

Giants Dugout. The Giants sell tickets at the ballpark and numerous Dugout locations, among them Four Embarcadero Center and 337 Geary Street near Union Square. A surcharge is added at locations other than the ballpark. ✉ *AT&T Park, 24 Willie Mays Plaza, at 3rd St., SoMa* ☎ *415/947–3419, 800/734–4268* ⊕ *sanfrancisco.giants.mlb.com/sf/ ballpark/dugout_stores.jsp.*

Tickets.com. This service sells game tickets online and charges a per-ticket service charge. ✉ *San Francisco* ☎ *877/473–4849* ⊕ *www.tickets.com.*

BEACHES

Taking in a beachside sunset is the perfect way to end a busy day—assuming the fog hasn't blown in for the afternoon. Always bring a sweater because even the sunniest of days can turn cold and foggy without warning. Treacherous currents and icy temperatures make most waters too dangerous for swimming without a wet suit, but with a Frisbee, picnic fixings, and some good walking shoes, you can have a fantastic day at the beach.

17

Aquatic Park Cove. This urban beach, surrounded by Fort Mason, Ghirardelli Square, and Fisherman's Wharf, is a quarter-mile-long strip of sand. The gentle waters near shore are shallow, safe for kids to swim or wade, and fairly clean. Locals—including the seemingly ubiquitous older-man-in-Speedo—come out for quick dips in the frigid water. Members of the **Dolphin Club** and the **South End Rowing Club** come every morning for a swim, and a large and raucous crowd braves the cold on New Year's Day. **Amenities:** restaurants; restrooms; showers. **Best for:** sunsets; swimming; walking. ✉ *San Francisco Maritime National Historic Park, 499 Jefferson St., at Hyde St., Fisherman's Wharf* ⊕ *www.nps.gov/safr.*

Baker Beach. With its gorgeous views of the Golden Gate Bridge and the Marin Headlands, Baker Beach is a local favorite (with an established nudist area at the far north end). The pounding surf and strong currents discourage swimming, but the mile-long shoreline is ideal for fishing, building sand castles, or looking for sea lions. On warm days the entire beach is packed with bodies. Picnic tables, grills, restrooms, and drinking water are available. Rangers give tours of the 50-ton gun at Battery Chamberlin, overlooking the beach, on the first weekend of every month. **Amenities:** parking (no fee); toilets. **Best for:** jogging; kids; sunsets. ✉ *Gibson Rd. off Bowley St., southwest corner of Presidio, Presidio.*

AT&T Park: Where Giants Tread

CLOSE UP

The size of AT&T Park hits you immediately—the field, McCovey Cove, and the Lefty O'Doul drawbridge all look like miniature models. At only 13 acres, the San Francisco Giants' ballpark is one of the country's smallest. After Boston's Fenway, AT&T Park has the shortest distance to the wall; from home plate it's just 309 feet to the right field. But there's something endearing about its petite stature—not to mention its location, with yacht masts poking up over the outfield and the blue bay sparkling beyond.

From 1960 to 2000 the Giants played at Candlestick Park, which was in one of the coldest, windiest parts of the city. (Giants' pitcher Stu Miller was famously "blown off the mound" here during the 1961 All-Star Game.)

In 2000 the Giants played their first game at AT&T Park (then called Pacific Bell Park and later SBC Park). All told, $357 million was spent on the privately funded facility, and it shows in the retro redbrick exterior, the quaint clock tower, handsome bronze statues, above-average food, and tiny details like baseball-style lettering on no-smoking signs. There isn't a bad seat in the house and the park has an unusual level of intimacy and access. Concourses circle the field on one level, and in some ticketed areas you can stand inches from players as they exit the locker rooms. At street level, non-ticket-holders can get up close outside a gate in right field. The giant Coke bottle and mitt you see beyond the outfield are part of the Coca-Cola Fan Lot playground. Diehards may miss the grittiness of Candlestick, but it's hard not to love this park. It still feels new but has an old-time aura and has become a San Francisco institution. Park tours are led daily at 10:30 and 12:30 and cost $22.

THE FAMOUS "SPLASH HIT"

Locals show up in motorboats and inflatable rafts with fishing nets, ready to scoop up home-run balls that clear the right field wall and land in McCovey Cove. Hitting one into the water isn't easy: the ball has to clear a 25-foot wall, the elevated walkway, and the promenade outside. Barry Bonds had the first splash hit on May 1, 2000.

GETTING THERE

Parking is pricey ($38 and up), and 2,300 spaces for nearly 42,000 seats doesn't add up. Take public transportation. Muni lines N and T (to CalTrain/Mission Bay and Sunnydale, respectively) stop right in front of the park, and Muni bus lines 10, 30, 45, and 47 stop a block away. Or you can arrive in style—take the ferry from Jack London Square in Oakland (⊕ *www. sanfranciscobayferry.com*).

China Beach. One of the city's safest swimming beaches was named for the impoverished Chinese fishermen believed to have once camped here, though some maps label it James D. Phelan Beach. This 600-foot strip of sand is just west of the Presidio and Baker Beach and has gentle waters, as well as lots of amenities, like picnic tables and grills. China Beach is bordered by the multimillion-dollar homes of the Seacliff neighborhood, and the hike down to the beach is steep. **Amenities:** parking (no fee); showers; toilets. **Best for:** fishing; grilling; picnics. ⊠ *Sea Cliff Ave. and El Camino del Mar, Richmond.*

Ocean Beach. The city's largest beach stretches for 3 miles along the Great Highway south of the Cliff House, making it ideal for long walks and runs. This isn't the cleanest shore, but it's an easy-to-reach place to chill, hunt for sand dollars, or watch daredevil surfers ride the waves. Extremely dangerous currents mean swimming is not recommended. After sunset, bonfires form a string of lights along the beach in summer, though fires are permitted only on the stretch of beach alongside Golden Gate Park. Restrooms are at the south end. **Amenities:** parking (no fee); toilets. **Best for:** bonfires; kite flying; long walks. ⊠ *Great Hwy. between Point Lobos Ave. and Sloat Blvd.*

BICYCLING

San Francisco is known for its treacherously steep hills, so it may be surprising to see so many cyclists. This is actually a great city for biking—there are ample bike lanes, it's not hard to find level ground with great scenery (especially along the water), and if you're willing to tackle a challenging uphill climb, you're often rewarded with a fabulous view—and a quick trip back down.

San Francisco Bicycle Coalition. The San Francisco Bicycle Coalition has extensive information about the policies and politics of riding and lists local events for cyclists on its website. You can download (but not print) a PDF version of the *San Francisco Bike Map and Walking Guide.* ⊠ *1720 Market St.* ☎ *415/431–2453* ⊕ *www.sfbike.org.*

17

WHERE TO RENT

Angel Island. This former military garrison and beautiful state park has some steep roads and great views of the city and the bay. Bicycles must stay on roadways; there are no single-track trails on the island. There is a small café offering a wide variety of lunch options, or bring your own grub and grab one of the many picnic tables scattered around the island. You can rent bikes on the island for $13.50 an hour or $50 a day (rentals during winter months are weekends only). Segway tours are also available for $68 per person. ⊠ *Tiburon* ☎ *415/435–5390* ⊕ *www. angelisland.org.*

Bay City Bike. With four locations in Fisherman's Wharf and one in Haight Ashbury, Bay City Bike isn't hard to find. The shop has an impressive fleet of bikes—many sizes and types—and friendly staff to help you map your biking adventure. ⊠ *2661 Taylor St., at Beach St., Fisherman's Wharf* ☎ *415/346–2453* ⊕ *baycitybike.com.*

Bike Hut. Known for its mom-and-pop–style service, the Hut is a small rental, repair, and used-bike shop. Rentals begin at $6 an hour. ⊠ *Pier 40, SoMa* ☎ *415/543–4335* ⊕ *www.thebikehut.org* ☉ *Closed Mon. and Tues.*

Blazing Saddles. This outfitter with multiple locations around San Francisco rents bikes for $8 to $9 an hour ($32 to $88 a day), depending on the type of bike, and shares tips on sights to see along the paths. ⊠ *2715 Hyde St., near Beach St., Fisherman's Wharf* ☎ *415/202–8888* ⊕ *www.blazingsaddles.com.*

WHERE TO BIKE

A completely flat, sea-level route, the Embarcadero hugs the eastern and northern bay and gives a clear view of open waters, the Bay Bridge, and sleek high-rises. The route from Pier 40 to Aquatic Park takes about 30 minutes to ride, and there are designated bike lanes the entire way. As you ride west, you'll pass the Bay Bridge, the Ferry Building, Coit Tower (look inland near Pier 19), and historic ships at the Hyde Street Pier. At Aquatic Park there's a nice view of Golden Gate Bridge. If you're not tired yet, continue along the Marina and through the Presidio's Crissy Field. You may want to time your ride so you end up at the Ferry Building, where you can refuel with a sandwich, a gelato, or—why not?—fresh oysters. ■ TIP➔ Keep your eyes open along this route—cars move quickly here, and streetcars and tourist traffic can cause congestion. Near Fisherman's Wharf you can bike on the promenade, but take it slow and watch out for pedestrians.

> **NO UPHILL BATTLE**
>
> Don't want to get stuck slogging up 20-degree inclines? Then pick up a copy of the foldout *San Francisco Bike Map and Walking Guide* ($4), which indicates street grades by color and delineates bike routes that avoid major hills and heavy traffic. You can pick up a copy in bicycle shops, some bookstores, or at the San Francisco Bicycle Coalition's website (⊕ *www.sfbike.org*).

A beautiful maze of roads and hidden bike paths crisscrosses San Francisco's most famous park, winding past rose gardens, lakes, waterfalls, museums, horse stables, bison, and, at the park's western edge, spectacular views of the Pacific Ocean. John F. Kennedy Drive is closed to motor vehicles on Sunday (and sometimes Saturday), when it's crowded with people-powered wheels. ■ TIP➔ Get a map of the park before you go—it's huge.

As Fell Street intersects Stanyan Street at the park's eastern entrance, veer right to begin a 30- to 45-minute, 3-mile ride down John F. Kennedy Drive to the Great Highway, where land meets ocean. Take a break and watch the waves roll in at Ocean Beach, or cross the street for a drink or a bite to eat at the casual, tree-shrouded Park Chalet (behind the Beach Chalet). Extend your ride a few more miles by turning left, riding a few blocks, and connecting with a raised bike path that runs parallel to the Pacific, winds through fields of emerald-green plants, and, after 2 miles, leads to Sloat Boulevard and the San Francisco Zoo.

The Marina Green, a vast lawn at the edge of the northern bay front, stretches along Marina Boulevard, adjacent to Fort Mason. It's the starting point of a well-used, paved bike path that runs through the Presidio along Crissy Field's waterfront wetlands, then heads for the Golden Gate Bridge and beyond. To do this ride, first take the path from Aquatic Park through Fort Mason to the Marina Green. Continue into the Presidio, and you'll eventually reach the base of the bridge, a 60-minute ride round-trip. To view the bridge from underneath, stay at water level and ride to Fort Point (where Kim Novak leaped into the drink in the film *Vertigo*).

If you want to cross the bridge, take Lincoln Boulevard to reach the road-level viewing area and continue across the bridge (signs indicate which side you must use). Once you're across, turn right on the first road leading northeast, Alexander Avenue. After a 10-minute all-downhill ride, you'll arrive on Bridgeway in downtown Sausalito, where you can rest at a café. After a little shopping, board the ferry (the terminal is where Bridgeway hits Sausalito Point) with your bike for the half-hour ride back to Fisherman's Wharf. ■TIP➜ **If it's overcast, foggy, or windy, don't bother doing the Golden Gate Bridge bike ride—the wind can feel downright dangerous on the bridge, and the trip is only awe-inspiring when you can take in the view.**

BOATING AND SAILING

San Francisco Bay has year-round sailing, but tricky currents and strong winds make the bay hazardous for inexperienced navigators. However, on group sails you can enjoy the bay while leaving the work to the experts.

Adventure Cat Sailing Charters. Near Fisherman's Wharf, Adventure Cat takes passengers aboard a 55-foot-long catamaran. The kids can play on the trampoline-like net between the two hulls while you sip drinks on the wind-protected sundeck. A 90-minute bay cruise costs $45; sunset sails with drinks and hors d'oeuvres are $60. ✉ *Pier 39, Dock J, Fisherman's Wharf* ☎ *800/498–4228, 415/777–1630* ⊕ *www. adventurecat.com.*

Rendezvous Charters. This operator offers individually ticketed trips on large sailing yachts, including sunset sails ($45) and Sunday brunch cruises on a schooner ($75). Ticketed trips tend to close from mid-October through March (although they continue to do private chartered sails throughout the year), so call in advance to confirm availability. ✉ *Pier 40, Suite 4, South Beach Harbor, Embarcadero* ☎ *415/543–7333* ⊕ *www.rendezvouscharters.com.*

SF Bay Adventures. Nautical tours, such as full-moon sails are the specialty on the company's *Freda B* schooner, along with Friday-night sails and sunset cruises. This outfit is based in Sausalito, but some boats depart from San Francisco. ✉ *Schooner Freda B Slip 907, 100 Bay St., Sausalito* ☎ *415/331–0444* ⊕ *www.sfbayadventures.com.*

Stow Lake. If you prefer calm freshwater, you can rent rowboats and pedal boats at Stow Lake in Golden Gate Park. Remember to bring bread for the ducks. ■TIP➜ **The lake is open daily from 10 to 5 for boating, rentals stop one hour before closing.** ✉ *50 Stow Lake Dr. E, off John F. Kennedy Dr., Golden Gate Park* ☎ *415/386–2531* ⊕ *www. stowlakeboathouse.com.*

17

FOOTBALL

San Francisco 49ers. The state-of-the-art Levi's Stadium, 45 miles south of San Francisco, has more than 13,000 square feet of HD video boards. Home games usually sell out far in advance. **Ticketmaster** (*www.ticketmaster.com*) and **StubHub!** (*www.stubhub.com*) are sources for single-game tickets. ⊠ *Levi's Stadium, 4900 Marie P. DeBartolo Way, from San Francisco, take U.S. 101 south to the Lawrence Expressway and follow signs, Santa Clara* ☎ *800/745–3000 Ticketmaster, 866/788–2482 StubHub!, 415/464–9377 Santa Clara stadium* ⊕ *www.49ers.com.*

HIKING

Hiking options in and around San Francisco include everything from the easygoing Golden Gate Promenade along the city's waterfront to the more rigorous sections the Bay Area Ridge Trail. And there are plenty of great hikes to be had in the Presidio.

Bay Area Ridge Trail. Hills and mountains—including Mt. Tamalpais in Marin County and Mt. Diablo in the East Bay, which is thought to have the second-longest sight lines anywhere in the world after Mt. Kilimanjaro—form a ring around the Bay Area. In San Francisco the Ridge Trail winds through the center of the city to the Golden Gate Overlook in the Presidio, offering up the most spectacular views. The Bay Area Ridge Trail is an ongoing project to connect all of the region's ridgelines. The trail is currently 367 miles long, but when finished it will extend more than 550 miles, stretching from San Jose to Napa and encompassing all nine Bay Area counties. One of the trail's most impressive ridgelines can be found on Mt. Tamalpais, in Marin County. ⊠ *San Francisco* ⊕ *www.ridgetrail.org.*

Golden Gate National Recreation Area (GGNRA). This huge, protected area encompasses the San Francisco coastline, the Marin Headlands, and Point Reyes National Seashore. It's veined with hiking trails, and guided walks are offered in some places. You can find current schedules at visitor centers in the Presidio and Marin Headlands; they're also online at *www.nps.gov/goga.* For descriptions of locations within the recreation area—along with rich color photographs, hiking information, and maps—pick up a copy of *Guide to the Parks,* available in local bookstores or online from the **Golden Gate National Parks Conservancy** (*www.parksconservancy.org*). ⊠ *Bldg. 201, Fort Mason* ☎ *415/561–3000* ⊕ *www.nps.gov/goga.*

Golden Gate Promenade. This great walk passes through Crissy Field, taking in marshlands, kite-flyers, beachfront, and windsurfers, with the Golden Gate Bridge as a backdrop. The 4.3-mile walk is flat and easy—it should take less than two hours round-trip. If you begin at Aquatic Park, you'll end up practically underneath the bridge at Fort Point Pier. ■**TIP→ If you're driving, park at Fort Point and do the walk from west to east.** It can get blustery, even when it's sunny, so be sure to layer. ⊠ *San Francisco.*

Presidio. Hiking and biking trails wind through nearly 1,500 acres of woods and hills in the Presidio, past old redbrick military buildings and jaw-dropping scenic overlooks with bay and ocean views. Rangers and docents lead guided hikes and nature walks throughout the year. Pick up a copy of the park's visitors guide at the Visitor Center (*105 Montgomery St.*) or online at www.nps.gov/prsf. The promenade at Crissy Field leads north past views of Golden Gate Bridge. If it's open, fortify yourself with coffee or snacks at the **Warming Hut** (*983 Marine Dr., off Long Ave.*) before following the paved road that continues on to the Civil War–era Fort Point, which sits under the bridge. ⊠ *Presidio Visitors Center, 105 Montgomery St. at Lincoln Blvd.* ☎ *415/561–4323* ⊕ *www.nps.gov/prsf.*

KAYAKING

Surrounded by water on three sides, San Francisco has plenty of opportunities for kayaking enthusiasts of all skill levels.

City Kayak. City Kayak operates bay tours along the waterfront and beneath the Bay Bridge starting from $44; the company also runs full-moon night paddles and trips to Treasure Island. Rentals are $38 per hour for a single kayak or stand-up paddleboard. Trips depart daily and no prior experience is necessary. ⊠ *South Beach Waterfront, Pier 40* ⊕ *citykayak.com.*

Sea Trek. This company offers trips around Angel Island and the Golden Gate Bridge, moonlight paddles, and many trips in Marin County. Three-hour trips cost from $75 to $120, full-day trips start at $95. Most excursions leave from Sausalito. ⊠ *Bay Model, 2100 Marinship Way, Sausalito* ☎ *415/332–8494* ⊕ *www.seatrek.com.*

17

RUNNING

San Francisco is spectacular for running. There are more than 7 miles of paved trails in and around **Golden Gate Park**; circling **Stow Lake** and then crossing the bridge and running up the path to the top of Strawberry Hill is a total of 2½ miles. An enormously popular route is the 2-mile raised bike path that runs from Lincoln Way along the ocean, at the southern border of Golden Gate Park, to Sloat Boulevard, which is the northern border of the San Francisco Zoo. (Stick to the park's interior when it's windy, as ocean gusts can kick up sand.) From Sloat Boulevard you can pick up the **Lake Merced** bike path, which loops around the lake and the golf course, to extend your run another 5 miles.

The paved path along the **Marina** provides a 1½-mile (round-trip) run along a flat, well-paved surface and has glorious bay views. Start where Laguna Street meets Marina Boulevard, then run west along the Marina Green toward the Golden Gate and St. Francis yacht clubs, near the docks at the northern end of Marina Boulevard. On weekends beware: you'll have to wind through the crowds—but those views are worth it. You can extend your Marina run by jogging the paths through the restored wetlands of Crissy Field, just past the yacht harbor, then up the hill to the Golden Gate Bridge.

The *San Francisco Bike Map and Walking Guide (see Bicycling)*, which indicates hill grades on city streets by color, is a great resource. Online, check the **San Francisco Road Runners Club** site (⊕ *www.sfrrc.org*) for some recommended routes and links to several local races.

EVENTS

Bay to Breakers. First run in 1912, the 12K Bay to Breakers race, held on the third Sunday in May, is one of the world's largest footraces—but in true San Francisco fashion there's nothing typical about it. About a third of the more than 50,000 runners are serious athletes; the rest are "fun runners" who wear famously wacky costumes—or attempt to wear no costumes at all. The race makes its way from the Embarcadero at the bay to the Pacific Ocean, passing through Golden Gate Park. ⊠ *San Francisco* ☎ *415/231–3130* ⊕ *www.baytobreakers.com*.

San Francisco Marathon. The marathon, usually held on a Sunday in late July, starts and finishes at the Embarcadero. Thousands of runners pass through downtown, the Marina, the Presidio, and Golden Gate Park and cross the Golden Gate Bridge, tackling some of the city's milder hills along the way. ⊠ *San Francisco* ☎ *888/958–6668 ext. 1* ⊕ *www. thesfmarathon.com*.

SKATING

Church of 8 Wheels. Dance or roll along to disco-era tunes at this retro-themed skating rink inside an old church. Weekend days are open to anyone; Friday and Saturday nights is adults only. ⊠ *554 Fillmore St. (at Fell), Hayes Valley* ☎ *415/752–1967* ⊕ *www.churchof8wheels.com* ⊠ *$10, skate rental $5*.

WHALE-WATCHING

Between January and April, hundreds of gray whales migrate along the coast; the rest of the year humpback and blue whales feed offshore at the Farallon Islands. The best place to watch them from shore is Point Reyes, in Marin County *(see Chapter 19)*.

For a better view, head out on a whale-watching trip. Seas around San Francisco can be rough, so pack motion-sickness tablets. You should also dress warmly, wear sunscreen, and pack rain gear and sunglasses; binoculars come in handy, too. Tour companies don't provide meals or snacks, so bring your own lunch and water. Make reservations at least a week ahead.

California Whale Adventures. California Whale Adventures has year-round whale-watching trips ($100), weekends only, and reservations are highly encouraged. In the fall you can take a great-white-shark tour ($200 per person, weekends only). All trips leave from Fisherman's Wharf. ⊠ *Fisherman's Wharf* ☎ *650/579–7777* ⊕ *www.californiawha-leadventures.com*.

SHOPPING
AND SPAS

Updated by
Jerry James
Stone

With its grand department stores and funky secondhand boutiques, San Francisco summons a full range of shopping experiences. From the anarchist bookstore to the mouthwatering specialty-food purveyors at the gleaming Ferry Building, the local shopping opportunities reflect the city's various personalities. Visitors with limited time often focus their energies on the high-density Union Square area, where several major department stores tower over big-name boutiques. But if you're keen to find unique local shops, consider moving beyond the square's radius.

Each neighborhood has its own distinctive finds, whether it's 1960s housewares, cheeky stationery, or vintage Levi's. If shopping in San Francisco has a downside, it's that real bargains can be few and far between. Sure, neighborhoods such as the Lower Haight and the Mission have thrift shops and other inexpensive stores, but you won't find many discount outlets in the city, where rents are sky-high and space is at a premium.

Seasonal sales, usually in late January and late July or August, are good opportunities for finding deep discounts on clothing. The *San Francisco Chronicle* and *San Francisco Examiner* advertise sales. For smaller shops, check the free *SF Weekly*, which can be found on street corners every Wednesday. Sample sales are usually held by individual manufacturers, so check your favorite company's website before visiting.

SHOPPING

UNION SQUARE AND CHINATOWN

UNION SQUARE

Serious shoppers head straight to Union Square, San Francisco's main shopping area and the site of most of its department stores, including Macy's, Neiman Marcus, Barneys, and Saks Fifth Avenue. Nearby are such platinum-card international boutiques as Yves Saint Laurent, Cartier, Emporio Armani, Gucci, Hermès, and Louis Vuitton.

The **Westfield San Francisco Shopping Centre,** anchored by Bloomingdale's and Nordstrom, is notable for its gorgeous atriums and its top-notch dining options.

■TIP➔ Most retailers in the square don't open until 10 am or later, so there isn't much advantage to getting an early start unless you're grabbing breakfast nearby. If you're on the prowl for art, be aware that many galleries are closed on Sundays and Mondays.

ART GALLERIES

Fodor's Choice ★ **Berggruen Gallery.** Twentieth-century American and European paintings are displayed throughout three airy floors. Some recent exhibitions have included the works of Robert Kelly and Isca Greenfield-Sanders. Look for thematic shows here, too; past exhibits have had titles such as Summer Highlights and Four Decades. ✉ *10 Hawthorne St., at Howard St., Union Sq.* ☎ *415/781–4629* ⊕ *www.berggruen.com.*

The Bond Latin Gallery. The charming owners of this Latin American art gallery will alone make you want to return. Cozy yet light, some of the vibrant works on show come from such artists as Diego Rivera, Laura Hernandez, and Francisco Toledo. ✉ *251 Post St., Suite 610, Union Sq.* ☎ *415/362–1480* ⊕ *www.bondlatin.com* ☽ *Closed Sun.*

Fodor's Choice ★ **Fraenkel Gallery.** This renowned gallery represents museum-caliber photographers or their estates, including Nicholas Nixon, Nan Goldin, Richard Misrach, and Garry Winogrand. Recent shows have included work by Robert Adams, Idris Khan, and Hiroshi Sugimoto. Most shows feature one or two artists, but the annual Several Exceptionally Good Recently Acquired Pictures showcases the range of works the gallery exhibits. ✉ *49 Geary St., 4th fl., between Kearny St. and Grant Ave., Union Sq.* ☎ *415/981–2661* ⊕ *fraenkelgallery.com* ☽ *Closed Sun. and Mon.*

Hackett-Mill Gallery. This gallery prides itself on its friendly staffers who will educate you about the art or leave you alone, whichever you prefer. Some of the artists here include Conrad Marca-Relli, Esteban Vincente, Kenzo Okada, and Robert De Niro Sr. The specialties here are American modern, postwar abstract expressionist, and Bay Area figurative art. ✉ *201 Post St., Suite 1000, at Grant Ave., Union Sq.* ☎ *415/362–3377* ⊕ *www.hackettmill.com* ☽ *Closed Sat.–Mon.*

Hang Art. A spirit of fun imbues this inviting space that showcases emerging artists. Prices range from a few hundred dollars to several thousand, making it an ideal place for novice collectors to get their feet wet. ✉ *567 Sutter St., 2nd fl., near Mason St., Union Sq.* ☎ *415/434–4264* ⊕ *www.hangart.com.*

18

Hespe Gallery. Priced between $3,000 and $50,000, the paintings and sculptures here by mid-career artists, many of them Californians, are primarily representational. Owner Charles Hespe is an instantly likable art enthusiast who delights buyers and browsers. ⊠ *251 Post St., Suite 210, between Stockton St. and Grant Ave., Union Sq.* ☎ *415/776–5918* ⊕ *www.hespe.com* ☽ *Closed Sun. and Mon.*

Meyerovich Gallery. Sculpture and works on paper by masters such as Pablo Picasso, Robert Motherwell, David Sultan, and Helen Frankenthaler are the attraction. Guy Dill's whimsical contemporary sculptures draw the eye from across the room. ⊠ *251 Post St., Suite 400, 4th fl., between Stockton St. and Grant Ave., Union Sq.* ☎ *415/421–7171* ⊕ *www.meyerovich.com* ☽ *Closed Sun.*

Modernism. Multimodal exhibits are on a seven-week rotation and span an impressive arc of multimedia, photography, performance, painting, and sculpture. Featured artists have included Le Corbusier and Erwin Blumenfeld. ⊠ *Monadnock Bldg., 685 Market St., Suite 290, Union Sq.* ☎ *415/541–0461* ⊕ *www.modernisminc.com.*

Robert Tat Gallery. Old meets new in Robert Tat's meticulously selected photography collection. Early 20th-century modernist works hang adjacent to contemporary pieces. A visit takes you back in time and around the world as well. ⊠ *49 Geary St., Suite 410, Union Sq.* ☎ *415/781–1122* ⊕ *www. robertat.com* ☽ *Closed Sun. and Mon.; Tues. by appointment only.*

Fodor's Choice ★ **Serge Sorokko Gallery.** This big, bright open space is a welcoming retreat from the racing pulse of Geary Street. The friendly, knowledgeable staff will answer your questions as you stroll past walls and podiums decorated by the works of some very famous contemporary artists, including the paintings of Hunt Slonem and porcelain flowers of Vladimir Kanevsky. It's the perfect place to get lost, and to spend a few thousand to tens of thousands of dollars, if you're so inclined. ⊠ *55 Geary St., between Kearny St. and Grant Ave., Union Sq.* ☎ *415/421–7770* ⊕ *www.sorokko.com.*

BEAUTY

The Art of Shaving. Looking for a silver-tip badger brush? A polished-teak shaving-soap bowl? Or even sandalwood-infused pre-shave oil? You can pick up all of these items here, while the master barbers in the back provide anything from a moustache trim to the 45-minute "Royal Shave" (including hot towel and after-shave mask). ⊠ *287 Geary St., at Powell St., Union Sq.* ☎ *415/677–0871* ⊕ *www.theartofshaving.com.*

Fresh. The cosmetics line's only Northern California store occupies a quaint historic structure built just after the 1906 earthquake. Indulge in oval milk soaps from France, sugar-lemon lotion, and pomegranate conditioner. Fresh is most popular for its body-care sets, the Umbrian Clay being one of them. During the holiday season, the Seaberry Restorative Body Cream can be hard to come by. ⊠ *301 Sutter St., at Grant Ave., Union Sq.* ☎ *415/248–0210* ⊕ *www.fresh.com.*

Lush. Towers of bulk soap, which can be cut to order, and mountains of baseball-size fizzing "bath bombs" are some of the first items you'll see in this tightly packed and extremely fragrant little boutique, which resembles a cheese shop more than a Sephora. Some potions are so fresh (and perishable) that they're stored in a refrigerator and come with an expiration date. ⊠ *240 Powell St., between O'Farrell and Geary Sts., Union Sq.* ☎ *415/693–9633* ⊕ *www.lushusa.com.*

CLOTHING: MEN AND WOMEN

The Archive. The closest thing to Savile Row in San Francisco, this small, cutting-edge, men-only boutique has everything from handmade suits to large handmade silver belt buckles from top-shelf Japanese and Italian designers. ⊠ *317 Sutter St., near Grant Ave., Union Sq.* ☎ *415/391–5550* ⊕ *archivesf.com* ⊗ *Closed Sun.*

Cable Car Clothiers. This classic British menswear store, open since 1939, is so fully stocked that a whole room is dedicated to hats, pants are cataloged like papers in file cabinets, and entire displays showcase badger-bristle shaving brushes. ■TIP➔ **The cable-car logo gear, from silk ties to pewter banks, makes for dashing souvenirs.** ⊠ *110 Sutter St., Suite 108, Union Sq.* ☎ *415/397–4740* ⊕ *www.cablecarclothiers. com* ⊗ *Closed Sun.*

Gucci. The gold-label designer exudes luxe elegance in a palatial temple of black lacquer, bronze, and marble. Fine jewelry, handbags, and luggage dominate the first floor, and shoes rule the second. If you make it to the third floor without maxing out your credit card, you'll be rewarded with a flute of champagne for trying on an evening gown or dinner coat. ⊠ *240 Stockton St., Union Sq.* ☎ *415/392–2808* ⊕ *www.gucci.com.*

Levi's. A massive flagship for 501s, this is quite possibly the biggest place to buy your favorite pair of five-pocket jeans. Every style, size, color, and cut of the original denim brand is here. You can even get a custom fitting if you book ahead of time. ⊠ *815 Market St., at 4th St., Union Sq.* ☎ *415/501–0100* ⊕ *us.levi.com.*

Fodor'sChoice
★ **Margaret O'Leary.** If you can only buy one piece of clothing in San Francisco, make it a hand-loomed cashmere sweater by this Irish-born local legend. The perfect antidote to the city's wind and fog, the sweaters are so beloved by San Franciscans that some of them never wear anything else. Pick up an airplane wrap for your trip home, or a media cozy to keep your tech toasty. Another store is in Pacific Heights, at 2400 Fillmore Street. ⊠ *1 Claude La., at Sutter St., just west of Kearny St., Union Sq.* ☎ *415/391–1010* ⊕ *www.margaretoleary.com.*

Metier. For boutique shopping that's anything but hit or miss, browse through this unusual selection of jewelry by artists like Arielle de Pinto, Philip Crangi, and Gillian Conroy. The one-of-a-kind rings, charms, and pendants have won this boutique an obsessively loyal following. ⊠ *546 Laguna St., between Linden St. and Hayes St., Union Sq.* ☎ *415/590–2998* ⊕ *www.metiersf.com.*

Scotch & Soda. With clean, tailored lines and deep solid colors, there is something elegant yet cutting-edge for every age here. Based on Amsterdam couture, and carrying European labels, this hive of a shop is cool but friendly; it also has an old but new feel to it. The Bodycon Peplum dress is a classic, as is the men's stretch wool blazer. This is a good place to visit if you're looking for a new pair of denims, or a cool shirt for a night out. ⊠ *59 Grant Ave., between Geary and O'Farrell Sts., Union Sq.* ☎ *415/644–8334* ⊕ *www.scotch-soda.com.*

18

Tory Burch. The East Coast socialite–turned–designer has brightened staid Maiden Lane with her outpost for Bergdorf Blondes, inspired by designs from the '60s and '70s. The carpet is a rich avocado, walls are magenta among other colors, and velvet curtains frame floor-to-ceiling mirrors in other candy colors. In addition to her ubiquitous ballet flats, Burch's signature tunics, silk blouses, and suits are on offer. ⊠ *50 Maiden La., between Kearny St. and Grant Ave., Union Sq.* ☎ *415/398–1525* ⊕ *www.toryburch.com.*

DEPARTMENT STORES

Bloomingdale's. The black-and-white checkerboard theme, the abundance of glass, and the sheer size might remind you of Vegas. This department store emphasizes American labels like Diane von Furstenberg and Jack Spade. The well-planned layout defines individual departments without losing the grand and open feel. ⊠ *845 Market St., between 4th and 5th Sts., Union Sq.* ☎ *415/856–5300* ⊕ *www.bloomingdales.com.*

Fodor's Choice
★

Gump's. It's a San Francisco institution, dating to the 19th century, and it's a strikingly luxurious one. The airy store exudes a museumlike vibe, with its large decorative vases, sumptuous housewares, and Tahitian-pearl display. It's a great place to pick up gifts, such as the Golden Gate Bridge note cards or silver-plated butter spreaders in a signature Gump's box. ⊠ *135 Post St., near Kearny St., Union Sq.* ☎ *415/982–1616* ⊕ *www.gumps.com.*

Neiman Marcus. The surroundings, which include a Philip Johnson–designed checkerboard facade, a gilded atrium, and a stained-glass skylight, are as ritzy as the goods showcased within. The mix includes designer men's and women's clothing and accessories as well as posh household wares. ■TIP➔ **Although the prices may raise an eyebrow or two, the Last Call sales—in January and July—draw big crowds.** After hitting the vast handbag salon, those who lunch daintily can order consommé and bread laden with strawberry butter in the Rotunda Restaurant. ⊠ *150 Stockton St., at Geary St., Union Sq.* ☎ *415/362–3900* ⊕ *www.neimanmarcus.com.*

Nordstrom. Somehow Nordstrom manages to be all things to all people, and this location, with spiral escalators circling a four-story atrium, is no exception. Whether you're an elegant lady of a certain age shopping for a new mink coat or a teen on the hunt for a Roxy hoodie, the salespeople are known for being happy to help. Nordstrom carries the best selections in town of designers such as Tory Burch, but its own brands have loyal followings, too. ■TIP➔ **The café upstairs is a superb choice for a shopping break.** ⊠ *Westfield Shopping Centre, 865 Market St., at 5th St., Union Sq.* ☎ *415/243–8500* ⊕ *shop.nordstrom.com.*

ELECTRONICS

Apple Store San Francisco. Apple's flagship San Francisco store has a new location and a lot more space. It's a two-level open-aired tech temple to Macs and the people who use them. Play with iPhones, laptops, and hundreds of geeky accessories, then watch a theater presentation or attend an educational workshop. ⊠ *300 Post St., at Stockton St., Union Sq.* ☎ *415/486–4800* ⊕ *www.apple.com.*

FOOD AND DRINK

William Glen & Son. The more than 400 whiskeys arranged along the back wall—mostly single-malt Scotches—are organized by their region of origin, so you can easily distinguish those made in Islay from those from Speyside or Lowland. The charming Scottish proprietor can tell you about his favorites, help you with the selection of tartan scarves or cashmere sweaters, or even equip you with a kilt. ⊠ *360 Sutter St., between Grant Ave. and Stockton St., Union Sq.* ☎ *415/989–5458* ⊕ *www.wmglen.com.*

FURNITURE, HOUSEWARES, AND GIFTS

Fodor'sChoice
★

Diptyque. The original Diptyque boutique in Paris has attracted a long line of celebrities. You can find the full array of scented candles and fragrances in this chic shop that would be at home on the boulevard St-Germain. Trademark black-and-white labels adorn the popular L'eau toilet water, scented with geranium and sandalwood. Candles come in traditional and esoteric scents, including lavender, basil, leather, and fig tree. Also available are Mariage Frères teas. ⊠ *73 Geary St., at Grant Ave., Union Sq.* ☎ *415/402–0600* ⊕ *www.diptyqueparis.com.*

Samuel Scheuer. Designers and other fans make their way here for luxurious bed and bath items and linens. The pretty tablecloths, runners, napkins, fragrant candles, and luxurious bath accessories are popular gifts. ⊠ *340 Sutter St., between Grant Ave. and Stockton St., Union Sq.* ☎ *415/392–2813* ⊕ *www.scheuerlinens.com.*

Williams-Sonoma. Behind striped awnings and a historic facade lies the massive mother ship of the Sonoma-founded kitchen-store empire. La Cornue custom stoves beckon you inward, and two grand staircases draw you upward to the world of dinnerware, linens, and chefs' tools. Antique tart tins, eggbeaters, and pastry cutters from the personal collection of founder Chuck Williams line the walls. ⊠ *340 Post St., between Powell and Stockton Sts., Union Sq.* ☎ *415/362–9450* ⊕ *www. williams-sonoma.com.*

HANDBAGS, LUGGAGE, AND LEATHER GOODS

Goyard. After more than a century of selling trunks, handbags, and pet leashes to Parisians, Goyard opened its second store here to offer San Franciscans a discreet alternative to Louis Vuitton. Rather than splash its name everywhere, the store signals luxury with a signature chevron pattern. Even if you walk away empty-handed, you'll be reminded of what travel used to mean. ⊠ *118 Grant Ave., at Geary St., Union Sq.* ☎ *415/523–8200* ⊕ *www.goyard.com.*

HANDICRAFTS AND FOLK ART

Britex Fabrics. Walls of Italian wool in deep rich colors, yards of Faille striped silk, and neat stacks of fresh cotton prints await your creative touch. A San Francisco institution, the multifloor Britex also sells a wide array of buttons, thread, and trim. If sewing is your thing, this will be a visit to paradise. ⊠ *146 Geary St., between Grant Ave. and Stockton St., Union Sq.* ☎ *415/392–2910* ⊕ *www.britexfabrics.com.*

18

JEWELRY AND COLLECTIBLES

Lang Antiques and Estate Jewelry. Dozens of diamond bracelets in the window attract shoppers to one of the city's best vintage jewelry shops, where rings, brooches, and other glittering items represent various eras and styles, from Victorian and Edwardian to art nouveau and Arts and Crafts. The shop has been selling fine jewelry, including engagement rings and a few vintage watches, since 1969. ⊠ *309 Sutter St., at Grant Ave., Union Sq.* ☎ *415/982–2213* ⊕ *www.langantiques.com.*

Shreve & Co. Along with gems in dazzling settings, San Francisco's oldest retail store—it's been at this location since 1852—carries watches by Jaeger-LeCoultre and others. On weekends well-heeled couples scope out hefty diamond engagement rings. ⊠ *150 Post St., at Grant Ave., Union Sq.* ☎ *415/421–2600* ⊕ *www.shreve.com.*

Tiffany & Co. This gray marble beauty towers over Union Square with almost as much leverage as its signature blue box. The company that all but invented the modern engagement ring makes more than just brides swoon with Elsa Peretti's sinuous silver and architect Frank Gehry's collection using materials like Pernambuco wood and black gold. ⊠ *350 Post St., between Powell and Stockton Sts., Union Sq.* ☎ *415/781–7000* ⊕ *www.tiffany.com.*

SHOES

Camper. The Spanish brand's whimsical footwear is wildly popular with young adults. Unexpected embroidered patterns (leaves, butterflies) adorn many of the pairs, sometimes beginning on one shoe and continuing on the other. Other styles are reminiscent of bowling and boxing shoes. ⊠ *39 Grant Ave., between O'Farrell and Geary Sts., Union Sq.* ☎ *415/296–1005* ⊕ *www.camper.com.*

SPORTING GOODS

Niketown. More glitzy multimedia extravaganza than true sporting-goods store, this emporium is nevertheless the best place in town to find anything and everything with the famous swoosh. ⊠ *278 Post St., at Stockton St., Union Sq.* ☎ *415/392–6453* ⊕ *store.nike.com.*

The North Face. The Bay Area–based national retailer is famous for its tents, sleeping bags, backpacks, and outdoor apparel, including rugged Gore-Tex jackets and pants. ⊠ *180 Post St., at Grant Ave., Union Sq.* ☎ *415/433–3223* ⊕ *www.thenorthface.com.*

CHINATOWN

The intersection of Grant Avenue and Bush Street marks the gateway to Chinatown. The area's 24 blocks of shops, restaurants, and markets are a nonstop tide of activity. Dominating the exotic cityscape are the sights and smells of food: crates of bok choy, tanks of live crabs, cages of live partridges, and hanging whole chickens. Racks of Chinese silks, colorful pottery, baskets, and carved figurines are displayed chockablock on the sidewalks, alongside fragrant herb shops where your bill might be tallied on an abacus. And if you need to knock off souvenir shopping for the kids and coworkers in your life, the dense and multiple selections of toys, T-shirts, mugs, magnets, decorative boxes, and countless other trinkets make it a quick, easy, and inexpensive proposition.

FOOD AND DRINK

Golden Gate Fortune Cookies. Nestled in a narrow alleyway, this tiny destination is impossible to find unless you have directions. This is the place to watch fortune cookies being made; the intricate process involves flattening, folding, and pressing patches of dough. You can purchase big bags of cookies in various flavors, shapes, and sizes to take home. ⊠ *56 Ross Alley, Chinatown* ☎ *415/781–3956.*

Great China Herb Co. Since 1922, this aromatic shop has been treating the city with its wide selection of ginseng, tea, and other herbs. You might even hear the click of an abacus as a purchase is tallied up. A Chinese doctor (who speaks English) is always on hand to recommend the perfect remedy. ⊠ *857 Washington St., between Grant Ave. and Stockton St., Chinatown* ☎ *415/982–2195.*

Fodor's Choice
★
Vital Tea Leaf. Tea enthusiasts will feel at peace in this bright, spacious, hardwood-floor haven for sipping. You'll find more than 400 different varieties of tea here, and the staff is extremely knowledgeable on the health benefits of each and every one. ⊠ *1044 Grant Ave., between Jackson St. and Pacific Ave., Chinatown* ☎ *415/981–2388* ⊕ *www.vitaltealeaf.net.*

FURNITURE, HOUSEWARES, AND GIFTS

The Wok Shop. The store carries woks, of course, but also anything else you could need for Chinese cooking—bamboo steamers, ginger graters, wicked-looking cleavers—plus accessories for Japanese cooking, including sushi paraphernalia and tempura racks. ⊠ *718 Grant Ave., at Sacramento St., Chinatown* ☎ *415/989–3797* ⊕ *www.wokshop.com.*

TOYS AND GADGETS

Chinatown Kite Shop. The kites sold here range from basic diamond shapes to box- and animal-shaped configurations. ■**TIP**➔ **Colorful dragon kites make great souvenirs.** ⊠ *717 Grant Ave., near Sacramento St., Chinatown* ☎ *415/989–5182* ⊕ *www.chinatownkite.com.*

18

SOMA AND CIVIC CENTER

SOMA

ANTIQUES

Antonio's Antiques. This SoMa maze of museum-quality English and French antiques and objets d'art might include an 18th-century French harp or delicate tortoise-shell miniatures. The shop's inventory leans toward items from the 17th and 18th centuries. ⊠ *701 Bryant St., at 5th St., SoMa* ☎ *415/781–1737.*

Grand Central Station Antiques. This large, three-story space stocks mostly 19th- and early-20th-century European and American storage pieces—armoires, highboys, buffets, and the occasional barrister bookcase—with an emphasis on the small and practical. Service is affable. ⊠ *360 Bayshore Blvd, at Flowers St., SoMa* ☎ *415/252–8155* ⊕ *www.gcsantiques.com.*

ART GALLERIES

Arthaus. This one-story gallery south of Market provides an intimate space for both local and New York artists to display their contemporary work. Gallery owners Annette Schutz and James Bacchi are very approachable and include a diverse range of mediums as well as rotating shows beneath their roof. ⊠ *411 Brannan St., between 3rd and 4th Sts., SoMa* ☏ *415/977–0223* ⊕ *www.arthaus-sf.com* ⊗ *Closed Sun. and Mon.*

Crown Point Press. What started as a print workshop in 1962 now includes studios as well as a large, airy gallery where etchings, intaglio prints, engravings, and aquatints by local and internationally renowned artists are displayed. ⊠ *20 Hawthorne St., between 2nd and 3rd Sts., SoMa* ☏ *415/974–6273* ⊕ *www.crownpoint.com* ⊗ *Closed weekends.*

San Francisco Camerawork. This nonprofit organization mounts thematic exhibits and has a well-stocked bookstore and a reference library. The lecture program includes noted photographers and critics. ⊠ *1011 Market St., 2nd fl., at 6th St., SoMa* ☏ *415/487–1011* ⊕ *www.sfcamerawork.org* ⊗ *Closed Sun. and Mon.*

Varnish Fine Art. Jen Rogers and Kerri Stephens's gallery specializes in thought-provoking works such as those by San Francisco–based artist Brian Goggin, known for his public art piece *Defenestration.* Ransom and Mitchell, two other noteworthy locals the gallery represents, blend photography and set design together to create a truly surreal visual experience. This gallery is open by appointment only, Tuesday through Saturday from 11 am to 6 pm. ⊠ *16 Jessie St., Suite C120, near 1st St., SoMa* ☏ *415/433–4400* ⊕ *www.varnishfineart.com* ⊗ *Closed Sun. and Mon.*

BOOKS

Alexander Book Co. The three floors here are stocked with literature, poetry, and children's books, with a focus on hard-to-find works by men and women of color. ⊠ *50 2nd St., between Jessie and Stevenson Sts., SoMa* ☏ *415/495–2992* ⊕ *www.alexanderbook.com.*

Fodor's Choice
★ **Chronicle Books.** This local beacon of publishing produces inventively designed fiction, cookbooks, art books, and other titles, as well as diaries, planners, and address books—all of which you can purchase at three airy and attractive spaces. The other stores are at 680 2nd Street, near AT&T Park, and 1846 Union Street, in Cow Hollow. ⊠ *Metreon Westfield Shopping Center, 165 4th St., near Howard St., SoMa* ☏ *415/369–6271* ⊕ *www.chroniclebooks.com.*

FOOD AND DRINK

Blue Bottle Coffee. The revered microroaster's practitioners brew their sacred beans in a $20,000 siphon bar from Japan with halogen-lighted glass globes that resemble a science experiment. A stop here makes for a perfect reprieve from shopping. ⊠ *66 Mint Plaza, off Mission St., SoMa* ☏ *415/495–3394* ⊕ *www.bluebottlecoffee.com.*

Bluxome Street Winery. Wineshops exist all over the city, but this is the only winery within city limits. Grapes are brought in from Russian River Valley, and all production takes place on-site, reviving an industry that was once thriving a hundred years ago in SoMa before Napa and Sonoma took it over. Come to the tasting room to sample light summery rosés, rich Pinot Noirs, or refreshing Sauvignon Blancs. On the last Saturday of each month, the space becomes a farmers' market with local vendors selling honey and eggs alongside the wine. ⊠ *53 Bluxome St., SoMa* ☏ *415/543–5353* ⊕ *www.bluxomewinery.com.*

K&L Wine Merchants. More than any other wine store, this one has an ardent cult following around town. The friendly staffers promise not to sell what they don't taste themselves, and weekly events—on Thursday from 5 pm to 6:30 pm and Saturday from noon to 3 pm—open the tastings to customers. The best-seller list for varietals and regions for both the under- and over-$30 categories appeals to the wine lover in everyone. ⊠ *855 Harrison St., at 4th St., SoMa* ☎ *415/896–1734* ⊕ *www.klwines.com.*

Wine Club. The large selection and great prices make up for this wine-shop's bare-bones ambience. At the self-serve wine bar you can taste wines for a modest fee, a great boon if you want to try before you buy. Caviar and wine paraphernalia, including Riedel wineglasses, books, openers, and decanters, are also sold here. ⊠ *953 Harrison St., between 5th and 6th Sts., SoMa* ☎ *415/512–9086* ⊕ *www.thewineclub.com.*

FURNITURE, HOUSEWARES, AND GIFTS
Mscape. The shop sells sleek furniture and accessories, such as low-slung couches with nary a curve in sight, and a variety of platform beds. Many items can be custom ordered. ⊠ *521 6th St., between Bryant and Brannan Sts., SoMa* ☎ *415/543–1771* ⊕ *mscapesf.com.*

HANDBAGS, LUGGAGE, AND LEATHER GOODS
Kate Spade. Punchy colors, retro shapes, and a cheeky sense of humor have made Kate Spade purses wildly popular among ladies of all ages. Case in point: the Over the Moon Rocket clutch is actually shaped as a rocket and contains 14-karat gold-plated hardware. The shop also stocks shoes, cosmetics cases, datebooks, and note cards. ⊠ *845 Market St., SoMa* ☎ *415/222–9638* ⊕ *www.katespade.com.*

JEWELRY AND COLLECTIBLES
San Francisco Museum of Modern Art Museum Store. The shop is known for its exclusive line of watches and jewelry, as well as artists' monographs and artful housewares. Posters, calendars, children's art sets and books, and art books for adults round out the merchandise. ⊠ *151 3rd St., between Mission and Howard Sts., SoMa* ☎ *888/357–0037* ⊕ *museumstore.sfmoma.org.*

SPORTING GOODS
REI. In addition to carrying a vast selection of clothing and outdoor gear of the Seattle-based co-op, the store rents camping equipment and repairs snowboards and bikes. ⊠ *840 Brannan St., between 7th and 8th Sts., SoMa* ☎ *415/934–1938* ⊕ *www.rei.com.*

CIVIC CENTER
FARMERS' MARKETS
Heart of the City Farmers' Market. Three times a week vendors sell heaps of cheap produce, along with baked goods, potted herbs, and the occasional live chicken. ⊠ *United Nations Plaza, between 7th and 8th Sts., Civic Center* ☎ *415/558–9455* ⊕ *heartofthecity-farmersmar.squarespace.com.*

FURNITURE, HOUSEWARES, AND GIFTS
Sur la Table. Everything the home chef could need is here, along with round aspic cutters, larding needles, and other things many cooks never knew existed. The store hosts cooking classes and jaw-dropping demonstrations. ⊠ *San Francisco Centre, 845 Market St., at 5th St., Civic Center* ☎ *415/814–4691* ⊕ *www.surlatable.com.*

18

THE TENDERLOIN

ART GALLERIES

John Pence Gallery. The 8,000-square-foot facility, San Francisco's largest gallery, exhibits drawings, paintings, and sculpture. Many of the works are by important contemporary academic realists. ✉ *750 Post St., between Leavenworth and Jones Sts., Tenderloin* ☎ *415/441–1138* ⊕ *www.johnpence.com* ⊙ *Closed Sun.*

Silverman Gallery. Fashion, music, performance, paintings, and photography collide here—literally. Every four to six weeks a new exhibit enters the space pushing the boundaries of content, concept, and form. The gallery also hosts talks with local and international artists. ✉ *488 Ellis St., between Jones and Leavenworth Sts., Tenderloin* ☎ *415/255–9508* ⊕ *jessicasilvermangallery.com* ⊙ *Closed Sun. and Mon.*

HAYES VALLEY

ANTIQUES

Another Time. Specializing in beautifully restored furniture from the 1930s through the 1960s, this store sells Heywood Wakefield tambour buffets, art-deco bars, and French art-deco desks. Jewelry, glassware, and lamps are on display, too. ✉ *1710 Market St., at Gough St., Hayes Valley* ☎ *415/553–8900* ⊕ *www.anothertimesf.com* ⊙ *Closed Mon. and Tues.*

BEAUTY

Nancy Boy. This sparse white-on-white locally owned store sells indulgent skin- and hair-care products for men, as well as a small selection of aromatherapy items, such as soy travel candles scented with essential oils. ✉ *347 Hayes St., between Franklin and Gough Sts., Hayes Valley* ☎ *415/552–3636* ⊕ *www.nancyboy.com.*

BOOKS

The Green Arcade. For environmental, political, sustainable, and über-green books, look no further. With deep roots in the community, energetic artwork, and an atmosphere that encourages reading, this is a good place to hide away; the comfy chairs and warm vibe make it hard to leave. ✉ *1680 Market St., at Gough St., Hayes Valley* ☎ *415/431–6800* ⊕ *www.thegreenarcade.com.*

Isotope Comic Book Lounge. For full-frontal nerdity in a chic modern setting, pay a visit SF's premier comic book lounge. You'll find a great selection of graphic novels and artwork by popular and local artists, as well as lively after-hours events. ✉ *326 Fell St., at Gough St., Hayes Valley* ☎ *415/621–6543* ⊕ *www.isotopecomics.com.*

CLOTHING: MEN AND WOMEN

Acrimony. A handblown-glass chandelier winks at you through the store's front window, while DJs do their thing in the back. Sandwiched in between are styles like Cameo miniskirts or Shona Joy's hip-hugging skinny pants. There's something special for men, too: double-layered muscle tees and Gitman Bros. blue oxfords and vintage chambray shirts. Think progressive and of-the-moment. ✉ *333 Hayes St., between Franklin and Gough Sts., Hayes Valley* ☎ *415/861–1025* ⊕ *www.shopacrimony.com.*

Azalea Boutique. With a dose of global flair, this boutique blends art, fun, and fashion. The deep-red walls provide a flattering backdrop both for patrons and the extensive denim collection (more than 100 different styles). Designers from Ariana Bohling to Freda Salvador and Pamela Love offer a true alternative from the ubiquitous department-store brands. At the nail bar here, you can indulge in natural services that include formaldehyde-free polish and organic cuticle creams. ⊠ *411 Hayes St., at Gough St., Hayes Valley* ☎ *415/861–9888* ⊕ *www.azaleasf.com.*

Dish. Many of the women's clothes displayed within this spare space are romantic, minus the frills. Look for the chic dresses of local designer Kathryn McCarron, as well as clothing and accessories by more widely known brands like Etten Eller and Zoe Chicco. ⊠ *541 Hayes St., between Laguna and Octavia Sts., Hayes Valley* ☎ *415/252–5997* ⊕ *www.dishboutique.com.*

Ver Unica. Though you can find a few items from the psychedelic '60s, beautifully preserved fashions from the '40s and '50s are the best reason for visiting. You can even track down purses and hard-to-find vintage shoes to go with that fur-trimmed jacket. ⊠ *526 Hayes St., between Gough and Octavia Sts., Hayes Valley* ☎ *415/621–6259.*

Welcome Stranger. Azalea's stylish sister store for men carries designer brands like Ontour, Filson, and Eastland Shoes. The styles range from rugged outdoors to urban chic, but somehow it all works—locals can't get enough of them. ⊠ *460 Gough St., between Hayes and Grove Sts., Hayes Valley* ☎ *415/864–2079* ⊕ *www.welcomestranger.com.*

FOOD AND DRINK

Arlequin Wine Merchant. If you like the wine list at Absinthe Brasserie, you can walk next door and pick up a few bottles from its highly regarded sister establishment. This small, unintimidating shop carries hard-to-find wines from small producers. Why wait to taste? Crack open a bottle on the patio out back. ⊠ *384 Hayes St., at Gough St., Hayes Valley* ☎ *415/863–1104* ⊕ *www.arlequinwinemerchant.com.*

Miette Confiserie. There is truly nothing sweeter than a cellophane bag tied with blue-and-white twine and filled with malt balls or chocolate sardines from this European-style apothecary. Grab a gingerbread cupcake or a tantalizing macaron or some shortbread. The pastel-color cake stands make even window-shopping a treat. ⊠ *449 Octavia Blvd., between Hayes and Fell Sts., Hayes Valley* ☎ *415/626–6221* ⊕ *www.miette.com.*

True Sake. Though it would be reasonable to expect a Japanese aesthetic at the first store in the United States dedicated entirely to sake, you might instead hear dance music thumping quietly in the background while you browse. Each of the many sakes is displayed with a label describing the drink's qualities and food-pairing suggestions. ⊠ *560 Hayes St., between Laguna and Octavia Sts., Hayes Valley* ☎ *415/355–9555* ⊕ *www.truesake.com.*

FURNITURE, HOUSEWARES, AND GIFTS

Flight 001. Ultrastylish travel accessories—retro-looking flight bags, supersoft leather passport wallets, and tiny Swiss travel alarm clocks—line the shelves of this brightly lighted shop, which vaguely resembles an airplane interior. High-tech travel gear and a small collection of guidebooks speed you on your way. ✉ *525 Hayes St., between Laguna and Octavia Sts., Hayes Valley* ☎ *415/487–1001* ⊕ *www.flight001.com.*

HANDICRAFTS AND FOLK ART

F. Dorian. In addition to cards, jewelry, and other crafts from Central and South America, Asia, the Middle East, and Africa—a carved wooden candle holder from Ivory Coast is one example—this store carries brightly colored glass and ceramic works by local artisans and whimsical mobiles. ✉ *370 Hayes St., between Franklin and Gough Sts., Hayes Valley* ☎ *415/861–3191.*

Polanco. Devoted to showcasing the arts of Mexico, this gallery sells everything from antiques and traditional folk crafts to fine contemporary paintings. Brightly painted animal figures and a virtual village of *Day of the Dead* figures share space with religious statues and modern linocuts and paintings. ✉ *334 Gough St., at Hayes St., Hayes Valley* ☎ *415/252–5753* ⊕ *www.polancogallery.com.*

SHOES

Gimme Shoes. From the chunky to the sleek, the shoes carried here—including those by Chie Mihara, Dries Van Noten, Loeffler Randall, and Sydney Brown—are top notch. And if $600 seems steep for a pair of black boots, perhaps you haven't seen the perfect pair by Fiorentini + Baker. ✉ *416 Hayes St., at Gough St., Hayes Valley* ☎ *415/864–0691* ⊕ *www.gimmeshoes.com.*

Paolo Shoes. Looking for gorgeous handcrafted Italian leather shoes? (Who isn't?) This is *the* place in San Francisco to find them. From knee-high boots to contoured heel pumps, Paolo Iantorno's designs will make your heart miss a beat. The prices might as well; they hover around the $300 mark, but all shoes are made in quantities of 25 or fewer pairs. ✉ *524 Hayes St., between Octavia and Laguna Sts., Hayes Valley* ☎ *415/552–4580* ⊕ *paoloshoes.com.*

NOB HILL AND POLK GULCH

CLOTHING: OUTLET AND DISCOUNT

Christine Foley. Discounts of up to 50% apply to the hand-loomed cotton sweaters with fanciful, intricate designs. There's also a large selection of colorful sweaters for children. Pillows, stuffed animals, and assorted knickknacks are also on offer in this small showroom. ✉ *Fairmont Hotel, 950 Mason St., at California St., Nob Hill* ☎ *415/399–9938* ⊕ *www.christinefoley.com.*

CLOTHING: WOMEN'S

Cris. This upscale designer consignment shop (the locals' best-kept secret) is full of nearly new items for a lot less than new prices. Chloe and Chanel are a couple of the many designers to grace the racks. Not only is this shop brimming with one-of-a-kind tops, dresses, and coats, but it smells like a spring garden. And to top it all off, they include a fresh flower with every purchase. ✉ *2056 Polk St., at Broadway St., Polk Gulch* ☎ *415/474–1191* ⊕ *www.crisconsignment.com.*

JEWELRY AND COLLECTIBLES

Velvet da Vinci. Each contemporary piece of jewelry here is one of a kind or a limited edition. The beautiful, unusual items might be sculpted out of resin, hammered from copper, or woven with silver wires. ⊠ *2015 Polk St., between Broadway St. and Pacific Ave., Polk Gulch* ☎ *415/441–0109* ⊕ *www.velvetdavinci.com.*

NORTH BEACH

ANTIQUES

Aria Antiques. Get a gift for your favorite globe-trotter at this oasis for the unordinary. You'll find maps, boxes, vases, and vintage furniture, as well as European artifacts. ⊠ *1522 Grant Ave., between Union and Filbert Sts., North Beach* ☎ *415/433–0219* ⊕ *Closed Sun.*

Schein & Schein. This tiny spot sells antique maps and engraved prints, many with a local focus, from inexpensive prints to genuine collectors' pieces. Whether you're looking for a chart of the world from the 13th century or a map of the Barbary Coast, this shop just might have it. The helpful owners will enthrall you with their historical anecdotes and vast knowledge. ⊠ *1435 Grant Ave., between Green and Union Sts., North Beach* ☎ *415/399–8882* ⊕ *www.scheinandschein.com* ☉ *Closed Sun.; open by appointment only Mon. and June–Aug.*

BOOKS

City Lights Bookstore *See North Beach chapter.*

CLOTHING: MEN AND WOMEN

AB fits. The friendly staff can help guys and gals sort through the jeans selection, one of the hippest in the city (check out the Dope & Drakker organic denim). Salespeople pride themselves on being able to match the pants to the person. ⊠ *1519 Grant Ave., between Filbert and Union Sts., North Beach* ☎ *415/982–5726* ⊕ *abfits.com* ☉ *Closed Mon.*

FOOD AND DRINK

Graffeo Coffee Roasting Company. Forget those fancy flavored coffees if you're ordering from this emporium, open since 1935 and one of the best-loved coffee stores in a city devoted to its java. The shop sells dark roast, light roast, and dark roast–decaf beans only. ⊠ *735 Columbus Ave., at Filbert St., North Beach* ☎ *415/986–2420* ⊕ *www.graffeo.com.*

Fodor's Choice ★ **Molinari Delicatessen.** This store has been making its own salami, sausages, and cold cuts since 1896. Other homemade specialties include meat and cheese ravioli, tomato sauces, and fresh pastas. ■TIP➔ Do like the locals: grab a made-to-order sandwich for lunch and eat it at one of the sidewalk tables or over at Washington Square Park. ⊠ *373 Columbus Ave., at Vallejo St., North Beach* ☎ *415/421–2337* ⊕ *www. molinarisalame.com.*

Victoria Pastry Co. In business since the early 1900s and a throwback to the North Beach of old, this bakery has display cases full of Italian pastries, cookies, and St. Honoré cakes. ⊠ *700 Filbert St., between Columbus Ave. and Powell St., North Beach* ☎ *415/781–2015.*

18

XOX Truffles. The decadent confection comes in 27 bite-size flavors here, from the traditional (cocoa-powder-coated Amaretto) to the unusual (flavored with rum-coconut liqueur and coated with coconut flakes or enrobing a bit of caramel). There's something yummy for everyone, even vegans (soy truffles). ⊠ *754 Columbus Ave., between Greenwich and Filbert Sts., North Beach* ☎ *415/421–4814* ⊕ *www.xoxtruffles.com.*

FURNITURE, HOUSEWARES, AND GIFTS

Biordi Art Imports. Hand-painted Italian pottery, mainly imported from Tuscany and Umbria, has been shipped worldwide by this family-run business since 1946. Dishware sets can be ordered in any combination. ⊠ *412 Columbus Ave., at Vallejo St., North Beach* ☎ *415/392–8096* ⊕ *www.biordi.com* ☉ *Closed Sun.*

MUSIC: MEMORABILIA

San Francisco Rock Posters and Collectibles. The huge selection of rock-and-roll memorabilia, including posters, handbills, and original art, takes you back to the 1960s. Also available are posters from more recent shows—many at the legendary Fillmore Auditorium—featuring such musicians as George Clinton and the late Johnny Cash. ⊠ *1851 Powell St., between Filbert and Greenwich Sts., North Beach* ☎ *415/956–6749* ⊕ *rockposters.com.*

PAPER AND STATIONERY

Lola of North Beach. A section of this intimate North Beach store is devoted to the various stages of a relationship: friendship, I like you, I love you, I miss you, I'm sorry, and I'm here for you. The shop also carries an impressive collection of baby clothes, including some adorable tees. ⊠ *1415 Grant Ave., at Green St., North Beach* ☎ *415/781–1817* ⊕ *lolaofnorthbeach.com.*

THE WATERFRONT

FISHERMAN'S WHARF

CLOTHING: MEN AND WOMEN

Helpers' Bazaar. Arguably the city's best-dressed philanthropist, Joy Bianchi, along with other volunteers, runs this store to benefit the mentally disabled. A red Bill Blass cocktail dress, a Chanel suit, or a Schiaparelli hat are among the vintage masterpieces you might expect to find here—to see the good stuff, all you have to do is ask nicely. Don't miss a look at Bianchi's "mouse couture," a clever fund-raiser display in which designers like Armani and Carolina Herrera dress up 4-inch stuffed mice. ⊠ *Ghirardelli Sq., 900 N. Point St., Fisherman's Wharf* ☎ *415/441–0779.*

EMBARCADERO

Four sprawling buildings of shops, restaurants, offices, and a popular independent movie theater—plus the Hyatt Regency hotel—make up the Embarcadero Center, downtown at the end of Market Street. Most of the stores are branches of upscale national chains, such as Ann Taylor and Banana Republic. Also in this area is the Ferry Building, with a focus on local food and other vendors.

BOOKS

Book Passage. Windows at this modest-size bookstore frame close-up views of the docks and San Francisco Bay. Commuters snap up magazines by the front door as they rush off to their ferries, while shoppers leisurely thumb through the thorough selection of cooking and travel titles. Author events take place several times a month. ⊠ *Ferry Building Marketplace, 1 Ferry Bldg. #42, at foot of Market St., Embarcadero* ☎ *415/835–1020* ⊕ *www.bookpassage.com.*

FARMERS' MARKETS

Fodor's Choice
★

Ferry Plaza Farmers' Market. The partylike Saturday edition of the city's most upscale and expensive farmers' market places baked goods, gourmet cheeses, smoked fish, and fancy pots of jam alongside organic basil, specialty mushrooms, heirloom tomatoes, handcrafted jams, and juicy-ripe locally grown fruit. On Saturday about 100 vendors pack in along three sides of the building, and sandwiches and other prepared foods are for sale in addition to fruit, vegetable, and other samples free for the nibbling. Smaller markets take place on Tuesday and Thursday. (The Thursday one doesn't operate from about late December through March.) ⊠ *Ferry Plaza, at Market St., Embarcadero* ☎ *415/291–3276* ⊕ *www.ferrybuildingmarketplace.com.*

FOOD AND DRINK

Fodor's Choice
★

Cowgirl Creamery Artisan Cheese. Fantastic organic-milk cheeses—such as the mellow, triple-cream Mt. Tam and *bocconcini* (small balls of fresh mozzarella)—are produced at a creamery an hour's drive north of the city. These and other carefully chosen artisanal cheeses and dairy products, including a luscious, freshly made crème fraîche, round out the selection at the in-town store. ⊠ *Ferry Building Marketplace, 1 Ferry Bldg. #17, at foot of Market St., Embarcadero* ☎ *415/362–9354* ⊕ *www.cowgirlcreamery.com.*

McEvoy Ranch. This is the only retail outpost of this Sonoma County ranch, a producer of outstanding organic, extra-virgin olive oil. ■TIP➔ If you stop by in fall or winter, don't miss the Olio Nuovo, the days-old green oil produced during the harvest. ⊠ *Ferry Building Marketplace, 1 Ferry Bldg. #16, at foot of Market St., Embarcadero* ☎ *415/291–7224* ⊕ *www.mcevoyranch.com.*

Recchiuti Confections. Michael and Jacky Recchiuti began making otherworldly chocolates in 1997, using traditional European techniques. Now considered among the best confectioners in the world, they stock their store here (there's also a smaller one in the Dogpatch neighborhood) with their full chocolate line, including several unique items inspired by the surrounding gourmet markets. ⊠ *Ferry Building Marketplace, 1 Ferry Bldg., Suite 30, Embarcadero at foot of Market St., Embarcadero* ☎ *415/834–9494* ⊕ *www.recchiuti.com.*

FURNITURE, HOUSEWARES, AND GIFTS

The Gardener. Artful, functional home and garden accessories are the lure here, from woven baskets and teak salad bowls to beautifully illustrated books. Although there's only a small selection of actual gardening items, such as seeds, bulbs, and tools, there are plenty of bath and body items with which to pamper yourself after a day in the yard. ⊠ *Ferry*

18

Building Marketplace, 1 Ferry Bldg., Suite 26, at foot of Market St., Embarcadero ☎ *415/981–8181* ⊕ *www.thegardener.com.*

SPORTING GOODS

FAMILY **Exploratorium.** The educational gadgets and gizmos sold here are so much fun that your kids—whether they're in grade school or junior high—might not realize they're learning while they're playing with them. Space- and dinosaur-related games are popular, as are science videos and CD-ROMs. ⊠ *Piers 15, at Embarcadero at Green St., Embarcadero* ☎ *415/528–4390* ⊕ *www.exploratorium.edu.*

FINANCIAL DISTRICT

BOOKS

William Stout Architectural Books. Architect William Stout began selling books out of his apartment 25 years ago. Today the store is a source for Bay Area professionals looking for serious-minded tomes on architecture and design. Head down into the crumbling whitewashed basement for beautifully illustrated coffee-table books. Stout is the sole distributor of the popular IDEO method cards, which offer and inspire design solutions. ⊠ *804 Montgomery St., between Gold and Jackson Sts., Financial District* ☎ *415/391–6757* ⊕ *www.stoutbooks.com* ☉ *Closed Sun.*

THE MARINA

The Marina is an outstanding shopping nexus, with stylish boutiques and mainstream and specialty housewares stores. On sunny weekends on the main commercial drag, Chestnut Street, the point seems to be as much about seeing and being seen as shopping—at least among the neighborhood's grown-up sorority sisters and frat boys.

CLOTHING: MEN AND WOMEN

dress. This quaint boutique offers up fashions by dozens of brands, among them Kathy Kamei and Ulla Johnson. The clothes have been thoughtfully selected with entire wardrobes in mind. Items don't crowd the racks, and the service is friendly without being overwhelming. ■TIP➜ You can sometimes find good bargains here. ⊠ *2271 Chestnut St., between Scott and Avila Sts., Marina* ☎ *415/440–3737* ⊕ *www. dresssanfrancisco.com.*

CLOTHING: OUTLET AND DISCOUNT

My Roommate's Closet. Fed by more than 25 boutiques in San Francisco, New York, and Los Angeles, the Closet carries clothing and accessories by designers like BB Dakota, Current Elliot, and Alexander McQueen, all at least 50% off the retail price. ⊠ *3044 Fillmore St., at Union St., Marina* ☎ *415/447–7703* ⊕ *myroommatescloset.com.*

PAPER AND STATIONERY

FLAX art & design. In addition to paints, brushes, and art supplies, this sprawling creators' playground sells beautifully made photo albums and journals, fine pens and pencils, crafts kits, stationery, and inspiring doodads for kids. ⊠ *Fort Mason, 2 Marina Blvd., Bldg. D, Marina* ☎ *415/530–3510* ⊕ *flaxart.com.*

COW HOLLOW

CLOTHING

Fodor'sChoice **Marmalade.** Filled with bright dresses and patterned tops, this Cow
★ Hollow beacon of style has a real Californian feel. Designers both
local and from Southern California are represented, and the owner
and her staff are happy to help you match things, including ear-
rings and sweaters and jeans and simple T-shirts. ⊠ *1843 Union St.,
between Octavia and Laguna Sts., Cow Hollow* ☎ *415/757–8614*
⊕ *marmaladesf.com.*

FOOD AND DRINK

PlumpJack Wines. A small selection of imported wines complements the
well-priced, well-stocked collection of hard-to-find California wines
here. Gift baskets—such as the Italian market basket, containing wine,
Italian foods, and a cookbook—are popular hostess gifts. Noe Valley
has a sister store. ⊠ *3201 Fillmore St., at Greenwich St., Cow Hollow*
☎ *415/346–9870* ⊕ *www.plumpjackwines.com.*

FURNITURE, HOUSEWARES, AND GIFTS

Topdrawer. The Japanese company's first U.S. store sells everything from
patterned *furoshiki* (a Japanese wrapping cloth) to bright, and very
realistic, cupcake-shaped erasers. There's an extensive selection of colorful stationery, leather-bound journals, daisy-printed masking tape,
and cards, many of which are made by local artists. ⊠ *1840 Union
St., between Octavia and Laguna Sts., Cow Hollow* ☎ *415/771–1108.*

JEWELRY AND COLLECTIBLES

Union Street Goldsmith. This local favorite prides itself on its selection of
rare gemstones, such as golden sapphires and violet tanzanite. Custom
work is a specialty: the no-pressure design consultants are happy to
discuss how to make the jewelry of your dreams a reality. ⊠ *2118
Union St., at Fillmore St., Cow Hollow* ☎ *415/776–8048* ⊕ *www.
unionstreetgoldsmith.com.*

PET FASHIONS

Moulin Pooch. Button-down sweaters, lace-trimmed dresses, sunhats,
sequined leashes—who knew dogs could dress this well? This shop
also sells gourmet canine cookies, some with liver-flavored icing. The
staffers will help you find just the right outfit for your pooch and can
direct you to the full-service grooming facility in back. ⊠ *1750 Union
St., between Gough and Octavia Sts., Cow Hollow* ☎ *415/440–7007*
⊕ *www.moulinpooch.com.*

SPORTING GOODS

Lululemon Athletica. This yoga-inspired company makes all kinds of
athletic gear out of Luon fabric—it's nonchafing, moisture-wicking,
preshrunk, and best of all it can be washed in warm water. The pants
have a rep as the best thing in town for a yogi's derriere. ⊠ *1981 Union
St., between Laguna and Buchanan Sts., Cow Hollow* ☎ *415/776–5858*
⊕ *www.lululemon.com.*

18

TOYS AND GADGETS

ATYS. Gadgets with a sleek modern design are imported from Scandinavia, Italy, Germany, and Japan. Among the eye-catching items are fancy German watches that tell time in words and Japanese knives that could pass for sculptures. ✉ *2149B Union St., between Fillmore and Webster Sts., Cow Hollow* ☎ *415/441–9220* ⊕ *www.atysdesign.com.*

THE RICHMOND

BOOKS

Fodor'sChoice ★ **Green Apple Books.** This local favorite with a huge used-book department also carries new books in every field. It's known for its history room and rare-books collection. Two doors down, at 520 Clement Street, is a fiction annex that also sells CDs, DVDs, comic books, and graphic novels. ✉ *506 Clement St., at 6th Ave., Richmond* ☎ *415/387–2272* ⊕ *www.greenapplebooks.com.*

SUNSET DISTRICT

FOOD AND DRINK

San Francisco Wine Trading Company. Owner and noted wine expert Gary Marcaletti stocks hard-to-find wines and hosts Saturday-afternoon tastings that usually start at 2 pm. ✉ *250 Taraval St., at Funston Ave., Sunset* ☎ *415/731–6222* ⊕ *www.sfwtc.com.*

FURNITURE, HOUSEWARES, AND GIFTS

General Store. New and vintage goods sit stylishly side by side in this fun, well-lit Outer Sunset space that sells books, lotions, hats, cups, dog leashes, and other items, most of them designed by local artists. Don't miss the greenhouse in back. ✉ *4035 Judah St., between 45th and 46th Aves., Sunset* ☎ *415/682–0600* ⊕ *shop-generalstore.com.*

Wishbone. If you're into the quirky and whimsical—bacon-flavored lip gloss, daisy pushpins, wacky snow globes, and cutesy toys and games—you'll enjoy browsing through Wishbone, which also has an extensive selection of unusual cards. ✉ *601 Irving St., at 7th Ave., Sunset* ☎ *415/242–5540* ⊕ *wishbonesf.com.*

THE HAIGHT, THE CASTRO, AND NOE VALLEY

THE HAIGHT

It's a sign of the times (and has been for a while) that a Gap store sits at the corner of Haight and Ashbury Streets, the geographic center of the Flower Power movement. Don't be discouraged: it's still possible to find high-quality vintage clothing, funky shoes, folk art from around the world, and used records and CDs in this always-busy neighborhood.

BOOKS

Booksmith. This fine bookshop sells current releases, children's titles, and offbeat periodicals. Authors passing through town often make a stop at this neighborhood institution. ✉ *1644 Haight St., between Cole and Clayton Sts., Haight* ☎ *415/863–8688* ⊕ *www.booksmith.com.*

Bound Together Anarchist Book Collective. This old-school collective, around since 1976, stocks books on anarchist theory and practice, as well as titles about gender issues, radicalism, and various left-leaning topics. A portion of the revenue supports anarchist projects and the Prisoners' Literature Project. ✉ *1369 Haight St., between Masonic and Central Aves., Haight* ☎ *415/431–8355* ⊕ *boundtogetherbooks. wordpress.com.*

CLOTHING: MEN AND WOMEN

Buffalo Exchange. Men and women can find fashionable, high-quality, used clothing at this national chain. Among the items: Levi's, leather jackets, sunglasses, and vintage lunch boxes. Some new clothes are available, too. ✉ *1555 Haight St., between Clayton and Ashbury Sts., Haight* ☎ *415/431–7733* ⊕ *www.buffaloexchange.com.*

Held Over. The extensive collection of clothing from the 1920s through 1980s is organized by decade, saving those looking for flapper dresses from having to wade through lime-green polyester sundresses of the '70s. Shoes, hats, handbags, and jewelry complete the different looks. ✉ *1543 Haight St., between Ashbury and Clayton Sts., Haight* ☎ *415/864–0818.*

Cookin': Recycled Gourmet Appurtenances. People trek here for the impressive collection of vintage Le Creuset cookware and bakeware in discontinued colors. If you can't make sense of this store's jumble of used cooking items—stacked ceiling-high in some places—ask the helpful owner, who will likely interrogate you about what you're preparing to cook before leading you to the right section, be that the corner with hundreds of ramekins or the area containing a bewildering selection of garlic presses. ✉ *339 Divisadero St., between Oak and Page Sts., Haight* ☎ *415/861–1854.*

MUSIC

Fodor's Choice ★ **Amoeba Music.** With more than 2.5 million new and used CDs, DVDs, and records at bargain prices, this warehouselike offshoot of the Berkeley original carries titles you can't find on Amazon. No niche is ignored—from electronica and hip-hop to jazz and classical—and the stock changes daily. ■ TIP➔ **Weekly in-store performances attract large crowds.** ✉ *1855 Haight St., between Stanyan and Shrader Sts., Haight* ☎ *415/831–1200* ⊕ *www.amoeba.com.*

Recycled Records. A Haight Street landmark, this store buys, sells, and trades used records, including hard-to-find imports and sides by obscure alternative bands. The CD collection is large, but the vinyl is the real draw. ✉ *1377 Haight St., between Masonic and Central Aves., Haight* ☎ *415/626–4075* ⊕ *www.recycled-records.com.*

SHOES

Fodor's Choice ★ **John Fluevog.** The trendy but sturdily made footwear for men and women is among the best in the city. Club girls go gaga over the Double Dutch boots, handing over a pretty penny. They have another small store near Union Square, at 253 Grant Avenue. ✉ *1697 Haight St., at Cole St., Haight* ☎ *415/436–9784* ⊕ *www.fluevog.com.*

18

THE CASTRO
CLOTHING: MEN

Rolo. Selling hard-to-find men's denim, sportswear, shoes, and accessories with a distinct European influence, this store includes clothes designed by Fred Perry, James Tudor, and Tre Noir. There's another location in SoMa at 1301 Howard Street. ✉ *2351 Market St., at Castro St., Castro* ☎ *415/431–4545* ⊕ *www.rolo.com.*

JEWELRY AND COLLECTIBLES

Brand X Antiques. The vintage jewelry, mostly from the early part of the 20th century, includes a wide selection of estate pieces and objets d'art. With rings that range in price from $5 to $30,000, there's something for everyone. ✉ *570 Castro St., between 18th and 19th Sts., Castro* ☎ *415/626–8908* ⊘ *Closed Sun.*

NOE VALLEY
BOOKS

Omnivore Books on Food. Love to eat? Love to read? Then this place is paradise. The shelves are bursting with books on growing and cooking food. The store stocks cookbooks on such diverse subjects as colonial Jamaican and Victorian England cuisine or 1940s creole cooking. And if you're after a signed first edition by Julia Child or James Beard, you'll find that, too. ✉ *3885A Cesar Chavez St., at Church St., Noe Valley* ☎ *415/282–4712* ⊕ *www.omnivorebooks.com.*

CHILDREN'S CLOTHING

FAMILY **Small Frys.** The colorful cottons carried here are mainly for infants, with some articles for older children. Brands include OshKosh and many Californian and French labels. A few shelves of organic and eco-friendly toys as well as whimsical finger puppets round out the selection. ✉ *4066 24th St., between Castro and Noe Sts., Noe Valley* ☎ *415/648–3954* ⊕ *www.smallfrys.com.*

CLOTHING: WOMEN'S

Ambiance. A well-loved destination for fashion-conscious locals, this is a fun place to find 1920s-inspired dresses, velvet scarves, and dangling silver jewelry. The store has some jaw-dropping sales. There are additional locations on 9th Avenue, Union, Haight, and Irving Streets. ✉ *3979 24th St., between Sanchez and Noe Sts., Noe Valley* ☎ *415/647–5800* ⊕ *www.ambiancesf.com.*

Two Birds. A fresh place to find a lacy top or a soft pair of jeans, Two Birds stocks Erin Kleinberg, Tracy Reese, and Frame Denim. Staying in touch with their city roots, owners Susanna Taylor and Audrey Yang carry sleek jewelry, handbags, and dresses by local designers, too. ✉ *1309 Castro St., between Jersey and 24th Sts., Noe Valley* ☎ *415/285–1840* ⊕ *www.2birds1store.com.*

FURNITURE, HOUSEWARES, AND GIFTS

Wink. Cards, toasters, aprons, books, candles, and even superhero Pez candy line the shelves. You'll also find fridge magnets, wisdom-spouting bags, and bakery-shape pencil erasers. And if you've misplaced your stainless-steel water bottle, the shop stocks a rainbow of colors. ✉ *4107 24th St., at Castro St., Noe Valley* ☎ *415/401–8881* ⊕ *www.winksf.com.*

HANDICRAFTS AND FOLK ART

Xela Imports. Africa, Southeast Asia, and Central America are the sources for the handicrafts sold at Xela (pronounced *shay*-la). They include jewelry, religious masks, fertility statuary, and decorative wall hangings. ⊠ *3925 24th St., between Sanchez and Noe Sts., Noe Valley* ☎ *415/695–1323* ⊕ *xelaimports.com.*

TOYS AND GADGETS

MISSION DISTRICT

The aesthetic of the hipsters and artist types who reside in the Mission contribute to the individuality of shopping here. These night owls keep the city's best thrift stores, vintage-furniture shops, alternative bookstores, and increasingly, small clothing boutiques afloat. As the Mission gentrifies though, bargain hunters find themselves trekking farther afield in search of truly local flavor.

ART GALLERIES

Southern Exposure. An artist-run, nonprofit gallery, this is an established venue for cutting-edge art. In addition to exhibitions, lectures, performances, and film, video screenings take place. ⊠ *3030 20th St., at Alabama St., Mission District* ☎ *415/863–2141* ⊕ *soex.org* ⊙ *Closed Sun. and Mon.*

BOOKS

Dog Eared Books. An eclectic group of shoppers—gay and straight, fashionable and practical—wanders the aisles of this pleasantly ramshackle bookstore. The diverse stock, about 85% of it used, includes quirky selections like vintage children's books, remaindered art books, and local zines. A bin of free books just outside the front door is fun to browse. ⊠ *900 Valencia St., at 20th St., Mission District* ☎ *415/282–1901* ⊕ *www.dogearedbooks.com.*

CLOTHING: MEN AND WOMEN

Schauplatz. A narrow store on a hip Mission block, Schauplatz sells vintage clothing from the 1920s to the 1980s. Some of the dramatic women's wear—go-go boots, pillbox hats, faux Chanel suits—is suitable for street wear or dress-up, depending on your style, while the menswear tends more toward fashionably retro jackets and button-up shirts from the classic to the gaudy. ⊠ *791 Valencia St., at 19th St., Mission District* ☎ *415/864–5665* ⊙ *Closed Tues.*

Self Edge. Hanging from metal rods on perfectly separated wooden hangers are dozens of pairs of Japanese selvage denim. The industrial-weight fabric that makes up these jeans will run you between $180 and $450, but alterers will hem them for free on a vintage chain-stitching machine. ⊠ *714 Valencia St., at 18th St., Mission District* ☎ *415/558–0658* ⊕ *www.selfedge.com.*

Sunhee Moon. A rack is designated for each color of the rainbow, and clothes are hung by gradation, making entry into Moon's shops a crayon-color dreamscape. The San Francisco–based designer uses only American-made fabrics and manufactures all of her clothes in the Mission. Her Berkeley aesthetic is coupled with Audrey Hepburn's simple, practical elegance. End result: lots of corduroy, solids accented with

18

an occasionally lively print, and well-placed large buttons. ✉ *3167 16th St., at Guerrero St., Mission District* ☎ *415/355–1800* ⊕ *www. sunheemoon.com.*

FURNITURE, HOUSEWARES, AND GIFTS

Aldea Home. A visit here is like being in someone's home and being able to buy everything you see, from the organic sheets to the chairs to the shampoo in the shower. The aesthetic is modern, with bright references to Mexico, India, Turkey, and Japan. Aldea is the perfect place to find a hostess gift or to deck out a corner that's missing something special. Nearby Aldea Niños (at 1017 Valencia) sells green products for kids. ✉ *890 Valencia St., at 20th St., Mission District* ☎ *415/865–9807* ⊕ *aldeahome.com.*

Casa Bonampak. This bright, authentic, fair-trade artisan store sells the work of Mexican artists, as well as decorations for various Mexican festivities. If you're looking for traditional sugar skulls, papel picado banners, or even Dia de los Gigantes (Day of the Giants, in honor of the hometown baseball team winning the World Series on the Day of the Dead in 2010) tees, look no further. The friendly owner and welcoming vibe will beckon you in. ✉ *1051 Valencia St., between Hill and 22nd Sts., Mission District* ☎ *415/642–4079* ⊕ *www.casabonampak.com.*

De Angelis. The trendy vintage furniture sold here will fit right in any space. With items that include Tommi Parzinger wall sconces, Hans Olsen's "Fried Egg" chairs, and even bronze coffee tables, the selection at De Angelis is truly inspirational. ✉ *573 Valencia St., at 17th St., Mission District* ☎ *415/861–9800.*

Fodor's Choice ★ **Paxton Gate.** Elevating gardening to an art, this serene shop offers beautiful earthenware pots, amaryllis and narcissus bulbs, decorative garden items, and coffee-table books such as *An Inordinate Fondness for Beetles.* The collection of taxidermy and preserved bugs provides more unusual gift ideas. A couple of storefronts away is too-cute Paxton Gate Curiosities for Kids, jam-packed with retro toys, books, and other stellar finds. ✉ *824 Valencia St., between 19th and 20th Sts., Mission District* ☎ *415/824–1872* ⊕ *www.paxtongate.com.*

Therapy. Housewares range from ever-practical refrigerator magnets to such downright silly items as a soap-on-a-rope tribute to the cartoon character Strawberry Shortcake. A retro theme runs to stationery and other reasonably priced items, and the adjacent annex sells retro-style furniture. ✉ *545 Valencia St., between 16th and 17th Sts., Mission District* ☎ *415/865–0981* ⊕ *www.shopattherapy.com.*

TOYS AND GADGETS

FAMILY **826 Valencia.** The brainchild of author Dave Eggers is primarily a center established to help kids with their writing skills via tutoring and storytelling events. But the storefront is also "San Francisco's only independent pirate supply store," a quirky space filled with eye patches, spyglasses, and other pirate-themed paraphernalia. Eggers's quarterly journal, *McSweeney's,* and other publications are available here. Proceeds benefit the writing center. ✉ *826 Valencia St., between 18th and 19th Sts., Mission District* ☎ *415/642–5905* ⊕ *826valencia.org.*

POTRERO HILL

ART GALLERIES

Catharine Clark Gallery. Although nationally known artists—like Masami Teraoka and Andy Diaz Hope—display their sculptures, paintings, photographs, and installation artwork here, emerging artists with a Bay Area connection get the spotlight, among them Chester Arnold and Josephine Taylor. ⊠ *248 Utah St., Potrero Hill* ☎ *415/399–1439* ⊕ *cclarkgallery.com* ⊗ *Closed Sun. and Mon.*

FURNITURE, HOUSEWARES, AND GIFTS

Fodor's Choice ★ **Heath Ceramics.** Sleek, glossy tiles for the home, newly spun dinnerware in rich earth colors, locally inspired cookbooks, and simple bamboo spoons stand stacked on shelves and tables in this factory showroom. ▬**TIP→ This is worth a stop if you're interested in seeing how plates and bowls are made.** Nearby Blue Bottle Coffee serves coffee and light snacks for people and dogs. ⊠ *2900 18th St., at Florida St., Potrero Hill* ☎ *415/361–5552* ⊕ *www.heathceramics.com.*

HANDBAGS, LUGGAGE, AND LEATHER GOODS

Rickshaw Bagworks. This San Francisco–based company will custom-make you your favorite bag. Choose from a variety of shapes and sizes to fit your MacBook, iPad, or Kindle. Totes, duffels, and messenger bags can also be designed to fit your unique lifestyle. You can also select from a variety of prints and colors, as well as eco-friendly materials; local artisans in their Dogpatch warehouse craft all bags. ⊠ *904 22nd St., between Indiana and Minnesota Sts., Potrero Hill* ☎ *415/904–8368* ⊕ *www.rickshawbags.com.*

HANDICRAFTS AND FOLK ART

Collage Gallery. The studio-gallery showcases handmade purses, painted candlesticks, jewelry, and other items by Bay Area artists. There are also a few small antiques, such as charming Westclox alarm clocks. ⊠ *1345 18th St., between Missouri and Texas Sts., Potrero Hill* ☎ *415/282–4401* ⊕ *www.collage-gallery.com.*

SPORTING GOODS

Fodor's Choice ★ **Sports Basement.** This sprawling store rewards intrepid shoppers with significant discounts on name-brand sportswear, accessories, and camping and outdoor gear. Helpful salespeople, more knowledgeable than you would expect at a discount warehouse, will help you find just the right running shoes, biking shorts, or yoga tights. Check out their location in the Presidio on Old Mason Street as well. ⊠ *1590 Bryant St., between 15th and 16th Sts., Potrero Hill* ☎ *415/575–3000* ⊕ *www.sportsbasement.com.*

BERNAL HEIGHTS

FURNITURE, HOUSEWARES, AND GIFTS

Succulence Life and Garden. Take a deep breath and exhale into the peacefulness of this indoor-outdoor garden shop bursting with lush, succulent greenery. There are bookcases full of plants, and even a "plant bar" where you can make your own plant/pot blending. There's also a host of classes you can enroll in if you're so inclined; the Vertical

Gardening DIY class starts at $65. If you're more of a traditionalist, there's a vibrant nursery in the back that will feed all your gardening needs. ✉ *402 Cortland Ave., between Wool and Bennington Sts., Bernal Heights* ☎ *415/282–2212* ⊕ *www.thesucculence.com.*

DOGPATCH

FOOD AND DRINK

The Wine House. The highly informed and friendly staffers here are willing to help you find the perfect wine for any occasion. The Burgundy, Bordeaux, and Rhône selections are especially good, and the assortment of California wines is small but well chosen. Prices are reasonable. ✉ *829 26th St., between Tennessee and 3rd Sts., Dogpatch* ☎ *415/355–9463* ⊕ *www.winesf.com* ☉ *Closed Sun.*

PACIFIC HEIGHTS AND JAPANTOWN

PACIFIC HEIGHTS

BEAUTY

BeneFit Cosmetics. You can find this locally based line of cosmetics and skin-care products at Macy's and Sephora, but it's much more fun to come to one of the eponymous boutiques. No-pressure salespeople dab you with whimsical makeup such as Ooh La Lift concealer and Tinted Love, a stain for lips and cheeks. ✉ *2117 Fillmore St., between California and Sacramento Sts., Pacific Heights* ☎ *415/567–0242* ⊕ *www.benefitcosmetics.com.*

Kiehl's. Fans swear by this company's high-quality, simply packaged skin- and hair-care products. Its spacious store stocks oceans of lotions, potions, and soaps. ✉ *1971 Fillmore St., between Wilmot and Pine Sts., Pacific Heights* ☎ *415/359–9260* ⊕ *www.kiehls.com.*

CHILDREN'S CLOTHING

FAMILY **Dottie Doolittle.** Pacific Heights mothers shop here for charming silk dresses and other special-occasion outfits for their little ones. Less pricey togs for infants, boys to size 12, and girls to size 16, are also for sale. ✉ *3680 Sacramento St., at Spruce St., Pacific Heights* ☎ *415/563–3244* ⊕ *www.dottiedoolittle.com.*

CLOTHING: MEN AND WOMEN

Elizabeth Charles. Parlaying the city's obsession with international designers, this intimate boutique stocks Caroline Constas, Kinder Aggugini, Isabel Marant, and Timo Weiland, with an emphasis on the very finest fabrics. ✉ *2056 Fillmore St., between California and Pine Sts., Pacific Heights* ☎ *415/440–2100* ⊕ *www.elizabeth-charles.com.*

HeidiSays Collections. Fanciful windows brimming with bright and festive prints draw passersby into this store. Perky salespeople help you choose between Elizabeth and James and M Missoni and other fashions. ✉ *2426 Fillmore St., between Washington and Jackson Sts., Pacific Heights* ☎ *415/749–0655* ⊕ *www.heidisays.com.*

FOOD AND DRINK

D&M Wines and Liquors. At first glance this family-owned business appears to be just another neighborhood liquor store, but it's actually a rare and wonderful specialist. In a city obsessed with wine, these spirits devotees distinguish themselves by focusing on rare, small-production Armagnac, Calvados, and Champagne. ⊠ *2200 Fillmore St., at Sacramento St., Pacific Heights* ☎ *415/346–1325* ⊕ *dandm.com.*

FURNITURE, HOUSEWARES, AND GIFTS

Nest. A cross between a Parisian antiques show and a Jamaican flea market, this store could get even the most monochrome New Yorker excited about color. You can turn up the volume on your SF souvenirs with vibrant handmade quilts, Chan Luu jewelry, Les Indiennes hand-blocked cotton fabrics, and M. Sasek's cheerfully illustrated book *This is San Francisco.* ⊠ *2300 Fillmore St., at Clay St., Pacific Heights* ☎ *415/292–6199* ⊕ *www.nestsf.com.*

Sue Fisher King Company. When Martha Stewart or the buyers at Williams-Sonoma need inspiration, they come to see how Sue has set her sprawling table or dressed her stately bed. (Her specialty is opulent linens for every room.) And when Pacific Heights residents are looking for an impeccable hostess or bridal gift, they come by for a hand-embroidered velvet pillow or a piece of Nicholas Newcomb Hudson Valley pottery. ⊠ *3067 Sacramento St., between Baker and Broderick Sts., Pacific Heights* ☎ *415/922–7276* ⊕ *www.suefisherking.com.*

JEWELRY AND COLLECTIBLES

Goldberry Jewelers. The former longtime girlfriend of Bob Dylan, Margie Rogerson opened this store to showcase her platinum-only designs. While she carries a large selection of engagement rings, her specialty is colored stones: rubies, sapphires, and emeralds. Their colors really sparkle against the background of this all white and Lucite space. By appointment only. ⊠ *3516 Sacramento St., between Laurel and Locust Sts., Pacific Heights* ☎ *415/921–4389* ⊕ *www.goldberry.com.*

PAPER AND STATIONERY

Paper Source. Beautiful handmade papers, cards, envelopes, ribbons, and bookbinding materials line the walls of this shop, which embodies the Bay Area's do-it-yourself spirit. Assembly is required here and that's the fun of it. ⊠ *1925 Fillmore St., at Pine St., Pacific Heights* ☎ *415/409–7710* ⊕ *www.papersource.com.*

JAPANTOWN

Unlike shops in the ethnic enclaves of Chinatown, North Beach, and the Mission, the 5-acre Japan Center (⊠ *Bordered by Laguna, Fillmore, and Post Sts. and Geary Blvd.* is under one roof. The three-block complex includes a reasonably priced public garage and three shop-filled buildings. Especially worthwhile are the Kintetsu and Kinokuniya buildings, where shops sell things like bonsai trees, tapes and records, jewelry, antique kimonos, *tansu* (Japanese chests), electronics, and colorful glazed dinnerware and teapots.

18

CLOSE UP

Antiques Blitz Tour

Whether hunting for Japanese porcelain or American art-deco lamps, serious antiques hounds could spend days poking around San Francisco. But if you have only one day to indulge your passion, with your walking shoes on your feet and cab fare in hand, you can hit some of the highlights.

Start your day in the city's preeminent antiques neighborhood, tree-lined Jackson Square, centered on Jackson Street between Montgomery and Sansome Streets. Although you would do well to pop into any shop on these few blocks, try **Antonio's Antiques**, which has two stories of furniture and objets d'art, most French and Italian, from the 17th and 18th centuries. (Take a cab to its larger SoMa store after leaving if you like what you see here.)

A short cab ride away (or a brief stroll to the Embarcadero and a ride on the F-line Muni streetcar), the more affordable shops lining Market Street appeal to a broader crowd. Ask the cabbie to ferry you south of Market, where the turn-of-the-20th-century Belgian oak beds and French armoires at **Grand Central Station Antiques** on 9th Street draw shoppers with slightly more traditional sensibilities.

BOOKS

Kinokuniya Bookstore. The selection of English-language books about Japanese culture—everything from medieval history to origami instructions—is one of the finest in the country. Kinokuniya is the city's biggest seller of Japanese-language books. Dozens of glossy Asian fashion magazines attract the young and trendy; the manga and anime books and magazines are wildly popular, too. ⊠ *Kinokuniya Bldg., 1581 Webster St., at Geary Blvd., Japantown* ☎ *415/567–7625* ⊕ *www.kinokuniya.com/us.*

FOOD AND DRINK

Crown & Crumpet Tea Salon. This is the perfect spot for all things British; C&C serves traditional afternoon tea starting at 11 am, complete with cucumber sandwiches and scones. The shop also sells china cups and other teatime accessories such as candies, clocks, and coasters. ⊠ *1746 Post St., 2nd fl., Japantown* ☎ *415/771–4252* ⊕ *www.crownandcrumpet.com.*

HANDICRAFTS AND FOLK ART

Soko Hardware. Open since 1925, this shop specializes in beautifully crafted Japanese tools for gardening and woodworking. In addition to the usual hardware-store items, you can find seeds for Japanese plants and books about topics such as making shoji screens. ⊠ *1698 Post St., at Buchanan St., Japantown* ☎ *415/931–5510.*

MALL

FAMILY **New People.** Japanese pop culture has never been so neatly organized as it is here at this state-of-the-art mini mall divided into four shiny levels: the cinema/café downstairs; MARUQ (selling Tokyo's hot fashion right here in SF!) on the first floor; clothing shops like Baby, the Stars Shine Bright, and Sou-Sou on the second floor; and the Superfrog Gallery on the third floor. Expect to see a rotation of emerging artists in the gallery and make sure you try the superstrong coffee and vegan donuts on sale in the café. ⊠ *1746 Post St., at Webster St., Japantown* ☎ ⊕ *www.newpeopleworld.com.*

WESTERN ADDITION

SPAS

Like the restaurant scene, spas in San Francisco are focused on natural, organic products and deeply reflect the various neighborhoods around the city.

SOMA

Remède Spa. All treatments at the St. Regis Hotel's très chic spa incorporate a line of high-end French skin-care products. Offerings include custom skin therapy, massage, body scrubs, seaweed wraps, and a variety of mani-pedi, facial, and waxing options. Prices range from $18 for a lip wax to $330 for a four-hands massage. ✉ *St. Regis Hotel, 125 3rd St., at Mission St., SoMa* ☎ *415/284–4060* ⊕ *remede.com/spa.html.*

HAYES VALLEY

Earthbody. A destination for organic products, cleansing, and relaxation—not to mention massage treatments to melt for—this eco-spa offers transformative workshops and rituals that help you heal from within. The Goddess Treatment, a client favorite, includes body exfoliation, a hot-oil scalp treatment, and massage using products infused with wildflower blossoms. ✉ *534 Laguna St., between Hayes and Fell Sts., Hayes Valley* ☎ *415/552–7200* ⊕ *www.earthbody.net.*

NOB HILL

Nob Hill Spa. Warning: after experiencing this serene and luxurious spa's treatments, you'll start to *expect* champagne after your massage. Unique features include the eucalyptus steam bath and a gorgeous infinity pool that overlooks the city through a glass wall. After your treatments, you can hang here all day: relax in the Zen room, get a green-tea body scrub, or just read on the sundeck. Regulars love the 80-minute Nourishing Seaweed facial, the 50-minute Organic Lavender Sugar Scrub skin-exfoliation treatment, and the Table Thai massage, 80 minutes of pure indulgence. ✉ *Huntington Hotel, 1075 California St., at Mason St., Nob Hill* ☎ *415/474–5400* ⊕ *www.nobhillspa.com.*

COW HOLLOW

Spa Radiance. Elegant but casual Spa Radiance specializes in facials and draws the occasional celebrity. Try the warm cocoa butter body treatment, or the "Nature's Kiss" spa escape—an organic detox facial followed by a warm lavender salt scrub and hot stone massage. A well-deserved treat is the very fine Swiss Oxygen 52 Vitamin facial. ✉ *3011 Fillmore St., between Union and Filbert Sts., Cow Hollow* ☎ *415/346–6281* ⊕ *www.sparadiance.com.*

18

PACIFIC HEIGHTS AND JAPANTOWN

International Orange. Treatments at this spa and yoga studio include the signature IO Massage, which incorporates Swedish, acupressure, Thai, and Shiatsu techniques. The more straightforward Hot Stone Massage is done with International Orange's own Anoint Oil—grape-seed oil infused with green tea and scented with white lotus and jasmine flower. For a city spa, this is a large space, but it's tranquil and even has a bamboo garden. ⊠ *2044 Fillmore St., 2nd fl., between Pine and California Sts., Pacific Heights* ☎ *415/563–5000* ⊕ *www.internationalorange.com.*

Kabuki Springs & Spa. Traditional sit-down Japanese showers and communal bathing are two out-of-the-ordinary experiences at the Kabuki. The renowned Javanese Lulur Treatment includes a combination massage with jasmine oil, exfoliation with turmeric and ground rice, a yogurt application, and a candlelight soak with rose petals. Men and women are welcome every day for private treatments, but call ahead regarding communal bathing schedules; the baths are coed only on Tuesday. Clothing is optional except on coed days. ⊠ *1750 Geary Blvd., at Fillmore St., Japantown* ☎ *415/922–6000* ⊕ *www.kabukisprings.com.*

Therapeia Massage. Massages at this oasis of calm near Japantown include and hot-stone options. Acupuncture and facials are also available. The focus is on cleansing and calming the mind as well as the body. ⊠ *1801 Bush St., lower level, Japantown* ☎ *415/885–4450* ⊕ *www. therapeiamassage.com.*

THE BAY AREA

WELCOME TO THE BAY AREA

TOP REASONS TO GO

★ **Bite into the "Gourmet Ghetto":** Eat your way through this area of North Berkeley, starting with a slice of perfect pizza from Cheese Board Pizza (just look for the line).

★ **Find solitude at Point Reyes National Seashore:** Hike beautifully rugged—and often deserted—beaches at one of the most beautiful places on Earth, period.

★ **Sit on a dock by the bay:** Admire the beauty of the Bay Area from the rocky, picturesque shores of Sausalito or Tiburon.

★ **Go bar-hopping in Oakland's hippest hood:** Spend an evening swinging through the watering holes of Uptown, Oakland's artsy-hip and fast-rising corner of downtown.

★ **Walk among giants:** Walking into Muir Woods, a mere 12 miles north of the Golden Gate Bridge, is like entering a cathedral built by God.

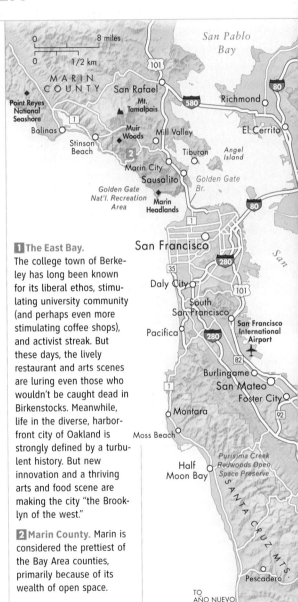

1 The East Bay. The college town of Berkeley has long been known for its liberal ethos, stimulating university community (and perhaps even more stimulating coffee shops), and activist streak. But these days, the lively restaurant and arts scenes are luring even those who wouldn't be caught dead in Birkenstocks. Meanwhile, life in the diverse, harborfront city of Oakland is strongly defined by a turbulent history. But new innovation and a thriving arts and food scene are making the city "the Brooklyn of the west."

2 Marin County. Marin is considered the prettiest of the Bay Area counties, primarily because of its wealth of open space.

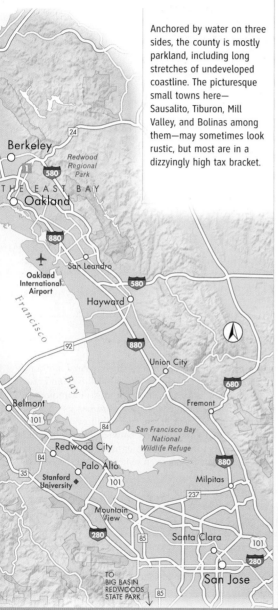

Anchored by water on three sides, the county is mostly parkland, including long stretches of undeveloped coastline. The picturesque small towns here—Sausalito, Tiburon, Mill Valley, and Bolinas among them—may sometimes look rustic, but most are in a dizzyingly high tax bracket.

GETTING ORIENTED

East of the city, across the San Francisco Bay, lie Berkeley and Oakland, in what most Bay Area residents refer to as the East Bay. These two towns have distinct personalities, but life here feels more relaxed than in the city—though every bit as vibrant.

Cross the Golden Gate Bridge and head north to reach Marin County's rolling hills and green expanses, where residents enjoy an haute-suburban lifestyle. Farther afield, the wild landscapes of the Muir Woods, Mt. Tamalpais, Stinson Beach, and Point Reyes National Seashore await.

19

Updated by
A. K. Carroll

It's rare for a metropolis to compete with its suburbs for visitors, but the view from any of San Francisco's hilltops shows that the Bay Area's temptations extend far beyond the city limits. East of the city are the energetic urban centers of Berkeley and Oakland. Famously radical Berkeley is also comfortably sophisticated, while Oakland has an arts and restaurant scene so hip that it pulls San Franciscans across the bay. To the north is Marin County with its dramatic coastal beauty and chic, affluent villages.

PLANNING

WHEN TO GO

As with San Francisco, you can visit the rest of the Bay Area any time of year, and it's especially nice in late spring and fall. Unlike San Francisco, though, the surrounding areas are reliably sunny in summer—it gets hotter as you head inland. Even the rainy season has its charms, as otherwise golden hills turn a rich green and wildflowers become plentiful. Precipitation is usually the heaviest between November and March. Berkeley is a university town, so it's easier to navigate the streets and find parking near the university between semesters, but there's also less buzz around town.

GETTING HERE AND AROUND

BART TRAVEL

Using public transportation to reach Berkeley or Oakland is ideal. The under- and aboveground BART (Bay Area Rapid Transit) trains make stops in both towns. Trips to either take about a half hour one-way from the center of San Francisco. BART does not serve Marin County.

Contacts BART. ☎ 510/465-2278 ⊕ www.bart.gov.

BOAT AND FERRY TRAVEL

For sheer romance, nothing beats the ferry; there's service from San Francisco to Sausalito, Tiburon, and Larkspur in Marin County, and to Alameda and Oakland in the East Bay.

The Golden Gate Ferry crosses the bay to Larkspur and Sausalito from San Francisco's Ferry Building (⊠ *Market St. and the Embarcadero*). Blue & Gold Fleet ferries depart daily for Sausalito and Tiburon from Pier 41 at Fisherman's Wharf; weekday commuter ferries leave from the Ferry Building for Tiburon. The trip to either Sausalito or Tiburon takes from 25 minutes to an hour. Purchase tickets from terminal vending machines.

The Angel Island–Tiburon Ferry sails to the island daily from April through October and on weekends the rest of the year.

The San Francisco Bay Ferry runs several times daily between San Francisco's Ferry Building or Pier 41 and Oakland's Jack London Square by way of Alameda. The trip lasts from 25 to 45 minutes, and leads to Oakland's waterfront shopping and restaurant district. Purchase tickets on board.

Boat and Ferry Lines Angel Island–Tiburon Ferry. ☎ 415/435–2131 ⊕ www.angelislandferry.com. **Blue & Gold Fleet.** ☎ 415/705–8200 ⊕ www.blueandgoldfleet.com. **Golden Gate Ferry.** ☎ 415/921–5858 ⊕ www.goldengateferry.org. **San Francisco Bay Ferry.** ☎ 707/643–3779, 800/643–3779 ⊕ sanfranciscobayferry.com.

BUS TRAVEL

Golden Gate Transit buses travel north to Sausalito, Tiburon, and elsewhere in Marin County from the Transbay Temporary Terminal (located at Howard and Main, two blocks south of Market) and other points in San Francisco. For Mt. Tamalpais State Park and West Marin (Stinson Beach, Bolinas, and Point Reyes Station), take any route to Marin City and then transfer to the West Marin Stagecoach. San Francisco Muni buses primarily serve the city, though the 76X does cross the Golden Gate and end at the Marin Headlands Visitors Center on weekends.

Though less speedy than BART, over 30 AC Transit bus lines provide service to and from the Transbay Temporary Terminal and throughout the East Bay, even after BART shuts down. The F and FS lines will get you to Berkeley, while lines C, P, B, and O take you to Oakland and Piedmont.

Bus Lines AC Transit. ☎ 510/891–4777 ⊕ www.actransit.org. **Golden Gate Transit.** ☎ 511 ⊕ www.goldengatetransit.org. **San Francisco Muni.** ☎ 311 ⊕ www.sfmta.com. **West Marin Stagecoach.** ☎ 511 ⊕ www.marintransit.org.

CAR TRAVEL

To reach the East Bay from San Francisco, take Interstate 80 East across the San Francisco–Oakland Bay Bridge. For U.C. Berkeley, merge onto Interstate 580 West and take exit 11 for University Avenue. For Oakland, merge onto Interstate 580 East. To reach downtown, take Interstate 980 West from Interstate 580 East and exit at 14th Street. Travel time varies depending on traffic, but should take about 30 minutes (or an hour if it's rush hour).

19

For all points in Marin, head north on U.S. 101 and cross the Golden Gate Bridge. Sausalito, Tiburon, the Marin Headlands, and Point Reyes National Seashore are all accessed off U.S. 101. The scenic coastal route, Highway 1, also called Shoreline Highway and Panoramic for certain stretches, can be accessed off U.S. 101 as well. Follow this road to Muir Woods, Mt. Tamalpais State Park, Muir Beach, Stinson Beach, and Bolinas. From Bolinas, you can continue north on Highway 1 to Point Reyes.

RESTAURANTS

The Bay Area is home to many popular and innovative restaurants, such as Chez Panisse in Berkeley and Commis in Oakland—for which reservations must be made well in advance. There are also countless casual but equally tasty eateries to test out; expect an emphasis on organic seasonal produce, locally raised meats, craft cocktails, and curated wine menus. Marin's dining scene trends toward the sleepy side, so be sure to check hours ahead of time.

HOTELS

With a few exceptions, hotels in Berkeley and Oakland tend to be standard-issue, but many Marin hotels package themselves as cozy retreats. Summer in Marin is often booked well in advance, despite weather that can be downright chilly. Check for special packages during this season. *Hotel reviews have been shortened. For full information, visit Fodors.com.*

WHAT IT COSTS				
	$	$$	$$$	$$$$
Restaurants	under $16	$16–$22	$23–$30	over $30
Hotels	under $151	$151–$199	$200–$250	over $250

Restaurant prices are the average cost of a main course at dinner or, if dinner is not served, at lunch. Hotel prices are the lowest cost of a standard double room in high season.

TOURS

Fodor's Choice ★ **Best Bay Area Tours.** Morning and afternoon tours of Muir Woods and Sausalito include at least 90 minutes in the redwoods before heading on to Sausalito. On returning to the city, tours make a scenic stop in the Marin Headlands to enjoy fantastic views. Knowledgeable guides lead small tours in comfortable vans, and hotel pickup is included, though park entrance is not. Another tour option includes a visit to Muir Woods and Wine Country exploration. ☎ 877/705–8687 ⊕ *bestbayareatours.com* ⊠ *From $60.*

Dylan's Tours. Spend three hours exploring San Francisco in a small group led by a city-savvy local guide, before heading to Sausalito for lunch, and then Muir Woods for an hour among giant redwoods. This family-owned company makes sure to leave its customers in the know about the culture and history of the area. ⊠ *782 Columbus Ave., North Beach* ☎ *415/932–6993* ⊕ *www.dylanstours.com* ⊠ *From $75.*

Great Pacific Tour Co. Morning and afternoon tours to Muir Woods and Sausalito run three to four hours, and include hotel pickup and drop-off in 14-passenger vans. Price includes park entrance fee. ☎ *415/626–4499* ⊕ *www.greatpacifictour.com* 🖃 *From $65.*

THE EAST BAY

To many San Franciscans, the East Bay is a world away. But don't fall into that trap, because there's much to see on the other side of the Bay Bridge—industrial-chic Emeryville, the rolling hills of Orinda, and the upscale shopping suburb of Walnut Creek to name a few. Add on Berkeley, with its world-class university, and edgy Oakland, with its booming arts culture, nightlife, and restaurant scenes, and you've got plenty of reasons to venture east.

BERKELEY

2 miles northeast of Bay Bridge.

Berkeley is the birthplace of the Free Speech Movement, the radical hub of the 1960s, the home of arguably the nation's top public university, and a frequent site of protests and political movements. The city of 115,000 is also a culturally diverse breeding ground for social trends, a bastion of the counterculture, and an important center for Bay Area writers, artists, and musicians. Berkeley residents, students, and faculty spend hours nursing coffee concoctions while they read, discuss, and debate at the dozens of cafés that surround campus. It's the quintessential university town, with numerous independent bookstores, countless casual eateries, myriad meetups, and thousands of cyclists.

Oakland may have Berkeley beat when it comes to ethnic diversity and cutting-edge arts, but unless you're accustomed to sipping hemp milk lattes while planning a protest prior to yoga, you'll likely find Berkeley charmingly offbeat.

19

GETTING HERE AND AROUND

BART is the easiest way to get to Berkeley from San Francisco. Exit at the Downtown Berkeley station, and walk a block up Center Street to get to the western edge of campus. AC Transit buses F and FS lines stop near the university and 4th Street shopping. By car, take Interstate 80 East across the Bay Bridge, merge onto Interstate 580 West, and take the University Avenue exit through downtown Berkeley or take the Ashby Avenue exit and turn left on Telegraph Avenue. Once you arrive, explore on foot. Berkeley is very pedestrian-friendly.

ESSENTIALS

Visitor Information Koret Visitor Center. ⊠ *2227 Piedmont Ave., at California Memorial Stadium* ☎ *510/642–5215* ⊕ *visit.berkeley.edu.* **Visit Berkeley.** ⊠ *2030 Addison St. , Suite 102* ☎ *510/549–7040, 800/847– 4823* ⊕ *www.visitberkeley.com.*

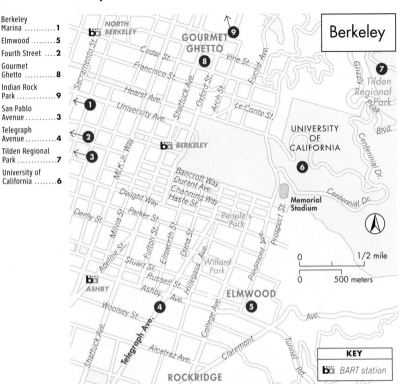

EXPLORING

TOP ATTRACTIONS

4th Street. Several blocks centering on 4th Street north of University Avenue have evolved from light industrial uses into an upscale shopping and dining district. The compact area is busiest on bright weekend afternoons. The Stained Glass Garden, Builders Booksource, and the Apple Store are among shoppers' favorites, along with a slew of boutiques, a fascinating reptile-filled Vivarium, and several wonderful paper stores. ⊠ *4th St. between University Ave. and Cedar St.* ⊕ *www.fourthstreet.com.*

QUICK BITES

Cheese Board Pizza. A jazz combo entertains the line that usually snakes down the block outside Cheese Board Pizza; it's that good. The cooperatively owned takeout spot and restaurant draws devoted customers with the smell of just-baked garlic on the pie of the day. **Known for:** vegetarian pizza by the slice or slab; live music performances. ⊠ *1504–1512 Shattuck Ave., at Vine St.* ☎ *510/549-3183* ⊕ *cheeseboardcollective.coop/pizza.*

Fodor's Choice **Gourmet Ghetto.** The success of Alice Water's Chez Panisse defined Cali-
★ fornia cuisine and attracted countless other food-related enterprises to a stretch of Shattuck Avenue now known as the Gourmet Ghetto. Foodies will do well to spend a couple of hours here poking around the shops, grabbing a quick bite, or indulging in a full meal.

The line stretches down the block in front of **Cheese Board Pizza** (*1512 Shattuck*), where live jazz bands serenade diners who spill out onto the sidewalk and median. Next door is the **Cheese Board Collective** and its fabulous bakery and cheese counter. Nearby, César (*1515 Shattuck*) wine bar and tapas house provides afternoon quaffs and late-night drinks, while the food stands of the **Epicurious Garden** (*1509–1513 Shattuck*)

A TASTING TOUR

For an unforgettable foodie experience, book a **Culinary Walking Tour** with Edible Excursions (*415/806–5970 www.edible-excursions.net*). Come hungry for knowledge and noshing. Tours ($105) take place on Thursdays at 11 and Saturdays at 10.

sell everything from sushi to gelato. In the back of the upscale food court, a small terraced garden winds up four levels to the **Imperial Tea Court**, a zenlike teahouse rife with imports and tea ware.

Across Vine, the **Vintage Berkeley** (*2113 Vine*) wineshop offers regular tastings and a great selection of reasonably priced bottles within the walls of a historic former pump house. Coffee lovers can head to the original **Peet's Coffee & Tea** at the corner of Walnut and Vine (*2124 Vine*) or venture to No. 1600 for a cup of Philz custom-blend coffee.

South of Cedar Street is the art-filled **Guerilla Cafe** (No. 1620), a breakfast and lunch spot beloved for its waffles (and Blue Bottle Coffee). Also look for the **Local Butcher Shop** (No. 1600), which sells locally sourced meat and hearty made-to-order sandwiches. For high-end food at takeout prices, try the salads, sandwiches, and signature potato puffs at **Grégoire**, around the corner on Cedar Street (No. 2109) or pastrami, latkes, and other Jewish deli fair at local favorite **Saul's Restaurant and Delicatessen** (No. 1475). **Masse's Pastries** with its delicate tortes, dainty eclairs, and decadent desserts (No. 1469) is a museum of edible artwork. We could go on, but you get the idea. ✉ *Shattuck Ave. between Delaware and Rose Sts., North Berkeley* ⊕ *www.gourmetghetto.org*.

19

FAMILY
Fodor'sChoice
★
Tilden Regional Park. Stunning bay views, a scaled-down steam train, and a botanic garden that boasts the nation's most complete collection of California plant life are the hallmarks of this 2,000-acre park in the hills just east of the U.C. Berkeley campus. The garden's visitors center offers tours, as well as information about Tilden's other attractions, including its picnic spots, Lake Anza swimming site, golf course, and hiking trails (the paved **Nimitz Way**, at Inspiration Point, is a popular hike with wonderful sunset views). ■**TIP**➔ Children love Tilden's interactive Little Farm and vintage carousel. ✉ *Tilden Regional Park, 2501 Grizzly Peak Blvd., Tilden Park* ☎ *510/544–2747 Park Office* ⊕ *www.ebparks.org/parks/tilden* ✉ *Free to park and botanic garden.*

University of California. Known simply as "Cal," the founding campus of California's university system is one of the leading intellectual centers in the United States and a major site for scientific research. Chartered in 1868, the university sits on 178 oak-covered acres split by Strawberry Creek; it's bound by Bancroft Way to the south, Hearst Avenue to the north, Oxford Street to the west, and Gayley Road to the east. Campus highlights include bustling and historic **Sproul Plaza** (*Bancroft Way and*

The University of California is the epicenter of Berkeley's energy and activism.

Sather Rd.), the seven floors and 61-bell carillon of **Sather Tower** (*Campanile Esplanade*), the nearly 3 million artifacts in the **Phoebe A. Hearst Museum of Anthropology** (Kroeber Hall), hands-on **Lawrence Hall of Science** (*1 Centennial Dr.*), the vibrant 34-acre **Botanical Gardens** (*200 Centennial Dr.*), and the eclectic and extensive collections housed in the **Art Museum & Pacific Film Archive** (*2155 Center*). ✉ *Berkeley* ☏ *510/642–6000* ⊕ *www.berkeley.edu*.

University of California Botanical Garden. Thanks to Berkeley's temperate climate, over 10,000 types of plants from all corners of the world flourish in the 34-acre University of California Botanical Garden. Free garden tours are given regularly. Benches and shady picnic tables make this a relaxing place for a snack with a breathtaking view. ✉ *200 Centennial Dr.* ☏ *510/643–2755* ⊕ *botanicalgarden.berkeley.edu* ◪ *$10.*

WORTH NOTING

FAMILY
Fodor'sChoice
★

Berkeley Marina. Enjoy spectacular views of San Francisco and Angel Island, as well as grassy expanses that are perfect for a picnic. The marina houses three restaurants and connects to bike paths and running trails. On sunny days, the 90-acre **César E. Chávez Park**, at the marina's northern tip, fills with kite flyers, dog walkers, and families grilling and riding bikes. ✉ *University Ave. , ½ mile west of I–80* ☏ *510/981–6740* ⊕ *www.ci.berkeley.ca.us/marina*.

Elmwood. Shops and cafés pack this pleasant neighborhood centered on College Avenue, just south of the U.C. campus. You'll know you're here when you spy the **historic Elmwood theater**, near College and Ashby Avenues, or notice the long line snaking outside nearby **Ici Ice Cream**, at 2948 College. Check out the architectural details of pre–World War II storefronts and the century-old shingled houses that line the tree-shaded streets. ⊠ *College Ave., between Dwight Way and Alcatraz Ave., Elmwood.*

OFF THE
BEATEN
PATH

Indian Rock Park. An outcropping of nature in a sea of North Berkeley homes, this is an unbeatable spot for a sunset picnic. Look for amateur rock climbers, after-work walkers, and cuddling couples, all watching the sun sinking beneath the Golden Gate Bridge. Come early to grab a spot. ⊠ *950 Indian Rock Ave., at Shattuck Ave.* 🖼 *Free.*

Peet's. When this Berkeley-born coffee chain opened at Vine and Walnut Streets in 1966, the unparalleled dark roast java was roasted in-store and brewed by the cup. Enjoy a splash while viewing a small exhibit in the back room that chronicles the company's evolution. ⊠ *2124 Vine St., at Walnut St.* ☎ *510/841–0564* ⊕ *www.peets.com.*

San Pablo Avenue. Berkeley's diversity is front and center along this evolving north–south artery in West Berkeley, where the old and new stand side by side: sari shops and a Mexican grocery do business near a hipster dive bar, a bait-and-tackle store, a typewriter store, and a dozen cool boutiques, all cheek by jowl in a melting pot microhood.

Start at **Bartavelle Coffee & Wine Bar** (No. 1603) off of Cedar. Order a handcrafted cappuccino and the best avocado toast this side of town. Journey a couple of blocks south to the **Albatross Pub** (No. 1822), a neighborhood favorite where grad students have been playing darts and eating free popcorn for 50 years. Tuck into solid Pakistani food at **Indus Village** (No. 1920) and stop by the **Halal Food Market** (No. 1964), then cross University Avenue. Duck into **Mi Tierra Foods** (No. 2082) for piñatas and chorizo—notice the Mission District–like mural—and **Middle East Market** (No. 2054) for rose water and rockin' baklava. **Café Venezuela** (No. 2056) has authentic arepas, and pretty much everyone loves the loaded thin-crust pies at **Lanesplitter Pizza & Pub** (No. 2033). The coffee at **Highwire** (No. 2049) is strong and delicious, and can be enjoyed indoors or on the back patio.

Long-running **Country Cheese** (No. 2101) has hundreds of cheeses, of course, but it also carries great bulk foods. Nearby industrial-cute **Gaumenkitzel** (No. 2121) serves up schnitzel, spaetzle, and other traditional German fare. Not to be confused with the fresh-baked loaves that come from **Acme Bread** (No. 1601), craft cocktails and curated whiskey flights are the most popular daily offerings at **Acme Bar & Company** (No. 2115).

As you move south, you'll pass lots of home-decor shops. Witness the chic renovation genius on display at **Mignonne Décor** (No. 2447) or venture into **Ohmega Salvage** (Nos. 2400–2403) and browse though its claw-footed tubs and pricey Victorian window frames.

At the corner of Dwight Way, stop for more caffeine at **Caffè Trieste** (No. 2500), Berkeley's homey branch of the North Beach bohemian coffee bar. Arousing browsing of erotic products can be had at sex-positive **Good Vibrations** (No. 2504). Find wonderful gifts for crafty soap and candle makers at **Juniper Tree Supplies** (No. 2520), and one-of-a-kind jewelry at **Kiss My Ring** (No. 2522). ⊠ *San Pablo Ave. , between Gilman St. and Ashby Ave.*

19

Telegraph Avenue. Cafés, bookstores, poster shops, and street vendors line Berkeley's student-oriented thoroughfare, a four-block corridor just south of campus. T-shirt sellers and tarot-card readers come and go, but **Rasputin Music** (No. 2401), **Amoeba Music** (No. 2455), and **Moe's Books** (No. 2476) are neighborhood landmarks worth checking out. College culture and copious caffeine have long been found at **Cafe Milano** (*2522 Bancroft Way*); meanwhile, fab food comes quickly from nearby Korean-Japanese fusion hot spot **Koja Kitchen** (2395) and grilled-cheese grandmasters at **The Melt** (2400). Polish off a visit with an indulgent cookie ice-cream sandwich from **CREAM** (2399). ✉ *Berkeley* ✥ *South of the Cal-Berkeley campus from Bancroft to Dwight Ways.*

WHERE TO EAT

Dining in Berkeley may be low-key when it comes to dress, but it's top-of-class in quality, even in less-refined spaces. Late diners beware: Berkeley is an "early to bed" kind of town.

$ CAFÉ

🍴 **1951 Coffee.** The first java spot of its kind, 1951 Coffee Company is a nonprofit coffee shop inspired and powered by refugees. In addition to crafting high-caliber coffee drinks and dishing out local pastries and sandwiches, this colorful café also serves as an inspiring advocacy space for refugees. Just three blocks south of campus, it's a favorite meet-up spot for locals and students alike. **Known for:** Verve coffee; Starter Bakery pastries; chai latte. [$] *Average main: $7* ✉ *2410 Channing Way, at Dana St.* ☎ *510/848–6252 ext. 270* 🌐 *1951coffee.com.*

$$ SOUTHERN

🍴 **Angeline's Louisiana Kitchen.** Exposed brick walls, maps of Louisiana, ceiling fans, and New Orleans music create a festive atmosphere at Angeline's. Specialties include Voo Doo Shrimp, crawfish étouffée, and buttermilk fried chicken. **Known for:** jambalaya; spicy gumbo; melt-in-your-mouth beignets. [$] *Average main: $20* ✉ *2261 Shattuck Ave., near Kittredge St.* ☎ *510/548–6900* 🌐 *www.angelineskitchen.com* 🕒 *No lunch Mon.*

$ DINER FAMILY

🍴 **Bette's Oceanview Diner.** Checkered floors, vintage burgundy booths, and an old-time jukebox set the scene at this retro-chic diner. The wait for a seat at breakfast can be quite long; luckily Bette's To Go is always an option. **Known for:** soufflé pancakes; spicy scrambles; meatloaf and gravy. [$] *Average main: $13* ✉ *1807 4th St., near Delaware St., 4th Street* ☎ *510/644–3230* 🌐 *www.bettesdiner.com* 🕒 *No dinner.*

$$$ SPANISH

🍴 **César.** Spanish-inspired small plates and craft cocktails are served late at César, Berkeley's premier tapas spot. Couples spill out from street-level windows on warm nights, or rub shoulders at the polished bar and communal table. **Known for:** lively bar with outstanding drinks; grilled bocadillos. [$] *Average main: $25* ✉ *1515 Shattuck Ave., at Vine St., North Berkeley* ☎ *510/883–0222* 🌐 *www.cesarberkeley.com.*

$$$$ MODERN AMERICAN Fodor's Choice ★

🍴 **Chez Panisse Café & Restaurant.** Alice Waters's legendary eatery is known for its locally sourced ingredients, formal prix-fixe menus, and personal service, while its upstairs café offers simpler fare in a more casual setting. Both menus change daily and legions of loyal fans insist that Chez Panisse lives up to its reputation. **TIP→ Reservations are practically essential.** **Known for:** sustainably sourced meats; inventive use of seasonal ingredients. [$] *Average main: $125* ✉ *1517 Shattuck Ave., at Vine St., North Berkeley* ☎ *510/548–5525 restaurant, 510/548–5049 café* 🌐 *www.chezpanisse.com* 🕒 *Closed Sun. No lunch in the restaurant.*

Innovative Berkeley restaurant Chez Panisse focuses on seasonal local ingredients.

$$ MODERN MEXICAN Fodor's Choice ★ 🍴 **Comal.** Relaxed yet trendy, Comal's cavernous indoor dining space and intimate back patio and fire pit draw a diverse, decidedly casual crowd for creative Mexican-influenced fare and well-crafted cocktails. The menu centers on small dishes that lend themselves to sharing and are offered alongside more than 100 tequilas and mezcals. **Known for:** margaritas and mezcal; fresh fish tacos; wood-fired entrées. [$] *Average main: $16* ✉ *2020 Shattuck Ave., near University Ave., Downtown* ☎ *510/926–6300* 🌐 *www.comalberkeley.com* ⏲ *No lunch.*

$$$ MODERN ITALIAN 🍴 **Corso.** This lively spot serves up a seasonal menu of excellent Florentine cuisine and Italian wines in a sparse but snazzy space. The open kitchen dominates a room, which includes closely spaced tables and festive flickering candles. **Known for:** handcrafted pasta; house-made salumi; Northern Italian specialties; extensive wine list. [$] *Average main: $24* ✉ *1788 Shattuck Ave., at Delaware St., North Berkeley* ☎ *510/704–8004* 🌐 *www.corsoberkeley.com* ⏲ *No lunch.*

$$ MODERN AMERICAN 🍴 **Gather.** All things local, organic, seasonal, and sustainable reside harmoniously under one roof at Gather. This haven for vegans, vegetarians, and carnivores alike is a vibrant, well-lit space that boasts funky light fixtures, shiny wood furnishings, and banquettes made of recycled leather belts. **Known for:** sustainable Californian cuisine; wood-fired pizzas; crispy brussels sprouts. [$] *Average main: $22* ✉ *2200 Oxford St., at Allston Way* ☎ *510/809–0400* 🌐 *www.gatherrestaurant.com.*

$$$ JAPANESE Fodor's Choice ★ 🍴 **Ippuku.** More Tokyo street chic than standard sushi house, this *izakaya*—the Japanese equivalent of a bar with appetizers—is decked with bamboo-screen booths. Servers pour an impressive array of sakes and *shōchū* and serve up surprising fare. **Known for:** shōchū selection; charcoal-grilled yakitori skewers. [$] *Average main: $25* ✉ *2130*

Center St., Downtown ☎ *510/665–1969* ⊕ *www.ippukuberkeley.com* ⊘ *Closed Mon. No lunch.*

$$$
MEDITERRANEAN
✕ **Lalime's.** Inside a charming flower-covered house, this restaurant serves dishes that reflect the entire Mediterranean region. The menu, constantly changing and unfailingly great, depends on the availability of fresh seasonal ingredients, and the two-level dining room is cheerful and light. **Known for:** seasonal Mediterranean-inspired specialties; California wines; cozy bungalow ambience. $ *Average main: $25* ✉ *1329 Gilman St., at Tevlin St., North Berkeley* ☎ *510/527–9838* ⊕ *www.lalimes.com* ⊘ *Closed Mon. No lunch.*

$
BAKERY
✕ **Nabolom Bakery.** A local favorite since 1976, Nabolom Bakery is a bright, bustling workspace where politics, pizza, and pastries collide. Fresh-baked favorites can be devoured on-site or taken to go. **Known for:** daily vegetarian pizza; cheese danish; cinnamon twists. $ *Average main: $7* ✉ *2708 Russell St., at College Ave.* ☎ *510/845–2253* ⊕ *www.nabolombakery.com* ⊘ *Closed Mon. and Tues.*

$
MEXICAN
FAMILY
✕ **Picante.** A barnlike space full of cheerful Mexican tiles and folk-art masks, Picante is a find for anyone seeking good Cal-Mex food for a song. The masa is freshly ground for the tortillas and tamales, the salsas are complex, and the flavor combinations are inventive. **Known for:** tamales and tacos; supernachos; large outdoor patio and fountain. $ *Average main: $14* ✉ *1328 6th St., near Camelia St.* ☎ *510/525–3121* ⊕ *www.picanteberkeley.com.*

$
AMERICAN
FAMILY
✕ **Rick & Ann's.** Haute comfort food and childhood favorites are the focus at this charming dining nook across from the Claremont hotel. Mac and cheese and free-range chicken potpie play second fiddle to brunches of cornmeal pancakes and gingerbread waffles, which are best enjoyed on the outdoor patio. **Known for:** weekend brunch; grown-up comfort food; mom's macaroni and cheese. $ *Average main: $14* ✉ *2922 Domingo Ave., at Ashby Ave., Claremont* ☎ *510/649–8538* ⊕ *www.rickandanns.com* ⊘ *No dinner.*

$$$
MODERN
AMERICAN
✕ **Rivoli.** Italian-inspired dishes using fresh California ingredients star on a menu that changes regularly. Inventive offerings are served in a tight modern dining room with captivating views of the lovely back garden. **Known for:** line-caught fish and sustainably sourced meats; curated wine list. $ *Average main: $28* ✉ *1539 Solano Ave., at Neilson St.* ☎ *510/526–2542* ⊕ *www.rivolirestaurant.com* ⊘ *No lunch.*

$
AMERICAN
FAMILY
Fodor's Choice
★
✕ **Saul's.** High ceilings and red-leather booths add to the friendly, retro atmosphere of Saul's deli, a Berkeley institution that is well known for its homemade sodas and enormous sandwiches. Locals swear by the pastrami sandwiches, stuffed-cabbage rolls, and challah French toast. ■ TIP→ Don't overlook the glass deli case, where you can order food to go. **Known for:** pastrami sandwich; deli hash. $ *Average main: $15* ✉ *1475 Shattuck Ave., near Vine St., North Berkeley* ☎ *510/848–3354* ⊕ *www.saulsdeli.com* ⊘ *Closed Thanksgiving and Yom Kippur.*

WHERE TO STAY

For inexpensive lodging, investigate University Avenue, west of campus. The area can be noisy, congested, and somewhat dilapidated, but it does include a few decent motels and chain properties. All Berkeley lodgings, except for the swanky Claremont, are strictly mid-range.

$$
HOTEL

⬚ **The Bancroft Hotel.** Renovated in 2012, this eco-friendly boutique hotel—across from the U.C. campus—is quaint, charming, and completely green. **Pros:** closest hotel in Berkeley to U.C. campus; friendly staff; many rooms have good views. **Cons:** some rooms are quite small; despite renovation, the building shows its age with thin walls; no elevator. *$ Rooms from: $160 ⊠ 2680 Bancroft Way ☎ 510/549–1000, 800/549–1002 toll-free ⊕ bancrofthotel.com ⤵ 22 rooms ⦿ Breakfast.*

$$$$
HOTEL
FAMILY
Fodor's Choice
★

⬚ **Claremont Resort and Spa.** Straddling the Oakland–Berkeley border, this amenities-rich Fairmont property—which celebrated its centennial in 2015—beckons like a gleaming white castle in the hills. **Pros:** amazing spa; supervised child care; solid business amenities; excellent dining and bar options; nearby hiking trails. **Cons:** parking is pricey; mandatory facilities charge. *$ Rooms from: $299 ⊠ 41 Tunnel Rd., at Ashby and Domingo Aves., Claremont ☎ 510/843–3000, 800/257–7544 reservations ⊕ www.fairmont.com/claremont-berkeley ⤵ 276 rooms ⦿ No meals.*

$
HOTEL
FAMILY

⬚ **Holiday Inn Express.** Convenient to the freeway and 4th Street shopping, this peach-and-beige hotel provides good bang for the buck. **Pros:** good breakfast; short walk to restaurant options on San Pablo and University; free Internet in rooms; free parking. **Cons:** area can be noisy and congested with traffic during commute hours; neighborhood can feel sketchy after dark. *$ Rooms from: $140 ⊠ 1175 University Ave., at Curtis St. ☎ 510/548–1700 ⊕ www.hiexberkeley.com ⤵ 70 rooms ⦿ Breakfast.*

$$$
HOTELHOTEL
Fodor's Choice
★

⬚ **Hotel Shattuck Plaza.** This historic boutique hotel sits amid Berkeley's downtown arts district, just steps from the U.C. campus and a short walk from the Gourmet Ghetto. **Pros:** central location near public transit; special date night and B&B packages; modern facilities; good views; great restaurant; pet friendly; free pass to nearby YMCA. **Cons:** public and street parking only; limited on-site fitness center. *$ Rooms from: $209 ⊠ 2086 Allston Way, at Shattuck Ave., Downtown ☎ 510/845–7300 ⊕ www.hotelshattuckplaza.com ⤵ 199 rooms ⦿ No meals.*

NIGHTLIFE AND PERFORMING ARTS

NIGHTLIFE

Fodor's Choice
★

Freight & Salvage Coffeehouse. Some of the most talented practitioners of folk, jazz, gospel, blues, world-beat, and bluegrass perform in this nonprofit coffeehouse, one of the country's finest folk music and story-telling venues. Most tickets cost less than $30. ⊠ 2020 Addison St., between Shattuck Ave. and Milvia St. ☎ 510/644–2020 ⊕ www.thefreight.org.

Fodor's Choice
★

Tupper & Reed. Housed in the former music shop of John C. Tupper and Lawrence Reed, this music-inspired cocktail haven features a symphony of carefully crafted libations, which are mixed with live music performed by local musicians. The historic 1925 building features a reservations-only balcony bar, cozy nooks, antique fixtures, a pool table, and romantic fireplaces. ⊠ 2271 Shattuck Ave., at Kitteredge St., Downtown ☎ 510/859–4472 ⊕ www.tupperandreed.com.

19

PERFORMING ARTS

Berkeley Repertory Theatre. One of the region's most highly respected and innovative repertory theaters, Berkeley Rep performs the work of classic and contemporary playwrights. Well-known pieces such as *Tartuffe* and *Macbeth* mix with world premieres and edgier fare like Green Day's *American Idiot* and Lemony Snicket's *The Composer Is Dead*. The theater's complex is in the heart of downtown Berkeley's arts district, near BART's Downtown Berkeley station. ⊠ *2025 Addison St., near Shattuck Ave.* ☎ *510/647–2949* ⊕ *www.berkeleyrep.org.*

Berkeley Symphony Orchestra. Fresh interpretations of classical works are a focus of this prominent orchestra, but commissioned new music and traditional pieces are also performed. BSO plays a handful of concerts each year, in Zellerbach Hall and other locations. ⊠ *1942 University Ave., Suite 207* ☎ *510/841–2800* ⊕ *www.berkeleysymphony.org.*

Cal Performances. Based out of U.C. Berkeley, this series runs from September through May. It features a varied bill of internationally acclaimed artists ranging from classical soloists to the latest jazz, world-music, theater, and dance ensembles. Past performers include Alvin Ailey American Dance Theatre, the National Ballet of China, Peter Sellars, and Yo-Yo Ma. ⊠ *101 Zellerbach Hall, Suite 4800, Dana Str. and Bancroft Way* ☎ *510/642–9988* ⊕ *calperformances.org.*

SHOPPING

Fodor's Choice
★

Amoeba Music. Heaven for audiophiles and movie collectors, this legendary Berkeley favorite is *the* place to head for new and used CDs, vinyl, cassettes, VHS tapes, Blu-ray discs, and DVDs. The massive and ever-changing stock includes thousands of titles for all music tastes, as well as plenty of Amoeba merch. There are branches in San Francisco and Hollywood, but this is the original. ⊠ *2455 Telegraph Ave., at Haste St.* ☎ *510/549–1125* ⊕ *www.amoeba.com.*

Body Time. Founded in Berkeley in 1970, this local chain uses premium-quality ingredients to create face, body, hair-care, and aromatherapy products. Essential oils and perfume oils can be combined to create personal fragrances. Tiare, gardenia, and China Rain are a few favorite scents. ⊠ *1950 Shattuck Ave., at Berkeley Way* ☎ *510/841–5818* ⊕ *www.bodytime.com.*

Kermit Lynch Wine Merchant. Credited with taking American appreciation of Old World wines to a higher level, this small shop is a great place to peruse as you educate your palate. The friendly salespeople will happily direct you to the latest French and Italian bargains. ⊠ *1605 San Pablo Ave., at Cedar St.* ☎ *510/524–1524* ⊕ *www.kermitlynch.com* ⊙ *Closed Sun. and Mon.*

Moe's Books. The spirit of Moe—the creative, cantankerous, cigar-smoking late proprietor—lives on in this world-famous four-story house of new and used books. Students and professors come here to browse the large selection, which includes literary and cultural criticism, art titles, and literature in foreign languages. ⊠ *2476 Telegraph Ave., near Haste St.* ☎ *510/849–2087* ⊕ *www.moesbooks.com.*

Rasputin Music. A huge selection of new music for every taste has been drawing crowds to this independent brand since 1971. Only in a town that also contained Amoeba Music could Rasputin's stock of used CDs, DVDs, collectibles, and vinyl be surpassed. ✉ *2401 Telegraph Ave., at Channing Way* ☎ *510/704–1146* ⊕ *www.rasputinmusic.com.*

OAKLAND

East of Bay Bridge.

In contrast to San Francisco's buzz and beauty and Berkeley's storied counterculture, Oakland's allure lies in its amazing diversity. Here you can find a Nigerian clothing store, a Gothic revival skyscraper, a Buddhist meditation center, and a lively salsa club, all within the same block.

Oakland's multifaceted nature reflects its colorful and tumultuous history. Once a cluster of Mediterranean-style homes and gardens that served as a bedroom community for San Francisco, the town had a major rail terminal and port city by the turn of the 20th century. Already a hub of manufacturing, Oakland became a center for shipbuilding and industry when the United States entered World War II. New jobs in the city's shipyards, railroads, and factories attracted thousands of laborers from across the country, including sharecroppers from the Deep South, Mexican Americans from the southwest, and some of the nation's first female welders. Neighborhoods were imbued with a proud but gritty spirit, along with heightened racial tension. In the wake of the civil rights movement, racial pride gave rise to militant groups like the Black Panther Party, but they were little match for the economic hardships and racial tensions that plagued Oakland. In many neighborhoods the reality was widespread poverty and gang violence—subjects that dominated the songs of such Oakland-bred rappers as the late Tupac Shakur. The highly publicized protests of the Occupy Oakland movement in 2011 and 2012 and the #BlackLivesMatter movement of 2014 and 2015 illustrate just how much Oakland remains a mosaic of its past.

Oakland's affluent reside in the city's hillside homes and wooded enclaves like Claremont, Piedmont and Montclair, which provide a warmer, more spacious alternative to San Francisco, while a constant flow of newcomers ensures continued diversity, vitality, and growing pains. Many neighborhoods to the west and south of the city center have yet to be touched by gentrification, but a renovated downtown and vibrant arts scene has injected new energy into the city. Even San Franciscans, often loath to cross the Bay Bridge, come to Uptown and Temescal for the nightlife, arts, and restaurants.

Everyday life here revolves around the neighborhood. In some areas, such as Piedmont and Rockridge, you'd swear you were in Berkeley or San Francisco's Noe Valley. Along Telegraph Avenue just south of 51st Street, Temescal is littered with hipsters and pulsing with creative culinary and design energy. These are perfect places for browsing, eating, or relaxing between sightseeing trips to Oakland's architectural gems, rejuvenated waterfront, and numerous green spaces.

19

GETTING HERE AND AROUND

Driving from San Francisco, take Interstate 80 East across the Bay Bridge, then take Interstate 580 East to the Grand Avenue exit for Lake Merritt. To reach downtown and the waterfront, take Interstate 980 West from Interstate 580 East and exit at 12th Street; exit at 18th Street for Uptown. For Temescal, take Interstate 580 East to Highway 24 and exit at 51st Street.

By BART, use the Lake Merritt Station for the Oakland Museum and southern Lake Merritt; the Oakland City Center–12th Street Station for downtown, Chinatown, and Old Oakland; and the 19th Street Station for Uptown, the Paramount Theatre, and the north side of Lake Merritt.

By bus, take the AC Transit's C and P lines to get to Piedmont in Oakland. The O bus stops at the edge of Chinatown near downtown Oakland.

Oakland's Jack London Square is an easy hop on the ferry from San Francisco. Those without cars can take advantage of the free Broadway Shuttle, which runs from the Jack London Square to 27th Street via downtown on weekdays and Friday and Saturday nights.

Be aware of how quickly neighborhoods can change. Walking is safe downtown and in the Piedmont and Rockridge areas, but avoid walking west and southeast of downtown, especially at night.

Shuttle Contact Broadway Shuttle. ⊕ *www.meetdowntownoak.com.*

ESSENTIALS

Visitor Information Visit Oakland. ⊠ *481 Water St., near Broadway, Jack London Square* ☎ *510/839–9000* ⊕ *www.visitoakland.org.*

EXPLORING

TOP ATTRACTIONS

FAMILY

Fodor's Choice

★

Oakland Museum of California. This museum surveys the state's art, history, and natural wonders in three galleries of absorbing, interactive exhibits. Travel through myriad ecosystems, from the sand dunes of the Pacific to the volcanic Mt. Shasta, and discover over 2,000 species in the expansive Gallery of California Natural Sciences. Explore disparate integrated stories in the rambling Gallery of California History, which includes everything from Ohlone baskets to Gold Rush era artifacts. Of particular interest in the Gallery of California Art are photographs by Dorothea Lange and paintings by members of the Bay Area figurative school. Stop by the Blue Oak café for a snack or relax for a minute in the flower gardens, which are open to the public at no charge during hours of operation. ■TIP➔ On Friday evenings the museum gets lively, with live music, food trucks, and half-price admission. ⊠ *1000 Oak St., at 10th St., Downtown* ☎ *510/318–8400, 888/625–6873 toll-free* ⊕ *museumca.org* ⊡ *$16, free 1st Sun. of month* ☉ *Closed Mon. and Tues.*

Fodor's Choice

★

Paramount Theatre. A glorious art-deco specimen, the Paramount operates as a venue for concerts and performances of all kinds, from the Oakland Symphony to Jerry Seinfeld and Elvis Costello. The popular classic movie nights start off with a 30-minute Wurlitzer concert. ■TIP➔ Docent-led tours, offered the first and third Saturday of the month, are fun and informative. ⊠ *2025 Broadway, at 20th St., Uptown* ☎ *510/465–6400* ⊕ *www.paramounttheatre.com* ⊡ *Tour $5.*

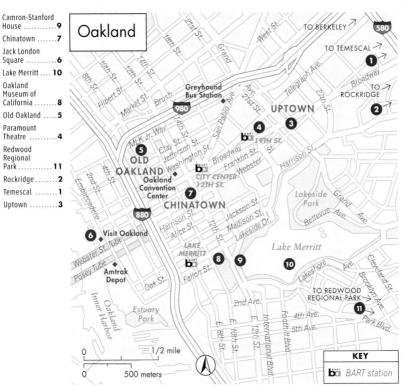

FAMILY
Fodor'sChoice
★
Rockridge. This fashionable upscale neighborhood is one of Oakland's most desirable places to live. Explore the tree-lined streets that radiate out from **College Avenue** just north and south of the Rockridge BART station for a look at California Craftsman bungalows at their finest. By day College Avenue between Broadway and Alcatraz Avenue is crowded with shoppers buying fresh flowers, used books, and clothing; by night the same folks are back for handcrafted meals, artisan wines, and locally brewed ales. With its specialty-food shops and quick bites to go, **Market Hall,** an airy European-style marketplace at Shafter Avenue, is a hub of culinary activity. ⊠ *College Ave., between Alcatraz Ave. and Broadway, Rockridge* ⊕ *www.rockridgedistrict.com.*

Fodor'sChoice
★
Temescal. Centering on Telegraph Avenue between 40th and 51st Streets, Temescal (the Aztec term for "sweat house") is a low-pretension, money-eyed-hipster hood with young families and middle-aged folks thrown into the mix. A critical mass of excellent eateries draws folks from around the Bay Area; there's veteran **Doña Tomás** (*5004 Telegraph Ave.*) and favorites **Pizzaiola** (*5008 Telegraph Ave.*) and **Aunt Mary's** (*4640 Telegraph Ave.*) as well as **Bakesale Betty** (*5098 Telegraph Ave.*), where folks line up for the fried-chicken sandwich, and **Doughnut Dolly** (*482B 49th St.*), where treats are fried to order. Old-time dive bars and smog-check stations share space with the trendy children's clothing

19

shop **Ruby's Garden** (*5026 Telegraph Ave.*) and the stalwart **East Bay Depot for Creative Reuse** (*4695 Telegraph Ave.*), where you might find a bucket of buttons or 1,000 muffin wrappers among birdcages, furniture, lunch boxes, and ribbon.

Around the corner, **Temescal Alley** (*49th St.*), a tucked-away lane of tiny storefronts, crackles with the creative energy of local makers. Surprising finds can be had at **Crimson Horticultural Rarities** (*No. 470*) or at the home-decor shop at **Bounty and Feast** (*No. 482*). Don't miss grabbing a sweet scoop at **Curbside Creamery** (*No. 482*). ⊠ *Telegraph Ave., between 40th and 51st Sts., Temescal* ⊕ *www.temescaldistrict.org.*

Fodor's Choice **Uptown.** This is where nightlife and cutting-edge art happens in
★ Oakland, along the Telegraph Avenue/Broadway corridor north of downtown. Dozens of galleries cluster around Telegraph, showing everything from photography and site-specific installations to glasswork and fiber arts. The first Friday of each month, thousands descend for **Art Murmur** (*oaklandartmurmur.org*), a late-night gallery event that has expanded into **First Friday** (*oaklandfirstfridays.org*), a veritable neighborhood festival featuring food trucks, street vendors, and live music along Telegraph Avenue.

Lively restaurants with a distinctly urban vibe make Uptown a dining destination every night of the week. Favorites include craft cocktails and eclectic Japanese-inspired fare at **Hopscotch** (*1915 San Pablo Ave.*), beautiful beverages and stylish cuisine at art-deco **Flora** (*1900 Telegraph Ave.*), tasty tapas and modern Spanish fare at trendy **Duende** (*468 19th*), upscale Southern comfort food at elegant **Picán** (*2295 Broadway*), and innovative Oaxacan fare and mezcal magic at **Calavera** (*2337 Broadway*) just to name a few.

Toss in the bevy of bars and there's plenty within walking distance to keep you busy for an entire evening: **Cafe Van Kleef** (*1621 Telegraph Ave.*), the friendly jumble that started it all Uptown; **Bar Three Fifty-Five** (*355 19th St.*), a house of great cocktails; strikingly beautiful but low-key **Dogwood** (*1644 Telegraph Ave.*), which has tasty nibbles; **Drake's Dealership** (*2325 Broadway*), with its spacious hipster-friendly beer garden; **Lost and Found** (*2040 Telegraph Ave.*), home of draft brews and cornhole boards; and **Somar** (*1727 Telegraph Ave.*), a bar, music lounge, and gallery in one. Uptown's shopping is exploding as well, with local goods at the fore; be sure to stop by **Oaklandish** (*1444 Broadway*) for T-shirts, jeans, and everything Oaktown. The **Paramount Theatre** (*2025 Broadway*), **Fox Theater** (*1807 Telegraph Ave.*), and other art-deco architectural gems distinguish this neighborhood. ⊠ *Oakland* ⊕ *Telegraph Ave. and Broadway from 14th to 27th Sts.*

WORTH NOTING

Camron-Stanford House. A proud reminder of the days when Oakland was a wealthy bedroom community, the Camron-Stanford House exudes dignity from its foundation up to its ornate widow's walk. Built in 1876, the Victorian served as the home of the Oakland Museum from 1910 to 1967, and a room containing documents and original artifacts chronicles the museum's history. Six painstakingly redecorated period rooms occupy the upper floor—a tribute to the craftsmanship and dedication that went into the 1978 restoration; this is the only remaining 19th-century Lake Merritt mansion. ■TIP➔ Tea and tour package ($40 per person) are available to groups of 10 or more, and there are free, guided tours every Sunday at 1, 2, and 3 pm. ✉ *1418 Lakeside Dr.* ☎ *510/874–7802* ⊕ *www.cshouse.org* ⌲ *$5* ⊘ *Closed Mon.–Sat.*

Chinatown. A densely packed, bustling neighborhood, Oakland's Chinatown, unlike its San Francisco counterpart, makes no concessions to tourists. You won't find baskets of trinkets lining the sidewalk and souvenir displays in the shop windows, but supermarkets such as **Yuen Hop Noodle Company and Asian Food Products** (*824 Webster St.*), open since 1931, overflow with delicacies, and the line for sweets, breads, and towering cakes snakes out the door of **Napoleon Super Bakery** (*810 Franklin St.*). Don't miss an enlightening tour of **The Fortune Cookie Factory** (*261 12th St.*), bubble tea and egg puffs at **Shooting Star Cafe** (*1022 Webster St.*), or a walk through the lovely **Chinese Garden Park** (*7th St.*). ✉ *Oakland* ✛ *Between Broadway and Fallon St. and between 6th and 12th Sts.* ⊕ *oakland-chinatown.info.*

Jack London Square. Shops, minor historic sites, restaurants, recreation, and the venerable **Yoshi's** (*510 Embarcadero W*) jazz club line Jack London Square, named for the author of *The Call of the Wild, The Sea Wolf,* and other works. London, who was born in San Francisco, also lived in Oakland, where he spent many a day boozing and brawling in the waterfront area, most notably at **Heinold's First and Last Chance Saloon** (*48 Webster St., at Embarcadero W*). The wonderful little saloon has been serving since 1883. Next door is the Klondike cabin in which London spent a summer in the late 1890s. The cabin was moved from Alaska and reassembled here in 1970.

Weekends at the square are lively, with diners and drinkers filling the many outdoor patios and bars, and shoppers perusing Sunday's farmers' market, from 9 am to 2 pm. Catch a movie at **Regal Jack London** (*100 Washington St.*), sample local wines at **Rosenblum Cellars** (*10 Clay St.*), play some bocce in **Plank's** beer garden (*98 Broadway*), or plan an adventure with **California Canoe & Kayak** (*409 Water St.*). ✉ *Oakland* ✛ *Embarcadero W at Broadway* ☎ *510/645–9292* ⊕ *www.jacklondonsquare.com.*

FAMILY **Lake Merritt.** Runners, joggers, and power walkers charge along the 3.4-mile path that encircles this 155-acre heart-shaped natural saltwater lake. Crew teams glide across the water and boatmen guide snuggling couples in authentic Venetian gondolas (*fares start at $60 per couple for 30 mins; 510/663–6603, gondolaservizio.com*), while yogis, jugglers, and picnickers look on from the shore. **Lakeside Park,** which surrounds the north side of Lake Merritt, has several outdoor attractions, including the small children's park, **Children's Fairyland** (*699 Bellevue Ave.*), and the **Lake Merritt Wildlife Sanctuary,** a water and air fowl haven that was also North America's first wildlife refuge. ■TIP➔ Don't miss the nearby Grand Lake neighborhood, centering on the parallel strips of Lakeshore Avenue and Grand Avenue, for good browsing and even better eating. ✉ *Lakeside Park, Bellevue and Grand Aves.* ⊕ *www.lakemerritt.org.*

19

Old Oakland. The restored Victorian storefronts that line the four historic blocks of Oakland's original downtown now contain restaurants, cafés, offices, shops, galleries, and a Friday morning farmer's market. Architectural consistency distinguishes the area from surrounding streets, giving it a distinct neighborhood feel. Old World–inspired **Caffè 817** (*817 Washington St.*) serves poached eggs and polenta, fresh-pressed panini, and bowls of café latte in an artsy atmosphere. Stop in for a deli sandwich at **Ratto's International Market** (*827 Washington St.*), an Italian grocery that's been in business for more than a century, or head over to the renovated **Swan's Market** (*538 9th St.*), where you can choose from an array of high-caliber multicultural eateries that offer takeout. **Pacific Coast Brewing Company** (*902 Washington St.*) pours a mean microbrew, while The **Trappist** (*460 8th St.*) wins loyalty for its exhaustive selection of Belgian ales. Various pop-up boutiques and permanent shops throughout the neighborhood are reinvigorating the storefront scene. ⊠ *Oakland* ⊹ *bordered by 6th St., 10th St., Clay St., and Broadway* ⊕ *old-oakland.com.*

FAMILY **Redwood Regional Park.** *Sequoia sempervirens,* or coastal redwoods, grow to 150 feet tall in Redwood Regional Park, one of the few spots in the Bay Area that escaped timber-hungry loggers in the 19th century. The 1,830-acre park has forested picnic spots and myriad hiking trails, including part of the 32-mile **East Bay Skyline National Trail**, which links Redwood to four other parks in the Berkeley–Oakland hills. ■TIP➔ Also check out adjacent Joaquin Miller Park for beautiful East Bay views and lush forested trails. ⊠ *7867 Redwood Rd.* ⊹ *From downtown Oakland take I–580 E for Hayward; take exit 24 for 35th Ave.; continue on 35th, which turns into Redwood Rd.; watch for a park entrance on the left in 3 to 4 miles.* ☎ *888/327–2757* ⊕ *www.ebparks. org/parks/redwood* 🖾 *Free; $5 per vehicle fee at some major entrances.*

WHERE TO EAT

$$ **✕ À Côté.** This Mediterranean hot spot is all about seasonal small plates,
MEDITERRANEAN cozy tables, family-style eating, and excellent wine. Heavy wooden tables, intimate dining nooks, natural light, and a heated patio make this an ideal destination for couples, families, and the after-work crowd. **Known for:** Pernod mussels; exquisite small plates; global and regional wine list. $ *Average main: $22* ⊠ *5478 College Ave., at Taft Ave., Rockridge* ☎ *510/655–6469* ⊕ *acoterestaurant.com* ☾ *No lunch.*

$ **✕ Brown Sugar Kitchen.** Influenced by Tanya Holland's African American
SOUTHERN heritage and French culinary education, the menu at this bustling little West
FAMILY Oakland dining destination features local, organic ingredients and sweet
Fodor'sChoice and savory dishes paired with sumptuous wines. The dining room is small,
★ but inviting with a long, sleek counter, red-leather stools, and spacious booths and tables. **Known for:** fried chicken and cornmeal waffles; bacon-cheddar-scallion biscuits; smoked chicken and shrimp gumbo. $ *Average main: $15* ⊠ *2534 Mandela Pkwy., at 26th St., West Oakland* ☎ *510/839–7685* ⊕ *www.brownsugarkitchen.com* ☾ *Closed Mon. No dinner.*

$$$ **✕ Calavera.** This Oaxacan-inspired hot spot offers inventive and
MODERN elevated plates in an industrial-chic space with lofty ceilings, warm
MEXICAN wooden tables, exposed brick walls, and heated outdoor dining. Innovative cocktails like the salted-air margarita come from a beautiful bar

with a library of over 100 agaves. **Known for:** innovative and beautiful cocktails; wide selection of tequilas and mezcal; carnitas tacos served in nixtamal heirloom corn tortillas; fresh ceviche. $ *Average main: $25* ✉ *2337 Broadway, at 24th St., Uptown* ☎ *510/338–3273* ⊕ *calaveraoakland.com* ⊗ *Closed Mon.*

$$$$ ✕ **Camino.** Russell Moore cooked at Chez Panisse for two decades before
AMERICAN he and Allison Hopelain opened this restaurant, which focuses on simple, seasonal, straightforward dishes that are cooked in an enormous, crackling *camino* (Italian for "fireplace"). Served on redwood tables in a Craftsman-meets-refectory-style dining room, the ever-changing menu has only three entrées—each cooked over its own open fire—that feature top-notch ingredients and pair perfectly with creative craft cocktails. **Known for:** wood-fired dishes; craft cocktails. $ *Average main: $32* ✉ *3917 Grand Ave., at Boulevard Way, Grand Lake* ☎ *510/547–5035* ⊕ *www.caminorestaurant.com* ⊗ *Closed Tues. No lunch* ⌤ *No tipping.*

$$ ✕ **Chop Bar.** The walls and tables are made of reclaimed wood at this
AMERICAN small, stylish roadside gathering space whose knowing, tattooed bartenders serve potent cocktails. A great neighborhood joint for every meal of the day (including brunch), Chop Bar implements a farm-to-table concept and serves upmarket gastropub grub. **Known for:** oxtail poutine; house-made burgers; pork confit. $ *Average main: $20* ✉ *247 4th St., at Alice St., Jack London Square* ☎ *510/834–2467* ⊕ *www.oaklandchopbar.com.*

$$$$ ✕ **Commis.** A slender, unassuming storefront houses the only East Bay
AMERICAN restaurant with a Michelin star (two of them, in fact). The room is mini-
Fodor's Choice malist and polished: nothing distracts from the artistry of chef James
★ Syhabout, who creates a multicourse dining experience based on the season and his distinctive vision. **Known for:** inventive multicourse tasting menu; Michelin-winning execution. $ *Average main: $149* ✉ *3859 Piedmont Ave., at Rio Vista Ave., Piedmont* ☎ *510/653–3902* ⊕ *commisrestaurant.com* ⊗ *Closed Mon. and Tues. No lunch.*

$$ ✕ **Doña Tomás.** A neighborhood favorite with bright red walls, authen-
MEXICAN tic Mexican artwork, and a festive outdoor patio, this sunny spot in Oakland's Temescal District serves seasonal Mexican fare to a hip but low-key crowd. Margaritas and horchata abound; brunch is served on weekends. **Known for:** chiles rellenos and carnitas; courtyard patio; margaritas. $ *Average main: $21* ✉ *5004 Telegraph Ave., near 51st St., Temescal* ☎ *510/450–0522* ⊕ *www.donatomas.com* ⊗ *Closed Mon. No dinner Sun. No lunch weekdays.*

$$ ✕ **Juhu Beach Club.** All the color, flavor, and fun of Mumbai's Juhu Beach
INDIAN is contained within the brightly colored walls of this festive funky Temescal eatery. Childhood memories, Indian street food, and family recipes have inspired Preeti Mistry's menu of spicy starters, savory sliders, inventive drinks, and edgy modern main courses. **Known for:** pav slider sandwiches; modern takes on traditional street food; refreshing drinks (both boozy and booze-free). $ *Average main: $22* ✉ *5179 Telegraph Ave., at 51st St., Temescal* ☎ *510/652–7350* ⊕ *juhubeachclub.com.*

$ ✕ **Le Cheval Restaurant.** This cavernous yet classy restaurant is a lunch-
VIETNAMESE time favorite and a good place to sample *pho*, a classic Hanoi-style beef noodle soup fragrant with star anise. An extensive menu of sautéed

19

entrées and rice and noodle dishes is complemented by a full bar and selection of regional wines. **Known for:** affordable lunch specials; Vietnamese classics and Asian noodle dishes. $ *Average main: $12* ⊠ *1007 Clay St., at 11th St., Old Oakland* ☎ *510/763–8495* ⊕ *www.lecheval. co* ⊗ *No lunch Sun.*

$$ ✕ **Luka's Taproom & Lounge.** Hip and urban, with an unpretentious vibe,
AMERICAN   Luka's is a real taste of Uptown with its Belgian-inspired California
Fodor's Choice   comfort food and plentiful selection of Trappist ales, local drafts, and
★   international bottles of beer. The late-night menu is a favorite of bar-hoppers, and DJs in the adjacent lounge keep the scene going well past last call. **Known for:** plentiful pints; late-night noshing. $ *Average main: $22* ⊠ *2221 Broadway, at W. Grand Ave., Uptown* ☎ *510/451–4677* ⊕ *www.lukasoakland.com.*

$$$$ ✕ **Oliveto Cafe & Restaurant.** Some of Oakland's finest chefs have come
ITALIAN   through the ranks of this locally renowned eatery that anchors Market Hall in the Rockridge neighborhood. The elegant upstairs dining room serves a daily menu of high-caliber Italian cuisine, while the downstairs marketplace café and bar offers everything from a morning espresso to pizza or a full-blown Italian meal. **Known for:** regional Italian food made with locally sourced ingredients; handmade pasta; whole animal butchery. $ *Average main: $32* ⊠ *5655 College Ave., at Shafter Ave., Rockridge* ☎ *510/547–5356* ⊕ *www.oliveto.com* ⊗ *No lunch weekends in restaurant.*

$$ ✕ **Pizzaiolo.** Chez Panisse alum Charlie Hallowell helms the kitchen of this
ITALIAN   rustic-chic Oakland institution. Diners of all ages perch on wooden chairs
FAMILY   with red-leather backs and nosh on farm-to-table Italian fare from a daily changing menu. **Known for:** seasonal wood-fired pizza; delicious daily breakfast pastries; rustic California-Italian entrées. $ *Average main: $22* ⊠ *5008 Telegraph Ave., at 51st St., Temescal* ☎ *510/652–4888* ⊕ *www. pizzaiolooakland.com* ⊗ *Closed Sun. No lunch.*

$$$ ✕ **Shakewell.** Two *Top Chef* vets opened this stylish Lakeshore restaurant,
MEDITERRANEAN   which serves creative and memorable Mediterranean small plates in a
Fodor's Choice   lively setting that features an open kitchen, wood-fired oven, communal
★   tables, and snug seating. As the name implies, well-crafted cocktails are shaken (or stirred) and poured with panache. **Known for:** wood-oven paella; Spanish and Mediterranean small plates; craft cocktails. $ *Average main: $25* ⊠ *3407 Lakeshore Ave., near Mandana Blvd.* ☎ *510/251–0329* ⊕ *www.shakewelloakland.com* ⊗ *Closed Mon. No lunch Tues.*

$$$$ ✕ **Wood Tavern.** Expect a warm welcome and a lively atmosphere at this
AMERICAN   longtime Rockridge favorite. A neighborhood gem in the truest sense, Wood Tavern serves contemporary American brasserie food with quality wine, well-crafted drinks, and refined service. **Known for:** cheese boards; modern American classics; an impressive yet approachable wine list; meat selections from the butcher block. $ *Average main: $32* ⊠ *6317 College Ave., near 63rd St., Rockridge* ☎ *510/654–6607* ⊕ *www.woodtavern.net* ⊗ *No lunch Sun.*

WHERE TO STAY

$$ ⊡ **Best Western Plus Bayside Hotel.** Sandwiched between the serene Oak-
HOTEL   land Estuary and an eight-lane freeway, this all-suites property has handsome accommodations with balconies or patios, many overlooking

the water. **Pros:** attractive, budget-conscious choice; free parking; free shuttle to and from airport, Jack London Square, and downtown; scenic water views. **Cons:** not within walking distance of anything of interest; freeway-side rooms can be loud. $ *Rooms from: $159* ✉ *1717 Embarcadero, off I–880, at 16th St. exit* ☎ *510/356–2450* ⊕ *hotelsinoakland ca.h.bestwestern.com* ⤴ *81 rooms* ❙◯❙ *Breakfast.*

$$$$ ⊡ **Oakland Marriott City Center.** A good choice downtown for business
HOTEL travelers—and not bad for leisure ones, either—the Marriott, conveniently located near the Old Oakland and Uptown neighborhoods, provides comprehensive services and amenities including a fitness center, pool, and second-floor restaurant. **Pros:** convenient location; ergonomically designed work areas; online discounts often available off-season; weekend discounts at half the weekday rate. **Cons:** daily Internet fee; steep fee for parking. $ *Rooms from: $359* ✉ *1001 Broadway, at 11th St., Downtown* ☎ *510/451–4000* ⊕ *www.marriott.com* ⤴ *494 rooms* ❙◯❙ *No meals.*

$$ ⊡ **Waterfront Hotel.** This thoroughly modern, pleasantly appointed Joie
HOTEL de Vivre property sits among the many high-caliber restaurants of Jack
FAMILY London Square. **Pros:** great location; lovely views; dog-friendly; excellent hotel restaurant, Lungomare; complimentary wine-and-cheese hour during the week; free shuttle service to downtown (limited hours); easy access to the ferry. **Cons:** passing trains can be noisy on city side; parking is pricey. $ *Rooms from: $180* ✉ *10 Washington St., Jack London Square* ☎ *510/836–3800 front desk, 888/842–5333 reservations* ⊕ *www.jdvhotels.com* ⤴ *145 rooms* ❙◯❙ *No meals.*

NIGHTLIFE AND PERFORMING ARTS

Back when rent was still relatively cheap, artists flocked to Oakland, giving rise to a cultural scene—visual arts, indie music, spoken word, film—that's still buzzing, especially in Uptown. Trendy new spaces pop up regularly and the beer-garden renaissance is already well-established. Whether you're a self-proclaimed beer snob or just someone who enjoys a cold drink on a sunny day, there's something for everyone. Oakland's nightlife scene is less crowded and more intimate than what you'll find in San Francisco. Music is just about everywhere, though the most popular venues are downtown.

19

NIGHTLIFE

BARS **Café Van Kleef.** Long before Uptown got hot, the late Peter Van Kleef
Fodor's Choice was serving stiff fresh-squeezed greyhounds, telling tales about his col-
★ lection of pop culture mementos, and booking live music at Café Van Kleef, a funky café-bar that crackles with creative energy—there's still live music every weekend. This local favorite still serves some of the stiffest drinks in town. ✉ *1621 Telegraph Ave., between 16th and 17th Sts., Uptown* ☎ *510/763–7711* ⊕ *cafevankleef.com.*

The Layover Music Bar and Lounge. Bright, bold, and unabashedly bohemian, this hangout filled with recycled furniture is constantly evolving because everything is for sale, from the artwork to the pillows, rugs, and lamps. The busy bar serves up signature organic cocktails, and live entertainment includes comedy shows, storytelling, and local DJs. ✉ *1517 Franklin St., near 15th St., Uptown* ☎ *510/834–1517* ⊕ *www.oaklandlayover.com.*

Make Westing. This sprawling industrial-chic space is always abuzz with hipsters playing bocce, the post-work crowd sipping old-fashioneds, or pretheater couples passing mason jars of Dungeness crab dip. The patio's your best bet for a conversation on a busy evening. ⊠ *1741 Telegraph Ave., at 18th St., Uptown* ☎ *510/251–1400* ⊕ *makewesting.com.*

BREWPUBS
AND BEER
GARDENS

Beer Revolution. Hard-core beer geeks: with hundreds of bottled beers and 50 taps, this craft beer and bottle shop is for you. Tear yourself away from the beer lists and grab a table on the patio. ⊠ *464 3rd St., at Broadway, Jack London Square* ☎ *510/452–2337* ⊕ *www.beer-revolution.com.*

Brotzeit Lokal. If you want a water view with your brew, head to this spot east of Jack London Square and enjoy a bretzel and obatzda (a soft German pretzel with Bavarian cheese dip), a selection of local wurst, or some Wiener schnitzel with your German or Belgian beer. ⊠ *1000 Embarcadero, near 8th St., Jack London Square* ☎ *510/645–1905* ⊕ *brotzeitbiergarten.com* ⊗ *Closed Mon.*

FAMILY
Fodor's Choice
★

Lost & Found. The diversions on the spacious, succulent-filled patio include Ping-Pong, cornhole, and community tables full of chilled-out locals. The beer selection ranges from blue collar to Belgian and a seasonal menu focuses on internationally inspired small bites. ⊠ *2040 Telegraph Ave., at 21st St., Uptown* ☎ *510/763–2040* ⊕ *www.lostand-found510.com* ⊗ *Closed Mon.*

The Trappist. Brick walls, dark wood, soft lighting, and a buzz of conversation set a warm and mellow tone inside this old Victorian space that's been renovated to resemble a traditional Belgian pub. The setting (which includes two bars and a back patio) is definitely a draw, but the real stars are the artisan beers—more than a hundred Belgian, Dutch, and North American brews. Light fare includes bar snacks and meat and cheese boards. ⊠ *460 8th St., near Broadway, Old Oakland* ☎ *510/238–8900* ⊕ *www.thetrappist.com.*

Telegraph. Hipsters hold court at Telegraph (aka Beeryland), where giant murals and bike wheel rims decorate the largely cement and mostly graffitied outdoor beer garden. Expect great burgers and home-made sausages paired with alcoholic slushies and beers that change daily. ⊠ *2318 Telegraph Ave., at 23rd St., Uptown* ☎ *510/444–8353* ⊕ *telegraphoakland.com.*

ROCK, POP,
HIP-HOP,
FOLK, AND
BLUES CLUBS

Fox Theater. This renovated 1928 theater, Oakland's favorite performance venue, is a remarkable feat of Mediterranean Moorish architecture and has seen the likes of Willie Nelson, Counting Crows, Rebelution, and B.B. King, to name a few. The venue boasts good sight lines, a state-of-the-art sound system, brilliant acoustics, and a restaurant and bar, among other amenities. ⊠ *1807 Telegraph Ave., between 18th and 19th Sts., Uptown* ☎ *510/302–2250* ⊕ *thefoxoakland.com.*

Fodor's Choice
★

Yoshi's. Opened in 1972 as a sushi bar, Yoshi's has evolved into one of the area's best jazz and live music venues. The full Yoshi's experience includes traditional Japanese and Asian fusion cuisine in the adjacent restaurant. ⊠ *510 Embarcadero W, between Washington and Clay Sts., Jack London Square* ☎ *510/238–9200* ⊕ *www.yoshis.com* ⌐ *$20–$80.*

SPORTS AND THE OUTDOORS

BASEBALL

FAMILY **Oakland A's.** Billy Beane of *Moneyball* fame is the executive vice president and titular head of this American League baseball team. Same-day tickets can usually be purchased at the **O.co Coliseum** box office (Gate D). To get to the game, take a BART train to the Coliseum station. ✉ *O.co Coliseum, 7000 Coliseum Way, off I–880, north of Hegenberger Rd.* ☎ *510/638–4900, 877/493–2255 tickets* ⊕ *www.athletics.com* ✉ *$10–40.*

BASKETBALL

FAMILY **Golden State Warriors.** Steph Curry and the beloved "Dubs" play basketball at the **Oracle Arena** from late October into April. BART trains serve the arena; get off at the Coliseum station. Purchase single tickets through Ticketmaster (*800/653–8000, www.ticketmaster.com*). ✉ *Oracle Arena, 7000 Coliseum Way, off I–880, north of Hegenberger Rd.* ☎ *888/479–4667 tickets* ⊕ *www.nba.com/warriors.*

FOOTBALL

Oakland Raiders. Known for their intensely loyal (and occasionally violent) fans, this NFL team currently plays at the O.co Coliseum. Catch them here while you can. Tickets are available through Ticketmaster (*800/653–8000, www.ticketmaster.com*). ✉ *O.co Coliseum, 7000 Coliseum Way, off I–880, north of Hegenberger Rd.* ☎ *510/864–5020 tickets, 800/724–3377 general Raiders info* ⊕ *www.raiders.com.*

SHOPPING

Pop-up shops and stylish, locally focused stores are scattered throughout the funky alleys of Old Oakland, Uptown, Rockridge, and Temescal, while the streets around Lake Merritt and Grand Lake offer more modest boutiques.

Atomic Garden. Get all your last-minute gifts at this hipster-chic Rockridge boutique, which carries high-end provisions from hand-forged scissors and linen napkins to meditation thread and aromatherapy sprays and oils. ✉ *5453 College Ave., between Taft and Kales Aves., Rockridge* ☎ *510/923–0543* ⊕ *atomicgardenoakland.com.*

Diesel. Wandering bibliophiles collect armfuls of the latest fiction and nonfiction at this revered shop. The loftlike space, with its high ceilings and spare design, encourages contemplation, and on chilly days a fire burns in the hearth. Past participants in the excellent authors' events have included Ian Rankin, Annie Leibovitz, and Michael Moore. ✉ *5433 College Ave., at Kales Ave., Rockridge* ☎ *510/653–9965* ⊕ *www.dieselbookstore.com.*

Maison d'Etre. Close to the Rockridge BART station, this store epitomizes the Rockridge neighborhood's funky-chic shopping scene. Look for high-end housewares and impulse buys like whimsical watches, imported fruit-tea blends, and funky slippers. ✉ *5640 College Ave., at Keith Ave., Rockridge* ☎ *510/658–2801* ⊕ *maisondetre.com.*

Fodor's Choice ★ **Oaklandish.** This is the place for Oaktown swag. What started in 2000 as a public art project of local pride has become a celebrated brand around the bay, and a portion of the proceeds from hip Oaklandish brand T-shirts and accessories supports grassroots nonprofits committed to bettering the local community. It's good-looking stuff for a good cause. ✉ *1444 Broadway, near 15th St., Uptown* ☎ *510/251–9500* ⊕ *oaklandish.com.*

19

MARIN COUNTY

Marin is, quite simply, a knockout—its abundance of protected parkland, open-space preserves, and rugged coastline are some of the most breathtaking and ecologically diverse in the world. The territory ranges from chaparral, grassland, and coastal scrub to broadleaf, redwood, and evergreen forest. It's well worth the drive over the Golden Gate Bridge to explore the stunning Marin Headlands and the sprawling beauty of Point Reyes National Seashore and its 80 miles of shoreline.

While Cyra McFadden's literary soap opera, *The Serial*, depicted Marin county as a bastion of hot-tubbing and "open" marriages, increasingly jet-set Marinites spend more time on outdoor activities, including surfing, cycling, kayaking, and hiking. Adrenaline junkies mountain bike down Mt. Tamalpais, while solitary folk wander along Point Reyes's empty beaches. Artists and musicians who arrived in the 1960s set a boho tone for mellow country towns, but much of Marin is undeniably chic, with high-tech companies making their mark in the local economy; this *is* one of the wealthiest counties in the nation.

After exploring Marin's natural beauty, consider a stop in one of its lovely villages. Most cosmopolitan is Sausalito, the town just over the Golden Gate Bridge from San Francisco. Across the inlet from Sausalito, Tiburon and Belvedere are lined with grand homes that regularly appear on fund-raising circuits, and to the north, landlocked Mill Valley is a hub of wining and dining and tony boutiques. Book Passage, a noted bookseller in the next town, Corte Madera, hosts regular readings by top-notch authors, and Larkspur, San Anselmo, and Fairfax beyond have walkable downtown areas, each a bit folksier than the next but all with good restaurants and shops and a distinct sense of place.

In general, the farther west you go, the more rural things become. Separated from the inland county by the slopes and ridges of giant Mt. Tamalpais, West Marin beckons to mavericks, artists, ocean lovers, and free spirits. Stinson Beach has tempered its isolationist attitude to accommodate out-of-towners, as have Inverness and Point Reyes Station. Bolinas, on the other hand, would prefer to keep to itself.

VISITOR INFORMATION

Contact **Marin Convention & Visitors Bureau.** ✉ *1 Mitchell Blvd., Suite B, San Rafael* ☎ *415/925–2060* ⊕ *www.visitmarin.org.*

THE MARIN HEADLANDS

Due west of the Golden Gate Bridge's northern end.

The term *Golden Gate* has become synonymous with the world-famous bridge, but it was first given to the narrow waterway that connects the Pacific and the San Francisco Bay. To the north of the Golden Gate Strait lies the Marin Headlands, part of the Golden Gate National Recreation Area (GGNRA), which boasts some of the area's most dramatic scenery.

GETTING HERE AND AROUND

Driving from San Francisco, head north on U.S. 101. Just after you cross the Golden Gate Bridge, take exit 442 for Alexander Avenue. Keep left at the fork and follow signs for "San Francisco/U.S. 101 South"), go through the tunnel under the freeway, and turn right up the hill. Muni bus 76X runs hourly from Sutter and Sansome Streets to the Marin Headlands Visitor Center on weekends and major holidays only.

EXPLORING

TOP ATTRACTIONS

FAMILY
Fodor's Choice
★

Marin Headlands. The headlands stretch from the Golden Gate Bridge to Muir Beach. Photographers perch on the southern headlands for spectacular shots of the city and bridge. Equally remarkable are the views north along the coast and out to the ocean, where the Farallon Islands are visible on clear days.

The headlands' strategic position at the mouth of San Francisco Bay made them a logical site for military installations from 1890 through the Cold War. Today you can explore the crumbling concrete batteries where naval guns once protected the area. The headlands' main attractions are centered on Fts, Barry and Cronkhite, which are separated by Rodeo Lagoon and Rodeo Beach, a dark stretch of sand that attracts sand-castle builders and dog owners.

The visitor center is a worthwhile stop for its exhibits on the area's history and ecology, and kids enjoy the "please touch" educational sites and small play area inside. You can pick up guides to historic sites and wildlife, and get information about programming and guided walks. ⊠ *Golden Gate National Recreation Area, Visitors Center, Fort Barry Chapel, Ft. Barry, Bldg. 948, Field and Bunker Rds., Sausalito* ☎ *415/331–1540* ⊕ *www.nps.gov/goga/marin-headlands.htm.*

FAMILY **Marine Mammal Center.** If you're curious about the rehabilitation of marine mammals from the Pacific—and the human practices that endanger them—stop by this research hospital and rehabilitation center for rescued aquatic creatures. An observation area overlooks pools where sea lions and seals convalesce, and informational exhibits explain the center's history and work. ■ TIP→ **You'll learn even more—and get closer to the animals—on a 45-minute docent-led tour.** ⊠ *Ft. Cronkhite, 2000 Bunker Rd., Sausalito* ☎ *415/289–7325* ⊕ *www.marinemammal-center.org* ⊠ *$9 tour fee (register online).*

Fodor's Choice
★

Nike Missile Site SF-88. The only fully restored site of its kind in the United States, the museum at SF-88 provides a firsthand view of menacing Cold War–era Hercules and Ajax missiles and missile-tracking radar, the country's last line of defense against Soviet nuclear bombers. It's worth timing your visit to take the guided tour, which features period uniforms and vehicles and includes a visit to the missile-launching bunker. ■ TIP→ **On the first Saturday of the month the site holds an open house during which Nike veterans describe their experiences.** ⊠ *Field Rd., off Bunker Hill Rd.* ☎ *415/331–1453* ⊕ *www.nps.gov/goga/nike-missile-site.htm* ☉ *Closed Sun.–Wed.*

19

FAMILY **Point Bonita Lighthouse.** A restored beauty that still guides ships to safety with its original 1855 refractory lens, the lighthouse anchors the southern headlands. Half the fun of a visit is the steep half-mile walk from the parking area through a rock tunnel, across a suspension bridge, and down to the lighthouse. Signposts along the way detail the bravado of surfmen, as the early lifeguards were called, and the tenacity of the "wickies," the first keepers of the light. ■TIP→ Call about 90-minute full-moon tours. ⊠ *End of Conzelman Rd., Ft. Barry, Bldg. 948, Sausalito* ☎ *415/331–1540* ⊕ *www.nps.gov/goga/pobo.htm* ♡ *Closed Tues.–Fri.*

WORTH NOTING

Hawk Hill. At 923 feet tall, craggy Hawk Hill is the best place on the West Coast to watch the migration of eagles, hawks, and falcons as they fly south for winter. The main migration period is from September through October, and the modest Hawk Hill viewing deck is about 2 miles up Conzelman Road from U.S. 101; look for a Hawk Hill sign and parking right before the road becomes one way. In September and October, on rain- and fog-free weekends, docents from the Golden Gate Raptor Observatory give free lectures on Hawk Hill; call ahead of time for details. ⊠ *Golden Gate National Recreation Area, Conzelman Rd., Sausalito* ⊕ *www.ggro.org.*

Headlands Center for the Arts. The campus, which is comprised of rehabilitated military buildings, features contemporary art in a rustic natural setting. An artist-renovated space called the Key Room contains objects found and created by residents, including interesting glass bottles filled with collected items, and other unusual ephemera. Stop by the Project Space studios and galleries, two flights up, to see what select artists in residence are up to—most of the work is quite contemporary. ⊠ *Ft. Barry, 944 Simmonds Rd., Sausalito* ☎ *415/331–2787* ⊕ *www.headlands.org* ♡ *Closed Fri. and Sat.*

SAUSALITO

2 miles north of Golden Gate Bridge.

Bougainvillea-covered hillsides and an expansive yacht harbor give Sausalito the feel of an Adriatic resort. The town sits on the northwestern edge of San Francisco Bay, where it's sheltered from the ocean by the Marin Headlands; the mostly mild weather here is perfect for strolling and outdoor dining. Nevertheless, morning fog and afternoon winds can roll over the hills without warning, funneling through the central part of Sausalito once known as Hurricane Gulch.

South of Bridgeway, which snakes between the bay and the hills, a waterside esplanade is lined with restaurants on piers that lure diners with good seafood and even better views. Stairs along the west side of Bridgeway and throughout town climb into wooded hillside neighborhoods filled with both rustic and opulent homes, while back on the northern portion of the shoreline, harbors shelter a community of over 400 houseboats. As you amble along Bridgeway past shops and galleries, you'll notice the absence of basic services. Find them and more on Caledonia Street, which runs parallel to Bridgeway and inland a couple of blocks. While

Rowers enjoy a sunny day on the Sausalito waterfront.

ferry-side shops flaunt kitschy souvenirs, smaller side streets and narrow alleyways offer eccentric jewelry and handmade crafts.

■ TIP→ The ferry is the best way to get to Sausalito from San Francisco; you get more romance (and less traffic) and disembark in the heart of downtown.

Sausalito developed its bohemian flair in the 1950s and '60s, when creative types, including artist Jean Varda, poet Shel Silverstein, and madam Sally Stanford, established an artists' colony and a houseboat community here (this is Otis Redding's "Dock of the Bay"). Both the spirit of the artists and the neighborhood of floating homes persist. For a close-up view of the quirky community, head north on Bridgeway, turn right on Gate Six Road, park where it dead-ends, and enter through the unlocked gates.

GETTING HERE AND AROUND

From San Francisco by car or bike, follow U.S. 101 north across the Golden Gate Bridge and take exit 442 for Alexander Avenue, just past Vista Point; continue down the winding hill to the water to where the road becomes Bridgeway. Golden Gate Transit buses will drop you off in downtown Sausalito, and the ferries dock downtown as well. The center of town is flat, with plenty of sidewalks and bay views. It's a pleasure and a must to explore on foot.

ESSENTIALS

Visitor Information Sausalito Chamber of Commerce. ⊠ 1913 Bridgeway ☎ 415/331–7262 ext. 10 ⊕ www.sausalito.org. Sausalito Information Kiosk. ⊠ El Portal St. ⚓ At the foot of El Portal St. at the Ferry Pier ☎ 415/331–1093 ⊕ www.oursausalito.com.

Marin
County

0   5 mi
0   5 km

EXPLORING

FAMILY **Bay Area Discovery Museum.** Sitting on 7½ acres of national park land
at the base of the Golden Gate Bridge, this indoor-outdoor nonprofit
children's museum offers entertaining and enlightening hands-on exhibits for younger children. Kids can stretch their creativity and develop
early STEM skills as they navigate wind tunnels, fish from a boat at
the indoor wharf, configure oversized foam blocks in the Imagination
Playground, and play outdoors among the tide pools, gravel pits, ship-
wrecks, and caves of Lookout Cove. At the multisensory Tot Spot, toddlers and preschoolers dress in animal costumes and crawl through
miniature tunnels. ⊠ 557 McReynolds Rd., at East Rd. off Alexander
Ave. ☎ 415/339–3900 ⊕ bayareadiscoverymuseum.org ⊇ $14, free 1st
Wed. of the month ☉ Closed Mon.

FAMILY **Bay Model.** This one-of-a-kind education center focuses on a sprawling
1½-acre model of the entire San Francisco Bay and Sacramento–San
Joaquin River delta system, complete with flowing water. Now open for
public exploration, the model has been used by the U.S. Army Corps of
Engineers to reproduce the rise and fall of tides, the flow of currents,
and the other physical forces at work on the bay. ⊠ 2100 Bridgeway, at
Marinship Way ☎ 415/332–3871, ⊕ www.spn.usace.army.mil/Missions/
Recreation/Bay-Model-Visitor-Center ⊇ Free ☉ Closed Sun. and Mon.

Sally Stanford Drinking Fountain. There's an unusual historic landmark on the Sausalito Ferry Pier—a drinking fountain inscribed "Have a drink on Sally" in remembrance of Sally Stanford, the former San Francisco brothel madam who became Sausalito's mayor in the 1970s. Sassy Sally would have appreciated the fountain's eccentric attachment: a knee-level basin with the inscription "Have a drink on Leland," in memory of her beloved dog. ⊠ *Sausalito Ferry Pier, Anchor St. at Humboldt St., off the southwest corner of Gabrielson Park ⊕ www.oursausalito.com/ sausalito-ferry-1.html.*

QUICK
BITES

Hamburgers Sausalito. Patrons queue up daily outside this tiny street-side shop for organic Angus beef patties that are made to order on a wheel-shaped grill. Brave the line (it moves fast) and take your food to the esplanade to enjoy fresh air and bay-side views. Known for: legendary burgers. ⊠ 737 Bridgeway, at Anchor St. ☎ 415/332–9471 ☾ No dinner.

Sausalito Ice House Visitors Center and Museum. The local historical society operates this dual educational exhibit and visitor center, where you can get your bearings, learn some history, and find out what's happening in town. ⊠ *780 Bridgeway, at Bay St. ☎ 415/332–0505 ⊕ www.sausalito-historicalsociety.com ☾ Closed Mon.*

Viña del Mar Plaza and Park. The landmark Plaza Viña del Mar, named for Sausalito's sister city in Chile, marks the center of town. Adjacent to the parking lot and ferry pier, the plaza is flanked by two 14-foot-tall elephant statues, which were created for the San Francisco Panama–Pacific International Exposition in 1915. It also features a picture-perfect fountain that's great for people-watching. ⊠ *Bridgeway and El Portal St. ⊕ www.oursausalito.com/parks-in-sausalito/ vina-del-mar-park.html.*

WHERE TO EAT

$
INTERNATIONAL
✕ **Avatar's.** "Purveyors of ethnic confusions," this family-run Marin minichain offers California Indian fusion combinations that locals revere. The warmth of service, willingness to cater to dietary needs, creativity of the food, and reasonable prices more than make up for the uninspired space. **Known for:** Punjabi enchiladas, especially curried pumpkin; savory masala chaas smoothies. Ⓢ *Average main: $14* ⊠ *2656 Bridgeway, at Coloma St. ☎ 415/332–8083 ⊕ www.enjoyavatars.com ☾ Closed Sun.*

$$
AMERICAN
✕ **Bar Bocce.** Nothing elevates wood-fired food more than beachside tables and a blazing fire pit... except maybe a game of bocce. Modern Californian cuisine, local beer, and signature sangria are served inside the snazzy bar and out on the patio, which opens to Richardson Bay. **Known for:** sourdough pizza crust; signature house meatballs. Ⓢ *Average main: $18* ⊠ *1250 Bridgeway, between Pine and Turney Sts. ☎ 415/331–0555 ⊕ www.barbocce.com.*

$$
SEAFOOD
FAMILY
Fodor's Choice
★
✕ **Fish.** If you're looking for fresh sustainably caught seafood, head to this gleaming dockside fish house a mile north of downtown. Order at the counter—cash only—and then grab a seat by the floor-to-ceiling windows or at a picnic table on the pier, overlooking the yachts and fishing boats. **Known for:** fish of the day; barbecued oysters; sustainably

19

caught, fire-grilled entrées. $ *Average main: $20* ⊠ *350 Harbor Dr., at Gate 5 Rd., off Bridgeway* ☎ *415/331–3474* ⊕ *www.331fish.com* ▭ *No credit cards* ☞ *Cash only.*

$$$
FRENCH
✕ **Le Garage.** Brittany-born Olivier Souvestre serves traditional French bistro fare in a relaxed, bay-side setting that feels more sidewalk café than the converted garage that it is. The restaurant seats only 35 inside and 15 outside, so make reservations or arrive early. **Known for:** PEI mussels and house-cut fries; weekend brunch. $ *Average main: $26* ⊠ *85 Liberty Ship Way , Suite 109* ☎ *415/332–5625* ⊕ *www.legaragebistrosausalito.com* ☞ *No reservations for weekend brunch.*

$
SCANDINAVIAN
✕ **Lighthouse Cafe.** A cozy spot with a dose of Scandinavian flair and a long counter bar that abuts an open kitchen, this local diner has been a favorite breakfast (served all day) and brunch destination for decades. Expect a wait, but rest assured it's worth it. **Known for:** Norwegian salmon omelet; loaded fruit pancakes; Danish lunch plate. $ *Average main: $13* ⊠ *1311 Bridgeway, between Locust and Turney Sts.* ☎ *415/331–3034* ⊕ *www.lighthouse-restaurants.com* ◷ *No dinner.*

$$$
ITALIAN
✕ **Poggio.** A hillside dining destination, Poggio serves modern Tuscan-style comfort food in a handsome, Old World–inspired space whose charm spills onto the sidewalks. An extensive and ever-changing menu of antipasti, pasta, hearty entrées, and pizzas emerges from the open kitchen's wood-fired oven. **Known for:** fresh local ingredients and traditional Northern Italian dishes; rotisserie chicken with property-grown organic herbs and vegetables; polpettini meatballs. $ *Average main: $30* ⊠ *777 Bridgeway, at Bay St.* ☎ *415/332–7771* ⊕ *www.poggiotrattoria.com.*

$$$
JAPANESE
Fodor's Choice
★
✕ **Sushi Ran.** Sushi aficionados swear that this tiny, stylish restaurant—in business for more than three decades—is the Bay Area's best option for raw fish, but don't overlook the excellent Pacific Rim fusions, a melding of Japanese ingredients and French cooking techniques. Book in advance or expect a wait, which you can soften by sipping one of the bar's 45 by-the-glass sakes. **Known for:** fish imported from Tokyo's famous Tsukiji market; local miso glazed black cod. $ *Average main: $30* ⊠ *107 Caledonia St., at Pine St.* ☎ *415/332–3620* ⊕ *www.sushiran.com* ◷ *No lunch weekends.*

WHERE TO STAY

$$$$
HOTEL
▦ **Casa Madrona & Spa.** This 19th-century landmark mansion first opened as an inn in 1906, expanding over the decades to include modern hotel rooms, private cottages, and mansion suites, along with a 3,000-foot full-service spa, all tiered down a hill in the center of Sausalito. **Pros:** contemporary modern furniture with rich Victorian touches; 11 varieties of room type from bay-side guest rooms to upper hillside cottage suites; central location; on-site fitness center and world-class spa. **Cons:** stairs required to access some cottages; breakfast is not included. $ *Rooms from: $319* ⊠ *801 Bridgeway* ☎ *415/332–0502, 800/288–0502* ⊕ *www.casamadrona.com* ⇆ *64 rooms* ⦿ *No meals.*

$$$$
HOTEL
▦ **Cavallo Point.** Set in the Golden Gate National Recreation Area, this luxury hotel and resort with a one-of-a-kind location on a former army post contains well-appointed, eco-friendly rooms that range from restored officers' quarters to modern spaces. **Pros:** stunning views;

activities include a cooking classes, yoga classes, and nature walks; spa with a tea bar; art gallery; accommodating staff. **Cons:** isolated from urban amenities; coffee and pastries provided, but not a full breakfast. [$] *Rooms from: $400* ✉ *601 Murray Circle* ☎ *415/339–4700* 🌐 *www.cavallopoint.com* 🛏 *142 rooms* 🍴 *No meals.*

$$ B&B/INN **Hotel Sausalito.** Handcrafted furniture and tasteful original art and reproductions give this Mission Revival-style inn the feel of a small European hotel. **Pros:** great staff; central location; solid mid-range hotel; vouchers to nearby Cafe Tutti provided. **Cons:** no room service; some rooms are small; daily public parking fee. [$] *Rooms from: $175* ✉ *16 El Portal, at Bridgeway* ☎ *415/332–0700* 🌐 *www.hotelsausalito.com* 🛏 *16 rooms* 🍴 *No meals.*

$$$$ B&B/INN **The Inn Above Tide.** The balconies at the Inn Above Tide literally hang over the water, and each of its rooms has a perfect-10 view that takes in wild Angel Island as well as the city lights across the bay. **Pros:** great complimentary breakfast; minutes from restaurants and attractions; central but tranquil setting. **Cons:** costly daily parking; some rooms are on the small side; five rooms have no balcony. [$] *Rooms from: $380* ✉ *30 El Portal* ☎ *415/332–9535, 800/893–8433* 🌐 *www.innabovetide.com* 🛏 *31 rooms* 🍴 *Breakfast.*

PERFORMING ARTS

Sausalito Art Festival. This annual juried fine-arts show, held over Labor Day weekend, features more than 270 artists and attracts more than 30,000 people to the Sausalito waterfront. Blue & Gold Fleet ferries from San Francisco dock at the pier adjacent to the festival. ✉ *2400 Bridgeway, # 220* ☎ *415/332–3555* 🌐 *www.sausalitoartfestival.org* 🎟 *$25.*

SPORTS AND THE OUTDOORS

KAYAKING

Sea Trek Kayaking and SUP Center. The center (SUP stands for stand-up paddleboarding) regularly offers guided three-hour scenic Sausalito tours and Saturday-evening starlight paddle trips, both appropriate for beginners. Additional trips could include a journey underneath the Golden Gate Bridge or to Angel Island, depending on the currents. Trips for experienced kayakers, classes, and rentals are also available. ✉ *2100 Bridgeway, off Bridgeway and Marinship Way* ☎ *415/332–8494* 🌐 *www.seatrek.com* 🎟 *From $25 per hr for rentals, $75 for 3-hr guided trip.*

SAILING

SF Bay Adventures. Expert skippers conduct sunset and full-moon sails around the bay, as well as fascinating Sunday-morning ecotours with the possibility of viewing whales and sharks. If you're interested, the company can arrange a private charter for you to barbecue on Angel Island or even spend the night in a lighthouse. ✉ *1001 Bridgeway, Suite B2A* ✥ *At Caledonia St.* ☎ *415/331–0444* 🌐 *www.sfbayadventures.com* 🎟 *Starting at $59* ☞ *Find tours at schoonerfredab.com.*

TIBURON

7 miles north of Sausalito, 11 miles north of Golden Gate Bridge.

On a peninsula that was named Punta de Tiburon (Shark Point) by 18th-century Spanish explorers, this beautiful Marin County community retains the feel of a village—it's more low-key than Sausalito—despite the encroachment of commercial establishments from the downtown area. The harbor faces Angel Island across Raccoon Strait, and San Francisco is directly south across the bay—which means the views from the decks of harbor restaurants are major attractions. Since 1884, when the San Francisco and North Pacific Railroad relocated their ferry terminal facilities to the harbor town, Tiburon has centered on the waterfront. ■TIP→ The ferry is the most relaxing (and fastest) way to get here, and allows you to skip traffic and parking problems.

GETTING HERE AND AROUND

Blue & Gold Fleet ferries travel between San Francisco and Tiburon daily. By car, head north from San Francisco on U.S. 101 and get off at CA 131/Tiburon Boulevard/East Blithedale Avenue (Exit 447). Turn right onto Tiburon Boulevard and drive just over 4 miles to downtown. Golden Gate Transit serves downtown Tiburon from San Francisco; watch for changes during evening rush hour. Tiburon's Main Street is made for wandering, as are the footpaths that frame the water's edge.

ESSENTIALS

Visitor Information Tiburon. ⊠ *Town Hall, 1505 Tiburon Blvd.* ☎ *415/435–7373* ⊕ *www.destinationtiburon.org.*

EXPLORING

FAMILY **Ark Row.** The second block of Main Street is known as Ark Row and has a tree-shaded walk lined with antiques and specialty stores. Some of the buildings are actually old 19th-century ark houseboats that floated in Belvedere Cove before being beached and transformed into stores. ■TIP→ If you're curious about architectural history, the Tiburon Heritage & Arts Commission has a self-guided walking-tour map, available online and at local businesses. ⊠ *Ark Row, Main St. , south of Juanita La.* ⊕ *tiburonheritageandarts.org.*

Old St. Hilary's Landmark and John Thomas Howell Wildflower Preserve. The architectural centerpiece of this attraction is a stark-white 1888 Carpenter Gothic church that overlooks the town and the bay from its hillside perch. Surrounding the church, which was dedicated as a historical monument in 1959, is a wildflower preserve that's spectacular in May and June, when the rare black or Tiburon jewel flower blooms. Expect a steep walk uphill to reach the preserve. The Landmarks Society will arrange guided tours by appointment. ■TIP→ The hiking trails behind the landmark wind up to a peak that has views of the entire Bay Area. ⊠ *201 Esperanza St., off Mar West St. or Beach Rd.* ☎ *415/435–1853* ⊕ *landmarkssociety.com/landmarks/st-hilarys/* ⊗ *Church closed Mon.–Sat. and Nov.–Mar.*

WHERE TO EAT

$$$ AMERICAN 🍴 **The Caprice.** For more than 50 years this Tiburon landmark that overlooks the bay has been the place to come to mark special occasions with local wines and European-American comfort food. The views are spectacular, and soft-yellow walls and starched white tablecloths help to make the space bright and light. **Known for:** seared sea scallops; shellfish risotto; rack of lamb; California wines. [$] *Average main: $28* ✉ *2000 Paradise Dr.* ☎ *415/435–3400* 🌐 *www.thecaprice.com* 🕒 *No lunch.*

$$$ SICILIAN 🍴 **Luna Blu.** Friendly, informative staff serve Sicilian-inspired seafood in this lively sliver of an Italian restaurant just a stone's throw from the ferry. Take a seat on the heated patio overlooking the bay, or cozy up with friends on one of the high-sided booths near the bar. **Known for:** sustainably caught seafood and local, organic ingredients; weekend English tea service. [$] *Average main: $25* ✉ *35 Main St.* ☎ *415/789–5844* 🌐 *lunablurestaurant.com* 🕒 *Closed Tues. No lunch weekdays.*

$ AMERICAN FAMILY 🍴 **New Morning Cafe.** Omelets and scrambles are served all day long at this homey triangular bay-side café with sunny outdoor seating. If you're past morning treats, choose from the many soups, salads, and sandwiches, best enjoyed at picnic tables. **Known for:** hearty American breakfast fare. [$] *Average main: $13* ✉ *1696 Tiburon Blvd., near Juanita Ln.* ☎ *415/435–4315* 🕒 *No dinner.*

$$$ AMERICAN 🍴 **Sam's Anchor Cafe.** Open since 1920, this casual dockside restaurant, rife with plastic chairs and blue-checked oilcloths, is the town's most famous eatery. Most people flock to the deck for beers, views, sunsets, and exceptionally tasty seafood. **Known for:** cioppino; Painted Hills natural beef burgers; patio beverages. [$] *Average main: $24* ✉ *27 Main St.* ☎ *415/435–4527* 🌐 *www.samscafe.com.*

WHERE TO STAY

$$$ HOTEL 🏨 **The Lodge at Tiburon.** Framed by stone pillars and sloped rooftops, the Lodge at Tiburon has the feel of a winter ski chalet, though the outdoor pool and its cabanas provide a summery counterpoint. **Pros:** free self-parking; spacious work desks; room service from the Tiburon Tavern; business and fitness centers; SkyDeck open-air lounge. **Cons:** breakfast not included; no bay views. [$] *Rooms from: $229* ✉ *1651 Tiburon Blvd., at Beach St.* ☎ *415/435–3133* 🌐 *lodgeattiburon.com* 🛏 *103 rooms* 🍽 *No meals.*

$$$$ B&B/INN 🏨 **Waters Edge Hotel.** Checking into this stylish downtown hotel feels like tucking away into an inviting retreat by the water—the views are stunning and the lighting is perfect. **Pros:** complimentary wine and cheese for guests every evening; restaurants/sights are minutes away; free bike rentals for guests; pet-friendly; free Wi-Fi. **Cons:** downstairs rooms lack privacy and balconies; paid self-parking; fitness center is off-site. [$] *Rooms from: $279* ✉ *25 Main St., off Tiburon Blvd.* ☎ *415/789–5999, 877/789–5999* 🌐 *www.marinhotels.com* 🛏 *23 rooms* 🍽 *Breakfast.*

MILL VALLEY

2 miles north of Sausalito, 4 miles north of Golden Gate Bridge.

Chic and woodsy Mill Valley has a dual personality. Here, as elsewhere in the county, the foundation is a superb natural setting. Virtually surrounded by parkland, the town lies at the base of Mt. Tamalpais and contains dense redwood groves traversed by countless creeks. But this is no lumber camp. Smart restaurants and chichi boutiques line streets that have been traversed by more rock stars than one might suspect.

The rustic village flavor isn't a modern conceit, but a holdover from the town's early days as a center for the lumber industry. In 1896, the Mt. Tamalpais Scenic Railroad—dubbed "The Crookedest Railroad in the World" because of its curvy tracks—began transporting visitors from Mill Valley to the top of Mt. Tam and down to Muir Woods, and the town soon became a vacation retreat for city slickers. The trains stopped running in the 1930s, as cars became more popular, but the old railway depot still serves as the center of town: the 1929 building has been transformed into the popular Depot Bookstore & Cafe, at 87 Throckmorton Avenue.

The small downtown area has the constant bustle of a leisure community; even at noon on a Tuesday, people are out shopping for fancy cookware, eco-friendly home furnishings, and boutique clothing..

GETTING HERE AND AROUND

By car from San Francisco, head north on U.S. 101 and get off at CA 131/Tiburon Boulevard/East Blithedale Avenue (Exit 447). Turn left onto East Blithedale Avenue and continue west to Throckmorton Avenue; turn left to reach Lytton Square, then park. Golden Gate Transit buses serve Mill Valley from San Francisco. Once here, explore the town on foot.

ESSENTIALS

Visitor Information Mill Valley Chamber of Commerce and Visitor Center. ⊠ *85 Throckmorton Ave.* 🖀 *415/388–9700* ⊕ *www.millvalley.org.*

EXPLORING

FAMILY **Lytton Square.** Mill Valley locals congregate on weekends to socialize in the coffeehouses and cafés near the town's central square, but it bustles most of the day. Shops, restaurants, and cultural venues line the nearby streets. ⊠ *Miller and Throckmorton Aves.*

OFF THE BEATEN PATH

Marin County Civic Center. A wonder of arches, circles, and skylights just 10 miles north of Mill Valley, the Civic Center was Frank Lloyd Wright's largest public project and has been designated a national and state historic landmark, as well as a UNESCO World Heritage Site. One-hour docent-led tours leave from the café on the second floor Wednesday mornings at 10:30. Or grab a self-guided tour map from the center's gift shop or website. ⊠ *3501 Civic Center Dr., off N. San Pedro Rd., San Rafael* 🖀 *415/473–3762 Visitor Services Office* ⊕ *www.marincounty. org/depts/cu/tours* 🖾 *Free admission; $10 tour fee.*

WHERE TO EAT

$$$
AMERICAN

✗ **Balboa Café.** With intimate lighting, rich wood accents, and fresh-pressed white linens, this modern California café offers an upscale dining experience complete with classic cocktails, an extensive wine list, and beautiful bistro-inspired dishes that feature locally sourced ingredients. The bar is always bustling, with a daily happy hour that extends into dinner; brunch is served on the weekends. **Known for:** Balboa burger; local wines; huevos rancheros; Dungeness crab risotto; Japanese himachi crudo. $ *Average main: $24* ⊠ *38 Miller Ave., at Sunnyside Ave.* ☎ *415/381–7321* ⊕ *balboacafemv.com* ⊗ *No lunch Mon.*

$$$
AMERICAN

✗ **Buckeye Roadhouse.** House-smoked meats and fish, grilled steaks, classic salads, and decadent desserts bring locals and visitors back again and again to this 1937 lodge-style roadhouse. Enjoy a Marin martini at the cozy mahogany bar or sip local wine beside the river-rock fireplace. **Known for:** oysters dingo; chili-lime "brick" chicken; smoked beef brisket. $ *Average main: $30* ⊠ *15 Shoreline Hwy., off U.S. 101* ☎ *415/331–2600* ⊕ *www.buckeyeroadhouse.com.*

$$$$
CONTEMPORARY

✗ **El Paseo.** Rock & Roll Hall of Famer Sammy Hagar helped to restore this 1947 California Mission–style restaurant, which reopened in 2011 with a Spanish-influenced California cuisine menu. The secluded brick walkway, bougainvillea-framed courtyard, and candlelit dining room provide the perfect setting for a romantic night out. **Known for:** deviled eggs with crispy chorizo; Akaushi steak frites; patio-side paella; daily happy hour. $ *Average main: $32* ⊠ *17 Throckmorton Ave., at E. Blithedale Ave.* ☎ *415/388–0741* ⊕ *www.elpaseomillvalley. com* ⊗ *No lunch.*

$
MEXICAN
FAMILY

✗ **Joe's Taco Lounge.** A colorful, quirky lounge loaded with Latino tchotchkes, chatty patrons, agave margaritas, and bottles of hot sauce, Joe's is a fun place to go for cheap Mexican eats and a dive-bar-meets-living-room feel. A sizable street-food-influenced menu includes tacos, burritos, Mexican pizzas, and selections for kids of all ages. **Known for:** fish and carnitas tacos; antojito sampler; street burgers. $ *Average main: $15* ⊠ *382 Miller Ave., and Montford Ave.* ☎ *415/383–8164* ⊕ *www.joestacolounge.com.*

$$$$
CONTEMPORARY
Fodor's Choice
★

✗ **Molina.** A cozy and clean aesthetic, a convivial vibe, and impeccable cuisine have turned this snug neighborhood spot into a destination restaurant. Owner-chef (and DJ) Todd Shoberg creates a modest nightly menu of small plates, entrées, and desserts that focus on wood-fired offerings and the freshest local ingredients. **Known for:** California coastal dishes; curated wine menu. $ *Average main: $32* ⊠ *17 Madrona St., between Lovell and Throckmorton Aves.* ☎ *415/383–4200* ⊕ *www. molinarestaurant.com* ⊗ *No lunch.*

WHERE TO STAY

$$$$
B&B/INN

🏠 **Mill Valley Inn.** The only hotel in downtown Mill Valley is comprised of a main building, the Creek House, with smart-looking European-inspired rooms, and two small cottages tucked among the trees. **Pros:** minutes from local shops and restaurants; some rooms have balconies, soaking tubs, and fireplaces; free parking; free mountain bikes. **Cons:** limited room service; dark in winter because of surrounding trees; some

19

rooms are not accessible via elevator. [$] *Rooms from: $289* ✉ *165 Throckmorton Ave., near Miller Ave.* ☎ *415/389–6608, 855/334–7946* 🌐 *www.marinhotels.com* 🛏 *25 rooms* 🍴 *Breakfast.*

$$ B&B/INN 🏨 **Mountain Home Inn.** Abutting 40,000 acres of state and national parks, this airy wooden inn sits on the skirt of Mt. Tamalpais, where you can follow hiking trails all the way to Stinson Beach. **Pros:** amazing terrace and views; peaceful, remote setting; in-room massage available; cooked-to-order breakfast. **Cons:** nearest town is a 12-minute drive away; restaurant can get crowded on sunny weekend days; no on-site fitness option. [$] *Rooms from: $199* ✉ *810 Panoramic Hwy., at Edgewood Ave.* ☎ *415/381–9000* 🌐 *www.mtnhomeinn.com* 🛏 *10 rooms* 🍴 *Breakfast.*

NIGHTLIFE AND PERFORMING ARTS

NIGHTLIFE

BREWPUS AND BEERGARDENS **Mill Valley Beerworks.** A great place to rest your feet after shopping or hiking, this neighborhood taproom serves a rotating selection of local and imported drafts and bottles. A simple menu of small plates and mains includes locally sourced cheeses, brussels sprouts, and burgers. ✉ *173 Throckmorton Ave.* ☎ *415/888–8218* 🌐 *millvalleybeerworks.com.*

MUSIC VENUES **Sweetwater Music Hall.** With the help of part-owner Bob Weir of the Grateful Dead, this renowned nightclub and café reopened in a historical Masonic Hall in 2012. Famous as well as up-and-coming bands play on most nights, and local stars such as Bonnie Raitt and Huey Lewis have been known to stop in for a pickup session. ✉ *19 Corte Madera Ave., between Throckmorton and Lovell Aves.* ☎ *415/388–3850, 877/987–6487 tickets* 🌐 *www.sweetwatermusichall.com.*

PERFORMING ARTS

MUIR WOODS NATIONAL MONUMENT

12 miles northwest of the Golden Gate Bridge.

Climbing hundreds of feet into the sky, *Sequoia sempervirens* are the tallest living things on Earth—some are more than 1,800 years old. One of the last remaining old-growth stands of these redwood behemoths, Muir Woods is nature's cathedral: imposing, awe-inspiring, reverence-inducing, and not to be missed.

GETTING HERE AND AROUND

If you drive to Muir Woods on a weekend or during peak season, expect to find epic traffic jams around the tiny parking areas and adjacent roads. Do yourself a favor and take a shuttle if you can. Marin Transit's Route 66 Muir Woods shuttle (*$5 round-trip www.marintransit.org*) provides regular transport from the Sausalito ferry landing, as well as Marin City, on a seasonal schedule. Private bus tours run year-round. To drive directly from San Francisco by car, take U.S. 101 north across the Golden Gate Bridge to exit 445B for Mill Valley/Stinson Beach, then follow signs for Highway 1 north and Muir Woods.

EXPLORING

FAMILY

Fodor's Choice

★

Muir Woods National Monument. Nothing gives perspective like walking among some of the world's last old-growth redwoods. The 550 acres of Muir Woods National Monument contain some of the most majestic redwoods in the world—some more than 250 feet tall. Though much of California's 2 million acres of redwood forest were lost to the logging industry, this stand was saved from destruction by William and Elizabeth Kent, who purchased the land in 1905, and later gifted it to the federal government. Theodore Roosevelt declared the space a national monument in 1908 and Kent named it after naturalist John Muir, whose environmental campaigns helped to establish the national park system.

Part of the Golden Gate National Recreation Area, Muir Woods is a pedestrian's park. The popular 2-mile main trail, which begins at the park headquarters, has been covered by a wooden boardwalk, and provides easy access to streams, ferns, azaleas, and redwood groves. Summer weekends can prove busy, so if you prefer a little serenity, consider taking a more challenging route, such as the **Dipsea Trail** which climbs west from the forest floor to soothing views of the ocean and the Golden Gate Bridge. For a complete list of trails, which vary in difficulty and distance, check with rangers.

Picnicking and camping aren't allowed, and neither are pets. Crowds can be large, especially from May through October, so try to come early in the morning or late in the afternoon. The **Muir Woods Visitor Center** has books and exhibits about redwood trees and the woods' history; the **Muir Woods Trading Company** serves hot food, organic pastries, and other tasty snacks, and the gift shop offers plenty of souvenirs.

■TIP➔ Cell service in the park is limited, so plan directions and communication ahead of time. ✉ *1 Muir Woods Rd., off Panoramic Hwy., Mill Valley* ☎ *415/388–2595 park information, 511 Marin transit* ⊕ *www.nps.gov/muwo* 💲 *$10; free on government holidays.*

MT. TAMALPAIS STATE PARK

13 miles northwest of Golden Gate Bridge.

The view of Mt. Tamalpais from all around the bay can be a beauty, but that's nothing compared to the views *from* the mountain, which range from jaw-dropping to spectacular and take in San Francisco, the East Bay, the coast, and beyond—on a clear day, all the way to the Farallon Islands, 25 miles away.

GETTING HERE AND AROUND

By car, take U.S. 101 north across the Golden Gate Bridge and exit 445B for Mill Valley/Stinson Beach. Continue north on Highway 1, which will turn into Panoramic Highway. By bus, take Golden Gate Transit to Marin City; in Marin City transfer to the West Marin Stagecoach, Route 61, and get off at Pantoll Ranger Station (*415/226–0855* ⊕ *www. marintransit.org/stage.html*). Once here, the only way to explore is on foot or by bike.

EXPLORING

FAMILY

Fodor's Choice

★

Mt. Tamalpais State Park. Although the summit of Mt. Tamalpais is only 2,571 feet high, the mountain rises practically from sea level, dominating the topography of Marin County. Adjacent to Muir Woods National Monument, Mt. Tamalpais State Park affords views of the entire Bay Area and the Pacific Ocean to the west. The name for the sacred mount comes from the Coast Miwok tribe and means "west hill," though some have tied it to a folktale about the "sleeping maiden" in the mountain's profile. For years the 6,300-acre park has been a favorite destination for hikers. There are more than 200 miles of trails, some rugged but many developed for easy walking through meadows, grasslands, and forests and along creeks. Mt. Tam, as it's called by locals, is also the birthplace (in the 1970s) of mountain biking, and today many spandex-clad bikers whiz down the park's winding roads.

The park's major thoroughfare, Panoramic Highway, snakes its way up from U.S. 101 to the **Pantoll Ranger Station** and then drops down to the town of Stinson Beach. Pantoll Road branches off the highway at the station, connecting up with Ridgecrest Boulevard. Along these roads are numerous parking areas, picnic spots, scenic overlooks, and trailheads. Parking is free along the roadside, but there's an $8 fee (cash or check only) at the ranger station and additional charges for walk-in campsites and group use.

The **Mountain Theater,** also known as the Cushing Memorial Amphitheatre, is a natural 4,000-seat amphitheater that was reconstructed with stone by the Civilian Conservation Corps in the 1930s. It has showcased summer "Mountain Plays" since 1913.

The **Rock Spring Trail** starts at the Mountain Theater and gently climbs for 1½ miles to the **West Point Inn,** which was once a stop on the Mt. Tam railroad route. Relax at a picnic table and stock up on water before forging ahead, via Old Railroad Grade Fire Road and the Miller Trail, to Mt. Tam's Middle Peak, which is another 1½–2 miles depending on route.

19

Starting from the Pantoll Ranger Station, the precipitous **Steep Ravine Trail** brings you past stands of coastal redwoods and, in the springtime, small waterfalls. Take the connecting **Dipsea Trail** to reach the town of Stinson Beach and its swath of golden sand. ■TIP➔ If you're too weary to make the 3½-mile trek back up, Marin Transit Bus 61 takes you from Stinson Beach back to the ranger station. ⊠ *Pantoll Ranger Station, 3801 Panoramic Hwy., at Pantoll Rd.* ☎ *415/388–2070* ⊕ *www. parks.ca.gov.*

PERFORMING ARTS

FAMILY

Mountain Play. Every May and June, locals tote overstuffed picnic baskets to the Mountain Theater to see the Mountain Play, an annual theater tradition that began in 1913. Past productions have included popular musicals like *West Side Story, The Music Man,* and *My Fair Lady.* ■TIP➔ A free shuttle runs from Manzanita Parking Lot at the junction of Highway 101 and Highway 1, just beyond the Mill Valley/Stinson Beach exit off Highway 101 and from Tamalpais High School. ⊠ *Mt. Tamalpais, Pantoll Rd. and Ridgecrst Blvd. off Panoramic Hwy.* ☎ *415/383–1100* ⊕ *www.mountainplay.org* ⊠ *$40.*

BEACH TOWNS

The winds whip wildly around Marin County's miles of coastline. The unruly waves and cool breeze make it more of an adventure than your typical day at the beach. Still, the natural beauty, rocky shores, and stunning views are nothing to balk at.

GETTING HERE AND AROUND

If you're driving, take U.S. 101 north to exit 445B (Highway 1 toward Mill Valley/Stinson Beach) and follow signs. Public transit serves Stinson Beach and Bolinas, but not Muir Beach.

MUIR BEACH

12 miles northwest of Golden Gate Bridge, 6 miles southwest of Mill Valley.

Except on the sunniest of weekends, Muir Beach is relatively quiet, but the drive here can be quite the scenic adventure.

GETTING HERE AND AROUND

A car is the best way to reach Muir Beach. From Highway 1, follow Pacific Way southwest ¼ mile.

EXPLORING

Green Gulch Farm Zen Center. Giant eucalyptus trees frame the long and winding road that leads to this tranquil Buddhist practice center. Meditation programs, tea instruction, gardening classes, and various other workshops and events take place here; there's also an extensive organic garden. Visitors are welcome to roam the property and walk through the gardens that reach down toward Muir Beach. Public Sunday programs are especially geared toward visitors. ⊠ *1601 Shoreline Hwy., at Green Gulch Rd.* ☎ *415/383–3134 welcome center* ⊕ *www. sfzc.org* ⊠ *free.*

BEACHES

FAMILY **Muir Beach.** Small but scenic, this beach—a rocky patch of shoreline off Highway 1 in the northern Marin Headlands—is a good place to stretch your legs and gaze out at the Pacific. Locals often walk their dogs here; families and cuddling couples come for picnicking and sunbathing. At one end of the sand are waterfront homes (and occasional nude sunbathers) and at the other are the bluffs of the Golden Gate National Recreation Area. A land bridge connects directly from the parking lot to the beach, as well as a short trail that leads to a scenic overlook and connects to other coastal paths. **Amenities:** parking (free); toilets. **Best for:** solitude; sunsets; walking. ⊠ *100 Pacific Way, off Shoreline Hwy.* ⊕ *www.nps.gov/goga/plany- ourvisit/muirbeach.htm.*

WHERE TO STAY

$$$ 🛏 **Pelican Inn.** From its slate roof to its whitewashed plaster walls, this B&B/INN inn looks so Tudor that it's hard to believe it was built in the 1970s, but the Pelican is English to the core, with its cozy upstairs guest rooms (no elevator), draped half-tester beds, a sun-filled solarium, and bangers and grilled tomatoes for breakfast. **Pros:** five-minute

walk to beach; great bar and restaurant; peaceful setting. **Cons:** 20-minute drive to nearby attractions; rooms are quite small and rustic; remote location; limited amenities. [$] *Rooms from: $222* ✉ *10 Pacific Way, off Hwy. 1* ☎ *415/383–6000* 🌐 *www.pelicaninn.com* 🛏 *7 rooms* 🍴 *Breakfast.*

STINSON BEACH

20 miles northwest of Golden Gate Bridge.

This laid-back hamlet is all about the beach, and folks come from all over the Bay Area to walk its sandy, often windswept shore. Ideal day trip: a morning hike at Mt. Tam followed by lunch at one of Stinson's unassuming eateries and a leisurely beach stroll.

GETTING HERE AND AROUND

If you're driving, take U.S. 101 to the Mill Valley/Stinson Beach/Highway 1 exit and follow the road west and then north. By bus, take Golden Gate Transit to Marin City and then transfer to the West Marin Stagecoach (61) for Bolinas.

BEACHES

FAMILY **Stinson Beach.** When the fog hasn't rolled in, this expansive stretch of sand is about as close as you can get in Marin to the stereotypical feel of a Southern California beach. There are several clothing-optional areas, among them a section called Red Rock Beach. ⚠ **Swimming at Stinson Beach can be dangerous; the undertow is strong and sharks sightings, though infrequent, have occurred; lifeguards are on duty May–September.** On any hot summer weekend, roads to Stinson are packed and the parking lot fills, so factor this into your plans. The town itself—population 600, give or take—has a nonchalant surfer vibe, with a few good eating options and pleasant hippie-craftsy browsing. **Amenities:** food and drink; lifeguards; parking (free); showers; toilets. **Best for:** nudists; sunset; surfing; swimming; walking. ✉ *Hwy. 1, 1 Calle Del Sierra* ☎ *415/868–0942 lifeguard tower* 🌐 *www.stinsonbeachonline.com* ☞ *No pets allowed on the beach.*

19

WHERE TO EAT AND STAY

$$ AMERICAN FAMILY 🍴 **Parkside Cafe.** The Parkside is popular for its 1950s beachfront snack bar, but the adjoining café, coffee bar, market place, and bakery shouldn't be missed either. A full menu featuring fresh ingredients, local seafood, wood-fired pizzas, and just-baked breads is served. **Known for:** local seafood; clam chowder; rustic house-made breads. [$] *Average main: $21* ✉ *43 Arenal Ave., off Shoreline Hwy.* ☎ *415/868–1272* 🌐 *www.parksidecafe.com.*

$$ AMERICAN Fodor's Choice ★ 🍴 **Sand Dollar Restaurant.** Constructed from three barges that were floated over from Tiburon in the 1920s, this family-owned restaurant still attracts wayfarers from Muir Beach to Bolinas. Sip whiskey at the bar or nosh on local seafood and down a beer on the deck, preferably on warm summer weekends, when live jazz and blue grass draw a vibrant crowd. **Known for:** fresh seafood; local oysters; sunny patio for dining and drinking. [$] *Average main: $20* ✉ *3458 Shoreline Hwy.* ☎ *415/868–0434* 🌐 *www.stinsonbeachrestaurant.com.*

$$ ⊡ **Sandpiper Lodging.** Recharge, rest, and enjoy the local scenery at this
B&B/INN ultrapopular lodging that books up months, even years, in advance.
FAMILY **Pros:** beach chairs, towels, and toys provided; lush gardens with BBQ;
minutes from the beach and town; free resident car parking. **Cons:** walls
are thin; limited amenities. $ *Rooms from: $165* ⊠ *1 Marine Way,
off Arenal Ave.* ☎ *415/868–1632* ⊕ *www.sandpiperstinsonbeach.com*
⤴ *11 rooms* ⦿| *No meals.*

$ ⊡ **Stinson Beach Motel.** Built in the 1930s, this motel is surrounded by
B&B/INN flowering greenery, and rooms are clean, simple, and summery. **Pros:**
minutes from the beach; cozy, unpretentious rooms; kitchenettes in cot-
tages. **Cons:** smaller rooms are cramped. $ *Rooms from: $140* ⊠ *3416
Shoreline Hwy.* ☎ *415/868–1712* ⊕ *www.stinsonbeachmotel.com* ⤴ *8
rooms* ⦿| *No meals.*

BOLINAS

7 miles north of Stinson Beach.

The tiny town of Bolinas wears its 1960s idealism on its sleeve, attract-
ing potters, poets, and peace lovers to its quiet streets. With a funky
gallery, a general store selling organic produce, a café, and an offbeat
saloon, the main thoroughfare, Wharf Road, looks like a hippie-fied
version of Main Street, USA.

GETTING HERE AND AROUND

Bolinas isn't difficult to find, though locals have notoriously removed
the street sign for their town from the highway: heading north from
Stinson Beach, follow Highway 1 west and then north. Make a left at
the first road just past the Bolinas Lagoon (*Olema–Bolinas Rd.*), and
then turn left at the stop sign. The road dead-ends smack-dab in the
middle of town. By bus, take Golden Gate Transit to Marin City; in
Marin City, transfer to the West Marin Stagecoach 61. Walking is the
only way to see this small town.

WHERE TO EAT

$$ ✕ **Coast Cafe.** Decked out in a nautical theme with surfboards and buoys,
AMERICAN the Coast serves weekend brunch and dependably good American lunch
FAMILY and dinner fare, including local fresh fish, grass-fed steaks, and wonderfully fresh vegetarian and vegan dishes. Find patio seating in the
front and back and live music during dinner on Thursday and Sunday. **Known for:** locally sourced ingredients; fresh fish and sustainable
meat. $ *Average main: $18* ⊠ *46 Wharf Rd., off Olema–Bolinas Rd.*
☎ *415/868–2298* ⊙ *Closed Mon.*

POINT REYES NATIONAL SEASHORE

Bear Valley Visitor Center is 12 miles north of Bolinas.

With sandy beaches stretching for miles, a dramatic rocky coastline, a
gem of a lighthouse, and idyllic, century-old dairy farms, Point Reyes
National Seashore is one of the most varied and strikingly beautiful
corners of the Bay Area.

GETTING HERE AND AROUND

From San Francisco, take U.S. 101 north, head west at Sir Francis Drake Boulevard (Exit 450B) toward San Anselmo, and follow the road just under 20 miles to Bear Valley Road. From Stinson Beach or Bolinas, drive north on Highway 1 and turn left on Bear Valley Road. If you're going by bus, take one of several Golden Gate Transit buses to Marin City; in Marin City transfer to the West Marin Stagecoach (you'll switch buses in Olema). Once at the visitor center, the best way to get around is on foot.

EXPLORING

FAMILY **Bear Valley Visitor Center.** A life-size orca model hovers over the center's engaging exhibits about the wildlife and history of the Point Reyes National Seashore. The rangers at the barnlike facility are fonts of information about beaches, whale-watching, hiking trails, and camping. Restrooms are available, as well as trailhead parking and a picnic area with barbecue grills. Winter hours may be shorter and summer weekend hours may be longer; call or check the website for details. ⊠ *Bear Valley Visitor Center, 1 Bear Valley Visitor Center Access Rd., west of Hwy. 1, off Bear Valley Rd., Point Reyes Station* ☎ *415/464–5100* ⊕ *www.nps.gov/pore/planyourvisit.*

FAMILY **Duxbury Reef.** Excellent tide pooling can be had along the 3-mile shoreline
Fodor's Choice of Duxbury Reef; it's the most extensive tide pool area near Point Reyes
★ National Seashore, as well as one of the largest shale intertidal reefs in North America. Look for sea stars, barnacles, sea anemones, purple urchins, limpets, sea mussels, and the occasional abalone. But check a tide table (*tidesandcurrents.noaa.gov*) or the local papers if you plan to explore the reef—it's accessible only at low tide. The reef is a 30-minute drive from the Bear Valley Visitor Center. Take Highway 1 south from the center, turn right at Olema–Bolinas Road (keep an eye peeled; the road is easy to miss), left on Horseshoe Hill Road, right on Mesa Road, left on Overlook Drive, and then right on Elm Road, which dead-ends at the Agate Beach County Park parking lot. ⊹ *At Duxbury Point, 1 mile west of Bolinas* ⊕ *www.ptreyes.org/activities/tidepools.*

FAMILY **Palomarin Field Station & Point Reyes Bird Observatory.** Birders adore Point Blue Conservation Science, which maintains the Palomarin Field Station and the Point Reyes Bird Observatory (PRBO) that are located in the southernmost part of Point Reyes National Seashore. The Field Station, open daily from sunrise to sunset, has excellent interpretive exhibits, including a comparative display of real birds' talons. The surrounding woods harbor some 200 bird species. As you hike the quiet trails through forest and along ocean cliffs, you're likely to see biologists banding birds to aid in the study of their life cycles. ■ TIP→ Visit Point Blue's website for detailed directions and to find out when banding will occur. ⊠ *999 Mesa Rd., Bolinas* ☎ *415/868–0655 field station, use ext. 395 to check conditions, 707/781–2555 headquarters* ⊕ *www.pointblue.org.*

FAMILY **Point Reyes Lighthouse & Visitor Center.** In operation since December 1,
Fodor's Choice 1870, this lighthouse—which was decommissioned in 1975—is one of
★ the premier attractions of the Point Reyes National Seashore. It occupies the tip of Point Reyes, 21 miles from the Bear Valley Visitor Center, a

19

scenic 40-minute drive over hills scattered with longtime dairy farms. The lighthouse originally cast a rotating beam lighted by four concentric wicks that burned lard oil. Keeping the wicks lighted and the 6,000-pound Fresnel lens soot-free in Point Reyes's perpetually foggy climate was a constant struggle that reputedly drove a few early attendants to alcoholism and insanity.

■TIP➜ The lighthouse is one of the best spots on the coast for watching gray whales. On both legs of their annual migration, the magnificent animals pass close enough to see with the naked eye. Southern migration peaks in mid-January, and the whales head back north in March; see the slower mothers and calves in late April and early May. Humpback whales can be spotted feeding in the summer months.

On busy whale-watching weekends (from late December through mid-April), buses shuttle visitors from the Drakes Beach parking lot to the top of the stairs leading down to the lighthouse and the road is closed to private vehicles. However you've arrived, consider whether you have it in you to walk down—and up—the 308 steps to the lighthouse. The view from the bottom is worth the effort, but the whales are also visible from the cliffs above the lighthouse. Keep in mind that the parking lot is a quarter-mile trek from the visitor center and the lighthouse steps are open only during visitor center hours. ■TIP➜ Winds can be chilly, and food, water, gas, and other resources are scarce, so be sure to come prepared. ⊠ *Lighthouse Visitor Center, 27000 Sir Francis Drake Blvd., western end of Sir Francis Drake Blvd., Inverness* ☎ *415/669–1534 visitor center* ⊕ *www.nps.gov/pore/planyourvisit/lighthouse.htm* ☉ *Closed Tues.–Thurs.* ☞ *Fee for weekend shuttle.*

FAMILY
Fodor'sChoice
★
Point Reyes National Seashore. One of the Bay Area's most spectacular treasures and the only national seashore on the West Coast, the 71,000-acre Point Reyes National Seashore encompasses hiking trails, secluded beaches, and rugged grasslands as well as Point Reyes itself, a triangular peninsula that juts into the Pacific. The town of **Point Reyes Station** is a one-main-drag affair with some good places to eat and gift shops that sell locally made and imported goods.

When explorer Sir Francis Drake sailed along the California coast in 1579, he allegedly missed the Golden Gate and San Francisco Bay, but he did land at what he described as a convenient harbor. In 2012 the federal government conceded a centuries-long debate and officially recognized Drake's Bay, which flanks the point on the east, as that harbor, designating the spot a National Historic Landmark and silencing competing claims in the 433-year-old controversy. Today Point Reyes's hills and dramatic cliffs attract other kinds of explorers: hikers, whale-watchers, and solitude seekers.

The infamous San Andreas Fault runs along the park's eastern edge and up the center of Tomales Bay; take the short **Earthquake Trail** from the visitor center to see the impact near the epicenter of the 1906 earthquake that devastated San Francisco. A half-mile path from the visitor center leads to **Kule Loklo,** a reconstructed Miwok village that sheds light on the daily lives of the region's first inhabitants. From here, trails also lead to the park's hike-in campgrounds (no car camping).

■ **TIP→ In late winter and spring, take the short walk at Chimney Rock, just before the lighthouse, to the Elephant Seal Overlook.** Even from the cliff, the male seals look enormous as they spar, growling and bloodied, for resident females.

You can experience the diversity of Point Reyes's ecosystems on the scenic **Coast Trail,** which starts at the Palomarin Trailhead, just outside Bolinas. From here, it's a 3-mile trek through eucalyptus groves and pine forests and along seaside cliffs to beautiful and tiny Bass Lake. To reach the Palomarin Trailhead, take Olema–Bolinas Road toward Bolinas, turn right on Mesa Road, follow signs to Point Blue Conservation Science, and then continue until the road dead-ends.

The 4.7-mile-long (one-way) **Tomales Point Trail** follows the spine of the park's northernmost finger of land through a Tule Elk Preserve, providing spectacular ocean views from the high bluffs. Expect to see elk, but keep your distance from the animals. To reach the moderately easy hiking trail, take Sir Francis Drake Boulevard through the town of Inverness; when you come to a fork, veer right to stay on Pierce Point Road and continue until you reach the parking lot at Pierce Point Ranch. ✉ *Bear Valley Visitor Center, 1 Bear Valley Visitor Center Access Rd., west of Hwy. 1, off Bear Valley Rd., Point Reyes Station* ☎ *415/464–5100* 🌐 *www.nps.gov/pore.*

WHERE TO EAT

$$ PIZZA FAMILY

🍴 **Café Reyes.** Sunny patio seating, hand-tossed pizza, and organic local ingredients are the selling points of this laid-back café. The semi-industrial dining room, which is built around a brick oven, features glazed concrete floors, warm-painted walls, and ceilings high enough to accommodate full-size market umbrellas. **Known for:** wood-fired pizza; Drake's Bay fresh oysters; outdoor patio dining. [$] *Average main: $16* ✉ *11101 Hwy. 1, Point Reyes Station* ☎ *415/663–9493* ⏲ *Closed Mon. and Tues.*

$$ ITALIAN Fodor's Choice ★

🍴 **Osteria Stellina.** Chef-owner Christian Caiazzo's menu of "Point Reyes Italian" cuisine puts an emphasis on showcasing hyperlocal ingredients like Marin-grown kale and Sonoma cheese. Pastas, pizzas, and a handful of entrées are served in a rustic-contemporary space with a raw bar that serves local oysters all day long. **Known for:** locally sourced produce and seafood; fresh oysters; inventive pizzas; decadent desserts. [$] *Average main: $20* ✉ *11285 Hwy. 1, at 3rd St., Point Reyes Station* ☎ *415/663–9988* 🌐 *www.osteriastellina.com.*

$$$$ MODERN AMERICAN

🍴 **Sir and Star at the Olema.** With lovely garden views, creative and cryptically named dishes, and upscale-rustic decor that somehow incorporates taxidermied animals, this historic roadhouse (located within the Olema Inn) elicits both rants and raves, often from diners sharing the same table. The locally focused menu of California cuisine changes seasonally; a special prix fixe is offered by reservation on Saturday evenings. **Known for:** inventive presentation of local ingredients; avant-garde small plates. [$] *Average main: $35* ✉ *10000 Sir Francis Drake Blvd., at Hwy. 1, Olema* ☎ *415/663–1034* 🌐 *sirandstar.com* ⏲ *Closed Mon. and Tues. No lunch.*

19

DID YOU KNOW?

The majestic Point Reyes
National Seashore offers
many attractions for nature
lovers: hiking, bird-watching,
camping, or whale-watching,
depending on the season.
But flower picking isn't
an approved activity;
the wildflowers here are
protected.

$$ AMERICAN 🍴 **Station House Cafe.** In good weather, hikers fresh from the park fill the Station House's lovely outdoor garden as well as its homey indoor tables, banquettes, and bar stools, so prepare for a wait. The community-centric eatery is locally focused and serves a blend of modern and classic California dishes comprised of organic seasonal ingredients, sustainable hormone-free meats, and wild-caught seafood. **Known for:** signature popovers; hearty breakfast items; local fresh seafood. [$] *Average main: $22* ✉ *11180 Hwy. 1, at 2nd St., Point Reyes Station* ☎ *415/663–1515* 🌐 *www.stationhousecafe.com* 🕓 *Closed Wed.*

$$ AMERICAN FAMILY 🍴 **Tomales Bay Foods.** A renovated hay barn off the main drag houses this collection of upscale food shops, which showcase local organic fruits and vegetables, premium packaged foods, and an international selection of exquisite cheeses. Cowgirl Creamery cheese is made on-site. **Known for:** local and imported cheese. [$] *Average main: $16* ✉ *80 4th St., at B St., Point Reyes Station* ☎ *415/663–9335 cheese shop* 🕓 *Closed Mon. and Tues. No dinner.*

$$$ SEAFOOD FAMILY Fodor's Choice ★ 🍴 **Hog Island Oyster Co. Marshall Oyster Farm & the Boat Oyster Bar.** Take a short trek north on Highway 1 to the gritty mecca of Bay Area oysters—the Hog Island Marshall Oyster Farm. For a real culinary adventure, arrange to shuck and barbecue your own oysters on one of the outdoor grills (all tools supplied, reservations required), or for the less adventurous, the Boat Oyster Bar is an informal outdoor café that serves raw and BBQ oysters, local snacks, and tasty beverages. **Known for:** fresh, raw, and BBQ oysters. [$] *Average main: $25* ✉ *20215 Shoreline Hwy.* ☎ *415/663–9218* 🌐 *hogislandoysters.com/locations/marshall* 🕓 *Oyster Bar closed Tues.–Thurs. No dinner.*

WHERE TO STAY

$$ B&B/INN FAMILY 🏨 **Cottages at Point Reyes Seashore.** Amid a 15-acre valley on the north end of Inverness, this secluded getaway offers spacious one- and two-bedroom cabins with fireplaces and patios perfect for sunset barbecues and leisurely breakfasts. **Pros:** spacious accommodations; great place to bring kids; private 8-acre wildlife preserve with nature trails. **Cons:** simple no frills decor; small pool. [$] *Rooms from: $160* ✉ *13275 Sir Francis Drake Blvd., Inverness* ☎ *415/669–7250, 800/416–0405 reservations* 🌐 *www.cottagespointreyes.com* 🛏 *20 cabins* 🍽 *No meals.*

$$$$ B&B/INN 🏨 **Manka's Inverness Lodge.** Chef-owner Margaret Gradé takes rustic fantasy to extravagant heights in her historic cabins and suites (circa 1910), where mica-shaded lamps cast an amber glow, and bearskin rugs warm wide-planked floors. **Pros:** extremely romantic; remote and quiet. **Cons:** hands-off service sometimes comes off as rude; sounds from neighboring rooms are easily heard; some question the value for the price. [$] *Rooms from: $365* ✉ *30 Callendar Way, at Argyle St., Inverness* ☎ *415/669–1034* 🌐 *www.mankas.com* 🛏 *9 rooms* 🍽 *Breakfast.*

$$$ B&B/INN 🏨 **The Olema.** Built in 1876, this rustic inn and restaurant—a sister property to Manka's Inverness Lodge—retains all its 19th-century architectural charm with the added flair of Margaret Gradé's eccentric details. **Pros:** great restaurant; magnificent scenery; romantic foyer with a 7-foot-high fireplace; in-room breakfast. **Cons:** no elevator means carrying your luggage up the stairs; amenities and bathrooms are basic;

service is hit and miss. [$] *Rooms from: $250 ⊠ 10000 Sir Francis Drake Blvd., Olema* ☎ *415/663–1034* ⊕ *sirandstar.com* ⊗ *Restaurant closed Mon. and Tues. No lunch weekdays* ↻ *5 rooms* |○| *Breakfast.*

$$
B&B/INN

⊞ **Ten Inverness Way.** This is the kind of down-to-earth B&B where you sit around after breakfast and share tips for hiking Point Reyes or linger around the living room and its stone fireplace and library. **Pros:** great base for exploring the nearby wilderness; peaceful garden and friendly staff; exceptional breakfast. **Cons:** some rooms are on the small side; poor cell-phone reception. [$] *Rooms from: $195 ⊠ 10 Inverness Way, Inverness* ☎ *415/669–1648* ⊕ *www.teninvernessway. com* ↻ *5 rooms* |○| *Breakfast.*

SPORTS AND THE OUTDOORS

HORSEBACK RIDING

FAMILY **Five Brooks Stable.** Tour guides here lead private and group horse rides lasting from one to six hours; trails from the stable wind through Point Reyes National Seashore, over mountains, through meadows, and along white sandy beaches. ⊠ *8001 Hwy. 1, south of Olema, Olema* ☎ *415/663–1570* ⊕ *www.fivebrooks.com* ▦ *from $40.*

KAYAKING

Blue Waters Kayaking. This outfit rents kayaks and stand-up paddle-boards and offers tours and classes. Make a reservation for rentals to guarantee availability. ⊠ *Tomales Bay Resort, 12944 Sir Francis Drake Blvd., Inverness* ☎ *415/669–2600* ⊕ *www.bluewaterskayaking. com* ▦ *from $50.*

NAPA AND
SONOMA

WELCOME TO NAPA AND SONOMA

TOP REASONS TO GO

★ **Biking:** Cycling is one of the best ways to see the Wine Country—the Russian River and Dry Creek valleys, in Sonoma County, are particularly beautiful.

★ **Browsing the farmers' markets:** Many towns in Napa and Sonoma have seasonal farmers' markets, each rounding up an amazing variety of local produce.

★ **Wandering di Rosa:** Though this art and nature preserve is just off the busy Carneros Highway, it's a relatively unknown treasure. The galleries and gardens are filled with hundreds of artworks.

★ **Canoeing on the Russian River:** Trade in your car keys for a paddle and glide down the Russian River in Sonoma County. From May through October is the best time to be on the water.

★ **Touring wineries:** Let's face it: this is the reason you're here, and the range of excellent sips to sample would make any oeno-phile (or novice drinker, for that matter) giddy.

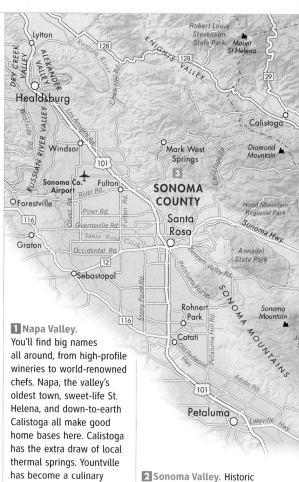

1 Napa Valley.
You'll find big names all around, from high-profile wineries to world-renowned chefs. Napa, the valley's oldest town, sweet-life St. Helena, and down-to-earth Calistoga all make good home bases here. Calistoga has the extra draw of local thermal springs. Yountville has become a culinary boomtown, while the tiny communities of Oakville and Rutherford are home to historic wineries such as Robert Mondavi and Ingle-nook. Rutherford in particu-lar is the source for outstanding Cabernet Sauvignon.

2 Sonoma Valley. Historic attractions and an unpreten-tious attitude prevail here. The town of Sonoma, with its picture-perfect central plaza, is rich with 19th-century buildings. Glen Ellen, meanwhile, has a special connection with author Jack London.

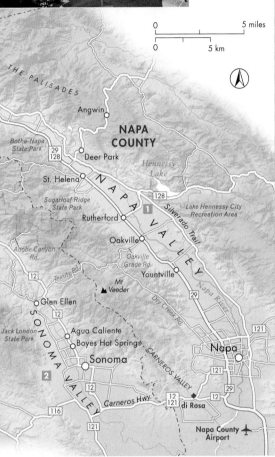

0 ——————— 5 miles

0 ——————— 5 km

GETTING ORIENTED

The Napa and Sonoma valleys run parallel, northwest to southeast , and are separated by the Mayacamas Mountains. Southwest of Sonoma Valley are several other important viticultural areas in Sonoma county, including the Dry Creek, Alexander, and Russian River Valleys. The Carneros, which spans southern Sonoma and Napa counties, is just north of San Pablo Bay.

20

3 Elsewhere in Sonoma. The winding, rural roads here feel a world away from Napa's main drag. The Russian River, Dry Creek, and Alexander valleys are all excellent places to seek out Pinot Noir, Zinfandel, and Sauvignon Blanc. The small town of Healdsburg gets lots of attention, thanks to its terrific restaurants, bed-and-breakfasts, and chic boutiques.

Updated by
Daniel Mangin

In California's premier wine region, the pleasures of eating and drinking are celebrated daily. It's easy to join in at famous wineries and rising newcomers off country roads, or at trendy in-town tasting rooms. Chefs transform local ingredients into feasts, and gourmet groceries sell perfect picnic fare. Yountville, Healdsburg, and St. Helena have small-town charm as well as luxurious inns, hotels, and spas, yet the natural setting is equally sublime, whether experienced from a canoe on the Russian River or the deck of a winery overlooking endless rows of vines.

The Wine Country is also rich in history. In Sonoma you can explore California's Spanish and Mexican pasts at the Sonoma Mission, and the origins of modern California wine making at Buena Vista Winery. Some wineries, among them St. Helena's Beringer and Rutherford's Inglenook, have cellars or tasting rooms dating to the late 1800s. Calistoga is a flurry of late-19th-century Steamboat Gothic architecture, though the town's oldest-looking building, the medieval-style Castello di Amorosa, is a 21st-century creation.

Tours at the Napa Valley's Beringer, Mondavi, and Inglenook—and at Buena Vista in the Sonoma Valley—provide an entertaining overview of Wine Country history. The tour at the splashy visitor center at St. Helena's Hall winery will introduce you to 21st-century wine-making technology, and over in Glen Ellen's Benziger Family Winery you can see how its vineyard managers apply biodynamic farming principles to grape growing. At numerous facilities you can play winemaker for a day at seminars in the fine art of blending wines. If that strikes you as too much effort, you can always pamper yourself at a luxury spa.

To delve further into the fine art of Wine Country living, pick up a copy of *Fodor's Napa and Sonoma*.

PLANNING

WHEN TO GO

High season extends from April through October. In summer, expect the days to be hot and dry, the roads filled with cars, and traffic heavy at the tasting rooms. Hotel rates are highest during the height of harvest, in September and October. Then and in summer book lodgings well ahead. November, except for Thanksgiving week, and December before Christmas are less busy. The weather in Napa and Sonoma is pleasant nearly year-round. Daytime temperatures average from about 55°F during winter to the 80s in summer, when readings in the 90s and higher are common. April, May, and October are milder but still warm. The rainiest months are usually from December through March.

GETTING HERE AND AROUND

AIR TRAVEL

Wine Country regulars often bypass San Francisco and Oakland and fly into Santa Rosa's Charles M. Schulz Sonoma County Airport (STS) on Alaska, Allegiant, and American, nonstop from several West Coast cities, Las Vegas, and Phoenix. Several major agencies rent cars here. ■ TIP→ Alaska allows passengers flying out of STS to check up to one case of wine for free.

BUS TRAVEL

Bus travel is an inconvenient way to explore the Wine Country, though it is possible. Take Golden Gate Transit from San Francisco to connect with Sonoma County Transit buses. VINE connects with BART commuter trains in the East Bay and the San Francisco Bay Ferry in Vallejo *(see Ferry Travel, below)*. VINE buses serve the Napa Valley and connect the towns of Napa and Sonoma.

CAR TRAVEL

Driving your own car is by far the most convenient way to get to and explore the Wine Country. In light traffic, the trip from San Francisco or Oakland to the southern portion of either Napa or Sonoma should take about an hour. Distances between Wine Country towns are fairly short, and in normal traffic you can drive from one end of the Napa or Sonoma valley to the other in less than an hour. Although this is a mostly rural area, the usual rush hours still apply, and high-season weekend traffic can often be slow.

Five major roads serve the region. U.S. 101 and Highways 12 and 121 travel through Sonoma County. Highway 29 and the parallel, more scenic, and often less crowded Silverado Trail travel north–south between Napa and Calistoga.

The easiest way to travel between the Napa Valley and Sonoma County is along Highway 12/121 to the south, or Highway 128 to the north. Travel between the middle sections of either area requires taking the slow, winding drive over the Mayacamas Mountains on the Oakville Grade, which links Oakville, in Napa, and Glen Ellen, in Sonoma.

20

■TIP→ If you're wine tasting, either select a designated driver or be careful of your wine intake—the police keep an eye out for tipsy drivers.

From San Francisco to Napa: Cross the Golden Gate Bridge, then go north on U.S. 101. Head east on Highway 37 toward Vallejo, then north on Highway 121, aka the Carneros Highway. Turn left (north) when Highway 121 runs into Highway 29.

From San Francisco to Sonoma: Cross the Golden Gate Bridge, then go north on U.S. 101, east on Highway 37 toward Vallejo, and north on Highway 121. When you reach Highway 12, take it north to the town of Sonoma. For Sonoma County destinations north of Sonoma Valley stay on U.S. 101, which passes through Santa Rosa and Healdsburg.

From Berkeley and Oakland: Take Interstate 80 north to Highway 37 west, then on to Highway 29 north. For the Napa Valley, continue on Highway 29; to reach Sonoma County, head west on Highway 121.

FERRY TRAVEL

The San Francisco Bay Ferry sails from the Ferry Building and Pier 41 in San Francisco to Vallejo, where you can board VINE Bus 11 to the town of Napa. Buses sometimes fill in for the ferries.

RESTAURANTS

Farm-to-table Modern American cuisine is the prevalent style in the Napa Valley and Sonoma County, but this encompasses both the delicate preparations of Thomas Keller's highly praised The French Laundry and the upscale comfort food served throughout the Wine Country. The quality (and hype) often means high prices, but you can also find appealing, inexpensive eateries, especially in the towns of Napa, Calistoga, Sonoma, and Santa Rosa, and many high-end delis prepare superb picnic fare. At pricey restaurants you can save money by having lunch instead of dinner. With a few exceptions (noted in individual restaurant listings), dress is informal.

HOTELS

The fanciest accommodations are concentrated in the Napa Valley towns of Yountville, Rutherford, St. Helena, and Calistoga; Sonoma County's poshest lodgings are in Healdsburg. The spas, amenities, and exclusivity of high-end properties attract travelers with the means and desire for luxury living. The cities of Napa and Santa Rosa are the best bets for budget hotels and inns, but even at a lower price point you'll still find a touch of Wine Country glamour. On weekends, two- or even three-night minimum stays are commonly required at smaller lodgings. Book well ahead for stays at such places during the busy summer or fall season. If your party will include travelers under age 16, inquire about policies regarding younger guests; some smaller lodgings discourage (or discreetly forbid) children. *Hotel reviews have been shortened. For full information, visit Fodors.com.*

WHAT IT COSTS				
	$	**$$**	**$$$**	**$$$$**
Restaurants	under $16	$16–$22	$23–$30	over $30
Hotels	under $201	$201–$300	$301–$400	over $400

Restaurant prices are the average cost of a main course at dinner or, if dinner is not served, at lunch. Hotel prices are for the lowest cost of a standard double room in high season.

TASTINGS AND TOURS

Many wineries require reservations for tours, seminars, and tastings, which in most cases are made through booking websites such as Cellar-Pass and VinoVisit. A good scheduling strategy is to book appointment-only wineries in the morning, saving the ones that allow walk-ins until the afternoon. That way, if lunch or other winery visits take longer than expected you won't be stressed about having to arrive at later stops at a precise time.

Many visitors prefer to leave the scheduling and driving to seasoned professionals. Whether you want to tour wineries in a van or bus along with other passengers or spring for a private limo, there are plenty of operators who can accommodate you. Tours generally last from five to seven hours and stop at four or five wineries. Rates vary from $80 per person to $250 or more, depending on the vehicle and whether the tour includes other guests. On most tours, at least one stop includes a behind-the-scenes look at production facilities and the chance to meet winemakers or others involved in the wine-making process. Most tour operators will pick you up at your hotel or a specified meeting place. You can also book a car and driver by the hour for shorter trips. Rates for limo generally run from $50 to $85 per hour, and there's usually a two- or three-hour minimum. ■TIP➜ Some tours include lunch and tasting and other fees, but not all do, so ask.

THE NAPA VALLEY

20

With more than 500 wineries and many of the biggest brands in the business, the Napa Valley is the Wine Country's star. With a population of about 79,000, Napa, the valley's largest town, lures with its cultural attractions and (relatively) reasonably priced accommodations. A few miles farther north, compact Yountville is densely packed with top-notch restaurants and hotels, and Rutherford and Oakville are renowned for their Cabernet Sauvignon–friendly soils. Beyond them, St. Helena teems with elegant boutiques and restaurants, and casual Calistoga, known for spas and hot springs, has the feel of an Old West frontier town.

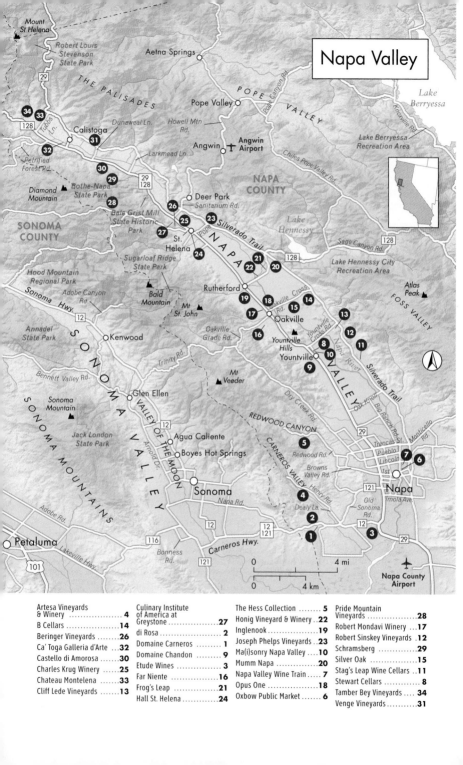

Napa Valley

NAPA

46 miles northeast of San Francisco.

After many years as a blue-collar burg detached from the Wine Country scene, the Napa Valley's largest town (population about 80,000) has evolved into one of its shining stars. Masaharu Morimoto and other chefs of note operate restaurants here, swank hotels and inns can be found downtown and beyond, and the nightlife options include the West Coast edition of the famed Blue Note jazz club. A walkway that follows the Napa River has made downtown more pedestrian-friendly, and the Oxbow Public Market, a complex of high-end food purveyors, is popular with locals and tourists. Nearby Copia, operated by the Culinary Institute of America, hosts cooking demonstrations and other activities open to the public and has a shop and a restaurant. If you establish your base in Napa, plan on spending at least a half a day strolling the downtown district.

GETTING HERE AND AROUND

Downtown Napa lies a mile east of Highway 29—take the 1st Street exit and follow the signs. Ample parking, much of it free for the first three hours and some for the entire day, is available on or near Main Street. Several VINE buses serve downtown and beyond.

EXPLORING
TOP ATTRACTIONS

Artesa Vineyards & Winery. From a distance the modern, minimalist architecture of Artesa blends harmoniously with the surrounding Carneros landscape, but up close its pools, fountains, and the large outdoor sculptures by resident artist Gordon Huether of Napa make a vivid impression. So, too, do the wines: mostly Chardonnay and Pinot Noir but also Cabernet Sauvignon, Merlot, and other limited releases like Albariño and Tempranillo. You can sample wines by themselves without a reservation or, at tastings for which a reservation is required, paired with chocolate, cheese, or tapas. ■ TIP➔ The tour, conducted daily, explores wine making and the winery's history. ✉ *1345 Henry Rd., off Old Sonoma Rd. and Dealy La., Napa* 🕾 *707/224–1668* ⊕ *www.artesawinery.com* 🗹 *Tastings $25–$60, tour $40 (includes tasting).*

20

Fodor's Choice ★ **di Rosa.** A formidable array of artworks from the 1960s to the present by Northern California artists is displayed on this 217-acre property. The works can be found not only in galleries and in the former residence of its late founder, Rene di Rosa, but also throughout the surrounding landscape. Some works were commissioned especially for di Rosa, among them Paul Kos's meditative *Chartres Bleu,* a video installation in a chapel-like setting that replicates a stained-glass window from the cathedral in Chartres, France. ■ TIP➔ You can view the current temporary exhibition and a few permanent works at the Gatehouse Gallery, but to experience the breadth of the collection you'll need to book a tour. ✉ *5200 Sonoma Hwy./Hwy. 121, Napa* 🕾 *707/226–5991* ⊕ *www.dirosaart.org* 🗹 *Gatehouse Gallery $5, tours $12–$15* ⊘ *Closed Mon. and Tues.*

Continued on page 356

WINE
TASTING *in*
NAPA *and*
SONOMA

Whether you're a serious wine collector making your annual pilgrimage to Nothern California's Wine Country or a newbie who doesn't know the difference between a Merlot and Mourvèdre but is eager to learn, you can have a great time touring Napa and Sonoma wineries. Your gateway to the wine world is the tasting room, where staff members are happy to chat with curious guests.

VISITING WINERIES

Tasting rooms range from the grand to the humble, offering everything from a few sips of wine to in-depth tours of facilities and vineyards. Many are open for drop-in visits, usually daily from around 10 am to 5 pm. Others require guests to make reservations. First-time visitors frequently enjoy the history-oriented tours at Charles Krug and Inglenook, or ones at Mondavi and J Vineyards that highlight the process as well. The environments at some wineries reflect their founders' other interests: art and architecture at Artesa and Hall St. Helena, movie making at Francis Ford Coppola, and medieval history at the Castello di Amorosa.

Many wineries describe their pourers as "wine educators," and indeed some of them have taken online or other classes and have passed an exam to prove basic knowledge of appellations, grape varietals, vineyards, and wine-making techniques. The one constant, however, is a deep, shared pleasure in the experience of wine tasting. To prepare you for winery visits, we've covered the fundamentals: tasting rooms, fees and what to expect, and the types of tours wineries offer.

Fees. In the past few years, tasting fees have skyrocketed. Most Napa wineries charge $25 or $30 to taste a few wines, though $40, $50, or even $75 fees aren't unheard of. Sonoma wineries are often a bit cheaper, in the $15 to $35 range, and you'll still find the occasional freebie.

Some winery tours are free, in which case you're usually required to pay a separate fee if you want to taste the wine. If you've paid a fee for the tour—generally from $20 to $40—your wine tasting is usually included in that price.

IN FOCUS WINE TASTING IN NAPA AND SONOMA

20

(opposite page) Carneros vineyards in autumn, Napa Valley. (top) Pinot Gris grapes. (bottom) Bottles from Far Niente winery.

MAKING THE MOST OF YOUR TIME

(top) Sipping and swirling in the DeLoach tasting room. (bottom) Learning about barrel aging at Robert Mondavi Winery.

■ **Call ahead.** Some wineries require reservations to visit or tour. It's wise to check before visiting.

■ **Come on weekdays.** Especially between June and October, try to visit on weekdays to avoid traffic-clogged roads and crowded tasting rooms. For more info on the best times of year to visit, see this chapter's Planner.

■ **Get an early start.** Tasting rooms are often deserted before 11 am or so, when most visitors are still lingering over a second cup of coffee. If you come early, you'll have the staff's undivided attention. You'll usually encounter the largest crowds between 3 and 5 pm.

■ **Schedule strategically.** Visit appointment-only wineries in the morning and ones that allow walk-ins in the afternoon. It'll spare you the stress of being "on time" for later stops.

■ **Hit the Trail.** Beringer, Mondavi, and other high-profile wineries line heavily trafficked Highway 29, but the going is often quicker on the Silverado Trail, which runs parallel to the highway to the east. You'll find famous names here, too, among them the sparkling wine house Mumm Napa Valley, but the traffic is often lighter and sometimes the crowds as well.

Domaine Carneros.

AT THE BAR

In most tasting rooms, you'll be handed a list of the wines available that day. The wines will be listed in a suggested tasting order, starting with the lightest-bodied whites, progressing to the most intense reds, and ending with dessert wines. If you can't decide which wines to choose, tell the server what types of wines you usually like and ask for a recommendation.

The server will pour you an ounce or so of each wine you select. As you taste it, feel free to take notes or ask questions. Don't be shy—the staff are there to educate you about the wine. If you don't like a wine, or you've simply tasted enough, feel free to pour the rest into one of the dump buckets on the bar.

TOURS

Tours tend to be the most exciting (and the most crowded) in September and October, when the harvest and crush-

Preston of Dry Creek bottles only estate-grown grapes.

ing are underway. Tours typically last from 30 minutes to an hour and give you a brief overview of the winemaking process. At some of the older wineries, the tour guide might focus on the history of the property.

■ TIP→ **If you plan to take any tours, wear comfortable shoes, since you might be walking on wet floors or dirt or gravel pathways or stepping over hoses or other equipment.**

MONEY-SAVING TIPS

■ Many hotels and B&Bs distribute coupons for free or discounted tastings to their guests—don't forget to ask.

■ If you and your travel partner don't mind sharing a glass, servers are happy to let you split a tasting.

■ Some wineries will refund all or part of the tasting fee if you buy a bottle. Usually one fee is waived per bottle purchased, though sometimes you must buy two or three.

■ Almost all wineries will also waive the fee if you join their wine club program. However, this typically commits you to buying a certain number of bottles on a regular basis, so be sure you really like the wines before signing up.

IN FOCUS WINE TASTING IN NAPA AND SONOMA

20

TOP 2-DAY ITINERARIES

First-Timer's Napa Tour

Start: Oxbow Public market, Napa. Get underway by browsing the shops selling wines, spices, locally grown produce, and other fine foods, for a taste of what the Wine Country has to offer.

Inglenook, Rutherford. The tour here is a particularly fun way to learn about the history

of Napa winemaking—and you can see the old, atmospheric, ivy-covered château.

Frog's Leap, Rutherford. Friendly, unpretentious, and knowledgeable staff makes this place great for wine newbies. (Make sure you get that reservation lined up.)

Dinner and Overnight: St. Helena. Splurge at Meadowood Napa Valley and you won't need to leave the property for

Carneros

di Rosa Preserve

Old Sonoma Rd.

121
12

Oxbow Public Market
Napa
29

KEY
First-Timer's Napa Tour
Wine Buff's Tour

N A P A
C O U N T Y

Robert Mondavi

Far Niente

Yountville

Oakville

Silverado Trail

Stag's Leap Wine Cellars

Wine Buff's Tour

Start: Stag's Leap Wine Cellars, Yountville, Napa. Famed for its Cabernet Sauvignon and Bordeaux blends.

Silver Oak, Oakville. Schedule a tour of this celebrated winery and taste the flagship Cabernet Sauvignon.

Mumm Napa, Rutherford. Come for the bubbly—which is available in

a variety of tastings—stay for the photography exhibits.

Dinner and Overnight: Yountville. Have dinner at one of the Thomas Keller restaurants. Splurge at Bardessono; save at Maison Fleurie.

Next Day: Robert Mondavi, Oakville. Spring for the reserve room tasting so you can sip the top-of-the-line wines, especially the Cabernet Sauvignon. Head across Highway 29 to the Oakville Grocery to pick up a picnic lunch.

an extravagant dinner at its restaurant. Save at El Bonita Motel with dinner at Gott's.

Next Day: Poke around St. Helena's shops, then drive to Yountville for lunch.

di Rosa, Napa. Call ahead to book a one- or two-hour tour of the acres of gardens and galleries, which are chock-full of thousands of works of art.

Domaine Carneros, Napa. Toast your trip with a glass of outstanding bubbly.

Sonoma Backroads

Far Niente, Oakville. You have to make a reservation and the fee for the tasting and tour is steep, but the payoff is an especially intimate winery experience. You'll taste excellent Cabernet and Chardonnay, then end your trip on a sweet note with a dessert wine.

Start: Iron Horse Vineyards, Russian River Valley. Soak up a view of vine-covered hills and Mount St. Helena while sipping a sparkling wine or Pinot Noir at this beautifully rustic spot.

Dutton-Goldfield Winery, Russian River Valley. A terrific source for Pinot Noir and Chardonnay, the stars of this valley.

Dinner and Overnight: Forestville. Go all out with a stay at the Farmhouse Inn, whose award-winning restaurant is one of the best in all of Sonoma.

Next Day: Westside Road, Russian River Valley. This scenic route, which follows the river, is crowded with worthwhile wineries like Arista and Rochioli—but it's not crowded with visitors. Pinot fans will find a lot to love. Picnic at either winery and enjoy the view.

Balletto Vineyards, Santa Rosa. End on an especially relaxed note with a walk through the vineyards and a patio tasting.

IN FOCUS WINE TASTING IN NAPA AND SONOMA 20

WINE TASTING 101

TAKE A GOOD LOOK.
Hold your glass by the stem, raise it to the light, and take a close look at the wine. Check for clarity and color. (This is easiest to do if you can hold the glass in front of a white background.) Any tinge of brown usually means that the wine is over the hill or has gone bad.

BREATHE DEEP.
1. **Sniff the wine once or twice** to see if you can identify any smells.

2. **Swirl the wine gently in the glass.** Aerating the wine this way releases more of its aromas. (It's called "volatilizing the esters," if you're trying to impress someone.)

3. **Take another long sniff.** You might notice that experienced wine tasters spend more time sniffing the wine than drinking it. This is because this step is where the magic happens. The number of scents you might detect is almost endless, from berries, apricots, honey, and wildflowers to leather, cedar, or even tar. Does the wine smell good to you? Do you detect any "off" flavors, like wet dog or sulfur?

Sniff

AT LAST! TAKE A SIP.
1. **Swirl the wine around your mouth** so that it makes contact with all your taste buds and releases more of its aromas. Think about the way the wine feels in your mouth. Is it watery or rich? Is it crisp or silky? Does it have a bold flavor, or is it subtle? The weight and intensity of a wine are called its body.

2. **Hold the wine in your mouth** for a few seconds and see if you can identify any developing flavors. More complex wines will reveal many different flavors as you drink them.

SPIT OR SWALLOW.
The pros typically spit, since they want to preserve their palate (and sobriety!) for the wines to come, but you'll find that swallowers far outnumber the spitters in the winery tasting rooms. Whether you spit or swallow, notice the flavor that remains after the wine is gone (the finish).

Sip

DODGE THE CROWDS

To avoid bumping elbows in the tasting rooms, look for wineries off the main drags of Highway 29 in Napa and Highway 12 in Sonoma. The back roads of the Russian River, Dry Creek, and Alexander valleys, all in Sonoma, are excellent places to explore. In Napa, try the northern end. Also look for wineries that are open by appointment only; they tend to schedule visitors carefully to avoid a big crush at any one time.

HOW WINE IS MADE

1. CRUSHING
Harvested grapes go into a stemmer-crusher, which separates stems from fruit and crushes the grapes to release "free-run" juice.

2. PRESSING
Remaining juice is gently extracted from grapes. Usually done by pressing grapes against the walls of a tank with an inflatable bladder.

3. FERMENTING
Extracted juice (and also grape skins and pulp, when making red wine) goes into stainless-steel tanks or oak barrels to ferment. During fermentation, sugars convert to alcohol.

4. AGING
Wine is stored in stainless-steel or oak casks or barrels, or sometimes in concrete vessels, to develop flavors.

5. RACKING
Wine is transferred to clean barrels; sediment is removed. Wine may be filtered and fined (clarified) to improve its clarity, color, and sometimes flavor.

6. BOTTLING
Wine is bottled either at the winery or at a special facility, then stored again for bottle-aging.

WHAT'S AN APPELLATION?

American Viticultural Area (AVA) or, more commonly, an appellation. What can be confusing is that some appellations encompass smaller subappellations. The Rutherford, Oakville, and Mt. Veeder AVAs, for instance, are among the Napa Valley AVA's 15 subappellations. Wineries often buy grapes from outside their AVA, so their labels might reference different appellations. A winery in the warmer Napa Valley, for instance, might source Pinot Noir grapes from the cooler Russian River Valley, where they grow better. The appellation listed on a label always refers to where a wine's grapes were grown, not to where the wine was made.

By law, if a label bears the name of an appellation, 85% of the grapes must come from it.

Wine and contemporary art find a home at di Rosa.

Domaine Carneros. A visit to this majestic château is an opulent way to enjoy the Carneros District—especially in fine weather, when the vineyard views are spectacular. The château was modeled after an 18th-century French mansion owned by the Taittinger family. Carved into the hillside beneath the winery, the cellars produce sparkling wines reminiscent of those made by Taittinger, using only Los Carneros AVA grapes. The winery sells flights and glasses of its sparklers, Chardonnay, Pinot Noir, and other wines. Enjoy them all with cheese and charcuterie plates, caviar, or smoked salmon. Seating is in the Louis XV–inspired salon or on the terrace overlooking the vines. The tour covers traditional methods of making sparkling wines. Both tours and tastings are by appointment only. ⊠ *1240 Duhig Rd., at Hwy. 121, Napa* ☎ *707/257–0101, 800/716–2788* ⊕ *www.domainecarneros.com* ⌲ *Tastings $10–$250, tour $50.*

Fodor's Choice ★ **Oxbow Public Market.** The market's two dozen stands provide an introduction to Northern California's diverse artisanal food products. Swoon over decadent charcuterie at the Fatted Calf (great sandwiches, too), slurp oysters at Hog Island, or chow down on duck or salmon tacos at C Casa. You can sample wine (and cheese) at the Oxbow Cheese & Wine Merchant, ales at Fieldwork Brewery's taproom, and barrel-aged cocktails and handcrafted vodkas at the Napa Valley Distillery. Napa Bookmine is among the few nonfood vendors here. ■ TIP➔ **If you don't mind eating at the counter, you can select a steak at the Five Dot Ranch meat stand and pay $8 above market price ($12 with two sides) to have it grilled on the spot, a real deal for a quality slab.** ⊠ *610 and 644 1st St., at McKinstry St., Napa* ⊕ *www.oxbowpublicmarket.com.*

WORTH NOTING

Etude Wines. You're apt to see or hear hawks, egrets, Canada geese, and other wildlife on the grounds of Etude, known for its sophisticated Pinot Noirs. Although the winery and its light-filled tasting room are in Napa County, the grapes for its flagship Carneros Estate Pinot Noir come from the Sonoma portion of Los Carneros, as do those for the rarer Heirloom Carneros Pinot Noir. Chardonnay, Pinot Blanc, Pinot Noir, and other wines are poured daily at the tasting bar and in good weather on the patio. Pinot Noirs from Carneros, the Sonoma Coast, Oregon, and Santa Barbara County are compared at the Study of Pinot Noir sessions ($50), for which reservations are required. ■TIP→ Single-vineyard Napa Valley Cabernets are another Etude emphasis; those from Rutherford and Oakville are particularly good. ✉ *1250 Cuttings Wharf Rd., 1 mile south of Hwy. 121, Napa* ☎ *707/257–5782* ⊕ *www.etudewines.com* ⌨ *Tastings $20–$50.*

The Hess Collection. About 9 miles northwest of Napa, up a winding road ascending Mt. Veeder, this winery is a delightful discovery. The limestone structure, rustic from the outside but modern and airy within, contains Swiss owner Donald Hess's world-class art collection, including large-scale works by contemporary artists such as Andy Goldsworthy, Anselm Kiefer, and Robert Rauschenberg. Cabernet Sauvignon is a major strength, and the 19 Block Cuvée, Mount Veeder, a Cabernet blend, shows off Malbec and other estate varietals. Tastings outdoors in the garden and the courtyard take place from spring to fall, with cheese or nuts and other nibbles accompanying the wines. ■TIP→ Among the wine-and-food pairings offered year-round, most of which involve a guided tour of the art collection, is a fun one showcasing locally made artisanal chocolates. ✉ *4411 Redwood Rd., west off Hwy. 29 at Trancas St./Redwood Rd. exit, Napa* ☎ *707/255–1144* ⊕ *www.hesscollection.com* ⌨ *Tastings $25–$175, art gallery free.*

Napa Valley Wine Train. Several century-old restored Pullman railroad cars and a two-story 1952 Vista Dome car with a curved glass roof travel a leisurely, scenic route between Napa and St. Helena. All trips include a well-made lunch or dinner. Guests on the Quattro Vino tour enjoy a four-course lunch and tastings at four wineries, with stops at one or two wineries incorporated into other tours. Murder-mystery plays are among the regularly scheduled special events. ■TIP→ It's best to make this trip during the day, when you can enjoy the vineyard views. ✉ *1275 McKinstry St., off 1st St., Napa* ☎ *707/253–2111, 800/427–4124* ⊕ *www.winetrain.com* ⌨ *From $146.*

Stag's Leap Wine Cellars. A 1973 Stag's Leap Wine Cellars S.L.V. Cabernet Sauvignon put this winery and the Napa Valley on the enological map by placing first in the famous Judgment of Paris tasting of 1976. The grapes for that wine came from a vineyard visible from the stone-and-glass Fay Outlook & Visitor Center, which has broad views of a second fabled Cabernet vineyard (Fay) and the promontory that gives both the winery and the Stags Leap District AVA their names. The top-of-the-line Cabernets from these vineyards are poured at the $45 Estate Collection Tasting. Among the other options are a cave tour and tasting and special wine-and-food pairings. ✉ *5766 Silverado Trail, at Wappo Hill Rd., Napa* ☎ *707/261–6410* ⊕ *www.cask23.com* ⌨ *Tasting $45, tours (with tastings by appointment only) $75 and up.*

20

WHERE TO EAT

$$$ MODERN AMERICAN Fodor's Choice ★ 🍴 **The Corner Napa.** Equal parts 21st-century gentleman's club and brooding urban loft, this downtown restaurant seduces with a suave palette of marble, leather, bronze, and polished walnut surfaces. Chef Dustin Falcon's cuisine similarly enchants, with pickled pearl onions, apple, sherry, and candied pecans elevating a garden beets salad, and Sicilian pistachio, Medjool dates, spiced yogurt, and fried naan balls playing well with each other and their dish's centerpiece, pan-seared Spanish octopus. **Known for:** contemporary decor; international wine list; specialty cocktails and rare spirits. [$] *Average main: $28* ✉ *660 Main St., near 5th St., Napa* ☎ *707/927–5552* 🌐 *www.cornerbarnapa.com* 🕐 *Closed Mon. No lunch Tues.–Sat.*

$$$ ECLECTIC 🍴 **Grace's Table.** A dependable, varied, three-squares-a-day menu makes this modest corner restaurant occupying a brick-and-glass storefront many Napans go-to choice for a simple meal. Iron-skillet corn bread with lavender honey and butter shows up at all hours, with chilaquiles scrambled eggs a breakfast favorite, savory fish tacos a lunchtime staple, and cassoulet and pork osso buco risotto popular for dinner. **Known for:** congenial staffers; good beers on tap; eclectic menu focusing on France, Italy, and the Americas. [$] *Average main: $24* ✉ *1400 2nd St., at Franklin St., Napa* ☎ *707/226–6200* 🌐 *www.gracestable.net.*

$$$$ MODERN AMERICAN Fodor's Choice ★ 🍴 **La Toque.** Chef Ken Frank's La Toque is the complete package: his imaginative modern American cuisine, served in a formal dining space, is complemented by a wine lineup that earned the restaurant a coveted *Wine Spectator* Grand Award. Built around seasonal local ingredients, the prix-fixe menu, which changes frequently, might include potato rösti with caviar, sole with eggplant and almond-hazelnut *picada* sauce, and five-spice Liberty Farm duck breast with black trumpet mushrooms. **Known for:** elaborate preparations; astute wine pairings. [$] *Average main: $80* ✉ *Westin Verasa Napa, 1314 McKinstry St., off Soscol Ave., Napa* ☎ *707/257–5157* 🌐 *www.latoque.com* 🕐 *No lunch.*

$$$ JAPANESE Fodor's Choice ★ 🍴 **Miminashi.** Japanese *izakaya*—gastropubs that serve appetizers downed with sake or cocktails—provided the inspiration for chef Curtis Di Fede's buzz-worthy downtown Napa restaurant. Ramen, fried rice, and yakitori anchor the menu, whose highlights include smoked-trout potato croquettes, crispy skewered chicken skin, and the ooh-inspiring *okonomiyaki* pancake with bacon and cabbage, topped by dried fermented tuna flakes. **Known for:** soft-serve ice cream for dessert and from to-go window; wines and sakes that elevate the cuisine. [$] *Average main: $28* ✉ *821 Coombs St., near 3rd St., Napa* ☎ *707/254–9464* 🌐 *miminashi.com* 🕐 *No lunch weekends.*

$$$$ JAPANESE 🍴 **Morimoto Napa.** *Iron Chef* star Masaharu Morimoto is the big name behind this downtown Napa hot spot where everything is delightfully overdone, right down to the desserts. Organic materials such as twisting grapevines above the bar and rough-hewn wooden tables seem simultaneously earthy and modern, creating a fitting setting for the gorgeously plated Japanese fare, from sashimi served with grated fresh wasabi to elaborate concoctions that include sea-urchin carbonara made with udon noodles. **Known for:** elaborate concoctions; gorgeous plating; omakase menu. [$] *Average main: $36* ✉ *610 Main St., at 5th St., Napa* ☎ *707/252–1600* 🌐 *www.morimotonapa.com.*

$$$$ MODERN AMERICAN Fodor's Choice ★

🍴 **Torc.** *Torc* means "wild boar" in an early Celtic dialect, and owner-chef Sean O'Toole, who formerly helmed kitchens at top Manhattan, San Francisco, and Yountville establishments, occasionally incorporates the restaurant's namesake beast into his eclectic offerings. O'Toole and his team enhance dishes such as roast chicken—recently prepared with Florence fennel, hedgehog mushroom, pickle lily, and bergamot—with style and precision. **Known for:** gracious service; specialty cocktails; Bengali sweet-potato pakora and deviled-egg appetizers. [$] *Average main: $33 ✉ 1140 Main St., at Pearl St., Napa ☎ 707/252–3292 🌐 www.torcnapa.com ⏲ Closed Tues. No lunch weekdays.*

$$$ SPANISH Fodor's Choice ★

🍴 **ZuZu.** At festive ZuZu the focus is on tapas, paella, the signature suckling pig, and other Spanish favorites often downed with cava or sangria. Regulars revere the paella, made with Spanish *bomba* rice, and small plates that might include white anchovies with sliced egg and rémoulade on grilled bread. **Known for:** singular flavors and spicing; Latin jazz on the stereo; sister restaurant La Taberna for bar bites three doors south. [$] *Average main: $29 ✉ 829 Main St., near 3rd St., Napa ☎ 707/224–8555 🌐 www.zuzunapa.com ⏲ No lunch weekends.*

WHERE TO STAY

$$$ HOTEL Fodor's Choice ★

🏨 **Andaz Napa.** Part of the Hyatt family, this boutique hotel with an urban-hip vibe has luxurious rooms with flat-screen TVs, laptop-size safes, and white-marble bathrooms stocked with high-quality bath products. **Pros:** proximity to downtown restaurants, theaters, and tasting rooms; access to modern fitness center; complimentary beverage upon arrival; complimentary snacks and nonalcoholic beverages in rooms. **Cons:** parking can be a challenge on weekends; unremarkable views from some rooms. [$] *Rooms from: $359 ✉ 1450 1st St., Napa ☎ 707/687–1234 🌐 andaznapa.com 🛏 141 rooms 🍽 No meals.*

$$$$ RESORT Fodor's Choice ★

🏨 **Carneros Resort & Spa.** Freestanding board-and-batten cottages with rocking chairs on each porch are simultaneously rustic and chic at this luxurious property made even more so by a $6.5 million makeover. **Pros:** cottages have lots of privacy; beautiful views from hilltop pool and hot tub; heaters on private patios. **Cons:** a long drive to destinations up-valley. [$] *Rooms from: $600 ✉ 4048 Sonoma Hwy./Hwy. 121, Napa ☎ 707/299–4900, 888/400–9000 🌐 www.thecarnerosinn.com 🛏 86 rooms 🍽 No meals.*

20

$$ B&B/INN Fodor's Choice ★

🏨 **Inn on Randolph.** A few calm blocks from the downtown action, the restored Inn on Randolph is a sophisticated haven celebrated for its gourmet gluten-free breakfasts and snacks. **Pros:** quiet residential neighborhood; gourmet breakfasts; sophisticated decor; romantic setting. **Cons:** a bit of a walk from downtown. [$] *Rooms from: $299 ✉ 411 Randolph St., Napa ☎ 707/257–2886 🌐 www.innonrandolph.com 🛏 10 rooms 🍽 Breakfast.*

$$ B&B/INN

🏨 **Napa River Inn.** Part of a complex of restaurants, shops, a nightclub, and a spa, this waterfront inn is within easy walking distance of downtown hot spots. **Pros:** wide range of room sizes and prices; near downtown action; pet friendly. **Cons:** river views could be more scenic; some rooms get noise from nearby restaurants. [$] *Rooms from: $299 ✉ 500 Main St., Napa ☎ 707/251–8500, 877/251–8500 🌐 www.napariverinn.com 🛏 66 rooms 🍽 Breakfast.*

NIGHTLIFE AND PERFORMING ARTS

Fodor's Choice   **Blue Note Napa.** The famed New York jazz room's West Coast club hosts
★   national headliners such as Chris Botti, Dee Dee Bridgewater, and Coco
Montoya, along with local talents such as Lavay Smith & Her Red Hot
Skillet Lickers. Chef Jessica Sedlacek, formerly of The French Laundry
and Bouchon in Yountville, supplies the culinary pizzazz—hearty entrées
such as boneless crispy chicken and a massive pork chop, and lighter fare
that includes raw oysters, chicken wings, and bacon-inflected potato frit-
ters (an instant hit). ✉ *Napa Valley Opera House, 1030 Main St., at 1st
St., Napa* ☎ *707/603–1258* ⊕ *www.bluenotenapa.com.*

Cadet Wine + Beer Bar. Cadet plays things urban-style cool with a long
bar, high-top tables, an all-vinyl sound track, and a low-lit, generally
loungelike feel. The two owners describe their outlook as "unabashedly
pro-California," but their lineup of 150-plus wines and beers circles the
globe. The crowd here is youngish, the vibe festive. ✉ *930 Franklin St.,
at end of pedestrian alley between 1st and 2nd Sts., Napa* ☎ *707/224–
4400* ⊕ *www.cadetbeerandwinebar.com.*

YOUNTVILLE

9 miles north of the town of Napa.

These days Yountville is something like Disneyland for food lovers.
You could stay here for a week and not exhaust all the options—several of them owned by The French Laundry's Thomas Keller—and the
tiny town is full of small inns and high-end hotels that cater to those
who prefer to walk (not drive) after an extravagant meal. It's also well
located for excursions to many big-name Napa wineries, especially
those in the Stags Leap District, from which big, bold Cabernet Sauvignons helped make the Napa Valley's wine-making reputation.

GETTING HERE AND AROUND

Downtown Yountville sits just off Highway 29. Approaching from the
south take the Yountville exit—from the north take Madison—and
proceed to Washington Street, home to the major shops and restaurants.
Yountville Cross Road connects downtown to the Silverado Trail, along
which many noted wineries do business. The free Yountville Trolley
serves the town daily from 10 am to 7 pm (on-call service until 11
except on Sunday).

EXPLORING
TOP ATTRACTIONS

Fodor's Choice   **Cliff Lede Vineyards.** Inspired by his passion for classic rock, owner and
★   construction magnate Cliff Lede named the blocks in his Stags Leap
District vineyard after hits by the Grateful Dead and other bands.
The vibe at his efficient, high-tech winery is anything but laid-back,
however. Cutting-edge agricultural and enological science informs
the vineyard management and wine making here. Architect Howard Backen designed the winery and its tasting room, where Lede's
Sauvignon Blanc, Cabernet Sauvignons, and other wines, along with
some from sister winery FEL, which produces much-lauded Anderson
Valley Pinot Noirs, are poured. ■TIP→ Walk-ins are welcome at the
tasting bar, but appointments are required for the veranda outside and

a nearby gallery that often displays rock-related art. ✉ *1473 Yountville Cross Rd., off Silverado Trail, Yountville* ☏ *707/944–8642* ⊕ *cliffledevineyards.com* 🍷 *Tastings $30–$50.*

Fodor's Choice
★ **Ma(i)sonry Napa Valley.** An art-and-design gallery that also pours the wines of about two dozen limited-production wineries, Ma(i)sonry occupies a manor house constructed in 1904 from Napa River stone. Tasting flights of wines by distinguished winemakers such as Heidi Barrett, Philippe Melka, and Thomas Rivers Brown can be sampled in fair weather in the sculpture garden, in a private nook, or at the communal redwood table, and in any weather indoors among the contemporary artworks and well-chosen *objets*—which might include 17th-century furnishings, industrial lamps, or slabs of petrified wood. ■TIP➡ Walk-ins are welcome, space permitting, but during summer, at harvest, and on weekends and holidays it's best to book in advance. ✉ *6711 Washington St., at Pedroni St., Yountville* ☏ *707/944–0889* ⊕ *www.maisonry.com* 🍷 *Tasting $35–$55.*

Fodor's Choice
★ **Stewart Cellars.** Three stone structures meant to mimic Scottish ruins coaxed into modernity form this complex that includes public and private tasting spaces, a bright outdoor patio, and a café with accessible vegan- and carnivore-friendly cuisine. The attention to detail in the ensemble's design mirrors that of the wines, whose grapes come from Stagecoach, Beckstoffer Las Piedras (for the intense Nomad Cabernet), and other coveted vineyards. Although Cabernet is the focus, winemaker Blair Guthrie, with input from consulting winemaker Paul Hobbs, also makes Chardonnay, Pinot Noir, and Merlot. ■TIP➡ On sunny days this is a good stop around lunchtime, when you can order a meal from the café and a glass of wine from the tasting room—for permit reasons this must be done separately—and enjoy them on the patio. ✉ *6752 Washington St., near Pedroni St., Yountville* ☏ *707/963–9160* ⊕ *www.stewartcellars.com* 🍷 *Tastings $35–$85.*

WORTH NOTING

Domaine Chandon. On a knoll shaded by ancient oak trees, this French-owned maker of sparkling wines claims one of Yountville's prime pieces of real estate. Chandon is best known for bubblies, but the still wines—Cabernet Sauvignon, Chardonnay, Pinot Meunier, and Pinot Noir—are also worth a try. You can sip by the flight or by the glass at the bar, or begin there and sit at tables in the lounge and return to the bar as needed; in good weather, tables are set up outside. For the complete experience, order a cheese board or other hors d'oeuvres on the lounge menu. ✉ *1 California Dr., off Hwy. 29, Yountville* ☏ *707/204–7530, 888/242–6366* ⊕ *www.chandon.com* 🍷 *Tastings $9–$40.*

Fodor's Choice
★ **Robert Sinskey Vineyards.** Although the winery produces a well-regarded Stags Leap Cabernet Sauvignon, two Bordeaux-style red blends (Marcien and POV), and white wines, Sinskey is best known for its intense, brambly Carneros District Pinot Noirs. All the grapes are grown in organic, certified biodynamic vineyards. The influence of Robert's wife, Maria Helm Sinskey—a chef and cookbook author and the winery's culinary director—is evident during the tastings, which are accompanied by a few bites of food with each wine. ■TIP➡ The Perfect Circle

20

Tour ($95), offered daily, takes in the winery's gardens and ends with a seated pairing of food and wine. Even more elaborate, also by appointment, is the Chef's Table ($175), on Friday and weekends. ✉ *6320 Silverado Trail, at Yountville Cross Rd., Napa* ☎ *707/944–9090* 🌐 *www.robertsinskey.com* 🎟 *Tastings $40–$70, tour $95.*

WHERE TO EAT

$$$$ MODERN AMERICAN Fodor's Choice ★

🍴 **Ad Hoc.** At this low-key dining room with zinc-top tables and wine served in tumblers, superstar chef Thomas Keller offers a single, fixed-price menu nightly, with a small but decadent Sunday brunch. The dinner selection might include smoked beef short ribs with creamy herb rice and charred broccolini, or sesame chicken with radish kimchi and fried rice. **Known for:** casual cuisine; great price for a Thomas Keller meal; don't-miss buttermilk-fried-chicken night. [$] *Average main: $55* ✉ *6476 Washington St., at Oak Circle, Yountville* ☎ *707/944–2487* 🌐 *www.adhocrestaurant.com* ⏲ *No lunch Mon.–Sat.; no dinner Tues. and Wed.* ☞ *Call a day ahead to find out the next day's menu.*

$$$ FRENCH Fodor's Choice ★

🍴 **Bistro Jeanty.** Escargots, cassoulet, *daube de boeuf* (beef stewed in red wine), and other French classics are prepared with the utmost precision at this country bistro whose lamb tongue and other obscure delicacies delight daring diners. Regulars often start with the rich tomato soup in a flaky puff pastry before proceeding to sole meunière or coq au vin, completing the French sojourn with warm apple tarte tatin and other authentic desserts. **Known for:** traditional preparations; oh-so-French ambience. [$] *Average main: $27* ✉ *6510 Washington St., at Mulberry St., Yountville* ☎ *707/944–0103* 🌐 *www.bistrojeanty.com.*

$$$ FRENCH Fodor's Choice ★

🍴 **Bouchon.** The team that created The French Laundry is also behind this place, where everything—the lively and crowded zinc-topped bar, the elbow-to-elbow seating, the traditional French onion soup—could have come straight from a Parisian bistro. Roasted chicken with leeks and oyster mushrooms and steamed mussels served with crispy, addictive *frites* (french fries) are among the perfectly executed entrées. **Known for:** bistro classics; rabbit and salmon rillettes. [$] *Average main: $27* ✉ *6534 Washington St., near Humboldt St., Yountville* ☎ *707/944–8037* 🌐 *www.bouchonbistro.com.*

$$ MODERN ITALIAN

🍴 **Ciccio.** The ranch of Ciccio's owners, Frank and Karen Altamura, supplies some of the vegetables and herbs for the modern Italian cuisine prepared in the open kitchen of this remodeled former grocery store. Seasonal growing cycles dictate executive chef Polly Lappetito's menu, with Tuscan kale and white-bean soup, wood-fired sardines with salsa verde, and a mushroom, Taleggio, and crispy-sage pizza among the frequent offerings. **Known for:** Negroni bar; prix-fixe chef's dinner; mostly Napa Valley wines, some from owners' winery. [$] *Average main: $19* ✉ *6770 Washington St., at Madison St., Yountville* ☎ *707/945–1000* 🌐 *www.ciccionapavalley.com* ⏲ *Closed Mon. and Tues. No lunch* ☞ *No reservations, except for prix-fixe chef's dinner (required; for 4–10 guests).*

$$$$ AMERICAN Fodor's Choice ★

🍴 **The French Laundry.** An old stone building laced with ivy houses chef Thomas Keller's destination restaurant. Some courses on the two prix-fixe menus, one of which highlights vegetables, rely on luxe ingredients such as *calotte* (cap of the rib eye); other courses take humble elements like fava beans and elevate them to art. **Known for:** signature starter "oysters and pearls"; intricate flavors; superior wine list. $ *Average main: $310* ⊠ *6640 Washington St., at Creek St., Yountville* ☎ *707/944–2380* ⊕ *www.frenchlaundry.com* ⊙ *No lunch Mon.–Thurs.* ⛰ *Jacket required* ⌕ *Reservations essential weeks ahead (call or check website for precise instructions).*

$$$
AMERICAN

✕**Mustards Grill.** Cindy Pawlcyn's Mustards fills day and night with fans of her hearty cuisine, equal parts updated renditions of traditional American dishes—what Pawlcyn dubs "deluxe truck stop classics"— and fanciful contemporary fare. Barbecued baby back pork ribs and a lemon-lime tart piled high with brown-sugar meringue fall squarely in the first category, with sweet corn tamales with tomatillo-avocado salsa and wild mushrooms representing the latter. **Known for:** roadhouse setting; convivial mood; hoppin' bar. $ *Average main: $27* ⊠ *7399 St. Helena Hwy./Hwy. 29, 1 mile north of Yountville, Napa* ☎ *707/944–2424* ⊕ *www.mustardsgrill.com.*

$
LATIN AMERICAN
Fodor'sChoice
★

✕**Protéa Restaurant.** A meal at Yountville's The French Laundry motivated Puerto Rico–born Anita Cartagena to pursue a career as a chef, which she did for several years at nearby Ciccio and elsewhere before opening this perky storefront serving Latin-inspired multi-culti fastfood cuisine. What's in season and the chef's whims determine the order-at-the-counter fare, but Puerto Rican rice bowls (often with pork), empanadas, and sweet-and-sour ramen stir-fries make regular appearances. **Known for:** patio and rooftop seating; beer and wine lineup; eager-to-please staff. $ *Average main: $13* ⊠ *6488 Washington St., at Oak Circle, Yountville* ☎ *707/415–5035* ⊕ *www.proteayv.com.*

$$$
MODERN
AMERICAN
Fodor'sChoice
★

✕**Redd.** Chef Richard Reddington's culinary influences include California, Mexico, Europe, and Asia, but his dishes, like his minimalist dining room, feel modern and unfussy. The glazed pork belly with apple puree, set amid a pool of soy caramel, is an example of the East-meets-West style, and the seafood preparations—among them petrale sole, clams, and chorizo poached in a saffron-curry broth—exhibit a similar transcontinental dexterity. **Known for:** five-course tasting menu; street-side outdoor patio; cocktails and small plates at the bar. $ *Average main: $30* ⊠ *6480 Washington St., at Oak Circle, Yountville* ☎ *707/944–2222* ⊕ *www.reddnapavalley.com.*

$$
ITALIAN

✕**Redd Wood.** Chef Richard Reddington's casual restaurant specializes in thin-crust wood-fired pizzas and contemporary variations on rustic Italian classics. With sausage soup laced with cabbage and turnip, pizzas such as the white anchovy with herb sauce and mozzarella, and the pork-chop entrée enlivened by persimmon, Redd Wood does for Italian comfort food what nearby Mustards Grill does for the American version: it spruces it up but retains its innate pleasures. **Known for:** industrial decor; easygoing service. $ *Average main: $21* ⊠ *North Block Hotel, 6755 Washington St., at Madison St., Yountville* ☎ *707/299–5030* ⊕ *www.redd-wood.com.*

WHERE TO STAY

$$$$
RESORT
Fodor'sChoice
★

🛏**Bardessono.** Although Bardessono bills itself as the "greenest luxury hotel in America," there's nothing spartan about its accommodations; arranged around four landscaped courtyards, the rooms have luxurious organic bedding, gas fireplaces, and huge bathrooms with walnut floors.

20

Pros: large rooftop lap pool; excellent spa, with in-room treatments available. **Cons:** expensive; limited view from some rooms. $ *Rooms from: $700 ☒ 6526 Yount St., Yountville ☎ 707/204–6000 ⊕ www. bardessono.com ☞ 62 rooms* ⦿*No meals.*

$$ ⌂ **Maison Fleurie.** A stay at this comfortable inn places you within easy
B&B/INN walking distance of Yountville's fine restaurants. **Pros:** smallest rooms a bargain; outdoor hot tub; pool (open in season); free bike rental. **Cons:** breakfast room can be crowded at peak times. $ *Rooms from: $219 ☒ 6529 Yount St., Yountville ☎ 707/944–2056, 800/788–0369 ⊕ www. maisonfleurienapa.com ☞ 13 rooms* ⦿*Breakfast.*

$$$ ⌂ **Napa Valley Lodge.** Clean rooms in a convenient motel-style setting
HOTEL draw travelers willing to pay more than at comparable lodgings in the city of Napa to be within walking distance of Yountville's tasting rooms, restaurants, and shops. **Pros:** clean rooms; filling continental breakfast; large pool area. **Cons:** no elevator; lacks amenities of other Yountville properties. $ *Rooms from: $350 ☒ 2230 Madison St., Yountville ☎ 707/944–2468, 888/944–3545 ⊕ www.napavalleylodge.com ☞ 55 rooms* ⦿*Breakfast.*

$$$$ ⌂ **North Block Hotel.** With chic Tuscan style, this 20-room hotel has
HOTEL dark-wood furniture and a brown-and-sage decor. **Pros:** extremely comfortable beds; attentive service; room service by Redd Wood restaurant. **Cons:** outdoor areas get some traffic noise. $ *Rooms from: $420 ☒ 6757 Washington St., Yountville ☎ 707/944–8080 ⊕ north-blockhotel.com ☞ 20 rooms* ⦿*No meals.*

SPORTS AND THE OUTDOORS

BALLOONING

Napa Valley Aloft. Between 8 and 12 passengers soar over the Napa Valley in balloons that launch from downtown Yountville. Rates include pre-flight refreshments and a huge breakfast. ☒ *V Marketplace, 6525 Washington St., near Mulberry St., Yountville ☎ 707/944–4400, 855/944–4408 ⊕ www.nvaloft.com* ⛅*From $220.*

BIKING

Fodor'sChoice **Napa Valley Bike Tours.** With dozens of wineries within 5 miles, this shop
★ makes a fine starting point for guided and self-guided vineyard and wine-tasting excursions. The outfit also rents bikes. ☒ *6500 Washington St., at Mulberry St., Yountville ☎ 707/944–2953 ⊕ www.napavalleybik-etours.com* ⛅*From $124 (½-day guided tour).*

SPAS

Fodor'sChoice **The Spa at Bardessono.** Many of this spa's patrons are hotel guests who
★ take their treatments in their rooms' large, customized bathrooms—all of them equipped with concealed massage tables—but the main facility is open to guests and nonguests alike. An in-room treatment popular with couples starts with massages in front of the fireplace and ends with a whirlpool bath and a split of sparkling wine. For the two-hour Yountville Signature treatment, which can be enjoyed in-room or at the spa, a shea-butter-enriched sugar scrub is applied, followed by a massage with antioxidant Chardonnay grape-seed oil and a hydrating hair-and-scalp treatment. The spa engages massage therapists skilled in Swedish, Thai, and several other techniques. In addition to massages,

the services include facials, waxing, and other skin-care treatments, as well as manicures and pedicures. ⊠ *Bardessono Hotel, 6526 Yount St., at Mulberry St., Yountville* ☎ *707/204–6050* ⊕ *www.bardessono.com/ spa* ⊡ *Treatments $60–$630.*

SHOPPING

V Marketplace. This two-story redbrick market, which once housed a winery, a livery stable, and a brandy distillery, now contains clothing boutiques, art galleries, a chocolatier, and food, wine, and gift shops. Celebrity chef Michael Chiarello operates a restaurant (Bottega), a tasting room for his wines, and Ottimo, with pizza, fresh mozzarella, and other stands plus retail items. Show some love to the shops upstairs, especially Knickers and Pearls (lingerie and loungewear), Montecristi Panama Hats (Johnny Depp found one he liked), and Lemondrops (kids' clothing and toys). ⊠ *6525 Washington St., near Mulberry St., Yountville* ☎ *707/944–2451* ⊕ *www.vmarketplace.com.*

OAKVILLE

2 miles northwest of Yountville.

A large butte that runs east–west just north of Yountville blocks the cooling fogs from the south, facilitating the myriad microclimates of the Oakville AVA, home to several high-profile wineries.

GETTING HERE AND AROUND

Driving along Highway 29, you'll know you've reached Oakville when you see the Oakville Grocery on the east side of the road. You can reach Oakville from the Sonoma County town of Glen Ellen by heading east on Trinity Road from Highway 12. The twisting route, along the mountain range that divides Napa and Sonoma, eventually becomes the Oakville Grade. The views on this drive are breathtaking, though the continual curves make it unsuitable for those who suffer from motion sickness.

EXPLORING

TOP ATTRACTIONS

B Cellars. The chefs take center stage in the open-hearth kitchen of this boutique winery's hospitality house, and with good reason: creating food-friendly wines is B Cellars's raison d'être. Visits to the Oakville facility—all steel beams, corrugated metal, and plate glass yet remarkably cozy—begin with a tour of the winery's culinary garden and caves. Most guests return to the house to sample wines paired with small bites, with some visitors remaining in the caves for exclusive tastings of Cabernet Sauvignons from several historic vineyards of Andy Beckstoffer, a prominent grower. Kirk Venge, whose fruit-forward style well suits the winery's food-oriented approach, crafts these and other wines, among them red and white blends and single-vineyard Cabernets from other noteworthy vineyards. ■TIP→ The B Cellars wine-and-food pairings, all strictly by appointment, are outstanding. ⊠ *703 Oakville Cross Rd., west of Silverado Trail, Oakville* ☎ *707/709–8787* ⊕ *www.bcellars.com* ⊡ *Tastings $37–$135.*

20

Fodor's Choice ★   **Far Niente.** Guests arriving at Far Niente are welcomed by name and treated to a glimpse of one of the Napa Valley's most beautiful properties. By appointment only, small groups are escorted through the historic 1885 stone winery, including some of the 40,000 square feet of aging caves, for a lesson on the labor-intensive method of making Far Niente's flagship wines: a Cabernet Sauvignon blend and a Chardonnay. Next on the agenda is a peek at the Carriage House, which holds a gleaming collection of classic cars. The seated tasting of wines and cheeses that follows concludes on a sweet note with Dolce, a late-harvest wine made from Semillon and Sauvignon Blanc grapes. ⊠ *1350 Acacia Dr., off Oakville Grade Rd., Oakville* ☎ *707/944–2861* ⊕ *www. farniente.com* 🖼 *Tasting and tour $75.*

Fodor's Choice ★   **Silver Oak.** The first review of this winery's Napa Valley Cabernet Sauvignon declared the debut 1972 vintage not all that good and, at $6 a bottle, overpriced. Oops. The celebrated Bordeaux-style Cabernet blend, still the only Napa Valley wine bearing its winery's label each year, evolved into a cult favorite, and Silver Oak founders Ray Duncan and Justin Meyer received worldwide recognition for their signature use of exclusively American oak to age the wines. At the Oakville tasting room, constructed out of reclaimed stone and other materials from a 19th-century Kansas flour mill, you can sip the current Napa Valley vintage, its counterpart from Silver Oak's Alexander Valley operation, and a library wine without an appointment. One is required for tours, private tastings, and food-wine pairings. ⊠ *915 Oakville Cross Rd., off Hwy. 29, Oakville* ☎ *707/942–7022* ⊕ *www.silveroak.com* 🖼 *Tastings $30–$75, tour $50 (includes tasting).*

WORTH NOTING

Opus One. In 1979 the Napa Valley's Robert Mondavi and France's Baron Philippe de Rothschild joined forces to produce a single wine: Opus One, a Bordeaux blend that was the first of Napa's ultrapremium wines. Tours here focus on the combination of agriculture, science, and technology required to create Opus One and conclude with a tasting of the current vintage. ■ TIP➔ **You can taste the wine without touring, but as with the tour you'll need a reservation.** ⊠ *7900 St. Helena Hwy./ Hwy. 29, at Oakville Cross. Rd., Oakville* ☎ *707/944–9442, 800/292–6787* ⊕ *www.opusonewinery.com* 🖼 *Tasting $50, tours $85–$140.*

Robert Mondavi Winery. The arch at the center of the sprawling Mission-style building frames the lawn and the vineyard behind, inviting a stroll under the arcades. You can head for one of the walk-in tasting rooms, but if you've not toured a winery before, the 90-minute Signature Tour and Tasting ($40, reservation recommended) is a good way to learn about enology, as well as the late Robert Mondavi's role in California wine making. Those new to tasting should consider the 45-minute Wine Tasting Basics experience ($25, by appointment). Serious wine lovers can opt for the appointment-only $55 Exclusive Cellar tasting, during which a server pours and explains limited-production, reserve, and older-vintage wines. ■ TIP➔ **Concerts take place in summer on the lawn; call ahead for tickets.** ⊠ *7801 St. Helena Hwy./Hwy. 29, Oakville* ☎ *888/766–6328* ⊕ *www.robertmondaviwinery.com* 🖼 *Tastings and tours $20–$55.*

RUTHERFORD

2 miles northwest of Oakville.

With its singular microclimate and soil, Rutherford is an important viticultural center, with more big-name wineries than you can shake a corkscrew at. Cabernet Sauvignon is king here. The well-drained, loamy soil is ideal for those vines, and since this part of the valley gets plenty of sun, the grapes develop exceptionally intense flavors.

GETTING HERE AND AROUND

Wineries around Rutherford are dotted along Highway 29 and the parallel Silverado Trail north and south of Rutherford Road/Conn Creek Road, on which wineries can also be found.

EXPLORING

TOP ATTRACTIONS

FAMILY
Fodor's Choice
★

Frog's Leap. John Williams, owner of Frog's Leap, maintains a sense of humor about wine that translates into an entertaining yet informative experience—if you're a novice, the tour here is a fun way to begin your education. You'll taste wines that might include Zinfandel, Merlot, Chardonnay, Sauvignon Blanc, and an estate-grown Cabernet Sauvignon. The winery includes a barn built in 1884, 5 acres of organic gardens, an eco-friendly visitor center, and a frog pond topped with lily pads. Reservations are required for all visits here. ■ TIP➜ The tour is recommended, but you can also just sample wines either inside or on a porch overlooking the garden. ✉ *8815 Conn Creek Rd., Rutherford* ☎ *707/963–4704, 800/959–4704* ⊕ *www.frogsleap.com* 🍷 *Tastings $20–$25; tour $25.*

Inglenook. Filmmaker Francis Ford Coppola began his wine-making career in 1975, when he bought part of the historic Inglenook estate. Over the decades he reunited the original property acquired by Inglenook founder Gustave Niebaum, remodeled Niebaum's ivy-covered 1880s château, and purchased the rights to the Inglenook name. The Inglenook Experience ($50), an escorted tour of the château, vineyards, and caves, ends with a seated tasting of wines paired with artisanal cheeses. Among the topics discussed are the winery's history and the evolution of Coppola's signature wine, Rubicon, a Cabernet Sauvignon–based blend. The Heritage Tasting ($45), which also includes a Rubicon pour, is held in the opulent Pennino Salon. Reservations are required for some tastings and tours, and are recommended for all. ■ TIP➜ Walk-ins can sip wines by the glass or bottle at The Bistro, a wine bar with a picturesque courtyard. ✉ *1991 St. Helena Hwy./Hwy. 29, at Hwy.128, Rutherford* ☎ *707/968–1100, 800/782–4266* ⊕ *www.inglenook.com* 🍷 *Tastings $45–$50, private experiences from $75.*

Mumm Napa. In Mumm's light-filled tasting room or adjacent outdoor patio you can enjoy bubbly by the flight, but the sophisticated sparkling wines, elegant setting, and vineyard views aren't the only reasons to visit. An excellent gallery displays original Ansel Adams prints and presents temporary exhibitions by premier photographers. Winery tours cover the major steps in making sparklers. For a leisurely tasting of several vintages of the top-of-the-line DVX wines, book an

20

Frog's Leap's picturesque country charm extends all the way to the white picket fence.

Oak Terrace tasting ($50; reservations recommended Friday through Sunday). ■TIP→ Carlos Santana fans may want to taste the sparklers the musician makes in collaboration with Mumm's winemaker, Ludovic Dervin. ⊠ *8445 Silverado Trail, 1 mile south of Rutherford Cross Rd., Rutherford* ☎ *707/967–7700, 800/686–6272* ⊕ *www.mummnapa.com* ✉ *Tastings $20–$50, tour $40 (includes tasting).*

WORTH NOTING

FAMILY **Honig Vineyard & Winery.** Sustainable farming is the big story at this family-run winery. The Eco Tour, offered seasonally, focuses on the Honig family's environmentally friendly farming and production methods, which include using biodiesel to fuel the tractors, monitoring water use in the vineyard and winery, and generating power for the winery with solar panels. The family produces only Sauvignon Blanc and Cabernet Sauvignon. By appointment, you can taste whites and reds at a standard tasting for $30; the reserve tasting ($60) pairs single-vineyard Cabernets with small bites. ⊠ *850 Rutherford Rd., near Conn Creek Rd., Rutherford* ☎ *800/929–2217* ⊕ *www.honig-wine.com* ✉ *Tastings $30–$60, tour $45.*

WHERE TO EAT AND STAY

$$$$ ✕**Restaurant at Auberge du Soleil.** Possibly the most romantic roost for a
MODERN dinner in all the Wine Country is a terrace seat at the Auberge du Soleil
AMERICAN resort's illustrious restaurant, and the Mediterranean-inflected cuisine
Fodor'sChoice more than matches the dramatic vineyard views. The prix-fixe dinner
★ menu, which relies largely on local produce, might include veal sweet-
breads and chanterelles in a caramelized shallot sauce or prime beef
pavé with hearts of palm, lobster mushrooms, and bok choy. **Known**

for: polished service; comprehensive wine list; over-the-top weekend brunch. $ *Average main: $115* ⊠ *Auberge du Soleil, 180 Rutherford Hill Rd., off Silverado Trail, Rutherford* ☎ *707/963–1211, 800/348–5406* ⊕ *www.aubergedusoleil.com.*

$$$
AMERICAN
Fodor's Choice
★

✕ **Rutherford Grill.** Dark-wood walls, subdued lighting, and red leather banquettes make for a perpetually clubby mood at this trusty Rutherford hangout. Many entrées—steaks, burgers, fish, succulent rotisserie chicken, and barbecued pork ribs—emerge from an oak-fired grill operated by master technicians. **Known for:** French dip sandwich; reasonably priced wine list. $ *Average main: $29* ⊠ *1180 Rutherford Rd., at Hwy. 29, Rutherford* ☎ *707/963–1792* ⊕ *www. rutherfordgrill.com.*

$$$$
RESORT
Fodor's Choice
★

▦ **Auberge du Soleil.** Taking a cue from the olive-tree-studded landscape, this hotel with a renowned restaurant and spa cultivates a luxurious look that blends French and California style. **Pros:** stunning views over the valley; spectacular pool and spa areas; the most expensive suites are fit for a superstar. **Cons:** stratospheric prices; least expensive rooms get some noise from the bar and restaurant. $ *Rooms from: $875* ⊠ *180 Rutherford Hill Rd., Rutherford* ☎ *707/963–1211, 800/348–5406* ⊕ *www.aubergedusoleil.com* ⤵ *50 rooms* ❏ *Breakfast.*

ST. HELENA

2 miles northwest of Oakville.

Downtown St. Helena is a symbol of how well life can be lived in the Wine Country. Sycamore trees arch over Main Street (Highway 29), a funnel of outstanding restaurants and tempting boutiques. At the north end of town looms the hulking stone building of the Culinary Institute of America at Greystone. Weathered stone and brick buildings from the late 1800s give off that gratifying whiff of history.

The town got its start in 1854, when Henry Still built a store. Still wanted company, so he donated land lots on his town site to anyone who wanted to erect a business. Soon he was joined by a wagon shop, a shoe shop, hotels, and churches. Dr. George Crane planted a vineyard in 1858, and was the first to produce wine in commercially viable quantities. A German winemaker named Charles Krug followed suit a couple of years later, and other wineries soon followed.

20

GETTING HERE AND AROUND
Downtown stretches along Highway 29, called Main Street here. Many wineries lie north and south of downtown along Highway 29. More can be found off Silverado Trail, and some of the most scenic spots are on Spring Mountain, which rises southwest of town.

EXPLORING
TOP ATTRACTIONS
Charles Krug Winery. A historically sensitive renovation of its 1874 Redwood Cellar Building transformed the former production facility of the Napa Valley's oldest winery into an epic hospitality center. Charles Krug, a Prussian immigrant, established the winery in 1861 and ran it until his death in 1892. Italian immigrants Cesare Mondavi and his wife, Rosa, purchased Krug in 1943, and operated it with their

sons Peter and Robert (who later opened his own winery). Krug, still run by Peter's family, specializes in small-lot Yountville and Howell Mountain Cabernet Sauvignons and makes Chardonnay, Merlot, Pinot Noir, Sauvignon Blanc, Zinfandel, and a Zinfandel port. The tour is by appointment only. ■ TIP→ To sample the small-lot Cabernets, book a Family Reserve & Limited Release Tasting ($40). ⊠ *2800 Main St./ Hwy. 29, across from the Culinary Institute of America, St. Helena* ☎ *707/967–2229* ⊕ *www.charleskrug.com* 🍷 *Tastings $20–$40, tour $60 (includes tasting).*

Fodor's Choice
★
Hall St. Helena. The Cabernet Sauvignons produced here are works of art and the latest in organic-farming science and wine-making technology. A glass-walled tasting room allows guests to see in action some of the high-tech equipment winemaker Steve Leveque employs to craft wines that also include Merlot, Cabernet Franc, and Sauvignon Blanc. Westward from the second-floor tasting area, rows of neatly spaced Cabernet vines capture the eye, and beyond them the tree-studded Mayacamas Mountains. The main guided tour takes in the facility, the grounds, and a restored 19th-century winery, passing by artworks—inside and out—by John Baldessari, Jaume Plensa, Jesús Moroles, and other contemporary talents. ■ TIP→ Among the engaging seminars here is the Ultimate Cabernet Experience ($125), the winery's flagship tasting of current and library releases, as well as wines still aging in barrel. ⊠ *401 St. Helena Hwy./Hwy. 29, near White La., St. Helena* ☎ *707/967–2626* ⊕ *www.hallwines.com* 🍷 *Tastings $40–$250, tours $40–$50.*

Fodor's Choice
★
Joseph Phelps Vineyards. An appointment is required for tastings at the winery started by the late Joseph Phelps, but it's well worth the effort—and all the more so since an inspired renovation of the main redwood structure, a classic of 1970s Northern California architecture. Known for wines crafted with grace and precision, Phelps does produce fine whites, but the blockbusters are red, particularly the Cabernet Sauvignon and the luscious-yet-subtle Bordeaux-style blend called Insignia. In good weather, one-hour seated tastings take place on a terrace overlooking vineyards and oaks. At 90-minute tastings as thoughtfully conceived as the wines, guests explore such topics as wine-and-cheese pairing, wine blending, and the role oak barrels play in wine making. Participants in the blending seminar mix the various varietals that go into the Insignia blend. ⊠ *200 Taplin Rd., off Silverado Trail, St. Helena* ☎ *707/963–2745, 800/707–5789* ⊕ *www. josephphelps.com* 🍷 *Tastings and seminars $75–$200.*

Pride Mountain Vineyards. This winery 2,200 feet up Spring Mountain straddles Napa and Sonoma counties, confusing enough for visitors but even more complicated for the wine-making staff: government regulations require separate wineries and paperwork for each side of the property. It's one of several amusing Pride Mountain quirks, but winemaker Sally Johnson's "big red wines," including a Cabernet Sauvignon that earned 100-point scores from a major wine critic two years in a row, are serious business. At tastings and on tours you can learn about the farming and cellar strategies behind Pride's acclaimed Cabs (the winery also produces Syrah, a Cab-like Merlot, Viognier, and Chardonnay among others). The tour, which takes in vineyards and caves, also includes tastings of wine still in barrel. ■TIP➔ **The views here are knock-your-socks-off gorgeous.** ✉ *4026 Spring Mountain Rd., off St. Helena Rd. (extension of Spring Mountain Rd. in Sonoma County), St. Helena* ☎ *707/963–4949* ⊕ *www.pridewines. com* ▢ *Tastings $20–$75.*

WORTH NOTING

Beringer Vineyards. Brothers Frederick and Jacob Beringer opened the winery that still bears their name in 1876. One of California's earliest bonded wineries, it is the oldest one in the Napa Valley never to have missed a vintage—no mean feat, given Prohibition. Frederick's grand Rhine House Mansion, built in 1884, serves as the reserve tasting room. Here, surrounded by Belgian art-nouveau hand-carved oak and walnut furniture and stained-glass windows, you can sample wines that include a limited-release Chardonnay, a few big Cabernets, and a Sauterne-style dessert wine. A less expensive tasting takes place in the original stone winery. Reservations are required for some tastings and recommended for tours. ■TIP➔ **The one-hour Taste of Beringer ($50) tour of the property and sensory gardens surveys the winery's history and wine making and concludes with a seated wine-and-food pairing.** ✉ *2000 Main St./Hwy. 29, near Pratt Ave., St. Helena* ☎ *707/963–8989, 866/708–9463* ⊕ *www.beringer.com* ▢ *Tastings $25–$125, tours $30–$50.*

Culinary Institute of America at Greystone. The West Coast headquarters of the country's leading school for chefs is in the 1889 Greystone Cellars, an imposing building once the world's largest stone winery. On the ground floor you can check out the quirky Corkscrew Museum and browse the Spice Islands Marketplace shop, stocked with gleaming gadgets and many cookbooks. The Bakery Café by illy serves soups, salads, sandwiches, and baked goods. One-day and multiday cooking and beverage classes take place weekly, public cooking demonstrations on weekends. Students run the Gatehouse Restaurant, which serves lunch and dinner except during semester breaks. ✉ *2555 Main St./Hwy. 29, St. Helena* ☎ *707/967–1100* ⊕ *www.ciachef.edu/california* ▢ *Museum free, cooking demonstrations $25, class prices vary.*

20

WHERE TO EAT

$$
MODERN
AMERICAN
Fodor'sChoice
★

✕ **Cindy's Backstreet Kitchen.** At her up-valley outpost, Cindy Pawlcyn serves variations on the comfort food she made popular at Mustards Grill, but spices things up with dishes influenced by Mexican, Central American, and occasionally Asian cuisines. Along with staples such as meat loaf with garlic mashed potatoes and beef and duck burgers served with impeccable fries, the menu might include a rabbit tostada or curried chicken salad. **Known for:** warm pineapple upside-down cake; ethereal parfait. $ *Average main: $22* ✉ *1327 Railroad Ave., at Hunt St., 1 block east of Main St., St. Helena* ☎ *707/963–1200* ⊕ *www. cindysbackstreetkitchen.com.*

$$
ITALIAN
Fodor'sChoice
★

✕ **Cook St. Helena.** A curved marble bar spotlit by contemporary art-glass pendants adds a touch of style to this downtown restaurant whose Northern Italian cuisine pleases with similarly understated sophistication. Mussels with house-made sausage in a spicy tomato broth, chopped salad with pancetta and pecorino, and the daily changing risotto are among the dishes regulars revere. **Known for:** top-quality ingredients; reasonably priced local and international wines; Cook Tavern two doors down for beer, wine, and cocktail-friendly small plates. $ *Average main: $22* ✉ *1310 Main St., near Hunt Ave., St. Helena* ☎ *707/963–7088* ⊕ *www.cooksthelena.com.*

$$$ ✕ **Farmstead at Long Meadow Ranch.** Housed in a high-ceilinged former
MODERN barn, Farmstead revolves around an open kitchen where executive chef
AMERICAN Stephen Barber's team prepares meals with grass-fed beef and lamb, fruits and vegetables, eggs, olive oil, wine, honey, and other ingredients from parent company Long Meadow Ranch. Entrées might include wood-grilled trout with fennel, brussels sprouts, pears, and hazelnuts, or a pork chop with broccolini, jalapeño grits, and apple chutney. **Known for:** Tuesday fried-chicken night; house-made charcuterie; seasonal cocktails. $ *Average main: $24* ✉ *738 Main St., at Charter Oak Ave., St. Helena* ☎ *707/963–4555* ⊕ *www.longmeadowranch.com/farmstead-restaurant.*

$$$ ✕ **Goose & Gander.** The pairing of food and drink at G&G is as likely to
MODERN involve cool cocktails as wine. Main courses such as grilled sturgeon,
AMERICAN pork loin with sweet-potato hash, and Wagyu beef with Bordelaise
Fodor's Choice sauce work well with starters that might include lamb merguez toast
★ and mushroom soup from wild and cultivated fungi. **Known for:** intimate main dining room with fireplace; alfresco dining on patio in good weather; basement bar among Napa's best drinking spots. $ *Average main: $29* ✉ *1245 Spring St., at Oak St., St. Helena* ☎ *707/967–8779* ⊕ *www.goosegander.com.*

$ ✕ **Gott's Roadside.** A 1950s-style outdoor hamburger stand goes upscale
AMERICAN at this spot whose customers brave long lines to order breakfast sandwiches, juicy burgers, root-beer floats, and garlic fries. Choices not available a half century ago include the ahi tuna burger and the chili-spice-marinated chicken breast served with Mexican slaw. **Known for:** tasty (if pricey) 21st-century diner cuisine; shaded picnic tables (arrive early or late for lunch to get one); second branch at Napa's Oxbow Public Market. $ *Average main: $13* ✉ *933 Main St./Hwy. 29, St. Helena* ☎ *707/963–3486* ⊕ *www.gotts.com* ☞ *Reservations not accepted.*

$$$$ ✕ **Press.** Few taste sensations surpass the combination of a sizzling steak
MODERN and a Napa Valley red, a union the chef and sommeliers at Press cel-
AMERICAN ebrate with a reverence bordering on obsession. Grass-fed beef cooked on the cherry-and-almond-wood-fired grill and rotisserie is the star—especially the rib eye for two—but the cooks also prepare pork chops, free-range chicken, fish, and even vegetarian dishes such as carrot and yellow-eye bean cassoulet. **Known for:** extensive wine cellar; impressive cocktails; casual-chic ambience. $ *Average main: $48* ✉ *587 St. Helena Hwy./Hwy. 29, at White La., St. Helena* ☎ *707/967–0550* ⊕ *www.pressthelena.com* ⊗ *Closed Tues. No lunch.*

$$$$ ✕ **The Restaurant at Meadowood.** Chef Christopher Kostow has garnered
MODERN rave reviews—and three Michelin stars for several years running—for
AMERICAN creating a unique dining experience. Patrons choosing the Tasting Menu
Fodor's Choice option ($275 per person) enjoy their meals in the dining room, its beau-
★ tiful finishes aglow with warm lighting, but up to four guests can select the Counter Menu ($500 per person) for the chance to sit in the kitchen

and watch Kostow's team prepare the food. **Known for:** complex cuisine; first-class service; romantic setting. $ *Average main: $275* ⊠ *900 Meadowood La., off Silverado Trail N, St. Helena* ☎ *707/967–1205, 800/458–8080* ⊕ *www.therestaurantatmeadowood.com* ⊗ *Closed Sun. No lunch* ⊂ *Jacket suggested but not required.*

$$$$

MEDITERRANEAN

Fodor'sChoice

★

✕ **Terra.** In an 1884 fieldstone building, chef Hiro Sone gives an unexpected twist to Italian and southern French cuisine, though for a few dishes, among them the signature sake-marinated black cod in a shiso broth, he draws on his Japanese background. Homey yet elegant desserts, courtesy of Sone's wife, Lissa Doumani, might include a chocolate mousseline with chocolate–peanut butter crunch and toasted marshmallow. **Known for:** prix-fixe menu; old-school romance and service; Bar Terra for cocktails, lighter fare à la carte. $ *Average main: $85* ⊠ *1345 Railroad Ave., off Hunt Ave., St. Helena* ☎ *707/963–8931* ⊕ *www.terrarestaurant.com* ⊗ *Closed Tues. No lunch.*

WHERE TO STAY

$

HOTEL

🛏 **El Bonita Motel.** The tidy rooms at this roadside motel are nice enough for budget-minded travelers, and the landscaped grounds and picnic tables put this property a cut above similar accommodations. **Pros:** cheerful rooms; hot tub; microwaves and mini-refrigerators. **Cons:** road noise is a problem in some rooms. $ *Rooms from: $196* ⊠ *195 Main St./Hwy. 29, St. Helena* ☎ *707/963–3216, 800/541–3284* ⊕ *www.elbonita.com* ⥽ *52 rooms* ⦿ *Breakfast.*

$$$

HOTEL

🛏 **Harvest Inn by Charlie Palmer.** Although this inn sits just off Highway 29, its patrons remain mostly above the fray, strolling 8 acres of landscaped gardens, enjoying views of the vineyards adjoining the property, partaking in spa services, and drifting to sleep in beds adorned with fancy linens and down pillows. **Pros:** garden setting; spacious rooms; well-trained staff. **Cons:** some lower-price rooms lack elegance; high weekend rates. $ *Rooms from: $354* ⊠ *1 Main St., St. Helena* ☎ *707/963–9463, 800/950–8466* ⊕ *www.harvestinn.com* ⥽ *78 rooms* ⦿ *Breakfast.*

$$$$

RESORT

Fodor'sChoice

★

🛏 **Meadowood Napa Valley.** Founded in 1964 as a country club, Meadowood has evolved into a five-star resort, a gathering place for Napa's wine-making community, and a celebrated dining destination. **Pros:** superb restaurant; hiking trails; gracious service; all-organic spa. **Cons:** very expensive; far from downtown St. Helena. $ *Rooms from: $650* ⊠ *900 Meadowood La., St. Helena* ☎ *707/963–3646, 800/458–8080* ⊕ *www.meadowood.com* ⥽ *85 rooms* ⦿ *No meals.*

20

CALISTOGA

3 miles northwest of St. Helena.

With false-fronted, Old West–style shops and 19th-century inns and hotels lining its main drag, Lincoln Avenue, Calistoga comes across as more down-to-earth than its more polished neighbors. Don't be fooled, though. On its outskirts lie some of the Wine Country's swankest (and priciest) resorts and its most fanciful piece of architecture, the medieval-style Castello di Amorosa winery.

Calistoga was developed as a spa-oriented getaway from the start. Sam Brannan, a gold rush–era entrepreneur, planned to use the area's natural hot springs as the centerpiece of a resort complex. His venture failed, but old-time hotels and bathhouses—along with some glorious new spas—still operate. You can come for an old-school mud bath, or go completely 21st century and experience lavish treatments based on the latest innovations in skin and body care.

GETTING HERE AND AROUND

Highway 29 heads east (turn right) at Calistoga, where in town it is signed as Lincoln Avenue. If arriving via the Silverado Trail, head west at Highway 29/Lincoln Avenue.

EXPLORING

TOP ATTRACTIONS

Ca' Toga Galleria d'Arte. The boundless wit, whimsy, and creativity of the Venetian-born Carlo Marchiori, this gallery's owner-artist, finds expression in paintings, watercolors, ceramics, sculptures, and other artworks. Marchiori often draws on mythology and folktales for his inspiration. A stop at this magical gallery may inspire you to tour **Villa Ca' Toga,** the artist's fanciful Palladian home, a tromp-l'oeil tour de force open for tours from May through October on Saturday mornings only, by appointment. ✉ *1206 Cedar St., near Lincoln Ave., Calistoga* ☎ *707/942–3900* ⊕ *www.catoga.com* ⊘ *Closed Tues. and Wed.*

Fodor's Choice   **Schramsberg.** On a Diamond Mountain site first planted to grapes
★   in the early 1860s, Schramsberg produces sparkling wines using the *méthode traditionnelle* (aka *méthode champenoise*). A fascinating tour covering Schramberg's history and wine-making techniques precedes the tasting. In addition to glimpsing the winery's historic architecture you'll visit caves, some dug in the 1870s by Chinese laborers, where 2 million–plus bottles are stacked in gravity-defying configurations. Tastings include generous pours of very different bubblies. To learn more about them, consider attending the session at which the wines are paired with cheeses; not held every day, this tasting focuses on the ways wine influences our experience of food and vice versa. All visits here are by appointment. ✉ *1400 Schramsberg Rd., off Hwy. 29, Calistoga* ☎ *707/942–4558, 800/877–3623* ⊕ *www.schramsberg. com* ✍ *Tastings and tours $65–$120.*

Fodor's Choice   **Venge Vineyards.** As the son of Nils Venge, the first winemaker to earn
★   a 100-point score from the wine critic Robert Parker, Kirk Venge had a hard act to follow. Now a consultant to exclusive wineries himself, Kirk is an acknowledged master of balanced, fruit-forward Bordeaux-style blends. At his casual ranch-house tasting room you can sip wines that might include the estate Bone Ash Cabernet Sauvignon, an Oakville Merlot, a Syrah from the Stagecoach Vineyard in the Vaca hills, and the Silencieux Cabernet, a blend of grapes from several appellations. Tastings are by appointment only. ■TIP➔ With its views of the well-manicured Bone Ash Vineyard and, west across the valley, Diamond Mountain, the ranch house's porch would make for a magical perch even if Venge's wines weren't works of art in themselves. ✉ *4708 Silverado Trail, 1½ miles south of downtown, near Dunaweal La., Calistoga* ☎ *707/942–9100* ⊕ *www.vengevineyards.com* ✍ *Tasting $25* ⊘ *Reservations recommended 3–4 wks in advance for weekend visits.*

WORTH NOTING

Castello di Amorosa. An astounding medieval structure complete with drawbridge and moat, chapel, stables, and secret passageways, the Castello commands Diamond Mountain's lower eastern slope. Some of the 107 rooms contain replicas of 13th-century frescoes (cheekily signed, "[the-artist's-name].com"), and the dungeon has an iron maiden from Nuremberg, Germany. You must pay for a tour to see most of Dario Sattui's extensive eight-level property, though with a basic tasting you'll have access to part of the complex. Bottlings of note include several Italian-style wines, including La Castellana, a robust "super Tuscan" blend of Cabernet Sauvignon, Sangiovese, and Merlot; and Il Barone, a deliberately big Cab made largely from Rutherford grapes. ■ TIP→ The two-hour Royal Food & Wine Pairing Tour by sommelier Mary Davidek ($85, by appointment only) is among the Wine Country's best. ⊠ 4045 N. St. Helena Hwy./Hwy. 29, near Maple La., Calistoga ☎ 707/967–6272 ⊕ www.castellodiamorosa.com 🖪 Tastings $25–$35, tours $40–$85 (include tastings).

Chateau Montelena. Set amid a bucolic northern Calistoga landscape, this winery helped establish the Napa Valley's reputation for high-quality wine making. At the pivotal Paris tasting of 1976, the Chateau Montelena 1973 Chardonnay took first place, beating out four white Burgundies from France and five other California Chardonnays, an event immortalized in the 2008 movie *Bottle Shock*. A 21st-century Napa Valley Chardonnay is always part of a Current Release Tasting ($25)—the winery also makes Sauvignon Blanc, Riesling, a fine estate Zinfandel, and Cabernet Sauvignon—or you can opt for a Limited Release Tasting ($50) focusing more on Cabernets. The walking Estate Tour takes in the grounds and covers the history of this stately property whose stone winery building was erected in 1888. Guests board a vehicle for the seasonal Vineyard Tour. Tours and some tastings require a reservation. ⊠ 1429 Tubbs La., off Hwy. 29, Calistoga ☎ 707/942–5105 ⊕ www.montelena.com 🖪 Tastings $25–$75, tours $40–$78.

Tamber Bey Vineyards. Endurance riders Barry and Jennifer Waitte share their passion for horses and wine at their glam-rustic winery north of Calistoga. Their 22-acre Sundance Ranch remains a working equestrian facility, but the site has been revamped to include a state-of-the-art winery with separate fermenting tanks for grapes from Tamber Bey's vineyards in Yountville, Oakville, and elsewhere. The winemakers produce three Chardonnays and a Sauvignon Blanc, but the stars are several subtly powerful reds, including the flagship Oakville Cabernet Sauvignon and a Yountville Merlot. A recent vintage of the top-selling wine, the Rabicano blend, contained Cabernet Sauvignon, Merlot, Petit Verdot, and Cabernet Franc. Visits to taste or tour require an appointment. ⊠ 1251 Tubbs La., at Myrtledale Rd., Calistoga ☎ 707/942–2100 ⊕ www.tamberbey.com 🖪 Tastings $35–$65, tour $10 extra.

20

WHERE TO EAT

$$$ ✕**Evangeline.** Brandon Sharp, formerly of nearby Solbar, opened this
MODERN restaurant whose gas-lamp-style lighting fixtures, charcoal-black hues,
AMERICAN and bistro cuisine evoke old New Orleans with a California twist.
Fodor'sChoice Executive chef Gustavo Rios puts a jaunty spin on dishes that might
★ include shrimp étouffée or grilled salmon with a chicory salad; the
elaborate weekend brunch, with everything from buttermilk waffles to
shrimp po'boys, is an up-valley favorite. **Known for:** outdoor courtyard;
palate-cleansing Sazeracs and signature old-fashioneds; gumbo ya-ya
and addictive fried pickles. $ *Average main: $24* ⊠ *1226 Washington
St., near Lincoln Ave., Calistoga* ☎ *707/341–3131* ⊕ *www.evangelin-
enapa.com* ☺ *No lunch weekdays.*

$$ ✕**Sam's Social Club.** Tourists, locals, and spa guests—some of the latter
MODERN in bathrobes after treatments—assemble at this resort restaurant for
AMERICAN breakfast, lunch, bar snacks, or dinner. Lunch options include pizzas,
sandwiches, an aged-cheddar burger, and entrées such as chicken pail-
lard, with the burger reappearing for dinner along with grilled salmon,
rib-eye steak frites, and similar fare, perhaps preceded by oysters and
other cocktail-friendly starters. **Known for:** casual atmosphere; active
patio scene; thin-crust lunch pizzas. $ *Average main: $22* ⊠ *Indian
Springs Resort and Spa, 1712 Lincoln Ave., at Wappo Ave., Calistoga*
☎ *707/942–4969* ⊕ *www.samssocialclub.com.*

$$$$ ✕**Solbar.** As befits a restaurant at a spa resort, the sophisticated menu
MODERN at Solbar is divided into "healthy, lighter dishes" and "hearty cuisine,"
AMERICAN with the stellar wine list's many half-bottle selections encouraging mod-
Fodor'sChoice eration, too. On the lighter side, grilled yellowfin tuna might come
★ with charred carrots, mole amarillo, and toasted pumpkin seeds, with
heartier options recently including a wood-grilled pork tenderloin with
jasmine rice, chili-laced cashews, and mustard greens. **Known for:** stylish dining room; festive outdoor patio; Sunday brunch. $ *Average main:
$33* ⊠ *Solage Calistoga, 755 Silverado Trail, at Rosedale Rd., Calistoga*
☎ *877/684–9146* ⊕ *www.solagecalistoga.com/solbar.*

WHERE TO STAY

$$$$ ▦ **Calistoga Ranch.** Spacious cedar-shingle lodges throughout this posh
RESORT wooded property have outdoor living areas, and even the restaurant,
Fodor'sChoice spa, and reception space have outdoor seating and fireplaces. **Pros:**
★ many lodges have private hot tubs on the deck; lovely hiking trails on
the property; guests have reciprocal privileges at Auberge du Soleil and
Solage Calistoga. **Cons:** innovative indoor-outdoor organization works
better in fine weather than in rain or cold. $ *Rooms from: $895* ⊠ *580
Lommel Rd., Calistoga* ☎ *707/254–2800, 855/942–4220* ⊕ *www.cal-
istogaranch.com* ⤳ *50 guest lodges* ❍l *No meals.*

$$ ▦ **Embrace Calistoga.** Extravagant hospitality defines the Napa Valley's
B&B/INN luxury properties, but Embrace Calistoga—the renamed Luxe Calistoga
Fodor'sChoice still run by the same attentive owners—takes the prize in the "small
★ lodging" category. **Pros:** attentive owners; marvelous breakfasts; res-
taurants, tasting rooms, and shopping within walking distance. **Cons:**
the hum of street traffic. $ *Rooms from: $269* ⊠ *1139 Lincoln Ave.,
Calistoga* ☎ *707/942–9797* ⤳ *5 rooms* ❍l *Breakfast.*

$$
RESORT

[hotel] **Indian Springs Resort and Spa.** Stylish Indian Springs—operating as a spa since 1862—ably splits the difference between laid-back and chic in accommodations that include lodge rooms, dozens of suites, 14 duplex cottages, three stand-alone bungalows, and two houses. **Pros:** palm-studded grounds with outdoor seating areas; on-site Sam's Social Club restaurant; enormous mineral pool. **Cons:** lodge rooms are small. [$] *Rooms from: $239* ✉ *1712 Lincoln Ave., Calistoga* ☎ *707/942–4913* 🌐 *www.indianspringscalistoga.com* 🛏 *113 rooms* 🍴 *No meals.*

$$$$
RESORT
Fodor's Choice ★

[hotel] **Solage Calistoga.** The aesthetic at this 22-acre property is Napa Valley barn meets San Francisco loft: guest rooms have high ceilings, polished concrete floors, recycled walnut furniture, and all-natural fabrics in soothingly muted colors. **Pros:** great service; complimentary bikes; separate pools for kids and adults. **Cons:** vibe may not suit everyone. [$] *Rooms from: $530* ✉ *755 Silverado Trail, Calistoga* ☎ *855/942–7442, 707/226–0800* 🌐 *www.solagecalistoga.com* 🛏 *89 rooms* 🍴 *No meals.*

SPAS

Fodor's Choice ★

Spa Solage. This eco-conscious spa has reinvented the traditional Calistoga mud and mineral-water therapies. Case in point: the hour-long "Mudslide," a three-part treatment that includes a mud body mask (in a heated lounge), a soak in a thermal bath, and a power nap in a sound-vibration chair. The mud here is a mix of clay, volcanic ash, and essential oils. Traditional spa services—combination Shiatsu-Swedish and other massages, full-body exfoliations, facials, and waxes—are available, as are fitness and yoga classes. ✉ *755 Silverado Trail, at Rosedale Rd., Calistoga* ☎ *707/226–0825, 855/790–6023* 🌐 *www.solagecalistoga.com/spa* 💆 *Treatments $110–$510.*

SPORTS AND THE OUTDOORS

Calistoga Bikeshop. Options here include regular and fancy bikes that rent for $28 and up for two hours, and there's a self-guided Cool Wine Tour ($110) that includes tastings at three or four small wineries. ✉ *1318 Lincoln Ave., near Washington St., Calistoga* ☎ *707/942–9687* 🌐 *www.calistogabikeshop.net.*

THE SONOMA VALLEY

The birthplace of modern California wine making—Count Aragon Haraszthy opened Buena Vista Winery here in 1857—Sonoma Valley seduces with its unpretentious attitude and pastoral landscape. Tasting rooms, restaurants, and historical sites, among the latter the last mission established in California by Franciscan friars, abound near Sonoma Plaza. Beyond downtown Sonoma, the wineries and attractions are spread out along gently winding roads. Sonoma County's half of the Carneros District lies within Sonoma Valley, whose other towns of note include Glen Ellen and Kenwood. Sonoma Valley tasting rooms are often less crowded than those in Napa or northern Sonoma County, especially midweek, and the vibe here, though sophisticated, is definitely less sceney.

All it needs is a fair maiden: Castello di Amorosa's re-created castle.

SONOMA

14 miles west of Napa, 45 miles northeast of San Francisco.

One of the few towns in the valley with multiple attractions not related to food and wine, Sonoma has plenty to keep you busy for a couple of hours before you head out to tour the wineries. And you needn't leave town to taste wine. There are about three dozen tasting rooms within steps of the tree-filled Sonoma plaza, some of which pour wines from more than one winery. The valley's cultural center, Sonoma was founded in 1835 when California was still part of Mexico.

GETTING HERE AND AROUND

Highway 12 (signed as Broadway near Sonoma Plaza) heads north into Sonoma from Highway 121 and south from Santa Rosa into downtown Sonoma, where (signed as West Spain Street) it travels east to the plaza. Parking is relatively easy to find on or near the plaza, and you can walk to many restaurants, shops, and tasting rooms. Signs point the way to several wineries a mile or more east of the plaza.

EXPLORING

TOP ATTRACTIONS

Gundlach Bundschu. "Gun lock bun shoe" gets you close to pronouncing this winery's name correctly, though everyone here shortens it to Gun Bun. The Bundschu family, which has owned most of this property since 1858, makes reds that include Cabernet Franc, Cabernet Sauvignon, Merlot, and a Bordeaux-style blend of each vintage's best grapes. Gewürztraminer, Chardonnay, and two rosés are also in the mix. Parts of the 1870 stone winery where standard tastings

($20) unfold are still used for wine making. For a more comprehensive experience, book a cave tour ($40), a Pinzgauer vehicle vineyard tour ($60), or a Heritage Reserve ($85) pairing of limited-release wines with small gourmet bites. Some tastings and all tours are by appointment only. ■TIP→ On some summer days you can enjoy the outdoor Vista Courtyard's broad vineyard views while tasting wines paired with cheese and charcuterie ($30). ⊠ *2000 Denmark St., at Bundschu Rd., off 8th St. E, 3 miles southeast of Sonoma Plaza, Sonoma* ☎ *707/938–5277* ⊕ *www.gunbun.com* ⊑ *Tastings $20–$30, tours $40–$85 (include tastings).*

Fodor's Choice ★ **Patz & Hall.** Sophisticated single-vineyard Chardonnays and Pinot Noirs are the trademark of this respected winery whose tastings take place in a fashionable single-story residence 3 miles southeast of Sonoma Plaza. It's a Wine Country adage that great wines are made in the vineyard—the all-star fields represented here include Hyde, Durell, and Gap's Crown—but winemaker James Hall routinely surpasses peers with access to the same fruit, proof that discernment and expertise (Hall is a master at oak aging) play a role, too. You can sample wines at the bar and on some days on the vineyard-view terrace beyond it, but to learn how food friendly these wines are, consider the Salon Tasting, at which they're paired with gourmet bites crafted with equal finesse. Tastings are by appointment only. ⊠ *21200 8th St. E, near Peru Rd., Sonoma* ☎ *707/265–7700* ⊕ *www.patzhall.com* ⊑ *Tastings $30–$60.*

Ram's Gate Winery. Stunning views, ultrachic architecture, and wines made from grapes grown by acclaimed producers make a visit to Ram's Gate an event. The welcoming interior spaces—think Restoration Hardware with a dash of high-style whimsy—open up to the entire western Carneros. In fine weather you'll experience the cooling breezes that sweep through the area while sipping sophisticated wines, mostly Pinot Noirs and Chardonnays, but also Pinot Blanc, Sauvignon Blanc, Cabernet Sauvignon, and Syrah. With grapes sourced from the Sangiacomo, Hudson, and other illustrious vineyards, winemaker Jeff Gaffner focuses on creating balanced wines that express what occurred in nature that year. All visits are by appointment only. ■TIP→ You can sip current releases at the tasting bar ($40), take a tour-and-taste ($65), or tour and enjoy wines paired with food ($90). ⊠ *28700 Arnold Dr./Hwy. 121, Sonoma* ☎ *707/721–8700* ⊕ *www. ramsgatewinery.com* ⊑ *Tastings $40–$90; tour $65 (includes tasting)* ⊙ *Closed Tues. and Wed.*

20

Fodor's Choice ★ **Scribe.** Andrew and Adam Mariani, sons of California walnut growers, established Scribe in 2007 on land first planted to grapes in 1858 by Emil Dresel, a German immigrant. Dresel's claims to fame include cultivating Sonoma's first Riesling and Sylvaner, an achievement the brothers honor by growing both varietals on land he once farmed. Using natural winemaking techniques they craft bright, terroir-driven wines from those grapes, along with Chardonnay, Pinot Noir, Syrah, and Cabernet Sauvignon. In restoring their property's 1915 Mission Revival–style hacienda the brothers preserved various layers of history—original molding and light fixtures, for instance, but also fragments of floral-print wallpaper

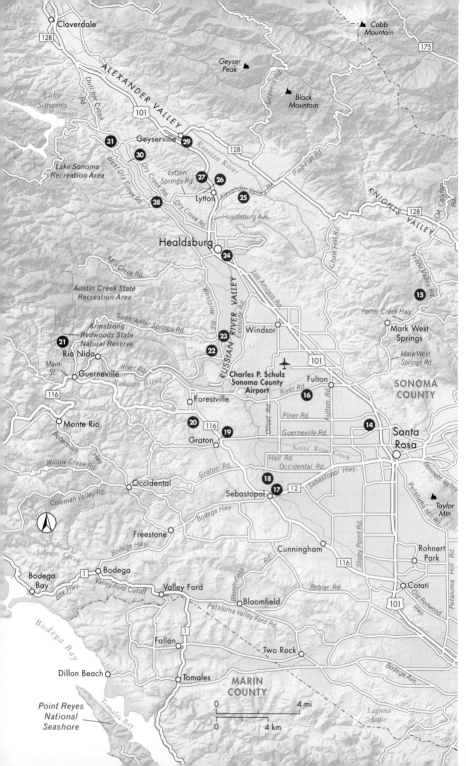

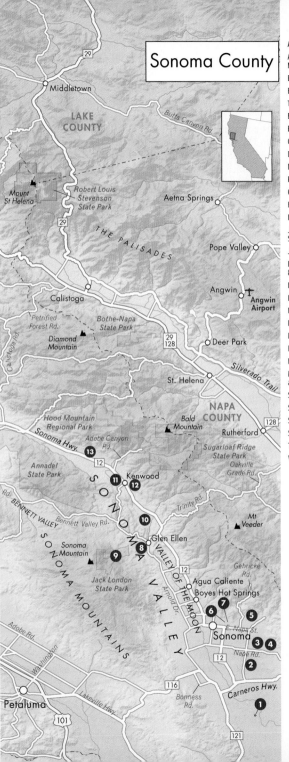

Sonoma County

and 1950s newspapers. Now a tasting space, the hacienda served during Prohibition as a bootleggers' hideout, and its basement harbored a speakeasy: two intriguing tales among many associated with this historic site. Tastings are by appointment only. ⊠ *2100 Denmark St., off Napa Rd., Sonoma* ☎ *707/939–1858* ⊕ *scribewinery.com* ⊠ *Tasting price varies; contact winery.*

Sonoma Mission. The northernmost of the 21 missions established by Franciscan friars in California, Sonoma Mission was founded in 1823 as Mission San Francisco Solano. It serves as the centerpiece of **Sonoma State Historic Park,** which includes several other sites in Sonoma and nearby Petaluma. Some early mission structures were destroyed, but all or part of several remaining buildings date to the days of Mexican rule over California. Worth a look are the **Sonoma Barracks,** a half block west of the mission at 20 East Spain Street, which housed troops under the command of General Mariano Guadalupe Vallejo, who controlled vast tracts of land in the region. **General Vallejo's Home,** a Victorian-era structure, is a few blocks west. ⊠ *114 E. Spain St., at 1st St. E, Sonoma* ☎ *707/938–9560* ⊕ *www.parks.ca.gov/?page_id=479* ⊠ *$3, includes same-day admission to other historic sites.*

Fodor's Choice   **Walt Wines.** You could spend a full day sampling wines in the tast-
★   ing rooms bordering or near Sonoma Plaza, but be sure not to miss Walt, which specializes in Pinot Noir from Sonoma County, Mendocino County (just to the north), California's Central Coast, and Oregon's Willamette Valley. Walk-ins are welcome to taste several wines inside a mid-1930s Tudor-inspired home or, weather permitting, at backyard tables beneath a tall, double-trunk redwood tree. To see how winemaker Megan Gunderson Paredes's wines pair with food—in this case small bites from The Girl & the Fig across the street—make a reservation for the Root 101: A Single Vineyard Exploration. At both tastings you'll learn about the origins of this sister winery to Hall St. Helena. ⊠ *380 1st St. W, at W. Spain St., Sonoma* ☎ *707/933–4440* ⊕ *www.waltwines. com* ⊠ *Tastings $30–$60.*

WORTH NOTING
Buena Vista Winery. The birthplace of modern California wine making has been transformed into an entertaining homage to the accomplishments of the 19th-century wine pioneer Count Agoston Haraszthy. Tours pass through the original aging caves dug deep into the hillside by Chinese laborers, and banners, photos, and artifacts inside and out convey the history made on this site. Reserve tastings ($40) include library and current releases, plus barrel samples. The rehabilitated former press house (used for pressing grapes into wine), which dates to 1862, hosts the standard tastings. Chardonnay, Pinot Noir, several red blends, and a vibrant Petit Verdot are the strong suits here. Tours are by appointment only. ■ TIP→ The high-tech Historic Wine Tool Museum displays implements, some decidedly low-tech, used to make wine over the years. ⊠ *18000 Old Winery Rd., off E. Napa St., Sonoma* ☎ *800/926–1266* ⊕ *www.buenavistawinery.com* ⊠ *Tastings $20–$50, tours $25–$40.*

WHERE TO EAT

$$$ ✕ **Cafe La Haye.** The dining room is compact, the open kitchen even
AMERICAN more so, but chef Jeffrey Lloyd turns out understated, sophisticated fare
Fodor'sChoice emphasizing local ingredients. Chicken, beef, pasta, and fish get deluxe
★ treatment without fuss or fanfare—the daily roasted chicken and the
risotto specials are always good. **Known for:** Napa-Sonoma wine list
with clever French complements; signature butterscotch pudding dessert; owner Saul Gropman on hand to greet diners. $ *Average main:*
$24 ✉ *140 E. Napa St., at 1st St. E, Sonoma* ☎ *707/935–5994* ⊕ *www.*
cafelahaye.com ⊗ *Closed Sun. and Mon. No lunch.*

$$$ ✕ **El Dorado Kitchen.** This restaurant owes its visual appeal to its clean
MODERN lines and handsome decor, but the eye inevitably drifts westward to the
AMERICAN open kitchen, where executive chef Armando Navarro's crew crafts
dishes full of subtle surprises. The menu might include ahi tuna tartare
with wasabi tobiko caviar as a starter, with paella awash with seafood
and dry-cured Spanish chorizo sausage among the entrées. **Known**
for: subtle tastes and textures; truffle-oil fries with Parmesan; spiced
crepes and other desserts. $ *Average main: $26* ✉ *El Dorado Hotel,*
405 1st St. W, at W. Spain St., Sonoma ☎ *707/996–3030* ⊕ *www.*
eldoradosonoma.com/restaurant.

$$$ ✕ **The Girl & the Fig.** At this hot spot for inventive French cooking inside
FRENCH the historic Sonoma Hotel bar you can always find a dish with owner
Fodor'sChoice Sondra Bernstein's signature figs on the menu, whether it's a fig-and-
★ arugula salad or an aperitif blending sparkling wine with fig liqueur.
Also look for duck confit, a burger with matchstick fries, and wild
flounder meunière. **Known for:** wine list emphasis on Rhône varietals;
artisanal cheese platters; croques monsieurs and eggs Benedict at Sunday brunch. $ *Average main: $24* ✉ *Sonoma Hotel, 110 W. Spain St.,*
at 1st St. W, Sonoma ☎ *707/938–3634* ⊕ *www.thegirlandthefig.com.*

$$$ ✕ **Harvest Moon Cafe.** Everything at this little restaurant with an odd,
AMERICAN zigzag layout is so perfectly executed and the vibe is so genuinely warm
Fodor'sChoice that a visit here is deeply satisfying. The ever-changing menu might
★ include homey dishes such as grilled half chicken with baked polenta
or pan-seared Hawaiian ono with jasmine rice and eggplant. **Known**
for: friendly service; back patio with central fountain. $ *Average main:*
$25 ✉ *487 1st St. W, at W. Napa St., Sonoma* ☎ *707/933–8160* ⊕ *www.*
harvestmooncafesonoma.com ⊗ *Closed Tues. No lunch.*

$$$$ ✕ **LaSalette Restaurant.** Born in the Azores and raised in Sonoma, chef-
PORTUGUESE owner Manuel Azevedo serves three- and five-course prix-fixe meals
Fodor'sChoice inspired by his native Portugal. The wood-oven-roasted fish is always
★ worth trying, and there are usually boldly flavored lamb and pork
dishes, along with soups, stews, salted cod, and other hearty fare.
Known for: authentic Portuguese cuisine; sophisticated spicing; olive-
oil cake with queijo fresco (fresh cheese) ice cream. $ *Average main:*
$55 ✉ *452 1st St. E, near E. Spain St., Sonoma* ☎ *707/938–1927*
⊕ *www.lasalette-restaurant.com.*

$$$$ ✕ **Oso Sonoma.** Chef David Bush, who achieved national recognition
MODERN for his food pairings at St. Francis Winery, owns this barlike small-
AMERICAN plates restaurant whose menu evolves throughout the day. Lunch
might see mole braised pork-shoulder tacos or an achiote chicken

20

sandwich, with dinner fare perhaps of steamed mussels, harissa roasted salmon, or roasted forest mushrooms with baby spinach and polenta. **Known for:** bar menu between lunch and dinner; Korean soju cocktails; decor of reclaimed materials. $ *Average main: $32* ⊠ *9 E. Napa St., at Broadway, Sonoma* ☎ *707/931–6926* ⊕ *www.ososonoma. com* ☾ *No lunch Mon.–Wed.*

$ ✕ **Sunflower Caffé.** Cheerful art and brightly painted walls set a jolly
AMERICAN tone at this casual eatery whose assets include sidewalk seating with Sonoma Plaza views and the verdant patio out back. Omelets and waffles are the hits at breakfast, with the smoked duck breast sandwich, served on a baguette and slathered with caramelized onions, a favorite for lunch. **Known for:** combination café, gallery, and wine bar; local cheeses and hearty soups; free Wi-Fi. $ *Average main: $13* ⊠ *421 1st St. W, at W. Spain St., Sonoma* ☎ *707/996–6645* ⊕ *www. sonomasunflower.com* ☾ *No dinner.*

WHERE TO STAY

$$ ⛳ **Inn at Sonoma.** They don't skimp on the little luxuries here: wine and
B&B/INN hors d'oeuvres are served every evening in the lobby, and the cheerfully painted rooms are warmed by gas fireplaces. **Pros:** last-minute specials are a great deal; free soda available in the lobby. **Cons:** on a busy street rather than right on the plaza. $ *Rooms from: $220* ⊠ *630 Broadway, Sonoma* ☎ *707/939–1340, 888/568–9818* ⊕ *www.innatsonoma.com* ⟿ *27 rooms* ❏ *Breakfast.*

$$$ ⛳ **MacArthur Place Hotel & Spa.** Guests at this 7-acre boutique prop-
HOTEL erty five blocks south of Sonoma Plaza bask in ritzy seclusion in plush
Fodor'sChoice accommodations set amid landscaped gardens. **Pros:** secluded garden
★ setting; high-style furnishings; on-site steak house. **Cons:** a bit of a walk from the plaza; some traffic noise audible in street-side rooms. $ *Rooms from: $399* ⊠ *29 E. MacArthur St., Sonoma* ☎ *707/938–2929, 800/722–1866* ⊕ *www.macarthurplace.com* ⟿ *64 rooms* ❏ *Breakfast.*

$ ⛳ **Sonoma Creek Inn.** The small but cheerful rooms at this motel-style inn
B&B/INN are individually decorated with painted wooden armoires, cozy quilts,
FAMILY and brightly colored contemporary artwork. **Pros:** clean, well-lighted bathrooms; lots of charm for the price; popular with bicyclists. **Cons:** office not staffed 24 hours a day; a 10-minute drive from Sonoma Plaza. $ *Rooms from: $145* ⊠ *239 Boyes Blvd., off Hwy. 12, Sonoma* ☎ *707/939–9463, 888/712–1289* ⊕ *www.sonomacreekinn.com* ⟿ *16 rooms* ❏ *No meals.*

SPAS

Willow Stream Spa at Fairmont Sonoma Mission Inn & Spa. With 40,000 square feet and 30 treatment rooms, the Wine Country's largest spa provides every amenity you could possibly want, including pools and hot tubs fed by local thermal springs. Although the place fills with patrons in summer and on some weekends, the vibe is always soothing. The signature bathing ritual includes an exfoliating shower, dips in two mineral-water soaking pools, an herbal steam, and a dry-salt sauna and rain tunnel. The regime draws to a close with cool-down showers. Other popular treatments involve alkaline baths, aloe-gel wraps, and massages in styles from Swedish to Thai. For a touch of the exotic designed to leave your skin luminous, try a caviar facial. The most requested room among couples is outfitted with a two-person copper bathtub. ⊠ *100 Boyes Blvd./Hwy. 12, 2½ miles north of Sonoma Plaza, Sonoma* ☎ *707/938–9000* ⊕ *www.fairmont.com/sonoma/willow-stream* ⊑ *Treatments $65–$528.*

SHOPPING

Sonoma Plaza is a shopping magnet, with tempting boutiques and specialty food purveyors facing the square or within a block or two.

G's General Store. The inventory of this "modern general store" runs the gamut from cute bunny LED nightlights and Euro-suave kitchen utensils to bright-print shirts and a log-and-leather sofa fit for a ski chalet. The owner used to buy for Smith & Hawken and Williams-Sonoma, so expect upscale merch presented with style. ⊠ *19 W. Napa St., near Broadway, Sonoma* ☎ *707/933–8082* ⊕ *www.ggeneralstore.com.*

Fodor'sChoice ★ **Sonoma Valley Certified Farmers Market.** To discover just how bountiful the Sonoma landscape is—and how talented its farmers and food artisans are—head to Depot Park, just north of the Sonoma Plaza, on Friday morning. This market is considered Sonoma County's best. ⊠ *Depot Park, 1st St. W, at the Sonoma Bike Path, Sonoma* ☎ *707/538–7023* ⊕ *www.svcfm.org.*

GLEN ELLEN

7 miles north of Sonoma.

Unlike its flashier Napa Valley counterparts, Glen Ellen eschews well-groomed sidewalks lined with upscale boutiques and restaurants, preferring instead its crooked streets, some with no sidewalks at all, shaded with stands of old oak trees. Jack London, who represents Glen Ellen's rugged spirit, lived in the area for many years; the town commemorates him with place names and nostalgic establishments. Hidden among sometimes-ramshackle buildings abutting Sonoma and Calabasas creeks are low-key shops and galleries worth poking through, and several fine dining establishments.

GETTING HERE AND AROUND

Glen Ellen sits just off Highway 12. From the north or south, take Arnold Drive west and follow it south less than a mile. The walkable downtown straddles a half-mile stretch of Arnold Drive.

20

EXPLORING

Fodor'sChoice ★ **Benziger Family Winery.** One of the best-known Sonoma County wineries sits on a sprawling estate in a bowl with 360-degree sun exposure, the benefits of which are explored on tram tours that depart several times daily. Guides explain Benziger's biodynamic farming practices and provide a glimpse of the extensive cave system. The regular tram tour costs $25; another tour costing $50 concludes with a seated tasting. Known for Chardonnay, Cabernet Sauvignon, Merlot, Pinot Noir, and Sauvignon Blanc, the winery is a beautiful spot for a picnic. ■ TIP➔ Reserve a seat on the tram tour through the winery's website or arrive early in the day on summer weekends and during harvest season. ⊠ *1883 London Ranch Rd., off Arnold Dr., Glen Ellen* ☎ *707/935–3000, 888/490–2739* ⊕ *www.benziger.com* ⊑ *Tastings $20–$40, tours $25–$50.*

Fodor's Choice
★
Jack London State Historic Park. The pleasures are pastoral and intellectual at author Jack London's beloved Beauty Ranch. You could easily spend the afternoon hiking some of the 30-plus miles of trails that loop through meadows and stands of oaks, redwoods, and other trees. Manuscripts and personal artifacts depicting London's travels are on view at the House of Happy Walls Museum, which provides an overview of the writer's life and literary passions. A short hike away lie the ruins of Wolf House, which burned down just before London was to move in. Also open to visitors are a few outbuildings and the restored Cottage, a wood-framed building where he penned many of his later works. He's buried on the property. ■TIP→ **Well-known performers headline the park's Broadway Under the Stars series, a hot ticket in summer.** ⊠ *2400 London Ranch Rd., off Arnold Dr., Glen Ellen* ☎ *707/938–5216* ⊕ *www.jacklondonpark.com* ⊠ *Parking $10 ($5 walk-in or bike), includes admission to museum; cottage $4.*

Fodor's Choice
★
Lasseter Family Winery. Immaculately groomed grapevines dazzle the eye at John and Nancy Lasseter's secluded winery, and it's no accident: Phil Coturri, Sonoma Valley's premier organic and biodynamic vineyard manager, tends them. Even the landscaping, which includes an insectary to attract beneficial bugs, is meticulously maintained. Come harvesttime, winemaker Julia Lantosca oversees gentle processes that transform the fruit into wines of purity and grace: a Semillon–Sauvignon Blanc blend, two rosés, and Bordeaux and Rhône reds. As might be expected of a storyteller as accomplished as John, whose screenwriting credits include *Toy Story, Cars,* and other Pixar features, evocative labels illustrate the tale behind each wine. These stories are well told on tours that precede tastings of wines, paired with local artisanal cheeses, in an elegant room whose east-facing window frames vineyard and Mayacamas Mountains views. All visits are by appointment only. ⊠ *1 Vintage La., off Dunbar Rd., Glen Ellen* ☎ *707/933–2814* ⊕ *www.lasseterfamilywinery.com* ⊠ *Tastings (some with tours) $25–$45.*

WHERE TO EAT

$$
ITALIAN
Fodor's Choice
★
✕ **Aventine Glen Ellen.** A Wine Country cousin to chef Adolfo Veronese's same-named San Francisco and Hollywood establishments, this Italian restaurant occupies an 1839 sawmill from California's Mexican period. Veronese's varied menu includes several pizzas (the seasonal one with black truffle honey, béchamel, and wild arugula is a savory masterpiece), an equal number of pasta dishes, a daily risotto, and several meat and fish entrées. **Known for:** chicken parmigiana the envy of local Sicilian grandmothers; outdoor patio overlooking Sonoma Creek. Ⓢ *Average main: $20* ⊠ *Jack London Village, 14301 Arnold Dr., ¾ mile south of downtown, Glen Ellen* ☎ *707/934–8911* ⊕ *www.aventinehospitality.com/glen-ellen* ⊘ *Closed Mon. and Tues.*

$$
FRENCH
✕ **The Fig Cafe.** The compact menu at this cheerful bistro, a Glen Ellen fixture, focuses on California and French comfort food—pot roast and duck confit, for instance, as well as thin-crust pizza. Steamed mussels are served with crispy fries, which also accompany the sirloin burger, and weekend brunch brings out locals and tourists for French toast, corned-beef hash, and pizza with applewood-smoked bacon and poached eggs. **Known for:** casual ambience; no corkage fee, so good

for enjoying your winery discoveries. $\boxed{\$}$ *Average main: $18* ⊠ *13690 Arnold Dr., at O'Donnell La., Glen Ellen* ☏ *707/938–2130* ⊕ *www. thefigcafe.com* ⊘ *No lunch weekdays.*

$$$ ✕ **Glen Ellen Star.** Chef Ari Weiswasser honed his craft at The French
ECLECTIC   Laundry, Daniel, and other bastions of culinary finesse, but at his Wine
Fodor's Choice   Country boîte he prepares haute-rustic cuisine, much of it emerging
★   from a wood-fired oven that burns a steady 600°F. Crisp-crusted, richly
sauced Margherita and other pizzas thrive in the torrid heat, as do
tender whole fish entrées and vegetables roasted in small iron skillets.
Known for: kitchen-view counter for watching chefs cook; enclosed
patio; Weiswasser's sauces, emulsions, and spices. $\boxed{\$}$ *Average main: $28*
⊠ *13648 Arnold Dr., at Warm Springs Rd., Glen Ellen* ☏ *707/343–
1384* ⊕ *glenellenstar.com* ⊘ *No lunch.*

WHERE TO STAY

$$ ⊡ **Gaige House.** Asian objets d'art and leather club chairs cozied up to
B&B/INN   the lobby fireplace are just a few of the graceful touches in this luxuri-
Fodor's Choice   ous but understated bed-and-breakfast. **Pros:** beautiful lounge areas;
★   lots of privacy; excellent service; full breakfasts, afternoon wine and
appetizers. **Cons:** sound carries in the main house; the least expensive
rooms are on the small side. $\boxed{\$}$ *Rooms from: $275* ⊠ *13540 Arnold
Dr., Glen Ellen* ☏ *707/935–0237, 800/935–0237* ⊕ *www.gaige.com*
⟿ *23 rooms* ⏀ *Breakfast.*

$$ ⊡ **Olea Hotel.** The husband-and-wife team of Ashish and Sia Patel oper-
B&B/INN   ate this boutique lodging that's at once sophisticated and down-home
Fodor's Choice   country casual. **Pros:** beautiful style; welcoming staff; chef-prepared
★   breakfasts; complimentary wine throughout stay. **Cons:** fills up quickly
on weekends; minor road noise in some rooms. $\boxed{\$}$ *Rooms from: $288*
⊠ *5131 Warm Springs Rd., west off Arnold Dr., Glen Ellen* ☏ *707/996–
5131* ⊕ *www.oleahotel.com* ⟿ *15 rooms* ⏀ *Breakfast.*

KENWOOD

3 miles north of Glen Ellen.

Tiny Kenwood consists of little more than a few restaurants and shops
and a historic train depot. But hidden in this pretty landscape of mead-
ows and woods at the north end of Sonoma Valley are several good
wineries, most just off the Sonoma Highway (Highway 12).

GETTING HERE AND AROUND

To get to Kenwood from Glen Ellen, drive north on Highway 12.

EXPLORING

Fodor's Choice   **B Wise Vineyards Cellar.** The stylish roadside tasting room of this pro-
★   ducer of small-lot reds sits on the valley floor, but B Wise's winery
and vineyards occupy a prime spot high in the Moon Mountain Dis-
trict AVA. B Wise made its name crafting big, bold Cabernets. One
comes from owner Brion Wise's mountain estate and another from
the nearby Monte Rosso Vineyard, some of whose Cabernet vines are
among California's oldest. These hearty mountain-fruit Cabs contrast
with a suppler one from the Napa Valley's Coombsville AVA. Mark Her-
old, known for several cult wines, makes the Cabernets with Massimo

Hitching a ride on the Benziger Family Winery tram tour

Monticelli, who's responsible for the rest of the uniformly excellent lineup: Sonoma Coast Chardonnay; Russian River Valley, Sonoma Coast, and Willamette Valley (Oregon) Pinot Noir; and estate Syrah, Petite Sirah, Petit Verdot, and Zinfandel. ⊠ *9077 Sonoma Hwy., at Shaw Ave., Kenwood* ☎ *707/282-9169* ⊕ *www.bwisevineyards.com* 🖾 *Tasting $20.*

Kunde Estate Winery & Vineyards. On your way into Kunde you pass a terrace flanked by fountains, virtually coaxing you to stay for a picnic with views over the vineyard. Family owned for more than a century, Kunde prides itself on producing 100% estate wines from its 1,850-acre property, which rises 1,400 feet from the valley floor. Kunde's whites include several Chardonnays and a Sauvignon Blanc, with Cabernet Sauvignon, Merlot, and a Zinfandel from 1880s vines among the reds. Two wines of note available only through the winery, both in the Destination Series, are the Red Dirt Red blend of seven varietals and the Dunfillan Cuvée, made from Cabernet and Syrah grapes. ■TIP→ **Make a reservation for the Mountain Top Tasting, a tour by luxury van that ends with a sampling of reserve wines.** ⊠ *9825 Sonoma Hwy./Hwy. 12, Kenwood* ☎ *707/833-5501* ⊕ *www.kunde.com* 🖾 *Tastings $15–$50, Mountain Top Tasting $50, grounds and cave tour free.*

St. Francis Winery. Nestled at the foot of Mt. Hood, St. Francis has earned national acclaim for its wine-and-food pairings. With its red-tile roof and bell tower and views of the Mayacamas Mountains just to the east, the winery's California Mission–style visitor center occupies one of Sonoma County's most scenic locations. The charm of the surroundings is matched by the mostly red wines, including rich, earthy Zinfandels from the Dry

Creek, Russian River, and Sonoma valleys. Chef Bryan Jones's five-course small bites-and-wine-pairings ($68)—Liberty duck breast cassoulet with one of the Zins, for example—are offered from Thursday through Monday; pairings with cheeses and charcuterie ($35) are available daily. ✉ *100 Pythian Rd., off Hwy. 12, Kenwood* ☎ *888/675–9463, 707/833–0242* ⊕ *www.stfranciswinery.com* ✉ *Tastings $15–$68.*

WHERE TO EAT AND STAY

$ ✕ **Café Citti.** Classical music in the background, a friendly staff, and a
ITALIAN roaring fire when it's cold outside keep this roadside café from feeling too spartan. Stand in line to order dishes such as roast chicken, pasta prepared with the sauce of your choice, and slabs of tiramisu for dessert, and someone will deliver your meal to a table indoors or on an outdoor patio. **Known for:** welcoming atmosphere; prepared salads and sandwiches; to-go winery picnics. $ *Average main: $14* ✉ *9049 Sonoma Hwy./Hwy. 12, Kenwood* ☎ *707/833–2690* ⊕ *www.cafecitti.com.*

$$$$ 🛏 **Kenwood Inn and Spa.** Fluffy feather beds, custom Italian furnishings,
B&B/INN and French doors opening onto terraces or balconies lend this inn's uncommonly spacious guest rooms a particularly romantic air. **Pros:** large rooms; lavish furnishings; romantic. **Cons:** road or lobby noise in some rooms; expensive. $ *Rooms from: $475* ✉ *10400 Sonoma Hwy./Hwy. 12, Kenwood* ☎ *800/353–6966* ⊕ *www.kenwoodinn.com* ⏎ *29 rooms* 🍽 *Breakfast.*

ELSEWHERE IN SONOMA

Sonoma County's northern and western reaches are a study in contrasts. Trendy hotels, restaurants, shops, and tasting rooms have transformed Healdsburg into a hot spot. Within a few miles, though, chic yields to bucolic, with only the occasional horse ranch, apple or peach orchard, or stand of oaks interrupting the rolling vineyard hills. The Russian River Valley is the grape-growing star, but Dry Creek and Alexander valleys and the Sonoma Coast also merit investigation. Office parks and tract housing diminish Santa Rosa's appeal, but wineries, cultural attractions, and solid budget lodgings can be found within its borders.

20

SANTA ROSA

8 miles northwest of Kenwood, 55 miles north of San Francisco.

With more than 170,000 people, Santa Rosa, the Wine Country's largest city, isn't likely to charm you with its malls, office buildings, and frequent traffic snarls. Its moderately priced lodgings, however, can come in handy, especially since Santa Rosa is roughly equidistant from Sonoma, Healdsburg, and notable Russian River wineries.

The location of Santa Rosa's former Northwestern Pacific Railroad depot—built in 1903 by Italian stonemasons and immortalized in Alfred Hitchcock's coolly sinister 1943 film *Shadow of a Doubt*—provides the name for the revitalized **Railroad Square Historic District** west of U.S. 101. The depot is now a visitor center, and 4th Street between Wilson and Davis streets contains restaurants, bar, and antiques and thrift shops worth checking out, as do nearby lanes.

GETTING HERE AND AROUND

Santa Rosa straddles U.S. 101, the route to take (north) from San Francisco. From the Sonoma Valley, take Highway 12 north. Sonoma County Transit buses serve the city and surrounding area.

EXPLORING

TOP ATTRACTIONS

Fodor'sChoice ★ **Balletto Vineyards.** A few decades ago Balletto was known for quality produce more than for grapes, but the new millennium saw vineyards emerge as the core business. About 90% of the fruit from the family's 650-plus acres goes to other wineries, with the remainder destined for Balletto's estate wines. The house style is light on the oak, high in acidity, and low in alcohol content, a combination that yields exceptionally food-friendly wines. On a hot summer day, sipping a Pinot Gris, rosé of Pinot Noir, or brut rosé sparkler on the outdoor patio can feel transcendent, but the superstars are the Chardonnays and Pinot Noirs. ■TIP→ **Look for the unoaked and Cider Ridge Chardonnays and the Burnside, Sexton Hill, and Winery Block Pinots, but all the wines are exemplary—and, like the tastings, reasonably priced.** ✉ *5700 Occidental Rd., 2½ miles west of Hwy. 12, Santa Rosa* ☎ *707/568–2455* ⊕ *www.ballettovineyards.com* 🍷 *Tasting $10.*

Fodor'sChoice ★ **Martinelli Winery.** In a century-old hop barn with the telltale triple towers, Martinelli has the feel of a traditional country store, but the sophisticated wines made here are anything but old-fashioned. The winery's reputation rests on its complex Pinot Noirs, Syrahs, and Zinfandels, including the Jackass Hill Vineyard Zin, made with grapes from 130-year-old vines. Noted winemaker Helen Turley set the Martinelli style—fruit-forward, easy on the oak, reined-in tannins—in the 1990s, and her successor, Bryan Kvamme, continues this approach. You can sample current releases at a Classic Tasting, but a better choice (which also doesn't require a reservation) is the Terroir Tasting, which focuses on how soil and other vineyard characteristics influence wines. Rarer and top-rated vintages are poured at appointment-only sessions. ✉ *3360 River Rd., east of Olivet Rd., Windsor* ☎ *707/525–0570, 800/346–1627* ⊕ *www.martinelliwinery.com* 🍷 *Tastings $12–$75.*

FAMILY **Safari West.** An unexpected bit of wilderness in the Wine Country, this African wildlife preserve covers 400 acres. Begin your visit with a stroll around enclosures housing lemurs, cheetahs, giraffes, and rare birds like the brightly colored scarlet ibis. Next, climb with your guide onto open-air vehicles that spend about two hours combing the expansive property, where more than 80 species—including gazelles, cape buffalo, antelope, wildebeests, and zebras—inhabit the hillsides. If you'd like to extend your stay, lodging in well-equipped tent cabins is available. ✉ *3115 Porter Creek Rd., off Mark West Springs Rd., Santa Rosa* ☎ *707/579–2551, 800/616–2695* ⊕ *www.safariwest.com* 🍷 *98–$115 ($45–$50 ages 4–12).*

WORTH NOTING

FAMILY **Charles M. Schulz Museum.** Fans of Snoopy and Charlie Brown will love this museum dedicated to the late Charles M. Schulz, who lived his last three decades in Santa Rosa. Permanent installations include a re-creation of the cartoonist's studio, and temporary exhibits often focus on a particular theme in his work. **TIP→ Children and adults can take a stab at creating cartoons in the Education Room.** ✉ *2301 Hardies La., at W. Steele La., Santa Rosa* ☎ *707/579–4452* 🌐 *www.schulzmuseum.org* 🎟 *$12 ($5 age 4–18).*

WHERE TO EAT AND STAY

$$$ ECLECTIC Fodor's Choice ★ 🍴 **Willi's Wine Bar.** Although this restaurant's name suggests a sedate spot serving wine and precious nibbles, boisterous crowds fill the warren of cozy enclaves here, snapping up small plates from the globe-trotting menu. Dishes such as the pork-belly pot stickers represent Asia, and Tunisian roasted local carrots and Moroccan-style lamb chops are among the Mediterranean-inspired foods. **Known for:** small plates; inspired wine selection; 2-ounce pours so you can pair a new wine with each dish; California-sourced cheese and charcuterie; covered patio. [$] *Average main: $29* ✉ *4404 Old Redwood Hwy., at Ursuline Rd., Santa Rosa* ☎ *707/526–3096* 🌐 *williswinebar.net* 🕒 *No lunch Sun. and Mon.*

$$ HOTEL 🏨 **Vintners Inn.** The owners of Ferrari-Carano Vineyards operate this oasis set amid 92 acres of vineyards that's known for its comfortable lodgings. **Pros:** spacious rooms with comfortable beds; jogging path through the vineyards; online deals pop up year-round. **Cons:** occasional noise from adjacent events center. [$] *Rooms from: $265* ✉ *4350 Barnes Rd., Santa Rosa* ☎ *707/575–7350, 800/421–2584* 🌐 *www.vintnersinn.com* 🛏 *38 rooms, 6 suites* 🍽 *No meals.*

RUSSIAN RIVER VALLEY

10 miles northwest of Santa Rosa.

The Russian River flows from Mendocino to the Pacific, but Russian River Valley wine making centers on a triangle with points at Healdsburg, Guerneville, and Sebastopol. Tall redwoods shade the two-lane roads of this scenic area, where, thanks to the cooling marine influence, Pinot Noir and Chardonnay are the king and queen of grapes.

GETTING HERE AND AROUND

Many Russian River Valley visitors base themselves in Healdsburg. You can find noteworthy purveyors of Pinots and Chards by heading west from downtown on Mill Street, which eventually becomes Westside Road. For Forestville and Sebastopol wineries, continue south and west along Westside until it intersects River Road and turn west. Turn south at Mirabel Road and follow it to Highway 116.

EXPLORING

TOP ATTRACTIONS

Fodor's Choice ★ **Arista Winery.** Brothers Mark and Ben McWilliams own this winery specializing in small-lot Pinot Noirs that was founded in 2002 by their parents. The sons have raised the winery's profile in several ways, most notably by hiring winemaker Matt Courtney, who has earned high praise from the *Wine Spectator* and other publications for his

balanced, richly textured Pinot Noirs. Courtney shows the same deft touch with Arista's Zinfandels, Chardonnays, and a Riesling. One tasting focuses the regions from which the Arista sources its grapes, another on small-lot single-vineyard wines. Tastings are by appointment only. ■TIP➔ Guests who purchase a bottle are welcome to enjoy it in the picnic area, near a Japanese garden that predates the winery. ⊠ *7015 Westside Rd., Healdsburg* ☎ *707/473–0606* ⊕ *www.aristawinery.com* ⊠ *Tastings $35–$65.*

FAMILY **Armstrong Redwoods State Natural Reserve.** Here's your best opportunity in
Fodor's Choice the western Wine Country to wander amid *Sequoia sempervirens,* also
★ known as coast redwood trees. The oldest example in this 805-acre state park, the Colonel Armstrong Tree, is thought to be more than 1,400 years old. A half mile from the parking lot, the tree is easily accessible, and you can hike a long way into the forest before things get too hilly. ■TIP➔ During hot summer days, Armstrong Redwoods' tall trees help the park keep its cool. ⊠ *17000 Armstrong Woods Rd., off River Rd., Guerneville* ☎ *707/869–2958 for visitor center, 707/869–2015 for park headquarters* ⊕ *www.parks.ca.gov* ⊠ *$8 per vehicle, free to pedestrians and bicyclists.*

Fodor's Choice **Dutton-Goldfield Winery.** An avid cyclist whose previous credits include
★ developing the wine-making program at Hartford Court, Dan Goldfield teamed up with fifth-generation farmer Steve Dutton to establish this small operation devoted to cool-climate wines. Goldfield modestly strives to take Dutton's meticulously farmed fruit and "make the winemaker unnoticeable," but what impresses the most about these wines, which include Pinot Blanc, Chardonnay, Pinot Noir, and Zinfandel, is their sheer artistry. Among the ones to seek out are the Angel Camp Pinot Noir, from Anderson Valley (Mendocino County) grapes, and the Morelli Lane Zinfandel, from grapes grown on the remaining 1.8 acres of an 1880s vineyard Goldfield helped revive. Tastings often begin with Pinot Blanc, a white-wine variant of Pinot Noir, proceed through the reds, and end with a palate-cleansing Chardonnay. ⊠ *3100 Gravenstein Hwy. N/Hwy. 116, at Graton Rd., Sebastopol* ☎ *707/827–3600* ⊕ *www.duttongoldfield.com* ⊠ *Tastings $20–$40.*

Fodor's Choice **Iron Horse Vineyards.** A meandering one-lane road leads to this winery
★ known for its sparkling wines and estate Chardonnays and Pinot Noirs. The sparklers have made history: Ronald Reagan served them at his summit meetings with Mikhail Gorbachev; George H.W. Bush took some along to Moscow for treaty talks; and Barack Obama included them at official state dinners. Despite Iron Horse's brushes with fame, a casual rusticity prevails at its outdoor tasting area (large heaters keep things comfortable on chilly days), which gazes out on acres of rolling, vine-covered hills. Regular tours take place on weekdays at 10 am. Tastings and tours are by appointment only. ■TIP➔ When his schedule permits, winemaker David Munksgard leads a private tour by truck at 10 am on Monday. ⊠ *9786 Ross Station Rd., off Hwy. 116, Sebastopol* ☎ *707/887–1507* ⊕ *www.ironhorsevineyards.com* ⊠ *Tasting $25, tours $30–$50 (includes tasting).*

Fodor's Choice ★ **Rochioli Vineyards and Winery.** Claiming one of the prettiest picnic sites in the area, with tables overlooking the vineyards, this winery has an airy little tasting room with a romantic view. Production is small and fans on the winery's mailing list snap up most of the bottles, but the winery is still worth a stop to sample the estate Chardonnay and Pinot Noir and, when available, the Sauvignon Blanc. Because of the cool growing conditions in the Russian River Valley, the flavors of the Chardonnay and Sauvignon Blanc are intense and complex, and the Pinot Noir, which helped cement the Russian River's status as a Pinot powerhouse, is consistently excellent. Tastings are by appointment only on Tuesday and Wednesday. ✉ *6192 Westside Rd., Healdsburg* ☎ *707/433–2305* 🌐 *www.rochioliwinery.com* 🎟 *Tasting $20.*

WORTH NOTING

The Barlow. A multibuilding complex on the site of a former apple cannery, The Barlow celebrates Sonoma County's "maker" culture with tenants who produce or sell wine, beer, spirits, crafts, clothing, art, and artisanal food and herbs. Only club members can visit the anchor wine tenant, Kosta Browne, but MacPhail, Wind Gap, and Marimar Estate have tasting rooms open to the public. Crooked Goat Brewing and Woodfour Brewing Company make and sell ales, and you can have a nip of vodka, gin, sloe gin, or wheat and rye whiskey at Spirit Works Distillery. An artist using traditional methods should be completing his five-year project to create the world's largest *thangka* (Tibetan painting). ■ **TIP→ During summer and early fall, the complex hosts a Thursday-night street fair, with live music and more vendors.** ✉ *6770 McKinley St., at Morris St., off Hwy. 12, Sebastopol* ☎ *707/824–5600* 🌐 *www.thebarlow.net* 🎟 *Complex free; tasting fees at wineries, breweries, distillery.*

WHERE TO EAT

$$$$ FRENCH Fodor's Choice ★ 🍴 **The Farmhouse Inn.** From the sommelier who assists you with wine choices to the servers who describe the provenance of the black truffles shaved over the intricate pasta dishes, the staff matches the quality of this restaurant's French-inspired prix-fixe meals. The signature dish, "Rabbit Rabbit Rabbit," a trio of confit of leg, rabbit loin wrapped in applewood-smoked bacon, and roasted rack of rabbit, is typical of preparations that are both rustic and refined. **Known for:** upscale accommodations with full-service spa; sophisticated cuisine; romantic dining. [$] *Average main: $95* ✉ *7871 River Rd., at Wohler Rd., Forestville* ☎ *707/887–3300, 800/464–6642* 🌐 *www.farmhouseinn.com* 🕒 *Closed Tues. and Wed. No lunch.*

$ MODERN AMERICAN FAMILY Fodor's Choice ★ 🍴 **Handline Coastal California.** Lowell Sheldon, who runs a fine-dining establishment (Peter Lowell's) a mile away, teamed up with farmer-partner Natalie Goble to convert Sebastopol's former Foster's Freeze location into a perky paean to coastal California cuisine. The lineup includes oysters raw and grilled, fish tacos, ceviches, tostadas, three burgers (beef, vegan, and fish), and, honoring the location's previous incarnation, chocolate and vanilla soft-serve ice cream for dessert. **Known for:** upscale comfort food; 21st-century roadside decor; lighthearted atmosphere. [$] *Average main: $12* ✉ *935 Gravenstein Hwy. S, near Hutchins Ave., Sebastopol* ☎ *707/827–3744* 🌐 *www.handline.com.*

20

WHERE TO STAY

$ HOTEL Fodor's Choice ★ **boon hotel+spa.** Redwoods, Douglas firs, and palms supply shade and seclusion at this lushly landscaped resort ¾ mile north of downtown Guerneville. **Pros:** memorable breakfasts; lush landscaping; on-site spa. **Cons:** lacks amenities of larger properties. [$] *Rooms from: $155* ✉ *14711 Armstrong Woods Rd., Guerneville* ☎ *707/869–2721* 🌐 *boonhotels.com* 🛏 *14 rooms* 🍴 *Breakfast.*

SPORTS AND THE OUTDOORS

CANOE TRIPS

Burke's Canoe Trips. You'll get a real feel for the Russian River's flora and fauna on a leisurely 10-mile paddle downstream from Burke's to Guerneville. A shuttle bus returns you to your car at the end of the journey, which is best taken from late May through mid-October and, in summer, on a weekday—summer weekends can be crowded and raucous. ✉ *8600 River Rd., at Mirabel Rd., Forestville* ☎ *707/887–1222* 🌐 *www.burkescanoetrips.com* 🎟 *$70 per canoe.*

HEALDSBURG

17 miles north of Santa Rosa.

Easily Sonoma County's ritziest town and the star of many a magazine spread or online feature, Healdsburg is located at the confluence of the Dry Creek Valley, Russian River Valley, and Alexander Valley AVAs. Several dozen wineries bear a Healdsburg address, and around downtown's plaza you'll find fashionable boutiques, spas, hip tasting rooms, and art galleries, and some of the Wine Country's best restaurants. Star chef Kyle Connaughton, who opened SingleThread Farms Restaurant in late 2016 to much fanfare, has motivated his counterparts all over town to up their game. Especially on weekends, you'll have plenty of company as you tour the downtown area. You could spend a day just exploring the tasting rooms and shops surrounding Healdsburg Plaza, but be sure to allow time to venture into the surrounding countryside.

GETTING HERE AND AROUND

Healdsburg sits just off U.S. 101. Heading north, take the Central Healdsburg exit to reach Healdsburg Plaza; heading south, take the Westside Road exit and pass east under the freeway. Sonoma County Transit Bus 60 serves Healdsburg from Santa Rosa.

EXPLORING

Fodor's Choice ★ **Hudson Street Wineries.** This under-the-radar joint tasting room of five family-run wineries provides a vivid snapshot of northern Sonoma small-lot production. Reds to look for include the Kaufman Sunnyslope Vineyard Pinot Noir from Willowbrook Cellars, the Enriquez Pinot Noir lineup plus Tempranillo, the Kelley & Young Malbec, the Shippey Petite Sirahs and Zinfandels, and the Owl Ridge Dry Creek Valley Zinfandel and Alexander Valley Cabernet Sauvignon. The Kelley & Young Sauvignon Blanc and Shippey Rosé of Petite Sirah stand out among the lighter wines. Locals, who appreciate the unfussy atmosphere and generous pours, often bring their out-of-town guests to this barnlike space about half a mile southeast of Healdsburg Plaza.

■ **TIP** → With most bottles costing between $20 and $30, the prices are beyond reasonable for wines of this quality. ⊠ *428 Hudson St., near Front St., Healdsburg* ☎ *707/433–2364* ⊕ *www.hudsonstreetwineries. com* ⊡ *Tasting $10* ☼ *Closed Tues. and Wed.*

WHERE TO EAT

$$$
SPANISH
Fodor'sChoice
★

✕ **Bravas Bar de Tapas.** Spanish-style tapas and an outdoor patio in perpetual party mode make this restaurant, headquartered in a restored 1920s bungalow, a popular downtown perch. Contemporary Spanish mosaics set a perky tone inside, but unless something's amiss with the weather, nearly everyone heads out back for flavorful croquettes, paella, jamón, *pan tomate* (tomato toast), duck egg with chorizo, pork-cheek sliders, skirt steak, and crispy fried chicken. **Known for:** casual small plates; specialty cocktails, sangrias, and beer; sherry flights. Ⓢ *Average main: $26* ⊠ *420 Center St., near North St., Healdsburg* ☎ *707/433–7700* ⊕ *www.barbravas.com.*

$$
ITALIAN
Fodor'sChoice
★

✕ **Campo Fina.** Chef Ari Rosen closed popular Scopa restaurant in 2017 but still showcases his contemporary-rustic Italian cuisine at this converted storefront that once housed a bar notorious for boozin' and brawlin'. Sandblasted red brick, satin-smooth walnut tables, and old-school lighting fixtures strike a retro note for a menu built around pizzas and Scopa gems such as Rosen's variation on his grandmother's tomato-braised chicken with creamy-soft polenta. **Known for:** outdoor patio and boccie court out of an Italian movie set; memorable lunch sandwiches. Ⓢ *Average main: $19* ⊠ *330 Healdsburg Ave., near North St., Healdsburg* ☎ *707/395–4640* ⊕ *www.campofina.com.*

$$
MODERN
AMERICAN
Fodor'sChoice
★

✕ **Chalkboard.** Unvarnished oak flooring, wrought-iron accents, and a vaulted white ceiling create a polished yet rustic ambience for executive chef Shane McAnelly's playfully ambitious small-plate cuisine. Starters such as pork-belly biscuits might seem frivolous, but the silky flavor blend—maple glaze, pickled onions, and chipotle mayo playing off feathery biscuit halves—signals a supremely capable tactician at work. **Known for:** chef's four-course tasting menu; pasta "flights" (choose three or six styles); The Candy Bar dessert. Ⓢ *Average main: $19* ⊠ *Hotel Les Mars, 29 North St., west of Healdsburg Ave., Healdsburg* ☎ *707/473–8030* ⊕ *www.chalkboardhealdsburg.com.*

$
FRENCH

✕ **Costeaux.** Breakfast, served all day at this bright-yellow French-style bakery and café, includes the signature omelet (sun-dried tomatoes, applewood-smoked bacon, spinach, and Brie) and French toast made from thick slabs of cinnamon-walnut bread. Croques, salads, smoked duck sandwiches, and an au courant Monte Cristo (turkey, ham, and Jarlsberg cheese) on that addictive cinnamon-walnut bread are among the lunch favorites. **Known for:** breads, croissants, and fancy pastries; quiche and omelets; front patio (arrive early on weekends). Ⓢ *Average main: $14* ⊠ *417 Healdsburg Ave., at North St., Healdsburg* ☎ *707/433–1913* ⊕ *www.costeaux.com* ☼ *No dinner.*

$$$
MODERN
AMERICAN

✕ **Shed Café.** With previous stints at top Wine Country restaurants, culinary director Perry Hoffman added farm-to-table sophistication to this combination café, coffee bar, and "fermentation bar" serving house-made kombucha, kefir water, and vinegar-based "shrub" sodas. A recent fall dish, Liberty Farms duck leg served with baba ganoush, black lentils, fairytale eggplant, and pistachio *dukkah* (an Egyptian-style

20

seed-nut mixture) hints at Hoffman's level of artistry. **Known for:** heirloom-grain Belgian waffles, Doug's eggs at breakfast; small lunch and dinner plates; four-course dinner option. $ *Average main: $25* ⊠ *25 North St., near Healdsburg Ave., Healdsburg* ☎ *707/431–7433* ⊕ *healdsburgshed.com/eat.*

$$$$ ✕ **SingleThread Farms Restaurant.** The seasonally oriented, multicourse
ECLECTIC Japanese dinners known as *kaiseki* inspired the prix-fixe vegetarian,
Fodor's Choice meat, and seafood menus at this restaurant from the internation-
★ ally renowned culinary artists Katina and Kyle Connaughton (she farms, he cooks), which debuted in late 2016. As Katina describes the endeavor, the 72 microseasons of their farm, 5 acres at a nearby vineyard plus SingleThread's rooftop garden of fruit trees and micro-greens, dictates Kyle's rarefied fare. **Known for:** culinary precision; spare, elegant setting; impeccable wine pairings. $ *Average main: $294* ⊠ *131 North St., at Center St., Healdsburg* ⊕ *www.singlethread-farms.com* ☾ *Closed Mon. No lunch.*

$$$$ ✕ **Valette.** Northern Sonoma native Dustin Valette opened this gor-
MODERN geously appointed homage to the area's artisanal agricultural bounty
AMERICAN with his brother, who runs a tight front-of-house ship. Charcuterie is an
Fodor's Choice emphasis, but also consider the cocoa nib–crusted Liberty duck breast
★ and day-boat scallops *en croûte* (in a pastry crust), a signature dish at Healdsburg's Dry Creek Kitchen when Valette served as its executive chef. **Known for:** intricate cuisine; "Trust me" (the chef) tasting menu; well-chosen mostly Northern California wines. $ *Average main: $31* ⊠ *344 Center St., at North St., Healdsburg* ☎ *707/473–0946* ⊕ *www.valettehealdsburg.com.*

$$$ ✕ **Willi's Seafood & Raw Bar.** The crowd at Willi's likes to enjoy spe-
SEAFOOD cialty cocktails at the full bar before sitting down to a dinner of small, mostly seafood-oriented plates. The warm Maine lobster roll with garlic butter and fennel remains a hit, and the ceviches, barbecued bacon-wrapped scallops, and "kale Caesar!" with toasted capers count among its worthy rivals. **Known for:** gluten-, dairy-, nut-, and seed-free options; Key lime cheesecake; caramelized banana split, and other desserts. $ *Average main: $25* ⊠ *403 Healdsburg Ave., at North St., Healdsburg* ☎ *707/433–9191* ⊕ *www.willisseafood.net* ☞ *Reservations not accepted Fri.–Sun.*

WHERE TO STAY

$ ⌃ **Best Western Dry Creek Inn.** Easy access to downtown restaurants,
HOTEL tasting rooms, and shopping, as well as outlying wineries and bicycle trails makes this California Mission–style motel near U.S. 101 a good budget option. **Pros:** laundry facilities; some pet-friendly rooms; frequent Internet discounts. **Cons:** thin walls; highway noise audible in many rooms. $ *Rooms from: $172* ⊠ *198 Dry Creek Rd., Healdsburg* ☎ *707/433–0300, 800/222–5784* ⊕ *www.drycreekinn.com* ⤳ *163 rooms* ⦿ *Breakfast.*

$$$ ⌃ **The Honor Mansion.** An 1883 Italianate Victorian houses this pho-
B&B/INN togenic hotel; guest rooms in the main home preserve a sense of the
Fodor's Choice building's heritage, whereas the larger suites are comparatively under-
★ stated. **Pros:** homemade sweets available at all hours; spa pavilions by pool available for massages in fair weather. **Cons:** almost a mile from

Healdsburg Plaza; walls can seem thin. $ *Rooms from: $325* ✉ *891 Grove St., Healdsburg* ☎ *707/433–4277, 800/554–4667* ⊕ *www.honormansion.com* ☾ *Closed 2 wks at Christmas* ☞ *13 rooms* ¡◯¡ *Breakfast.*

$$$$
HOTEL
Fodor's Choice
★
🔲 **Hôtel Les Mars.** This Relais & Châteaux property takes the prize for opulence with guest rooms spacious and elegant enough for French nobility, 18th- and 19th-century antiques and reproductions, canopy beds dressed in luxe linens, and gas-burning fireplaces. **Pros:** large rooms; just off Healdsburg's plaza; fancy bath products; room service by Chalkboard restaurant. **Cons:** very expensive. $ *Rooms from: $540* ✉ *27 North St., Healdsburg* ☎ *707/433–4211* ⊕ *www.hotellesmars.com* ☞ *16 rooms* ¡◯¡ *Breakfast.*

$$$
HOTEL
🔲 **h2hotel.** Eco-friendly touches abound at this hotel, from the plant-covered "green roof" to wooden decks made from salvaged lumber. **Pros:** stylish modern design; complimentary bikes. **Cons:** least expensive rooms lack bathtubs; no fitness facilities. $ *Rooms from: $322* ✉ *219 Healdsburg Ave., Healdsburg* ☎ *707/922–5251* ⊕ *www.h2hotel.com* ☞ *36 rooms* ¡◯¡ *Breakfast.*

$$$$
B&B/INN
Fodor's Choice
★
🔲 **SingleThread Farms Inn.** Although the physical elements, from the custom bedding and furnishings down to the trays on which breakfast is delivered, speak to husband-and-wife team Kyle and Katina Connaughton's phenomenal attention to detail, in the end it's the spirit of this rare place that astounds the most—that someone would *care* this much about the intricacies of understated service and comfort away from home and pull it off so flawlessly. **Pros:** high style; in-room amenities from restaurant; rooftop garden; multicourse breakfast. **Cons:** one must eventually check out. $ *Rooms from: $900* ✉ *131 North St., at Center St., Healdsburg* ⊕ *www.singlethreadfarms.com* ☞ *5 rooms* ¡◯¡ *Breakfast.*

SPAS

Fodor's Choice
★
Spa Dolce. Owner Ines von Majthenyi Scherrer has a good local rep, having run a popular nearby spa before opening this stylish facility just off Healdsburg Plaza. Spa Dolce specializes in skin and body care for men and women, and waxing and facials for women. Curved white walls and fresh-cut floral arrangements set a subdued tone for such treatments as the exfoliating Hauschka body scrub, which combines organic brown sugar with scented oil. There's a romantic room for couples to enjoy massages for two. ■ TIP➔ **Many guests come just for the facials, which range from a straightforward cleansing to an anti-aging peel.** ✉ *250 Center St., at Matheson St., Healdsburg* ☎ *707/433–0177* ⊕ *www.spa-dolce.com* ✑ *Treatments $50–$225.*

SPORTS AND THE OUTDOORS

Fodor's Choice
★
Wine Country Bikes. This shop several blocks southeast of Healdsburg Plaza is perfectly located for single or multiday treks into the Dry Creek and Russian River valleys. Bikes, including tandems, rent for $39–$145 per day. One-day tours start at $149. ■ TIP➔ **The owner and staff can help with bicycling itineraries, including a mostly gentle loop, which takes in Westside Road and Eastside Road wineries and a rusting trestle bridge, as well as a more challenging excursion to Lake Sonoma.** ✉ *61 Front St., at Hudson St., Healdsburg* ☎ *707/473–0610, 866/922–4537* ⊕ *www.winecountrybikes.com.*

20

SHOPPING

Healdsburg is a pleasant spot to window shop, with dozens of art galleries, boutiques, and high-end design shops on or near the plaza.

Fodor's Choice **Gallery Lulo.** A collaboration between a local artist and jewelry maker
★ and a Danish-born curator, this gallery presents changing exhibits of jewelry, sculpture, and objets d'art. ⊠ *303 Center St., at Plaza St., Healdsburg* ☏ *707/433–7533* ⊕ *www.gallerylulo.com.*

Fodor's Choice **The Shed.** Inside a glass-front, steel-clad variation on a traditional grange
★ hall, this shop-cum-eatery celebrates local agriculture. It stocks specialty foods, seeds and plants, gardening and farming implements, cookware, and everything a smart pantry should hold. ⊠ *25 North St., west of Healdsburg Ave., Healdsburg* ☏ *707/431–7433* ⊕ *healdsburgshed.com.*

DRY CREEK AND ALEXANDER VALLEYS

With its diverse terrain and microclimates, the Dry Creek Valley supports an impressive range of varietals. Zinfandel grapes flourish on the benchlands, whereas the gravelly, well-drained soil of the valley floor is better known for Chardonnay and, in the north, Sauvignon Blanc. Pinot Noir, Syrah, and other cool-climate grapes thrive on eastern-facing slopes that receive less afternoon sun than elsewhere in the valley. The Alexander Valley, which lies northeast of Healdsburg, is similarly rustic. Wineries here are known for Zinfandels, Chardonnays, and Cabernet Sauvignons.

GETTING HERE AND AROUND

To reach the Dry Creek Valley from Healdsburg, drive north on Healdsburg Avenue and turn west (left) on Dry Creek Road. To get to the Alexander Valley from the plaza, drive north on Healdsburg Avenue and veer right onto Alexander Valley Road. Follow it to Highway 128, where many of this appellation's best wineries lie.

EXPLORING

TOP ATTRACTIONS

Fodor's Choice **Jordan Vineyard and Winery.** A visit to this sprawling property north
★ of Healdsburg revolves around an impressive estate built in the early 1970s to replicate a French château. A seated one-hour Library Tasting of current Cabernet Sauvignon and Chardonnay releases takes place in the château itself, accompanied by small bites prepared by executive chef Todd Knoll. The tasting concludes with an older vintage Cabernet Sauvignon paired with cheese. The 90-minute Winery Tour & Tasting includes the above, plus a walk through part of the château. All visits are by appointment only. ■ TIP➔ **For a truly memorable experience, splurge on the three-hour Estate Tour & Tasting, whose pièce de résistance is the Cabernet segment, which unfolds at a 360-degree vista point overlooking 1,200 acres of vines, olive trees, and countryside.** ⊠ *1474 Alexander Valley Rd., 1½ miles east of Healdsburg Ave., Healdsburg* ☏ *800/654–1213, 707/431–5250* ⊕ *www.jordanwinery. com* ⊠ *Library tasting $30, winery tour and tasting $40, estate tour and tasting $120* ⊙ *Closed Sun. Dec.–Mar.*

Fodor'sChoice **Locals Tasting Room.** If you're serious about wine, Carolyn Lewis's tast-
★ ing room alone is worth a trek 8 miles north of Healdsburg Plaza to
downtown Geyserville. Connoisseurs who appreciate Lewis's ability
to spot up-and-comers head here regularly to sample the output of a
dozen or so small wineries, most without tasting rooms of their own.
There's no fee for tasting—extraordinary for wines of this quality—and
the extremely knowledgeable staff are happy to pour you a flight of
several wines so you can compare, say, different Cabernet Sauvignons.
✉ *21023A Geyserville Ave., at Hwy. 128, Geyserville* ☎ *707/857–4900*
⊕ *www.tastelocalwines.com* ✑ *Tasting free.*

Fodor'sChoice **Ridge Vineyards.** Ridge stands tall among California wineries, and
★ not merely because its 1971 Monte Bello Cab placed first in a 2006
Judgment of Paris rematch. The winery built its reputation on Cabernet Sauvignons, Zinfandels, and Chardonnays of unusual depth
and complexity, but you'll also find blends of Rhône varietals. Ridge
makes wines using grapes from several California locales—including the Dry Creek Valley, Sonoma Valley, Napa Valley, and Paso
Robles—but the focus is on single-vineyard estate wines, such as
the exquisitely textured Lytton Springs Zinfandel blend from grapes
grown near the tasting room. In good weather you can taste outside,
taking in views of rolling vineyard hills while you sip. ■TIP→ **The
$20 tasting option includes a pour of the top-of-the-line Monte Bello
Cabernet Sauvignon blend from grapes grown in the Santa Cruz
Mountains.** ✉ *650 Lytton Springs Rd., off U.S. 101, Healdsburg*
☎ *408/867–3233* ⊕ *www.ridgewine.com/visit/lytton-springs* ✑ *Tastings $5–$20, tours $30–$40.*

Truett Hurst Winery. When the weather's fine, few experiences rate more
sublime ("pure magic," is the common refrain from visitors here)
than sitting on Truett Hurst's sandy, tree-shaded Dry Creek shoreline, sipping a Pinot Noir or a Zinfandel rosé, chatting with friends,
and watching the water flow by. A few of Truett Hurst's half dozen
Zinfandels are always poured in the high-ceilinged tasting room.
Other wines to look for include Petite Sirah, Cabernet Sauvignon,
and the Dark Horse GPS (Grenache, Syrah, Mourvèdre, and Petite
Sirah). Picnickers are welcome creek-side or on the outdoor patio;
meats, smoked fish, cheeses, and spreads are available for sale on-site.
■TIP→ Bands—sometimes local, sometimes from beyond—liven things
up in the tasting room on weekend afternoons. ✉ *5610 Dry Creek Rd.,
2 miles south of Canyon Rd., Healdsburg* ☎ *707/433–9545* ⊕ *www.
truetthurst.com* ✑ *Tasting $10.*

WORTH NOTING

Dry Creek Vineyard. Sauvignon Blanc marketed as Fumé Blanc put Dry
Creek Vineyard on the enological map in the 1970s, but the winery
receives high marks as well for its Zinfandels, Bordeaux-style red
blends, and Cabernet Sauvignons. In the nautical-theme tasting room—
Dry Creek has featured sailing vessels on its labels since the 1980s—you
can choose an all–Sauvignon Blanc flight, an all-Zinfandel one, or a
mix of these and other wines. A vineyard walk and an insectary garden
enhance a visit to this historic producer, a fine place for a picnic under
the shade of a magnolia and several redwood trees. ■TIP→ You can

20

reserve a boxed lunch two days ahead through the winery, a time-saver on busy weekends. ✉ *3770 Lambert Bridge Rd., off Dry Creek Rd., Healdsburg* ☎ *707/433–1000, 800/864–9463* 🌐 *www.drycreekvineyard.com* 🎟 *Tastings $15–$50, tour $30.*

FAMILY **Francis Ford Coppola Winery.** The fun at what the film director calls his "wine wonderland" is all in the excess. You may find it hard to resist having your photo snapped standing next to Don Corleone's desk from *The Godfather* or beside other memorabilia from Coppola films (including some directed by his daughter, Sofia). A bandstand reminiscent of one in *The Godfather Part II* is the centerpiece of a large pool area where you can rent a changing room, complete with shower, and spend the afternoon lounging poolside, perhaps ordering food from the adjacent café. A more elaborate restaurant, Rustic, overlooks the vineyards. As for the wines, the excess continues in the cellar, where more than 40 varietal wines and blends are produced. ✉ *300 Via Archimedes, off U.S. 101, Geyserville* ☎ *707/857–1400* 🌐 *www.franciscoppolawinery.com* 🎟 *Tastings free–$25, tours $20–$75, pool pass $35.*

FAMILY **Preston of Dry Creek.** The long driveway at homespun Preston, flanked by vineyards and punctuated by the occasional olive tree, winds down to farmhouses encircling a large shady yard. Year-round, organic produce grown in the winery's gardens is sold at a small shop near the tasting room; house-made bread and olive oil are also available. Owners Lou and Susan Preston are committed to organic growing techniques and use only estate-grown grapes in their wines, which include a perky Sauvignon Blanc, Barbera, Petite Sirah, Syrah, Viognier, and Zinfandel. Tours, on Thursday and Friday only, are by appointment. ■ **TIP→ With several outdoor areas set up with tables (there's also a boccie court), Preston is a terrific place for a weekday picnic; weekends, though also good, can be crowded, and there's no boccie.** ✉ *9282 W. Dry Creek Rd., at Hartsock Rd. No. 1, Healdsburg* ☎ *707/433–3372* 🌐 *www.prestonvineyards.com* 🎟 *Tasting $10, tour $25.*

WHERE TO EAT AND STAY

$$ ITALIAN Fodor's Choice ★ 🍴 **Diavola Pizzeria & Salumeria.** A dining area with hardwood floors, a pressed-tin ceiling, and exposed-brick walls provides a fitting setting for the rustic cuisine at this Geyserville mainstay. Chef Dino Bugica studied with several artisans in Italy before opening this restaurant that specializes in pizzas pulled from a wood-burning oven and several types of house-cured meats, with a few salads and meaty main courses rounding out the menu. **Known for:** wood-fired pizzas; smoked pork belly, pancetta, and spicy Calabrese sausage. [$] *Average main: $19* ✉ *21021 Geyserville Ave., at Hwy. 128, Geyserville* ☎ *707/814–0111* 🌐 *www.diavolapizzeria.com.*

$ HOTEL 🏨 **Geyserville Inn.** Clever travelers give the Healdsburg hubbub and prices the heave-ho but still have easy access to outstanding Dry Creek and Alexander Valley wineries from this modest, family-run inn. **Pros:** pool; second-floor rooms in back have vineyard views; picnic area. **Cons:** occasional noise bleed-through from corporate and other events. [$] *Rooms from: $149* ✉ *21714 Geyserville Ave., Geyserville* ☎ *707/857–4343, 877/857–4343* 🌐 *www.geyservilleinn.com* 🛏 *41 rooms* 🍽 *No meals.*

TRAVEL SMART
SAN FRANCISCO

GETTING HERE AND AROUND

San Francisco encompasses 46.7 square miles. As a major metropolitan hub it has a fantastic public transportation system; however, if you stray from the main thoroughfares public transport can get tricky, and renting a car becomes a more practical option.

All the city's major attractions are easily accessible via Muni (buses and light-rail vehicles), BART (Bay Area Rapid Transit) trains, taxis, and cable cars; or if you have a comfy pair of shoes, you can always walk. It's exactly 8 miles from the west side of the city to the east side. The streets are neatly arranged along two grids that come together at Market Street, and with the area's well-known landmarks—the Golden Gate Bridge (north), Sutro Tower (south), the Bay Bridge (east), and the Pacific Ocean (west)—as a physical compass, it's difficult to lose your way.

The East Bay is also extremely accessible via public transport; BART is a good way to get where you want to go. And the North Bay is only a boat or bike ride away. Both are good choices, depending on the weather. A car only becomes necessary when you want to go farther north, for example, to Napa or Sonoma County. Keep in mind that rush-hour traffic isn't pleasant, so if you do rent a car try to take to the streets between 10 am and 3 pm, or after 7 pm.

▌ AIR TRAVEL

The least expensive airfares to San Francisco are priced for round-trip travel and should be purchased in advance. Airlines generally allow you to change your return date for a fee; most low-fare tickets, however, are nonrefundable. (But if you cancel, you can usually apply the fare to a future trip, within one year, to any destination the airline flies.)

Nonstop flights from New York to San Francisco take about 5½ hours, and with the 3-hour time change, it's possible to

leave JFK by 8 am and be in San Francisco by 10:30 am. Some flights may require a midway stop, making the total excursion between 8 and 9½ hours. Nonstop times are approximately 1½ hours from Los Angeles, 3 hours from Dallas, 4½ hours from Chicago, 4½ hours from Atlanta, 11 hours from London, 12 hours from Auckland, and 13½ hours from Sydney.

AIRPORTS

The major gateway to San Francisco is San Francisco International Airport (SFO), 15 miles south of the city. It's off U.S. 101 near Millbrae and San Bruno. Oakland International Airport (OAK) is across the bay, not much farther away from downtown San Francisco (via I–80 east and I–880 south), but rush-hour traffic on the Bay Bridge may lengthen travel times considerably. San Jose International Airport (SJC) is about 40 miles south of San Francisco; travel time depends largely on traffic flow, but plan on an hour and a half with moderate traffic.

Depending on the price difference, you might consider flying into Oakland or San Jose. Oakland's an easy-to-use alternative, because there's public transportation between the airport and downtown San Francisco. Getting to San Francisco from San Jose, though, can be time-consuming and costly via public transportation. Heavy fog is infamous for causing chronic delays into and out of San Francisco. If you're heading to the East or South Bay, make every effort to fly into Oakland or San Jose Airport, respectively.

At all three airports security check-in can take 30 to 45 minutes at peak travel times.

▌TIP➜ Count yourself lucky if you have a layover at SFO's International Terminal. The food served by branches of top local eateries beats standard airport fare: Italian pastries from Emporio Rulli, tacos at 24th & Mission Taco House, grilled sandwiches at Firewood Grill, Mediterranean fare from Amoura Cafe.

Long layovers needn't only be about sitting around or shopping. You can burn off vacation calories, too. Check out ⊕ *www.airportgyms.com* for lists of health clubs that are in or near many U.S. and Canadian airports.

Airport Information Oakland International Airport (OAK). ⊠ *1 Airport Dr., Oakland* ⊹ *2 miles west of I–880* ☎ *510/563–3300* ⊕ *www.flyoakland.com.* **San Francisco International Airport** (SFO). ⊠ *McDonnell and Link Rds.* ☎ *800/435–9736, 650/821–8211* ⊕ *www.flysfo.com.*

GROUND TRANSPORTATION
FROM SAN FRANCISCO INTERNATIONAL AIRPORT

Transportation signage at the airport is color-coded by type and is quite clear. A taxi ride to downtown costs around $60; rideshare companies like Lyft and Uber are a popular option and start around $25 for a shared ride into the city. Airport shuttles are inexpensive and generally efficient. Lorrie's Airport Service and SuperShuttle both stop at the lower level near baggage claim and take you anywhere within the city limits of San Francisco. They charge around $17 each way, depending on where you're going. Lorrie's also sells tickets online; you can print them out before leaving home.

Shuttles to the East Bay, such as BayPorter Express, depart from a lot near the lower level; expect to pay between $38 and $47. Inquire about the number of stops a shuttle makes en route to or from the airport; some companies, such as East Bay Shuttle, have nonstop service, but they cost a bit more. Marin Door to Door operates van service to Marin County starting at $40 for the first passenger, and $12 for each additional person. Marin Airporter buses cost $22 (cash only) and require no reservations but stop only at designated stations in Marin; buses leave every 30 minutes, on the half hour and hour, from 5 am to midnight.

You can take BART directly to downtown San Francisco; the trip takes about 30 minutes and costs less than $9. (There are both manned booths and vending machines for ticket purchases.) Trains leave from the international terminal every 15 or 20 minutes, depending on the day or time.

Another inexpensive way to get to San Francisco (though not as convenient as BART) is via two SamTrans buses: No. 292 (50 minutes) and the KX (35 minutes). Fares are $2.25 from SFO, $4 to SFO. Board the SamTrans buses on the lower level.

To drive to downtown San Francisco from the airport, take U.S. 101 north to the Civic Center/9th Street, 7th Street, or 4th Street/Downtown exits. If you're headed to the Embarcadero or Fisherman's Wharf, take I–280 north (the exit is to the right, just north of the airport, off U.S. 101) and get off at the 4th Street/King Street exit. King Street becomes the Embarcadero a few blocks east of the exit. The Embarcadero winds around the waterfront to Fisherman's Wharf.

FROM OAKLAND INTERNATIONAL AIRPORT

A taxi to downtown San Francisco costs around $80; rideshare companies like Lyft and Uber offer rides for around $50. BayPorter Express and other shuttles serve major hotels and provide door-to-door service to the East Bay and San Francisco. SuperShuttle operates vans to San Francisco and Oakland. Marin Door to Door serves Marin County for $50 for the first passenger, and $12 for each additional person.

The best way to get to San Francisco via public transit is to take BART, which is free upon boarding but requires ticket purchase at the Coliseum/Oakland International Airport BART station (BART fares vary depending on where you're going; the ride to downtown San Francisco from here costs $10.20).

If you're driving from Oakland International Airport, take Airport Drive east to I–880 north to I–80 west over the Bay Bridge. This will likely take at least an hour.

**FROM SAN JOSE
INTERNATIONAL AIRPORT**

A taxi to downtown San Jose costs about $20 to $25; a trip to San Francisco runs about $150 to $165. Rideshare companies like Lyft and Uber offer rides to downtown San Jose starting around $12; a trip to San Francisco starts around $55.

To drive to downtown San Jose from the airport, take Airport Boulevard east to Route 87 south. To get to San Francisco from the airport, take Route 87 south to I-280 north. The trip will take roughly two hours.

At $9.75 for a one-way ticket, there's no question that Caltrain provides the most affordable option for traveling between San Francisco and San Jose's airport. However, the Caltrain station in San Francisco at 4th and Townsend Streets isn't in a conveniently central location. It's on the eastern side of the South of Market (SoMa) neighborhood and not easily accessible by other public transit. You'll need to take a taxi or walk from the nearest bus line. From San Francisco it takes 90 minutes and costs $9.75 to reach the Santa Clara Caltrain station, from which a free shuttle runs every 15 minutes (every 30 minutes on nights and weekends), whisking you to and from the San Jose International Airport in 15 minutes.

Contacts American Airporter. ☏ 415/202–0733 ⊕ www.americanairporter.com. **Caltrain.** ☏ 800/660–4287 ⊕ www.caltrain.com. **East Bay Shuttle.** ☏ 925/800–4500 ⊕ www.eastbayshuttle.net. **GO Lorrie's Airport Shuttle.** ☏ 415/334–9000 ⊕ www.gosfovan.com. **Marin Airporter.** ☏ 415/461–4222 ⊕ www.marinairporter.com. **Marin Door to Door.** ☏ 415/457–2717 ⊕ www.marindoortodoor.com. **SamTrans.** ☏ 800/660–4287 ⊕ www.samtrans.com. **SuperShuttle.** ☏ 800/258–3826 ⊕ www.supershuttle.com.

▌ BART TRAVEL

BART (Bay Area Rapid Transit) trains, which run until midnight, travel under the bay via tunnel to connect San Francisco with Oakland, Berkeley, and other cities and towns beyond. Within San Francisco, stations are limited to downtown, the Mission, and a couple of outlying neighborhoods.

Trains travel frequently from early morning until evening on weekdays. After 8 pm weekdays and on weekends there's often a 20-minute wait between trains on the same line. Trains also travel south from San Francisco as far as Millbrae. BART trains connect downtown San Francisco to San Francisco International Airport; the ride costs $8.95.

Intracity San Francisco fares are $1.95; intercity fares are $3.20 to $11.45. BART bases its ticket prices on miles traveled and doesn't offer price breaks by zone. The easy-to-read maps posted in BART stations list fares based on destination, radiating out from your starting point of the current station.

During morning and evening rush hour, trains within the city are crowded—even standing room can be hard to come by. Cars at the far front and back of the train are less likely to be filled to capacity. Smoking, eating, and drinking are prohibited on trains and in stations.

Contacts Bay Area Rapid Transit (*BART*). ☏ 415/989–2278 ⊕ www.bart.gov.

▌ BOAT TRAVEL

Several ferry lines run out of San Francisco. Blue & Gold Fleet operates a number of routes, including service to Sausalito ($11.50 one-way) and Tiburon ($11.50 one-way). Tickets are sold at Pier 39, boats depart from Pier 41 nearby. Alcatraz Cruises, owned by Hornblower Cruises and Events, operates the ferries to Alcatraz Island ($35.50 including audio tour and National Park Service ranger-led programs) from Pier

33, about a half-mile east of Fisherman's Wharf. Boats leave 14 times a day (more in summer), and the journey itself takes 30 minutes. Allow at least 2½ hours for a round-trip jaunt. Golden Gate Ferry runs daily to and from Sausalito and Larkspur ($11.75 and $11 one-way), leaving from Pier 1, behind the San Francisco Ferry Building. The Alameda/Oakland Ferry operates daily between Alameda's Main Street Terminal, Oakland's Jack London Square, and San Francisco's Pier 41 and the Ferry Building ($6.60 one-way); some ferries go only to Pier 41 or the Ferry Building, so ask when you board. Purchase tickets on board.

Information Alameda/Oakland Ferry.
☎ 877/643–3779 ⊕ sanfranciscobayferry.com.
Alcatraz Cruises. ☎ 415/981–7625 ⊕ www.
alcatrazcruises.com. **Blue & Gold Fleet.**
☎ 415/705–8200 ⊕ www.blueandgoldfleet.
com. **Ferry Building Marketplace.** ⊠ 1 Ferry
Bldg., at foot of Market St. on Embarcadero
☎ 415/983–8030 ⊕ www.ferrybuildingmarket-
place.com. **Golden Gate Ferry.** ☎ 415/923–
2000 ⊕ www.goldengateferry.org.

BUS TRAVEL

Greyhound serves San Francisco with buses from many major U.S. cities; within California, service is limited to hub towns and cities only. The Greyhound depot is located at the Transbay Temporary Terminal, in the SoMa district. Tickets can be purchased online; seating is on a first-come, first-served basis. Cash, checks, and credit cards are accepted.

Contacts Greyhound. ⊠ Transbay Temporary Terminal, 200 Folsom St., at 1st St., SoMa
☎ 415/495–1569 ⊕ www.greyhound.com.

CABLE-CAR TRAVEL

Don't miss the sensation of moving up and down some of San Francisco's steepest hills in a clattering cable car. Jump aboard as it pauses at a designated stop, and wedge yourself into any available space. Then just hold on.

The fare (for one direction) is $7. You can buy tickets on board (exact change isn't required but operators can only make change up to $20) or at the kiosks at the cable-car turnarounds at Hyde and Beach Streets and at Powell and Market Streets.

The heavily traveled Powell–Mason and Powell–Hyde lines begin at Powell and Market Streets near Union Square and terminate at Fisherman's Wharf; lines for these routes can be long, especially in summer. The California Street line runs east and west from Market and California Streets to Van Ness Avenue; there's often no wait to board this route.

CAR TRAVEL

Driving in San Francisco can be a challenge because of the one-way streets, snarly traffic, and steep hills. The first two elements can be frustrating enough, but those hills are tough for unfamiliar drivers.

Be sure to leave plenty of room between your car and other vehicles when on a steep slope. This is especially important when you've braked at a stop sign on a steep incline. Whether with a stick shift or an automatic transmission, every car rolls backward for a moment once the brake is released. So don't pull too close to the car ahead of you. When it's time to pull forward, keep your foot on the brake while tapping lightly on the accelerator. Once the gears are engaged, let up on the brake and head uphill.

■TIP→ Remember to curb your wheels when parking on hills—turn wheels away from the curb when facing uphill, toward the curb when facing downhill. You can get a ticket if you don't do this.

Market Street runs southwest from the Ferry Building, then becomes Portola Drive as it rounds Twin Peaks (which lie just south of the giant radio-antennae structure, Sutro Tower). It can be difficult to drive across Market. The major east–west streets north of Market are Geary Boulevard (it's called Geary Street east of Van Ness Avenue), which runs to the Pacific Ocean; Fulton Street, which begins at the back of the Opera House and continues along the north side of Golden Gate Park to Ocean Beach; Oak Street, which runs east from Golden Gate Park toward downtown, then flows into northbound Franklin Street; and Fell Street, the left two lanes of which cut through Golden Gate Park and empty into Lincoln Way, which continues to the ocean.

Among the major north–south streets are Divisadero, which heading south becomes Castro Street at Waller Street and continues just past César Chávez Street; Van Ness Avenue, which heading south becomes South Van Ness Avenue after it crosses Market Street; and Park Presidio Boulevard, which heading south from the Richmond District becomes Crossover Drive within Golden Gate Park and empties into 19th Avenue.

GASOLINE

Gas stations are hard to find in San Francisco; look for the national franchises on major thoroughfares such as Market Street, Geary Boulevard, Mission Street, or California Street.

Aside from their limited numbers and high costs, everything else is standard operation at service stations. All major stations accept credit and debit cards; self-service pumps are the norm. Most gas stations are open seven days a week until 11 pm or midnight. Many national franchises on well-traveled streets are open 24/7.

PARKING

San Francisco is a terrible city for parking. In the Financial District and Civic Center neighborhoods parking is forbidden on most streets between 3 or 4 pm and 6 or 7 pm. Check street signs carefully to confirm, because illegally parked cars are towed immediately. Downtown parking lots are often full, and most are expensive. The city-owned Sutter-Stockton, Ellis-O'Farrell, and 5th-and-Mission garages have the most reasonable rates in the downtown area. Large hotels often have parking available, but it doesn't come cheap; many charge in excess of $40 a day for the privilege.

Garages 5th & Mission / Yerba Buena Garage. ⊠ *833 Mission St., at 5th St., SoMa* ☎ *415/982-8522* ⊕ *www.fifthandmission. com.* **City Park Opera Plaza.** ⊠ *601 Van Ness Ave., at Turk St., Civic Center* ☎ *415/771-4776.* **Ellis-O'Farrell Garage.** ⊠ *123 O'Farrell St., between Powell and Stockton Sts., Union Sq.* ☎ *415/986-4800.* **Embarcadero Center Garage.** ⊠ *1-4, Embarcadero Center, between Battery and Drumm Sts., Financial District* ☎ *415/772-0670* ⊕ *embarcaderocenter.com.* **Performing Arts Garage.** ⊠ *360 Grove St., between Franklin and Gough Sts., Civic Center* ☎ *415/252-8238.* **Pier 39 Garage.** ⊠ *2 Beach St., at Embarcadero, Fisherman's Wharf* ☎ *415/705-5418* ⊕ *www.pier39.com.* **Portsmouth Square Plaza Garage.** ⊠ *733 Kearny St., at Clay St., Chinatown* ☎ *415/982-6353* ⊕ *www.sfpsg.com.* **Sutter-Stockton Garage.** ⊠ *444 Stockton St., at Sutter St., Union Sq.* ☎ *415/982-7275.* **Vallejo Street Garage.** ⊠ *766 Vallejo St., between Powell St. and Stockton St., North Beach* ☎ *415/989-4490.* **Wharf Garage.** ⊠ *350 Beach St., between Taylor and Mason Sts., Fisherman's Wharf* ☎ *415/227-0114.*

ROAD CONDITIONS

Although rush "hours" are 6–10 am and 3–7 pm, you can hit gridlock on any day at any time, especially over the Bay Bridge and leaving and/or entering the city from the south. Sunday-afternoon traffic can be heavy as well, especially over the bridges.

The most comprehensive and immediate traffic updates are available through the city's 511 service, either online at ⊕ *www.511.org* (where real-time data shows you the traffic on your selected route) or by calling 511. On the radio, tune in to an all-news radio station such as KQED 88.5 FM or KCBS 740 AM/106.9 FM.

Be especially wary of nonindicated lane changes.

San Francisco is the only major American city uncut by freeways. To get from the Bay Bridge to the Golden Gate Bridge, you'll have to take surface streets, specifically Van Ness Avenue, which doubles as U.S. 101 through the city.

RULES OF THE ROAD

To encourage carpooling during heavy traffic times, some freeways have special lanes for so-called high-occupancy vehicles (HOVs)—cars carrying more than one or two passengers. Look for the white-painted diamond in the middle of the lane. Road signs next to or above the lane indicate the hours that carpooling is in effect. If the police stop you because you don't meet the criteria for travel in these lanes, expect a fine close to $500.

Drivers are banned from using handheld mobile telephones while operating a vehicle in California. The use of seat belts in both front and back seats is required in California. The speed limit on city streets is 25 mph unless otherwise posted. A right turn on a red light after stopping is legal unless posted otherwise, as is a left on red at the intersection of two one-way streets. Children must ride in a properly secured child passenger safety restraint in the backseat until they are eight years old or 4 feet 9 inches tall.

CAR RENTALS

When you reserve a car, ask about cancellation penalties, taxes, drop-off charges (if you're planning to pick up the car in one city and leave it in another), and surcharges (for being under or over a certain age, for additional drivers, or for driving across state or country borders or beyond a specific distance from your point of rental). All these things can add substantially to your costs. Request car seats and extras such as GPS when you book.

TAKE THE 511

Several transportation organizations—the Metropolitan Transportation Commission, the California Highway Patrol, the California Department of Transportation, and more—pool their data into a free, one-stop telephone (☎ 511) and Web (⊕ www. ☎ 511.org) resource for all nine Bay Area counties. The service provides the latest info on traffic conditions, route, and fares for all public transit and has info about bicycle and other transportation. The phone line operates 24/7 toll-free.

Rates are sometimes—but not always—better if you book in advance or reserve through a rental agency's website. There are other reasons to book ahead, though: for popular destinations, during busy times of the year, or to ensure that you get certain types of cars (vans, SUVs, exotic sports cars).

■TIP→ Make sure that a confirmed reservation guarantees you a car. Agencies sometimes overbook, particularly for busy weekends and holiday periods.

Car-rental costs in San Francisco vary seasonally, but generally begin at $50 a day and $275 a week for an economy car with air-conditioning, automatic transmission, and unlimited mileage. If you dream of driving with the top down, or heading out of town to ski the Sierra, consider renting a specialty vehicle. Most major agencies have a few on hand, but you have a better chance of finding one at Exotic Car Collection by Enterprise or the locally based City Rent-a-Car. The former specializes in high-end vehicles and arranges for airport pickup and drop-off. City Rent-a-Car likewise arranges airport transfers, and also delivers cars to Bay Area hotels. Both agencies also rent standard vehicles at prices competitive with those of the major chains. ■TIP→ When renting a specialty car, ask about mileage limits. Some companies stick you with per-mile charges if you exceed 100 miles a day.

Generally you must be at least 21 years old to rent a car, but some agencies won't rent to those under 25; check when you book. Super Cheap Car Rental is near the airport and rents to drivers under 21 for an extra fee.

ALTERNATIVE RENTALS

Carma and Zipcar are membership organizations for any person over 21 with a valid driver's license who needs a car only for short-term use. You must join their clubs beforehand, which you can do via their websites. They're especially useful if you only want to rent a car for part of the day (say four to six hours), find yourself far from the airport, or if you're younger than some rental agencies' 25-years-or-older requirement. The membership fee often allows you to use the service in several metropolitan areas. If using such a service, you can rent a car by the hour as well as by the day.

GoCar rents electric vehicles at Fisherman's Wharf and Union Square. These cars can travel between 25 and 35 mph and are very handy for neighborhood-based sightseeing, but they're not allowed on the Golden Gate Bridge. GoCars are electric, two-seater, three-wheeled, open convertibles with roll bars (so drivers must wear helmets) with GPS audio tours of the city. You can pick up a GoCar at locations in Fisherman's Wharf and Union Square.

Local Agencies Carma. ☎ 415/995–8588, ⊕ www.gocarma.com. **City Rent-a-Car.** ✉ 1433 Bush St., near Van Ness Ave., Polk Gulch ☎ 415/359–1331 ⊕ www.cityrentacar. com. **GoCar.** ☎ 800/914–6227 ⊕ www. gocartours.com. **Super Cheap Car Rental.** ✉ 10 Rollins Rd., at Millbrae Ave., Millbrae ☎ 650/777–9993 ⊕ www.supercheapcar.com. **Zipcar.** ☎ 866/494–7227 ⊕ www.zipcar.com.

Major Agencies Alamo. ☎ 800/462–5266 ⊕ www.alamo.com. **Avis.** ☎ 800/633–3469 ⊕ www.avis.com. **Budget.** ☎ 800/218–7992 ⊕ www.budget.com. **Hertz.** ☎ 800/654–3131 ⊕ www.hertz.com. **National Car Rental.** ☎ 877/222–9058 ⊕ www.nationalcar.com.

▌ MUNI TRAVEL

The San Francisco Municipal Railway, or Muni, operates light-rail vehicles, the historic F-line streetcars along Fisherman's Wharf and Market Street, buses, and the world-famous cable cars. Light rail travels along Market Street to the Mission District and Noe Valley (J line), the Ingleside District (K line), and the Sunset District (L, M, and N lines) while also passing through the West Portal, Glen Park, and Castro neighborhoods. The N line continues around the Embarcadero to the Caltrain station at 4th and King Streets; the T-line light rail runs from the Castro, down Market Street, around the Embarcadero, and south past Mission Bay and Hunters Point to Sunnydale Avenue and Bayshore Boulevard. Muni provides 24-hour service on select lines to all areas of the city.

On buses and streetcars the fare is $2.50. Exact change is required, and dollar bills are accepted in the fare boxes. For all Muni vehicles other than cable cars, 90-minute transfers are issued free upon request at the time the fare is paid. These are valid for unlimited transfers in any direction until they expire (time is indicated on the ticket). Cable cars cost $7 and include no transfers (see Cable-Car Travel).

One-day ($21), three-day ($32), and seven-day ($42) Passports valid on the entire Muni system can be purchased at several outlets, including the cable-car ticket booth at Powell and Market Streets and the visitor information center downstairs in Hallidie Plaza. A monthly ticket is available for $80, and can be used on all Muni lines (including cable cars) and on BART within city limits. The San Francisco CityPass ($86), a discount ticket booklet to several major city attractions, also covers all Muni travel for seven consecutive days.

The San Francisco Municipal Transit and Street Map ($5) is a useful guide to the extensive transportation system. You can buy the map at most bookstores and at the San Francisco Visitor Information Center, on the lower level of Hallidie Plaza at Powell and Market Streets.

BUS OPERATORS

Outside the city, AC Transit serves the East Bay, and Golden Gate Transit serves Marin County and a few cities in southern Sonoma County.

Bus and Muni Information San Francisco Municipal Transportation Agency (*Muni*). ☎ *311, 415/701–3000* ⊕ *www.sfmta.com.*

▌TAXI TRAVEL

Taxi service is notoriously bad in San Francisco, and finding a cab can be frustratingly difficult. Popular nightspots such as the Mission, SoMa, North Beach, and the Castro are the easiest places to hail a cab off the street; hotel taxi stands are also an option. If you're going to the airport, make a reservation or book a shuttle instead. Taxis in San Francisco charge $3.50 for the first 0.5 mile (one of the highest base rates in the United States), 55¢ for each additional 0.2 mile, and 55¢ per minute in stalled traffic; a $4 surcharge is added for trips from the airport. There's no charge for additional passengers; there's no surcharge for luggage. For trips further than 15 miles outside city limits, multiply the metered rate by 1.5; tolls and tip are extra.

That said, San Francisco's poor taxi service was a direct factor in the creation of ride-sharing services such as Uber and Lyft, which are easy to use and prominent throughout the city and its surrounding areas. San Franciscans generally regard taxis as a thing of the past and use ride-sharing on a day-to-day basis. If you're willing to share a car with strangers, a trip within the city can run as low as $4; rates go up for private rides and during peak demand times. These services are especially economical when going to or from the airport, where a shared ride will run you about $25 — half the cost of a cab.

Taxi Companies Flywheel Taxi. ☎ *415/970–1303* ⊕ *flywheeltaxi.com.* **Luxor Cab.** ☎ *415/282–4141* ⊕ *www.luxorcab.com.* **National Veterans Cab.** ☎ *415/321–8294* ⊕ *sfnationalcab.sftaxischool.com/index.html.* **Yellow Cab.** ☎ *415/333–3333* ⊕ *yellowcabsf.com.*

Complaints San Francisco Police Department Taxi Complaints. ☎ *415/701–4400.*

▌TRAIN TRAVEL

Amtrak trains travel to the Bay Area from some cities in California and the United States. The *Coast Starlight* travels north from Los Angeles to Seattle, passing the Bay Area along the way, but contrary to its name, the train runs inland through the Central Valley for much of its route through Northern California; the most scenic stretch is in Southern California, between San Luis Obispo and Los Angeles. Amtrak also has several routes between San Jose, Oakland, and Sacramento. The *California Zephyr* travels from Chicago to the Bay Area, and has spectacular alpine vistas as it crosses the Sierra Nevada range. San Francisco doesn't have an Amtrak train station but does have an Amtrak bus stop at the Ferry Building, from which shuttle buses transport passengers to trains in Emeryville, just over the Bay Bridge. Shuttle buses also connect the Emeryville train station with BART and other points in downtown San Francisco. You can buy a California Rail Pass, which gives you 7 days of travel in a 21-day period for $159.

Caltrain connects San Francisco to Palo Alto, San Jose, Santa Clara, and many smaller cities en route. In San Francisco, trains leave from the main depot, at 4th and Townsend Streets, and a rail-side stop at 22nd and Pennsylvania Streets. One-way fares are $3.75 to $13.75, depending on the number of zones through which you travel; tickets are valid for four hours after purchase time. A ticket is $7.75 from San Francisco to

Palo Alto, at least $9.75 to San Jose. You can also buy a day pass ($7.50–$27.50) for unlimited travel in a 24-hour period. It's worth waiting for an express train for trips that last from 1 to 1¾ hours. On weekdays, trains depart three or four times per hour during the morning and evening, only once or twice per hour during daytime non-commute hours and late night. Weekend trains run once per hour, though there are two bullet trains per day, one in late morning and one in early evening The system shuts down after midnight. There are no onboard ticket sales. You must buy tickets before boarding the train or risk paying up to $250 for fare evasion.

Information Amtrak. ☎ *800/872–7245* ⊕ *www.amtrak.com.* **Caltrain.** ☎ *800/660– 4287* ⊕ *www.caltrain.com.* **San Francisco Caltrain station.** ✉ *700 4th St., near Townsend St.* ☎ *800/660–4287.*

ESSENTIALS

▮ COMMUNICATIONS

INTERNET

The city of San Francisco now offers free Wi-Fi service in selected parks and areas in and around the city. For a detailed list of locations visit ⊕ *www6.sfgov. org.* All public libraries also provide Internet access and most hotels have a computer stationed in the lobby with free (if shared) high-speed access for guests. Some hotels can charge a small fee to provide a high-speed connection in the room, others offer it free of charge. In addition, many cafés throughout San Francisco, Marin County, and the East Bay offer free Wi-Fi, but a few continue to charge a fee. For a list of free Wi-Fi spots in San Francisco, check ⊕ *www. openwifispots.com.*

▮ DAY TOURS AND GUIDES

For walking-tour recommendations, see the Experience San Francisco chapter or the pull-out On-the-Go map.

BOAT TOURS

Blue & Gold Fleet operates a bay cruise that lasts an hour. Tickets may be purchased at Pier 39, near Fisherman's Wharf or online. The tour, on a ferryboat with outside seating on the upper deck, as well as inside seating, loops around the bay taking in the Bay Bridge, Alcatraz Island, and the Golden Gate Bridge. An audiotape tells you what you're seeing.

Information Blue & Gold Fleet. ☎ 415/705–8200 ⊕ www.blueandgoldfleet.com.

BUS AND VAN TOURS

In addition to bus and van tours of the city, most tour companies run excursions to various Bay Area and Northern California destinations, such as Marin County and the Wine Country, as well as to farther-flung areas, such as Monterey and Yosemite. City tours generally last 3½ hours and cost about $50 per person. The bigger outfits operate large buses, which tend to be roomy. Service is more intimate with the smaller companies, however, because they can fit only about 10 people per vehicle; the vans can be a little tight, but with the driver-guide right in front of you, you're able to ask questions easily and won't have to worry about interrupting someone on a microphone, as is the case with the big companies.

Centrally located in North Beach, Dylan's offers guided six-hour tours around San Francisco, which then move on to Sausalito and Muir Woods ($89) in modern air-conditioned mini buses. The company also leads electric bike tours starting at $69.

The Great Pacific Tour Company is a good small company that conducts city tours in passenger vans (starting at $65). Gray Line San Francisco operates tours in 28- to 50-passenger buses. For $19 more, Gray Line can supplement a city tour with a bay cruise.

Actors from the Antenna Theater company lead the tours for Magic Bus, a literal time machine that transports visitors back to 1960s San Francisco. The bus provides a space for music and film clips to both educate and entertain; once the bus stops, you arrive at the historic place you just saw on your screen. Tickets are $70 each and tours last about 2½ hours. Pickup is on Geary Street in Union Square facing the Macy's, drop-off back in Union Square. Book online, and in advance, to guarantee a seat.

Information Dylan's Tours. ✉ 782 Columbus Ave. ☎ 415/932–6993 ⊕ dylanstours.com. **Gray Line San Francisco.** ☎ 415/353–5310 ⊕ graylineofsanfrancisco.com. **The Great Pacific Tour Company.** ☎ 415/626–4499 ⊕ greatpacifictour.com. **Magic Bus.** ☎ 855/969–6244 ⊕ magicbussf.com.

HELICOPTER TOURS

San Francisco Helicopter Tours offers several options that give you a bird's-eye view of the city. Its Vista tour sweeps over the western shoreline, the Presidio, Union Square, AT&T Park, Alcatraz, and the Golden Gate Bridge; the tour lasts 20 minutes and costs $195 per person. The Vista Grande tour, which lasts 30 minutes and costs $250, takes in all of the above as well as Sausalito and Marin County. Longer tours, including trips to the Wine Country, also are available. The tours depart from San Francisco International Airport or the Sausalito heliport; a shuttle transports guests to and from the departure point, picking up and dropping off at downtown hotels and Fisherman's Wharf. Book at least 48 hours in advance.

Information San Francisco Helicopter Tours. ☎ 800/400–2404, 650/635–4500 ⊕ www.sfhelicoptertours.com.

▌ MONEY

San Francisco often finds itself near the top of lists rating the most expensive cities in the United States. Don't let that scare you off; those ratings are usually based on the cost of living. Local real-estate prices are out of this world—but a trip here doesn't have to cost the moon.

Payment methods are those standard to major U.S. cities. Plastic is king; hotels and most restaurants accept credit cards. Small, casual restaurants, though, may be cash-only operations. You can easily find ATMs in every neighborhood, either in bank branches, convenience stores, drugstores, supermarkets, and even some coffee shops.

Prices throughout this guide are given for adults. Substantially reduced fees are almost always available for children, students, and senior citizens.

▌ RESTROOMS

Public facilities are in forest-green kiosks throughout main areas of the city, including at Fisherman's Wharf, on Market Street at Powell Street, at Church and Market Streets, and at the Civic Center. There is no fee to use these facilities. They're self-cleaning but can occasionally be unpleasant. Most public garages have restrooms, large hotels usually have lobby-level facilities, and chain bookstores and coffee shops are another good bet.

▌ SAFETY

San Francisco is generally a safe place for travelers who observe all normal urban precautions. Use common sense and, unless you know exactly where you're going, steer clear of certain neighborhoods late at night, especially if you're walking alone. Below are certain areas to stay on alert, or avoid:

The Tenderloin. Thought to be named for a cut of steak, this neighborhood west of Union Square and above Civic Center can be a seedy part of town, with drug dealers, homeless people, hustlers, and X-rated joints. It's roughly bordered by Taylor, Polk, Geary, and Market Streets. Avoid coming here after dark, especially if you're walking.

Western Addition. Past incidents of gang activity have made this neighborhood somewhat sketchy. Don't stray too far off Fillmore Street.

Civic Center. After a show here, walk west to Gough Street; and avoid Market Street between 6th and 10th.

Some areas in Golden Gate Park. These include the area near the Haight Street entrance, where street kids often smoke and deal drugs, and around the pedestrian tunnels on the far west end of the park.

Like many large cities, San Francisco has many homeless people. Although most are no threat, some are more aggressive and can persist in their pleas for cash until it feels like harassment. If you feel uncomfortable, don't reach for your wallet.

■TIP→ Distribute your cash, credit cards, IDs, and other valuables between a deep front pocket, an inside jacket or vest pocket, and a hidden money pouch. Don't reach for the money pouch once you're in public.

▌ TAXES

The sales tax in San Francisco is 8.5%. Nonprepared foods (from grocery stores) are exempt. The tax on hotel rooms is 14%.

▌ TIME

San Francisco is on Pacific Time. Chicago is 2 hours ahead of San Francisco, New York is 3 hours ahead, and, depending on whether daylight saving time is in effect, London is either 8 or 9 hours ahead and Sydney is 17 or 18 hours ahead.

▌ TIPPING

TIPPING GUIDELINES FOR SAN FRANCISCO	
Bartender	About 15%, starting at $1 a drink at casual places
Bellhop	$1–$5 per bag, depending on the level of the hotel
Hotel concierge	$5 or more, if he or she performs a service for you
Hotel doorman, room service, or valet	$3–$4
Hotel maid	$5 a day (either daily or at the end of your stay, in cash)
Taxi driver	15%–20%, but round up the fare to the next dollar amount
Tour guide	10% of the cost of the tour
Waiter	18%–20%, with 20% being the norm at high-end restaurants

▌ VISITOR INFORMATION

The San Francisco Convention and Visitors Bureau can mail or email you brochures, maps, and festivals and events listings. Once you're in town, you can stop by the bureau's information center near Union Square. Information about Wine Country, redwood groves, and northwestern California is available at the California Welcome Center on Pier 39.

Berkeley's Visitor Information Center provides an extensive events calendar and detailed suggestions. The Oakland Convention & Visitors Bureau also has an informative website highlighting local events, restaurants, and hotels. For information about Marin County and the parks within it, visit the Marin County Convention & Visitors Bureau in San Rafael or online at ⊕ *www.visitmarin.org.*

The California Travel and Tourism Commission provides free visitor information and itinerary planners for the entire state.

Contacts San Francisco Visitor Information Center. ⊠ *Hallidie Plaza, lower level, 900 Market St., at Powell St., Union Sq.* ☎ *415/391–2000* ⊕ *www.sftravel.com.*

Metro Area Marin Convention & Visitors Bureau. ⊠ *1 Mitchell Blvd., Suite B, at Redwood Hwy., San Rafael* ☎ *415/925–2060, 866/925–2060* ⊕ *www.visitmarin.org.* **San Jose Convention & Visitors Bureau.** ⊠ *408 S. Almaden Blvd., near Balbach St., San Jose* ☎ *800/726–5673, 408/295–9600* ⊕ *www. sanjose.org.* **Visit Berkeley Information Center.** ⊠ *2030 Addison St., Suite 102, Berkeley ⊹ one block north of Downtown Berkeley BART station* ☎ *800/847–4823, 510/549–7040* ⊕ *www.visitberkeley.com.*

State California Travel and Tourism Commission. ☎ *877/225–4367, 916/444–4429* ⊕ *www.visitcalifornia.com.* **California Welcome Center.** ⊠ *Pier 39 , Beach St. and the Embarcadero , Bldg. B, 2nd level* ☎ *415/981–1280* ⊕ *www.visitcwc.com.*

ONLINE RESOURCES

This comprehensive website, ⊕ *www.sanfrancisco.com*, contains links to local restaurants, cultural institutions, and services in and around the city.

For local politics and news, there's the online presence of the major daily newspaper, ⊕ *www.sfgate.com*, as well as ⊕ *www.fogcityjournal.com*. Current arts and cultural events are detailed on the extensive events calendar of ⊕ *www.sfstation.com* or the *San Francisco Chronicle*'s online entertainment pages, ⊕ *www.sfgate.com/entertainment*.

For more cost-conscious, on-the-pulse guidance, visit ⊕ *sf.funcheap.com*. You can browse articles from *San Francisco Magazine,* a monthly glossy, at ⊕ *www.modernluxury.com/san-francisco*. The annual July issues on "bests" (restaurants, activities, and so on) are handy overviews. *SF Weekly*'s site, ⊕ *www.sfweekly.com*, makes for good browsing.

Where's the Wi-Fi? Click on ⊕ *www.wifi-freespot.com* to see where you can log on in the Bay Area for free.

THE FODORS.COM CONNECTION

Before your trip, be sure to check out what fellow travelers are saying in Travel Talk Forums on ⊕ *www.fodors.com*.

INDEX

PHOTO CREDITS

Front cover: Inge Johnsson / Alamy [Description: Transamerica building and skyline, San Francisco, California]. **Back cover, from left to right:** Jaspe | Dreamstime.com; errnovik | Dreamstime.com; Lunamarina | Dreamstime.com. **Spine:** holbox / Shutterstock. 1 and 2, Philip Dyer/istockphoto. 5, travelstock44/Alamy. **Chapter 1: Experience San Francisco:** 8-9, Prisma/Bildagentur AG/Alamy. 18 (left), Eli Mordechai/Shutterstock. 18 (top right), Andresr/Shutterstock. 18 (bottom right), Chee-Onn Leong/Shutterstock. 19 (top left), Chris Pancewicz/Alamy. 19 (right), Robert Holmes. 9 (bottom left), Brett Shoaf/Artistic Visuals Photography. 29, travelstock44/Alamy. 31, Brett Shoaf/Artistic Visuals Photography. 32, San Francisco Municipal Railway Historical Archives. **Chapter 2: Union Square & Chinatown:** 33, Rubens Abboud/Alamy. 35, Chee-Onn Leong/Shutterstock. 36, Steve Rosset/Shutterstock. 38, San Francisco Travel Association/Scott Chernis. 40, Sheryl Schindler/SFCVB. 41, Brett Shoaf/Artistic Visuals Photography. 42 (top), Arnold Genthe. 42 (bottom), Library of Congress Prints and Photographs Division. 43 (left), Sandor Balatoni/SFCVB. 43 (right), Library of Congress. 44, Brett Shoaf/Artistic Visuals Photography. **Chapter 3: SoMa and Civic Center:** 47, Walter Bibikow/age fotostock. 49, Robert Holmes. 50, Rafael Ramirez Lee/Shutterstock. **Chapter 4: Nob Hill and Russian Hill:** 57, SurangaSL / Shutterstock. 59, Brett Shoaf/Artistic Visuals Photography. 60, Traveltelly | Dreamstime.com. **Chapter 5: North Beach:** 65, TasFoto | Dreamstime.com. 67 and 68, Brett Shoaf/Artistic Visuals Photography. 70, M & J Miller / age fotostock. **Chapter 6: On the Waterfront:** 73, Jon Arnold Images/Alamy. 75, Musee Mecanique in San Francisco. 76, Robert Holmes. 85, Lewis Sommer/SFCVB. 86, Daniel DeSlover/Shutterstock.87 (left), POPPERFOTO/Alamy. 87 (center and right), wikipedia.org. 89, Eliza Snow/iStockphoto. 90, Steve Rosset/Shutterstock. **Chapter 7: The Marina and the Presidio:** 91, Carolina Garcia Aranda/iStockphoto. 93, Brett Shoaf/Artistic Visuals Photography. 94, CAN BALCIOGLU/Shutterstock. 95 (top), Zack Frank/Shutterstock. 95 (bottom), Steve Holderfield/Shutterstock. 96, javarman/Shutterstock. **Chapter 8: The Western Shoreline:** 103 and 105, Robert Holmes. 106, Brett Shoaf/Artistic Visuals Photography. 108, Chee-Onn Leong/Shutterstock. **Chapter 9: Golden Gate Park:** 111, California Travel and Tourism Co. 112, Robert Holmes. 113 and 114 (top), Brett Shoaf/Artistic Visuals Photography. 114 (center), Robert Holmes. 114 (bottom), Brett Shoaf/Artistic Visuals Photography. 115, Natalia Bratslavsky/iStockphoto. 116, Robert Holmes. 117 (top), Jack Hollingsworth/SFCVB. 117 (center), Robert Holmes. 117 (bottom), Brett Shoaf/Artistic Visuals Photography. 118 (top and bottom), RobertHolmes. 119 (top and bottom), Janet Fullwood. 120 (top), Donna & Andrew/Flickr. 120 (center and bottom), Robert Holmes. **Chapter 10: The Haight, the Castro, and Noe Valley:** 121, Robert Holmes. 123, Brett Shoaf/Artistic Visuals Photography. 124, SFCVB. 127, aprillilacs, Fodors.com member. **Chapter 11: Mission District:** 133, Kārlis Dambrāns/Flickr, [CC BY 2.0]. 135, Robert Holmes. 136, Brett Shoaf/ Artistic Visuals Photography. 138, Held Jürgen/Prisma/age fotostock. 140, Robert Holmes. **Chapter 12: Pacific Heights and Japantown:** 143, Robert Holmes. 145, ryan + sarah/Flickr. 146, Brett Shoaf/Artistic Visuals Photography. 148. Janet Fullwood. 149. (top) iStockphoto. 149. (bottom) Susanne Friedrich/ iStockphoto. 150, Rafael Ramirez Lee/iStockphoto. **Chapter 13: Where to Eat:** 155, OPENKITCHEN-Photography/Tartine. 156, San Francisco Travel Association/Scott Chernis. 157 (top), T photography / Shutterstock. 157 (bottom), Walleyelj | Dreamstime.com. 158, Eric Wolfinger/In Situ. **Chapter 14: Where to Stay:** 191, Argonaut Hotel. 192, Clift Hotel. **Chapter 15: Performing Arts:** 213, Erik Tomasson. 214, Max Kiesler/Flickr, [CC BY 2.0]. **Chapter 16: Nightlife:** 225, San Francisco Travel Association/Scott Chernis. 226, Robert Holmes. **Chapter 17: Sports and the Outdoors:** 247, Rich Vintage Photography/iStockphoto. 248, Robert Holmes. **Chapter 18: Shopping and Spas:** 257, Robert Holmes. 258, Flash2309 | Dreamstime.com. **Chapter 19: The Bay Area:** 287, Gary Crabbe / Alamy. 298, Jyeshern Cheng/iStockphoto. 290, Brett Shoaf/Artistic Visuals Photography. 296, California Travel and Tourism Commission / Bongo. 299, Nancy Hoyt Belcher / Alamy. 317, Robert Holmes. 327, Robert Holmes. 336, S. Greg Panosian/iStockphoto. **Chapter 20: Napa and Sonoma:** 339, Andrew Zarivny / Shutterstock. 341, Robert Holmes. 348, Warren H. White. 348, Robert Holmes. 349 (top), kevin miller/ iStockphoto. 349 (bottom), Far Niente+Dolce+Nickel & Nickel. 350 (top and bottom) Robert Holmes. 351 (top), Domaine Carneros. 351 (bottom), star5112/Flickr. 352 (top left), Rubicon Estate. 352 (top right and bottom) and 353 (top and bottom), Robert Holmes. 354 (top), Philippe Roy/Alamy. 354 (middle), Agence Images/Alamy. 354 (bottom), Cephas Picture Library/Alamy. 355 (top), Napa Valley Conference Bureau. 355 (second and third from top), Wild Horse Winery (Forrest L. Doud). 355 (fourth from top), Napa Valley Conference Bureau. 355 (fifth from top), Panther Creek Cellars (Ron Kaplan). 355 (sixth from top), Clos du Val (Marvin Collins). 355 (seventh from top), Panther Creek Cellars (Ron Kaplan). 355 (bottom), Warren H. White. 356, di Rosa. 368, Terry Joanis/Frog's Leap. 378, Castello di Amorosa. 388 and 392-393, Robert Holmes. **About Our Writers:** All photos are courtesy of the writer except for the following: Michele Bigley, courtesy of Tony Belko; Denise Leto, courtesy of Kevin Finney; Daniel Mangin, courtesy of J Rodby; Fiona G. Parrott, courtesy of William Rogue.

NOTES

NOTES

NOTES

ABOUT OUR WRITERS

Amanda Kuehn Carroll lives in the Bay Area but left her heart in Kansas City. She loves words, wonder, and tiny spoons and her writing covers food trends, local getaways, and artist profiles. Her work has appeared in *Edible East Bay, 7x7, Food Network,* and *San Francisco Magazine.* For this edition, Amanda updated the Bay Area chapter.

Longtime Fodor's writer and editor **Denise M. Leto** roams the city out of sheer love for SF, peeking down overgrown alleyways and exploring tucked-away corners from the Tenderloin to the Richmond, often with her three homeschooled kids in tow. She updated all the neighborhood chapters and updated our special features on cable cars, Chinatown, Golden Gate Park, Alcatraz, and the Golden Gate Bridge.

Rebecca Flint Marx is a San Francisco-based writer and editor who has written about food for publications including The *New York Times, San Francisco Magazine, The New Yorker,* and *WIRED.* She has won James Beard and IACP awards for her work.

Daniel Mangin returned to California, where he's maintained a home for three decades, after two stints at the Fodor's editorial offices in New York City, the second one as the Editorial Director of Fodors.com and the Compass American Guides. While at Compass he was the series editor for the *California Wine Country* guide and commissioned the *Oregon Wine Country* and *Washington Wine Country* guides. A wine lover whose earliest visits to Napa and Sonoma predate the Wine Country lifestyle, Daniel is delighted by the evolution in wines, wine making, and hospitality. With several dozen wineries less than a half-hour's drive from home, he often finds himself

transported as if by magic to a tasting room bar, communing with a sophisticated Cabernet or savoring the finish of a smooth Pinot Noir. For this edition, Daniel, the writer of Fodor's Travel Napa & Sonoma, updated the Wine Country and Where to Stay chapters.

Andrea Powell has lived in San Francisco for eight years. She is the former associate editor of *San Francisco* magazine and currently contributes to WIRED.

Jerry James Stone, author of *Holidazed: A Cocktail Cookbook for Getting Lit on Christmas*, has been eating and drinking his way through San Francisco for years now, focusing on the sustainable food and wine movement. You can find all his vegan and vegetarian recipes at Cooking Stoned (⊕ *www.cookingstoned.tv*). Jerry updated the Nightlife and the Performing Arts chapters in this year's guide. Follow him on Twitter @jerryjamesstone for mouthwatering recipe ideas.

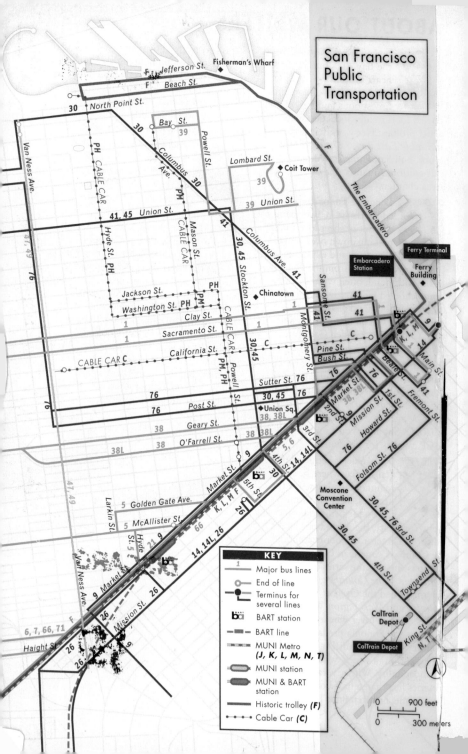